Buyer Behavior: Theoretical and Empirical Foundations

Advisor:
THOMAS ROBERTSON

Buyer Behavior: Theoretical and Empirical Foundations

Edited by

John A. Howard
Columbia University

and

Lyman E. Ostlund
Columbia University

Alfred A. Knopf
New York

To Lynn
and
To Lotta

This is a Borzoi Book
Published by Alfred A. Knopf, Inc.

Library of Congress Cataloging in Publication Data

Howard, John A   comp.
  Buyer behavior.

    1. Consumers—Addresses, essays, lectures.
I. Ostlund, Lyman E., joint comp. II. Title.
HC79.C6H67   658.8'34   72-13239
ISBN 0-394-31681-9

Manufactured in the United States of America

First Edition

98765432

Cover photo by Lynda Gianforte

Preface

Signs of increasing theoretical rigor in the study of buyer behavior are becoming evident on all sides. Certainly, academic research on buyer behavior has depended heavily upon concepts developed in behavioral disciplines and multivariate statistical techniques. Perhaps more important, however, is the clear evidence that the quality of academic research in buyer behavior is rising and serious attention is being given to the problems of carefully stating structural relationships among variables, operational definitions of concepts, disaggregative data analysis, and cautious statements, if any, concerning management implications. To an increasing degree, research projects are being structured to fill theoretical gaps, rather than pioneer new schools of thought. Although the importance of replication in research is still largely ignored in buyer behavior research, there are signs that this is changing as well.

The interest in buyer behavior theory extends into the classroom as well. To an increasing degree, graduate schools of business have added buyer behavior seminars or courses to their MBA curricula. Other schools have accomplished a similar objective by integrating theory within their several marketing management courses. Regardless of the approach, several difficulties exist in teaching buyer behavior. Students rapidly discover what their professors already know concerning buyer behavior theory: it is new, still fragmented, and seldom lends itself directly to prescriptive thoughts on marketing strategy. For these reasons and others, the subject does not lend itself to textbook packaging. At the same time, however, journal articles on the subject are often complicated and frustrating to the student for whom the subject is new. The organization of this book is directed at overcoming this difficulty.

The research activities surrounding buyer behavior theory have received strong support from many commercial market researchers. Not only have these market researchers been frequent contributors to professional journals, they have made available the data and/or the resources to facilitate much of the academic research on buyer behavior. Several leading marketers have set up special funds for this purpose, recognizing that they as major marketers will ultimately benefit from an investment in theoretical effort. While it must be said that the same receptivity does not exist on the part of all marketing managers, this is changing as well. Generally, the acceptance of behavioral research findings comes piecemeal, many times camouflaged under the topic of market segmentation.

Last but not least, there is a growing recognition by some public policy makers that so-called consumerism issues should be analyzed in the light of consumer information-processing and decision-making.

In contemplating this book, the editors have attempted to keep in mind several possible readers: the academic and commercial researcher, the student, the marketing manager, and the public policy maker. The opening chapter discusses the need for theory and presents a theory of buyer behavior that has undergone development, empirical investigation, and revision during the past decade. The chapters that follow are arranged in terms of elements of that model. Each chapter is intended to give a sampling of what is both known and unknown about a specific element from the theory. Readings have been selected to meet several criteria: (1) relevance to this theory and major research avenues in the field, (2) relevance to the practice of marketing, (3) clarity of exposition, and (4) conceptual accuracy. Not one of these four criteria is necessarily any more important than the remaining three; readings were selected that were thought to meet all four criteria. Recognizing that many of the readings would cause difficulties for readers, each chapter begins with a discussion of a theory element and refers to the readings that follow in that chapter in an attempt to focus attention on aspects of each reading that were considered important in its selection. At the same time, however, the responsibility for critically evaluating the reading is left in the hands of the reader.

We would like to thank Tom Robertson for his encouragement and helpful suggestions during the design and preparation of this book. Our research assistant Kjell M. Halvorsen contributed many useful ideas as well as considerable time to our literature search. And surely without the energies and patience of Thelma Ezzell and her daughter Marilyn the several revisions of our writing and the quest for releases would never have been completed so smoothly and on time!

J. A. H.
L. E. O.

Contents

Introduction

1

1

1. The model: current status of buyer behavior theory

john a. howard
& lyman e. ostlund

The architect can design a functional and appealing building that meets the needs of his client without necessarily knowing much about theoretical physics. Similarly, businessmen have put together product offerings with considerable success over the centuries without necessarily being conscious students of buyer behavior theory. In both cases, however, it is important to notice that some form of theory, elementary or complex, explicit or implicit, has governed decision-making. It is not correct to say that the marketer operates without a theory of buyer behavior, but rather that his theory is most always grossly incomplete and seldom made explicit. By the same reasoning, it makes no sense to claim that he can or should operate without theory, dismissing it is impractical. There is nothing more practical than a sound theory. The real issue is what constitutes a sound theory and how can it be developed.

It must be freely acknowledged that no current theory of buyer behavior satisfies the end requirements of either the marketer or the researcher. But progress toward that end, starting from a very modest beginning, has been rapid in the past ten years. A very important impetus has been the computer and multivariate statistical techniques. For the first time, large masses of data can be assembled and freely manipulated so as to facilitate the investigation of buyer decision-making as a highly complex, interactive process. There has also been increasing attention focused on the measurement difficulties that must be met in order for any set of hypotheses, whatever the theory, to be adequately tested. The headlong rush toward the establishment of large disaggregated information systems to guide and control marketing strategy has served to reinforce the idea articulated earlier that executive decision-making and organization will reflect the theory the executive holds of his environment (Howard, 1965). That is, the data requirements of an information system cannot be adequately specified until management makes explicit its theory of the marketplace and, later, proceeds to conduct validating research for improving an operational theory.

The student of marketing strategy, regardless of age, likewise improves upon his analytical batting average if his approach has some order and structure. Within a classroom, the analysis of marketing cases can be more meaningful learning experiences if primary and secondary questions are answered based upon an assumed explicit model, even if incomplete.

The marketer may say that he is simply testing his hunches when trying a new element of marketing strategy or commissioning a market research project. However, if the pursuit has been well planned we could instead credit him with refining his theory of buyer behavior. A marketing manager soon learns that he cannot simply ask a single question—for example, why do people buy this or that product? His question must be far more refined with respect to purpose and possible causal variables. If not, he will receive at best a superficial answer and perhaps waste a good deal of money in market research. But, as with any activity, if he is unwilling to attempt orderly experimentation and testing, he will have only his intuition for guidance. Moreover, he cannot evaluate the wisdom of a proposed advertising copy test or segmentation study unless he gives careful thought to what variables are relevant to his own theory of buyer behavior or communication effects, and whether or not they can be meaningfully measured.

Similar difficulties seem to exist in recent efforts to pass laws providing useful information to the consumer. Much of this legislation has been based upon how educated people *should* search for and process information rather than how generally less educated people *do* ignore or incompletely process much of the available information. An example of this appears to be the experience thus far with unit pricing and with truth-in-lending legislation (Angell, 1971). While both the concept of unit pricing and truth-in-lending laws may be justified on other grounds, studies have indicated that a large proportion of consumers pay relatively little attention to the additional information, either because it is not in a form that they can readily process, or because other evaluative criteria are far more important. On the other hand, most say they appreciate having it available.

Thus, it is not difficult to suggest applications for a sound theory of buyer behavior. It is, however, very difficult to derive one. How does one judge the soundness of theory? Without indulging in a philosophy of science discussion, a few simple but demanding criteria are set forth:

1. Theory must aid significantly in explaining buyer behavior, not merely describe it. We do not seek only to classify buyers into a number of subgroups as one does in market segmentation. Rather, we want to relate the various states of mind leading from awareness of a stimulus to behavior regarding that stimulus. We are then primarily concerned with processes of cognition and linkages between mental constructs. With this being the case, it must be recognized that several of the mental constructs involved with any theory of buyer behavior will not lend themselves to measurement; their existence and their importance in the model can only be assumed. Nevertheless, continuing research will narrow the range of conflicting explanations.
2. Toward the end of explaining buyer behavior, sound theory must incorporate mainstream thinking from principal avenues of research. Of necessity, a theory of buyer behavior must draw upon all the behavioral disciplines while still being cautious in accepting

their conclusions as relevant to buyer behavior. This borrowing process is not dangerous providing efforts are made to replicate the research conclusions in a context of buyer behavior. One would like to avoid borrowing until a substantial amount of supporting re- search has been done in the originating discipline, so that he can be assured that the emerging conclusions represent the mainstream of substantial investigation.

3. A sound theory of buyer behavior should have the property of sug- gesting clear avenues for fruitful research. It should serve as the catalyst in stimulating and directing research that would otherwise fly off in a multitude of directions. In this purpose, its relevance to buyer behavior should be obvious and persuasive to researchers.

4. To serve these criteria, operational measures or definitions of theory elements should be included. Providing operational measures is particularly difficult, given the measurement shortcomings that generally exist in the behavioral sciences. It is doubtful whether any theory of buyer behavior, including the one to be presented in this chapter, adequately meets this criterion to satisfy even the majority of interested researchers.

PAST THEORETICAL EFFORTS

In the past decade, there have been several notable attempts to set forth a theory of buyer behavior. Starting with the learning theory by Hull (1943, 1952) and adding cognitive structure, Howard (1963, 1965) opened early efforts directed at theory development (Figure 1). This theory was later expanded and refined by a stream of research known as the Columbia University Project on Buyer Behavior along with the research findings of many other researchers (Howard and Sheth, 1969). See Figure 2 for the Howard-Sheth model.

During the same period, other contributions were being made. Nicosia's (1966) theory of consumer decision processes was aimed specifically at the decision process surrounding new product delibera- tions (Figure 3). Nicosia's emphasis on decision-making as an ongoing process was an important advance.

A dramatic although frequently overlooked contribution to buyer behavior theory was made by Amstutz (1967) in his computer simulation of a total marketing environment (Figure 4). This simulation of truly enormous size was totally disaggregative and consisted of separate interacting simulations of the consumer, the retailer, the manufacturer and his sales force, competitors and their respective sales forces, dis- tributors, plus government constraints over certain marketing maneu- vers (e.g., pricing) and allowable forms of communications between the competitors. While the first concern of Amstutz was clearly that of deriving a workable simulation model, the effort is also notable in its contribution toward synthesizing research from a variety of dis- ciplines into a conceptual model, and from that going on to set forth operational definitions of variables, which in turn could be quantified for later simulation.

The Engel consumer decision-making model (Figure 5), bearing some similarity to the earlier Nicosia model, became the organizing framework for a textbook on consumer behavior (Engel, Kollat, and Blackwell, 1968).

AN UPDATED THEORY OF BUYER BEHAVIOR

In accordance with the criteria set forth earlier, there have been several recent developments that suggest that a revision in the theory of buyer behavior is timely. First of all, a third research project on buyer behavior is underway at Columbia, this time on an American heavy consumer durable market, which has forced some revision in certain theory elements, and which, more importantly, has brought about superior operational definitions of certain variables with a resulting improvement in their predictive ability and has led to the development of better testing methods. Whereas a test of the Howard and Sheth (1969) version of the model by Farley and Ring (1970) demonstrated consistent but modest overall predictive merit (based upon the instant

FIGURE 1 Extensive Problem Solving

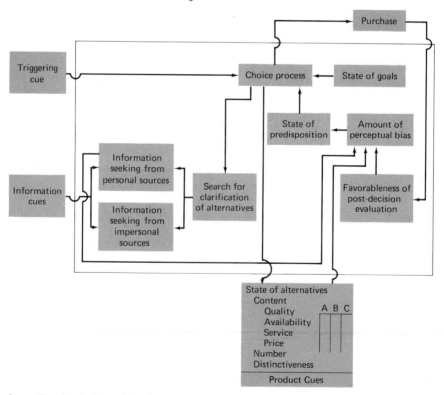

Source: Reproduced with permission from John A. Howard, *Marketing Management Analysis and Planning,* 1963.(Rev. Ed. Homewood, III: Richard D. Irwin, Inc.), p. 47.

breakfast market), the latest research effort promises an advance in predictive capability.

Furthermore, an effort has been made to take advantage of the work by other researchers, particularly concerning perception and the cognitive process generally. Last, but not the least important, is our interest in shaping and discussing the model such as to make it meaningful for the widest possible audience. It is only through this means that interest in its further testing and application to research and strategy issues will be stimulated beyond the confines of Columbia. Certain theory elements have been reformulated, and others combined in a manner that it is felt more clearly reflects mainstream thinking within the research community.

The remainder of this chapter is devoted to describing the updated theory of buyer behavior in terms of five primary divisions:

1. Exogenous variables that include the *institutional environment*, the *societal environment* and the buyer's *personal characteristics*.
2. Information processing, leading from *information sources* through *media selection* and *perceptual bias* to *information recalled*.
3. Motive-directed cognition leading to purchase satisfaction.
4. Levels of problem-solving and *overt search* to effect the information-processing function.
5. Operational measures for the variables.

FIGURE 2   A Simplified Description of the Theory of Buyer Behavior

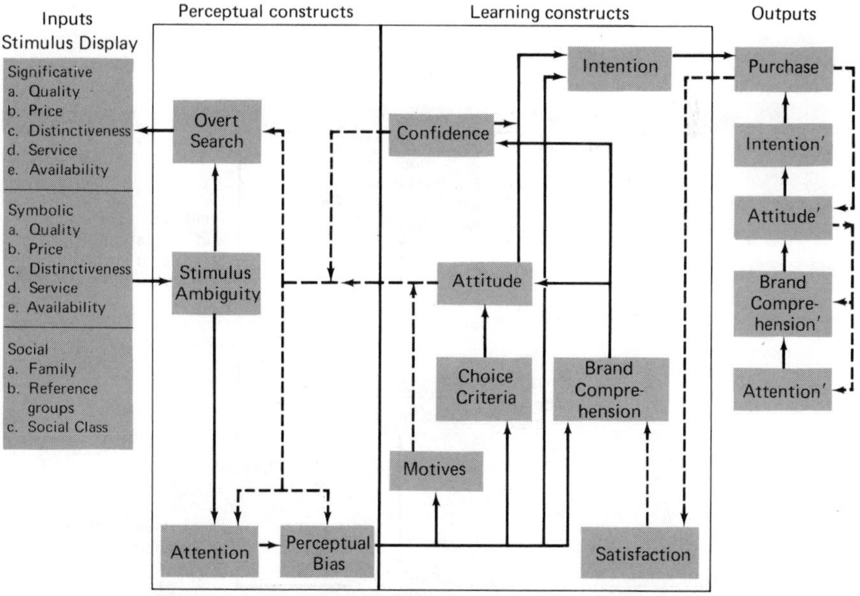

Solid lines indicate flow of information; dashed lines, feedback effects.

Source: Reprinted from John A. Howard and Jagdish N. Sheth, *The Theory of Buyer Behavior,* Copyright 1966, by permission of John Wiley & Sons, Inc. p. 30.

Figure 6 is a model of this theory. All elements of the model are printed in italics within this chapter, merely for clarity. The broken lines indicate feedback flows. An asterisk following a referenced study indicates its inclusion in this book. The remainder of this book takes up individual model elements within these primary divisions, in accordance with a scheme set forth at the close of this chapter.

EXOGENOUS VARIABLES

Institutional Environment

The *institutional environment* in which buyer behavior takes place is treated according to two primary classifications: *commercial* and *noncommercial institutions. Commercial institutions* include competing marketers, trade associations, and industry groups that provide a stream of information from what is termed *marketer-dominated information sources. Noncommercial institutions* include governmental agencies, consumer testing services, and the editorial content (nonadvertising content) of the mass media. Information from these noncommercial institutions is generally perceived as neutral, even though occasionally this is not true.

FIGURE 3   The Comprehensive Scheme: A Summary Flow Chart

Field one: From the Source of a Message to the Consumer's Attitude

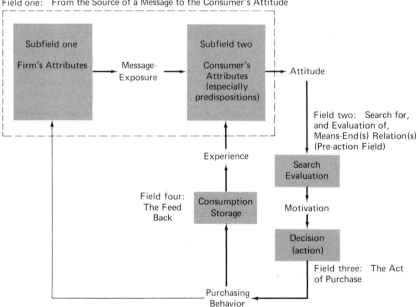

Source: Francesco M. Nicosia, *Consumer Decision Processes: Marketing and Advertising Implications,* © 1966. p. 156. Reprinted by permission of Prentice-Hall, Inc., Englewood Cliffs, N. J.

Societal Environment

The *societal environment* is divided into three elements: *time pressure, social-organizational setting,* and *culture. Time pressure* refers

FIGURE 4   Macro Flow Chart Example

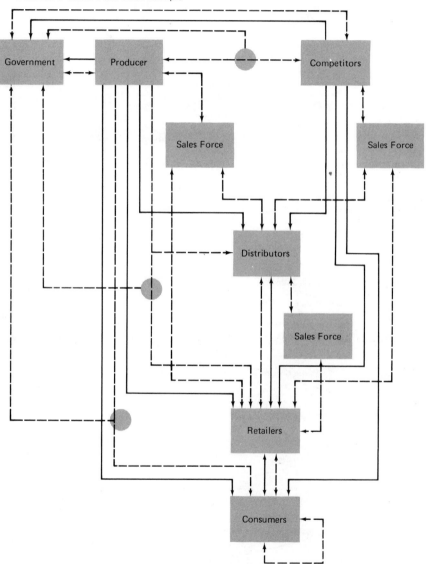

Source: Reprinted from *Computer Simulation of Competitive Market Response* by Arnold Amstutz by permission of the M.I.T. Press, Cambridge, Massachusetts. Copyright © 1967. p.17.

FIGURE 5   A Complete Model Showing Outcomes of the Purchasing Decision

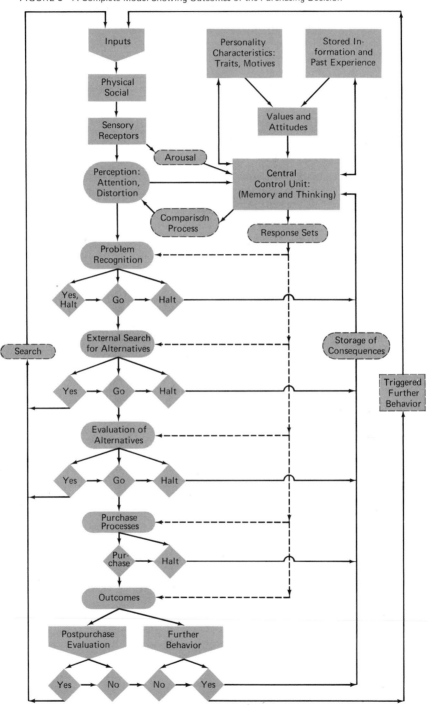

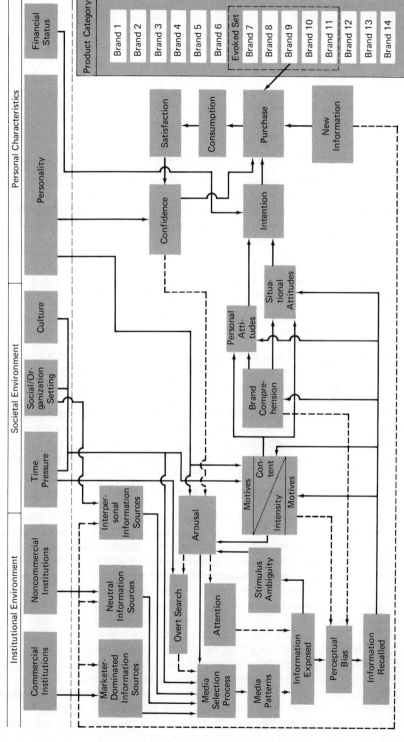

FIGURE 6   Theory of Buyer Behavior

to both the pace of life generally and the allotment of time given to the specific buying decision. Obviously, severe limitations on available time will affect the degree of information search and purchase deliberations generally. Since this theory is intended to apply for both consumer and industrial buyer behavior, the *societal environment* elements are intended to account for either context. Thus, *social-organizational setting* explicitly recognizes the interactions of societal norms and organizational constraints within either the organization of the family or the commercial enterprise. In a consumer context, differences in perception and behavior across social classes can be extreme, as Levy (1966)* documents. *Cultural* variations, both intranational and international can have a pronounced, although highly selective, impact on buyer behavior. Research by Bauer and Cunningham (1970) indicates that the impact of cultural variables on the behavior of blacks is largely a function of aspirations toward or away from finding a place within white middle-class America. Very recent work by Katona, Strumpel, and Zahn (1971) presents a fascinating contrast between consumer profiles in several Western countries. The article by Sommers and Kernan (1967)* examines some subtle differences between the cultures of the advanced English-speaking nations.

Personal Characteristics

Personal characteristics include *personality* and *financial status*. *Personality* is defined as an enduring disposition or quality of a person that accounts for his relative consistency in emotional, temperamental, and social behavior.

The application of *personality* characteristics in the study of buyer behavior has had an unfortunate history. Researchers have used personality tests freely without being critical of their measurement shortcomings, as discussed by Peterson (1965). Particularly in market segmentation, psychological or personality dimensions have been thrust into highly inappropriate and demanding roles, such that their potency as predictors of behavior has been found limited. These results should not have surprised researchers, even though they were often characterized in the literature as revelations. Personality characteristics should not be regarded as "direct" determinants of variations in behavior as is too commonly assumed, but rather as inputs to the cognitive process leading ultimately to behavior. As a result, selected personality measures will correlate with behavior in certain product categories and not in others. For example, contrast the findings of Frank, Massy, and Lodahl (1969)* with those of Sparks and Tucker (1971).* Even when personality characteristics do relate significantly with behavior, the proportion of variance explained is usually quite modest. While the authors take no firm position on which psychological characteristics are of greatest value in buyer behavior research, the following characteristics are mentioned only because of their frequent appearance in marketing literature and to more clearly indicate the types of enduring personality characteristics we have in mind: mental capacity, introversion-extroversion, venturesomeness, self-esteem (general self-confidence), dogmatism, and neuroticism. It should be pointed out that these dimensions have typically been derived in other behavioral disciplines. Their highly inappropriate customary application in marketing has led many researchers to call for the development of buyer behavior centered quasi-personality dimensions. So-called life style dimensions were developed as an outgrowth from this thinking. Life styles are not personality characteristics, however, since they are generally grounded in rather a specific situational environment of relatively short duration. An example of life style research is that by Wells and Tigert (1971).* Without doubt, rather narrowly defined life style dimensions have generally demonstrated greater predictive value when related directly to behavior. It should be noted, however, that if such life style dimensions are highly product category specific, they no longer carry the generality that is sought in constructing a theory of buyer behavior.

Financial status is the second form of *personal characteristic*, and is treated separately from *personality* for the obvious reason that it is neither a state of mind nor necessarily an enduring characteristic. Favorable or unfavorable *financial status* is determined relative to a proposed purchase (*intention*) and of course changes over time. The financial status of a buyer is a self-perception and would likely reflect an assessment not merely of current assets but also borrowing power.

INFORMATION-PROCESSING

The second division of the model concerns all elements of information-processing leading to *information recalled. Information sources* are considered in terms of the labels provided by Cox (1963). *Marketer-dominated information sources* originate from *commercial institutions* and are perceived by the buyer as informative though not necessarily unbiased. Thus, their greatest impact comes in generating awareness of product characteristics rather than being accepted as a source of unbiased evaluation. Bogart, Tolley, and Orenstein (1970)* provide evidence on the impact of even a single advertisement. A *neutral* information source is one that is generally perceived as unbiased. Of course, not all people will agree that a given source is neutral. *Inter-personal information sources* flow from the *social-organizational setting*. In the case of consumer behavior, this setting consists largely of family, friends, and acquaintances. Research by Berey and Pollay (1968), Davis (1970),* Myers (1966), Nicosia (1964),* and Ward and Wackman (1971) documents the potency of these influences. *Interpersonal information* can serve to create awareness and/or alter evaluative judgments. In industrial buying behavior there is the *social setting* that exists between fellow workers in joint purchase deliberations or between purchasing agent and salesman. There exists, however, the additional interpersonal information overlay that arises from the *organizational setting*. After all, a hierarchical structure exists that relates employees according to authority, thus the opinions of superiors are obviously perceived differently from those of peers.

Information from these two sources feeds into the *media selection process*, which can be regarded as a separate buying process determining the importance attached to each communication and thus each medium. One should bear in mind that the importance attached to a given communication or medium varies among persons, decisions, and situations.

We need to learn a great deal about how people process information. However, we do know that people look to different informational sources at each stage of their buyer deliberations. For example, physicians turn toward respected colleagues for appraising drugs of increasing perceived risk, rather than rely upon pharmaceutical salesmen whom they may esteem as friends (Bauer and Wortzel, 1966).* Similarly, Bucklin (1965) found that the likelihood of consumers consulting newspaper ads varied according to the type of purchase, existing knowledge, perceived risk, and other factors. *Time pressures* of the day or one's other obligations generally will affect the probability of exposure to media sources. If the decision must be made hurriedly, the time available for accidental or deliberate information exposure is commensurately reduced. Similarly, differences as to *social-organizational setting* as well as *culture* will affect the likelihood of exposure. For example, exposure to types of media varies by social class. Lower middle and lower classes devote greater attention to broadcast media, particularly passive involvement with television, than do upper middle and upper classes, who instead, in a relative sense, favor the written media. Also, the total exposure to informational sources varies directly with social class. Because of these variations the probability of exposure to a specific information source is similarly affected.

International *cultural* differences generate obvious differences in media patterns partly as a function of availability (e.g., lack of television) and differences in media quality. Intranational *cultural* variations interact with social class variables to also affect the media selection process. In the United States the exposure of certain minority groups to the print media, particularly newspapers, is far below the national average. The same is true for teenagers who, some parents would declare, constitute a separate culture. Over time, the exercise of this conscious or unconscious *media selection process* generates firm *media patterns*.

Exposure to a given information source, *information exposed*, results when *attention* is focused on the source. Prevailing *media patterns* determine the probability that a given source will fall within the scope of *attention*, as a result of accidental or deliberate means. *Attention* is thus defined as the degree of adjustment or "openness" of a sense receptor (e.g., eyes, ears) to a stimulus, relative to some optimal level for communication to the brain. Work by Krugman (1965, 1971), Hawkins (1970),* and Blackwell, Hensel, and Sternthal (1970)* examines aspects of how physiological states of receptors relate to stimulus reception. Note that *attention* is treated as a feedback mechanism. By feedback is meant an informational flow from one point in the model to a second point earlier in the total mental process, causing a recycling of that process or at least a recycling of a significant portion of the process. In effect, an oscillation is set up, which normally dampens toward an equilibrium position. In the case of *attention*, the state of receptors is caused by prior mental experience, thus it is a feedback flow.

As can be seen from the theory, *arousal* is determined by *personality* as a direct input, and *confidence* as a feedback input. This feedback, having an inverse effect, is crucially important because it enables the buyer to filter out information that is relevant to a brand but that he does not need because he is already well informed about it. *Personality* attributes, such as mental capacity, clearly affect the level of *arousal*. The role of *confidence* as the second determinant of *arousal* is discussed later.

If the buyer is in a relatively high state of *arousal* toward a problem, he may "conclude" that its solution will require more information than he currently has. We must be careful to remember, however, that most of these processes are largely unconscious. A high state of arousal triggers *overt search*, which refers to the deliberate search for new information that in turn flows into the long-term *media selection process* governing the information to which he is exposed. At the same time, *attention* is affected and his sensory receptors are more open; thus, when he is exposed to new information, he is more likely to perceive it. Either through accidental exposure or through *overt search*, the buyer may become aware of new information that will move him along on a motive-directed cognitive process leading to purchase. Survey work by Udell (1966) and experimental laboratory work by Green (1966) suggest that buyers are far from exhaustive in their information-seeking. Moreover, as the buyer accumulates experience, the amount of *overt search* before purchase tends to decrease, as learning theory would suggest (Bennett and Mandell, 1969).*

Information exposed does not directly become the *information recalled* and used in purchase deliberations. The buyer has the capability and does regularly alter his perception of information as to its meaning and importance for memory retention in the process of *perceptual bias. Information exposed* has two major characteristics, which Cox (1962b)* has labeled as "predictive value" and "confidence value." Information has predictive value to the degree it provides valid indicators or cues of relevant characteristics concerning a product or other object. However, predictive information may not be readily understood. Cox gives the example of a buyer attempting to decide which hi-fi stereo outfit to buy. The electronic specifications of each would provide highly predictive information were the buyer an electronics engineer and capable of evaluating them, but he isn't. So the buyer looks instead at the exterior finish and control knobs, something he can readily evaluate, and assumes the outfit's interior quality corresponds to its exterior. The exterior appointments thus furnish information cues of high confidence value.

Unfortunately, the predictive value aspect of information has not been well investigated; the confidence value, on the other hand, has under various rubrics a venerable history. We label it *stimulus ambiguity* and gather into it a number of important ideas and research approaches. First, it includes the physical aspects of a message, for example, static on radio broadcasts, snow on a television screen, and smudged printing in a newspaper. Second, it includes the meaning aspect of a message, for example, any vagueness or ambiguity concerning the intended meaning of words. Third, it includes source credibility aspects, as to how the particular source of a message alters its effects on an audience. Bauer (1965b)* discusses the evidence regarding source effect. Fourth, it includes such distinctions as "fantasy" versus "reality" in intended and perceived versions of a message.

Stimulus ambiguity affects *arousal* just as does any conflict in the buyer's mind, but the relationship is complex (Howard and Sheth, 1969). It perhaps should also be shown as a determinant of *perceptual bias* because to the extent that a message is ambiguous, it is likely to trigger a selective mechanism as contained in *perceptual bias*. The exact nature of this relationship is at the moment very unclear, and thus we omit it from the theory.

In the absence of accurate informational cues, which the buyer can judge with confidence, reliance may be placed on the brand name as an indicator of quality (Allison and Uhl, 1964;* Makens, 1965). Using price as an indicator of quality arises the same way (Jacoby, Olson, and Haddock, 1970; Gardner, 1971*).

The determinants of *perceptual bias* are two feedback flows from *motives* and *brand comprehension*, both of which are discussed later. The feedback of *motives* means, very simply, that "we see what is important for us and the rest tends to be filtered out." The effect of *motives* on *perceptual bias* is in terms of prior experience and is a process that extends throughout life. The impact of *motives* upon *perceptual bias* can thus be thought of as associative rather than discretely causal. *Personality* characteristics and influences from our *societal environment*, being determinants of *motives*, indirectly affect *perceptual bias*.

Information recalled is thus the resultant of *information exposed* after having passed through *perceptual bias*. This imperfect view of the world goes on to become an input to *motives, brand comprehension, personal attitudes*, and *situational attitudes*, all of which are next discussed.

MOTIVE-DIRECTED COGNITION LEADING TO PURCHASE SATISFACTION

Buyer behavior can best be understood as motive-directed behavior. However, motives are highly elusive and have not received the successful research attention that their importance would seem to dictate. *Motives* are derived from biogenic or psychogenic needs, wants, or desires of the buyer that are related, though not necessarily uniquely related, to buying and consuming a product class or category. We distinguish between two components of *motives*: *content* and *intensity*. *Content* refers to the goals toward which the buyer is striving and *intensity* refers to their relative importance or magnitude. This distinction is important in terms of how *motives* affect other model constructs: *arousal* and *personal* and *situational attitudes*.

First of all, *motives* reflect *personality* characteristics, both in terms of *content* and *intensity*. Notice that the arrow from *personality* to *motives* is drawn to the upper horizontal bar within the *motives* box, which indicates that it affects both *content* and *intensity*. Similarly, all elements of the *societal environment* affect both components of *motives*. *Information recalled* can affect both *intensity* and *content* of *motives*, or only the *content*. In the former case, the *information recalled* may be of a sort that not only heightens the *intensity* of a *motive* (e.g., need for achievement), but also indicates what constitutes meaningful achievement and its appropriate symbols (*content*). On the other hand, *information recalled* may not affect *intensity* of the *motive* but may merely suggest a new way for its appropriate satisfaction.

Nonevaluative elements of *information recalled* contribute to the buyer's *brand comprehension*, or his knowledge about the existence and characteristics of a set of brands within a category. *Brand comprehension* thus concerns the denotative meaning of a brand. It is particularly important, because to the extent that the buyer knows something about it, he has available the words to describe it in talking with others about how good it is, which in turn is a powerful determinant of his behavior.

It is known that the buyer generally focuses his primary attention on a small subgroup of brands within a product category, and many times is not even aware that other brands exist. The subset of brands can, of course, change over time as a result of accidental or deliberate information exposure. This subset of brands is referred to as the *evoked set* and has been shown to exist in research by Campbell (1969).* Notice that in Figure 6 *evoked set* is diagrammed as representing the subset of brands 7, 8, 9, 10, and 11 from within a product category. This is done to indicate that the buyer's ultimate purchase choice will be one of the five brands since those are the only ones that he considers.

Up to this point, we have not discussed the formation of preferences, or attitudes, toward brands. Remember that *brand comprehension* is strictly nonevaluative knowledge of brands, although some dimensions of a brand may be both descriptive and evaluative components. The model accounts for attitudes in terms of two sets of dimensions: *personal attitudes* and *situational attitudes*. As the term implies, *personal attitudes* are the preference evaluations of brands by the individual on each of several dimensions that in turn are weighted according to how much they are *valued* by the individual (not importance in the sense of prominence). It is perhaps worth emphasizing that "attitude" is a term whose existence in our vocabulary and whose definition is predicated on its usefulness for us in understanding human behavior (Bauer, 1966),* as is true for most of our constructs. In the discussion concerning attitudes and intention that follows, several simplifying assumptions are made. A few of these are given later.

Suppose that for judging automobiles, a buyer uses only three dimensions: prestige, speed, and value. Furthermore, let us assume that prestige is valued twice as much as either of the remaining two dimensions. If we imagine the buyer as allocating 100 points among the three dimensions, prestige would receive 50 points and speed and value each 25 points. Suppose his *evoked set* consists of brands 7, 8, 9, 10, and 11. If each dimension is scaled 0–10 in order of increasing favor, evaluations on each dimension might arise as indicated in Table 1. With value priorities attached to dimensions and evaluations attached to brands on each of the three dimensions, the relative preference among brands is determined by a multiplication process. In this hypothetical case, brand 10 is thus ranked first, and brand 11 ranked last.

So much for the *personal attitude* dimensions. What about *situational attitudes?* Suppose the same prospective buyer must consider his wife's opinions before making the purchase. Having discussed with her the proposed purchase, he knows something of her opinions toward automobiles and the automobile brands he has in his *evoked set*. Bear in mind it is his perceptions of those opinions that will count, even if they are partially in error. While he may not be aware of all the details as to why, his wife has tried to explain to him that she favors brand 9. The reasons why are depicted in Table 2. We see that she evaluates automobiles only as to their comfort and styling. Moreover, she values the first dimension with three times the importance of the second. Therefore, the priority values are shown as 75 and 25 respectively. The brand evaluations multiplied by the priorities yield an overall preference ranking with brand 9 coming out as her first choice.

Thus, the prospective automobile buyer must cope with two *situational attitudes* from his wife. In a moment of weakness, he has decided not to risk his wife's wrath and, in fact, decides to weight her overall preference score distribution equally with his. The results of this decision will be discussed later in Table 3, wherein his purchase *intention* probability distribution is derived.

The determinants of *personal attitudes* are *motive content, information recalled* as to evaluative or connotative information, and *brand comprehension*. That is, *motive content* largely determines the values attached to *personal attitude* dimensions, while connotative *information recalled*, along with denotative information from *brand comprehension* are processed to determine the evaluation of each brand on each attitude dimension. The same determinants hold true for *situational attitudes* except, of course, that different motives and items of information are involved.

In the case of industrial buying behavior, the buyer may have *personal attitudes* as to companies or salesmen with which he prefers to deal; however, he also has *situational attitudes*, such as obtaining the best value for his company, observing certain rules of professional ethics, and recognizing the opinions of his superiors in the organization (Wind, 1970).*

TABLE 1 Relative Preference Among Five Hypothetical Automobile Brands on Buyer's Three Personal Attitude Dimensions

Brand	Prestige			Speed			Value			Overall Preference	
	Evaluation	Priority	Preference Score	Evaluation	Priority	Preference Score	Evaluation	Priority	Preference Score	Score	Ranking
7	7	50	350	1	25	25	6	25	150	525	3
8	2	50	100	7	25	175	9	25	225	500	4
9	5	50	250	5	25	125	8	25	200	575	2
10	10	50	500	6	25	150	0	25	0	650	1
11	2	50	100	4	25	200	7	25	175	475	5

TABLE 2   Situational Attitudes from the Buyer's Wife

Brand	Comfort			Styling			Overall Preference	
	Evaluation	Priority	Preference Score	Evaluation	Priority	Preference Score	Score	Ranking
7	6	75	450	7	25	175	625	2
8	4	75	300	8	25	200	500	3
9	7	75	525	6	25	150	675	1
10	3	75	225	4	25	100	325	4
11	2	75	150	3	25	75	225	5

It must be remembered that buyer indifference toward which brand he buys may mean a very weak, nonpredictive attitude structure (Baber, 1968).*

The next link in the cognitive chain leading to purchase is *intention*. Intention refers to the likelihood of purchasing given brands, unless *new information* causes a deviation from his plan, including changes in his expected *financial status* that prevent him from acting upon his attitudes. Juster (1966) first suggested that a subjective probability assessment of buying intentions furnishes a superior measure, rather than merely asking someone which brand he will buy next. Gruber (1970), Ostlund (1969), and Stapel (1968)* have successfully employed scales similar to that by Juster. Thus, *intention* is conceptualized as the relative probability of purchase for brands within the *evoked set*. The probability measures are derived from the output of the *personal* and *situational attitudes*.

Table 3 continues the automobile example discussed earlier. The

TABLE 3   Intention: Relative Probability of Purchasing Specific Brands

Brand	Overall Preference Score		Total	Buyer's Intention Distribution
	Personal Attitudes (Buyer)	Situational Attitudes (Wife)		
7	525	625	1,150	.23*
8	500	500	1,000	.20
9	575	675	1,250	.25
10	650	325	975	.19
11	475	225	700	.13
Total Points			5,075	1.00

* Calculated: $\dfrac{1,150}{5,075} = .23$

overall preference scores from *personal* and *situational attitudes* are first combined. The point values in this case total 5,075. Brand 9 has the highest single point total (1,250) and its relative purchase probability becomes 1,250 divided by 5,075 or .25. Based solely upon this information, we would say that the most likely brand he will purchase is number 9. However, .25 is clearly much less than unity, thus another brand might ultimately be purchased.

What might cause such a deviation from plan? One or more of three factors, the first two of which are *new information* and *financial status*. Suppose that just prior to purchase he is exposed to *new information* of some form: a compelling advertisement for brand 7; a conversation with an irate current owner of a brand 9 automobile; or the latest issue of *Consumer Reports* containing a study on automobiles where brand 9 is given a low rating. Suddenly he has *new information* to digest, thus he must cycle through the entire information and motive-directed cognitive processes leading to a new *intention*. On the other hand, a suddenly depressed *financial* status might cause him to delay or terminate purchase deliberations, or settle for a cheaper brand.

A third factor enters into the question of whether his *intention* will be acted upon, and that is his *confidence*. As discussed earlier, *confidence* affects information-processing through *arousal*. It also has impact on whether or not the buyer will move from the final step in motive-directed cognition, *intention*, on to the behavioral step of *purchase*. Acting upon one's deliberations amounts to the hour of truth, and it is at that point where the buyer's *confidence* in his own ability to judge among alternatives is put to the test. It is often useful to think of *brand comprehension, personal attitudes,* and *confidence* as determining a brand concept.

Assuming that he confronts no new information which persuades him to alter his *intention*, that his financial status still allows it, and that his *confidence* is sufficiently positive, he becomes the proud owner of a brand 9 automobile. For his sake we hope it will outlast his car payments and his peers will think kindly of his decision.

The preceding discussion concerning *attitudes* and *intention* has occurred under an umbrella of several implicit simplifying assumptions, three of which are mentioned. First, it was assumed that attitudes are additive (prestige + speed + value). Second, it was assumed that evaluations on dimensions can be combined with value weightings of dimensions through simple multiplication of evaluations times weights in order to derive *intentions*. Third, it was assumed that the overall preference is derived from previously settled attitude dimensions, rather than vice versa. We recognize that these assumptions have not been found valid in all cases, but consider them sufficient and useful for purposes of simplifying the discussion of *attitudes* and *intentions*.

It should be remembered that unplanned or so-called impulse purchases can arise, particularly for relatively low-priced, frequently purchased products or for novelties. Much of this behavior is best regarded as simply deferred purchasing or purchasing for home inventory. That is, the buyer may decide that the next time it is convenient he will buy some razor blades. His home supply is reduced but not exhausted so there is no pressing need to make a special shopping trip. A few days later he happens by a display rack of razor blades near the check-out counter of a neighborhood supermarket, and suddenly remembers he should replenish his supply. For this reason, and others, a buyer frequently leaves a store with many more items than were on his shopping list (Kollat and Willett, 1967).*

Regardless of whether the eventual purchase is planned or unplanned, certain behaviors and mental processes occur at the point of purchase that are of interest. *New information* can be encountered from in-store advertising or from a salesman (Pennington, 1968).* Moreover, the physical location of a brand as to shelf position and size of display can affect the likelihood of noticing or even purchasing a brand (Frank and Massy, 1970).* Shopping can be a confusing experience, especially when it is difficult to judge the best value from several size-price combinations. Friedman (1966)* has advanced some measures of consumer confusion.

Consumption of the selected brand will furnish him with the next highly important source of information. His degree of *satisfaction* will be dependent upon how well the product performs in matching or exceeding expectations as contained in his *personal* and *situational attitudes*. For products such as automobiles, which involve a sizable financial or psychological commitment, a great deal of importance will be attached to the level of *satisfaction* obtained. In fact, if there is decided dissatisfaction, an entire chain of possible behaviors may be stimulated. Negative *satisfaction* or cognitive dissonance has been investigated in a series of buyer behavior studies since it was first conceptualized by Festinger (1957). Kassarjian and Cohen (1965)* submit evidence that cognitive dissonance apparently causes smokers to discredit the validity of studies claiming a causal linkage between lung cancer and cigarette smoking. Oshikawa (1969),* however, questions whether the theory of cognitive dissonance is valid in the natural market setting. Moreover, Hunt (1970)* attempted to test whether a marketer could make use of some management implications that have frequently been made from dissonance studies, and obtained negative results.

Should it happen that the product purchased fails to meet his expectations, the buyer may become uncertain as to his ability in selecting among brands within the specific product category, that is, his *confidence* in judging brands within that category may be shaken. His original level of *confidence* was a result, first of all, of his own *personality* characteristics, such as venturesomeness and general self-confidence, along with prior purchases within the product category, and the levels of satisfaction that resulted. Repeated disappointments from brands selected within a given product category, particularly if costly, will result in not only reduced *confidence* but also reduced future purchase incidence.

The *confidence* construct is essential to this buyer behavior theory (Howard, 1969).* Its validation is not complete, but some evidence of its existence has been generated. Atkinson (1964) summarized the *a priori* evidence regarding the relationship between *confidence* and *purchase* (pp. 274–276). From survey work relating intentions to purchases, Juster (1966) found that purchase was more likely among respondents who were highly confident in their expressed intention to make a consumer durable purchase. Moreover, Johnson (1968) found that buyer confidence in judging a brand increased the likelihood of purchase. The concept, specific self-confidence, as defined and investigated by Cox and Bauer (1964), Gergen and Bauer (1967), and Ostlund (see "Product Specific Self-Confidence Related to Buying Intentions," this volume), is highly similar to the *confidence* construct and furnishes additional support.

LEVELS OF PROBLEM-SOLVING

Discussion of the model thus far has been with respect to extensive problem-solving, in which the buyer does not have a firmly established attitude structure on individual brands. He must develop this in the process discussed earlier. In fact, he may not have the necessary attitude dimension for evaluating brands and, consequently, may lack a clearly defined category concept. For this reason, a great deal of learning must take place before his *brand comprehension, personal* and *situational attitudes,* and *confidence* are sufficiently well established to yield a purchase intention.

Genuine problem-solving of this nature is, however, relatively infrequent, as Katona (1953) has argued. Rather, past exposure to information concerning the product category, along with prior purchase decisions and levels of satisfaction, may well have generated a fairly unambiguous set of *personal* and *situational attitude* dimensions. He may seek information, primarily for *brand comprehension,* in order to complete an evaluation of brand alternatives. In any case, his search for additional information is far less exhaustive and he is said to be engaged in limited problem-solving.

With the passage of time, the buyer accumulates extensive information through the purchase of brands in a given product category, and thus the importance he attaches to the process diminishes. He may have found a brand that ideally suits his requirements. Instead, he may have concluded that all brands are pretty much alike and thus sticks to one brand simply from inertia, or switches brands frequently, based solely upon current price or availability. Under these circumstances, the information search is brief, the decision process swift, and the entire process is described as routinized response behavior. With an unambiguous set of *personal* and *situational attitude* dimensions, and with enough information within *brand comprehension,* the buyer sees no point in wasting his time on additional *overt search.* In fact, his *evoked set* may be decidedly reduced.

Therefore, purchase deliberation within a specific product category may at one point involve extensive problem-solving, but with additional experience may evolve to limited problem-solving. Some types of purchase decisions, being infrequent and/or involving large commitments (e.g., buying a home, a car, or a major appliance), may always involve extensive problem-solving. At the opposite end of the scale, routinized response behavior is characteristic of many, if not most, packaged goods purchases. The buyer may, however, feel that over time he has gotten into a rut, always buying the same brand, never experimenting to find something better. In an effort to break out of such monotony, he may engage in the psychology of complication, where he deliberately engages in *overt search* in order to open up the breadth of his *evoked set* and consider new alternatives. More common, of course, is the opposite mode of behavior, the psychology of simplification, where through repeated purchases and increased product knowledge, *personal* and *situational attitude* dimensions crystallize, *brand comprehension* is high, and, in the interest of time economy, the buyer lapses into routinized response behavior.

OPERATIONAL MEASURES

While a theory can be useful only if suitable operational measures of its elements exist, it should be recognized that at this stage in our knowledge securing these measures might better be regarded as a goal rather than an accomplishment. Nevertheless, we feel that it is important to indicate how we would state the measures of each model construct at this point in time.

Let us begin by returning to the three information sources: *marketer-dominated, neutral,* and *interpersonal.* Ideally the measurement of these sources would take the form of an "informational audit" of all information to which the buyer could possibly be exposed. While a reasonable job of this can be done for the *marketer-dominated information sources* through obtaining reprints of ads and scripts from the broadcast media together with the schedules for each, the other two information sources offer far greater difficulty. An audit of *neutral information sources* poses the primary difficulty of deciding what information sources are generally perceived as neutral. Moreover, since such sources can take very diverse forms, an audit might be impractical in a given case. However, interviews of buyers could at least inquire as to their recalled exposure to such sources regarding a given topic, and more specifically, whether they regularly read certain consumer testing publications, or for that matter, did they read a given issue of such a publication. Even greater difficulty is encountered when contemplating an adequate auditing process of *interpersonal information sources.* In commenting upon the importance of word-of-mouth communication in determining the fate of new products, several writers have suggested that this communication process be monitored (Bauer, 1965a; King, 1965; Lazer and Bell, 1966; and others). No one, however, has stated how this could be done without destroying or severely distorting the ongoing flow. When interpersonal communication takes place within the family, an audit or monitoring scheme is clearly unworkable. A remaining, though highly artificial approach, would be to simply ask people whether they have discussed with family or friends a given purchase question or set of brands. Projective techniques such as sentence completion or fill-in-the-dialogue cartoon strips could be used to probe for what interpersonal communication people might expect to take place if a product-centered conversation were initiated. This would, of course, be a highly imperfect surrogate measure of content from genuine product-centered conversation.

The *media selection process,* it too a "buying" process, is a function of the three informational sources just discussed, the *societal environment, overt search,* and *arousal.* We do not purport to understand the *media selection process,* but only suggest that it does go on and its output remains its only measurement: *media patterns,* that is, the relative importance attached to each medium at a given point in time as it affects a specific decision within buyer behavior. Remember that all media, even opinions from friends and family, are subjected to the media buying process, not just the mass media. The measurement of *media patterns* could be accomplished by use of simple bi-polar importance evaluation scales applied to each medium.

Information exposed poses severe measurement difficulties. It is a function of *media patterns* and *attention.* However, Krugman (1965) and others have discussed the low levels of audience involvement that exist for certain media, particularly television. The result is that while learning can take place, it is a very slow additive process that does not lend itself to ordinary measures of conscious recognition or noting. At the same time, the perceptual process is clearly not subliminal. We pose no answers for this difficulty but instead conclude that for the moment, *information exposed* must simply be deduced from an examination of the *media patterns*.

Perceptual bias poses another difficult measurement area. Recall that it is a process involving forms of perceptual distortion. Within laboratory conditions, these forms can be separately manipulated and measured. This, however, cannot usually be accomplished under field conditions, which for buyer behavior research is far more important. While it is generally conceded that a good deal of perceptual distortion goes on in the minds of humans, the process and the conditions under which it occurs are not fully understood. We do know, however, that *motives*, as they reflect one's self-concept and *personality*, can seriously alter what humans claim they see, and remember. Moreover, their degree of current knowledge (*brand comprehension*) determines what *information exposed* is regarded as new and thus perhaps added to *information recalled*. While the process of *perceptual bias* cannot itself be measured, an input-output comparison can be made in certain cases in terms of comparing known *information exposed* to *information recalled*. While this is still inadequate, it is the best we can currently suggest.

The next equally troublesome model element is that of *motives*. The *intensity* of *motives* can be assessed in terms of the importance people attach to the attainment of specific goals. Moreover, the *content* of *motives* can be assessed by a variety of techniques, such as depth interviewing or clinical analysis, but the validity and reliability of these techniques are open to question. All the more complex is the origin of *motives*. The model suggests that *motives* are a function of *societal environment*, *personality*, and *information recalled*. As observed earlier, the impact of *motives* on other mental constructs extends over a lifetime in an associative sense, and is not generally subject to abrupt directional changes. The same is true for the origin of *motives*, in that their *content* and *intensity* evolve over time.

The next model elements with two or more determinants are those of *personal* and *situational attitudes*. *Motive content*, *information recalled*, and *brand comprehension* are thought to determine these attitude dimensions. The separate roles of these several determinants related to attitude formation cannot be stated in a way that would apply generally. However, output measures of the attitude constructs themselves can be made. In fact, the earlier discussion that centered around Tables 1–3 indicated that the attitude constructs have been deliberately conceptualized in a manner that facilitates their measurement. Pragmatism such as this is essential, owing to the vital importance of *attitude* and *intention* measures in predicting behavior. The measurement of the two attitude constructs is thus in terms of output measures on weighted 0–10 brand evaluation scales.

The determinants of *intention* are, of course, *personal* and *situational attitudes*. Buying intentions have been measured by a variety of scales in the past. As mentioned earlier, it has been demonstrated by Juster

(1966), Gruber (1970), and Stapel (1968)* that a subjective probability scale (0–100) is generally a superior predictor of behavior, relative to asking the simple question: "Which brand will you buy next?" For this reason, the relative purchase probability measure, discussed earlier in connection with Table 3, becomes an appropriate measure of *intention*.

The *evoked set* can readily be measured by a simple question asking the buyer to list those brands within a product category that he would consider buying.

Satisfaction arises from the experience of consumption, against the background of expectations embodied in the *attitude* constructs. Its measurement can be accomplished by questions such as, "How satisfied were you with the brand of coffee you used last time?" with a response in terms of a scale such as "completely satisfied, mostly satisfied, slightly satisfied, slightly dissatisfied, mostly dissatisfied, completely dissatisfied." Note that this is not a measure of brand awareness.

Confidence, one's perceived ability to judge product alternatives within a category, is thought to be a function of the *information* he has received about the brand including his *satisfaction* from buying and consuming it, and *personality*, particularly self-esteem.

Confidence has been measured by Cox (1962b),* Arndt (1966), Barach (1967), and Ostlund (see "Product Specific Self-Confidence Related to Buying Intentions," this volume) in terms of rather direct questions such as, "How confident are you in judging Brand A?" While it is recognized that for certain products of high psychological content, a direct question of this sort could be very misleading, for most product categories relatively direct questions are perhaps satisfactory.

Arousal is a function of *personality, confidence,* the *intensity* of *motives,* and *stimulus ambiguity.* Stimulus ambiguity should be broadly treated to include physical ambiguity as well as the credibility of the message such as might come about because of an untrusted or incompetent source. *Arousal* plays a central role in regulating the inflow of information and in giving impetus to or energizing overt behavior, such as *purchase.* One aspect of its regulating information flows is to influence *attention.*

Overt search is determined by *arousal* and *time pressure.* It refers to the deliberate search for new information. Its measurement can be conducted in terms of direct questions concerning how much effort the buyer has made in seeking information before purchase in a given product category. Examples of such effort would be the number of stores shopped at or the number of people talked to in seeking information prior to making a given purchase.

CHAPTERS THAT FOLLOW

The remaining chapters of this book are intended to provide a sampling of the empirical foundations for a theory of buyer behavior. The selection of these readings is governed by our interest in indicating both what is and is not known concerning constructs of the model.

Chapters 2 through 15 are organized to conform with the theory already discussed. These chapters are: Culture, Social Class, and Life Style; Personality and Motivation; Marketer-Dominated Information Sources; Interpersonal Information Sources; Arousal and Attention; Overt Search and the Media Selection Process; Stimulus Ambiguity and Perceptual Bias; Brand Comprehension and Evoked Set; Attitudes; Intention: Planned Purchases; Unplanned Purchases; Behavior and Cognition During Purchase; Satisfaction and After Purchase Effects; and Confidence. The three remaining chapters, 16, 17, and 18, concern Purchase Patterns; Diffusion; and Buyer Behavior and Public Policy.

Purchase patterns refers to the regularity or relative frequency of the brands purchased by a buyer, substantially different from random order. Most of the research centered on purchase patterns has used the term "brand loyalty." The choice of this term is most unfortunate for it suggests that the explanation for consistent purchase patterns is buyer conviction of a given brand's superiority. Several alternative explanations have been found, such as local distribution patterns and buyer indifference or inertia, which often are more accurate. Nevertheless, the degree of regularity that has been uncovered is in itself interesting for it relates to the question of under what conditions one can expect limited problem-solving or, more particularly, routinized response behavior.

Research on the diffusion of innovations, long a major school of investigation in branches of sociology, has, within the past ten years, also become an important area of study within buyer behavior. The diffusion process can in a sense be regarded as a dynamic view of buyer behavior. That is, the adoption or rejection of an innovation by an initial small group of buyers propagates to affect the adoption or rejection likelihood of later buying groups and, in the process, generates an S-shaped cumulative adoption curve. Chapter 17 begins with a reading in which the principal areas of investigation within diffusion literature are related to elements of the buyer behavior model presented here. It is hoped that this effort will be a first step in stimulating "cross-pollenization" between the two areas of study.

With the increased interest in the study of "consumerism" issues, the need for developing and applying buyer behavioral theory to such public policy issues is pressing. In this connection, a final paper by the editors is included as an indication of how this effort might be structured.

REFERENCES

ALLISON, RALPH I. AND KENNETH P. UHL. "Influence of Beer Brand Identification on Taste Perception." *Journal of Marketing Research,* Vol. 1 (August 1964), 36–39.

AMSTUTZ, ARNOLD E. *Computer Simulation of Competitive Market Response.* Cambridge, Mass.: M.I.T. Press, 1967.

ANGELL, FRANK J. "Some Effects of the Truth-in-Lending Legislation." *Journal of Business,* Vol. 44 (January 1971), 78–85.

ARNDT, JOHAN. "Word of Mouth Advertising: The Role of Product Related Conversations to the Diffusion of a New Food Product." Unpublished Ph.D. dissertation, Graduate School of Business Administration, Harvard University, 1966.

ASSAEL, HENRY AND GEORGE S. DAY. "Attitudes and Awareness as Predictors of Market Share." *Journal of Advertising Research,* Vol. 8 (December 1968), 3–10.

ATKINSON, JOHN W. *An Introduction to Motivation.* New York: Van Nostrand, 1964, pp. 274–276.

BABER, CECIL. "If You Think I Care, You've Got Another Thing Coming." In *Attitude Research on the Rocks,* edited by Lee Adler and Irving Crespi, pp. 232–239. Chicago: American Marketing Association, 1968.

BARACH, JEFFREY A. "Self-Confidence and Reactions to Television Commercials." In *Risk Taking and Information Handling in Consumer Behavior,* edited by Donald F. Cox, pp. 428–441. Cambridge, Mass.: Harvard Business School, 1967.

BAUER, RAYMOND A. "Word of Mouth Communication in Marketing." Working paper, Harvard University, 1965a.

———. "A Revised Model of Source Effect." Presidential Address of the Division of Consumer Psychology, American Psychological Association Annual Meeting, Chicago, September, 1965b.

———. "Attitudes, Verbal Behavior, and Other Behavior." In *Attitude Research at Sea,* edited by Lee Adler and Irving Crespi, pp. 3–14. Chicago: American Marketing Association, 1966.

——— AND SCOTT M. CUNNINGHAM. "The Negro Market." *Journal of Advertising Research,* Vol. 10 (April 1970), 3–13.

BAUER, RAYMOND A. AND LAWRENCE H. WORTZEL. "Doctor's Choice: The Physician and His Sources of Information About Drugs." *Journal of Marketing Research,* Vol. 3 (February 1966), 40–47.

BENNETT, PETER D. AND ROBERT M. MANDELL. "Prepurchase Information Seeking Behavior of New Car Purchasers—The Learning Hypothesis." *Journal of Marketing Research,* Vol. 6 (November 1969), 430–433.

BEREY, LEWIS A. AND RICHARD W. POLLAY. "The Influencing Role of the Child in Family Decision-Making." *Journal of Marketing Research,* Vol. 5 (February 1968), 70–72.

BIRD, M. AND A. S. C. EHRENBERG. "Intentions to Buy and Claimed Brand Usage." *Operations Research Quarterly,* Vol. 17 (1966), 27–46.

BLACKWELL, ROGER D., JAMES S. HENSEL, AND BRIAN STERNTHAL. "Pupil Dilation: What Does It Measure?" *Journal of Advertising Research,* Vol. 10 (August 1970), 15–18.

BOGART, LEO, B. STUART TOLLEY, AND FRANK ORENSTEIN. "What One Little Ad Can Do." *Journal of Advertising Research,* Vol. 10 (August 1970), 3–13.

BUCKLIN, LOUIS P. "The Informational Role of Advertising." *Journal of Advertising Research,* Vol. 5 (September 1965), 11–15.

CAMPBELL, BRIAN MILTON. "The Existence of Evoked Set and Determinants of Its Magnitude in Brand Choice Behavior." Unpublished Ph.D. dissertation, Columbia University, 1969. (The abstract appears in this volume.)

CARMAN, JAMES M. "Correlates of Brand Loyalty: Some Positive Results." *Journal of Marketing Research,* Vol. 7 (February 1970), 67–76.

COX, DONALD F. "Information and Uncertainty: Their Effects on Consumers Product Evaluations." Unpublished Ph.D. dissertation, Cambridge, Mass.: Harvard Business School, 1962a.

———. "The Measurement of Information Value: A Study in Consumer Decision-Making." In *Proceedings of the American Marketing Association,* edited by William S. Decker (Fall 1962b), pp. 413–421.

————. "The Audience as Communicators." *Proceedings of the American Marketing Association,* edited by Stephen Greyser (Winter 1963), 58–72.

————, ed. *Risk Taking and Information Handling in Consumer Behavior.* Cambridge, Mass.: Harvard Business School, 1967.

———— AND RAYMOND A. BAUER. "Self-Confidence and Persuasibility in Women." *Public Opinion Quarterly* (Fall 1964), 453–466.

DAVIS, HARRY L. "Dimensions of Marital Roles in Consumer Decision Making." *Journal of Marketing Research,* Vol. 7 (May 1970), 168–177.

DOEHLERT, DAVID H. "Similarity and Preference Mapping: A Color Example." In *Marketing and the New Science of Planning,* edited by Robert L. King, pp. 250–258. Chicago: American Marketing Association, 1968.

DOLICH, IRA J. "Congruence Relationships Between Self Images and Product Brands." *Journal of Marketing Research,* Vol. 6 (February 1969), 80–84.

ENGEL, JAMES E., DAVID T. KOLLAT, AND ROGER D. BLACKWELL. *Consumer Behavior.* New York: Holt, Rinehart and Winston, 1968.

EVANS, FRANKLIN B. "Ford Versus Chevrolet: Park Forest Revisited." *Journal of Business,* Vol. 41 (1968), 445–459.

FARLEY, JOHN U. "Why Does 'Brand Loyalty' Vary Over Products?" *Journal of Marketing Research,* Vol. 1 (November 1964), 9–14.

———— AND L. WINSTON RING. "An Empirical Test of the Howard-Sheth Model of Buyer Behavior." *Journal of Marketing Research,* Vol. 7 (November 1970), 427–438.

FESTINGER, LEON. *A Theory of Cognitive Dissonance.* Stanford, Calif.: Stanford University Press, 1957.

FRANK, RONALD E. AND WILLIAM F. MASSY. "Shelf Position and Space Effects on Sales." *Journal of Marketing Research,* Vol. 7 (February 1970), 15–24.

————, AND THOMAS M. LODAHL. "Purchasing Behavior and Personal Attributes." *Journal of Advertising Research,* Vol. 9 (December 1969), 15–24.

FRIEDMAN, MONROE PETER. "Truth in Packaging in an American Supermarket." Part 1, *Fair Packaging and Labeling,* Hearings before the Committee on Interstate and Foreign Commerce, House of Representatives, Eighty-ninth Congress. Washington, D.C.: U.S. Government Printing Office (Serial No. 89–44), 1966, pp. 154–160.

GARDNER, DAVID M. "Is There a Generalized Price-Quality Relationship?" *Journal of Marketing Research,* Vol. 8 (May 1971), 241–243.

GERGEN, KENNETH J. AND RAYMOND A. BAUER. "The Interactive Effects of Self-Esteem and Task Difficulty on Social Conformity." In *Risk Taking and Information Handling in Consumer Behavior,* edited by Donald F. Cox, pp. 411–427. Cambridge, Mass.: Harvard Business School, Division of Research, 1967.

GRANBOIS, DONALD H. AND RONALD P. WILLETT. "An Empirical Test of Probabilistic Intentions and Preference Models for Consumer Durables Purchases." In *Marketing and the New Science of Planning,* edited by Robert L. King, pp. 401–408. Chicago: Proceedings of the Fall 1968 Conference, American Marketing Association.

GREEN, PAUL E. "Consumer Use of Information." In *On Knowing the Consumer,* edited by Joseph Newman, pp. 67–80. New York: Wiley, 1966.

GRUBER, ALIN. "Purchase Intent and Purchase Probability." *Journal of Advertising Research,* Vol. 10 (February 1970), 23–27.

HALL, EDWARD T. *The Silent Language.* Garden City, N.Y.: Doubleday, 1959.

HAWKINS, DEL. "The Effects of Subliminal Stimulation on Drive Level and Brand Preference." *Journal of Marketing Research,* Vol. 7 (August 1970), 322–326.

HOWARD, JOHN A. *Marketing Management: Analysis and Planning.* Rev. ed. Homewood, Ill.: Irwin, 1963.

————. *Marketing Theory.* Boston: Allyn & Bacon, 1965.

————. "Confidence as a Validated Construct." Paper presented before Third Annual Conference on Buyer Behavior, Graduate School of Business, Columbia University, May 22–23, 1969.

———— AND JAGDISH N. SHETH. *The Theory of Buyer Behavior.* New York: Wiley, 1969.

HULL, CLARK L. *Principles of Behavior.* New York: Appleton-Century, 1943.

————. *A Behavior System.* New Haven: Yale University Press, 1952.

HUNT, SHELBY D. "Post-transaction Communications and Dissonance Reduction." *Journal of Marketing,* Vol. 34 (July 1970), 46–51.

JACOBY, JACOB, JERRY C. OLSON, AND RAFAEL A. HADDOCK. "Price, Brand Name, and Product Composition Characteristics as Determinants of Perceived Quality." Purdue University Papers in *Consumer Psychology,* No. 3, 1970.

JOHNSON, ROBERT P. "Study of Intentions vs. Behavior." Unpublished manuscript, Graduate School of Business, Columbia University, 1968.

JUSTER, F. THOMAS. "Consumer Buying Intentions and Purchase Probability: An Experiment in Survey Design." *Journal of the American Statistical Association,* Vol. 61 (September 1966), 658–696.

KASSARJIAN, HAROLD H. AND JOEL B. COHEN. "Cognitive Dissonance and Consumer Behavior." *California Management Review,* Vol. 8 (1965), 55–64.

KATONA, GEORGE. "Rational and Economic Behavior." *Psychological Review,* Vol. 60 (September 1953), 307–318.

————, BURKHARD STRUMPEL, AND ERNEST ZAHN. "Profiles of Consumer Cultures." In *Aspirations and Affluence,* pp. 167–186. New York: McGraw-Hill, 1971.

KATZ, DANIEL. "The Functional Approach to the Study of Attitudes." *Public Opinion Quarterly,* Vol. 24 (1960), 163–204.

KING, CHARLES W. "Communicating with the Innovator in the Fashion Adoption Process." *Proceedings of the Fall 1965 Educators' Conference of the American Marketing Association,* pp. 425–439.

KOLLAT, DAVID T. AND RONALD P. WILLETT. "Customer Impulse Purchasing Behavior." *Journal of Marketing Research,* Vol. 4 (February 1967), 21–31.

KRUGMAN, HERBERT E. "The Impact of Television Advertising: Learning Without Involvement." *Public Opinion Quarterly* (Fall 1965), 349–356.

————. "Brain Wave Measures of Media Involvement." *Journal of Advertising Research,* Vol. 11 (February 1971), 3–9.

LAZER, WILLIAM AND WILLIAM E. BELL. "The Communication Process and Innovation." *Journal of Advertising Research,* Vol. 6 (September 1966), 2–7.

LEVY, SIDNEY J. "Social Class and Consumer Behavior." In *On Knowing the Consumer,* edited by Joseph Newman, pp. 146–160. New York: Wiley, 1966.

MAKENS, JAMES C. "Effect of Brand Preference Upon Consumers' Perceived Taste of Turkey Meat." *Journal of Applied Psychology,* Vol. 49 (1965), 261–263.

MYERS, JAMES C. "Patterns of Interpersonal Influence in the Adoption of New Products." In *Science, Technology and Marketing,* edited by Raymond M. Haas, pp. 750–757. Chicago: Proceedings of the 1966 Fall Conference of the American Marketing Association.

NICOSIA, FRANCESCO M. "Opinion Leadership and the Flow of Communication: Some Problems and Prospects." In *Reflections on Progress in Marketing,* edited by L. George Smith, pp. 340–358. Chicago: Proceedings of the American Marketing Association, 1964.

————. *Consumer Decision Processes: Marketing and Advertising Implications.* Englewood Cliffs, N.J.: Prentice-Hall, 1966.

OSHIKAWA, SADAOMI. "Can Cognitive Dissonance Theory Explain Consumer Behavior?" *Journal of Marketing,* Vol. 33 (October 1969), 44–49.

OSTLUND, LYMAN E. "Product Perceptions and Predispositional Factors as Determinants of Innovative Behavior." Unpublished Ph.d. dissertation, Harvard University, 1969.

————. "Predictors of Innovative Behavior." A revision of a paper presented at the Annual Conference of the Association of Consumer Research, University of Massachusetts, Amherst, August 30, 1970.

————. "Identifying Early Buyers." *Journal of Advertising Research,* Vol. 12 (April 1972), 25–30.

OZANNE, URBAN B. AND GILBERT A. CHURCHILL. "Adoption Research: Information Sources in the Industrial Purchasing Decision." In *Marketing and the New Science of Planning,* edited by Robert L. King, pp. 352–359. Chicago: Proceedings of the Fall 1968 Conference, American Marketing Association.

PENNINGTON, ALLAN L. "Customer-Salesman Bargaining Behavior in Retail Transactions." *Journal of Marketing Research,* Vol. 5 (August 1968), 255–262.

PETERSON, DONALD R. "Scope and Generality of Verbally Defined Personality Factors." *Psychological Review,* Vol. 72 (1965), 48–59.

ROBERTSON, THOMAS S. AND JAMES N. KENNEDY. "Prediction of Consumer Innovators: Application of Multiple Discriminant Analysis." *Journal of Marketing Research,* Vol. 5 (February 1968), 64–69.

ROTHMAN, JAMES. "Formulation of an Index of Propensity to Buy." *Journal of Marketing Research,* Vol. 1 (May 1964), 21–25.

SHAFFER, JAMES DUNCAN. "The Influence of 'Impulse Buying' or In-the-Store Decisions on Consumers' Food Purchases." *Journal of Farm Economics* (May 1960), 317–324.

SOMMERS, MONTROSE AND JEROME KERNAN. "Why Products Flourish Here, Fizzle There." *Columbia Journal of World Business,* Vol. 11 (1967), 89–97.

SPARKS, DAVID L. AND W. T. TUCKER. "A Multivariate Analysis of Personality and Product Use." *Journal of Marketing Research,* Vol. 8 (February 1971), 67–70.

STAPEL, JAN. "Predictive Attitudes." In *Attitude Research on the Rocks,* edited by Lee Adler and Irving Crespi, pp. 96–115. Chicago: American Marketing Association, 1968.

TUCKER, W. T. "The Development of Brand Loyalty." *Journal of Marketing Research,* Vol. 3 (August 1964), 32–35.

UDELL, JON G. "Prepurchase Behavior of Buyers of Small Electrical Appliances." *Journal of Marketing,* Vol. 30 (October 1966), 50–52.

WARD, SCOTT AND DANIEL B. WACKMAN. "Television Advertising and Intra-Family Influence: Children's Purchase Influence Attempts and Parental Yielding." In *Effects of Television on Children and Adolescents.* Cambridge, Mass.: Marketing Science Institute, July, 1971.

WEBSTER, FREDERICK E. AND FREDERICK VON PECHMANN. "A Replication of the 'Shopping List' Study." *Journal of Marketing,* Vol. 34 (April 1970), 61–63.

WELLS, WILLIAM D. AND DOUGLAS J. TIGERT. "Activities, Interests and Opinions." *Journal of Advertising Research,* Vol. 11 (August 1971), 27–35.

WILDING, JOHN AND RAYMOND A. BAUER. "Consumer Goals and Reactions to a Communication Source." *Journal of Marketing Research,* Vol. 5 (February 1968), 73–77.

WIND, YORAM. "Integrating Attitude Measures in a Study of Industrial Buying Behavior." In *Attitude Research on the Rocks,* edited by Lee Adler and Irving Crespi, pp. 58–77. Chicago: American Marketing Association, 1968.

————. "Industrial Source Loyalty." *Journal of Marketing Research,* Vol. 7 (November 1970), 450–457.

Exogenous Variables

2

2 CULTURE, SOCIAL CLASS, AND LIFE STYLE

We open our examination of empirical foundations in buyer behavior by focusing attention on exogenous variables. The first of these variables are culture, social class, and life style. Culture can be thought of as the dominant primary norms of learned behavior developed, shared, and transmitted among members of a particular society. Within a country that includes a relatively heterogeneous population, such as the United States, subcultures exist distinguished not only by certain obvious differences of language, religion, or skin color, but also by certain life styles or patterns of behavior. Figuratively speaking, whereas the United States has been referred to as the "great melting pot," it might more accurately be referred to as the "great casserole." That is, subcultures still abound, each of which is relatively consistent internally, within a total loosely defined American culture. Thus it is of interest to examine two kinds of cultural differences, intranational and international, as they affect buyer behavior.

Within any culture, there will evolve in time differences in social status or social class, even in so-called classless societies. These differences tend to reflect the dominant values of the culture, its goals, and the importance attached to various skills or contributions. It is far more difficult to adequately describe social class differences than it is to merely document the existence of the social class structure.

In buyer behavior theory, *culture* and *social/organizational setting* are said to affect the *media selection process* and *motives*. That is, these exogenous variables will in part determine the importance attached to different sources of information, and thus *information exposed*, and the goals toward which the buyer will shape his purchase decisions. In addition, since the *social/organizational setting* provides the *interpersonal information sources*, this variable provides a portion of the informational input to the *media selection process*.

Anthropologists have long provided fascinating contrasts of cultures throughout the world, both present and past. But differences between primitive and advanced cultures are obvious and of little real practical benefit to the marketer. It is of more interest to contrast the subtle but important differences in culture among basically similar advanced countries. The article by Sommers and Kernan (1967)* provides an excellent example of such analysis for America, Great Britain, Canada, and Australia. The differences examined clearly suggest their impact on motives and consequently on buying behavior.

Several approaches have been taken to the measurement of social class in the United States (Engel, Kollat, and Blackwell, 1968, pp. 274–283). For example, the well-known Warner system of classification relies on four indicators: occupation, source of income, residential area, and type of dwelling (Warner, Meeker, and Eells, 1960). It is important to understand, however, that Americans typically tend to classify themselves somewhere within the middle class even if they fall into the upper or lower extremes according to the Warner system. Centers (1949) allowed respondents to classify themselves according to one of four groups: upper class, middle class, lower class, or working class. Three percent of the population identified with the upper class, 43 percent with the middle class, 51 percent with the working class, and only 1 percent with the lower class.

Variations in life style, attitudes, values, self-perception, and behavioral patterns are related to social class distinctions as discussed by Levy (1966).* These effects are, however, consequences of the impact of social class on *interpersonal information sources*, the *media selection process*, and *motives* both with respect to *content* and *intensity*. But it should be understood that in a given instance, it may not be obvious whether a behavioral variation is due exclusively to a cultural factor or social class or a combination of both. There is obviously interaction between these two exogenous variables such that their separate effects cannot always be isolated. Moreover, as is true with the exogenous variable *personality*, one should not expect that variations in cognition or behavior due to social class or culture will be apparent in all product categories. Nevertheless, where variations are present, they are often of great magnitude.

Recently, growing attention has been focused on so-called life styles. Unfortunately, a consistent definition and operational measures of this concept do not currently exist. Although some might argue that life style measures should be used in marketing studies instead of personality measures, the two are certainly not identical concepts. Life style usually refers to a description of one's current opinions, activities, or interests as relevant to a given research interest, such as the study of automobile owners. Such personal characteristics reflect both personality and situational variables. *Personality*, on the other hand, should be viewed as a more basic, enduring set of psychological characteristics relatively independent of situational variables or particular research interest. Life style measures therefore reflect cultural and social class differences, and it is because of this that the concept is included within this chapter by means of the Wells and Tigert (1971)* article.

REFERENCES

1. CENTERS, RICHARD C. *The Psychology of Social Classes.* Princeton, N.J.: Princeton University Press, 1949.
2. ENGEL, JAMES, DAVID KOLLAT, AND ROGER BLACKWELL. *Consumer Behavior.* New York: Holt, Rinehart and Winston, 1968, pp. 274–283.
3. WARNER, W. LLOYD, MARCHIA MEEKER, AND KENNETH EELLS. *Social Class in America.* New York: Harper & Row, 1960.

2. Why products flourish here, fizzle there
montrose sommers & jerome kernan

Of the many forces that bear on buying decisions culture is perhaps the one most often taken for granted. Cultural values typically come in dead last in the parade of exhortations about economic variables, social class, buyers' psyches, and so on. This attitude probably stems from a common misconception regarding the relevance of culture to marketing, the consequence of which is almost always lost sales opportunities.

New products succeed; old products maintain entrenched market positions; promotional campaigns for diet foods, soft drinks, or kitchen appliances stand or fall in direct relation to how well marketers create products and product information which are meaningful and persuasive in the eyes of those who comprise markets. While it can always be said that consumers are individuals with different needs, motivations, or desires, it is also axiomatic that individuals within a culture generally rely on basic hard-core values for all types of decisions—those dealing with consumption as well as others.

This common core of values is reflected in this country in "the American way of life." Part of this way of life results in a characteristic approach to the evaluation of goods and services as well as the product information that supports them. For the marketing manager, a knowledge of this approach and its role in the consumer's evaluation of products and product claims is essential. It helps him to decipher the seemingly random success experience of both new and established products in this country. Further, the ability to compare the characteristics of a number of national markets results in guidelines for adapting domestic marketing strategies to other countries. It is such adaptations that facilitate successful overseas market expansion.

What are the value orientations that underlie characteristic market behavior? Talcott Parsons[1] and Seymour Martin Lipset[2] isolated six categories to help identify the relevant values. To these authors cultural patterns can be distinguished by the degree to which people: (1) are either egalitarian or elitist; (2) are prone to lay stress on accomplishment or inherited attributes; (3) expect material or non-material rewards; (4) evaluate individuals or products in terms of objective norms or subjective standards; (5) focus on the distinctiveness of the parts (intensiveness) rather than the general characteristics of the whole (extensiveness); and (6) are oriented toward personal rather than group gain.

IF THE PAIR FITS

Where do different cultures find themselves with respect to these paired attributes? Citizens of the U.S. for the most part share the attributes described by the first term of the paired groups discussed above and listed in the table on page thirty-nine. In the United States people are encouraged to improve their social position. They can expect: (1) to receive, within limits, recognition for their activities; (2) to be rewarded with material perquisites; (3) to be viewed objectively—what you can do—rather than subjectively—who you are; (4) to be judged in terms of those specific activities pertinent to the situation; and (5) to make evaluations in terms of personal gain. This does not mean that there are no elitist, qualitative, nonmaterial, subjective, extensive or collective values in American society. There very obviously are, but such traits cannot be called dominant in the sense that they are in the British system.

Although in Great Britain values are obviously in flux, the dominant ones are still elitist, qualitative, nonmaterial, subjective, extensive and collective. The British system does not encourage the individual to improve his social position; class structure is an acknowledged fact of life. Recognition is very much bound up with the question of class or category relationship—the right people or objects do the right things. The rewards the system offers for appropriate activity, while they include material perquisites, are to a very important degree positional or status rewards which confer power or prestige rather than tangible gain. The evaluation of an individual or an object is made not so much by an impersonal standard applied to specific activities or functions, but rather by more personal or subjective standards which again vary with group, category or class. Whereas Americans are more liable to apply an objective standard to a narrow range of activities or functions, the British apply a more subjective standard across a broader range of activities. Finally, the British tend to look at persons or objects less in terms of their uniqueness and distinctiveness (less intensively) than do Americans.

Australia and Canada stand between these two extremes for most of the paired variables. One exception is the Australian orientation toward equality. Australians are even more concerned with questions of equality and general worth than are Americans. It can be maintained that Australians, because of their overriding concern for equality, have value orientations that are more closely allied with those of Americans and that the orientations of Canadians generally parallel those of the British.

WHERE THE ACTION IS

In societies where performance, not origin, is key, a high premium is placed on doing things. The members of such a society seek new activities. In this sense, then, the reality of a contingency—that is, something that must be acted upon—is more basic to the United States than to Great Britain, where there is relatively little stress on action. Americans, for example, will go to great lengths to consume leisure time. The profusion of leisure-related products in the U.S. is an example of how this value orientation influences the marketing system.

Estimates of Rankings[a] of Countries According to Strength of the Six Pattern Variables (Ranked According to First Term in Each Pair)

Pattern Variable	United States	Australia	Canada	Britain
Equal—Elite	2	1	3	4
Performance—Quality	1	2.5	2.5	4
Material—Nonmaterial	1	3	2	4
Objective—Subjective	1	3	2	4
Intensive—Extensive	1	2.5	2.5	4
Individual—Collective	1	3	2	4

[a] Five of the pattern variable rankings are adapted from Lipset, *op. cit.*, p. 521; the sixth (material-nonmaterial) is from Parsons, *op. cit.*, pp. 101–112.

When this performance orientation is coupled with a predisposition to be intensive—i.e., to perceive many separate and distinct needs to be acted upon as well as a variety of ways in which these needs can be served—the probability of accepting new contingencies as real is greater than when an extensive value orientation prevails. Americans see more separate and distinct activities plus more separate and distinct products which can be used in their performance than do Canadians, Australians or Britons. Such a disposition supports the market for gadgets, the great array of household and kitchen appliances and accessories, as well as extras for autos, boats, and for almost any other standard item. Intensive evaluation results in specialization within activities and therefore in new products and services. This proliferation of activities is responsible for the long list of American "necessities" that are often viewed by others as frivolous and nonessential.

The pressing desire to solve problems appears most readily in a culture that has strong egalitarian, material and individual value orientations. In the U.S., the opportunity to perform is open to all. It is the superior performance of the individual that results in a superior reward. This kind of an orientation causes *contest mobility*, a situation where individuals compete for and win status and material rewards on the basis of performance. Superior performance in activities is facilitated by specialized products and services—the basic products, accessories and gadgets that are available in the American market.

Contest mobility applies to all and motivates people to search for new solutions. New problems are rapidly perceived, almost as challenges. In a world where performance is important, the more areas that one discovers need to be acted upon, the greater the opportunity to perform successfully. Real contingencies are conceived of as hurdles over which one must jump successfully, and possibly at an increasing rate, in order to achieve both improved status and material position.

The rewards for performance in any society can be increased status, material wealth, or both. Where an equalitarian value orientation is coupled with emphasis on individual performance, rewards tend to be material rather than positional in nature. In the United States, positional rewards are viewed as almost no rewards at all, whereas in Great Britain they are highly respected. Material goods facilitate problem solving and are therefore closely identified with performance. They are perhaps the most important symbols for communicating information about the activities of an individual and they symbolize wealth, position and competence.

In this light, then, we expect Americans (1) to accept or at least try new products and services, (2) to see where small tasks or activities can be successfully performed with specialized products, (3) to feel that everyone is entitled to acquire such products and services and (4) to feel that an individual's social worth will be significantly reflected in the products that he both owns and uses.

The British will not perceive problems and their solutions in the same way as do Americans. Relying more on status and quality, and being more elitist than egalitarian, the Briton lacks the American's contest mobility. His society places less emphasis on performance and therefore he is less disposed to recognize new contingencies as real. Old and established views and methods are more highly valued than the new. When the qualitative approach is joined to an extensive basis of evaluation—i.e., perceiving relatively few separate and distinct problems and solutions—the probability of accepting new contingencies is even further reduced. Thus while Americans view many special-purpose gadgets as necessary for the performance of specific jobs, Britons view the same products as perhaps useful but not particularly necessary because the jobs are not particularly pressing or necessary. At any rate, they are certainly not products which *all* people need, although they may be appropriate for some.

Since in Britain very frequently it is position not performance that results in rewards, the incentive for anything other than basic performance is partly removed and the desire to cope with new problems and to solve them successfully is not strong. Also, because of the emphasis on position, the ownership and use of products is not as infallible an indicator of a person's social role as it is in the United States. Status or position, while it can be recognized by the use of products and services, can also, and probably more easily, be recognized in nonmaterial factors such as family and education.

MATESHIP IN AUSTRALIA

In some ways the Australians are much like Americans and in others like the British, and the same observation can be made about the Canadians. Canadians are more likely to accept the existence of problems and the need for action than Australians because they place greater emphasis on material and objective values, although both countries score the same on performance orientation. And while the contest mobility theme is more limited in Canada than in the United

States it is stronger in Canada than in Australia because of the latter's emphasis on egalitarianism. The attitude of the Australians to one another is described by the term "mateship," which is "the uncritical acceptance of recognized obligations to provide companionship and material or ego support as required."[3] The mateship concept implies that an action is acceptable as long as it is not carried to an extreme— the extreme being behavior and appearance that are better than average. This concept is illustrated by the statement[4]: "In England, the average man feels he is inferior; in America he feels superior; in Australia he feels equal." This concern for equality, when added to other variables such as nonmaterialism and a subjective approach, tends to make Australians less aware of problems and their urgency than Canadians.

MINUTIA MINDERS

In countries where an intensive value orientation is strong, both people and products are scrutinized closely. Americans, for example, are most likely to notice small product differences—slight changes in style, design, coloring, packaging or instructions—and Britons are least likely. A person with a strong intensive orientation would comment: "But this is really different from the others," while a person with a strong extensive orientation would say: "But this is really the same as all the others."

In identifying product features, the relatively strong performance and objective orientation of the American leads him to ask: "What does it do?" or "What is it for?" The objective standards require specific information about performance—speed, precision, ease of operation or implementation, safety in use, etc. In Britain, the extensive value orientation disposes people to be less interested in these details and more concerned with overall classification. Those product features that are readily discernible to an American or Canadian are more likely to be ignored by an Australian or an Englishman, who tend to identify products and ascribe value to them in terms of the maker, the manufacturing process or the accepted use.

PROMOTION MUST ALSO CONFORM

The promotional information which supports products in culturally differentiated markets must also be individualized. The product claims made by promotional information can be thought of as including three components—the meaningful, the plausible and the verifiable. The cultural values of the market will strongly influence the kinds of topics that are meaningful. Similarly, they will control the types of product claims people are predisposed to entertain or consider plausible. Finally, they will influence the basis upon which claims can be rendered verifiable.

In introducing a product in the American market and making meaningful claims on its behalf, it is important to focus on the product in both descriptive and visual terms. The item should be appropriate for all Americans—a legitimate object of aspiration as well as an object that meets basic health and safety standards. At the same time, the product should enhance the individual so that the user will be recognized as influential, important, or as an authority because he appreciates the same functional product attributes as do other important or professional individuals.

Promoting the same product meaningfully in the British market calls for product claims that are based on how the product is related to traditionally performed and accepted tasks, products and materials. A product is not necessarily appropriate for all. The user does not gain more individual recognition but gains recognition as a particular type of person.

An illustration of the differences between American and British buying attitudes can be drawn from an experience of General Mills. The success of the Betty Crocker brand of cake mix in the United States can be attributed to the fact that the mix is designed so that any housewife can produce a "professional" or difficult type of cake that will win her the praise of her family, neighbors and friends. In Great Britain, the Betty Crocker brand (as well as a cheaper line) was introduced in 1959, was heavily promoted ($1,400,000 for both lines over four years), but was withdrawn by 1963. The failure of the program was attributed, in part, to the buying attitudes of the British housewife.

"Market observers here felt the product names might have played a part in their marketing failure. Angel cake and devil's food sounded too exotic for British housewives. And many housewives felt such expert-looking cakes as those on the Betty Crocker packs must be hard to make.

"Perhaps it was traditionalism that finally beat General Mills. The market leader, with 40 percent of the trade in this $10,000,000 field, is Stoddard & Hansforth, which sticks to simple products—its Viota brand of cake mixes features such old favorites as tea cakes, jam surprise, fruit cakes and cherry cakes."[5]

It is apparent from this that British and American housewives differ in their interpretations of what comprises a simple or an exotic product and of what it takes to be an expert or an authority.

BRITISH PRODUCT DESIGN LAGS

In contrasting British and American consumers, Boyd and Piercy comment that "attitudes and habits of many consumers even slow down the trends (toward Americanization) now under way"[6] and point out that a relative lack of desire for change, a willingness to put up with no small amount of inconvenience and conservative tastes still prevail. Such attitudes explain why British consumers think of American products in such terms as: "They're so novel . . . There's something for every occasion . . . What will Americans think of next?"[7] The result is that in clothing, furniture, chinaware, housewares and major and minor household appliances, British manufacturers have been noticeably deficient (relative to Americans) in product design.[8]

The British home is depicted as a private "castle" where nothing changes. "The middle-class (British) housewife is oriented more toward the traditional than the new in home furnishing. She regards the old styles as tried and trusted and, therefore, better than the new —the older the furniture, perhaps the better. Should it become necessary to replace it, she probably does so with the identical style and color."[9]

SAVING SOME FOR THE NEXT CHAP

Observers of the Australian scene are impressed with the similarity between Australians and Americans. One important difference is again the Australian attitude toward achievement. Illustrative of this attitude is a typical Australian comment to an aggressive salesman: "Don't be greedy, mate, you've had yours for this time. Reckon I've got to save some for the next chap. Fair shares for all, you know."[10] Many product claims that succeed in the United States can be used in Australia but themes that focus on the professional aspects of a product or its status enhancement are likely to fail because of the Australian sense of fair play. By the same token, claims of British origin that are based on exclusiveness are likely to run up against this same value orientation.

Claims about British and American products that are introduced into the Canadian market also require some adjustment. Executives of an American-owned Canadian affiliate comment that: "Possibly half of the U.S. prepared advertisements are usable in Canada, but almost never without some change being made in copy or one of the illustrations."[11] Canadians notice physical characteristics and components less and tend to respond to simpler forms and avoid the "gaudy and over-trimmed styling"[12] that are often attributed to American products. Somewhat like the British, they are predisposed to longer-lasting, more stable products that do not suffer from model-change and obsolescence. More than the Australian, Canadian character is: "... balance between the Old World and the New.... In matters of tradition, of moral values, of family sociological patterns, Canadians lean toward the point of view of Great Britain. In manner and custom... they incline toward the U.S. This sense of balance is shown throughout their way of life. It has often been said that Canadians are conservative in accepting extreme fashions. Yet any successful New York buyer will tell you that Canadian women have an instinctive 'feel' for good style—even though it is not exciting. They are not as eager (as Americans) to try new ideas; it is more difficult to switch them away from the tried and true. They do not respond to hyperboles; they do not like to be conspicuous in any way."[13]

Similar illustrations of the "plausibility" component can be applied to the U.S., British, Canadian, and Australian cultures. While Americans would find most plausible claims that feature opportunities for success, prestige or personal recognition, Canadians and Australians would find these somewhat less plausible, and Britons would see the least amount of relevance in them. Claims dealing with newness, better performance, and materials are most plausible to Americans, less so to Canadians and Australians, and least so for Britons. The claim that a product can be appropriate for all meets the approbation of both Australians and Americans but not so easily that of Canadians and even less that of the British.

VARIETIES OF VERIFICATION

Verifying claims is very much bound up with the use of authority figures and the presentation of information which is considered "proof" in each of these major markets. The authorities and prestige carriers will, of course, differ in each situation. The cultural hero used in an American testimonial is typically an individual who has become an expert in famous endeavors or succeeded in terms of achieving great social mobility. The professional athlete and the show business star have demonstrated both mobility and success or expertise. Similar types of authority or prestige carriers exist in the other countries but their influence is not so widespread. Australians, again because of their militant equalitarianism, would be predisposed toward accepting the American type of testimonial as proof. "... Australian advertisements and commercials are characterized by a wide use of Americanism ... television commercials prepared and used in the United States are often seen on Australian sets, advertising the same products as in the country of origin."[14]

FIRST COMES SALABILITY

The concepts of product, market, and promotion provide a basis for understanding the importance of cultural values. The significance of cultural determinants on buying decisions is directly related to the question of market expansion.

It is axiomatic that market expansion depends on salability. Salability in turn ultimately depends on what activities the members of a cultural group (a market) perform or anticipate performing, and what products they consider appropriate for coping with these contingencies. To understand cultural values is, in a very real sense, to know what products *can* be sold in that market. The issue of what products *will* be sold depends upon the ability of marketers to adapt their products and promotional efforts to the contingencies perceived by people in the market. The cultural variable, then, bears on the expansion decision in two distinct, but related ways. First, cultural values determine the position of sanctioned products in a market and thereby answer the question: "Is expansion into a given market advisable?" Second, the dominant value orientations in a market offer strategic clues as to how the product can be marketed.

The United States, British, Canadian and Australian markets are, anthropologically speaking, relatively similar. They share a fairly common linguistic and political heritage. Quite predictably, then, a study of the value orientations of other cultures with less common ground will manifest even greater dissimilarity.

It is well to recognize, however, that virtually any new market will exhibit ethnocentrism—specifically, the opinion that *its* cultural values are superior to all others. This means that overt commercial proselytization is not likely to be successful. For example, Canadians do *not* want to be "Americanized." They want to adopt certain features of American culture, but on their own terms.

In some situations expansion into new cultural markets can be accomplished by using the *same product and the same promotion.* The typical marketing for, say, Coca Cola is one case where an existing product will readily and immediately fit into the market's cultural inventory. This means that the established way of life in the market recognizes the reality of the contingency for which the product is suited. Also, recognition of the differences between the product and substitutes for it are already present in the culture. Finally, promotional product claims—their meaningfulness, plausibility, and verifiability—are universal enough to be acceptable to consumers. In effect, such claims are so innocuous that they benefit from a kind of cross-cultural impunity. What this means is that usually this type of expansion strategy is most appropriate when expanding into a cultural market that is similar to the firm's original market.

Probably more expansion situations involve the use of the *same product but different promotion.* There are two reasons for this strategy. First, the situation simply might be one where the existing product fits into the market's cultural inventory. Real contingencies can be met with it, and the product is recognized as a viable alternative to existing products in the inventory. All the product lacks is cultural sanctioning by people in the market. In this case product claims used in other cultural markets are inadequate, perhaps even disparaging, because they fail to meet one or more of the promotional tests. Promotion must be changed to conform to the particular value orientations of the market to guarantee product acceptance.

This strategy is also appropriate when the existing product fits into the market's cultural inventory, but in a way *different* from other markets, i.e., it is recognized as an acceptable product but it is used differently than in other markets. The same automobile, for example, may be a necessity to an American but is a distinct luxury to a European. Products that are used differently must be promoted differently. Promotional claims made in one market may be totally irrelevant in another market where cultural values define the product another way. The expansion strategy of *same product-different promotion,* whatever reasons prompt its use, tends to be appropriate in situations where the coveted market reflects a culture whose way of life is similar but where implementation of life styles is along different lines.

Another method of expansion must be used in markets that reflect life styles so different from those familiar to the firm that existing products are not included in their cultural inventories. Such markets, if they are to be captured, require different products. These products should be thought of in approximately the same light as their counterparts in other cultural markets. What this means is that in order to expand into Market X, the firm may have to alter its original product—perhaps its color, shape, size, package, etc.—but not the means of promotion. The *different product-same promotion* strategy is used in the multinational marketing of laundry detergents. Typically, the products differ among countries but the nature of promotional claims made in their behalf is similar. Laundering techniques may vary from culture to culture, but the "cleaningest" theme is universally subscribed to.

Finally, the expansion situation may be one where both the life styles and the way they are implemented are "foreign" to the firm's previous experience. The appropriate strategy in such situations is to use a *different product-different promotion* technique. This is the most risky kind of expansion because it involves more than extending the firm's existing production and marketing facilities and it often prompts firms to consider "buying their way into" such markets by acquiring existing firms in the market. This is what occurred when Walgreen acquired the Mexican restaurant-retail chain, Sanborn's.

Merely to admit the relevance of cultural values is not enough for market expansion. When contemplating new markets, management must assess the significance of the cultural attitudes and not just take into account comparative curiosities like polygamy and cannibalism, or merely study such consumer habits as the frequency with which people change their clothes. These approaches may be interesting but are not basic to the expansion decision. What is required is a structural scheme, such as the paired-variable approach discussed in this article.

If products, markets and promotion are thought of in terms of behavioral patterns, both the nature and extent of cultural influence on buying decisions and hence on market expansion are clear. Cultural values determine what activities people perform and what contingencies they perceive. Furthermore, the manner in which members of a culture approach their activities—how they cope with contingencies—determines the acceptance of products by the culture. Cultural values also determine the efficacy of promotional claims made in behalf of products. The extent to which a proposed market reflects different life styles or ways of implementing them should be taken into consideration. Expansion into a new market will be more successful if, based on the patterns discussed, combinations of old and new products and methods of promotion are then introduced.

NOTES

1. Talcott Parsons, *The Social System*, New York, The Free Press of Glencoe, 1964, pp. 101–112.
2. Seymour Lipset, "The Value Patterns of Democracy: A Case Study in Comparative Values," *American Sociological Review*, Vol. 28, August, 1963, pp. 515–531.

3. Ronald Taft and Kenneth F. Walker, "Australia," in Arnold M. Rose (ed.), *The Institutions of Advanced Societies*, Minneapolis, The University of Minnesota Press, 1958, pp. 144–145.
4. Cited in Lipset, *op.cit.*, p. 322.
5. "General Mills Withdraws from British Market," *Advertising Age*, May 20, 1963, p. 4. Excerpted in John Fayerweather, *International Marketing*, Englewood Cliffs, New Jersey, Prentice-Hall, Inc., 1965, p. 99.
6. Harper Boyd and Ivan Piercy, "Retailing in Great Britain," *Journal of Marketing*, Vol. 27, January, 1963, p. 35.
7. John Ewing, "Marketing in Australia," *Journal of Marketing*, Vol. 26, April, 1962, p. 58.
8. Harper Boyd and Ivan Piercy, "Marketing to the British Consumer," *Business Horizons*, Vol. 6, Spring, 1963, p. 79.
9. Harper Boyd and Ivan Piercy, "Retailing in Great Britain," *Journal of Marketing*, Vol. 27, January, 1963, p. 31.
10. John Ewing, "Marketing in Australia," *Journal of Marketing*, *op.cit.*, p. 56.
11. Jack R. Stone, "American-Canadian Co-Operation: Key to Successful Advertising," in Litvak and Mallen (eds.), *Marketing: Canada*, Toronto, Ontario, McGraw-Hill of Canada, Ltd., 1964, p. 262.
12. B. P. Ohlson, "The Challenge of New Product Development," *Ibid.*, p. 152.
13. Byrne Hope Sanders, "The Canadian Consumer," in Fox and Leighton (eds.), *Marketing in Canada*, Homewood, Illinois, Richard D. Irwin, Inc., 1958, p. 12.
14. John Ewing, "Marketing in Australia," *op.cit.*, p. 58.

3. Social class and consumer behavior

sidney j. levy

The study of market segmentation is a troublesome one. It raises many questions not easily answered. Numerous studies have sought to determine relationships between particular consumer variables and specific purchasing behavior. All too often these studies are frustrating because they mainly demonstrate that the variables most highly related to the behavior are those that are so close to the behavior as to be redundant in explaining it—or do not explain much at all. Diversity—almost a perversity of diversity—is the easiest generalization to fall back on. When we examine user groups, we find varieties of people, scores, and dimensions; when we examine sociological categories or groups, we find varieties of user behaviors. Either the person high in score on innovation does not show initiative in the area we want to study, or a dramatic example of high status values and philosophy in our sample turns out to be sociologically a lower status consumer. Although these may be exceptional cases, there are surely enough of them to muddy the waters and reduce correlations sharply; and science has the task of explaining exceptional cases in lawful terms also.

Thus, in trying to classify people as kinds of buyers we encounter the problem of the refusal of so many people to be consistent buyers, or at least consistent in the ways we seek to order their behavior.

But all this is to say that the study of market segmentation is certainly in no better condition than much of the behavioral sciences in trying to "explain" any human actions. And indeed the latter are worse off, because so few people are working to develop the multitudinous series of limited studies designed to test variable against variable which are tirelessly presented in social science journals. Nor are there enough workers governing basic investigations, building the intellectual edifice whose bricks are the little studies. As I understand it, this meeting was designed to serve some of that function; in a sense to boot-strap ourselves into having some of the kind of knowledge that comes from looking back over one's work and asking what have we found out.

In attempting to do this in the area of social class, I will start by saying, arrogant as the admission of my hope may be, that I did not find a Rosetta Stone of Social Class, or Newtonian Laws of Consumer Action and Reaction. I did not think it would be useful, either, to accumulate findings that show that people of one status or another are more or less apt to buy various classes of products, as facts in and of themselves. We would not be much furthered in our study simply by learning that lower status people buy relatively more hardware store items or Ann Page products, or that higher status people buy relatively more books or Crosse and Blackwell products. There are some such differences; and I would like to point out something of their general character and coherence.

Social class variations are variations in life style. Although social class groups are not sharply distinguished by their behavior in most studies, they do show behaviors that can be viewed as ranging along a continuum or as different patternings using common elements drawn from the core American culture. Differences are often subtle differences so that it is not easy to find truly marked and easily demonstrated contrasts even in such basic aspects as child rearing. This means that to many marketers such differences are not very important or useful, whereas other people do find them helpful in their thinking. Those who do not find these differences useful tend to be impressed by mass society and its increasingly homogeneous aspects, stressing the similarity between a prosperous lower class and an upper middle class kitchen, when both are well furnished with modern appliances, often of the same brands. However, even these "same kitchens" may have important differences in them, and have been arrived at through rather different marketing processes based on different values, thought processes, and purchasing actions.

Consumer actions are complexly interwoven with attitudes and feelings. The influence of social class on consumers may perhaps be interpreted by putting together a series of ideas which, taken together, show something of this complex; thus we gain by accumulation a sense of the importance of social class as pervasive—even if less meaningful in some areas than in others. Some generalizations are offered here that sum up findings from various specific studies carried out at Social Research over the past fifteen years. The emphasis is on differences, since there is a common tendency to gloss them over.

VALUES

Underlying the many other differences among social classes as consumer groups is the fact of differences in values. Lower status people value education less than middle class people do. This has repercussions in the market in various ways, since many products are consumed as part of gaining an education, as well as depending on having education. There is a sharper relative emphasis on morality, respectability, doing things right, among middle class people; they believe they can control their destinies and fortunes and achieve success by implementing these values. Lower status people are more apt to seek immediate gratifications, to rely on luck, and are less willing to risk their security. These are well-known sociological findings.[1] They are mentioned here to remind that such broad points of view as these have been repeatedly noted as characteristically varying among social

---

[1] Herbert H. Hyman, "The Value Systems of Different Classes: A Social Psychological Contribution of the Analysis of Stratification," in Bendix and Lipset (eds.), *Class, Status and Power: A Reader in Social Stratification,* 426–42. (Rev. ed. 1966, Free Press.)

classes. They suggest that social stratification produces different ways of seeing the world—and of consuming, since consuming is ultimately one of the ways in which people implement their values.

One study of femininity[2] indicated that the lower class woman, who feels doomed to the lower end of the economic scale, is not likely to feel proud of what she does. There is little to value because life seems dull and unrewarding.

> I lead a dog's life . . . work . . . I get up in the morning . . . cook all day . . . pick up after four children and a husband . . . sew . . . what would you call that—peaches and cream?
> I consider my life very dull.
> Dull and boring . . . I spend most of my time working and have nothing much to show for it.

Those who have achieved more economically show greater content and a more vigorous sense of acquisition; they feel they have gotten somewhere and do have something to show for it.

> I'm contented . . . more contented than I was 15 or 20 years ago. I collect . . . milk glass and copper things.
> I feel I lead a really happy life, I never had it so good. I collect salt and pepper shakers with a story behind them.

The higher one is in the social scale, the more comprehensive are one's values; there is a greater sense of one's participation in the community, as well as an increase in self-expressive activities. Self-fulfillment is more valued and more pursued as a real possibility.

> I sculpt, sail and love to dance. I like to read . . . I'm very active from dawn 'til dusk.

INTERPERSONAL ATTITUDES

Another broad factor influencing consumption is the nature of people's interpersonal attitudes. These are, of course, individually ramified in many ways, but some consistencies are visible. Attitudinal differences are seen at the most intimate levels, affecting sexual relations, the use of contraceptives, and conjugal roles. There are consequences in effectiveness of family planning and preferences in family size. For example, lower status people are much less likely to use diaphragms, since its use requires more interpersonal support from the husband than lower class men tend to give their wives.[3]

More generally, upper middle class women tend to regard their husbands as companions, to feel like a peer in money matters. They are likely to demand much of themselves for achievement: to be a good wife, mother, an intellectually stimulating being, home economist, child therapist, organization woman, etc., and also to be a person of composure and competence. As parents, upper middles need their chil-

---

[2] *Images of Femininity*, Social Research report, 1960.

[3] Lee Rainwater, *Family Design: Marital Sexuality, Family Planning and Family Limitation*, Chicago, Aldine Publishing Company, 1964.

dren to be bright, active, strong, lively, and precocious, and are given to characterizing their babies as active and alert. They look for products that will add to their success, competence, and proficiency as mothers and fathers.

By comparison, lower middle class parents are more apt to stress control and conformity, the meeting of values and requirements that relate to cleanliness, politeness, neatness, and order. These parents are most troubled by dirty diapers and the idea of things being messy. Most parents want "good" babies, but lower middles are particularly prone to want them well-behaved, well-scheduled, and manageable.

Working class fathers are relatively distant from their babies.

> I take little care of him, but help when I can. He laughs, and moves around, and seems to know me. (At five months)

Working class mothers strongly need to enjoy their babies, to get pleasure from them. They will tolerate difficulties with their babies, finding in them self-justification and interpersonal responsiveness. In sum, to simplify, the upper middle wants her child bright and alert; the lower middle wants him properly behaved; and the working class woman wants a gratifying possession.[4]

In terms of more general relationships, lower class women tend to say they dress to please themselves, possibly to excuse their bold dress up urges; lower middle class women give some emphasis to other women and much less to pleasing themselves. Upper middle class women have a broader sense of display and think of their audiences as spread among themselves, husbands, other women and men.[5]

The narrower interpersonal circles of working class people show themselves in many ways. They make less use of long distance.[6] They have a tendency to relate socially more to relatives than middle class people do; in spending vacations, working class people are distinctly more prone to visit relatives, to stay home, or have the husband go alone, than to follow the middle class custom of going away from home as a family group.[7]

SELF-PERCEPTIONS

Consumer behavior may reflect the varied self-perceptions, or self-images held by individuals, as such; and, to some degree, as they are characteristic of members of social class groups.

These views of oneself provide a source of consumer action, since they are the expressions of needs, of aims, and of the individual's internal logic, all of which find their objects in the market place. To the extent that people seek products and services that are congruent with

---

[4] *Babies and Baby Care Products*, Social Research report, 1960.

[5] *Chicagoland Women and Their Clothing*, Social Research report, 1960.

[6] *A Socio-Psychological Study of Telephone Users*, Social Research report, 1955.

[7] *Status of the Working Class in Changing American Society*, Social Research report, 1961.

their self-perceptions (as they are and as they would like to be), their self-perceptions are a guide to understanding their marketing behavior. Certainly, individual personality is diverse, more so than the general values held characteristically within a group; relating consumer behavior meaningfully to personality is, therefore, one of marketing research's more challenging tasks. However, that there are some systematic differences among classes is suggested from various directions. For example, in a study of sanitary protection, it was indicated that women of lower social status tend to have more sense of taboo about their bodies and less understanding of them.[8] They were prone to think of themselves as having menstrual problems. They were less receptive to the use of tampons, an instance of their lesser receptivity to important changes in behavior, their lesser scientific information, their more traditional ideas and feelings about sexual matters and interpersonal relations, etc.[9]

Compare the ideas and tone of these two women, the first a lower class, ethnic girl.

> I am Spanish, you see, and Spanish girls are not made like American girls and are not brought up the same. We would not be able to use anything like that . . . You see, we are closed up. American girls are opened up at birth, but Spanish girls are not and we are not opened until we are married and then we go to our husbands and he is the one who opens us.

The second is an upper middle class woman who commented on her use of tampons:

> I figured if I could accommodate one thing I could accommodate another.

Higher status people have more pride in their organisms. They think of themselves as fastidious people; upper middle class women express themselves less urgently when it comes to "needing a deodorant," not believing they smell so bad in the first place. The self-oriented aspects of grooming, of personal pride and self-esteem are prominent in the reactions of higher status women, less to the fore among lower middle status women where general social motives and self-consciousness tend to seem more pressing; lower class women respond more to immediate needs, thinking in terms of tonight's date and special occasions.[10, 11]

Definitions of men, what a "real man" should be to fit the goals, norms, and values of his social class reflect many variables, especially those relating to his physical being, and his effectiveness in vocational and familial relations. Some relative emphases are discernible among the social classes. Upper middle class people tolerate a much more "feminine" conception of a real man. They do not think that a real man

---

[8] *Attitudes toward Feminine Hygiene,* Social Research report, 1957.

[9] *Meanings and Motives in the Tampon Market,* Social Research report, 1958.

[10] *Toothpaste: A Socio-Psychological Study,* Social Research report, 1951.

[11] *Cleanliness and Personal Attraction,* Social Research report, 1955.

has to be crudely tough to be effective. They think that being clean, fastidious, and well-groomed, is part of being a successful person, and demonstrates the kind of narcissism one expects in a higher status person. They think of hygiene, grooming, and dress as especially related to one's career and how it is being lived up to. A higher status man may have distinctive specialized hobbies; some tendency to think of women as pals—and they think he should be a friend; and the idea that masculine know-how finds expression in knowing one's way about the world—in jet planes, restaurants, modern business.

Lower middle class people think a good man is particularly a good father, a responsible husband, a man who builds a solid home life. He is serious, earnest, somewhat depressed, eager for his children to do well in school so that they might become well-established, and fearful that they might be trespassed against by lower class people. He is the most conventional, generally, in dress, resistant to Ivy League and Continental influences, and hopeful that the double-breasted suit will come back to cover up his bulging middle.

Working class people think that a real man is a sturdy guy who can make a decent living. Lower class men like to have body know-how, physical adeptness and manual skills, to understand how things work. They want to get along, to get some fun out of life. They expect to work fairly hard and to relax as hard as they can, because they feel life uses them up faster than it does higher status people.[12-17] A study of age grading showed a trend for lower status people to think of themselves as mature and as old at younger ages than do higher status people.[18]

DAILY LIFE

According to differences of occupations and activities (as well as income differences, socially evaluated differences, etc.), the manner in which the whole day is lived includes both subtle and gross differences. Lower status women are apt to get up earlier in the morning and to feel they can make do with less sleep; in general, working class people are especially faced with the problem of needing to get to bed early and wanting to watch late movies on television. Middle class housewives are more likely than lower class women to plan things with some care, to enjoy trying out some new things, to feel a sense of mastery

---

[12] *Hair Product Preferences*, Social Research report, 1951.

[13] *Men's Clothing and Tailoring*, Social Research report, 1958.

[14] *German Men*, Social Research report, 1960.

[15] *Images of Masculinity*, Social Research report, 1961.

[16] *Marketing to Men*, Social Research report, 1963.

[17] S. J. Levy, "The Meanings of Work," *Notes and Essays on Education for Adults*, No. 39, The Center for the Study of Liberal Education for Adults, May, 1963.

[18] B. Neugarten and W. Peterson, "A Study of the American Age-Graded System," *Proceedings of 4th Congress of International Association of Gerontology*, Vol. 3, 497–502, 1957.

over household chores; lower class women are more prone to agree that "a woman's job is never done."

In general, with increasing status there is more activity outside the home and in the time spent in expressive activities—reading, art, and music, and helping the children do various things. The distribution and use of time shows class trends; for example, the time for the dinner hour varies systematically from class to class. About a fourth of the lower lowers in one sample were likely to be at dinner before five o'clock, and very few after seven o'clock, while more than half the upper middles were still at dinner after seven o'clock. Also, more time is spent at the meal as status rises. The television set is also much more likely to be on during dinner in lower class homes than in middle class homes.[19-21]

These four areas of values, interpersonal relations, self-perceptions, and daily life are broad in character. They reflect the basic facts that groups in our society do different kinds of work, have different types and amounts of financial reward, are evaluated differently along various dimensions of social esteem and importance to the community. As consequences, they think of themselves differently, behave differently, and want differently. In relation to some more specific marketing areas, these differences find further expression.

SHOPPING

Social status appears to affect how people feel about where they should shop. The tendencies here are for lower status people to prefer local, face-to-face places where they feel they will get a friendly reception, easy credit if needed, etc. As a consequence, the same products (and brands) may be purchased in different channels of distribution by members of different social classes. In the purchase of cosmetics, upper middle class women are more apt to shop in department stores than are lower status women who are, in turn, relatively more apt to shop in variety stores. Drug stores seem equally attractive or suitable to all. Studies of department stores also show that among the stores available, there are sharp differences in status reputation, and that consumers tend to sort themselves out in terms of where it is appropriate for themselves to shop. This is not a gross, either/or phenomenon. Most establishments will have customers of more than one social class. But their loadings will differ, and their purchasing patterns may differ. Upper middles characteristically go to Sears for certain kinds of goods, proportionately different from the array bought by lower status customers; and lower status people often go to Marshall Field's only to buy gifts, or even to acquire a gift wrapping. Food chains are similarly selected as varying in status suitability.

The upper middle class woman organizes shopping more purposefully and efficiently than women of lower status. She is more knowl-

[19] *Life Patterns of Mrs. Middle Majority*, Social Research report, 1949.

[20] *A Day in the Life of Mrs. Middle Majority*, Social Research report, 1949.

[21] *Attitudes toward Television*, Social Research report, 1964.

edgeable about what she wants, where she will go for it, when she will get it; her shopping is both selective and wide-ranging.

> I shop in Wanamakers, Lord and Taylor, Bonwit's, and Snellenberg, depending on what I want at the time I'm shopping. I go shopping with a specific thing in mind. I usually group my shopping for the coming season's needs for clothing for myself and the children. I shop for food regularly once a week at Penn Fruit.

Lower middle class women "work" more at their shopping, showing more anxiety about it, finding nonfood purchases especially demanding and tedious, and fraught with uncertainties. Their clothing purchases tend to be more piecemeal than upper middles' are, and there is more orientation to seeking out the best buy for the money.

> I'm always buying clothing for the family. I look around and buy the best I can for as little as I can. With supermarkets, I watch for ads on Thursdays. . . . For example, I just bought a blanket and I went to three stores to look. As it happened, we bought at Lits; they had the nicest blanket for the best price.

Lower class women are the most impulsive about shopping, the least organized. They often like to go out just to have a reason to get out of the house.

> My shopping is very broad and vague. I don't go anywhere in particular but for food and that I get at Best Market. For clothing, I usually go to one of the department stores or when they have an advertisement to show what is on sale and what is different than the usual run of things. I just shop wherever I find what I want.

The implications of these remarks overlap among women, but the continuum is discernible, and finds its most specific expression in the local, social orientation of the lower lower class shopper.

> Some people like to run around from store to store and buy in them large grocery chains. I sometimes buy can goods there, but the best place, the one I like best, is Greene's (a small grocery store in the block). They'll save things for me and I can always get what I want.

Thus, the goals, methods, and places of shopping form patterns that distinguish members of the different social classes in various ways.[22-26]

MEDIA

The fact that media are approached and used in contrasting (as well as similar) ways among social class groups is important for marketing understanding. At a rather simple level there are variations; for example, lower status people are less apt to *subscribe* to newspapers than

[22] *Hair Products and Cosmetics*, Social Research report, 1962.

[23] *Images of Seven Chicago Department Stores*, Social Research report, 1956.

[24] *Major Retailers in the Philadelphia Market*, Social Research report, 1958.

[25] *The American Drug Store: Image, Use and Function*, Social Research report, 1958.

[26] *Credit Buying and Its Motivations*, Social Research report, 1961.

are middle class people, and more likely to read and subscribe to *True Story*, for example; they are more likely to enjoy the comics freely, to embrace television, and to watch late movies. Upper middle class tastes on television are likely to run more actively to current events and drama; moving down the social scale, one finds a relative rise of interest in soap opera, quiz shows, situation comedy, and variety. Middle class people worry more about the effect of television on their children than do lower class people.

The different meanings of media have been explored in many studies. The media function in varied ways, and each also fits differentially into the lives of the social classes. There are (sometimes sharp) class preferences among the newspapers available in a community, in evaluating magazines, in selecting television shows, in listening to the radio, in how newspapers are read, in receipt and meaning of direct mail; and, in general, in the total volume of materials to which people are exposed and to which they attend in one or another of the media. Higher status people see more magazines, read more of the newspaper, and buy more newspapers. Lower class people tend to prefer the afternoon paper; middle class people tend to prefer the morning paper. Studies in the past three years of television in fifteen major cities show that upper middle class people consistently prefer the NBC channel, while lower middles prefer the CBS; and these preferences are in keeping with the images of the networks, and the characteristics of the social classes.[27-34]

ADVERTISING

Attitudes toward advertising are diverse, and reflect much individual variety. However, the many background factors already noted lead to social class differences in this sphere also. The expressly symbolic nature of advertising is particularly meaningful in aiming it toward the differentiated understandings of members of different groups. Broadly speaking, upper middle class people are more critical of advertising, suspicious of its emotional appeals, and questioning of its claims. They are trained in pursuing subtle meanings and usually dis-

---

[27] *The Meaning of Newspapers*, Social Research report, 1954.

[28] *Attitudes toward Television in [various cities]*, Social Research report, several years.

[29] *The Sunday Comics*, Social Research report, 1954.

[30] I. O. Glick and S. J. Levy, "Living with Television," Chicago, Aldine Publishing Company, 1962.

[31] *The Differing Meanings of Women's Magazines and Television*, Social Research report, 1954.

[32] *Magazine Readership as Related to Social Class, Age, and Sex*, Social Research report, 1962.

[33] *Newspapers in the Social World of Chicagoans*, Social Research report, 1963.

[34] *Patterns of Radio Listening in the New York Metropolitan Region*, Social Research report, 1962.

play an attitude of sophisticated superiority to advertising compared to the more straightforward, literal-minded, and pragmatic approach of lower middle and upper lower class people.

This does not mean that upper middle class people are unresponsive to advertising; although they insist on expressing detachment, they are more strongly appealed to by sheer difference, by approaches that seem somewhat individual in tone, that show some wit, that convey elements of sophistication, stylishness, that seem to appeal to good judgment, discriminating taste, that offer the kinds of objects and symbols that are significant of their status and self-expressive aims. Lower status people are relatively more receptive to advertising that is strongly visual in character, that shows activity, ongoing work and life, impressions of energy, and solutions to practical problems in daily requirements and social relationships.[35-37]

Some specific illustrations can be found in women's reactions to promotional advertising, offering coupons and special inducements. Upper lower class women are most receptive when the activity does not seem too difficult. They feel intrigued, economical, shrewd, that they would be fools not to take advantage of many offers that come their way, to cut costs, to get something a little extra.

> I think they are real nice. I like those coupons. I'm not rich enough to throw away 15 cents. I know some people think it is silly to save them, but I don't. Boy, they add up, you know.

Lower middle class women often feel the same attraction, but are more reserved in their reaction, feeling the need to question the utility of offers. They like to feel that they are sensible about their use of offers and promotions, that what they get is important or interesting enough to be worth the effort. They enjoy some sense of complexity, an enrichment of shopping in this kind of participation, but they can also be quite aloof.

> Another one of those. Not very interesting. Too much money to gamble on. If I wanted one of those I could go out and buy one. This doesn't interest me one little bit, I just wouldn't bother with it.

Upper middle class women feel the most remote, sensing lower class economic implications and looking down their noses at the quality of premiums, the size of savings, etc. Their interest vies with their sense of apartness.

> I have never used an offer. I see the coupons in all the papers. They are good for people with large families, they can save a lot if they use the coupons. I find them attractive but I never seem to use them.
>
> Sometimes they offer knives in a set, Cannon towels, dolls, jewelry, blouses. They might interest some people, not me.

In general, values, level and quality of education, the different social

---

[35] *A Study of Thematic Coherence in Advertising Approaches*, Social Research report, 1961.

[36] *The General Nature of Advertising Symbols*, Social Research report, 1949.

[37] *Attitudes toward Toilet Tissues and Their Advertising*, Social Research report, 1952.

aims, and socioeconomic variations produce such differences in characteristic reactions, although much of this is obscured by the volume of advertising learning that goes on, and the projective interpretation that can make the same advertisement mean different things to different people to suit their needs.[38-41]

The kinds of products people want to consume differ, and the reasons for which they consume the same products differ. Going up the social scale, one finds that gum chewing decreases and the reasons given for chewing gum tend to change; more services are used—hotels, motels, airplanes, telephones, dry cleaning, delivery, insurance, investments, etc.; taking of laxatives tends to decline.

There are general differences in whole areas of consumption. The use of food is a good example. Going up the social scale, one finds that food tends to be regarded and used in increasingly symbolic fashion, and going down the scale, one discovers that it is consumed more and more pragmatically. Also, it is apt to be used more self-indulgently at upper middle and lower class levels than at the lower middle, as is also true of drinking. Interest in furniture tends to take different forms. Upper middle class people prefer to search out furniture that is stylish and in keeping with some specified personal or family esthetic; lower class people are more apt to emphasize sturdiness, comfort, and maintenance; lower middles have the characteristic "middle" anxiety about doing what is "right," respectable, neat, pretty, etc.[42-45]

Although the points and summary statements offered above would (when elaborated) have interest in themselves, and did so to various study sponsors in specific instances, they also gain interest for their contribution to a cumulative understanding. They imply a coherence in the marketplace that functions with a consistency that is at least potentially available for continued study. There is suggested a social class structure that may start (or end) with variations in income, but which operates more meaningfully than in terms of amount of money available for spending. However, it has come about that the individual person (or family) exists in and is a manifestation of a milieu that has certain limitations and certain opportunities. The results have recognizable and usually quite logical consequences.

Upper lower class people tend to be defined in their total patterning of personality and ways of living by the fact that society allots them, so to speak, a manual, physical, body-focused assignment. Being the doers, the handlers, they are expected to *act* or *behave* overtly, to

---

[38] *The Meanings and Influence of Promotional Advertising*, Social Research report, 1960.

[39] *A Study of Stamps*, Social Research report, 1963.

[40] S. J. Levy, "Symbols of Source, Substance, and Sorcery," *Art Direction Magazine*, 1960.

[41] S. J. Levy, "Symbols for Sale," *Harvard Business Review*, Vol. 37, No. 4, 1959.

[42] *Chewing Gum and the Consumer*, Social Research report, 1961.

[43] *The Laxative and Antacid Market*, Social Research report, 1952.

[44] *Contemporary Patterns of Food Logic and Consumption*, Social Research report, 1961.

[45] *The Kroehler Report*, Social Research report, 1958.

accomplish in ways that emphasize locomotor activity. In law they are its concrete, physical expression, found driving cars, pounding on doors, laying on sticks and handcuffs. In commerce they sell, serve, retail, handle things, make change, wrap packages. In physical production, they are the mechanics and manipulators, using their hands and muscles with or without skill to produce concrete objects. Such workers, trained to their world, become generally restricted in ego functions. Their orientation is local, concrete, face-to-face, relatively deprived of long range considerations or larger horizons. Immediate gratifications and readiness to express impulses tend to be observed in these people, since they do not usually perceive meaningful incentives to do otherwise.

Lower middle class people characteristically have "the cultural assignment" of applying known principles to defined problems in an accurate manner. Ideally speaking, they are expected to implement laws, regulations, systems, etc., to be caretakers, and intermediary supervisors. As such, in law they deal with its principles as lawyers and clerks; in commerce they may be bookkeepers, accountants, seeing to it that financial methods are systematically and precisely applied. In production, they are supervisors and engineers, again implementing and using known systems and generalizations about physical processes and structures. Such workers, trained to their world, become oriented to a functional and pragmatic view, coupled with anxiety about achieving respectability and success through virtuous performance. This gives them a larger perspective than that found in the lower class, reinforces the importance of education and of deferring gratifications in favor of long range goals.

Upper middle class people have the cultural assignment of initiating knowledge, establishing policy, of exerting judgment, and deciding on the methods and procedures to be used. They embody the intellectual, professional, and managerial point of view. In law they are judges and legislators; in commerce they are managers, controllers, determining the content of the procedures and actions to be carried out by workers of lower status. In a production hierarchy, they may be chiefs, physicists, and scientists. Such workers, trained to their world, emphasize ego processes, an awareness of more distant horizons, large social events and concern with individuality and achievement. They use more integrated and varied means of satisfying their aims, feeling free to satisfy impulses frowned on by lower middle class people, and are able to organize their lives from a point of view beyond the power of lower class people.

The differences listed in the earlier series of points that relate more or less closely to marketing have their roots in the differences suggested in these brief descriptions of three main social classes. These differences seem "real" differences, in that they are not simply the result of variations in income, but are expressions of the profoundly varied forms of experience that become available to members of each social class. They may be obscured by the commonalities in human aims and in American experience, and by the superficial significance of much consumption, but they seem consistent and persistent in governing, where relevant, the consumers' approaches to the market.

4. Activities, interests and opinions

william d. wells & douglas j. tigert

In the early 1950s advertising and marketing were host to an extended and lively fad that came to be known as Motivation Research. Armed with "projective techniques" from clinical psychology and some exciting notions from psychoanalysis, MR practitioners penetrated deeply into the consumer's psyche, revealing for the first time to their astounded clients the "real" reasons people buy products.

The research establishment's reaction was predictable. Conventional researchers insisted that MR was unreliable, invalid, unobjective, too expensive, liable to be misleading, and altogether an instrument of the Devil—and whatever was good about motivation research had long been standard practice anyway. The motivation researchers replied that conventional research was sterile, dull, shallow, rigid, and superficial.

The controversy rolled on through the '50s until everything that could be said had been said too often. As the contestants and the audience wearied, the spotlight moved from MR and the couch to OR [Operations Research] and the computer.

But MR left a legacy. Before MR, advertising and marketing research had in fact been a vast wasteland of percentages. The marketing manager who wanted to know why people ate the competitor's cornflakes was told "32 per cent of the respondents said taste, 21 per cent said flavor, 15 per cent said texture, 10 per cent said price, and 22 per cent said don't know or no answer." The copywriter who wanted to know his audience was told: "32.4 years old, 12.62 years of schooling, 90 per cent married with 2.1 children."

To this desert MR brought people. In addition to the exotic (and largely unworkable) projective tests, motivation researchers employed long, free-flowing narrative interviews, and through these interviews marched an array of mothers who worried about getting the kids to school on time, old ladies whose feet hurt, fretful young housewives who didn't know how to make a good pie crust, fathers who felt guilty about watching television when they should be painting the porch and skinny kids who secretly, but sincerely, believed that The Breakfast of Champions had something to do with their batting averages. For the first time, research brought the marketing manager and the copywriter face to face with an audience or a group of customers instead of a bunch of decimals. The marketing manager and the copywriter thought they were—and they probably were in fact—aided in their task of communication.

Reprinted by permission from the *Journal of Advertising Research*, Vol. 11, pp. 27–35 © Copyright 1971, by the Advertising Research Foundation.

Data used in this article were provided by Market Facts, Inc. and the Leo Burnett Company, Inc. The analysis was made possible by a grant from the Ford Foundation to the Graduate School of Business, University of Chicago.

The rise of OR and the computer did nothing to change this need to have some sensible contact with believable humans. As the mathematical models proliferated, percentages and averages turned into dots, arrows, brackets, boxes, asterisks, and squiggles. The humans who used to show up in motivation research reports disappeared into the computer and emerged as regression coefficients and eigenvalues. The copywriter and the marketing manager, especially the copywriter, still needed some way to appreciate the consumer.

It begins to appear that this need will now be met at least in part by research that focuses on consumers' activities, interests, prejudices, and opinions. Variously called "psychographic" research, "life style" research and even (incorrectly) "attitude" research, it resembles motivation research in that a major aim is to draw recognizably human portraits of consumers. But it also resembles the tougher-minded, more conventional research in that it is amenable to quantification and respectable samples.

This paper is about this new and slightly more sanitary version of motivation research. It starts with a specific example. It mentions various uses. It describes some of the techniques of data gathering and analysis. It ends with a discussion of some criticisms and problems, and the usual rosy but cautious predictions about developments in the future.

DESIGN

One thousand questionnaires were mailed to homemaker members of Market Facts' mail panel. In addition to the usual demographics and questions about a variety of products, the questionnaires contained 300 "activity, interest, and opinion" statements to which the respondent indicated degree of agreement on a six-point scale. For instance, the first statement was, "When I set my mind to do something I usually can do it," and the respondent answered on a scale that ran from 1 (definitely disagree) to 6 (definitely agree). The statements covered a wide variety of topics—including day-to-day activities; interests in media, the arts, clothes, cosmetics and homemaking; and opinions on many matters of general interest.

SWINGING EYE MAKE-UP USER

One of the products on the questionnaire was eye make-up. Respondents were asked how often they use it on a seven-step scale ranging from "never" to "more than once a day."

The demographic questions showed that eye make-up users tend to be young and well-educated, and tend to live in metropolitan areas. Usage rates were much higher for working wives than for full-time homemakers, and substantially higher in the West than in other parts of the country.

Cross-tabulation with other products showed the user of eye make-up to be a heavy user of other cosmetics—liquid face make-up base, lipstick, hair spray, perfume, and nail polish, for example. Perhaps less predictably, she also turned out to be an above-average cigarette smoker and an above-average user of gasoline and the long distance telephone.

On television, she liked the movies, the Tonight Show, and Run For Your Life; she didn't like panel programs or Westerns. She read fashion magazines, news magazines and *Life* and *Look;* she didn't read *True Confessions* or *Successful Farming.*

Thus, eye make-up is clearly not an isolated product. Instead, it is part of a behavior pattern, a pattern that suggests an organized set of tastes and values.

Cross-tabulation of eye make-up with the activity, interest, and opinion questions added significant detail to this emerging picture. Compared with the non-user of eye make-up, the user appeared to be much more interested in fashion. For instance, she was more apt to agree with statements like: "I often try the latest hairdo styles when they change;" "I usually have one or more outfits that are of the very latest style;" "An important part of my life and activities is dressing smartly;" and "I enjoy looking through fashion magazines."

Secondly, she said in a number of ways that being attractive to others, and especially to men, is an important aspect of her self image. (All the respondents in this study were homemakers. The large majority were married.) More than the non-user of eye make-up, the user said, "I like to feel attractive to all men;" "Looking attractive is important in keeping your husband;" "I want to look a little different from others;" and "I like what I see when I look in the mirror."

She indicated that she is very meticulous about her person: "I comb my hair and put on my lipstick first thing in the morning;" "I take good care of my skin;" "I do not feel clean without a daily bath;" and "Sloppy people feel terrible."

More than the non-user she said, "I would like to make a trip around the world;" "I would like to spend a year in London or Paris;" "I enjoy going through an art gallery;" and "I like ballet."

She said, "I like parties where there is lots of music and talk;" "I like things that are bright, gay and exciting;" and "I do more things socially than do most of my friends." Not surprisingly, she said "no" to "I am a homebody."

As far as household chores are concerned, she conceded that she is not a compulsive housekeeper. She said "yes" to "I would like to have a maid to do the housework" and "no" to: "I like to go grocery shopping" and "I enjoy most forms of housework."

Her reaction to her home was style-conscious rather than utilitarian: "I like to serve unusual dinners;" "I am interested in spices and seasonings;" "If I had to choose I would rather have a color television set than a new refrigerator." She said "no" to "I furnish my home for comfort, not for style;" "I try to arrange my home for my children's convenience;" and "It is more important to have good appliances in the home than good furniture."

Finally, she ascribed to a number of statements that suggest accept-ance of the contemporary and rejection of traditional ideas. More than the non-user she tended to agree with, "I like to think I am a bit of a swinger;" "I like bright, splashy colors;" and "I really do believe that blondes have more fun." She rejected statements like, "Women should not smoke in public;" "There is too much emphasis on sex today;" "Spiritual values are more important than material things;" and "If it was good enough for my mother, it is good enough for me."

THE HEAVY USER OF SHORTENING

In the same study, another product—shortening—produced a vividly contrasting picture. Compared with the heavy user of eye make-up, the heavy user of shortening was not as young, had a larger family and was much less likely to have a job outside the home. She was also much more apt to be living outside a metropolitan area, and to be liv-ing in the South, especially the Southeast.

The clues continued in the product use pattern. Heavy users of shortening tended to be heavy users of flour, sugar, laundry detergent, canned lunch meat, canned vegetables, cooked pudding, mustard, and catsup—all products that go with large families. They were not heavy users of eye make-up or any of the cosmetics that go with it.

In the activity, interest, and opinion questions the contrast deepened. Almost none of the items that correlated with use of eye make-up also correlated with use of shortening. When the same question did cor-relate with both products, the correlations were usually in opposite directions.

Compared with the light user of shortening, the heavy user expressed a much stronger interest in cooking and baking. With much greater frequency she said "yes" to, "I love to bake and frequently do;" "I save recipes from newspapers and magazines;" "I always bake my cakes from scratch;" and "The kitchen is my favorite room." She also said, "I love to eat" and "I love candy."

Instead of disliking the job of keeping house, she said she likes it: "I enjoy most forms of housework;" "Usually I have regular days for washing, cleaning, etc. around the house;" "I am uncomfortable when my house is not completely clean." She *disagreed* with "I would like to have a maid to do the housework" and "My idea of housekeeping is 'once over lightly.'"

She said she sews: "I often make my own or my children's clothes" and "I like to sew and frequently do."

She indicated heavy involvement with her children and with the positive emotional tone of her family: "I try to arrange my home for my children's convenience," a statement that correlated *negatively* with eye make-up use. She also said, "Our family is a close-knit group;" "There is a lot of love in our family;" and "I spend a lot of time with my children talking about their activities, friends, and problems."

An unexpected and certainly non-obvious finding was that she is unusually health conscious, and this frame of mind extends to a personal interest in fresh air and exercise: "Everyone should take walks, bicycle, garden, or otherwise exercise several times a week;" "Clothes should be dried in the fresh air and sunshine;" "I love the fresh air and out-of-doors;" "It is very important for people to wash their hands before eating each meal;" and "You should have a medical checkup at least once a year."

Finally, she said she is not a party-goer, and she is definitely not cosmopolitan: "I would rather spend a quiet evening at home than go to a party" and "I would rather go to a sporting event than a dance." She said "No" to "Classical music is more interesting than popular music;" "I like ballet;" and "I'd like to spend a year in London or Paris."

These two sharply contrasting portraits—the eye make-up user and the shortening user—show how recognizable humans emerge from quantified activity, interest and opinion data.

PORTRAITS OF TARGET GROUPS

Perhaps the most obvious use of this kind of research is the one already mentioned—portraits of target groups in the advertising and marketing of products. If it is granted that all forms of advertising and marketing are in some sense communication, and if it is granted that a communicator can usually do a better job when he can visualize his audience than when he cannot, it seems obvious that this level of descriptive detail is a significant improvement over the rather sparse and sterile demographic profiles that have been traditional in marketing research.

The target group is often, but by no means always, the product's heavy user. The target group may be the light user or the non-user. It may be some special segment, such as smokers of mentholated cigarettes. It may be some demographic segment, such as young married men with a college education. If a target group can be specified and identified, a useful portrait is at least a possibility.

MEDIA VALUES NOT IN THE NUMBERS

Media representatives insist that an audience's quality, as well as its size, should be considered. Activity, interest, and opinion questions provide some insight into audience quality by drawing a portrait of the medium's user. The *Playboy* reader, for instance, turns out to be pretty much the male counterpart of the swinging eye make-up user, while the male *Reader's Digest* reader emerges as the soul of conservative middle class values—pro-business, anti-government welfare, anti-union power, interested in politics, interested in community projects and activities. The *Time*-only reader, compared with the *Newsweek*-only reader, emerges as less concerned about job security, less worried about government and union power, less worried about the peril of communism and more favorably disposed toward advertising (Tigert, 1969).

Media analysts know that, compared with magazines, television is a very "blunt" medium. Since magazine audiences select themselves in accordance with the magazine's specialized editorial content, while television program audiences are usually very large and very heterogeneous, it is usually much easier to find distinct demographic differences among the readers of different magazines than among the viewers of different television programs. But work with activity, interest, and opinion variables suggests that television program audiences may be more different than some suspect.

Before Brand Rating Index, Simmons, and other syndicated product-media services became widely available, it was customary to match media with products by demographic "profile": "Our product is used by young, upscale housewives, so we want to be in a book that appeals to young, upscale housewives." It has sometimes been suggested that the psychographic profile be substituted for the demographic profile as a link between product and media: "Our product is used by women with a certain activity, interest, and opinion pattern, so we want to be in books or on TV programs that appeal to people who match that description." But this intuitively appealing idea has the same drawbacks as demographic profile matching. The correlations that link products to media through psychographics are no stronger than the correlations that link products to media through demographics, so a product and a medium can have similar activity, interest, and opinion profiles without being much related to each other. It is always safer to use the direct product-medium link in selecting media than to try to infer this link through some third set of variables.

Where psychographics can be of help in media selection is in improving the analyst's understanding of the product-medium linkages that are found through direct cross-tabulation. For instance, if direct cross-tabulation shows that many heavy users of home permanents are devoted readers of *True Story*, the activities, interests, and opinions of the women who *both use the product and read the magazine* will help explain the reasons behind this relationship by showing what, exactly, home permanent users and *True Story* readers have in common. That sort of understanding if often of great help in making sensible decisions.

OTHER VARIABLES

Questions about activities, interests, and opinions can shed light on topics other than products and media. They can give additional meaning to the standard demographic classifications by showing how the executive's wife differs from the homemaker in a blue-collar household. They can further define the generation gap. They can add to what is known about sex differences. They can further describe the opinion leader, the new product tryer, the television addict, the trading stamp saver, the discount shopper, the political activist, the lady who thinks there is too much advertising to children on television. For almost any identifiable type of behavior there is at least the possibility of new insight when the behavior is viewed in the context of opinions, interests, and activities. Topics studied in this way include age and social class (Tigert, 1970), opinion leadership and information seeking (Reynolds and Darden, 1971), fashion interest and leadership (Summers, 1970), reactions to new product concepts (Nelson, 1971), furniture store choice and preferences for furniture styles (Good and Suchsland, 1970) and Stone's concept of "shopping orientations" (Darden and Reynolds, 1971).

GETTING THE DATA

Since activity, interest, and opinion items are self-administering to literate respondents, data can be obtained through either personal contact or established mail panels. Personal contact permits probability samples. It can also, with enough effort, reach hard-to-find respondents like young single males, transients, hippies, and prisoners. For many purposes, however, established mail panels yield a satisfactory return at a good cost. Because activity, interest, and opinion questions are in general so very interesting to respondents, mail questionnaires as long as 25 pages have yielded usable returns from 75 to 80 per cent of mail panel samples.

Good items come from intuition, hunches, conversations with friends, other research, reading, head scratching, day-dreaming, and group or individual narrative interviews. Appendix 1 is a list of items that came from these sources and from Wilson (1966), Pessemier and Tigert (1966), and a set of unpublished studies by Social Research, Inc. for MacFadden-Bartell Corporation. The items are grouped into "scales" through factor analysis.

INDIVIDUAL ITEMS VS. SCALES

The user of activity, interest, and opinion material has the option of employing a large, highly diversified collection of statements that cover as many different topics as possible, or of using a more limited number of multi-item scales. The multi-item scale approach is favored by psychometric tradition because properly constructed scales are invariably more reliable than individual items.

Unhappily, however, scales have four important disadvantages: (1) They limit coverage because they reduce the number of topics covered by any given number of items, and the longer the scales, the greater the reduction. (2) The shorthand of the scale name (e.g., "Credit User," "Fashion Conscious") encourages the analyst to think only in terms of the name rather than the richness of detail in the individual items. (3) Since scale items are never exact duplicates of each other, there are times when the scale as a whole correlates with some other variable but individual items do not, and there are times when individual items correlate with some other variable but the scale as a whole does not. Thus, the scale approach sometimes misses some potentially useful relationships. (4) Use of pre-established scales limits the findings to dimensions the analyst thought would be important, thereby precluding discovery of the unexpected.

The alternative is to throw a wide net and hope to catch something interesting, a practice sometimes disparagingly referred to as a fishing expedition. While this criticism should not be taken lightly, it should also be borne in mind that going on a fishing expedition is one of the best ways to catch fish. The items listed in Appendix 1, and the items cited in the examples, typify items that have worked well in past studies. An item library too large for reproduction here is available from the authors.

FORCED CHOICE VS. SCALAR RESPONSES

As an alternative to having the respondent mark a scale position to indicate his answer, some analysts prefer to present two AIO statements and ask the respondent to indicate which he agrees with more. Others prefer to ask the respondent to rank a set of statements from most to least agreement. When carefully applied, these alternatives can help suppress the undesirable effects of "yeasaying," social desirability, and other troublesome response styles, and they force discrimination among items that might otherwise be marked at the same scale position. On the other hand, forced-choice and ranking questions are often difficult to administer and difficult for the respondent to handle, and analysis of the data presents certain sticky problems. Studies that used the forced-choice approach successfully are described by Nelson (1969, 1971). The analysis problems are described by Hicks (1970).

CLINICAL VS. AIO VARIABLES

Some of the earliest attempts to use this sort of material in advertising and marketing research employed standardized inventories designed to measure general personality traits, with results that were usually somewhat disappointing (Evans, 1959; Westfall, 1962). Much of the later work has tended to move away from general personality traits toward variables that are more closely related to the behavior under consideration—homemaking activities and interests for household products, sociability items for cosmetics, and so on. As a result, it has often been ·found that significant relationships emerged where none had been found before, and it has often been easier to visualize uses for the relationships that were uncovered.

Nevertheless, the use of general personality traits has not been abandoned. Their value, especially when combined with activity, interest, and opinion items, is clearly demonstrated in studies by Nelson (1969) and Ziff (1971).

ANALYSES

When the sample is large and responses are well scattered, the simplest way to look at AIO material is ordinary cross-tabulation. For instance if the AIO scale has six steps, and the product use scale has seven, the relationship between each AIO and the product would appear in an ordinary 6 x 7 table.

But when the sample is small, or when either AIO or product responses are highly skewed, a 6 x 7 table will have many empty or nearly empty cells. In these common situations, it is best to condense the data beforehand by grouping scale steps to embrace reasonable numbers of respondents. When using a six-step scale, a strategy that usually works satisfactorily is to group steps 1–2, 3–4, 5–6.

If many relationships must be considered, for instance 100 products × 300 AIO items, the analyst who orders a complete cross-tabulation will find 30,000 tables on his desk before he can shut off the computer. One alternative is to order a product's × AIO's correlation matrix, and to have only those product-AIO correlations that are statistically significant cross-tabulated. This strategy may throw away some significant and potentially interesting curvilinear relationships, but it avoids the stupefying effect of 30,000 tables. A more detailed description of this approach can be found in an article by Plummer (1971).

Once the significant relationships have been found, the problem is to organize and understand them. Here the analyst's skill, experience, and ingenuity come to work, just as they did in the analysis of motivation research interview data. Factor analysis is a great help. R factor analysis can help condense AIO data by putting related statements together into categories. Q factor analysis can further simplify the problem by grouping respondents into types with similar response patterns. Neither of these procedures is automatic or fool-proof, however, and there is little danger that the computer will replace the experienced and insightful analyst in the bridge between data gathering and application.

APPLICATIONS

Here are three examples of the way relationships between products and AIO items have been turned into action. They are derived from real situations, but, for obvious reasons, they are heavily disguised.

A new car wax is a significant improvement over products now on the market. The plan is to present this new wax in the context of fantastic and futuristic space gadgetry, a product so much better than anything now available that it belongs in the twenty-first century. An examination of the AIO profile of the target group shows no special interest in the future, in fantasy, in science, or in space. Instead the potential customer appears to be preoccupied with the here and now, and to be most impressed by facts, by proof, by the testimony of others he trusts and by demonstration. The campaign is reoriented to take account of this disposition.

A product traditionally advertised in folksy, homey, small town settings is found to be most heavily used by young housewives with an AIO profile almost as swinging as that of the eye make-up user. This finding fosters consideration of new advertising, and produces recommendations for changes in promotion and packaging.

The advertising for a heavy duty floor cleaner has been emphasizing its ability to remove visible dirt such as mud, dog tracks, and spilled food. The AIO profile of the target group shows great concern about germs and odors, and unusual preoccupation with the appearance of surfaces. The recommendation is to place special emphasis on the product's germicidal qualities and to feature the shiny surface the product leaves when the job is finished.

Further examples of actual and potential uses of AIO material can be found in Husted and Pessemier (1971), Nelson (1971), Plummer (1971) and Tigert (1969, 1971).

CRITICISMS AND PROBLEMS

It has been said that the relationships between AIOs and products or media are merely surface manifestations of the more familiar, more "basic" demographics. The psychographic profile of the *Playboy* reader, for instance, might be thought of as merely a sign that *Playboy*'s readers are young, relatively well-educated males. While this assertion is in part correct, two considerations suggest that it would be wrong to depend on demographics only. First, two products with very similar demographic profiles sometimes turn out to have usefully different psychographic profiles. Fresh oranges and fresh lemons are one example, as noted later in this paper.

Second, a demographic bracket in itself means little unless one has a clear picture of its life style implications. Everyone has some idea of what it means to be a young mother with a college education, or a middle-aged male with a blue-collar job, but such designations can be richly supplemented by information about the activities, interests, and opinions that go with them. Plummer's (1971) study of bank charge card users shows explicitly how AIO data can produce results that did not emerge when only demographic data were available.

LOW CORRELATIONS

When expressed as product-moment correlations, the relationships between AIO items and products or media are low—often around .2, and seldom higher than .3 or .4. Thus, they do not "explain the variance" very well, even when put together in a prediction equation.

It should be remembered, however, that the variance "explained" is the variance in the behavior of individuals, not the variance in the average behavior of groups, so a product-moment correlation of .2 is deceptively small. Consider the following cross-tabulation table. The product-moment correlation is .2—4 per cent of the variance "explained"—yet the relationship is obviously meaningful.

This point has been discussed in detail by Bass, Tigert, and Lonsdale (1968), so it will not be belabored here. Perhaps it is sufficient to say that anyone who refuses to look at the relationships between AIOs and products, or AIOs and media, must also—to be consistent—refuse

to look at the relationships between products or media and demographics, because the correlations are the same size, or smaller. Further, anyone who rejects the relationships between AIOs and products,
or AIOs and media, must also reject the use of media selection models
that depend upon relationships between media use and product use.
These relationships, too, when expressed as product-moment correlations, are rarely higher than .3.

TABLE 1   Cross-Tabulation of Shortening Use and Degree of Agreement with
"I Save Recipes from Newspapers and Magazines"*

	Once a Week or Less (286)	Few Times a Week (296)	Once a Day or More (204)
Definitely Agree	42%	52%	63%
Generally Agree	24%	25%	19%
Moderately Agree	20%	12%	14%
Moderately, Generally or Definitely Disagree	14%	11%	4%

* To avoid small cell frequencies both variables are condensed by combining adjacent
categories.

OVERLAPPING PORTRAITS

AIO portraits do not always differ as much as the portraits of the eye
make-up user and the shortening user. Many cosmetics are much alike.
The heavy user of sugar looks like the heavy user of shortening and
heavy user of flour. These overlaps occur because products themselves
overlap, forming families that denote life styles (Wells, 1968).

But even similar portraits sometimes show useful differences, like
the differences between heavy users of fresh oranges and heavy users
of fresh lemons. Both groups of respondents show a strong interest in
cooking and baking, especially with unusual recipes. Both also show
unusual interest in community activities. However, the heavy user of
fresh oranges, but *not* the heavy user of fresh lemons, is distinguished
by a strong need for cleanliness: "A house should be dusted and
polished at least three times a week." "It is very important for people
to brush their teeth at least five times a day." "Odors in the house
embarrass me." The heavy user of fresh lemons, but *not* the heavy
user of fresh oranges, is distinguished by an unusual interest in fresh
air and exercise: "I love the fresh air and out-of-doors." "I bowl, play
tennis, golf or other active sports quite often." And the heavy user of
fresh oranges, but *not* the heavy user of fresh lemons, indicates she is
a bargain hunter: "I usually watch the advertisements for announcements of sales," and "I'm not a penny-pincher but I love to shop for
bargains."

Thus, the two groups are much alike, but they also differ along
interesting and actionable dimensions.

ARE HEAVY USERS ALL ALIKE?

Certain products may be heavily used for two or more quite different purposes. For instance, mouthwash may be used as a precaution against colds, or as a cosmetic. Since the cold user and the cosmetic user have very different life styles (Nelson, 1969), the picture presented by "the heavy user" will be a jumble of the two. It is important to be aware of this possibility and to separate users into subgroups whenever there is reason to suspect that the product plays a variety of roles.

THIN PRODUCTS

Not all products correlate significantly with a large number of activity, interest, and opinion items. In one typical study, of 127 products, 32 correlated significantly with fewer than ten of the 300 AIO items, 67 correlated significantly with more than 10 but fewer than 30, and 35 correlated significantly with more than 30. Since portraits provided by fewer than ten correlations are usually not very helpful, a general rule of thumb would be that the chances of drawing a blank are about one in four.

It is hard to know why some products are so "thin." It is not because "rich" products are used by small, way-out segments of the population, while "thin" products are used by people in general. Instant coffee, cat food, laxatives, and cold cereal have all shown few AIO associations; laundry detergent, stomach remedies, gasoline, and floor wax have shown many. The potential user should be aware that "rich" results are not automatic.

THE FUTURE

In a recent issue of this Journal, James Benson, chairman of Ogilvy and Mather, was quoted: "There is more similarity between the consumer in New England and the consumer in Old England than there is between the consumer in New England and the consumer in New Orleans. Increasingly, markets will need to be segmented more on psychological, social and attitudinal criteria than on the traditional bases of geography and demography."

Partly as a result of such urging, the use of psychographics and related techniques is gaining considerable momentum. A substantial number of large scale proprietary studies have been conducted, with enough success that at least some of the sponsors have come back to ask for more. The approach has sparked interest among academic researchers, and papers on it or using it are beginning to appear.

The danger, of course, is that this somewhat novel way of sizing up consumers will be oversold, and that users will be disappointed when it does not turn out magic answers to all conceivable questions. Readers who respond "definitely agree" to the statement, "Most people have a lot of common sense," will hope that that won't happen.

REFERENCES

BASS, FRANK M., DOUGLAS J. TIGERT, AND RICHARD T. LONSDALE. Market Segmentation: Group Versus Individual Behavior. *Journal of Marketing Research*, Vol. 5, No. 3, August 1968, pp. 264–70.

DARDEN, WILLIAM R. AND FRED D. REYNOLDS. Shopping Orientations and Product Usage Rates. *Journal of Marketing Research*. Forthcoming, 1971.

EVANS, FRANKLIN B. Psychological and Objective Factors in the Prediction of Brand Choice: Ford vs. Chevrolet. *Journal of Business*, Vol. 32, October 1959, pp. 340–369.

GOOD, WALTER S. AND OTTO SUCHSLAND. Consumer Life Styles and Their Relationship to Market Behavior Regarding Household Furniture. Research Bulletin, No. 26, Michigan State University, 1970.

HICKS, LOU E. Some Properties of Ipsative, Normative, and Forced Choice Measures. *Psychological Bulletin*, Vol. 74, No. 3, 1970, pp. 167–184.

HUSTED, THOMAS P. AND EDGAR A. PESSEMIER. Segmenting Consumer Markets with Activity and Attitude Measures. Paper No. 298, Institute for Research in the Behavioral, Economic and Management Sciences, Krannert Graduate School of Industrial Administration, Purdue University, March, 1971.

NELSON, ALAN R. A National Study of Psychographics. Paper presented at the 52nd International Marketing Congress, American Marketing Association, Atlanta, Georgia, June, 1969.

NELSON, ALAN R. New Psychographics: Action-Creating Ideas, Not Lifeless Statistics. *Advertising Age*, June 28, 1971, pp. 1, 34.

PESSEMIER, EDGAR A. AND DOUGLAS J. TIGERT. In J. S. Wright and J. L. Goldstucker (Eds.). *New Ideas for Successful Marketing*, Chicago, Ill.: American Marketing Association, 1966.

PLUMMER, JOSEPH T. Life Style and Advertising: Case Studies. Paper given at 54th Annual International Marketing Congress, American Marketing Association, San Francisco, California, April, 1971.

PLUMMER, JOSEPH T. Life Style Patterns and Commercial Bank Credit Card Usage. *Journal of Marketing*, Vol. 35, No. 2, 1971, pp. 35–41.

REYNOLDS, FRED D. AND WILLIAM R. DARDEN. Mutually Adaptive Effects of Interpersonal Communication. *Journal of Marketing Research*. Forthcoming, 1971.

SUMMERS, JOHN O. The Identity of Women's Clothing Fashion Opinion Leaders. *Journal of Marketing Research*, Vol. 7, 1970, pp. 178–185.

TIGERT, DOUGLAS J. Life Style Correlates of Age and Social Class. Paper presented at the first annual meeting of the Association for Consumer Research, Amherst, Mass., August, 1970.

TIGERT, DOUGLAS J. A Psychographic Profile of Magazine Audiences: An Investigation of a Media's Climate. Paper presented at the American Marketing Association Consumer Behavior Workshop, Ohio State University, Columbus, Ohio, 1969.

WELLS, WILLIAM D. In J. Arndt (Ed.). *Insights into Consumer Behavior*. New York: Allyn and Bacon, 1968.

WESTFALL, RALPH. Psychological Factors in Predicting Product Choice. *Journal of Marketing*, Vol. 26, April 1962, pp. 34–50.

WILSON, CLARK C. In J. S. Wright and J. L. Goldstucker (Eds.). *New Ideas for Successful Marketing*, Chicago, Ill.: American Marketing Association, 1966.

ZIFF, RUTH. Psychographics for Market Segmentation. *Journal of Advertising Research*, Vol. 11, No. 2, pp. 3–9.

APPENDIX 1

PRICE CONSCIOUS
I shop a lot for "specials."

I find myself checking the prices in the grocery store even for small items.

I usually watch the advertisements for announcements of sales.

A person can save a lot of money by shopping around for bargains.

FASHION CONSCIOUS
I usually have one or more outfits that are of the very latest style.

When I must choose between the two I usually dress for fashion, not for comfort.

An important part of my life and activities is dressing smartly.

I often try the latest hairdo styles when they change.

CHILD ORIENTED
When my children are ill in bed I drop most everything else in order to see to their comfort.

My children are the most important thing in my life.

I try to arrange my home for my children's convenience.

I take a lot of time and effort to teach my children good habits.

COMPULSIVE HOUSEKEEPER
I don't like to see children's toys lying about.

I usually keep my house very neat and clean.

I am uncomfortable when my house is not completely clean.

Our days seem to follow a definite routine such as eating meals at a regular time, etc.

DISLIKES HOUSEKEEPING
I must admit I really don't like household chores.

I find cleaning my house an unpleasant task.

I enjoy most forms of housework. (Reverse scored)

My idea of housekeeping is "once over lightly."

SEWER
I like to sew and frequently do.

I often make my own or my children's clothes.

You can save a lot of money by making your own clothes.

I would like to know how to sew like an expert.

HOMEBODY
I would rather spend a quiet evening at home than go out to a party.

I like parties where there is lots of music and talk. (Reverse scored)

I would rather go to a sporting event than a dance.

I am a homebody.

COMMUNITY MINDED
I am an active member of more than one service organization.

I do volunteer work for a hospital or service organization on a fairly regular basis.

I like to work on community projects.

I have personally worked in a political campaign or for a candidate or an issue.

CREDIT USER
I buy many things with a credit card or a charge card.

I like to pay cash for everything I buy. (Reverse scored)

It is good to have charge accounts.

To buy anything, other than a house or a car, on credit is unwise. (Reverse scored)

SPORTS SPECTATOR
I like to watch or listen to baseball or football games.

I usually read the sports page in the daily paper.

I thoroughly enjoy conversations about sports.

I would rather go to a sporting event than a dance.

COOK
I love to cook.

I am a good cook.

I love to bake and frequently do.

I am interested in spices and seasonings.

SELF-CONFIDENT

I think I have more self-confidence than most people.

I am more independent than most people.

I think I have a lot of personal ability.

I like to be considered a leader.

SELF-DESIGNATED OPINION LEADER

My friends or neighbors often come to me for advice.

I sometimes influence what my friends buy.

People come to me more often than I go to them for information about brands.

INFORMATION SEEKER

I often seek out the advice of my friends regarding which brand to buy.

I spend a lot of time talking with my friends about products and brands.

My neighbors or friends usually give me good advice on what brands to buy in the grocery store.

NEW BRAND TRYER

When I see a new brand on the shelf I often buy it just to see what it's like.

I often try new brands before my friends and neighbors do.

I like to try new and different things.

SATISFIED WITH FINANCES

Our family income is high enough to satisfy nearly all our important desires.

No matter how fast our income goes up we never seem to get ahead. (Reverse scored)

I wish we had a lot more money. (Reverse scored)

CANNED FOOD USER

I depend on canned food for at least one meal a day.

I couldn't get along without canned foods.

Things just don't taste right if they come out of a can. (Reverse scored)

DIETER

During the warm weather I drink low calorie soft drinks several times a week.

I buy more low calorie foods than the average housewife.

I have used Metrecal or other diet foods at least one meal a day.

FINANCIAL OPTIMIST

I will probably have more money to spend next year than I have now.

Five years from now the family income will probably be a lot higher than it is now.

WRAPPER

Food should never be left in the refrigerator uncovered.

Leftovers should be wrapped before being put into the refrigerator.

WIDE HORIZONS

I'd like to spend a year in London or Paris.

I would like to take a trip around the world.

ARTS ENTHUSIAST

I enjoy going through an art gallery.

I enjoy going to concerts.

I like ballet.

3 PERSONALITY AND MOTIVATION

Personality traits have received considerable attention in marketing, more recently under the rubric of psychographics. Both terms in practice tend to be used loosely; for example, psychographics sometimes includes any internal variable such as attitude. Typically, by "trait" we mean a *consistent pattern of behavior.*

Personality traits serve two purposes. Most of the attention has been in terms of their use as market segmenting criteria. Haire with his 1950 shopping list study, described by Webster and Pechman (1970),* created considerable interest in this possibility, but his approach was highly inferential. Evans was probably the first to attack this problem systematically in marketing. His original study in 1959 of *personality* traits and car purchasing showed limited relationships, and these were roughly confirmed by a similar study in the same geographic area eight years later. Frank, Massy, and Lodahl (1969)* also show disappointing results. The *personality* variables contribute little additional explanation of purchasing behavior of ongoing products.

The second important use of *personality* traits is in attempting to understand the total purchasing process, as used by Farley and Ring (1970). While this approach has greater theoretical appeal, *personality* traits again are found to make a relatively small contribution toward explaining behavior.

The confusing state of research regarding *personality* traits is due largely to the earlier practice of bivariate analysis. That is, the researcher merely related, one at a time, given *personality* traits to a given type of behavior. While the level of association was often found to be statistically significant, the relationship seldom was very revealing. The multivariate approach of Sparks and Tucker (1971)* represents a more promising approach, which has the potential of yielding richer insight into the ultimate impact of personality on behavior, whether or not a multi-stage intervening mental process is specified. Nevertheless, Sparks and Tucker find from their analysis only modest predictive value for personality traits.

If we are to arrive at a useful understanding of buyer behavior, we cannot be satisfied with knowing merely that certain traits are related to purchase: we must know the underlying cognitive process, the paths of causation by which these effects occur. In the future it may well be concluded that *personality* traits are more useful in explaining how buyers take in and process information than in predicting purchases.

Motives reflect *personality* traits and arise from both biogenic and psychogenic needs, wants, or desires of the buyer. Their impact is felt upon both information-processing and the formation of *attitude* dimensions for product evaluation. Two components of *motives* are considered: *content* and *intensity*. It is generally postulated that an equilibrating process is involved: a need of some kind stimulates a certain *motive content* and *intensity* (importance) that triggers *arousal* (Chapter 6), which, in turn, energizes action in a direction that is expected to satisfy the need. If successful, *motive intensity* declines and consequently so does *arousal*, establishing a new equilibrium.

Motives operate upon information-processing not only through *arousal* but also through *perceptual bias*, which can distort or filter the true content of information to which the buyer is exposed. This can have a massive effect on *information recalled*, which later affects other state-of-mind measures.

While motives are postulated to be a source of attitude dimensions, researchers have given relatively little attention to assessing the closeness of this relationship. Rather, the study of the relationship of *personality* traits to purchase behavior has been more popular, even if often discouraging.

REFERENCE

1. FARLEY, JOHN AND WINSTON L. RING. "An Empirical Test of the Howard-Sheth Model of Buyer Behavior." *Journal of Marketing Research*, Vol. 7 (November 1970), 427–438.

5. A replication of the "shopping list" study

frederick e. webster, jr. &
frederick von pechmann

Mason Haire's classic "shopping list" study is one of the most familiar and most often quoted pieces of research in marketing.[1] That study, reported in 1950, supported three general conclusions. First, many products (such as instant coffee) have meaning and significance for consumers that go far beyond the physical attributes of the products themselves. Second, these hidden values in products are a major influence on the consumer's purchase decisions. Third, the identification and assessment of such motives require indirect approaches, such as projective techniques. To these conclusions drawn by Professor Haire can also be added the observation that convenience foods, such as instant coffee, carry a certain opprobrium. However, if asked directly why they did not purchase instant coffee, people had been found to say "I don't like the flavor." This is a much more acceptable explanation than "People will think I am lazy and not a good wife."

The authors' hypothesis was that the differences between the "Maxwell House (Drip Grind)" housewife and the "Nescafé Instant" housewife which Haire identified in 1950 would not be found in 1968. There is strong evidence that convenience foods in general and instant coffee in particular have become much more acceptable to the American housewife. Soluble (i.e., instant) coffee sales have increased from less than 20% in 1955 to over 30% of total U.S. coffee sales in 1965. Well over half of the products on grocery store shelves in 1968 were not available to the consumer in 1957. The majority of new products offered to the housewife have been convenience items such as boil-in-the-bag frozen foods, baking mixes, prepared foods, snacks, canned meats, and dietetic foods.[2]

THE HAIRE STUDY

Haire conducted personal interviews with a sample of 100 housewives in the Boston area. The following verbal instructions were given to each respondent:

> Read the shopping list below. Try to project yourself into the situation as far as possible until you can more or less characterize the woman who brought home the groceries. Then write a brief description of her personality and character. Wherever possible indicate what factors influenced your judgment.

Reprinted by permission from *Journal of Marketing*, Vol. 34 (April, 1970), pp. 61–77, published by the American Marketing Association.

[1] Mason Haire, "Projective Techniques in Marketing Research," *Journal of Marketing*, Vol. 14 (April, 1950), pp. 649–656.

[2] "New Items in the Food Industry," *Progressive Grocer*, Vol. 46 (June, 1967), pp. 55–62.

Two shopping lists were used. Each one was given to 50 respondents. The respondents were not aware of the existence of two shopping lists.

SHOPPING LIST I	SHOPPING LIST II
Pound and a half of hamburger	Pound and a half of hamburger
2 loaves of Wonder bread	2 loaves of Wonder bread
Bunch of carrots	Bunch of carrots
1 can Rumford's Baking Powder	1 can Rumford's Baking Powder
Nescafé Instant Coffee	1 lb. Maxwell House Coffee (Drip Grind)
2 cans Del Monte peaches	2 cans Del Monte peaches
5 lbs. potatoes	5 lbs. potatoes

Strict coding procedures, which required virtually literal interpretation of the stories, were used to analyze responses. Nothing was "read into" the responses. For example, if a respondent described the shopper as "careful and thrifty," this response was recorded as "careful" and "thrifty," not as "budget conscious" or "conscientious."

THE 1968 STUDY

The authors attempted to duplicate Haire's methodology as closely as possible. Questionnaires were delivered to a judgment sample of urban and suburban housewives in the Hartford, Connecticut area. A total of 44 questionnaires were delivered in person and 42 of these were returned by mail. The following instructions were placed at the top of each questionnaire:

> After the two questions [asking for the respondent's age and marital status] there is a shopping list. Please read the list. Try to project yourself into the situation as far as possible until you can more or less characterize the woman who bought the groceries. Then write a brief description of her personality and character. Wherever possible, indicate what factors influenced your judgment. This is a test to see how well you can size up another person's personality on the basis of very little information.

These instructions are virtually the same as those used by Haire, except that the last sentence ("This is a test....") was given verbally in the Haire research. The authors corresponded with Professor Haire during the conduct of this research to minimize differences in methodology. The major differences between the two studies are in location and in sample size. The authors obtained 22 responses to the Nescafé list and 20 responses to the Maxwell House list, whereas Haire obtained 50 responses to each shopping list. While a larger sample would have been better, sample size was not felt to be a serious limitation given that neither sample was a true probability sample and that projective techniques are the methodology. The present study followed the same careful, literal coding policies as used in the Haire study.

RESULTS

The findings of the two studies are presented in Table 1. The results of the 1968 study confirm the hypothesis which guided the research.

TABLE 1   Percentage of Respondents Ascribing Characteristics to Shoppers

Ascribed Characteristics	Haire Study			1968 Study		
	Nescafé shopper (n=50)	Maxwell House shopper (n=50)	chi square	Nescafé shopper (n=22)	Maxwell House shopper (n=20)	chi square
Lazy	48%	4%	22.921[d]	18%	10%	0.010
Poor planner	48	12	13.762[d]	27	25	0.034
Thrifty	4	16	2.778[a]	36	55	0.813
Spendthrift	12	0	4.433[b]	23	5	1.436
Bad wife	16	0	6.658[c]	18	5	0.706
Good wife	4	16	2.778[a]	18	25	0.026
Overweight				18	10	0.010
Time-saver				32	10	1.808
Does not enjoy homemaking				18	10	0.010
Enjoys homemaking				27	40	0.298
No imagination				41	30	0.172
Single girl, busy				18	10	0.010
Brand of coffee mentioned				50	35	0.447

[a] Significant at .10 level.
[b] Significant at .05 level.
[c] Significant at .01 level.
[d] Significant at 0.001 level.

There are *no* significant differences between characteristics ascribed to the Maxwell House shopper and those for the Nescafé shopper in 1968. In the Haire study, the six characteristics listed first in Table 1 were all found to be significantly different for the Maxwell House and Nescafé shoppers. (While Professor Haire did not report his statistical analysis, the authors have compared his reported data with their data by using a chi-square test for two independent samples.[3]) None of these characteristics was found to be significantly different for the two classes of shoppers in the 1968 study.

While the Nescafé housewife of 1968 tends to be differentiated from the Maxwell House housewife on the same dimensions as in the 1950 study, the differences have diminished to the point where they are no

[3] Sidney Seigel, *Nonparametric Statistics* (New York: McGraw-Hill, 1956), pp. 104–110.

longer statistically significant. (This may also reflect differences in sample size to some extent.)

DISCUSSION

There are at least two kinds of explanations for the results of the 1968 study. The authors are comfortable with the explanation, offered by their hypothesis, that convenience foods are more acceptable to the American housewife today than they were in 1950. The Nescafé shopper receives a more favorable assessment today. On the other hand, it is important to note that the Maxwell House shopper has taken on more negative characteristics. There are increases in the percentage of respondents describing the Maxwell House shopper as "lazy," "poor planner," and "thrifty." Subjective interpretation of the responses suggests that this reflects the "old-fashioned" nature of the shopping list itself. This is also consistent with the authors' hypothesis about the role of convenience foods. Forty-one percent of the Nescafé and 30% of the Maxwell House respondents described the shopper as having "no imagination."

Thus, not only is the Nescafé shopper more acceptable today, but *both* the Nescafé and the Maxwell House shopper are seen in a more negative light than in 1950 due to the influence of such items as a bunch of carrots, baking powder, and a bag of potatoes on the list. The modern housewife's shopping list might find these items replaced with carrots and peas in butter sauce, brown 'n' serve rolls, and instant potatoes au gratin.

The 1968 Nescafé shopper is more likely to be characterized as busy, single, interested in saving time, and lacking in imagination. Respondents also described the Nescafé shopper as quick, energetic, fast-working, out-going, friendly, physically active, and on-the-move. Many of these comments were stated in a positive way—the 1968 Nescafé shopper is seen by many as a busy girl, not necessarily a bad wife.

By contrast, the Maxwell House shopper was seen as more likely to enjoy homemaking, more in the mold of the traditional housewife. Twenty percent of the respondents who saw the Maxwell House shopping list actually described the shopper as living on a farm. She was also described as "dull, phlegmatic," and as having "no spirit of adventure" and "no elegance of taste." But, these comments about the Maxwell House shopper often seemed to be more influenced by the other items on the list than the Maxwell House Drip Grind coffee. As one respondent stated, "This list strains neither the brains nor the budget." Apparently, the existence of Nescafé instant coffee on the shopping list helped to counteract this tendency. While convenience foods were viewed with caution and mild disfavor at the time Haire conducted his study, they now may be taken as a sign that the shopper is "with it."

CONCLUSIONS

Today, the shopper who buys instant coffee is more typical than the consumer who buys "drip grind" coffee. The findings of the study are quite consistent with the observation that convenience foods enjoy a large degree of acceptance today, acceptance that was just beginning in the late 1940s. This replication of Haire's famous study also is interesting because of the similarity of results obtained from a very unstructured research technique used by two different research teams. While the purpose of this study was not the validation of projective techniques, it is important to note that literal coding procedures still produced essentially similar response categories from data collected in similar fashion.

6. Purchasing behavior and personal attributes

ronald e. frank,
william f. massy,
& thomas m. lodahl

To what extent is household purchasing behavior correlated with the personality characteristics of husband or wife? With demographic characteristics? With measures of socioeconomic status? What do personality characteristics *add* (over and above demographic and socioeconomic characteristics) to our ability to understand and predict purchasing behavior?

This paper summarizes the results of an extensive analysis of these questions in the context of data for three product categories: coffee, tea, and beer.

IMPORTANCE OF INVESTIGATION

Knowledge of the correlates of behavior are important because they may be used as surrogates for original behavioral variables. Consider the case of a coffee advertiser. If he wants to reach heavy users and knows that family size and stage in life cycle are important correlates of usage, he can use published media statistics giving reach and frequency figures for these socioeconomic classes. Thus, a media strategy can be devised without recourse to statistics relating media coverage directly to coffee usage.

Correlates of purchasing behavior may be useful in another way. Situations arise where it is not possible to physically direct promotional efforts to members of a particular target market segment. When this happens, it may be desirable to broadcast the promotion to a wider audience than would be suggested by segmentation analysis but with the message designed so the promotion will be self-selected by the target groups. Knowledge of purchasing behavior correlates may be invaluable in designing promotional messages, and it is here that personality correlates should be important. If it were found that— other things being equal—heavy coffee users exhibit identifiable personality traits, it might be possible to tailor a promotional message to be more visible to people with these traits than to the public at large.

Finally, it should be noted that knowledge of the personality and socioeconomic correlates of consumer buying behavior may be useful

Reprinted by permission from the *Journal of Advertising Research,* © Copyright 1969, by the Advertising Research Foundation.

A debt of gratitude is owed the J. Walter Thompson Company from whose panel these data originally came. Funds for support of the project were supplied by the Graduate School of Business, Stanford University, under a grant from the Ford Foundation. Computer time was subsidized by the Stanford Computer Center under National Science Foundation Grant No. GP-948.

in a purely scientific sense in addition to whatever immediate practical use such knowledge can be put in the process of devising market segmentation strategies. More should be known about the underlying structure of the purchasing process. It may also be of interest to examine the behavioral implications of differences in socioeconomic characteristics or personality patterns—as economists or psychologists rather than as marketing scholars. The correlates of purchasing behavior can shed light on these questions, though, of course, statistical analyses can never provide the last word on behavioral cause-effect relations.

PSYCHOLOGICAL VS. DEMOGRAPHIC AND SOCIOECONOMIC CORRELATES

The need for contrasting the relative efficacy of socioeconomic and psychological characteristics is especially important because of growing dissatisfaction with socioeconomic characteristics as a basis for predicting members of particular market segment groups.

The idea that psychological characteristics should play a more prominent role in segmentation analyses is summed up in *Grey Matter* (1965):

> To most marketers, "market segmentation" means cutting markets into slices—demographically, geographically, according to economic status, race, national origin, education, sex and other established criteria. But the idea of relating marketing strategy to psychological differences among customers has been slow to germinate. We call it "Psychographic Market Segmentation." . . . The profit potential in psychographic segmentation of market is greater than is generally realized and those advertisers who see these opportunities clearly, and exploit them skillfully, are scoring and will score triumphs, while those who continue to dissipate competitive energy only on established notions of market segmentation may find themselves on a "me too" merry-go-round.

In spite of the relatively strong positions that have been taken in favor of segmentation based on psychological characteristics of customers, there has been relatively little research published that provides an empirical basis for these conjectures. In addition, what has been published supports the notion that when effects of psychological characteristics do exist, they are relatively small.

Gottlieb (1958) found only slight differences in personality characteristics of heavy and light users of a proprietary medication. With respect to compulsiveness (one dimension of personality studied) he concluded, "It is probably not possible to address oneself to a clearly delineated compulsive group. What one should do is to address himself to the compulsiveness in all of us." Evans (1959) and Westfall (1962) report an attempt to predict customer automobile ownership based on knowledge of socioeconomic and personality characteristics. Like Gottlieb, they found only a modest association between personality and customer buying behavior.

Similar findings are reported by Koponen (1960), the Advertising

Research Foundation (1964) as well as other researchers. Both the Koponen and ARF studies used data from the J. Walter Thompson consumer panel.

Method

The J. Walter Thompson consumer panel served as the source of the data used in this investigation. Household purchase records from July 1956 through June 1957 for three frequently purchased grocery products—beer, coffee, and tea—were studied. For each purchase of a given product made by a household, a record was made of the month and year of purchase, brand, quantity, package size, cost, and whether or not a deal was involved. (A "deal" is defined as any special offer made to a household, such as a cents-off label or a coupon offering a discount or premium.) There were 230,000 purchase transactions for the three products combined from monthly diaries of about 5,000 households.

Socioeconomic and personality information were also available for each household in the sample. The socioeconomic variables included: (1) sex, age, income, and occupation of the household head; (2) level of education for both the husband and wife; (3) ownership of home, TV, and automobiles; and (4) geographic region and market size in which the household was located. The personality characteristics were based on the results of the Edwards Personal Preference Schedule, which was administered separately to both the husband and wife. Details of the method by which the test was administered and a discussion of the general personality statistics exhibited by the sample may be found in Koponen (1957).

The Edwards test provided measures of the following personality needs: achievement, compliance, order, exhibition, autonomy, association, analysis, dependence, dominance, self-depreciation, assistance, change, endurance, heterosexuality, and aggression.

The analyses presented for each product category are based on fewer than the 5,000 households included in the study because: (1) some of the households did not continuously turn in reports; (2) none of the products was purchased by 100 per cent of the sample; (3) some of the analyses required the deletion of households with low purchase rates; and (4) the sample was split into two parts at the initiation of the study for reasons which are discussed in the following paragraphs.

There were 15 measures used to describe household purchasing behavior which served as alternative dependent variables (see Exhibit). In addition, there were 29 independent variables (24 personality measures and five demographic and socioeconomic characteristics). Multiple regression analysis served as the principal statistical technique. For each product, 15 regressions were run, each with the same set of 29 independent variables.

The process which led to the final model was an elaborate set of statistical analyses. A detailed report of these analyses and results can be found in Massy, Frank, and Lodahl (1968).

At the start of the investigation, there was no body of theory sufficiently well-developed to provide a guide for specifying the nature and extent of relationships between various aspects of household buying behavior (e.g., total consumption of a product or brand loyalty) and household socioeconomic and personality characteristics.

We did, however, have some thoughts about where to start. But we were not sure how many experiments would have to be tried before we would arrive at what, in our judgment, would be a satisfactory basis for specifying the set of interrelationships we had chosen to study. We recognized that the process of intensive experimentation with a given set of data can easily lead to erroneous interpretations. Even if a set of data are in fact uncorrelated sequences of random numbers, for example, the performance of a sufficient number of experiments using different combinations of explanatory variables will eventually lead to a statistically significant association.

Data were divided into two parts to eliminate erroneous statistical conclusions. One set of data was an analysis sample, consisting of approximately one-third of the households in the sample. The other set of data was the validation sample, consisting of the remaining two-thirds of the sample respondents. Households were assigned at random to the two groups. Experiments were performed on the analysis sample. Once a reasonable model was developed, the second set of data provided a check on the stability of results by re-estimating the relationships by using the validation sample. This procedure provided an important form of insurance against arriving at spurious conclusions.

Work on the analysis sample proceeded in three stages: (1) dependent variable specification; (2) independent variable specification; and (3) experiments on alternative models of the relationship between the independent and dependent variables.

DEPENDENT VARIABLE SPECIFICATION

To develop a set of measures of household buying behavior that would be both parsimonious and efficient, a list was made of 29 different measures of household purchasing behavior for each product. These included such variables as dollars spent, number of transactions, number of brands purchased, number of stores shopped in, per cent of purchases devoted to the most frequently purchased brand as well as the most frequently visited store and per cent of purchases spent on deals. The list included all variables which previously had been recorded in literature as measures of total consumption as well as brand and store loyalty.

Exhibit
Variable Dictionary

I. *DEPENDENT VARIABLES*
  A. ACTIVITY MEASURES
    1. *Activity factor score* (coffee and beer only): Amount of activity exhib- ited by families with respect to the product— combines total units and number of trips.
    2. *Activity in trips factor*

score (tea only): Amount of activity exhibited by families with respect to the product, as measured by the total number of trips on which purchases were made.

3. *Number of units purchased.*

4. *Number of shopping trips on which product was purchased.*

5. *Average number of units purchased per trip.*

6. *Activity in unit factor score* (tea only).

B. BRAND LOYALTY MEASURES

7. *General loyalty factor score:* Overall tendency for loyalty to stores and brands combined.

8. *Brand loyalty factor score:* Tendency for a household to be brand loyal. Combines measures such as number of brands purchased, per cent spent on most frequently purchased brand, per cent spent on second most frequently purchased, etc.

9. *Number of brands purchased.*

10. *Per cent spent on most often purchased brand.*

11. *Consistency of purchases for second and third most popular brands factor score:* Tendency for the purchases of these brands to be clustered together in time rather than occurring at irregular intervals.

C. STORE LOYALTY

12. *Store loyalty factor score:* Same as No. 8 except for stores.

13. *Number of stores in which product was purchased.*

14. *Per cent spent in most frequently shopped in store.*

15. *Per cent purchases spent on deals.*

II. *INDEPENDENT VARIABLES*

A. PERSONALITY (Variables 1–12 are women's scores and 13–24 men's)

1. *Deference:* To get suggestions from others.

2. *Order:* To have things organized.

3. *Exhibition:* To be the center of attention.

4. *Autonomy:* To be independent of others making decisions.

5. *Affiliation:* To be loyal to friends.

6. *Intraception:* To analyze one's feelings and moods.

7. *Succorance:* To have others provide help when in trouble.

8. *Abasement:* To feel guilty when one does something wrong.

9. *Nurturance:* To help friends when they are in trouble.

10. *Change:* To experiment and try new things.

11. *Endurance:* To keep a job until it is finished.

12. *Aggression:* To criticize others publicly.

13–24. Same as Nos. 1–12 except for men.

B. DEMOGRAPHIC AND SOCIOECONOMIC

25. *Age of wife.*

26. *Size of family.*

27. *Car ownership:* Presence or absence of car.

28. *Size of metropolitan area.*

29. *Income-occupation factor score.*

These 29 measures were then submitted to a factor analysis. After interpreting the loadings of each variable on each factor (which allowed identification of the information contained in each factor) the factor scores of each sample household on each factor were calculated. In addition, raw variables were retained where no factor included equivalent information or where a check on findings was desired.

Separate factor analyses of these 29 measures were conducted for each of the three products. Initial differences could be attributed to the nature of the buying process across products or to the differences in such items as the average number of transactions per household as well as the distribution of number of transactions over households.

In order to clarify this source of ambiguity, a simulation model was developed. The model was used to generate artificial purchase sequences for individual households. The advantage of the model was to permit a generation of artificial household purchase histories which could control the nature of the buying process, the average number of transactions per household, and the distribution of transactions over households within each product.

These analyses yielded a set of 15 measures of household purchasing behavior.

INDEPENDENT VARIABLE SPECIFICATION

Initially, a series of three factor analyses which included the following variables were run: (1) Household demographic and socioeconomic characteristics, (2) men's personality scores, and (3) women's personality scores.

The problem of adequately characterizing the personality variables was more complex than that posed by the demographic and socioeconomic characteristics. Two statistical analyses were conducted to determine if a household's purchasing behavior depends on the sum of the effects of the husband's and wife's personalities or if it depends on the personality structure of the household (i.e., on the relationship between the personality of husband and wife). First, a factor analysis was run which included both the husband's and wife's scores. Second, a canonical correlation analysis was run in which the association between the full set of husband's personality scores and the corresponding set of scores for the wife was measured.

The canonical correlation analysis proved the more useful of the two. It was used to compute a series of household personality measures which were linear combinations of the husband's and wife's raw scores. These "canonical variates" served as an alternative to the original scores which were used to measure personality one person at a time (i.e., ignoring household personality structure).

EXPERIMENTS WITH ALTERNATIVE MODELS

An extensive set of stepwise regressions then were run on the purchasing variables as well as on a wide range of alternative specifications of demographic, socioeconomic, and personality measures. These included the original measures of the independent variables as well as the

TABLE 1   Predictive Power of Personality and Socioeconomic Variables Against Purchasing Behavior: Validation Sample Only

	Coffee				Tea				Beer				#	#
	R^2 (1)	F (2)	R^2SES (3)	FAD (4)	R^2 (5)	F (6)	R^2SES (7)	FAD (8)	R^2 (9)	F (10)	R^2SES (11)	FAD (12)	Sig. (13)	Sig. (14)
Activity factor score (coffee and beer)	.059	2.69*	.030*	1.61*	—	—	—	—	.074	1.25	.034*	.80	2	1
Activity in trips factor score (tea)	—	—	—	—	.068	2.18*	0.38*	.118	—	—	—	—	1	0
Number of units purchased	.066	3.04*	.029*	2.30	.072	2.31*	.041*	.119	.074	1.25	.012	1.25	2	0
Number of shopping trips	.047	2.10*	.023*	1.31	.055	1.74*	.017*	.146	.074	1.25	.022*	1.07	2	0
Average number of units purchased per trip	.048	2.16*	.018*	1.64*	.043	1.34	.018*	.94	.101	1.76*	.012	1.87*	2	2
Activity in units factor score (tea only)	—	—	—	—	.075	2.42*	.035*	1.57*	—	—	—	—	1	1
General loyalty factor score	.054	2.44*	.024*	1.62*	.056	1.78*	.025*	1.19	.083	1.41	.038*	.71	2	1
Brand loyalty factor score	.050	2.42*	.024*	1.63*	.044	1.38	.014*	1.14	.083	1.43	.022	1.27	1	1
Number of brands purchased	.070	3.13*	.042*	1.39	.054	1.70*	.017*	1.40	.104	1.70*	.017*	1.40	3	0
Per cent spent on most often purchased brand	.045	2.05*	.026*	1.09	.047	1.46	.012	1.30	.093	1.61*	.026*	1.41	2	0
Consistency of purchases for second and third most popular brand	.070	3.25*	.021*	3.02*	.028	.88	.007	.61	.079	1.34	.032	.97	1	1
Store loyalty factor score	.045	2.05*	.018*	1.47	.055	1.75*	.028*	1.05	.070	1.17	.018	1.04	2	0
Number of stores in which product was purchased	.044	1.97*	.025*	1.04	.038	1.17	.021*	.63	.052	.87	.016	1.55*	1	1
Per cent spent in most frequently shopped in stores	.034	1.50*	.012*	1.58*	.047	1.48*	.025*	.82	.058	.96	.96	.015	2	1
Per cent purchases spent on deals	.038	1.68*	.011*	1.45	.095	3.13*	.062*	1.30	—	—	—	—	2	0
Sample size		1282				899				485				

* Significant at the .05 level.

canonical variates. In addition, experiments were performed on a number of nonlinear models, i.e., to test the hypothesis that income's effect on total consumption would decrease as income increased and the hypothesis that only extremes in personality would have any effect on purchasing behavior.

Results

All of the analyses discussed in the previous section were performed on the "analysis" sample. The list of variables reported in the Exhibit represents the outcome of this work. The results reported in this section were generated from the "validation" sample which, in effect, constituted a fresh set of data.

The set of predictors after experimentation with the analysis sample was reduced to 24 personality variables and five measures of socioeconomic status. For measures of purchasing behavior, there remained 13 for the coffee sample, 14 for the tea sample, and 12 for the beer sample. Using an ordinary multiple regression program, the 29 predictors were regressed against each of the dependent variables. Results of this analysis are summarized in terms of predictive power in Tables 1, 2, and 3.

Table 1 shows that the values of R^2 for the total predictive battery against the purchasing behavior variables generally are quite low (Columns 1, 5, and 9). While all values of F are significant for the coffee sample, the predictor battery accounts for only three to seven per cent of the variance in purchasing behavior for coffee. The same conclusion generally is true for the tea and beer samples, although sample sizes are smaller. While these significance levels are high enough (at least for coffee and tea) to give confidence in the battery's predictive power, the relationships are rather weak. Thus, purchasing behavior is not well-predicted by the best combinations of personality scores and traditional socioeconomic indices.

Columns 4, 8, and 12 of Table 1 show the values of F (labeled Fad) obtained in a test to determine the significance of the variance added

TABLE 2   Number and Per Cent of Significant (.05 Level) Predictions by Type of Purchasing Behavior

		Activity Variables	Brand Behavior Variables	Store Behavior Variables	Total
Total battery	N	9	9	7	25
(SES + Personality)	%	69	60	64	64
SES only	N	11	12	8	31
	%	85	80	73	78
Variance added by	N	5	3	2	10
personality (FAD)	%	38	20	18	26
Number of significant					
predictions		25	24	17	66
Per cent significant		64	53	51	56

by the personality data to the overall prediction, given the amount of variance already accounted for by the socioeconomic indicators.

Table 2 sheds light on the patterns of prediction in Table 1. It shows the percentage of significant predictions for each of the three major groups of purchasing behavior variables: activity variables, brand behavior, and store behavior. The columns of Table 2 show that activity variables are the best predicted by the battery, with 64 per cent of the predictions on activity reaching significance at the five per cent level or beyond. Brand and store behavior variables are about equally well predicted by the battery with 53 and 51 per cent of the predictions reaching the five per cent level, respectively. Table 2 also shows that although 64 per cent of the predictions for the total battery reached significance at the five per cent level, 78 per cent of the predictions using only socioeconomic variables reached significance, and in only 26 per cent of the cases did personality variables add a significant increment to predictive efficacy based on socioeconomic data alone. Personality variables seem to add considerably more to the prediction of activity variables than they do for either brand or store behavior.

Table 3 gives a breakdown of predictive power by products. It is

TABLE 3   Number and Per Cent of Significant (.05 Level) Predictions by Product

		Coffee	Tea	Beer	Total
Total battery (SES + Personality)	N	13	9	3	25
	%	100	64	25	64
SES only	N	13	12	6	31
	%	100	86	50	78
Variance added by personality (FAD)	N	7	1	2	10
	%	54	7	17	26
Number of significant predictions		33	22	11	66
Per cent significant predictions		84	52	31	56
Sample size		1282	899	485	

shown that coffee is by far the best predicted of the three products with 84 per cent of the predictions reaching significance at the five per cent level, tea is second with 52 per cent, and beer is a poor third with 31 per cent. The personality variables add a significant increment to the prediction from socioeconomic data alone in 54 per cent of the cases for coffee, but only in seven and 17 per cent of the cases for tea and beer, respectively. Beer purchasing behavior, however, is relatively poorly predicted by all of the measures in the battery. (Part of this is due to the lower power of the F test with smaller sample sizes.)

To summarize conclusions on predictive power: (1) purchasing behavior is poorly predicted by the battery; (2) socioeconomic data alone has the best prediction record for purchasing behavior with 78 per cent of the predictions reaching significance; (3) and personality scores add a significant increment to the prediction from socioeconomic data in only 26 per cent of the cases, with most of these clustered on coffee on the product breakdown and on activity variables in the purchasing behavior breakdown.

One major question in this study was whether personality data add enough predictive power for the understanding of purchasing behavior to justify added expense and collection difficulty. Given the results summarized above, it appears that they do not; but it should be noted that socioeconomic data alone do a poor job of prediction on an absolute basis. Taken together, they account for between one and four per cent of the variance in purchasing behavior for coffee and also for tea and beer. If this small proportion of variance in any set of behavioral data can be understood with socioeconomic data, then it seems worthwhile to try new predictors in an effort to understand behavior more thoroughly, at least for research purposes.

The following is a summary of the relationships of brand loyalty, store loyalty, and activity.

For brand loyalty it was found that:

1. High incomes and big markets generally mean low loyalty.
2. Husband's endurance score is associated with high loyalty for all three product classes. This is the most stable relationship between personality and brand behavior.
3. Husband and wife's personality scores on the same personality dimension relate differently to the dependent variables and, therefore, have to be treated as separate entities.
4. Brand loyalty may have two different psychological bases in the wife's personality scores: one based on independence (autonomy score) and one based on resistance and fear of change (deference and succorance scores).
5. Husband's preferences may play a strong role in brand behavior in families, considering the number and strengths of the relationships between husbands' personality scores and brand behavior.
6. Switching behavior may have a psychological basis in needs for affiliation and deference on the part of the husband, suggesting that husbands in high-switching families are more susceptible to persuasive communications.

For store loyalty, principal conclusions were:

1. Market size and income, as in brand loyalty, are associated with low store loyalties.
2. Husband's endurance score is again strongly and consistently related to high store loyalty.
3. Husband's deference score and wife's change score are again associated with low store loyalty.

Concerning personality, the preceding seems to suggest a two-factor interpretation of high loyalty patterns. It would seem that there is a "strength" pattern which includes high scores on husband's need for endurance, wife's need for autonomy, and wife's need for endurance. Since this can be an almost impenetrable combination, these people might be referred to as "unreachables." Once they are won over to a brand, it would seem very difficult to dislodge them. They tend to have high loyalty, high consistency, and to some extent fairly long run lengths. It is not clear where they stand on dealing behavior. There is also a "resistance-fear pattern" which includes wife's need for deference and succorance and husband's need for succorance. It may be somewhat easier to devise promotional strategies for reaching this group. On the other hand, wife's deference is associated with low dealing behavior and with long run lengths; this highly brand-loyal person would probably need to be very sure about the qualities of the new brand before deciding to try it out.

The low loyalty pattern, on the other hand, seems to have somewhat clearer strategic implications. Low loyalty appears to be associated with high scores on wife's need for change and with high husband's deference and affiliation scores. These are also associated with high propensities to purchase on deal, with short-run lengths, and with low consistency on second and third brands. It would seem easier to switch this person, but it might be equally easy to switch him out of the new brand and into yet another. Most of the foregoing comments are based on the brand analysis for coffee, although elements of the low loyalty pattern also appear in the data for tea.

The high store-loyal family is one in which the husband has a high need for endurance. One strategic implication is that to maintain this kind of loyal clientele, the store should retain a relatively stable shelf and product organization, since this person has relatively high completion needs.

Concerning activity, results indicate that families who purchase much coffee are big families, have a car, and live in large market areas. Heavy tea purchasing families tend to be large, but unlike the heavy coffee drinkers, they tend not to have cars, and they live in smaller market areas. Heavy consumers of beer tend to be low in income; they live in larger market areas.

The personality results on activity are relatively more stable across the four dependent variables than are brand or store behavior, but they appear to be somewhat less stable across products. Considering the results for coffee, the family that consumes much coffee tends to have a husband who is high on need for intraception and a wife who is high on needs for endurance. Intraception is a need to be analytical about oneself and others, and this finding reinforces the stereotype of the coffee drinker as an intellectual. Endurance needs in the high coffee drinking wife are needs for completion and closure.

Heavy coffee drinking families also have husbands who are low in needs for deference, order, and affiliation. The latter finding is of interest since it contradicts the stereotyped coffee drinker as hearty, sociable, and friendly. On balance, the picture of the heavy coffee drinking family is one in which the husbands are analytical, independent, have low needs for order, and are not very friendly; the wife is a lady with strong completion needs.

The heavy tea drinking family is characterized almost exclusively by the husband's personality scores. In this family the husband is high on needs for affiliation, endurance, and aggression. He is a friendly guy with strong completion needs who is not afraid to criticize others in public.

The family with higher beer consumption has a wife with high needs for endurance (like the heavy coffee drinking families), high needs for succorance, and a husband with low needs for deference.

In summary, the relationships between personality data and consumption for coffee, tea, and beer seem useful in characterizing heavy users of these products. To some degree, these findings have contradicted the more commonly held stereotypes of the coffee and tea drinkers; the heavy coffee drinking husband turns out to be cool, detached, and analytical; the heavy tea drinking husband is a friendly, aggressive person with high needs for closure. Heavy coffee drinking is a big-city practice, while heavy tea drinking is a small-town pattern. The husband in the high beer consuming family is low in needs for deference. The wife has high needs to be taken care of by others and high needs for closure.

Conclusions

The degree of association between socioeconomic, demographic, and personality variables with household purchasing behavior is extremely modest. In addition, the incremental contribution of personality variables to prediction or knowledge of socioeconomic and demographic characteristics is extremely small.

Admittedly, this research has several limitations. As with all secondary analyses, the data were not collected specifically for the purposes for which they were used. The lack of data on environmental events was particularly limiting. In classic psychological terms, the stimulus part of the stimulus-organism-response prediction model is missing. Without this, it was necessary to use a trait-psychology model, where only data on organism (personality and SES) and response (purchasing behavior) were available. It is clear from the results that this model is inadequate for understanding purchasing behavior.

Finally, it must be noted that results are limited to three product classes—all of them beverages. This decision was necessary because of the availability of data in sufficient quantities and because coffee especially is a well researched product in other studies.

In a sense, findings generate more problems than they resolve. The various measures of buying behavior that were used are relatively reliable phenomena. (The coefficients of determination between the measures of household purchasing behavior based on the first six month period with the same measures based on the last six month period ranged from .47 to .93 with a median of .78.) The sample was large, nationally distributed, and carefully selected for the best combination of predictor and dependent measures using data from the analysis sample. No other known study has been done on as large a scale, and it must be concluded that understanding of purchasing behavior is much more limited than generally has been thought.

If socioeconomic and general personality characteristics are not important determinants of household buying behavior, then what variables are likely to make a difference? In order to answer this question, two additional pieces of information should be kept in mind: (1) Though reliable, these measures of buying behavior (except for store loyalty) have relatively low correlations from one product to the next; and (2) a person's personality, as measured by the Edwards test, presumably reflects enduring needs of the individual—that is, needs that are "common denominators" of behavior regardless of the nature of the problem and/or situation.

The presence of relatively high reliability leads us in the direction of believing that a large component of household buying behavior is systematic in nature and potentially amenable to understanding and prediction. In spite of this fact, personality and socioeconomic characteristics have low correlations with buying behavior. The low intercorrelations of purchasing behavior across products provides a possible insight into this anomaly. The more stable household purchasing behavior is from one product or situation to the next, the more importance can be attached to enduring characteristics of an individual as determinants of such behavior. The logic of this argument leads us to believe that one of the most fruitful directions for future research is the study of characteristics (including attitudes, valuation criteria, physical distribution) that are idiosyncratic to both the customer and the product and not to the customer alone as in the case of general personality characteristics. In addition to obtaining measurements of attitudes, use opportunities and marketing and physical distribution variables, it may be desirable to construct special-purpose personality measures for this kind of study. Our results do not indicate that personality variables do not predict—they clearly do—but perhaps a general-purpose test like the Edwards is not as adequate to the job as a battery of instruments specifically constructed for this purpose would be.

Second, it is very clear from our results that more work needs to be done on family decision-making patterns. Husband's personality scores clearly correlate significantly with loyalty and activity variables, but how and at what point his influence is exerted remains a mystery. When such a study is done, it will probably be found that this varies considerably over products; if so, this would also help account for our low "loyalty-proneness" correlations and the low stability of our personality correlations over products.

Another line of attack for future research is suggested by the fact that our study is cross-sectional rather than longitudinal. Our purchasing behavior· variables are obtained by averaging or aggregating a one-year time series of buying data for each household in the sample. While these variables do tap many of the dynamic characteristics of purchasing behavior, no attempt has been made to deal with time changes, per se, or to relate them to changes in environmental variables. It may be that while personality characteristics are not very important determinants of average household buying behavior, as it exists at a particular point in time, they may still play a key role in predicting how different households will adjust their activity and loyalty patterns to temporal changes in the environment—e.g., advertising campaigns, changes in retail availability, entrance of new brands, shifts in reference group orientations, etc.

A program of research aimed at evaluating the effects of personality needs (and socioeconomic status) on response to environmental changes would have to begin with the development of response measures that are either household-specific or are defined over small strata that are relatively homogeneous in the relevant explanatory variables. This requires both panel data on household purchases and time series data on environmental events. Numerous studies have analyzed differences in the response to promotional efforts of households with different socioeconomic characteristics. Unfortunately, the panel data used in these studies do not include measures of personality.

In spite of the obvious limitations, many of the relationships exhibit reasonable stability. They add an increment to knowledge about household-to-household variations in purchasing behavior. For example, endurance needs turned out to be a significant correlate of brand and store loyalty, and the two-factor interpretation of the personality basis of loyalty should stand up with further study. The interpretation of the affiliation-deference low loyalty pattern as susceptibility to influence also is an interesting topic for future work. Nevertheless, it is felt this study is definitive in showing that temporal averages of purchasing behavior are measures not predictable in any simple and direct way from personality and socioeconomic status variables.

REFERENCES

ADVERTISING RESEARCH FOUNDATION. *Are There Consumer Types?* New York: Advertising Research Foundation, 1964.

EVANS, F. B. Psychological and Objective Factors in the Prediction of Brand Choice. *Journal of Business*, Vol. 32, No. 4, October 1959, pp. 340–369.

GOTTLIEB, M. J. in L. Stockman (ed.). *Advancing Marketing Efficiency.* Chicago: American Marketing Association, 1958.

GREY ADVERTISING AGENCY. Herd Hysteria: A Mounting Marketing Hazard. *Grey Matter*, Vol. 36, 1965.

KOPONEN, A. Personality Characteristics of Purchasers. *Journal of Advertising Research*, Vol. 1, No. 1, September 1960, pp. 6–12.

KOPONEN, A. *The Influence of Demographic Factors on Responses to the Edwards Personal Preference Schedule* (Unpublished Ph.D. Dissertation, Columbia University, 1957).

MASSY, W. F., R. E. FRANK AND T. M. LODAHL. *Purchasing Behavior and Personal Attributes.* Philadelphia: University of Pennsylvania Press, 1968.

WESTFALL, R. Psychological Factors in Predicting Choice. *Journal of Marketing*, Vol. 26, No. 2, April 1962, pp. 34–40.

7. A multivariate analysis of personality and product use

david l. sparks
& w. t. tucker

INTRODUCTION

Despite the general failure of empirical studies over the past ten or more years to locate important relationships between personality and consumptive behavior, there remains among students of marketing this item of faith: behavior in the marketplace is critically reflective of individual personality. The corollary of that belief is that the measuring instruments or statistical techniques (or both) that have been commonly used in empirical work are incapable of giving more than glimpses of the structures and processes involved.

Statistical Techniques

Most of the work attempting to relate personality to consumer behavior has used bivariate inferential techniques or regression including multiple correlation. This implies the view (probably not held by any researcher) of personality as a bundle of discrete and independent traits which either do not interact or do so only in the simple sense that a number of diverse forces can be resolved into a *single* vector.

A recent study by Kernan notes that canonical analysis, alone or in conjunction with hierarchical grouping, can suggest the existence of molar personality types that are essentially synthesized out of the individual traits of a simple personality test [6]. Since Kernan's data delivered only one significant canonical root (at the .10 level), he could not use that technique to draw inferences about the complexity of personality trait interaction; but a hierarchical clustering of subjects based on choice strategies in a game playing situation posited four synthetic character types in which total personalities rather than specific traits seemed to be the operant variables.

The present study parallels the Kernan research with the intention of using hierarchical grouping in the same way, unless canonical analysis infers several significant roots.

In effect, the statistical techniques used in many previous studies relating personality to consumer behavior [2, 3, 7, 8, 9, 10] probably constitute a part of the "inadequate theoretical framework" referred to by Brody and Cunningham [1].

Reprinted by permission from *Journal of Marketing Research*, Vol. 8 (February 1971), pp. 67–70, published by the American Marketing Association.

David L. Sparks is Assistant Professor of Marketing, University of Richmond and W. T. Tucker is Professor of Marketing Administration, University of Texas at Austin. The authors express their appreciation to Professor Grady D. Bruce for his valuable suggestions during the course of this study.

Measuring Instruments

Psychologists are no more elated than those in marketing with current personality theory or the attendant measuring instruments. There is no persuasive theoretical basis for preferring one sort of personality test to another, despite a great variety of tests. On one hand, instruments like the Edwards or the California Personality Inventory measure a host of individual traits; on the other, the I-O scale locates everyone at some point on a unidimensional continuum. (Clinical techniques requiring subjective judgments are disregarded here for operational reasons.)

Additionally, instruments may be roughly categorized into two subclasses, those asking largely for: (1) direct reports on thoughts and feelings, and (2) reports of activities, actual or preferred. Preferences for one or the other of these subclasses will in some measure depend upon the way the experimenter regards personality. It is legitimate to think of personality as an intimate aspect of the cognitive and affective organization of the central nervous system (or the total organism). It is equally legitimate to regard it as a verbal construct describing behavioral regularities. When someone is described as anti-intraceptive or rigid, it is the cognitive and affective organization that is the principal reference. To call someone sociable or kleptomaniac is to classify him behaviorally with little regard for central processes. This dichotomy is not rigorous; a number of personality tests, Cohen's CAD for instance [2], ask for cognitive evaluations of behavior or otherwise provide mixed cases.

RESEARCH DESIGN

A sample of 190 college students (173 of whom accurately completed forms) chosen for their availability in introductory marketing classes were used to explore the relationship between consumer behavior and personality. The choice of such a sample (in this case all of the males present in particular classes on a particular day) seems appropriate when the effort is to locate the existence of relationships rather than to describe or define them for particular universes. Beyond this, the sample method was essentially that of Kernan [6] and Tucker and Painter [9]. Both previous studies showed that the frequency distributions on the Gordon Personal Profile [5] and Gordon Personal Inventory [4] for such a sample varied little from those of groups on which the test was normed.

The use of the Gordon tests was based on several considerations: (1) the bias of the authors toward the behaviorally-oriented rather than the cognitively-oriented test as relevant to consumer behavior, (2) the previous and partially successful use of that test [6, 9], and (3) the short time required for subjects to complete the tests. The fact that eight traits isolated by the test are not fully independent is of concern but seems of less consequence than the test's demonstrated ability to differentiate people with regard to the kinds of behavior under study.

The instrument to measure the subjects' product use had 17 multiple-choice questions. The products, considered to be typical for this subject group, were: headache remedies, mouthwash, men's cologne, hair spray, shampoo, antacid remedies, *Playboy*, alcoholic beverages, complexion aids, vitamins, cigarettes, coffee, chewing gum, and after-shave lotion. In addition, subjects were asked how often they brushed their teeth and had their hair cut. Another question asked about their adoption of new clothing fashions. Response categories were, generally: never, less than once a week, about once a week, more than once a week but less than once a day, and about once a day. For five of the products, dichotomous or specially worded response categories were required. While these products were not a complete inventory of typical products, they did represent a reasonable number and were considered sufficient for this investigation.

A pretest of the 17-item product-use questionnaire with 62 male undergraduates led to minor changes in the question wording and response categories. A varimax factor analysis of the pretest data showed the 17 questions to be almost completely independent, the last of the 17 factors extracting nearly as much variance as the first. While desirable in one sense, independence as extensive as this raises critical issues which will be discussed later.

FINDINGS

A correlation analysis of the data (Table 1) shows essentially the same weak and spotty relationships between personality traits and particular product use reported previously. It may lead one to conclude that some two percent of the variance in the use of mouthwash may be accounted for by cautiousness or that some six percent of the variance in the use of men's cologne is associated with sociability. The total of 18 significant but low correlations in a matrix where seven would be expected to occur by chance may be persuasive that something is responsible, but the findings seem to be of minimal value.

Canonical analysis provides both a more persuasive case for the relationship under study and some hints concerning the kinds of personality structures involved. That is far from saying that canonical analysis illuminates the field; it is notoriously difficult to interpret beyond the significance levels of R's associated with particular roots.

Table 2 shows the first three canonical roots with R's of .606, .548, and .413. These have significance levels of .0001, .0002, and .0752 respectively, leaving little doubt that there are significant relationships involved. More interesting, since the basic relationship involved has not really been in doubt, is the nature of the relationship suggested. The meanings of the roots can be crudely approximated by extracting the items with heavy loadings from the predictor and criterion sets, somewhat simplifying the picture. In this case, items with coefficients above .30 are used.

The first root is associated with the use of shampoo, alcoholic beverages, cigarettes, and early fashion adoption. Those involved are best

TABLE 1   Correlation Matrix: Product Use and Personality Trait

Product	Ascend-ancy	Responsi-bility	Emotional stability	Socia-bility	Cautious-ness	Original thinking	Personal relations	Vigor
Headache remedy	.0254	−.1391	−.2104ᵃ	.1490	−.0073	−.0649	−.0875	−.0907
Mouthwash	.0702	−.0983	−.1308	.1125	.1501ᵃ	−.0242	.0443	−.1238
Men's cologne	.1473	−.1066	−.1222	.2599ᵃ	.1247	.0715	−.0459	.0008
Hair spray	−.0580	−.1241	−.0725	.0388	−.0824	−.0668	−.0664	−.0159
Shampoo	.1735ᵃ	−.1420	.0729	.1459	−.0449	.0757	.0412	.0116
Antacid remedy	.0217	−.1521ᵃ	−.2692ᵃ	.0393	−.1222	−.0974	−.1119	−.0886
Playboy	.1293	−.0218	.0787	.2621ᵃ	−.1038	.0650	.0169	.1185
Alcoholic beverages	.2001ᵃ	−.1605ᵃ	.0159	.1973ᵃ	−.2861ᵃ	.0041	−.1436	.0261
Brush teeth	−.1324	−.0418	.0196	−.0624	−.0663	−.1645ᵃ	.0329	−.1074
Fashion adoption	.2892ᵃ	−.1647ᵃ	−.0628	.3858ᵃ	−.0919	.0924	.0838	.0557
Complexion aids	.0065	−.0591	−.0106	.0845	−.1131	−.0826	−.0667	−.0902
Vitamin capsules	.1384	−.1197	−.1759ᵃ	.1288	−.0855	.0963	−.0414	.0016
Haircut	−.0587	.0616	.0655	−.0774	−.0670	−.0247	−.0394	−.0311
Cigarettes	.0869	−.1465	−.1213	.0954	−.1313	.1408	−.0376	−.0305
Coffee	−.0413	−.0265	−.1478	−.0185	.0403	−.0781	−.0683	−.0734
Chewing gum	.1645ᵃ	−.1035	−.1165	.2581ᵃ	−.1209	−.0447	.0433	−.0446
After-shave lotion	.0506	.1016	.0429	.0751	.0091	.1288	.0168	.0676

ᵃ Indicates correlation coefficient is significant at the .05 level.

TABLE 2   Results of Canonical Analysis

Variables	Canonical coefficients		
	1	*2*	*3*
Criterion set (product use)			
Headache remedy	−.0081	−.4433	.1123
Mouthwash	−.1598	−.4538	.2809
Men's cologne	.2231	−.1935	−.2121
Hair spray	.0664	.0706	.0857
Shampoo	.3784	.1587	−.0063
Antacid remedy	−.1421	−.1746	−.3226
Playboy	.1511	.1591	.5220
Alcoholic beverages	.4639	.3098	−.1329
Brush teeth	−.1879	−.0152	.2341
Fashion adoption	.3226	−.3993	.0856
Complexion aids	−.0243	.0925	.1799
Vitamin capsules	.2870	−.0599	−.4975
Haircut	−.1698	.1855	−.0170
Cigarettes	.4065	.0551	−.2894
Coffee	−.2441	−.2453	.1330
Chewing gum	.2051	−.1320	.1342
After-shave lotion	−.0270	.3022	.0108
Predictor set (personality traits)			
Ascendancy	.0182	−.0517	−.4375
Responsibility	−.5125	.0777	−.1688
Emotional stability	.4309	.6405	.4880
Sociability	.6072	−.3597	.6199
Cautiousness	−.2869	−.5959	.2438
Original thinking	.2377	.1620	−.3076
Personal relations	−.1245	−.0567	.0369
Vigor	.1681	.2592	.0481
Roots	.3671	.3000	.1711
Canonical R	.606	.548	.413
χ^2	72.7419	56.7026	29.8417
d.f.	24	22	20
Probability	.0000	.0002	.0752

described as sociable, emotionally stable, and irresponsible (minus responsibility). The relationships are intuitively acceptable, although they are certainly not the only ones that would be so. Nevertheless, it makes sense to think that early fashion adopters are those particular sociables who are also emotionally stable (not easily upset) and also somewhat irresponsible (responsibility has previously been associated with modal behavior [9]).

The second root is associated with (again converting signs verbally for ease of expression) the use of headache remedies and mouthwash, late fashion adoption, and infrequent use of after-shave lotion. The personality characteristics are sociability, cautiousness, and emotional instability. At this point there emerges a clear advantage to the methodology. Both early and late fashion adoption are related to sociability, but in different personality contexts.

This seems to be exactly the kind of relationship personality theory implies: not a simple connection between sociability and early fashion adoption, but a more complex one in which sociability combined with emotional stability and irresponsibility is oriented toward one sort of action while sociability combined with emotional instability and cautiousness is oriented toward its opposite.

In the third root (with the marginal significance level of .075) sociability again characterizes the individual, but in this context the relationship with fashion adoption is very low and there is an association with light or no use of cigarettes, again a reversal of the variate-to-variate relationship suggested by the first root.

The most obvious explanation for these findings lies in the notion that it is the person in some gestalt in which the entire personality and the entire situation form a particular configuration, who acts, not the individual personality trait. But this view includes the possibility that the most useful approach to the subject is to measure individual personality characteristics and synthesize the molar personality from such measures. The relationships of the above canonical analysis suggest that even a simple model based on trait interaction could prove more predictive than a trait-by-trait approach. Nevertheless, some of the relationships suggested could stem in large part from nonlinearity. Further, canonical analysis is a linear technique which can only indi-

TABLE 3   Results of Cluster Analysis

	Cluster					
	1	2	3	4	5	6
Personality trait: Kernan's study[a]						
Ascendancy	81.0	19.0	81.0	43.0		
Responsibility	43.0	11.0	19.0	80.0		
Emotional stability	40.0	15.0	40.0	77.0		
Sociability	77.0	12.0	77.0	39.0		
Cautiousness	54.0	31.0	5.0	69.0		
Original thinking	72.0	31.0	45.0	43.0		
Personal relations	70.0	10.0	54.0	57.0		
Vigor	81.0	13.0	38.0	63.0		
Personality trait: present study[a]						
Ascendancy	66.6	54.9	50.8	52.3	49.4	63.0
Responsibility	44.2	55.2	49.2	47.6	61.7	41.1
Emotional stability	43.7	57.4	54.3	50.7	47.8	44.4
Sociability	63.6	49.1	42.9	37.9	36.4	59.8
Cautiousness	40.2	45.1	46.6	51.5	62.2	33.5
Original thinking	52.2	54.5	53.1	48.3	43.9	51.0
Personal relations	49.4	42.3	45.5	48.7	40.3	39.3
Vigor	49.4	61.2	61.5	54.1	44.3	52.3

[a] Mean percentile scores.

rectly suggest the presence of certain possible nonlinear associations while leaving others occult.

The present study parallels that of Kernan [6] closely enough that there is some interest in seeing whether a hierarchical clustering of subjects on the basis of their reported product-use behavior approximates the interesting personality profiles that related to particular game playing strategies. Table 3 shows the four clusters Kernan located and the six clusters that seem to best describe the present data. No persuasive case can be made for similarities in grouping, although the imaginative mind can perceive parallels. Nor does the cluster analysis, when compared with product use, add to the conclusions available through canonical analysis alone in this case. It seems possible that the near-fantasy situation of game playing in relative isolation may give freer play to personality expression than consumption patterns which operate under social, economic, and habitual constraints.

The annoying fragmentation of 17 questions into 17 factors of approximately equal magnitude is not readily explained. It is difficult to conceive that the frequency of use of mouthwash, men's cologne, hair spray, shampoo, and after-shave lotion are essentially independent behaviors not tied together. The problem may lie in the methodology, although it is difficult to understand how the response categories could mask associations when most were used by fairly large numbers of subjects. Yet on both pretest and test the same lack of structure appeared. The kind of post hoc explanations that come to mind do little to reassure one that there are not large areas of dissociated events in consumer behavior that will require explanatory models far more complex or far more numerous than one would wish.

CONCLUSIONS

The association of identical personality traits (within different sets of personality traits) with diverse consumer behavior suggests that trait interactions or nonlinear relationships may compose a significant portion of the personality-behavior relation. This may partially explain the difficulty in empirically demonstrating the commonly accepted hypothesis that personality influences consumer activities. Inferential techniques do not generally lend themselves to the location of the sorts of relationships implied by these findings.

The apparent lack of correlation among product-use patterns suggested by factor analyses of questionnaire responses leads to the conclusion that a general model applicable to all consumer behavior would prove extremely complex. The alternative of exploring personality in connection with particular behavior or particular products seems therefore the only current application to practical marketing problems.

The particular relationships among traits suggested by this study should be considered as merely representative of the sorts of interrelations that can occur. In all probability a study of other subjects, and other products, or other sorts of behavioral differences would show the relevance of different trait combinations.

REFERENCES

1. BRODY, ROBERT P. AND SCOTT M. CUNNINGHAM. "Personality Variables and the Consumer Decision Process," *Journal of Marketing Research*, 5 (February 1968), 50–7.
2. COHEN, JOEL B. "An Interpersonal Orientation to the Study of Consumer Behavior," *Journal of Marketing Research*, 4 (August 1967), 270–8.
3. EVANS, FRANKLIN B. "Psychological and Objective Factors in the Prediction of Brand Choice: Ford Versus Chevrolet," *Journal of Business*, 32 (October 1959), 340–69.
4. GORDON, LEONARD V. *Gordon Personal Inventory*. New York: Harcourt, Brace, & World, 1963.
5. ————. *Gordon Personal Profile*. New York: Harcourt, Brace, & World, 1963.
6. KERNAN, JEROME B. "Choice Criteria, Decision Behavior, and Personality," *Journal of Marketing Research*, 5 (May 1968), 155–64.
7. KOPONEN, ARTHUR. "Personality Characteristics of Purchasers," *Journal of Advertising Research*, 1 (September 1960), 6–12.
8. PESSEMIER, EDGAR A., PHILIP C. BURGER, AND DOUGLAS J. TIGERT. "Can New Product Buyers be Identified?" *Journal of Marketing Research*, 4 (November 1967), 349–55.
9. TUCKER, W. T. AND JOHN J. PAINTER. "Personality and Product Use," *Journal of Applied Psychology*, 45 (October 1961), 325–9.
10. WESTFALL, RALPH. "Psychological Factors in Predicting Product Choice," *Journal of Marketing*, 26 (April 1962), 34–40.

Information-processing

3

4 MARKETER-DOMINATED INFORMATION SOURCES

Obviously, the buyer receives information from many sources, some interpersonal and others marketer-dominated. Marketing tends to emphasize the latter when discussing advertising and sales force effects. Our discussion here will be confined mainly to advertising, not because sales force effort is unimportant but because more systematic research is available on advertising effects.

Even with advertising, can you answer the question, "How do you describe an ad?" We have not done nearly enough in developing ways of describing ads: each ad tends to be almost a unique entity, and this state of affairs handicaps effective research. This point may become more concrete when we discuss *stimulus ambiguity* in Chapter 8. Here, we will leave "advertising" largely undefined as an introduction to what is, in effect, a vast and exciting area, especially in this period of sharp consumer criticism of advertising practices.

One of the topics around which heated discussions often occur is how effective is advertising. Vance Packard's writings (1957) illustrate one extreme, and the objective researcher, who finds it impossible to prevent the "noise" of the many market forces operating on the buyer from engulfing and hiding the effects of advertising, represents the other. Bogart, Tolley, and Orenstein (1970)* focus on this problem, showing that in the situation studied, few people were affected, but these were affected enough to buy. This conclusion raises many interesting questions to be treated in later chapters, such as how is the buyer able to be unconsciously selective in the information he assimilates.

Does the nature of the ad itself, for example, make any difference in whether it is consciously perceived? If not, a lot of salaries are being wasted on copywriters and artists in advertising agencies. But this question can be given serious thought only if we can meaningfully describe an ad in its environment, some of which Bauer (1967)* discusses under source effect. "Source" here can best be understood as a part of the Lasswell paradigm, "Who says what to whom through which medium with what effect?" "Who" is, of course, the source. Bauer not only does a splendid job of setting forth these dimensions, which are relevant here where we are dealing with marketer-dominated sources, but he also illustrates well how social science, or any science, evolves by stringing pieces of past evidence together into a rationale that can effectively guide the generation of new evidence. The four dimensions of the source effects given by Bauer are competence, trust, likability, and power.

REFERENCE

1. PACKARD, VANCE. *The Hidden Persuaders*. New York: McKay, 1957.

8. What one little ad can do

leo bogart, b. stuart tolley, & frank orenstein

What can a single ad or commercial accomplish with the multitudes who really couldn't care less about what the advertiser wants to tell them, and whose attention is diverted by the clamor of innumerable distractions in daily life?

Advertising men generally assume that even those messages which leave virtually no discernible memory trace at all may, through the force of repetition, turn out to have a residual effect.

The common theory has it that consumers carry around in their heads an enormous assortment of brand images of varying clarity, intensity, and favorability; these brand images are activated at the time of purchase decisions. A brand's image is not merely the accumulated result of many casual exposures to its name and its advertising; it reflects experience. This suggests the hypothesis that if the consumer "set" toward a brand is apt to be built more out of actual use than out of casual, unwanted advertising exposures, an advertisement's duty may *not* merely be to add its trivial mite to the pile of previous trivial exposures, but also to produce an *immediate* effect on the very few people who were already (whether they knew it or not) "ready to buy" and predisposed to attend to the message with more than casual interest.

Huge markets are made up of small numbers of buying decisions made on any one day. In a 30 hour period, the study reported on here found only six per cent of the housewives buying coffee, yet these purchases add up to an annual volume of over $2.5 billion dollars. The brand choices made by these six women in 100 may be influenced by advertising, but to what extent are they influenced directly by messages which reach them when coffee is a salient subject for them?

The job-hunter reads the classified ads with a purpose and with his attention strongly focused. Perhaps at not quite the same level of intensity, the woman who is in the market for a new fall suit will study ads to get ideas on the specifics of style and pricing before she goes on her shopping trip. Most retail advertising is designed to have this kind of immediate effect, but retailers recognize that an ad must be exposed to vast numbers of people in order to produce a direct response from the very few who will buy the advertised item. Retailers can measure the pull of an ad from mail and phone orders or from the increased volume of traffic at the sales counters. An ad can pull traffic but not sales if the merchandise does not live up to the promises.

The sales effects of an ad may be delayed for days or even weeks, and the customer brought to the store by an ad for one item can end up buying others as well. Apart from the direct sales response, the cumulative effect of advertisements for many different items helps to build a store's overall reputation and thus its traffic. All these side-effects make it hard even for retailers to measure the exact yield from a single ad.

Unlike the retailer, the national advertiser rarely expects that any individual advertisement will produce a visible sales response unless it announces a radically new product, or represents a special offer of limited duration, or has a strong fashion or fad appeal. Rather, he expects that the individual ad, along with others in the campaign, will produce a cumulative effect when they are exposed repeatedly to the same people.

Because national advertisers generally acknowledge that the impressions created by a single product advertisement are at a low level of intensity, field studies of advertising effects normally try to measure the impact of a whole campaign, rather than that of any one individual message. The more directly one focuses the attention of experimental subjects on the communications being studied, the easier it is to measure responses which disappear in the confusion of the real marketing world. But can traceable effects be measured for a single national ad under *normal* conditions of exposure?

THE RESEARCH DESIGN[1]

This study had two principal objectives: (1) To see whether it was possible, under field conditions, to measure short-run direct sales responses to individual national advertisements for specific products, and (2) to look at the relationship between measures of sales response and measures of communication response which are less expensive, easier to obtain, and, hence, more commonly used to determine whether or not an ad is successful.

The study reported here sought to combine the best features of field and laboratory research. In the laboratory, one can not only describe relationships but also determine cause and effect. Tight controls can be exercised over the communications input. The number of variables that might influence the outcome can be limited.

In field experiments, there are inevitably unanticipated complications, and many extraneous variables (competitive activities, pricing, distribution, etc.) apart from the advertising under study may affect the results.

Generally, a laboratory test is conducted with a specially selected population. This may make the experiment easier to control, but the

[1] The research described in this article was sponsored by the Newsprint Information Committee, and field work and tabulations were conducted by Opinion Research Corporation under the project direction of Reuben Cohen, assisted by Herbert Abelson. (Both are now associated with Response Analysis Corporation.) B. Stuart Tolley was the Bureau of Advertising's project director responsible for the analysis of the data. The study was conducted in technical consultation with the Advertising Research Foundation.

sample is often atypical. A field experiment, by contrast, commonly deals with a broad cross-section of real people functioning in a normal environment. In the field experiment, advertising appears in its usual context and is exposed to the audience under normal conditions. As a result it often takes a long period of time to obtain traceable effects. In laboratory experiments, the test audience may be subjected to unusual advertising pressure in order to obtain faster results within a shorter time period.

The spontaneous memory of an individual ad is short indeed, given the number of competing messages which crowd the customer's attention on any one day. Therefore, this study was limited to what happened in a period of one and a half days after exposure. In adapting laboratory requirements to field conditions, it was necessary to control potential exposure to each individual ad and to make certain that those possibly exposed and those definitely unexposed were comparable people living in the same market with identical conditions of product distribution and brand position.

To avoid findings limited to one ad in one place, the same ads were placed in different communications environments, in newspapers of different bulk, on different days of the week, and with different editorial matter and advertising on the page spread.

The experiment was run in June 1968, in six cities of different sizes in different parts of the country: Amarillo, Los Angeles, Pittsburgh, Providence, Roanoke, and Wichita.

Each of the papers in these cities on any one day carries many hundreds of advertisements. Some carry dozens of national advertisements. How could one possibly measure the effects of this highly variable communications impact on the consumer purchases made by readers in the day and a half after the ads appeared? This problem was solved by experimentally introducing a series of identical ads into all these papers, unbeknownst not only to the subscribers but to the boys who delivered the papers. A total of 2,438 home interviews was conducted with housewives on the day after delivery of the morning newspaper (an average of 30 hours later). By using morning papers, the respondents were given a whole day to look through their papers and then go shopping before the interviewers arrived the next day.

In each city we selected matched samples of home delivery routes, two for each of two successive days. We used two days rather than one simply because of the difficulty of finding and training enough interviewers to handle a study of the intended dimensions within a single day.

The production of a newspaper is an extremely complicated job of manufacturing and distribution and the mere mechanics of inserting the test pages and controlling their delivery to the right homes was in itself a prodigious project. A key part of the procedure was the production of test pages which, when produced in the newspapers, are virtually indistinguishable by the reader from other pages. For five of the cities these test pages were produced by photo-offset in an outside printing shop some days ahead of time, using the appropriate dateline and the paper's own typographical format and editorial material of a timeless, feature character.

The test pages were inserted just after the real copies came off the presses, and the papers were delivered to subscribers in the normal way.

The test pages were inserted into each paper in a four-page sheet and a single two-page sheet so that each of the six test pages faced a real page. This made possible the simultaneous testing of a range of products and creative treatments which might not ordinarily occur in any day's issue of a given newspaper.

The test pages were generally accepted by respondents as a normal part of the paper. In every interview, respondents were asked, "Would you say that this issue of the newspaper was pretty much the same as other issues of the (day and newspaper), or was it different or unusual in any way?" If "different," they were asked, "In what way?" Only 1.1 per cent referred to something which could be pinned to the test pages. For instance, some said there were no page numbers.

Two sets of test pages were created for each day, with different ads in each set. Since two matched groups were set up for the same day, each was a control for the other. In each city personal interviews were carried out with approximately 100 housewives in each of the two matched groups. Because each ad was exposed in each of the six cities, this meant a total of at least 600 respondents per ad.

Ads from a wide variety of sources were used for insertion into the newspapers. Some were newspaper ads, some were taken out of magazines, and one was developed by the Bureau of Advertising. Several of the magazine ads were originally in color and had to be adapted to black and white for inclusion in the test newspapers.

Ads for durables, mostly high-ticket items, were also included, even though no direct relationship to immediate sales could be anticipated. These ads were considerably larger than the packaged-goods ads, as is generally the case.

The average packaged-goods ad tested took up 686 lines of newspaper space, about a quarter of the average 2400-line page. This size unit reflected actual advertiser practice rather than any arbitrary judgment of what the proper size unit should be.

To find out what specific purchases the respondent had made since the newspaper had entered her home, a three-screen, pyramiding sequence of questions was used, starting with what was easiest to remember. After she had begun to recreate the experience, the interview moved to the specifics of product and brand.

The first set of questions asked what stores she had been in or had phoned either "yesterday" or the day of the interview, and the time each store was shopped. A list of 15 types of stores was used to remind her of the possibilities. For food and grocery stores there was a list of product categories to jog the consumer's memory of what she had bought, and finally she was asked about specific brands. At every step of the process there were probes to permit mentions of types of stores and products other than those pre-listed. (See Figure 1.)

A similar procedure—but with somewhat less detail—was used to get at the respondent's purchase plans for the remainder of the interview day and the next day.

These measurements made it possible to compare shopping, purchases, and plans to buy, among those who could and could not have been exposed to the test ads.

FIGURE 1   Example of a Typical Shopping Experience

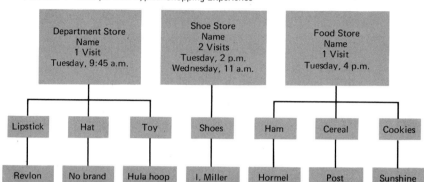

Since shifts in attitude might be expected among the general public even when sales response might be hard to detect, each respondent was asked to use a four-position scale to rate three brands. One of the three brands was represented by a test ad in the paper received the day before; usually the second brand was represented by a test ad in the same product category—to which she could *not* have been exposed. The third was for the other most important competing brand in the product category. The positions on the scale were:

> A brand I would probably buy the next time I buy that product
> One of two or three brands I would probably consider buying the next time I buy that product
> Not a brand I would consider buying
> Never heard of the brand.

The heart of the field experiment was the comparison of those women in the "test" sample (who had the test ads in newspapers delivered to their homes, and who may *or may not* have paid attention to them) with those in the "control" sample who *could not* have seen the test ads. (Each matched sub-sample was a test group for some ads and a control group for others.)

Not every measure was used for each type of ad. For instance, the comparison of sales was made only on the 24 high-volume packaged goods ads. The seven durables were not included in this, since one-day movement of large, expensive items was too small for measurement even with a large sample base. However, the durables could be included in the comparisons of test and control group attitudes. (See Figure 2.)

For 18 of the 24 packaged goods, a test ad for one brand was paired against a test ad for another brand of the same product category. Half of the sample received a test ad for Kraft American Cheese and the other half an ad for Borden's American Cheese. Thus the same respondents were the experimental group for one brand and the control group for the other brand.

In most cases both ads were the same size and the same shape. Usually they were placed on the same page of the paper (as delivered) and in the same position. In the case of these paired ads, *both* test and control groups were exposed to advertising for the product, so the

FIGURE 2

Measurement of:

Type of Ad (and average number of lines)	Attitudes	Brand Sales	Product Sales
7 Durables (1589) — — — — — — — — —	X		
24 Packaged Goods (686) 18 ads in 9 pairs of competing brands (692) — — — — — — — — —	X	X	
6 ads not paired against competing brands (664) — — — — — — — — —	X	X	X
Total 31 Ads (889)			

effect of the advertisements could be measured for each *brand*, but not for over-all sales of the *product*.

However, the design permitted product sales effects to be measured, too. The remaining six packaged goods ads were *not* paired. (For instance, the experimental group received a test ad for Dash Laundry Detergent, but the control group received no test ad for laundry detergent.) For these six test ads, comparisons could be made between newspaper advertising and *no* newspaper test advertising for the product category that day.

(The six products advertised in the no-pair group are not exactly comparable to those in the paired group. For example, the no-pair brands had only half the average purchase rates of the paired brands and the total purchase rates for the products were also about one-third lower, on average. Furthermore, the purchase rates of brands in a no-ad situation might be different from those in a situation where there was an ad for a competing brand of the same product.)

In the day and a half between delivery of the test paper and the interview, respondents were of course exposed to a variety of advertisements in all the test product categories and in all media, but these could be assumed to carry equal weight in the test and control groups. We were interested in measuring the effects of a single ad over and above the normal flow of advertising messages.

The readership portion of the study came after the questions on consumption and attitude. It covered page opening, recognition, and proven recall of the test ads and ads on the adjacent real pages of the same newspapers. To establish proven recall, respondents were asked to describe ads for specific advertisers and items. Recall was considered "proven" by the playback of any actual copy or layout features of the advertisement. The recall questions were asked before respondents were shown the newspaper for the page-opening and ad-recognition measures.

In addition to these standard measures, two other measurements were added: (1) Product focus or recall of brand-related content. (This referred to playback of product message as part of the proven recall, as opposed to references to ad technique.) (2) Personal "connections" between ad content and the reader's own life. This is a measure of an ad's ability to arouse involvement with the product. The concept was originally defined by Krugman (1966) as "... conscious bridging experiences or personal references ... that the subject makes between the content of the persuasive stimulus and the content of his own life."

In summary, for each ad a series of measurements was obtained that reflected different dimensions of its ability to communicate and to be remembered, and at the same time a number of measurements of response at the level of actual purchase or disposition to purchase.

ADVERTISING COMMUNICATION AND ADVERTISING EFFECTS

How advertising relates to sales and attitudes can be studied by first considering *only* those people who had the opportunity to receive each test ad in their home-delivered newspaper. If they paid attention and absorbed the copy points of an ad, are they also more likely to buy the advertised product?

To answer this question we compared purchases of the advertised brand by people with varying degrees of exposure and memory of the advertising. The group who best remembered the ad were those who could prove recall by playing back a spontaneous description. Of these, the ones who "connected" with it were the ones to whom it communicated best; others, when the ad was actually shown to them, remembered noting or reading it; still others who had stopped to read something on the page did not remember the test ad. Then there were those who remembered opening the spread but had not read the ad or any other ad or article on the page. Finally, there were the "unexposed" who said that they had not opened the page on which the ad appeared in the paper.

Table 1 shows that the people who could prove recall reported buying far more of the advertised brands in the thirty-hour period between receipt of the paper and the interview than did those who did not read anything on the page. The percentages buying any individual adver-

TABLE 1   Purchase of the Advertised Brand, Among Those Who Recall It to Varying Degrees

Among those who:	(Base Number of Instances)	Number/1000 subscribers who bought advertised brand
Made a "Connection" with ad message	(129)	8
Proved recall of ad	(682)	9
Recognized ad (when shown)	(2,565)	4
Read something on page other than ad	(8,649)	3
Opened page, read nothing	(7,896)	2
Did not open page with ad	(6,003)	2

(X^2 for "proved recall" against "did not open page" = 10.50; $P < .002$)

tised brand are tiny in every case, but this reflects the extraordinary thinness of the market for any product on any given day and the tremendous challenge the advertiser faces in getting his message to the very few people who are ready to buy. The differences between the unexposed and those with proven recall of the ad are significant at the *.0017* level. That is, they could occur by chance only once in about 600 times.

As Table 2 shows, first choice preference for the advertised brand

TABLE 2 Preference for the Advertised Brand, Among Those Who Recall It to Varying Degrees

Among those who:	(Base Number of Instances)	% Who would pick advertised brand "Next Time"
Made a "Connection" with ad message	(163)	35%
Proved recall of ad	(910)	25%
Recognized ad (when shown)	(3,265)	27%
Read something on page other than ad	(10,095)	21%
Opened page, read nothing	(9,643)	19%
Did not open page with ad	(7,117)	19%

(X^2 for "proved recall" against "did not open page" = 18.73; P < .001)

also tends to go up as the strength of communication increases.

The relationship is equally strong when we "turn the tables on their sides." Proven recall of a brand's advertisement is higher among those who consider that brand acceptable (Table 3). Among those who recall

TABLE 3 Ad Recall and Brand Choice

	Per cent of those potentially exposed who prove ad recall	Bases (Number of Instances)
Brand 1 would pick	6.2%	(3,632)
One of 2 or 3	6.2%	(3,994)
Not consider next time	4.0%	(6,156)
All others	3.4%	(5,635)

(For preferred brand versus "not consider," X^2 = 24.11; P < .001)

the ad, the proportion who make connections goes up as brand acceptability increases (Table 4), but the proportion whose spontaneous playback focuses on the product or brand rather than on technique is not strikingly greater (Table 5). (This suggests that Krugman's concept of "connections"—which looks at *whether* the reader relates to the ad—represents a more rewarding device for content-analyzing responses to advertisements than the more conventional classification in terms of *what* the reader remembers.)

The findings thus far presented would at first glance seem to demonstrate conclusively that advertising communication is strongly linked

TABLE 4   "Connections" and Brand Choice

Among those who:	"Connections" as percent of proven recall	Bases (Number of Instances)
Would pick brand	26%	(224)
One of 2 or 3 to consider	18%	(237)
Would not consider next time	13%	(237)
All others	15%	(195)

(X^2 = 12.13, P < .001)

playback focuses on the product or brand rather than on technique is not strikingly greater (Table 5). (This suggests that Krugman's

TABLE 5   Product Focus and Brand Choice

Among those who:	Percent of all ad recallers who focus on product or brand	Bases (Number of Instances)
Would pick or consider brand	61%	(471)
All others	56%	(439)

(X^2 = 2.25, P = .144)

to sales effects. However, a skeptic might still legitimately ask, "Do they buy the brand because they remember the ad message, or do they remember the message because they are (perhaps for totally extraneous reasons) customers for the product?"

Had the study rested its case solely on people's memory of the advertising they had read, there would still be strong doubt on the subject of cause and effect. Fortunately this question had been anticipated in the experimental research design, which made it possible to compare the brand purchases of those readers receiving a paper with the test ads and those whose newspapers carried ads for other brands instead.

Taking the aggregate of all the ads and brands under study, we found that in comparison with the control group, the test group showed 14 per cent more purchases of the advertised brand (a difference that could occur by chance only once in eight times), a 10 per cent greater brand share (a difference that could occur by chance only once in six times), 15 per cent more sales of any brand of the advertised product for the six cases where this comparison could be made (a difference which could occur by chance only once in twelve times), and four per cent more first choices of the advertised brand for purchase "next time," about the same for the 24 packaged goods and the seven durables, and for those who are in the immediate market for a product and those who are not (a difference which could occur by chance only once in eight times). (The details are presented in Table 6.)

TABLE 6   Comparison of Test and Control Samples

24 Packaged goods	Control		Test		Difference	P*
	Percent	(Base Number of Instances)	Percent	(Base Number of Instances)		
Purchases of test brand today or yesterday	.44	(22,603)	.50	(22,548)	+14%	.123
Brand share of test brand	10.6	(938)	11.7	(958)	+10%	.156
Plans to buy test brand today or tomorrow	.84	(22,603)	.69	(22,548)	−18%	.104
6 Non-paired packaged goods						
Purchases of the product today or yesterday	2.9	(4,955)	3.3	(4,905)	+15%	.083
All 31 brands in test						
Would pick brand "next time I buy product"	19.2	(26,858)	20.0	(26,855)	+ 4%	.119

* Probability values were computed by a comparison of six replicated subsamples for both test and control groups, with the sampling variance for each sample based on the formula $S^2_p = \frac{1}{6}\left[\frac{E(p_i - \bar{p})^2}{11}\right]$ where, p_i is the percentage for ith sub-sample, and $\bar{p}$ is the overall study percentage for all 12 sub-samples.

There *was* one finding which ran counter to expectations. We antici-pated that any direct action by consumers as the result of exposure to an ad would already have been taken within the thirty hours that elapsed between delivery of the paper and the time of the interview. Did any of the after-effects persist in the form of plans to buy the test brand "today or tomorrow?" ("Planning to buy" is obviously a more vague and less satisfactory measure than a report of actual purchase.) When the test and control groups were compared, it was found that fewer women said they planned to purchase the test brand. Perhaps a partial explanation is that the ads worked to trigger faster buying action on the part of women who were otherwise vaguely "in the market." By converting purchase intentions into actual buying, they may have temporarily reduced the pool of potential purchasers of the test brands. Unfortunately, there is no way to corroborate or disprove this speculation from the data.

Two other observations are worth making about this analysis. First, if it is assumed that the findings for the six no-pair ads can be gener-alized—i.e., that an ad for one brand also provides a promotional push for the whole product category, it would follow that the 14 per cent greater rate of test brand purchases in the experimental group repre-sents an understatement because the product category was being promoted in the control group, too, for the 18 paired brands. (If one takes the two increases literally, they would cumulate to 21 per cent greater sales of the test brands the day after the ad appeared.)

Then, too, the rate of actual purchases among those in the experi-mental group who *reported not* opening the page was almost identical with that in the control group who *could not* have been exposed (.43 per cent versus .44 per cent). The purchase rate among those in the test sample who opened the page was .53 per cent, or 20 per cent more than among the unexposed.

The over-all consistency of the experimental findings corroborates the earlier conclusion that advertising communications cause sales, quite apart from whether the reverse is also true. None of the observed differences hit the magic probability level of .05, but the true test of causality for a scientist is whether or not the data fit together.

Denton E. Morrison and Ramon E. Henkel, writing in the May 1969 issue of *The American Sociologist*, comment that, "Even if the general logic of statistical inference provided a sound basis for judging scien-tific hypotheses . . . it would not make sense to insist on arbitrary, con-sistently high levels of significance in scientific work. Significance exists on a probabilistic continuum. . . . The only way a significance level can be decided upon rationally is in the situation where the cost of a wrong decision can be calculated. . . . To insist on the .05 or .01 level is, then, to talk about the science of business, not the business of science." In a recently published magazine-television media test run by General Foods (1970), in markets differences were considered "probably favorable" if they could occur between a third and a sixth of the time by chance alone and "definitely favorable" if they could occur by chance less than one time in six.

The percentage changes we found could, of course, have been

greater or smaller if 31 different ads had been used in the test. Bigger ads, better ads, ads for more interesting products might have produced substantially greater demonstrations of effect than those actually obtained.

EVALUATING SPECIFIC ADS

The data thus far presented deal with the aggregate results rather than with those for individual ads, simply because the subsamples (of about 600 respondents) exposed to each individual ad were not large enough to provide statistically meaningful comparisons of sales results in a thin 30-hour market. Although this limitation is acknowledged, it was nonetheless possible to look at the variability of performance among the advertisements measured, in terms of all the available measurements of readership and sales effects.

The first conclusion that emerges from this analysis is that while on balance and over the long haul advertising promotes sales and improves reputation, individual ads may not merely fail to produce results; they may produce *negative* results, as was found in the case of three ads in this test.

There is a common idea that advertising pressure always works in a favorable direction, that mere exposure of consumers to the advertiser's message is bound to attract rather than to repel them. Yet copy tests of individual ads or commercials often show negative effects when people are unconvinced or when their attention is distracted by technique. An ad may convey unintended communications which arouse irrelevant fantasies. Copy, visuals, models, background, all convey symbolic meanings which may or may not enhance the product message. One might even infer that a bad ad or commercial which might simply disappear down the "memory hole" of the average reader or viewer would arouse more visible negative effects on the part of a real live prospect whose mind was already on the product and who was really paying attention to the message. On the other hand, a strong advertisement heightens awareness not only of the advertised brand but of the generic product category, so it may add strength to the competition in an inelastic market.

There is always great resistance on the part of advertising practitioners to the evidence that a good deal of advertising fails to do the job or is actually harmful. Yet, one knows, such null or negative results are commonly encountered in field surveys and are as commonly explained away on the grounds that the evidence is statistically inconclusive. Since single ads may have a reverse effect, the risks are less when the advertising researcher measures a campaign, in which, on balance, the results are more likely to show movement in the desired direction.

Even so, carefully conducted field experiments of continuing advertising campaigns, such as those reported by the Milwaukee Advertising Laboratory (1969), provide striking examples which show that specific (TV) advertisements can be counter-productive.

If some ads work against the advertiser's interests, this should only heighten interest in techniques which might help to distinguish good ads from bad ones. For this purpose, all the ads were ranked in terms of each performance variable on which there were data. We had already looked at the relationship between sales effects and readership among the women interviewed in the study, and found the expected positive results. But one can also consider the data for the sample of *ads*, rather than of *people*, to see whether an individual ad that ranked high by one measure would also rank high by other measures.

Findings indicated that in a pair of competitive ads, one may be superior by some yardsticks of communication, the other by different yardsticks. Figure 3 shows two illustrations of this variability.

Figure 3

This is not the place to diagnose the two pairs of ads used to illustrate the point: suffice it to say that in each case, the ad with the higher recognition score fails to maintain its dominance by the criterion of recall or connections.

This does not mean that the various measures of readership are unrelated. Table 7 shows that recognition and recall rank orders are

TABLE 7   Spearman Rank-Order Correlations Among Performance Measures

		Number of Brands Ranked
Readership		
Recognition—Recall	+.73	(31)
Effects		
Brand Sales—Brand Preference	+.42	(24)
Readership—Effects		
Recognition—Sales	+.13	(24)
Recognition—Brand Preference	+.22	(31)
Recall—Sales	+.03	(24)
Recall—Brand Preference	+.32	(31)

closely (but not perfectly) correlated, just as they were shown to be (at the +.92 level between recognition and aided recall) in the ARF's P.A.R.M. study conducted over a decade ago. Brand preference, not unexpectedly, shows a moderate relationship both with sales on the one hand and with proven recall on the other.

The key question is whether any measures of ad *readership* can tell whether an ad is serving the advertiser's *sales* objectives? Table 7 shows that there is almost no relationship between an ad's sales performance—when compared with other ads—and its comparative readership performance, as measured either by recognition or recall. The rank correlation with recognition is .13, with recall .03.

It is apparent that an ad may arouse widespread attention and high readership without persuading the few people in the immediate market who are ready to buy. Conversely, an ad may rank low in its appeal to the general reader and still have a strong sales effect upon the very few prospective customers in the immediate market. Obviously, it is in the interest of any advertiser to win maximum attention, but his task does not end at that point.

At a time when advertising communications proliferate rapidly, there is a strong temptation for advertising craftsmen to resort to the gimmickry and technical virtuosity which arouse attention through their ingenuity, startle effect, or entertainment value; in the process the brand's identity and the basic persuasive story may be lost.

Evidence in support of this assertion comes from a secondary study we conducted among 83 advertising decision-makers (company brand and advertising managers, agency account executives, creative, media and research men) in New York, Boston, Cincinnati, Detroit, and Los Angeles.

This secondary study was conducted in October 1968, with fieldwork by Creative Research Services, Inc. It was not part of the major study which underwent A.R.F. consultation. The study used a folder of scaled-down reproductions of the test ad pages to get the experts' ratings of how consumers would respond to the ads, in terms of sales effects, effects on brand attitudes, proven recall and recognition. By assigning scale ratings to the predictions, it was possible to correlate the experts' judgments against the actual results for the ads in the field experiment.

As Table 8 indicates, the experts did very well in predicting reader-

TABLE 8   Spearman Rank-Order Correlations Between Experts' Ratings and Field Results

Proven Recall	+.64
Recognition	+.55
Brand Acceptability	−.06
Brand Choice*	+.69
Sales Results	+.06

* Brand Choice reflects those who would "pick next time" among those who consider the brand acceptable.

ship performance, their record in predicting attitude change was mixed, and they could not predict which ads would sell more of the brand. The last, and critically important finding, follows logically from our earlier discovery that sales results had only a chance relationship to the ads' ability to win attention. But it is precisely the prediction of attention-value which is the adman's stock in trade, which in effect makes him an expert. Only the pretesting of an ad's persuasive power (as opposed to its attention value), and pretesting among consumers actively in the market, can be expected to reduce the level of random error that even the most talented of advertising professionals introduces into his predictive judgments of advertising performance.

CONCLUSION

Even a large and carefully designed communications experiment like this one leaves many questions unanswered. Hindsight shows that samples of both respondents and advertisements should have been much larger, but while a much bigger and costlier experiment might have reduced the statistical tolerances, we do not believe it would alter the basic conclusion, which is that advertising really works. Not merely newspaper advertising, we hasten to add, because the research also found parallel 30-hour results for a sample of television commercials which were measured as a by-product of the basic experimental design.

Advertising works for national brands, the evidence seems to say, not merely by creating or reinforcing a brand's reputation among the general public, but by directly and rather quickly motivating or activating the very small number of people who may already be potential customers, and who are, albeit at some remote level of sub-awareness, receptive to a reminder of what the advertiser wants to tell them. Obviously every advertisement that exerts its minuscule, imperceptible pressure on the consumer is matched and met by counterpressures from competitive forces. The consumer is continually pushed, pressured, and battered from every direction, though she is so inured to it all that she scarcely notices. But no advertiser should be under the illusion that each little nudge doesn't count, just because it's so hard to see the customer jump when he pushes. Something is happening out there, and frequent coverage of all the potential customers is still the way to make it happen more often.

REFERENCES

GENERAL FOODS. A Major Advertiser Tests the Effectiveness of General Magazines—*Life, Look, Reader's Digest*—and Television. 1970.

GIBSON, LAWRENCE D. If I Don't Want to Loan You the Plow . . . , Advertising Research Foundation *Proceedings, 14th Annual Conference.* New York: 1968, pp. 37–43.

KRUGMAN, HERBERT E. The Measurement of Advertising Involvement, *Public Opinion Quarterly,* Winter, 1966.

ULE, G. MAXWELL. The Milwaukee Advertising Laboratory—A Continuing Source of Advertising Serendipity. Advertising Research Foundation *Proceedings, 15th Annual Conference.* New York: 1969, pp. 71–76.

9. A revised model of source effect

raymond a. bauer

Not so long ago in a paper entitled "The Obstinate Audience" (Bauer, 1964) I introduced the notion that communication research had unwittingly slipped largely into the trap of treating the recipients of communications as though their only concerns were defense of their own ego or the ingratiation of other persons. I concluded that we ought to take a "full-blown problem-solving" approach to the audience. I would like to continue the same line of thought and spell out its implications for our model of source effect in communication.

To date, our model of source effect has had, explicitly or implicitly, the same defect from which our communication model in general has tended to suffer. Discussions of the credibility of sources of communication have failed to draw a distinction between those characteristics of the source that bear on an individual's motivation to ingratiate others or defend his ego (which I will call the psycho-social game), and those characteristics that bear on his motivation to cope with problems of the real world other than the problem of social relations (I will call this the problem-solving game).

Let me give my impression of how we got into this trap. My comments will be historical in form even though they are not based on systematic historical information. If you choose (as do I) you may call this an historical reconstruction.

A good point of departure is to consider what distinguishes the social psychologist from other scholars. It may seem like a trivial observation but psychology is an area of systematic study because we do not understand as much about how people behave as we would like. But there is a peculiar circumstance associated with behavior that is not understood, namely, that it tends to be labeled "irrational." Thus skills and concepts of the social scientist in general are called upon when "people aren't behaving the way they are supposed to." What this means is that their behavior is inexplicable in terms of someone's commonsense model of how rational people are supposed to behave.

The distinctive contribution of the social sciences has been to make sense out of supposedly irrational behavior. As a result, we have a chosen set of variables such as reference groups, compliance, emulation, social norms, ego-defense, imitation, reenforcement, and so on. While some of us study decision making and problem solving, these concepts seldom find their way into our discussions of social behavior. This observation is certainly not original with me. The following is a quotation from Bruner, Goodnow, and Austin (1962, p. 79):

Presidential Address of the Division of Consumer Psychology, American Psychology Association Annual Meeting, Chicago, Illinois, September, 1965. Reprinted by permission.

Psychology has been celebrating the role of "emotional factors" and "unconscious drives" in behavior for so long now that man's capacity for rational coping with his world has come to seem like some residual capacity that shows its head only when the irrational lets up.

The result, as I commented in "The Obstinate Audience," is that we have acted as though there were two unrelated models of human behavior: the "rational" model used by people such as economists and the "nonrational" model used by behavioral scientists and especially by psychologists. Sometimes they have even been treated as competing models whereas only the two taken together form a complete model.

There is an immense seductiveness to the behavioral science model. It is much more interesting to explain preference for breakfast foods as due to the influence of reference groups than in terms of taste or price. It is much more interesting to study the reasons a man reads automobile ads after he buys a car than before. But the fact of the matter is that although a person's choice of breakfast foods may be influenced by his or her reference groups even to the extent of choosing a breakfast food which he does not like best, there is no reason to believe that he would regularly eat food he thought was unpalatable nor that he would pay really outlandish prices. And, the man who reads ads to reduce postdecision dissonance almost certainly reads ads or got information from some source *before* buying his automobile. But, try to spice up a cocktail party with those sorts of facts!

My case, of course, will be that failure to consider *both* the problem-solving aspects and the psycho-social aspects of source effects has kept us from understanding as much of the process as is possible.

The literature on source effect has a continuous history since Aristotle's *Rhetoric* in which one main theme has been played throughout: The more credible a source of information is, the more effective will be the messages emanating from that source. Credibility, by and large, has been regarded as a unitary phenomenon. Sometimes the word "prestige" has been used, on some occasions as a substitute for credibility and sometimes as an explanation of *why* a source is credible. In other studies a credible source was also seen as "trustworthy" or "likable," and in one instance even rated by subjects on the dimension of being "dynamic" (Berlo and Lemert, 1961). But the study which used this dimension of credibility—"dynamic"—had the title "An empirical test of a *general* [my emphasis] construct of validity." There has been only a groping progress toward realization that credibility may be something other than a "general" or "unitary" phenomenon, nor has there been a visible thread of suspicion that source credibility is ever anything except a "good thing."

The basis for suspecting that something was afoot has existed for some time. In studying communication effects, for example, it has long been recognized that one must distinguish between the retention of information and shift in attitude. As long as the source of the message was one of low "credibility," it made sense that one might remember what such a person had said but refuse to adopt his position on the issue. But over a decade ago, Kelman and Hovland produced a paradoxical finding. I will quote from the discussion of this experiment in the Hovland, Janis, and Kelley (1953) volume:

> An interesting . . . finding was that recall was significantly better when the communication was given by a neutral source than either the positive or negative source. The authors suggest that affective response may adversely influence the amount of material learned and recalled, and that both the positive and negative communicators were responded to with greater affect than the neutral one. An emotional reaction to the communicator may focus attention upon him to the detriment of attending to his conclusions and learning his arguments.

Thus well over a decade ago, there was evidence that a favored source could have an unfavorable effect, namely, reducing the amount of information that the audience would retain. The mechanism postulated was that *any* emotional involvement, whether negative or positive, interfered with the subjects' efforts to learn the content of the communication.

About one decade later, Galen R. Rarick (1963), in a doctoral thesis done at Stanford University, took a decisive step forward. Noting there had been persistent findings that a low credibility source did not necessarily interfere with retention of information and that a high credibility source had, on at least one occasion, done so, he posited that there were really two components to source credibility which he labeled the cognitive and affective components.

The items he used for identifying the cognitive component were ones that might be described as involving prestige, power, competence and so forth. The items associated with the affective component were ones involving trust and likability. He hypothesized that attitude change is positively related to both the cognitive and affective components of source credibility. But, he argues, learning of information is negatively correlated with the affective component of source credibility. That is, when the source is seen as either high or low on a combination of trustworthiness and likability (these are my words, not his), the subjects will not remember as much as if the source were neutral. In other words, he was proposing a direct test of the hypothesis suggested by Kelman and Hovland, and attempted to link the "interference" to learning directly to one component of the source, that which he labeled "affective."

For the most part, we may say that Rarick's hypotheses were confirmed, even though one portion of the data was somewhat weaker than the others. He thus raised for the first time the idea that a source of communications might be regarded as having more than one component and that these components acted differently on attitude change and on retention of information.

Without further ado, therefore, I propose to present a model for the components of a communication source that is compatible with the propositions I introduced earlier, namely, that people are engaged not only in the psycho-social game, which has furnished almost all the explanatory concepts of communication research, but they also are engaged in problem solving. I will introduce several pieces of work that support the distinctions made in this model, acknowledge some complications, and spell out what I can see in the way of implications both for further research and for application.

Imagine for yourself a 2 × 2 table with four cells, two across the top and two down the side (Exhibit 1). In the top row we have two entries:

EXHIBIT 1

The Game	Components		Type of Attitude Change
Problem Solving	Competence	Trust	Internalization
Psycho-Social	Power	Likability	Compliance Identification

competence and trust. In the bottom row, we have two entries: power and likability. The top row components of competence and trust are pertinent to the problem-solving game. They provide answers to the questions: Does this person know what he is talking about? And: Should I believe him? The bottom two cells of power and likability are associated with the psycho-social game. They answer the general question: Is there any reason why I should ingratiate this person? Then there are two subquestions. The component of power is related to: What can he do for, or to, me? And the component of likability is related to: Do I want to please him apart from what he can do to, or for, me?

Let me comment on these components. You will note that I did not use the ubiquitous term "prestige." This is because it is itself a compound variable. In the problem-solving game, competence gives prestige, and in the psycho-social game power gives prestige. To the extent that the term prestige has other connotations they do not seem relevant in this context.

Furthermore, I would admit freely that in the real world these variables are not independent of each other. Likability and trust are associated. As we performed manipulations of the image of trustworthiness of a source, we found as we increased the rating on trust, likability increased although we had not said anything to indicate that the person was in any way more pleasant. We are *inclined* to like a person we trust and trust a person we like; and powerful people *tend* to be competent and competent people to be powerful. They, however, are different variables. We can say: I like him but in this situation I wouldn't trust him; or, I hate his guts, but at least you can trust him; or, he doesn't carry much weight around here, but he knows what he is talking about; or, he can make or break you around here, but he is stupid. Hence, the desirability of being sure which aspect we are dealing with, even though we know they tend to be intercorrelated.

You may have noticed that this model makes no explicit provision for ego-defense. It seems to me that the various devices of ego-defense that have been identified in connection with communicative behavior are *not* directly involved with the audience's relationship to the source, at least insofar as these four components are concerned *per se*. Devices of ego-defense arise *via* the interaction of *other* elements in the communication situation and the source. I will give some examples later.

Before continuing to spell out the details of this model, perhaps it would be well to present some data to support at least part of what has been said. Is this distinction between playing the problem-solving game and playing the psycho-social game a meaningful one? There are two studies which seem to bear rather directly on this topic and one which is less direct but illustrates the role which ego-defense may play.

Back and Gergen (1963) draw essentially the same distinction which I have drawn in connection with responses in an interview situation.

> On the one side we have the models of survey research which think that the respondent is motivated for information-giving, and on the other clinically-oriented ones which consider each answer to an interview an intense interpersonal manipulation.

When, they ask, will the respondent in an interview act so as to give information, and when will he act so as to ingratiate himself with the respondent? They argue that given his choice, the average respondent will try to some extent to ingratiate himself with the interviewer. One of the devices which is used to prevent the respondent from playing the psycho-social game is to deprive the respondent of cues whereby he can tell which type of answer is likely to please the interviewer. However, as a lengthy interview proceeds, the respondent becomes increasingly aware of the thrust of the investigation, and thereby has better cues as to the type of answer that is likely to be preferred. By using essentially the same question both early and late in a lengthy interview on mental health problems, they found that answers given late in the interview were more likely to be "o.k." responses from the point of view of established mental health thinking. For example, the later answers to a question about the handling of a delinquent boy were less oriented toward punishment and much more oriented toward giving the boy mental health treatment.

Thus, in asking under what circumstances a respondent would play "the information game," and under what circumstances they would play "the ingratiation game," they demonstrated that it was possible to specify circumstances under which there would be some appreciable shift from one game to another.

By using a combination of techniques to evoke the "ingratiation game" they were able to shift the proportion of mental health-oriented responses from 22% to 79%. This was on a sample of 4,000, and none of the techniques employed was different from standard survey practice. Certainly it is more than a trivial matter to know which game the respondent is playing.

An earlier study of mine involved the same issue. I was concerned with the strong bias of studies of source effect or personal influence toward explanations involving ingratiation or compliance. Therefore, I analyzed (Bauer, 1961) the relative role of two sources of influence on physicians' choice of drug: the doctor's preference for a particular drug company and his preference among the detailmen—the salesmen—of various drug firms. My reasoning was that when the drug for which he had to make a choice was less risky, there would be more of a tendency to play the psycho-social game. Thus, with less risky drugs, his preference for the detailman would be a more important correlate of his drug preference than it would be with more risky drugs. With more risky drugs, the doctor ought to be more involved with the problem-solving game and the role of his preference for a particular company would be more important. The data bore this out. With the more risky drug, the role of the company's reputation was twice as important as that of the detailman; with the less risky drug, the two sources played an equal role. This finding suggests that the importance of the cognitive task serves as a constraint against playing the psycho-social game. As the importance of the decision decreases, the individual is freer to play the psycho-social game.

Of course, if the cognitive task is excessively important, the subject may flee the field, or invoke one or another of a variety of defenses. We are all familiar with early studies which showed that as fear-arousing communications became threatening beyond a certain point they proved less effective rather than more effective. Hewgill, and Miller (1965) provide an interesting variant on this phenomenon. With a source of low credibility they found the pattern that had been found before; namely, that a message with a mild threat appeal was more effective than one with a severe threat appeal. However, with a source of *high* credibility, this phenomenon did not occur; the strong fear appeal was more effective than the mild one.

This I would regard as no more than a modification of my earlier proposition that the importance of the problem serves as a constraint holding the subject to playing the problem-solving game. A more highly credible source serves as a constraint against a person discounting the urgency of the issue and thereby giving himself a rationale for shifting the game.

Thus, these three studies illustrate that there are apparently two games which the subject can play: that this is at least partially predictable and manipulable, that the shift from one game to another can produce results of considerable importance, and that the source itself can influence which game will be played or, in fact, whether the subject will flee the field. Obviously, a person faced with a very serious problem and a totally incompetent source of information will be motivated to forget the whole matter.

Now, I would like to return to spelling out more of the details of the model. We have our four components: competence and trust, associated with the problem-solving game; and power and likability, associated with the psycho-social game. In addition to being associated with two different types of games the respondent may be playing, they ought also be associated with different types of attitude change although direct evidence for this is presently lacking.

Kelman has for some time pointed out that there are three significantly different types of attitude change: compliance, identification, and internalization. (See Kelman, 1961.) Compliance is behavioral conformity aimed at ingratiating a person whom one likes, fears, or seeks a favor from. The respondent will admit that there is no change in his own beliefs that correspond to the change in behavior. It is clearly associated with the psycho-social game. I can conceive of no way in which it is relevant to the problem-solving game. It is a purely behavioral adjustment to improve one's social relations.

With identification—using Kelman's term—the individual in some meaningful way has changed his attitude, but he has done so to stabilize his relations to some other person. This is characteristic of the socialization of the child in which he learns his parents' attitudes in order to please them and stay out of trouble. Insightfully, Kelman points out that up to a point these attitudes are unstable since they are contingent on the significant other person continuing to remain in one's life space. In accordance with his prediction, he was able to demonstrate that the individual's attitudes snapped back to their original position under circumstances in which the other person ceased to play an important role. By definition, attitude change of the sort that Kelman labels identification is, in essence, associated with the psycho-social game. It is true that after a while such attitudes may become stably internalized because they take on positive functions for the individual; but here we are concerned only with the initial circumstances of change.

Thus, compliance and identification are associated with the psycho-social game, but not with problem solving. If a person is seeking information that is relevant to some problem he has, and he accepts and uses that information, then whatever change in state has taken place is meaningfully "his." Any new attitude ought to be internalized in the sense that Kelman uses the term, namely, that it constitutes a change in belief rather than mere overt behavioral compliance and the change in belief is not related to and dependent on one's relationship to some other person. We shall soon see that there are some vital variations even in such internalized attitudes.

Once more, having pushed the theoretical argument along a few steps, I would like to turn to some data. Essentially we are returning to an extension of Rarick's experiment but one which is based upon the sort of thinking I have been putting forth. Let us rephrase Rarick's findings in my language. Suppose a person is confronted with an important and complex problem and is offered a solution by a person whom he regards as highly competent and highly trustworthy. He may accept the solution without examining the evidence carefully. Now suppose he is confronted with a highly competent person whom he does not trust. His response might be phrased in these terms: This guy ought to know what he is talking about but is he trying to put something over on me? Under such circumstances we ought to get the pattern of results that Rarick obtained. A group confronted with a highly competent, highly trusted, source will exhibit a good deal of attitude change but relatively little retention of factual information or supporting arguments, since they were willing to accept the solution without examining the evidence. But, the group faced with a highly competent source which is not trusted should show less attitude change but better retention of evidence since they ought to be motivated to examine it more closely. *If* the subjects are playing the problem-solving game, then I have restated Rarick's position but in terms that are more precise and which suggest a further, more interesting experiment.

A person confronted with a very complex problem and exposed to a communication from a source which he perceives to be both competent and trustworthy may accept the source's answer to the problem without examining it critically. If this were to happen, the literature on sleeper effects indicates that he will gradually dissociate his new opinion from the source from which he garnered it. This would mean that at some later point in time, the person who had been exposed to the "best" source would be peculiarly vulnerable to counter-propaganda since he had not examined the basis for adopting his opinion and he had forgotten the source of it. While Kelman and Hovland, and later Rarick, had demonstrated that even a positively valued source might interfere with learning of factual information, this new formulation gives the first hint that I know of that a very good source, high on both competence and trustworthiness, may have some vulnerability with respect to opinion change.

These propositions were tested in a doctoral thesis by Murray Hilibrand (1964). The topic chosen for Hilibrand's experiment was civil defense. A strong, pro-civil defense message was written. Then four separate descriptions of the author of the message were written to correspond to all four combinations of high and low competence and trust. The low competence, low trust source was described as a politician who had slipped into a civil defense position after failing to get reelected. The low competence, high trust source was a lawyer of impeccable reputation but who had no background of a technical nature. The high competence, low trust source was presented as a man of great technical competence but who had left the Atomic Energy Commission after a tiff with his superiors, who felt that he had lost his sense of perspective in his passionate advocacy of civil defense. The high competence, high trust source was described like the last man as far as technical background was concerned, but as being very fairminded and objective. A panel of judges was used to evaluate these descriptions which were revised a couple of times until we were convinced that they did in fact draw the contrasting pictures for which we were striving.

The messages, together with a covering letter from the State Director of Civil Defense, and the description of the purported author and a short questionnaire, were mailed to a randomly selected portion of the employees of two departments of the state government of Massachusetts. The covering letter from the director stated that he was asking a group of citizens to evaluate a number of civil defense messages and requested that they read the description of the author and the message and then fill out the accompanying questionnaire and return it to him. Our major reason for including the questionnaire was to increase the probability of the experimental material being read.

Two and one-half weeks later, these people who had received the messages were convened in the auditorium of their office building under a pretext that had no overt relationship to the message that had been sent to them. Subjects who had been exposed to each type of source were identified by the color of the cards they carried with them to the auditorium and assigned to separate areas of the auditorium. Then, with appropriate controls for the interaction of before-and-after measures, a measure was made of the effects of the original mailing, the subjects were given an anti-civil defense message to read, and a measure was made of their attitudes toward civil defense after exposure to counter-propaganda.

Note their situation: There were absolutely no cues that we know of that linked their presence in the auditorium to the earlier mailing nor was any reference made to it. Furthermore, civil defense is an issue of such seriousness that this factor in itself should be a constraint against playing the psycho-social game. We may assume they were interested primarily in the problem for its own sake.

The attitude measure made before exposure to counter-propaganda produced a familiar pattern: The better the source the more favorable the opinions toward civil defense. Those exposed to the high competence, high trust source had the most favorable opinions, and those exposed to the low competence, low trust source had the least favorable opinions. Those exposed to the other two sources fell neatly in between in a virtual tie with each other.

But, of course, the crucial test was the measure of opinion after exposure to counter-propaganda. The group exposed to the high competence, high trust source proved so vulnerable to counter-propaganda that the initial advantage of that source was so thoroughly offset that this group ended up with the least favorable attitude toward civil defense. I repeat: The effect of counter-propaganda was not only greater on this group but great enough to more than offset the initial advantage. After counter-propaganda, the "best" source was the worst source.

The best source *after* counter-propaganda was that characterized as high competence, low trust. A best guess as to how the process worked would be that subjects confronted with a message on a topic of importance from a source which they regarded as highly competent but not necessarily to be trusted will think the matter through carefully, and that this process of thinking their position through serves as inoculation against later counter-propaganda. While both sets of opinions could be said to be internalized, internalization of the conclusion with and without the supporting evidence has considerable importance for the stability of that opinion.

To make sure that the time dimension, the intervening two-and-one-half weeks, in which it was assumed the subjects' opinions would become dissociated from the source was important, the entire procedure was replicated with a group of subjects who read the counter-statement immediately after they read the pro-civil defense message and answered a questionnaire on their attitudes toward civil defense. Certain patterns which emerged from this portion of the study are difficult to interpret and may actually be a result of a certain amount of confusion which occurred at that time in the auditorium. One thing that does emerge clearly, however, is that when there is immediate exposure to counter-propaganda, the group exposed to the high competence, high trust source is least vulnerable to counter-propaganda. The passage of time does seem to be an essential ingredient to the generation of vulnerability in this group.

As a bow to conventional criteria for evaluating findings, I hereby announce that all the findings reported here are statistically significant at levels accepted as proper by journals of the APA.

There is an inconvenient limitation on this experiment in that with a topic such as civil defense it is impossible to write material that permits a clear distinction between attitudes and supporting evidence, since almost all data and arguments in favor of civil defense have a built-in bias such that even if they were not *remembered*, a person favorable to civil defense will choose them in a multiple-choice situation. I can report, however, that as items got closer to being strictly factual, there was a progressive tendency for the subjects exposed to the high competence, *low* trust source to select more correct items.

Further experimentation is required, using a topic which is more suitable for the distinction between attitude and factual information.

The experiment just reported suggests that by making a clear distinction among the components of a source and the type of game played, and constructing an experiment in which it was highly probable that the subjects would be playing the problem-solving game, we were led to some rather novel findings. It seems to me highly doubtful that we would have had the particular set of hypotheses if we had thought of the subjects as motivated to ingratiate the source of the message. As a matter of fact, I am ready to predict that with a topic of seriousness such as civil defense, and if the design rules out the playing of the psycho-social game, any variation in the perceived power or likability of the source will not have any influence on either attitude change—except as variation in these components have a halo effect on competence and trustworthiness. By this I mean that if an increased level of likability produces an increase in trust, care must be taken to calibrate the levels of trust for sources of varying likability.

To pose the matter more frontally, I am asserting that the notion of "emotional involvement" with the source invoked by previous investigators is irrelevant.

There are other experiments conducted by my colleagues or myself and one by Nisbett and by Gordon (1966) at Columbia which—taken together—make sense only if we assume that the subjects were trying to solve a problem rather than playing the psycho-social game. Cox (see Cox and Bauer, 1964) asked women to compare two identical stockings and then exposed them to a recorded message from an allegedly experienced so-called salesgirl favoring one of the bogus brands. Those subjects who were relatively more confident in their ability to judge the stockings were less likely to follow the salesgirl's suggestion. Gergen and I paralleled Cox's experiment (Gergen and Bauer, 1966). As a task we asked subjects to compare pairs of abstract pictures on dimensions which we specified. They too were exposed to the judgments of a stooge. We gave them two tasks, one of which was easier than the other. There was less persuasibility with the easier task. Barach (1966) found that persons exposed to five T.V. commercials were less influenced as they were more confident of their ability to judge products.

Findings of this sort are not unusual, since a considerable number of investigators in the past have reported greater persuasibility among subjects faced with difficult tasks or who were convinced in some way that they were not doing well. There are some differences in these recent studies, however, that bear on the circumstances under which a person will accept assistance from a source. We have indicated, as others have, that they are more likely to accept assistance as they are having difficulty with the task. There would be, by the way, no sensible explanation for these findings if we assumed that subjects were either trying to ingratiate themselves or salve their egos. One might try to ingratiate himself with someone in a physical position to help him out of a tough situation by actually doing a job for him. But in these experiments the source of the message was in no position to help except to offer information. And in the experiments by Cox, and by Gergen and myself, there was no plausible reason for thinking that accepting the stooge's suggestion would in any way ingratiate the experimenter.

There has been another tradition of research on persuasibility, that which correlates persuasibility with variables like generalized self-confidence. The persistent finding has been that there is a linear relationship between low self-confidence and persuasibility among men, and no relationship with generalized self-confidence among women, although women as a group are more persuasible across the board.

The experiments by Cox, Gergen and myself, and Barach, as well as by Nisbett and Gordon, mentioned previously, have all produced a curvilinear relationship between self-confidence and persuasibility. People of medium self-confidence have been most persuasible. Barach subjects were women watching T.V. commercials, and their shift in product preference was measured. He found a curvilinear shift in product preference for five separate commercials in five different product categories. I will now repeat: For the first time relationships have been found between generalized self-confidence and persuasibility among women; and in four separate experiments a curvilinear relationship has been found for the first time. One of these experiments, the one at Columbia, was carried out with predominantly, but not exclusively, male college subjects. And the other subjects have ranged from female college students to middle-aged, middle-class housewives.

Why suddenly all these curvilinear relationships when they have never been reported before—and also with women? I will try to grope my way toward a possible explanation.

In those experiments that I am personally acquainted with the subjects seemed clearly to be playing the problem-solving game. This may explain the fact that we are finally finding a relationship between persuasibility and self-confidence in women in that, in the earlier experiments, the topics—as Janis had suggested—were not ones that particularly were likely to get women involved in the substance of the issue. Hence, on an across-the-board basis, the women in the earlier experiments may have decided to "just go along."

There is evidence in the data of these recent experiments that a certain degree of need for additional information is required before the personality variable plays a role. For example, Cox found that the women relatively confident in their ability to handle the task not only were less persuasible, but that the correlation of persuasibility with self-confidence washed out. Or, to rephrase this in our terms, when the subjects have enough evidence on which to make their own judgments they do not have to face the decision of whether or not to accept the "help" of a "source."

Thus it would appear that a person must be involved with the difficulty of the task beyond some critical point before he has to face the very personal question, "Will I rely on someone else's advice or not?" Beyond that point, and only beyond that point, does the decision, to accept or not accept help, relate to his or her generalized self-confidence.

In all honesty, the experiments by Barach and by Gergen and myself do not reflect the flattening out of the relationship between self-confidence and persuasibility. But there are several possible reasons for this, one of which may be that the "easy" situation was not easy enough to pass below the critical point. In any event, Cox's data are so strong, and with a large sample, that I feel we must continue to entertain this hypothesis. It is easy and obvious to understand that people high on self-confidence might prefer their judgment to that of others. But why should the data be curvilinear? Why should people very low on self-confidence be less persuasible than those of medium self-confidence? The obvious answer is defensiveness and Cox's experiment, which has the data most adequate for testing this notion, supports it. The low self-confidence group had by a factor of more than two the largest proportion to shift in the direction opposite to that suggested. None of the other data I have seen contradicts this and tends, at least to some extent, to support it.

However, McGuire (1966) offers another reason for curvilinearity, one cited by Nisbett and Gordon, and which furnishes basis for some of their main hypotheses. McGuire contends that a curvilinear relationship may result from two offsetting linear trends. Minimally, in order to be persuaded by a communication a person must understand it. Self-confidence or self-esteem according to McGuire's argument is correlated with ability to comprehend a message, and hence with at least the opportunity to be persuaded. Low self-confidence or self-esteem, on the other hand, is related to a tendency to "yield" to persuasive messages. Hence, a person low in self-confidence might be disposed to "yield" to a persuasive message, but lack the capacity to comprehend that to which they are disposed to yield. According to this argument, in many persuasive situations, the most persuasible persons should be those neither very high nor very low in self-confidence or self-esteem—i.e., those persons with sufficient capacity to comprehend, but low enough in self-esteem to be compliant.

I am inclined, however, to reject this explanation of curvilinearity for the particular experiments with which I am most closely acquainted (Cox and Bauer, Gergen and Bauer) since it does not seem plausible to me that in these experiments the subjects low in self-esteem could have had difficulty in comprehending the messages, since the messages were far from complex. Certainly in the experiment conducted by Gergen and myself the crucial "message" to which the subjects might yield was sufficiently simple that if the subjects could not understand it fully they could not have participated in the experiment.

Attributing the lower persuasibility to persons of low self-esteem to low ability to comprehend the message *might* be invoked as an explanation for the counter-persuasibility of the women in Cox's experiment—e.g., they moved in the direction opposite to that suggested because they failed to understand what they were supposed to "yield" to! However, this explanation seems scarcely more plausible than our suggestion that these women were "defensive," and thus systematically counter-persuasible. It may be argued that the data are consistent with either interpretation. If so, neither scheme of explanation, therefore, should be rejected at this time.

McGuire's notion that ability to be persuaded is dependent upon ability to comprehend (a position consistent with many research findings on the relationship of intelligence and/or education to reactions to communications), and that ability to comprehend is related to self-esteem is worth serious consideration. The experiment of Nisbett and Gordon involved one set of messages which consisted of reasonable elaborate, fact-filled arguments. For this set of messages, they found not a curvilinear relationship of persuasibility to self-esteem, but a linear relationship in the direction opposite to that ordinarily found! That is to say it was persons *high* in self-esteem who were most persuaded, and persons low in self-esteem who were least persuaded!

Nisbett and Gordon interpret this finding as reflecting McGuire's postulated positive linear relationship of self-esteem to ability to comprehend the message, arguing that there will be some messages sufficiently difficult that this trend will mask the counter-trend of persons low in self-esteem being more disposed to yield.

In any event, investigators now have found both curvilinear trends in the data on persuasibility, and one linear trend in the direction opposite to that previously found.

Next, we have to ask the question of why we have this sudden rash of curvilinear and "counter linear" relationships. This frankly bothers me. I cannot dismiss the earlier findings. The researchers are too competent and the results too clear-cut.

It is possible that the difference is due to precisely what I have stressed throughout this paper between the problem-solving and the psycho-social game. Summoning up all my intuition and censoring nothing, I can envisage the following: Faced with a problem of substantial importance to them, people of really low self-confidence may freeze when confronted with another input. Their conscious or subconscious verbalizations of this situation might be one of these: "Look, I'm having enough trouble figuring this out. Go away and leave me alone." Or: "Don't push me around. Nobody's going to tell me what to do." The latter response in particular may account for the counter-suggestibility.

Now let's try my intuition on the psycho-social game. Suppose the same person, low in generalized self-confidence, is facing the issue of whether he will "go along" with some powerful and/or liked person. Possibly again, he could become defensive and rigid. But the tests of generalized self-confidence have been based generally on the individual's confidence *vis-a-vis* other persons. Without having had the opportunity to do a systematic review of the instruments which have been used, I have the impression that "low self-confidence" on these instruments is weighted not only toward acquiescent persons but toward persons who freely admit their tendency toward acquiescence in a social situation (Cox and Bauer, 1964). Hence, it would follow that "persuasibility" would be a linear phenomenon if the subjects were playing the psycho-social game.

I trust that I have in no sense contributed an impression of disbelief in the existence or importance of the psycho-social game. I am thoroughly convinced of its importance and equally convinced of the importance of knowing when it is, and is not, being played. Apart from any particular proposition I have put forward, if the model I have proposed makes any sense there are jobs to be done. Most specifically, we have to learn more about how we can deliberately determine the "game" that our subjects are playing; or to detect which game is being played if we have not controlled it by experimental manipulation.

If my proposal that the two models of human behavior which have evolved as tacit competitors are merely complimentary portions of a sensible overall model, then this well established area of research—the role which source credibility plays in the communication process—offers a fruitful area in which to explore the benefits of this more complete model.

REFERENCES

BACK, KURT W. AND K. J. GERGEN, "Idea Orientation and Ingratiation in the Interview: A Dynamic Model of Response Bias." *Proceedings of the Social Statistics Section of the American Statistical Association,* 1963; pp. 284–288.

BARACH, J. A., "Self-confidence and Reactions to Television Commercials," unpublished manuscript, Harvard University, 1965. Doctoral dissertation in progress; 1966.

BAUER, RAYMOND A., "The Obstinate Audience," *American Psychologist,* May, 1964.

BAUER, RAYMOND A., "Risk Handling in Drug Adoption: Role of Company Preference," *Public Opinion Quarterly,* Winter, 1961.

BAUER, RAYMOND A., AND DONALD F. COX, "Rational v. Emotional Communications: A New Approach." Arons and May, editors: *Television and Human Behavior.* New York: Appleton-Century-Crofts, 1963; pp. 140–154.

BERLO, DAVID K., AND J. LEMERT, "An Empirical Test of a General Construct of Credibility." Paper presented at SAA Convention, New York City, 1961.

BRUNER, JEROME S., J. GOODNOW, AND G. AUSTIN, *A Study of Thinking.* New York: Science Editions, Inc., 1962, p. 79.

Cox, Donald F. and Raymond A. Bauer, "Self-confidence and Persuasibility in Women," *Public Opinion Quarterly*, Fall, 1964; pp. 453–466.

Gergen, K. J., and R. A. Bauer, "The Interactive Effects of Self-esteem and Task Difficulty on Social Conformity," Harvard University; unpublished, 1966.

Hewgill, Murray N. and Gerald R. Miller, "Source Credibility and Response to Fear-arousing Communications," *Speech Monographs*, June, 1965, pp. 95–101.

Hilibrand, Murray, *Source Credibility and the Persuasive Process*. Boston, Harvard Graduate School of Business Administration, Doctoral thesis, May, 1964.

Hovland, Carl I., Irving Janis, and Harold Kelley, *Communication and Persuasion*. New Haven, Yale University Press, 1953; pp. 37–38.

Kelman, H. C., "Processes of Opinion Change," *Public Opinion Quarterly*, Spring, 1961.

Kelman, Herbert C. and Jonas Cohler, "Reactions to Persuasive Communication as a Function of Cognitive Needs and Styles." Paper read at meetings of Eastern Psychological Association, April 3, 1959.

McGuire, W. J., "Personality and Susceptibility to Social Influence," in E. F. Borgatta and W. W. Lambert, eds., *Handbook of Personality Theory and Research*; Chicago, Rand McNally Company, 1966.

Nisbett, Richard E. and Andrew Gordon, "Self-esteem and Susceptibility to Social Influence," Department of Social Psychology, Columbia University, 1966; unpublished manuscript.

Rarick, G. R., "Effects of Two Components of Communicator Prestige," unpublished paper based on doctoral thesis presented to the Session on Communication Theory, Pacific Chapter, American Association for Public Opinion Research, Asilomar, California, January, 1963.

5 INTERPERSONAL INFORMATION SOURCES

In almost every instance of buyer decision-making, interpersonal information sources are somehow present. The intended degree of influence can range from mild to dominant and can vary in content from exclusively factual to exclusively persuasive.

Considerable investigation has centered on the effects of mass communications through the filtering network of so-called opinion leaders. Nicosia (1964)* briefly reviews the history of such research and what characteristics opinion leaders are thought to have in common. He goes on to report on a study of auto insurance opinion leaders and raises some doubts concerning the designation of leaders, their behavioral attributes, such as degree of mass media exposure, and their product knowledge. It should be understood, however, that regardless of problems surrounding the opinion leader concept, the frequently strong impact of word-of-mouth communication itself is not denied. Most of our knowledge concerning word-of-mouth communications has originated from studies of voting patterns or the diffusion (propagation) of innovations in the form of products or merely ideas. Consequently, research on consumer word-of-mouth communications began with replications of such earlier studies. Due to this fact, certain of the studies referred to in Chapter 17 are equally relevant to Chapter 5.

Family role structure in decision-making for auto and furniture purchases was studied by Davis (1970).* His work clearly shows the great variation in influence between husband and wife across different aspects of the purchase question. By and large, the degree of influence by each mate reflects a rather logical specialization of roles according to skills. Nevertheless, the variability in the influence pattern across households is substantial. But in any case, a high level of consensus appears to exist within each household as to the decision roles of husband and wife.

Although virtually no research has centered on the impact of interpersonal information flows in an industrial marketing context, their presence within the purchasing company and between friendly purchasing companies is well known and taken into account by the skilled industrial salesman. The Ozanne and Churchill (1968)* study within Chapter 17 at least demonstrates that interpersonal communication sources are very important between the decision-maker and the salesman.

10. Opinion leadership and the flow of communication: some problems and prospects

francesco m. nicosia

The diffusion of ideas has always attracted the curiosity of people for varied reasons. While poets like Homer and Virgil have attempted to portray its image analogically, some of us in the social sciences are now trying to understand its nature and causes. The questions we ask are: How do people come to accept a new style of life as expressed by the purchase and use of new products, brands and services? What social and *psychological* mechanisms describe diffusion and the individual's acceptance of an innovation?

Work done over the years has revealed the complexity of these questions, and has served to highlight several promising approaches. One of these has been the study of the flow of interpersonal communication (i.e., information and influence) and has led to the concept of "horizontal" opinion leadership. Today, I should like to discuss some problems and prospects related to this approach. The first of these problems concerns the choice of a research strategy for the study of concepts that still need some clarification—in our case, horizontal opinion leadership. The second problem concerns this concept itself—its explication, its operational definition, and its role in the flow of communication. To communicate more clearly the ideas I have in mind, I shall refer to a specific set of data on opinion leadership in the field of auto insurance.* This material is introduced for expository or illustrative rather than analytical purposes.

Research on the flow of communication through personal channels has rapidly increased during the last twenty years. The number of theoretical approaches, research strategies, and measuring problems has increased proportionally. Some background information, therefore, is necessary to put in perspective the two main areas of this report.

Reprinted by permission from L. George Smith, ed., *Reflections on Progress in Marketing*, Proceedings of the Fall Conference, 1964, pp. 340–358, published by the American Marketing Association.

* These data are currently undergoing a secondary analysis at our Consumer Behavior Program, sponsored jointly by the School of Business Administration and the Survey Research Center, University of California at Berkeley. Mr. R. J. Lawrence, working with a grant from the Research Program in Marketing of the Institute of Business and Economic Research, has been most helpful in all phases of the investigation. The results of an earlier analysis of the same data by my former student, H. D. Roberts, have also been helpful. The constructive criticism of Rodney Stark has been invaluable, and I hope that some of his ideas on the present topic will be tested in the future. His suggestions and those of the other members of the new generation of "young Turks" (especially R. Wenkert), and by the still young Turk Charles Y. Glock have been as stimulating as ever.

SOME BACKGROUND INFORMATION

In this section I shall set the stage for the following discussion by first summarizing the major features of research on opinion leaders, and then describing the available data and the way I have approached them for this discussion.

Opinion Leaders and the Flow of Interpersonal Communication

During the last few decades several ideas pertaining to the flow of communication through personal channels have been proposed. Some of these have not yet been extensively investigated, such as the concepts of innovator elaborated by Katona and Mueller, taste makers proposed by the Opinion Research Corporation, and those of reference groups and reference idols.[1] Another idea, current for some time although not rigorously explored, is the notion that information and influence flow "vertically"; that is, they filter through a social group, from top to bottom.[2]

The concept of the horizontal opinion leader, differently, has caused a great deal of interest since its early formulation by Lazarsfeld, *et al.*, and Lazarsfeld and Katz.[3] These researchers have studied the communication flow in small, face-to-face, informal groups of peers. As a convenient contrast to the vertical view, the flow is here seen as horizontal and confined within distinct social groups.

A stream of encouraging research has stemmed from these early formulations. The findings are well known. Opinion leaders are equals within their own social groups; they tend to specialize in different products; leaders in one product area differ from those in other areas according to socio-economic and demographic characteristics. Messages channeled through mass media, books, conventions, shows, and other sources, tend to reach mass audiences in two stages: first, they are noted by opinion leaders; and second, are transmitted by the

---

[1] G. Katona and E. Mueller, "A Study of Purchase Decisions," in *Consumer Behavior*, L. H. Clark, Editor. (New York: New York University Press, 1954); Opinion Research Corporation, *America's Tastemakers*, 1959, and *The Initiators*, 1960 (Princeton: Opinion Research Corporation); and the summary in H. H. Hyman, "Reflections on Reference Groups," *Public Opinion Quarterly*, Fall, 1960, pp. 383–96.

[2] For a serious review and rebuttal of this idea, see C. W. King, "Fashion Adoption: A Rebuttal of the 'Trickle Down' Theory," in *Toward Scientific Marketing*, Stephen A. Greyser, Editor. (Chicago: American Marketing Association) pp. 108–25.

[3] P. F. Lazarsfeld, et al., *The People's Choice* (New York: Columbia University Press, 1948); P. F. Lazarsfeld and E. Katz, *Personal Influence* (New York: Free Press, 1955). For a complete statement of the research designs used in this research tradition, see E. Katz, "The Two-Step Flow of Communication: an Up-to-Date Report on an Hypothesis," *Public Opinion Quarterly*, Spring 1957, pp. 61–78. For the work done by rural sociologists, see a little known publication by the Foundation for Research on Human Behavior, *The Adoption of New Products: Process and Influence* (Ann Arbor, Michigan, 1959). For a thorough recent review of the work done on opinion leaders, see E. M. Rogers, *Diffusion of Innovations* (New York: Free Press, 1962).

opinion leaders to members of their social milieu through direct contact in its many forms, from casual conversations to deliberate advice seeking. Finally, while in some communities (or product areas) opinion leaders tend to enact the role of early adopters of new products and ideas, in other communities their decision to adopt an innovation follows that of the early adopters.[4]

These well known findings are potentially valuable in improving communication techniques employed by business firms, advertising and public relations agencies, etc., and in obtaining a better understanding of social behavior in general. Advertising campaigns would be more effectively conducted if opinion leaders in the field of the product, brand, or service advertised could be economically identified. Media planning or choice of themes, for instance, would benefit greatly from such information. As far as I know, however, there is only a minimum of marketing and advertising applications of these ideas. There are several conceptual and operational difficulties that may account for this, some of which I shall discuss in this report.

The Auto Insurance Data

Many studies have produced evidence that opinion leaders affect the flow of communication concerning movies, breakfast food, fashion, new farm equipment and practices, and ethical drugs. A set of survey data held by the library of our Consumer Behavior Program lends itself to an investigation of opinion leadership in the field of auto insurance. These data, together with a motivation research study, were gathered in a project designed to test the effectiveness of an intensive trial advertising campaign by a large insurance company operating through the agency system. This campaign introduced a new auto insurance policy, "Plan X," in a midwestern city of about 500,000 people during the late spring and early summer of 1961. The survey evaluated the campaign's results in terms of the recognition (aided and unaided) of several advertisements concerning both Plan X and local independent agents, and the image of each created by the campaign.

The sample consisted of heads of households who were assumed to be the major family decision makers in regard to auto insurance. An attempt was made to confine the sample to white middle-income groups that were considered the primary potential purchasers of Plan X, and at whom the campaign had been directed. Sampling was done on a geographic basis (census tracts) with subjects in the $6,000 to $8,000 income range, with emphasis on suburban and semi-suburban areas. The data were gathered by means of 45-minute personal interviews conducted by a professional survey firm. Usable interviews provided a group of 481 heads of households, of whom 37 were women and 444 were men.

These data are currently undergoing a secondary analysis. One of the purposes of this analysis is to find whether the data reveal auto

---

[4] For a tentative explanation of this finding based on the consideration of different community norms (progressive *versus* conservative) and their impact on opinion leaders, see H. Menzel, "Innovation, Integration, and Marginality: A Survey of Physicians," *American Sociological Review*, October 1960, pp. 704–13.

insurance opinion leaders. To put the matter in different and perhaps more modest terms, the purpose is to see whether the dimensions that have identified opinion leaders in other products apply also to the auto insurance field. The dimensions used in *Personal Influence* (Katz and Lazarsfeld, *op. cit.*) were chosen as the most appropriate to the data available for three reasons.

First, although the Decatur housewives are obviously different from the principally male head-of-households of our data, it may be assumed that they are relatively more akin to our population than doctors and farmers. Second, with respect to the product, it is reasonable to assume that the choice of auto insurance is relatively closer to the choice of the products studied in *Personal Influence* than to that of ethical drugs and farm practices and equipment. Finally, recognizing the inherent limitations of secondary analyses, the Decatur study was selected because some of its critical dimensions of opinion leadership were present also in the auto insurance data.

In summation, the critical dimensions of opinion leadership in *Personal Influence* and available in my data are self-designation, exposure to mass media, factual awareness about a particular product, and awareness of general events. (The indicators and the questions used to measure them are listed below.) Having selected these dimensions as the starting point of my investigations, I was confronted with a choice of a research strategy. I believe this choice not only affects the analysis of the auto insurance data, but also plays a critical role in the other reports presented in this session and more generally in the study of phenomena not adequately understood.

THE CHOICE OF A RESEARCH STRATEGY

The methods underlying the construction of research designs for studying real life situations and the analysis of the data so collected are relatively new. Over the years, analysis of survey data has become strongly dependent on a series of data elaborations. These consist, for example, of cross tabulations that attempt to build variables (e.g., assessment of the reliability and validity of indicators, and construction of indices and typologies), and to analyze interactions among variables (e.g., cases of spuriousness, interpretation, and specification). Statistical procedures such as tests of significance, statistics of relations, etc., if necessary and applicable, are employed only after the possibilities of elaborations have been exhausted.

There is disagreement among researchers concerning the relative advantages and the use-sequence of these two procedures (i.e., from elaborations to statistics of relations; or from statistics of relations to elaborations). From the point of view of survey research, neither sequence is inherently preferable to the other. They appear to complement each other.[5] However, there are situations where their use-

---

[5] A seminar directly concerned with such an issue was held during the year 1961–62 ("General Analysis Program," Survey Research Center, University of California at Berkeley, H. Selvin in charge). The seminar ended with an experiment where the

sequence makes a difference; the situation confronting me at the beginning of the investigation is an example. Let me illustrate.

According to the Decatur study, we find that (a) some people designate themselves as opinion leaders, and, in relation to non-opinion leaders, are (b) more likely to be exposed to mass media, (c) to be more aware of current events, and, above all, (d) to have more factual knowledge about the product of their competence. We can ask whether the same findings are true for auto insurance. But how are we going to ask this question of our data? In other words, which research strategy shall we follow? I believe that we can choose from essentially two, both current in the literature.

The first strategy consists of what we may call an "objective" or "neutral" approach to the data—implying the immediate and direct use of one or more of the algorithms available in multivariate statistics. For example, a researcher following this strategy could look at the extent to which the three variables—mass media exposure, awareness of general events, and awareness of auto insurance—explain (statistically) the variable opinion leadership (yes: OL; no: $\overline{\text{OL}}$). Or a researcher could construct an index by ranking our respondents according to whether they score high, medium, or low in media exposure, general awareness, and auto insurance awareness; and then he would ask whether the self-designated opinion leaders are significantly more likely than non-leaders to be in the top half of the index, and conversely, whether non-leaders are significantly more likely to be in the lower half. Or, he could be more ambitious and attack the problem in a truly "Panzer Divisionen" fashion, passing through a discriminant analysis algorithm not only the above four variables but also all other variables describing our respondents (and in a 45-minute interview you may well guess that there was a multitude of respondent attributes). After getting the results, he then attempts to interpret them—hoping that these *ad hoc* interpretations will be useful to management.

The second research strategy we can follow suggests, however, that often several things should be clarified before we engage in statistical operations. That is, survey research methods suggest that we should assess the reliability and validity of the measuring instruments and of the indicators to be used as measures of our variables. And, more generally, we should attempt to understand the phenomenon under study as conceptualized by, and thus filtered through, a specific research design, and as then reflected in the data thus collected. In a word, this second strategy recommends that if a researcher has theoretical and/or methodological reservations, he ought to check them before using the powerful statistical methods currently available.

My prefatory remarks have already implied that I have some reserva-

---

same set of survey data was given to different researchers, who approached the data either on the basis of the traditional survey analysis or on the basis of statistical procedures such as factor analysis and analysis of variance. The results of the experiments and the ensuing discussions, I believe, showed these two strategies to be complementary. Apropos of some major problems in the analysis of survey data, see the thoughtful discussion by J. M. Morgan and J. A. Sunquist, "Problems in the Analysis of Survey Data," *Journal of the American Statistical Association*, June 1963, pp. 415–36.

tions about the concept of horizontal opinion leadership. Further, the very exploratory nature of my investigation—opinion leaders as components of communication concerning auto insurance—stresses the need for a cautious approach to available data. Such considerations have led me to choose the second strategy.

The remarks presented in the next two sections stem from this second strategy. I believe I would not have been able to see some qualities of my data had I initially chosen the paths of the first strategy. To illustrate, very recently Mr. Lawrence and I, following the first strategy, constructed an index based on the aggregation of respondent scores in media exposure, general awareness, auto insurance awareness, and preference for "technical" and "social" personal channels of communications.[6] We found that self-designated leaders are significantly more likely to score higher than the non-leaders on this total index (this is significant at the level between 0.05 and 0.10). Now, the researcher familiar with survey methods well knows that even for the construction of such indices the second strategy is imperative. But what I want to stress here is that had I begun with this or any other path suggested by the first strategy, I would not have been able to see some of the "disappointing" tables I shall show in a moment and to develop the considerations I shall later suggest.

SOME OBSERVATIONS DRAWN FROM A CASE STUDY

As mentioned earlier, in marketing and advertising there is a lack of application of the ideas formulated by research on opinion leadership. Some of the problems accounting for this can be grouped under three major headings: (1) those concerning the identification of opinion leaders, especially the self-designation question; (2) those concerning the behavioral attributes distinguishing leaders from non-leaders (i.e., in our case, auto insurance awareness, general awareness, and mass media exposure); and (3) those concerning the social and psychological mechanisms that lead a subject to enact the role of leader in a certain product field. The tables drawn from the auto insurance data here presented readily illustrate these problems, and set the stage for the remarks developed in the last section.

Self-designation

In the Decatur study, respondents were asked whether they had given or received advice about certain products.[7] Our auto insurance ques-

---

[6] In following the second strategy, I found that this latter dimension also discriminates between leaders and non-leaders; see below and also the paper by King in these proceedings.

[7] The respondents were then asked to name the advisors or advisees; these were subsequently also interviewed to confirm each adviser-advisee dyad. Only 54 per cent of these dyads were fully confirmed. However, the authors report that the analysis of only the confirmed pairs produced the same results as the analysis based on the self-designation question alone (Katz and Lazarsfeld, *op. cit.*, p. 237, fn. 3).

tionnaire contained a self-designation question, that read: "Have you influenced *two* or more of your friends, relatives, neighbors about their buying of auto insurance?"[8] The mention of a single influence was not acceptable for a "yes" to be recorded by the interviewers. Of the 481 respondents, 96 put themselves on record as influentials. The percentage of self-designated opinion leaders in both studies is shown in Table 1.

TABLE 1   Self-designation as Opinion Leader

	Percent of Total Sample
Auto Insurance Study	20
Decatur Study	
marketing	24
fashion	22
movie-going	17 (or 28*)

* as a percent of those in the sample who went to the movies at least once a month.

Behavioral Attributes of Opinion Leaders

The Decatur study reveals that self-designated opinion leaders differ from non-leaders in at least the three attributes mentioned earlier. In the auto insurance survey we have indicators for each of these.

As for the general awareness attribute, our survey involved a question that ran: "Here is a list of some recent events that you may have heard or read about. Would you please tell me whether or not you have heard or read about each one?"[9] We have prepared a tentative index of general awareness, and shown the distribution of our leaders and non-leaders along this index in Table 2.

In the auto insurance survey there are five questions each dealing with some factual aspect of auto insurance.[10] An index of auto insurance awareness has been tentatively prepared on the basis of these indicators, and the relative position of our self-designated opinion leaders on this index was computed. The results are presented in Table 3.

[8] This question is somewhat different from that asked in Personal Influence (Q. 5., p. 147). For the consequences of this difference, see the comparison of the two sets of responses in Table 1.

[9] The list included national and international events of a non-commercial nature, two commercial events, and a false event (i.e., an event that had not happened). Specifically, they dealt with the: death of Hemingway, Soviet pressure on Berlin, new Ford Falcon Futura, investigation of drug prices by the Kefauver Committee, death of Gary Cooper, Carolyn Kennedy's rescue from the pool, Plan X, tractor exchange with Cuba, Bradley kidnapping case (false event), and Eichmann trial. The item of Plan X was not included in the index of general awareness mentioned in the text.

[10] These questions indicate whether the respondents had heard or read of Plan X; whether they knew what Plan X was about; whether they recognized the symbol of Plan X and the trade mark of the independent insurance agents used in the advertising campaign; and, finally, whether they knew the difference between a direct writer and an independent insurance agent.

TABLE 2   Index of General Awareness: Opinion Leaders and Non-Leaders

Index of General Awareness	Self-designated Opinion Leaders	Self-designated Non-Leaders
High	50	44
Medium	42	40
Low	8	16
	100%	100%
	(96)	(385)

TABLE 3   Index of Auto Insurance Awareness: Opinion Leaders and Non-Leaders

Index of Auto Insurance Awareness	Self-designated Opinion Leaders	Self-designated Non-Leaders
High	29	18
Medium	55	60
Low	16	22
	100%	100%
	(96)	(385)

Finally, we have a measure of our subjects' exposure to mass media (TV, radio, newspapers, and magazines) in the questionnaire. An index of mass media exposure has been tentatively prepared, and the subjects' position on this index is shown in Table 4.

TABLE 4   Index of Exposure to Mass Media: Opinion Leaders and Non-Leaders

Media Exposure	Self-designated Opinion Leaders	Self-designated Non-Leaders
High	34	34
Medium	32	39
Low	34	27
	100%	100%
	(96)	(385)

As one would expect from the hypothesis of two- or multi-step communication flow, self-designated opinion leaders (OL) tend to know more about auto insurance and general events compared to our self-designated non-leaders ($\overline{\text{OL}}$) (at least, this is true on the basis of the indicators we have used for these dimensions). There is only a small difference between the OL and the $\overline{\text{OL}}$ in the case of low exposure to mass media. The meaning of these tables is far from being self-evident. Independent of whether or not the relationships revealed by the tables pass a statistical test of significance, several elaborations are necessary before reaching an interpretation. Here, I shall not report on most of the elaborations I have made thus far because their importance would be limited to the field of auto insurance.[11]

The only point I would like to emphasize is that in all three tables there exist sizable numbers of OL who tend to behave like $\overline{OL}$, and vice versa. For example, 16 per cent of OL have a very low knowledge of auto insurance, while 18 per cent of $\overline{OL}$ have a high knowledge of the same.

The analyst who chooses to look at his indicators and measuring instruments before subjecting the data to statistical operations usually becomes concerned when the absolute number of "deviant" cases is large. The reasons for this concern are independent of whether a relation passes a statistical test of significance; these reasons go beyond the fact that the number of deviant cases has an effect, for example, on the amount of unexplained variance in an analysis of variance. The presence of these cases is always a direct challenge to the researcher's theory of a phenomenon's structure (and his theory is reflected by the types of questions he asks of the data). Furthermore, analyses focused on deviant cases often lead to clarifications, and sometimes to reformulations of the theory guiding the analysis and use of research methods and techniques. I shall suggest below some possible clarifications of this apparent lack of sharp differentiation between leaders and non-leaders with respect to these behavioral attributes.

Processes Accounting for Opinion Leadership

Several processes may describe how an individual comes to enact a leadership role. I cannot report today on the role of personality traits and social, contextual factors in such processes. Our data, however, permit an investigation of some of the ways in which our OL and $\overline{OL}$ acquire their awareness of auto insurance. For instance, our subjects can acquire information about auto insurance either through selective exposure to mass media, or as a result of their general awareness, or both. Let us then see whether the OL differ from the $\overline{OL}$ according to these processes.

A few elaborations show that the effects of general awareness and of media exposure on the respondent's auto insurance awareness is slightly greater in the OL group than in the $\overline{OL}$ group. But again we find some disappointing similarities between the two groups. Although the score of our auto insurance awareness index reaches its maximum among the leaders, its minimum is practically the same for both groups.

A lack of sharp differentiation between the two groups is noticeable also when we look at the process through which they learn of a specific aspect of auto insurance marketing. One of the questions used to establish the degree of auto insurance awareness was: "Do you think that a direct writer and an independent insurance agent are different

---

[11] Some elaborations are presented in F. M. Nicosia, "Advertising, Buying of Auto Insurance, and Opinion Leaders: A Progress Report," Working Paper No. 12, Research Program in Marketing, Institute of Business and Economic Research, University of California at Berkeley, August 31, 1964. Unpublished.

or are they the same?" This question was followed by another which ran: "Where or from whom did you learn that the independent agent is different from (similar to) the direct writer?" Among those who got the correct answer, 72 were self-designated OL and 213 were non-leaders.[12] Table 5 indicates the channels of information from which the

TABLE 5   The Channels Through Which Knowledge of the Difference Between the Direct Writer and the Insurance Independent Agent Is Acquired

Channels of Information	Opinion Leaders	Non-Leaders
1. Mass media		
Television	13	14
Radio	4	4
Newspapers	1	2
Magazines	—	1
Direct mail, window displays	—	—
Flyers on windshields, billboards	3	1
Total mass media	21	21
2. Personal channels		
Friend, relative	19	11
Contact by insurance salesman	15	24
Car dealer, banker, lawyer	1	—
Total personal channels	35	35
3. Other sources	31	28
No answer	13	16
	100%	100%
	(72)	(213)

two groups of respondents learned of this specific difference of marketing auto insurance policies.

Both groups have learned the difference more from personal channels than mass media. Among the latter, television dominates; this probably reflects the consequence of the advertiser's budget allocation that emphasized TV over other mass media. Differences between the two groups exist only in personal channels. Friends and relatives are more frequently mentioned by OL than by $\overline{\text{OL}}$, while the reverse is true for insurance salesmen. I am not prepared to report now on the elaborations performed thus far to interpret these differences.

Table 5, however, reminded me of a finding by Coleman, Katz and Menzel.[13] In their study of physicians, they found that the impact of "technical" personal channels (in our case, these would be independent agents, direct writers, car dealers, lawyers, and bankers) on the

---

[12] The "don't knows" (DK) and the wrong answers in the two groups were as follows:

	Opinion Leaders	Non-Leaders
Percentage of DK	16	25
Percentage of wrong answers	9	16

[13] J. Coleman, E. Katz and H. Menzel, "The Diffusion of an Innovation among Physicians," *Sociometry*, December, 1957, pp. 253–70.

adoption decision is greater than that of "social" personal channels (i.e., friends, relatives, neighbors). I have pursued this lead and asked whether this distinction between personal channels has an effect on auto insurance awareness. Using the responses to the question, "If you were looking for information and advice on buying auto insurance, who of the following would you ask first? Who would you ask next? And next?" I determined the subjects' preferences for exclusively technical or social channels, and then computed the auto insurance awareness scores for each group. Table 6 shows the results.

TABLE 6   Auto Insurance Awareness by Opinion Leaders and Non-Leaders and by Preferences for Types of Personal Channels of Information (Auto Insurance Awareness—mean score of group)

Preferences for Personal Channels	Self-designated	
	Opinion Leaders (55)	Non-Leaders (223)
Only technical	1.917 (36)	1.621 (144)
Only social	1.658 (19)	1.272 (79)

For both OL and $\overline{\text{OL}}$ exclusive reliance on technical channels is associated with higher knowledge of auto insurance and, as expected, the highest score is for OL. But again note that in Table 6 a large number of $\overline{\text{OL}}$ prefer technical channels alone (60%) and more than one third of OL prefer social channels (34%). On the basis of the concept of horizontal opinion leadership, we would have expected these two percentages to be very small.

SOME PROBLEMS AND PROSPECTS

In discussing research strategies, I have mentioned that had we begun the analysis by relying only on the first strategy, we would have found that leaders and non-leaders are statistically different in their total score of auto insurance awareness, general awareness, mass media exposure, and preference for personal channels either exclusively technical or social in nature. I noted also that in this way we would have missed the opportunity of closely observing the nature of our data.

The preceding tables (as well as others not presented here) have resulted from the second research strategy. I believe that these make my point. On the one hand, it appears that on the basis of the statistical test Mr. Lawrence and I made, we cannot reject the hypothesis that the critical dimensions revealed by the Decatur study apply as well to auto insurance. On the other hand, our cross tabulations consistently reveal a large number of deviant cases for each of the four dimensions among both the leaders and non-leaders.

We should accept the challenge coming from these tables. What, then, can we say about our results in the field of auto insurance? And can we make observations that apply to opinion leadership in general? This, I believe, is possible, and I would like to suggest the following.

Let me initially note that, as in the physical and natural sciences, a major problem in the social sciences is defining a concept (variable) amenable to measurement and other operations. An operational definition, as we know, implies that the researcher must make a *choice* of the concept's dimensions he believes relevant to a particular problem; and subsequently, it implies a *choice* of the indicator(s) for each dimension and the measuring instrument(s) of each indicator. The freedom in making such choices is a serious handicap in social science research, especially when conducted in non-laboratory settings. For my purposes, the main difficulty is that a standardized definition of opinion leadership has not yet been agreed upon. Though all the operational definitions used in past studies identify concepts of horizontal opinion leaders, there remain methodological problems that deserve consideration. I shall discuss a few of them.[14]

The Identification of Opinion Leaders

The first group of methodological problems is met by the researcher who attempts identification of opinion leaders in real life situations. His procedures are essentially three. The procedure of early studies relies on a self-designation question; for example, "Have you recently tried to convince anyone of your political ideas?" Another procedure employed in later studies consists of the self-designation question, followed by a confirmation of the leaders' influence through interviews of the subjects who have supposedly been influenced. Both of these procedures have been applied to a sample, and thus the researchers have been unable to observe all possible leader-follower pairs. The third procedure, aimed in part at overcoming this limitation, consists of asking each member of a population a sociometric question, for example, to name three or four best friends. An illustration of this third procedure is the well known study of doctors' decisions to adopt a new ethical drug; here the researchers interviewed all physicians of a community.[15]

Looking at past studies of opinion leadership, I believe that the self-designation question has several limitations. To begin with, the lack of sharp differentiation between the behavior of the leaders and non-

---

[14] For other ideas that point to methodological and substantive clarifications see, for example, R. A. Bauer, "Risk Handling in Drug Adoption: The Role of Company Preference," *Public Opinion Quarterly*, Winter, 1961, pp. 546–59; D. F. Cox, "The Audience as Communicators," pp. 58–72, and C. W. King, *op. cit.*, pp. 108–28, both in *Toward Scientific Marketing*, Stephen A. Greyser, Editor. (Chicago: American Marketing Association, Winter Conference, December, 1963); S. Polgar, H. Dunphy and B. Cox, "Diffusion and Farming Advice," *Social Forces*, October, 1963, pp. 104–12; D. C. Barnlund and C. Harland, "Propinquity and Prestige as Determinants of Communication Networks," *Sociometry*, December, 1963, pp. 467–79; S. Cunningham, "Perceived Risk as a Factor in Product-Oriented Word-of-Mouth Behavior," and C. W. King, "Discriminants of Innovative Consumer Behavior," both in these proceedings.

[15] In a study of 159 full-time farmers, the sociometric choice gives a .56 correlation with the ranking of a local county extension agent, whereas the self-designation question correlates .41. The corrected contingency coefficient between sociometric

leaders in Tables 2 through 6 may depend on whether or not the self-designation question is a reliable and valid measuring instrument. Beside the known interview biases, the use of the self-designation question alone does not permit control of the respondent's self-perception.[16] Furthermore, interpersonal flow of information and influence may occur even if the subjects are not aware of it, and here the question is totally inadequate. Even if we strengthen the question by confirming the influential-follower relationship, it seems to me that this instrument is not yet satisfactory.

The discriminating power of the self-designation question, moreover, may vary a great deal from product to product. This power may be very low in auto insurance and in similar cases when opportunities for interpersonal communications are rare over a period of time. For auto insurance, most likely this opportunity arises only in case of accidents or at the time of policy renewal. Apropos of this latter case, the motivation research study done together with the survey reveals that most of the recent "switchers" acted not on an understanding of the policy's merits but on the advice of their insurance agent (and a few other "switchers" were not even aware that their policy had been changed!).[17]

The final point is that the wording of the self-designation question in the auto insurance study partitions only influentials from non-influentials. There can be a difference, however, between a non-influential and a follower. This limitation of the wording, then, possibly explains why the behavior of many non-leaders differs from that expected of followers; but this does not explain why many of the leaders deviate substantially and consistently from the expected norm.

All in all, my argument does not reject the self-designation question in favor of the sociometric procedure. Indeed, not many marketing and advertising problems could be approached with the latter. Further, the cost of the sociometric procedure is unwarranted in a large number of situations. These limitations of the sociometric procedure urge the adoption of the self-designation question, provided it is improved through *ad hoc* controls in research design and the use of additional indicators.

The Behavioral Attributes of Opinion Leaders

The second group of methodological problems concerns the determination of the behavioral attributes that characterize an opinion leader. Past evidence has consistently pointed to at least three attributes: a

choice and self-rated influentials is .37; see R. Mason, "The Use of Information Sources by Influentials in the Adoption Process," *Public Opinion Quarterly*, Fall, 1963, pp. 455–66.

[16] B. Abu-Laban, "Self-Conception and Appraisal by Others, A Study of Community Leaders," *Sociology and Social Research*, October, 1963, pp. 32–37.

[17] With reference to the role of personal sources of influence in consumer decisions, recent research shows most interesting interplays among the difficulty of a decision, the ensuing cognitive processes, and personality traits; see R. Bauer, "Psychology on the Fringe: The Interrelationship of Theory and Application," paper delivered to the Maritime Psychological Association, September 10, 1964; mimeograph.

high degree of exposure to mass media,[18] knowledge about the product whose acceptance they influence, and awareness of general events.

This evidence suggests a generalized picture of the networks through which communication flows. Opinion leaders are seen as "hooked into" mass media networks; within these, they become informed and then they operate like switchboards passing information and influence on to their peers through a series of social networks. The deviations observed in our data suggest, however, a more complicated picture. By considering the three attributes, we can generate eight types of opinion leaders. To illustrate, type (8.) in Table 7 reminds us that

TABLE 7   Some Dimensions of the Concept of Opinion Leader and Types of Empirical Studies

		Exposure to Mass Media			
		Opinion Leaders are Exposed		Opinion Leaders are not Exposed	
		OL are Informed	OL are not Informed	OL are Informed	OL are not Informed
General Awareness	Opinion Leaders are High	1.	2.	3.	4.
	Opinion Leaders are Low	5.	6.	7.	8.

there can be respondents who influence others despite their lack of mass media exposure and their ignorance of that about which they are talking. If we consider our findings on leaders' preferences for exclusively social or technical channels, it is possible to generate a greater number of types.

It appears that past research has tended to concentrate on type (1.). However, all possible types of leaders may be important to marketing and advertising management. The choice of the ways to reach leaders, the kinds of messages to transmit to them, and other factors may be different for each type of leader. Let us not forget also that the prerequisites for dealing effectively with these choices are manifold—the identification of possible leader types operating in a given product field, the assessment of the absolute number of subjects comprising

---

[18] Patterns of mass media exposure of leaders and non-leaders, however, may vary only over a period of time. That is, the leaders may have higher exposure than non-leaders at the introduction of an innovation. Once they have passed information to the non-leaders, the usual phenomenon of self-exposure may operate among the non-leaders so that their exposure, too, becomes high. For suggestions on this point, see the results in Foundation for Research on Human Behavior, *op. cit.*, and in Mason, *op. cit.*, as well as the Decatur study.

each type, and the evaluation of the relative role each type has in the adoption of new products or the switching between established brands. Future applications, therefore, may well depend on our success in differentiating leader types.

Processes Accounting for Opinion Leadership

The variety of social and psychological processes that determine an opinion leader constitutes the third group of methodological problems. Past studies have indicated that one of the ways a leader may acquire expertise in a product field is through his exposure to mass media and to other leaders (i.e., in the case of multi-step flow of interpersonal communication). In these studies it appears that the subject's correlates can be socio-economic and demographic, and that the nature of the product generally determines which of these attributes is important.

These findings suggest a contextual view of opinion leadership. However, many studies of leadership in all its facets point to the importance of personality traits. At the present time, I find it difficult to bring this latter consideration to bear because the field studies we have discussed have not explicitly involved an investigation of the contribution of personality traits to opinion leader formation. Besides the intrinsic value of studying opinion leadership from both the contextual and the traitist points of view, the interplay between the two may explain some of the leader types listed in Table 7. For example, with respect to type (8.), while an individual may live in a social milieu that deprives him of information,[19] yet his personality may be sufficiently assertive for his peers to accept him as a leader.

We turn our attention now to the other side of the dyad—the receivers of information and influence. I have not been able to find either theoretical or operational distinctions between these two aspects of communication in opinion leadership studies. But it is clear from communication research that cognitive and affective items of a message may have a different impact on the receiver.[20] As far as I know, past studies of opinion leadership have also overlooked the receiver's perception of a communication source and, more generally, the variations in his behavior and attitude change caused by the known source effect. In addition, often overlooked is the fact that this strength of influence depends on the receiver's own predispositions. This is quite clear in contingency tables used by McPhee[21] and others in simulating

---

[19] R. Stark, "Deprivation and Cultural Sophistication," Survey Research Center, University of California at Berkeley, Unpublished. Always on the role of structural factors in the flow of communication, see the hypotheses discussed in Menzel, *op. cit.*

[20] J. T. Klapper, *The Effects of Mass Communication* (New York: Free Press, 1960), *passim;* A. R. Cohen, *Attitude Change and Social Change* (New York: Basic Books, Inc., 1964), *passim.*

[21] W. N. McPhee, *Formal Theories of Mass Behavior* (New York: Free Press, 1963); and "Note on a Campaign Simulator," *Public Opinion Quarterly,* Summer, 1961, pp. 184–93.

political and other behaviors. Even if we cannot reach the sophistication of communication research in commercial surveys, it is apparent that a receiver's reaction can vary according to whether a source tells him something in favor or against a brand, or to adopt or not adopt a brand. All in all, the standard self-designation question as well as other indicators used in past studies do not collect data concerning the direction (or sign) of a message—i.e., whether the communication is pro or con a brand and its adoption. Shortage of time, resources, or other constraints on a project often compel us to assume that the direction of influence has a symmetrical impact, but it may not necessarily be so.

In conclusion, there are several problems in opinion leadership research that might benefit from further clarification. Both researchers and administrators would gain from future efforts aimed at finding better ways to identify opinion leaders and uncover their behavioral characteristics. Effort should be invested also in the study of the social and psychological mechanisms that lead an individual to enact the role of leader and in the attempt to capture more clearly leadership roles in communication networks.

While we refine the concept of opinion leadership, we should investigate its relationships to the concepts mentioned at the beginning of my report. In the long run, I believe efforts could be profitably directed toward uncovering the types of communication networks and their dynamics, particularly the interplay between mass media and interpersonal networks. If we pursue research in these directions, hopefully one day we may be able to visualize and map some of the major aspects of a society's communication process, and thus begin to understand the diffusion of ideas, products, brands, and services—that is, a great deal of our present and future way of life.

11. Dimensions of marital roles in consumer decision making

harry l. davis

INTRODUCTION

The literature on family role structure is characterized by diverse theories about the structure of marital roles in decision making. At one extreme are those researchers who assume unidimensionality, and whose studies describe families as "matriarchal," "patriarchal," and "companionship," e.g., Burgess and Locke [2], or who use "global influence questions," e.g., Heer [6] and "overall power scores," e.g., Blood and Wolfe [1]. Other sociologists recognize at least two power hierarchies within the family—e.g., the distinction between "instrumental" and "expressive" roles [15] or Farber's [3] dichotomy between "policy" and "routine household" decisions. Herbst [8] suggests four bases for role differentiation: (1) household duties; (2) child control and care; (3) social activities; and (4) economic activities. At the other extreme is the even more highly differentiated role structure implicit in the marketing literature. For example, Sharp and Mott [17] report that husbands exert more influence than wives in the purchase of automobiles, less influence than wives in deciding how much to spend on food, and equal influence in deciding about vacations and housing. Other studies [11, 19] suggest a further factoring of decisions for single purchases into numerous components.

These alternative views of family role structure undoubtedly reflect the different orientations of sociological and marketing research. Measurement of family authority is usually a first step in many sociological studies, and it is used as the independent or dependent variable in subsequent analyses. This may explain why the dimensionality of roles itself has been the subject of such little *empirical* research. While the sociological literature is strong on theory and somewhat weak on data, the literature in marketing is just the reverse. Measurement of purchase influence for specific products is often the only objective of such research.

Both of these approaches leave important questions unanswered. Sociologists, for example, often establish typologies on an *a priori* basis and then "force" data into these classifications. Whether Herbst's economic activities do, in fact, represent a unidimensional area of family structure has not been subject to adequate empirical testing.

Reprinted by permission from *Journal of Marketing Research*, Vol. 7 (May 1970), pp. 168–177, published by the American Marketing Association.

Harry L. Davis is Assistant Professor of Marketing, University of Chicago. He is grateful to Alvin J. G. Silk and Harry V. Roberts for their valuable assistance.

The absence of any explicit theory in the marketing literature, on the other hand, seriously limits generalizations. The roles of husband, wife, or children are discussed only on a product-by-product basis. Researchers have not questioned whether decision making influence within the family could be described in terms of a fewer number of dimensions that would subsume several products or several steps in the decision process for a single product. The answer to this question has implications for market research in suggesting what kinds of questions need to be asked, to whom, and with what degree of specificity.

Contributing to these alternative conceptualizations is the use of widely differing sources of information about purchase influence. A sampling of research shows that data have been collected from wives only, husbands only, a matched group of husbands and wives, husbands and wives within the same family, and children.

The extent to which wives can accurately report purchase influence is subject to considerable confusion in the literature. Some researchers stress the similarity between husbands' and wives' responses. Wolgast found a high level of agreement in husbands' and wives' reports about relative influence in four economic decisions. She concludes that "husbands and wives reflect one another's judgments almost perfectly" [21, p. 153]. Blood and Wolfe justify the use of wives as sole respondent by the fact that "other studies show that husbands and wives usually agree sufficiently to make it possible to rely on one partner's responses" [1, p. 273]. Heer also concludes that the agreement between husband and wife is "substantial though not unanimous" [6, p. 66]. Others emphasize the inconvenience and cost associated with interviewing more than one respondent per family. Scanzoni [16], for example, reasons that the decision to obtain data from both spouses often necessitates a smaller sample size, which, in turn, will lower the generalizability of results.

At the same time, the literature also contains studies that point to the considerable disagreement between husband and wife in their reporting of purchase influence. Ferber obtained independent assessments of relative influence in eight consumer decisions from the adult members of 237 families. Finding little correspondence between husbands' and wives' answers (R^2 ranging from .02 to .29) he concluded that "the reliability of ratings of relative influence of different family members, or different sexes, on purchases obtained by direct questioning of one member of the family is highly limited" [4, p. 232]. Several other studies [5, 12, 16] have found that the percentage of couples whose responses agree averages only slightly more than 50%. And more recently, Morgan [14] has observed that couples are likely to agree more about each other's personality than they do in reporting who decided about specific purchase decisions.

There is clearly a need to resolve the apparent confusion about the sufficiency of wives' responses. An answer is important for research on family decision making since role consensus itself may be related to the balance of power between husband and wife. An answer is equally important to market researchers who must decide whether to interview both spouses or only the wife.

This article is a response to these difficult problems surrounding the description and measurement of family role structure. Specifically, this article will consider these questions:

1. What are the dimensions of husband-wife roles in two consumer purchase decisions?
2. To what extent do husbands and wives agree in their perception of roles?

METHOD

The data reported are drawn from a questionnaire administered to 100 families living in four Chicago suburbs. A small convenience sample was obtained by contacting families through three churches (two Protestant and one Catholic) and a grade school P.T.A. Couples were solicited by means of a letter asking their cooperation in a research project on "family living" and "decision making." Both husband and wife were requested to come to the church or school at the same time in order to participate. Each spouse was directed to a separate room in order to fill out the questionnaire, making collaboration impossible.

Couples were asked a series of questions about the relative influence of husband and wife in two durable goods purchases—an automobile and living room furniture. Several interrelated decisions were included for each product. For the last automobile purchased, husband and wife were asked to report who decided: (1) when to purchase; (2) how much money to spend; (3) make; (4) model; (5) color; and (6) where to purchase. Similar decisions were investigated for the furniture purchase—who usually decides: (1) what furniture to purchase; (2) how much to spend; (3) where to purchase; (4) when to purchase; (5) style; and (6) color and fabric. The questions were rated on a 5-point scale (husband decided=1; husband more influence than wife=2; equal influence=3; wife more influence than husband=4; wife decided=5). Since these five categories refer only to the roles of husband and wife, the response to any given question represents a respondent's perception of *relative* influence in the decision.

The selection of these two products and the techniques used to measure marital roles can be justified because both purchases represent important family decisions. Also, they usually involve substantial financial outlay, extended period of ownership, social importance, and joint use by several family members. In terms of other consumer research, both would undoubtedly be classified as "policy" or "major economic" decisions. Moreover, it is meaningful to speak of *marital* roles in reference to both decisions. Other studies [11, 19] have found that husbands and wives are the major participants in these purchases. This finding also supports the use of a simple rating scale limited to a measure of husband-wife influence.

The data presented in this paper differ in several ways from other studies. Whereas existing research has investigated marital roles across several economic decisions or for a single product purchase, these data can be analyzed both across and within product purchase decisions because of the use of the same question for each of the two product purchases and the same measure of influence for all 12 decisions. There are also responses to the same questions from both husband and wife, permitting comparison of husbands' responses as a group with wives', as well as between husband and wife within the same family. The extent of agreement can also be calculated for each of 12 decisions to determine whether the nature of the decision significantly affects the level of consensus.

Reliance on this small sample seems warranted in light of the exploratory nature of this study. No attempt is made to generalize the particular distribution of relative influence for any decision to all families. The interest is to consider the relationship between husbands' and wives' responses and between decisions within the same families. At the same time, the small sample size and the use of volunteer subjects urge caution in generalizing the findings.

FINDINGS

Relative Influence in Purchase Decisions

Tables 1 and 2 show the distribution of husbands' and wives' responses

TABLE 1   Marital Roles in Selected Automobile and Furniture Purchase Decisions As Perceived by Husbands (N=97)

Who decided:	Patterns of Influence (%)		
	Husband has more influence than wife	Husband and wife have equal influence	Wife has more influence than husband
When to buy the automobile?	68	29	3
Where to buy the automobile?	62	35	3
How much to spend for the automobile?	62	37	1
What make of automobile to buy?	60	32	8
What model of automobile to buy?	41	50	9
What color of automobile to buy?	25	50	25
How much to spend for furniture?	22	47	31
When to buy furniture?	16	45	39
Where to buy the furniture?	7	53	40
What furniture to buy?	3	33	64
What style of furniture to buy?	2	26	72
What color and fabric to select?	2	16	82

to questions about relative influence in 12 automobile and furniture purchase decisions.[1] The individual questions are listed in order of

[1] To simplify presentation, the original 5-point scale was collapsed by combining the categories "husband decided" with "husband more than wife," and "wife decided" with "wife more than husband." The distribution of responses between the two "extreme" response categories (1 and 2; 4 and 5) provides no additional insights for the purpose of the first analysis.

TABLE 2   Marital Roles in Selected Automobile and Furniture Purchase Decisions As Perceived by Wives (*N*=97)

Who decided:	Patterns of Influence (%)		
	Husband has more influence than wife	Husband and wife have equal influence	Wife has more influence than husband
When to buy the automobile?	68	30	2
Where to buy the automobile?	59	39	2
How much to spend for the automobile?	62	34	4
What make of automobile to buy?	50	50	—
What model of automobile to buy?	47	52	1
What color of automobile to buy?	25	63	12
How much to spend for furniture?	17	63	20
When to buy the furniture?	18	52	30
Where to buy the furniture?	6	61	33
What furniture to buy?	4	52	44
What style of furniture to buy?	2	45	53
What color and fabric to select?	2	24	74

increasing wife influence based on the average score for each decision. Data from husbands are reported in Table 1; the wives' responses are shown in Table 2.

The tables reveal considerable variability in husband-wife roles in these decisions, and it would be misleading to generalize about husband and wife roles in any absolute sense. For example, conclusions about which spouse makes "the furniture purchase decision" would necessarily depend on which particular decision was being made. Marked differences in the wife's influence can be seen by comparing decisions about how much to spend and when to buy with those concerning style, color and fabric. The same thing can be seen for the automobile purchase decisions. The percentage of husband-dominant families decreases from 60% in the decision about what make of automobile to buy to 25% in the decision about what color to select.

Also, one cannot generalize about roles in a particular decision without reference to the product being purchased. For example, compare the percentage of husband-dominant families in two decisions— where to buy the automobile and where to buy furniture. The former is characterized by a large proportion of husband-dominant families while in the latter, less than 10% of the families are husband-dominant. The same is true when comparing the decision about how much to spend for the automobile and furniture. The modal response is husband-dominant for automobiles but joint for furniture.

Finally, note the substantial variability in roles for individual decisions. Only three decisions have more than 65% of the families in any one of the three influence types. For the other decisions there is a considerable spread over two (and in some cases, three) categories. Reliance on the modal response in such cases to classify *decisions* as either husband-dominant, joint, or wife-dominant would actually conceal the considerable amount of variability in roles that exists between families.

Patterns of Relative Influence

The discussion in the previous section has been limited to the distribution of relative influence for each decision. In this section consider the distribution of relative influence across all six automobile and furniture decisions simultaneously. The emphasis here is upon the *pattern* of husband-wife influence across several decisions. Under the assumption of unidimensionality, all families should fall into one of three different patterns—husband-dominant, wife-dominant or joint—across all decisions. Alternatively, a pattern might reflect a division of labor between husband and wife (e.g., some decisions shared while others the responsibility of one spouse) common to a large number of families.[2] The number of patterns and their frequency will tell more about the variability in marital roles across decisions and may suggest a way of classifying families into various influence or decision "types."

For the purpose of this analysis, the 5-point scale of relative influence was again collapsed into 3 points by combining "husband decided" with "husband more than wife" (scale positions 1 and 2) and "wife decided" with "wife more than husband" (scale positions 4 and 5). In addition, automobile and furniture decisions were considered separately, so that each pattern included only 6 decisions. Both of these actions should make any regularities in the data more apparent.

Even with these modifications, the data show considerable variability in the number of unique patterns. Husbands' and wives' responses to the 6 automobile decisions yielded 52 and 38 patterns respectively. Similar results were found for furniture decisions—50 patterns (husbands' responses) and 46 patterns (wives' responses). Since the total number of respondents was 97 for the automobile purchase and 98 for the furniture purchase, a different pattern of relative influence is found for about every two respondents.

A few patterns do account for considerably more than two respondents each. Three patterns account for 32% of all families in the case of the automobile purchase (husbands' responses). Two of these—all joint ($N=6$) and all husband-dominant ($N=13$)—indicate unidimensionality. The other pattern ($N=12$) is husband-dominant with the exception of one joint decision ("What color of automobile to buy"). These same three patterns account for 45% of all families when the wives' responses are analyzed. The furniture purchase reveals somewhat more variability on this same criterion although four patterns continue to account for a large percentage of all families—31% (husbands' responses) and 41% (wives' responses). The most frequent pattern as reported by both husbands and wives is wife dominance for all six decisions ($N=14$ and $N=12$ respectively). Six other unique patterns (with frequencies of five or more) occur only once.

---

[2] The analysis of these patterns across three or more decisions does not lend itself to the usual factor analytic or clustering techniques which begin with a matrix of intercorrelations between pairs of variables. Such techniques could conceal the presence of meaningful regularity in relative influence across decisions.

This analysis provides little basis for developing family "types" based upon patterns of relative influence since one would have to overlook more than 50% of the sample. The variability described in the previous section when roles were examined by decision across families is also apparent when families are studied across decisions.

Dimensions of Decision Roles

The discussion to this point has emphasized the variability of marital roles in two consumer purchases. In this section consider the interrelationship of roles between these decisions and then group decisions together on the basis of their similarities. The objective is to identify and delineate "dimensions" of decision roles.

Tables 3 (husbands' responses) and 4 (wives' responses) show the association between roles in 12 automobile and furniture purchase decisions. Gamma coefficients were computed from 5×5 contingency tables showing the distribution of relative influence for every pair of decisions.

Tables 3 and 4 reveal the same patterns for husbands and wives. The triangle in the upper left-hand corner of the two matrices shows the association between relative influence in six automobile purchase decisions. Relative influence in all of these decisions is positively associated. Moreover, the degree of association is generally high. Data from husbands yield gammas ranging from .21 to .74. The degree of association reported by wives is even stronger, ranging from .42 to .92. The same pattern characterizes the association between relative influence in furniture purchase decisions (see the triangle in the lower right-hand corner of each matrix). Although there is some variability in the size of these gammas, one would conclude that decision roles within these product purchases are strongly and positively related.

The relationship between relative influence in automobile and furniture decisions can be seen in the square or lower left-hand portion of the matrices in Tables 3 and 4. In contrast to the association among decision roles *within* each of the two product categories, there is little relationship *across* product categories. The majority of signs are negative, indicating an inverse relationship between influence in automobile purchase decisions and influence in the purchase of furniture. Moreover, the magnitude of gammas is low. The degree of association ranges from .00 to .26 for wives and from .01 to −.38 for husbands, showing that purchase influence for automobiles is not related to purchase influence for furniture.

In an effort to more adequately delineate dimensions of decision roles, both matrices were analyzed using a clustering technique developed by McQuitty [13]. This technique groups decisions into clusters so that the associations between pairs of decisions within a given cluster are high, while the associations between decisions in different clusters are low. First the two decisions in the matrix having the highest association are combined, and then the association between this "new" two-decision cluster and each of the remaining decisions is

TABLE 3 Association (Gamma) Between Relative Influence in Selected Automobile and Furniture Purchase Decisions—Husbands' Responses (N=97)

Decisions	Automobile decisions						Furniture decisions					
	1	2	3	4	5	6	7	8	9	10	11	12
Automobile decisions:												
1. When to buy?												
2. Where to buy?	.44											
3. How much to spend?	.69	.44										
4. What make to buy?	.36	.74	.49									
5. What model to buy?	.21	.63	.57	.74								
6. What color to buy?	.24	.52	.37	.54	.59							
Furniture decisions:												
7. How much to spend?	.15	−.34	−.05	−.38	−.34	−.14						
8. When to buy?	.30	−.12	.25	−.14	−.09	−.06	.53					
9. Where to buy?	−.06	−.17	−.10	−.20	−.06	.13	.62	.59				
10. What to buy?	.17	−.14	−.10	−.17	−.11	.01	.61	.47	.64			
11. What style to buy?	.01	−.17	−.23	−.23	−.27	−.01	.48	.20	.59	.80		
12. What color and fabric to select?	.01	.09	.05	−.09	−.04	.33	.33	.23	.54	.71	.81	

TABLE 4   Association (Gamma) Between Relative Influence in Selected Automotive and Furniture Purchase Decisions—Wives' Responses (N=97)

Decisions	Automobile decisions						Furniture decisions					
	1	2	3	4	5	6	7	8	9	10	11	12
Automobile decisions:												
1. When to buy?												
2. Where to buy?	.78											
3. How much to spend?	.79	.69										
4. What make to buy?	.73	.78	.51									
5. What model to buy?	.70	.71	.55	.92								
6. What color to buy?	.52	.65	.42	.72	.66							
Furniture decisions:												
7. How much to spend?	.13	−.01	.14	.10	.08	.13						
8. When to buy?	.02	−.11	.26	−.18	.01	−.10	.77					
9. Where to buy?	.12	−.12	−.04	−.03	.01	.05	.67	.56				
10. What to buy?	.01	−.14	−.07	−.07	.03	−.09	.75	.60	.77			
11. What style to buy?	.00	−.10	−.17	−.14	−.09	−.10	.46	.26	.65	.75		
12. What color and fabric to select?	.03	−.07	.01	.05	.08	.04	.55	.40	.67	.71	.85	

determined.[3] The matrix is thus reduced by one row and one column. The same procedure is applied as many times as there are columns in the

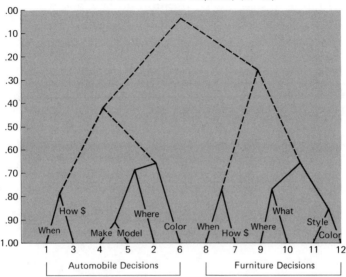

FIGURE 1. A Classification of Roles in Selected Automobile and Furniture Purchase Decisions (Wives' Responses) (N = 97)

original matrix, each time beginning with the two decisions (or two clusters) having the highest association. The association between the final two clusters is by definition the lowest gamma in the original matrix.

The results of this analysis can be seen in Figures 1 and 2, which give a graphic representation of how various decisions join together to form clusters. In addition, the height at which decisions or clusters merge represents the degree of association between them. Decisions were ordered along the x-axis to avoid intersecting lines as they were brought together.

Looking first at the wives' responses (Figure 1), four clusters of decisions are evident,[4] two of which represent product-related deci-

---

[3] An example illustrating this procedure may be useful. In Table 4 decisions about make and model of automobile are the most highly associated (.92). The association between this cluster and the remaining ten decisions is in each case determined by the pair with the lowest association. For example, the association between make of automobile and when to buy is .73; the association between model of automobile and when to buy is .70. To satisfy the classification assumption as specified by McQuitty—i.e., the three automobile decisions about make, model and when to buy must have as many common characteristics as the pair with the fewest—.70 is selected.

[4] The stopping criteria for forming clusters of decisions is based upon the degree of association between decisions and/or clusters. The interrelationship of decisions through the formation of four clusters is high—greater than .60 for wives and .50 for husbands. Beyond this point, however, the association is markedly lower. In Figure 2, for example, the relationship between the two clusters of automobile decisions is only .21; the association between the two clusters of furniture decisions is also low—.20. It seems reasonable, therefore, to describe roles in these twelve purchase decisions in terms of four major dimensions.

sions in the purchase of automobiles and furniture. One cluster includes four automobile decisions—what make and model of automobile
to buy, where to buy it, and what color to select. Similar subdecisions
also cluster together for the furniture purchase—what style and what
color and fabric to select, what furniture to buy, and where to buy it.
Decisions about the timing and expense of each purchase form the
remaining two clusters. With one exception, the same dimensions of
decision roles are present in the analysis of husbands' responses
(Figure 2).[5]

Thus, two bases for role differentiation can be seen in these two
product purchases—one basis being the product itself. Decision roles
in the purchase of automobiles are not related to decision roles in the
purchase of furniture. Within each of these product categories, roles

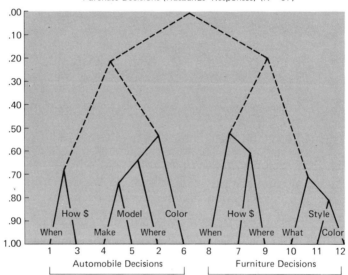

FIGURE 2   A Classification of Roles in Selected Automobile and Furniture
Purchase Decisions (Husbands' Responses) (N = 97)

are further differentiated by the nature of the decision. Roles in
"product-selection" decisions (e.g., model, make, color) differ from
roles in "allocation" or "scheduling" decisions (e.g., how much to
spend and when to buy).

Role Consensus

The discussion to this point has considered the responses to questions
about purchase influence separately for husbands and for wives. In

[5] The one exception is seen in the furniture decision clusters. Three decisions—
what furniture to buy, what style and what color to select—form one cluster. The
remaining three decisions (i.e., when to buy furniture, how much to spend and
where to buy) group together into another. In contrast to the wives' perception
of similarity between what furniture to buy and where to buy it, husbands perceive roles in deciding where to buy furniture as being more similar to the decision of how much to spend.

this section turn to the question of whether or not husbands and wives considered as groups and as individual families agree in their perception of roles.

Table 5 is a summary of Tables 1 and 2 and shows the average rela-

TABLE 5   Average Relative Influence in Selected Automobile and Furniture Purchase Decisions As Perceived by Husbands and Wives

Who decided:	Mean response from:		Difference in means
	Husbands (N=97)	Wives (N=97)	
When to buy the automobile?	1.95	1.83	+.12
Where to buy the automobile?	1.97	1.95	+.02
How much to spend for the automobile?	2.05	1.98	+.07
What make of automobile to buy?	2.13	2.11	+.02
What model of automobile to buy?	2.41	2.17	+.24
What color of automobile to buy?	2.95	2.73	+.22
How much to spend for furniture?	3.17	3.04	+.13
When to buy the furniture?	3.27	3.18	+.09
Where to buy the furniture?	3.45	3.35	+.10
What furniture to buy?	3.80	3.55	+.25
What style of furniture to buy?	3.91	3.68	+.23
What color and fabric to select?	4.17	3.92	+.25

tive influence in the 12 purchase decisions as reported by husbands and wives. As before, the individual decisions are listed in order of increasing wife influence.

This table reveals a high level of agreement in husband-wife perception when viewed in these aggregate terms. Note first that the rank ordering of decisions in terms of increasing wife influence is identical for husbands and wives. Moreover, the differences between husbands' and wives' responses are not statistically significant on the basis of a multivariate test which considers all 12 decisions simultaneously ($F=$ .9041; $df=12, 187$; $p<.54$). It is not likely that the conclusions reached by advertisers would differ at all depending on whether they had examined the husbands' responses or the wives'.

Two noteworthy patterns can be detected in these data. First, the direction of differences between the mean response of husbands and wives is consistent across all 12 decisions. Either one or both spouses seem to be modest in the assessment of their own influence. That is, husbands attribute more influence to their wives than wives attribute to themselves, and/or vice-versa. Secondly, the largest disagreements between husbands and wives occur for decisions that involve what might be termed "aesthetic" considerations (e.g., what model and color of automobile to buy, what furniture, what style and what color of furniture to buy). One reason may be, for example, that a husband's assessment of his wife's importance in decisions requiring aesthetic skills tends to be biased upward as a result of cultural expectations about the "appropriate" role for women. Alternatively, a wife might bias downward her husband's participation in such decisions for the same reason.

The data contained in Table 5, of course, do not provide any evidence of the extent to which husbands and wives *within the same family* agree in their role perception. In an extreme case, husbands and wives could exhibit perfect agreement as groups but perfect disagreement on an intrafamily comparison.[6] What can be said about the extent of role consensus within families? Is there the same high level of agreement that was characteristic of the aggregate comparisons?

Table 6 shows the extent of agreement between husbands and wives

TABLE 6   Extent of Husband-Wife Agreement in Selected Automobile and Furniture Purchase Decisions (*N* = 97)

Who decided:	Husband attributes less influence to wife than she attributes to herself		Husband and wife agree	Husband attributes more influence to wife than she attributes to herself	
	−2 %	−1 %	%	+1 %	+2 %
When to buy the automobile?	2	14	66	16	2
How much to spend for the automobile?	1	22	63	12	2
What make of automobile to buy?	—	20	64	15	1
What model of automobile?	—	14	59	25	2
What color of automobile?	—	14	59	26	1
Where to buy the automobile?	—	18	68	13	1
What furniture to buy?	—	10	59	30	1
How much to spend for furniture?	1	18	57	21	3
Where to buy the furniture?	—	16	63	19	2
When to buy the furniture?	1	21	48	25	5
What style of furniture to buy?	—	10	62	28	—
What color and fabric to select?	—	9	75	16	—

in the 6 automobile and 6 furniture decisions. The determination of whether or not a couple agrees was based upon a comparison of a 3-point (as opposed to the 5-point) scale. Disagreements, therefore, indicate a significant difference in perception. At the extreme, a difference of two scale points means that one spouse perceived a decision as husband-dominant while the other perceived it as wife-dominant. A disagreement between whether a decision was husband-dominant or

---

[6] The distinction between these two definitions of agreement is sometimes confused in the literature. For example, Hill bases a decision to utilize the wife as respondent on Wolgast's study of economic decision making. She found, according to Hill, "the wife equally well informed, and more accurate in predicting plans than the husband" [9, p. 73]. This is hardly accurate, however, since Wolgast's findings were based upon a comparison of husbands as a group with wives as a group—who, incidentally, were rarely from the same family.

joint (and wife-dominant or joint) is represented by a difference of one scale point.

The percentage of couples who agree about their roles in decision making averages 63% for the 6 automobile purchase decisions and 61% for the 6 furniture purchase decisions. The range of agreement is somewhat greater for the furniture decisions. Although these percentages are higher than the 33% expected by chance, these results raise considerable doubt about the validity of assuming that wives' responses are sufficient. In a large number of cases—ranging from 25% to 52% of the families—one would obtain a *different* assessment of relative influence by asking the husband. To rely only on wives' responses would be both incomplete and possibly misleading. Hence, the similarity between husbands' and wives' responses when viewed in aggregate terms is clearly not present on a within-family comparison.

What can be said about the nature of the disagreements? Perhaps role consensus varies in some predictable ways by families, decisions, or relative influence. It is also possible that the disagreements are more or less random, reflecting an inherent ambiguity in questions about purchase influence.

The nature of the distribution of disagreements for each decision provides some evidence for this latter explanation. Notice that the great majority of disagreements are only one scale point. Moreover, the shape of the distributions tends to be symmetrical. Only in the case of three or four furniture purchase decisions is there any tendency for the disagreeing couples to overrepresent those in which husbands attribute *more* influence to the wife than the wife attributes to herself. If there were a consistent bias in the way couples responded to these questions, it is likely that these distributions would have been more highly skewed.

Another possible explanation for disagreement is the presence of real conflict surrounding the decision. If a husband and wife disagreed about what make of car to buy and had reached a compromise, an assessment of "who decided" might be difficult since it would be subject to different interpretations. One might, therefore, anticipate a positive relationship between reported conflict and the extent of disagreement about who actually made the decision. The data do not conform to this expectation, however. While the six automobile decisions tend to be seen as relatively conflict-free, each furniture decision involves "some disagreement" in about 40% of the families on the average.[7] If different perceptions of roles really do arise from such conflicts, one should find lower consensus for furniture decisions than for automobile decisions. As seen in Table 6, this is not apparent. In fact, it is the similarity in the magnitude of role consensus across these decisions rather than any difference that is noteworthy.

A third possibility is that relative influence is itself related to the

---

[7] Using husbands' responses, the percentage of families who report disagreement in automobile decisions ranges from 3% to 13%. Disagreement is even less according to wives—from 2% to 8%. The percentage of families who report disagreement in furniture decisions ranges from 40% to 61% (husbands' responses) and from 25% to 51% (wives' responses).

magnitude of role consensus. It might be, for example, that disagreeing couples share decisions more equally. Couples with highly specialized roles (i.e., husband-dominant or wife-dominant), on the other hand, might display high consensus given less ambiguity about "who decides." In order to examine this possible relationship a comparison was made of average relative influence in each decision for three groups: (1) couples who agreed; (2) wives who disagreed with their husbands; and (3) husbands who disagreed with their wives. Differences in the mean values among these groups were not large. The only noteworthy pattern was the tendency for "disagreeing husbands" to attribute consistently more influence to wives than do their wives or the couples who agree. This finding suggests that the bias described earlier is due primarily to husbands rather than wives. It also suggests that relative influence has no relationship to the degree of consensus in the light of the husbands' consistent upward bias over both product categories.

Finally, is there any evidence that families tend to agree or disagree across several decisions? One simple test is merely to plot the number of disagreements (from 0 to 6) for each product. A bimodal distribution would be found if one group of families consistently agreed and another group consistently disagreed about their roles in these decisions. Regularity could also be represented by a relatively flat distribution in which couples formed a scale from high to low consensus. Rather than finding either of these two distributions, however, the data showed unimodal distributions for both automobile and furniture decisions with the mode in each case at two disagreements. Knowing that a couple disagreed about their roles in one decision does not increase the ability to predict whether they will agree or disagree about others.

The search for systematic differences in families, decisions, or relative influence as a basis for explaining the disagreement in spouses' perception of relative influence has produced largely negative results. It seems much more likely that disagreement reflects measurement error.

DISCUSSION

The multidimensional role structure evident in these two purchase decisions contrasts with the unidimensional or bidimensional authority structures posited in much of the existing sociological literature. Instrumental decisions, in Parson's [15] terminology, or economic decisions, as defined by Herbst [8], of which the automobile and furniture decisions would seem to be a part, can be differentiated much further.[8] This finding also raises doubts about the common practice of summing over individual decisions in order to construct an "overall" power score for a family. There should be prior evidence that the decisions are, in

---

[8] This conclusion is consistent with several sociological studies that have found considerable role specialization within the family (Levinger [10]; Tharp [18]; and Wilkening and Bharadwaj [20]).

fact, unidimensional. From a marketing point of view, the analysis suggests a *less* differentiated structure than that which is often implicit in the literature. It is possible to subsume several decisions under a more general category and hence begin to generalize about roles in consumer decisions. Of interest in future research is whether the same two clusters of product-related and allocation-related decisions are found for other product categories and whether these dimensions are sensitive to the demographic and social characteristics of families.

These results regarding role consensus have one direct implication for research. If the purpose of a study is merely to describe the relative influence of husbands and wives in various purchase decisions, then interview only one spouse. The conclusions reached by an advertiser in determining the appropriate audience for his message would not differ depending upon whether he had collected data from husbands or wives. If, on the other hand, a study uses purchase influence as a basis for classifying families for the purpose of further investigation, then the extent of within-family agreement becomes critical. The responses of one spouse may consistently provide better predictions of other aspects of a family's consumption behavior. Moreover, independent reports from husband and wife provide a basis for estimating the validity of measures used in a study.

How can the level of role consensus be increased? The findings of this study suggest that the use of specific, as opposed to global, measures of purchase influence is not the answer. It would appear that disagreement reflects each spouse's differing interpretations about the meaning of influence rather than any systematic bias inherent in these questions, whether general or specific. Attempts to increase consensus about roles will require more attention to the dynamics of the decision process. Information about the nature and frequency of discussion prior to each decision, length of the planning period, importance of each decision, and details about search activities may permit construction of meaningful classifications. Even with improved methodological procedures, however, one should consider that each spouse may have different but *equally legitimate* perceptions of relative influence. If this is true, the now common search for one "objective reality" or for the spouse who is "right" is misguided.

REFERENCES

1. BLOOD, ROBERT O. AND DONALD M. WOLFE, *Husbands and Wives: The Dynamics of Married Living*, Glencoe, Illinois: The Free Press, 1960.
2. BURGESS, ERNEST W. AND HARVEY J. LOCKE, *The Family*, New York: American Book Company, 1960.
3. FARBER, BERNARD, "A Study of Dependence and Decision-Making in Marriage," unpublished Doctoral dissertation, University of Chicago, September 1949.
4. FERBER, ROBERT, "On the Reliability of Purchase Influence Studies," *Journal of Marketing*, 19 (January 1955), 225–32.
5. HABERMAN, PAUL W. AND JACK ELINSON, "Family Income Reported in Surveys: Husbands Versus Wives," *Journal of Marketing Research*, 4 (May 1967), 191–4.

6. HEER, DAVID M., "Husband and Wife Perceptions of Family Power Structure," *Marriage and Family Living*, 36 (February 1962), 65–7.

7. ———, "Dominance and the Working Wife," *Social Forces*, 36 (May 1958), 341–7.

8. HERBST, P. G., "The Measurement of Family Relationships," *Human Relations*, 5 (February 1952), 3–35.

9. HILL, REUBEN, "Patterns of Decision-Making and the Accumulation of Family Assets," in Nelson Foote, ed., *Household Decision-Making*, New York: New York University Press, 1961, 57–80.

10. LEVINGER, GEORGE, "Task and Social Behavior in Marriage," *Sociometry*, 27 (December 1964), 433–48.

11. *Male vs. Female Influence on the Purchase of Selected Products as Revealed by an Exploratory Depth Interview Study with Husbands and Wives*, New York: Fawcett Publications, 1958.

12. McCANN, GLEN C., "Consumer Decisions in the Rural Family in the South," paper presented at the annual meeting of the American Sociological Association, New York, August, 1960 (mimeographed).

13. McQUITTY, LOUIS L., "Hierarchical Syndrome Analysis," *Educational and Psychological Measurement*, 20 (Summer 1960), 293–304.

14. MORGAN, JAMES T., "Some Pilot Studies of Communication and Consensus in the Family," *Public Opinion Quarterly*, 32 (Spring 1968), 113–21.

15. PARSONS, TALCOTT AND ROBERT F. BALES, *Family, Socialization, and Interaction Process*, Glencoe, Illinois: The Free Press, 1955.

16. SCANZONI, JOHN, "A Note on the Sufficiency of Wife Responses in Family Research," *Pacific Sociological Review*, 8 (Fall 1965), 109–15.

17. SHARP, HARRY AND PAUL MOTT, "Consumer Decisions in the Metropolitan Family," *Journal of Marketing*, 21 (October 1956), 149–56.

18. THARP, ROLAND C., "Dimensions of Marriage Roles," *Marriage and Family Living*, 25 (November 1963), 389–404.

19. *Time Magazine*, "Family Decision-Making," Research Report 1428, 1967.

20. WILKENING, EUGENE A. AND LAKSCHMI BHARADWAJ, "Dimensions of Aspirations, Work Roles, and Decision-Making of Farm Husbands and Wives in Wisconsin," *Journal of Marriage and the Family*, 29 (November 1967), 703–11.

21. WOLGAST, ELIZABETH H., "Do Husbands or Wives Make the Purchasing Decisions?" *Journal of Marketing*, 23 (October 1958), 151–8.

6 AROUSAL AND ATTENTION

Because the two topics of *arousal* and *attention* are so intimately related to motivation, let us begin by laying a motivational background. Motivation is generally acknowledged to be one of the central processes of learning to buy and, also, of the actual act of buying once the buyer's pattern of brand choice has become established. Interpretations differ somewhat because of our lack of knowledge, and a particular position is taken here: motivation is both energizing and directive, but marketer activity probably serves only to energize.

Arousal is the point at which the central aspects of buying behavior converge, as we saw in Chapter 1. Arousal can be thought of as having two effects, one concerned with regulating information input and the second concerned with triggering information-seeking. To highlight the role of *arousal* in regulating the flow of information input, we are grouping it here with *attention* for which *arousal* is the antecedent condition.

A second effect of *arousal* is to energize and so be an influence to bring about *overt search*, discussed in Chapter 7. Obviously, *overt search*, too, is a process that must be learned, including the specific search directions it takes: Does the buyer seek his information from ads, friends, a newspaper, or television? The first and second effects have to do with his information, and a third effect is to energize the purchase act.

Given these consequences of *arousal*, what are its determinants? *Motive intensity* has already been mentioned as one. Some past pupil dilation research centered on this aspect. It was alleged that when people are confronted by items or pictures of items that they like, their eye pupils tend to dilate. This reported finding stimulated considerable hope that eye pupil dilation, a measure of visual *attention*, could be used as the measure of advertising copy effectiveness as referred to by Blackwell, Hensel, and Sternthal (1970).* As they nicely show, *arousal* can be stimulated by other factors than *motive intensity* (shown via preference). The complexity of the stimulus, that is, *stimulus ambiguity*, and *confidence* in judging the brand concept are also antecedent conditions of *arousal*.

Motive intensity is obviously important. In practice, for example, we would expect the buyer to search more for information about brands with which he is deeply involved. We should speak more correctly of degree of involvement in the product class.

Turning to a topic related to attention, in the late 1950s considerable concern was expressed over the feasibility and social dangers of subliminal advertising. The idea was that a stimulus of intensity below the awareness threshold level would "sneak up on the buyer and get through his defenses." Hawkins (1970)* finds that a subliminal stimulus can intensify a motive, specifically thirst, but he finds no evidence that it will give predictable direction to that energized behavior, hence no tendency to direct the buyer to a particular brand.

12. Pupil dilation: what does it measure?

roger d. blackwell, james s. hensel, & brian sternthal

A popular and allegedly valid nonverbal measure of psychological response to visual stimuli is the pupillometer. Developed as an academic research tool to monitor and measure the linkage of pupil dilation and constriction to ongoing mental activity, it was later adopted for commercial use.

Typical application has been to problems of evaluating advertising materials, packages, and products, which has led to a growing conviction that in many areas of consumer research one might make better predictions of behavior from pupil responses than from verbal or opinion data.

Unfortunately, in the field of consumer research in general and advertising research in particular, the need for objective measures of psychological responses to various stimuli materials often leads to the practice of adopting a technique as a useful predictor of human behavior without first thoroughly investigating the technique.

The utilization of the pupil dilation technique as a measure of the effectiveness of advertisements is a prime example of this fallacious strategy on the part of advertising researchers. The slim ray of hope that the pupil dilation technique offers to researchers in their search for objective measures of ad effectiveness has perhaps in turn led to application of the technique to managerial problems before a systematic investigation of its utility and constraints has been conducted.

As a result, both unfounded optimism and ill-timed skepticism abound about the potential usefulness of the pupillometer in measuring advertising effectiveness. This polarity in attitudes is in itself an inhibiting factor in increasing understanding of the technique.

The purpose of the following discussion, however, is to clarify existing knowledge about pupil dilation.

The physiological mechanism of pupillary reactions can be divided into the following main categories (Lowenstein and Lowenfeld, 1962):

The Light Reflex: The response of the pupil to stimulation of the retina by an increase of light.

The Reaction to Near Vision: The contraction of the pupil which coincides with convergence of the eyes and accommodation of the lens upon viewing a near object.

Pupillary Reflex Dilation: Pupillary dilation elicited by sensory or emotional stimuli, or by spontaneous thoughts or emotions.

The Darkness Reflex: The pupillary response brought about by short interruption of a steady level of light-adaptation.

The Lid-Closure Reflex: Pupillary movements which accompany spontaneous, intentional, or reactive short closing of the eyelids.

Reprinted by permission from *Journal of Advertising Research,* Vol. 10, pp. 15–18, © copyright 1970, by the Advertising Research Foundation.

Pupillary "Unrest" and "Hippus": Apparently spontaneous oscillations of the pupil under steady conditions of illumination.

Although advertising and psychological researchers are primarily interested in the pupillary reflex dilation elicited by sensory or emotional stimuli, or by spontaneous thoughts or emotions, the other pupillary reactions are of major concern in terms of operational procedures and potential methodological artifacts.

It should be noted that much of the confusion and conflicting evidence that abounds in pupil dilation literature seems to be a direct result of the lack of constancy in the various experiments with regard to these reactions.

With respect to the psychological factors causing the pupillary reflex dilation, Hess and his associates (1960) have reported increases in the size of the pupil of the eye accompanying emotionally-toned or interesting visual stimuli. While the pupil is capable of changes from two to eight millimeters in response to light, the variation of pupil diameter is usually within ten per cent and often two per cent.

In addition to pupillary reactions to interesting visual stimuli, difficulty of mental arithmetic problems and pleasantness of stimuli have also been experimentally demonstrated as causing pupil responses (Hess and Polt, 1964; Hess, 1965). Moreover, Hess contends that pupil response acts as a bi-directional indicator of positive and negative affect of visually presented stimuli.

In other words, pupil response for a given stimulus can range from extreme dilation (positive affect) to extreme constriction (negative affect), depending upon whether the material shown is pleasant and interesting or unpleasant and distasteful to the viewer.

Hess and Polt (1960) describe these reported increases in the size of the pupil accompanying the viewing of emotionally-toned or interesting visual stimuli as being explained by the role of the sympathetic division of the autonomic nervous system.

Although they admit that the role of the sympathetic division in determining pupil size is quite complex, their argument is based on Kuntz's inference that "strong emotional states are accompanied by general sympathetic stimulation" and that "deep emotions of pleasure as well as fear are commonly accompanied by pupillary dilation."

This line of thinking about the psychological processes being monitored by pupil dilation seems logical until one is confronted with the many studies which have contradicted Hess's inferences.

Several studies, for example, have found no relationship between pupil diameter and pleasantness of the viewed stimuli. In one study, it was found that pupil size is not systematically related to the rated affect of visually presented words (Peavler and McLaughlin, 1967). In another study, by Pavio and Simpson, although dilation was found to reflect the cognitive difficulty of generating mental images to words, it did not vary with word pleasantness and unpleasantness.

On another aspect of Hess's work, there has been disagreement with the idea of pupil response as a bi-directional indicator of affect and interest. In a study conducted by Peavler and McLaughlin, the hypothesis that pupil diameter acts as a bi-directional indicator of positive and negative affect of visually presented stimuli was completely disproven.

The whole concept of constriction to a stimulus, provided adequate light controls are employed, has been questioned by Lowenfeld (1966). She argues, as a result of extensive physiological investigations, that all psychological and sensory stimuli, other than luminance increments, can dilate the pupil, while none of them cause it to constrict. Moreover, the constriction reported by Hess may be artifactual.

Woodmansee (1966) has noted that control stimulus baseline diameter frequently varies for different test-control stimulus combinations. A delayed dilation response to a test stimulus during a control stimulus may inflate the control baseline value to such an extent as to bias its use as a neutral comparison for the succeeding test stimulus.

Thus, "constriction" to a test stimulus could be observed when, in fact, the pupil change reflected a return to the appropriate diameter for the existing light conditions. Other than the work of Hess, the literature shows no evidence for the aversion-constriction hypothesis. Woodmansee has failed to demonstrate is existence in repeated attempts.

Just as contradiction has occurred in understanding the relationship between pupil dilation and the affect-arousing characteristics of various stimuli, there has also arisen another interpretation of the psychological process being monitored by pupillary responses.

Hess and Polt initiated this interpretation when they suggested that the pupillary response provides a sensitive peripheral indicator of the effort exerted during problem solving. Additional work has confirmed that suggestion and has further indicated that changes of pupil size may follow rapid variations in attention during a single task.

Thus, in a short-term memory task, a pupillary dilation occurs as the subject attends to, and presumedly rehearses, a string of digits or words (Beatty and Kahneman, 1966). When a person performs a transformation on a string of digits, the dilation is substantially larger than when he merely repeats the string. The peak is attained during the reporting phase, which is also the time when the transformed string is produced and the processing load on the subject is maximal.

Transient pupillary responses also reflect the different kinds of effort involved in thinking about concrete or abstract words or in recalling a familiar association (Kahneman and Beatty, 1966). In the latter case, a very steep dilation occurs immediately after the presentation of the cue to report, and further work has shown that the pupillary response to the effort of recalling an item diminishes as the item is overlearned (Kahneman and Beatty, 1967).

Although the foregoing results suggest a correlation between pupillary diameter and such constructs as arousal, alertness, or attention, it is apparent that the correlation is in need of additional specification.

A person is certainly in a relatively heightened state of alertness when he is watching for a faint signal, intent on a melody, attempting to recall his wedding anniversary, or doing arithmetic in his head. Though all these states are presumedly similar in some respects, they appear to differ in others.

Consequently, there is a need to make more specific the relations between physiological indicators and various kinds of attention. An important distinction has lately been drawn between attention directed outward, as in listening to a melody, and that directed inward, as in solving a problem (Lacey, et al., 1963). Distinct physiological patterns of autonomic activation are correlated with these two states. The evidence available suggests that pupillary dilations occur whenever attention is directed to the active processing of information, but the evidence concerning pupillary behavior when attention is directed to the passive acceptance of stimulation is either lacking or confusing.

Based on this type of thinking, Kahneman and Beatty conducted a study where pupils were measured while observers made pitch judgments of musical tones under the method of constant stimuli.

A substantial dilation occurred immediately after the presentation of the comparison tone, and the size of this response was closely correlated to the difficulty of the discrimination. In addition, baseline changes occurred within each block of trials, but had little effect on the magnitude of dilations. Responses to redundant stimuli, including the standard itself, decreased during the experimental session. These results not only supported the major hypothesis that pupillary measurements are a valid index of processing load even in cases where the verbal content of the process is presumably minimal, but they also pointed out that reduction of pupillary response is a correlate of reduced psychological significance of the stimulus, and is not the effect of mere repetition. Similar conclusions have been reached by Cohen and Walter (1964) in the description of the evoked potentials that accompany psychologically significant events.

In their discussion of the results of the pitch discrimination study, Kahneman and Beatty reinforce this argument:

> The present research adds to the growing evidence that pupillary dilations are closely related to the demands that mental tasks of various kinds place on the information-processing capacity of the organism. The magnitude of the responses observed above is clearly not determined by the arousing characteristics of any stimulus; rather, it corresponds to what the organism does with the information conveyed by a particular stimulus. The pupillary responses dealt with in the above-mentioned study are probably linked to the EEG correlates of specific mental activity that have recently been described in the literature. The frequent use of the concept of processing load in the present paper has been guided by a simple analogy: consider a houseful of electrical devices that are variously put in operation by manual switches or by their own internal governor systems. The total Amperage demanded by the entire system at any one time may easily be read on the appropriate electrical instrument outside the house. Processing load is here construed as analogous to an aggregate demand for power, and there is ground for hope that the pupil may function as a useful approximation to the relevant measuring device. There is an important difference between the contexts in which the concept of load and the more familiar concept of arousal would be applied. An organism may be said to be aroused by a stimulus; an organism is placed under load by its own responses.

It appears that Hess and his associates have attempted to interpret all pupillary changes in terms of an emotional response. Even the more obvious processing load responses can be explained as reflecting changing levels of anxiety that accompany performance.

This type of interpretation is hard to disprove, since it is probably true that the performance of more difficult tasks is generally accompanied by a higher level of anxiety. However, the proponents of such a view may have to broaden the concept of anxiety to the point that it becomes virtually meaningless or else a synonym of processing load.

In particular, it is certainly the case that some people find the challenge of dealing with mental problems altogether attractive and pleasant, and yet respond to these activities by major pupillary dilations.

The authors' current impression is that pupillary dilations probably accompany any substantial increase in mental activity, regardless of the pleasantness of this activity.

The empirical research seems to indicate that the pupil dilation measure can be useful in determining the effectiveness of advertising. The literature seems to leave some doubt, however, as to just what psychological processes, and thus advertising responses, are being monitored by pupillary responses.

If Hess and his associates are correct, pupil dilation should be a measure of the arousal quality of the stimuli, and thus emotional value of the stimuli itself. However, if Kahneman and Beatty's analysis of pupil dilation as a valid index of mental activity resulting from the processing of incoming stimuli is correct, pupillary responses can be expected to monitor the degree of mental activity accorded by the organism to the incoming stimuli and, thus, awareness of the ad.

REFERENCES

BEATTY, JACKSON AND DANIEL KAHNEMAN. Pupillary Changes in Two Memory Tasks. *Psychonomic Science*, Vol. 5, 1966, pp. 371–72.

COHEN, J. AND W. G. WALTER. The Interactions of Responses in the Brains to Semantic Stimuli. *Psychophysiology*, Vol. 144, 1964, pp. 182–83.

HESS, E. H. AND J. M. POLT. Pupil Size as Related to Interest Value of Visual Stimuli. *Science*, Vol. 132, 1960, pp. 349–50.

HESS, E. H. AND J. M. POLT. Pupil Size in Relation to Mental Activity During Simple Problem Solving. *Science*, Vol. 143, 1964, pp. 1190–92.

HESS, E. H. Attitude and Pupil Size. *Scientific American*, Vol. 212, 1965, pp. 46–54.

KAHNEMAN, D. AND J. BEATTY. Pupil Diameter and Load on Memory. *Science*, Vol. 154, 1966, pp. 1583–85.

KAHNEMAN, D. AND J. BEATTY. Pupillary Responses in a Pitch-Discrimination Task. *Perception and Psychology*, Vol. 2, 1967, pp. 101–105.

LACEY, J. L., *et al.* In P. H. Knopp (ed.). *Expression of the Emotions of Man.* New York: International Universities Press, 1963.

LOWENFELD, I. E. Pupil Size. *Opthomology*, Vol. 11, 1966, pp. 291–94.

LOWENSTEIN, O. AND I. E. LOWENFELD. The Pupil. In H. Dawson (ed.). *The Eye.* New York: Academic Press, 1963.

PAVIO, A. AND H. M. SIMPSON. The Effect of Word Abstractness and Pleasantness on Pupil Size During an Imagery Test. *Psychonomic Science*, Vol. 5, 1966, pp. 55–56.

PEAVLER, W. S. AND J. P. MCLAUGHLIN. The Question of Stimulus Content and Pupil Size. *Psychonomic Science*, Vol. 8, 1967, pp. 505–06.

13. The effects of subliminal stimulation on drive level and brand preference

del hawkins

With a few exceptions, interest and experimentation by the marketing profession in the field of subliminal stimulation has been virtually non-existent since the brief flurry of publicity and experiments in 1957–59. However, the field of marketing should maintain an *active* interest in this area. The potential utilization of subliminal stimulation as an advertising technique has not been completely eliminated, although both procedural and ethical considerations make such an approach unlikely at the present time. Furthermore, there is the untested possibility that many of those advertisements which are easily "available" to the average individual's sensing devices never enter into his realm of awareness and may in fact function as subliminal messages [2]. Thus, it seems essential that the marketing profession understand this phenomenon as fully as possible.

This article attempts: (1) to clarify certain concepts and definitions associated with subliminal research; (2) to propose a theoretical explanation for certain properties of the phenomenon; and (3) to report the findings of two experiments designed to test the theory and to clarify the nature of the effects which a subliminal message may have on the respondent.

CONCEPTS AND DEFINITIONS

The most prevalent term related to the phenomenon under consideration is *subliminal perception*, which refers to the registration of a stimulus below the threshold of perception. However, the concept of a perceptual threshold is subject to at least three interpretations. There is a *registration threshold* below which a stimulus is presumed to have no effect on the organism. Many early studies in the area utilized the concept of an *absolute threshold*, the length of intensity of exposure at which the stimulus is correctly identified 50% of the time. Most current investigations utilize the *recognition threshold*, the length or intensity of exposure on which a stimulus is correctly reported for the first time in a series of exposures of increasing duration or intensity. However, none of the above thresholds represents an absolute point.

Reprinted by permission from *Journal of Marketing Research*, Vol. 7 (August 1970), pp. 322–326, published by the American Marketing Association.

Del Hawkins is Assistant Professor of Marketing, Southern Illinois University. He is grateful to Professors W. T. Tucker and Grady Bruce for their constructive criticism in all phases of the research on which this article is based.

Instead, all three vary with individuals, experimental conditions, characteristics of the stimuli, and transient psychological and physiological conditions of the subject. This variability has led to the concept of a range of exposure conditions bounded at one end by a stimulus intensity providing zero information to the perceiver and at the other end by an intensity providing maximum information [14]. The actual threshold under consideration falls somewhere along this continuum depending on the operation of the variables mentioned above.

The term *subception* is frequently used interchangeably with *subliminal perception*. However, a recent article aimed at providing a consistent set of definitions for this area recommended that: (1) *subception* be used "only in connection with experiments involving discrimination without awareness (employ only subliminal stimuli)"; (2) *subliminal perception* be used only for experiments "in which a supraliminal or masking stimulus is used in connection with a subliminal stimulus"; and (3) *subliminal stimulation* be used as "a general classificatory term for experiments dealing with both procedures" [11].

Obviously, the concept of awareness occupies a critical position in the study of subliminal stimulation. The terms *awareness* and *consciousness* are often used interchangeably in studies of subliminal stimulation. However, the distinction made by Eriksen [6] equating awareness with the psychological quality of the phenomenon and consciousness with the state of physiological alertness of the individual will be utilized in this article.

Awareness and unawareness are generally treated as dichotomous categories defined in terms of the subject's ability to give a correct verbal report of the stimulus. However, there are a number of problems associated with using such an operational definition. Thus, experiments studying the same effect in the same way may vary in the adequacy of the questioning of the subject concerning his awareness of the stimulus, in his motivation to respond with the care and precision required, in the effects of the interrogation itself on the process of awareness, etc. [6]. Nonetheless, a definition of awareness in terms of verbal report is the only practical alternative for most experimental conditions.

THEORETICAL BACKGROUND

In several experiments, subliminal stimulation has been successful in increasing subjective hunger ratings [5, 16] or in influencing the emotional reaction to a neutral stimulus [12, 15]. Any theoretical explanation of these findings and the fact that the influence appears to have been limited to simple arousal must account for how the stimuli enter the system without the subject's awareness and explain why only certain effects are obtained. A theory meeting these conditions may be developed by utilizing two basic concepts proposed by Clark Hull: the reaction threshold and the fractional goal response.

Hull conceives of the threshold concept in general as a "... quantum of resistance or inertia which must be overcome by an opposing force before the latter can pass into action" [9, p. 323]. The reaction threshold is defined as the "...minimal effective reaction potential which will evoke observable reaction" [9, p. 324]. The effective reaction potential is basically a function of habit strength, the stimulus, drive, and inhibitory potential.

Hull proposes that "all minimal stimulus thresholds in psychophysics are the sum of the true initial threshold plus an artifact of undetermined magnitude which arises from the action of the oscillation function" [9, p. 325]. This function, which serves to weaken effective reaction potential, is to a considerable extent asynchronous. Hull states that "One of the ultimate physiological or submolar causes of molar behavioral oscillation lies in the variability of the molecular constituents of the nervous system, the neurons" [9, p. 309]. Thus he sees the momentary effective reaction potential as the effective reaction potential modified by the oscillation function. From this concept and that of the reaction threshold, he postulates: "The momentary effective reaction potential must exceed the reaction threshold before a stimulus will evoke a given reaction" [9, p. 344].

Hull's second major concept to be used in explaining the effects of subliminal communications is the fractional antedating goal reaction and its associated stimulus, the fractional goal stimulus. Hilgard and Bower explain the creation of fractional antedating goal reactions [7, p. 148]:

> Many of the stimuli present at the time the goal is reached are also present earlier. These include the stimuli from the drive, environmental stimuli both earlier and during reinforcement, traces from earlier stimuli persisting to the goal, as well as stimuli aroused by the animal's own movements. Hence, in repeating a sequence of acts leading to a goal... there are always enough of these stimuli conditioned to the goal response to elicit fractions to the goal response prior to reaching the goal.

The fractional goal response is credited with producing a continuous stimulus (the fractional goal stimulus) characteristic of the consumption of the goal substance. Although Hull generally avoids references to consciousness or awareness, he does state [9, p. 151]:

> The fact that the fractional goal reaction occurs in an antedating manner at the beginning of the behavior chain or sequence *constitutes on the part of the organism a molar foresight or knowledge of the not-here and the not-now.*

By using Hull's concepts of the reaction threshold and the fractional goal stimulus, an explanation of a stimulus' ability to influence behavior without the subject's awareness can be developed. The first essential proposal is that there exists a reaction threshold for stimulating the afferent nervous system and the fractional goal response related to the stimulus that is lower than the reaction threshold for awareness. Two types of evidence lend credence to this proposal. The first is physiological investigations which have demonstrated that "... the frequency of the neural waves or impulses emitted by a receptor is slow with weak stimulation and fast with strong stimulation" [8, p. 41].

Thus, while a subliminal stimulus may not produce frequent enough impulses to trigger the reaction of awareness, they may be frequent enough to evoke other responses which have a lower reaction threshold, such as a well-established fractional goal response. The second type of support comes from the frequent finding that subjects can learn to recognize previously "subliminal" levels of stimulation, which indicates that levels capable of activating the receptor mechanisms do not necessarily result in awareness of the nature of the stimulus.

METHODOLOGY

Two experiments were conducted to test the validity of the theoretical explanation described above and to ascertain the extent to which messages received subliminally by the subject (whether or not such was the intention of the sender) are effective in influencing behavior. Both experiments relied on a three-channel tachistoscope[1] to present the messages subliminally. This is an electronic device for illuminating a maximum of three stimulus cards in a preselected pattern for predetermined time intervals, and is capable of mixing the three images optically to produce the appearance of a single image [13].

Experiment 1

The major purposes of this experiment were to: (1) determine whether subjective thirst ratings could be influenced by a subliminal stimulus as predicted by the theory; (2) compare the effects of the subliminal and supraliminal presentation of the same stimulus; and (3) compare the effects of the subliminal presentation of a simple thirst stimulus with a more complex form of the same stimulus.

Four experimental groups of 24 subjects each were differentiated by the subliminal message they received. The presentation of the subliminal stimuli took place during a cover experiment which had the stated purpose of establishing recognition thresholds for various brand names. Group I, the control group, received the nonsense syllable NYTP at the subliminal exposure time of 2.7 milliseconds (a pretest with different subjects indicated only slightly better than chance forced-choice recognition of "something" or "nothing" when either the stimulus card or a blank card was shown). Group II received the same subliminal nonsense syllable but was "forced" to recognize and repeat aloud five times the word COKE in the cover experiment (the other three groups were recognizing automotive brand names). Group III was subliminally presented with the word COKE and Group IV with the subliminal command DRINK COKE. The basic stimulus word COKE was used on the assumption that it has acquired a generic meaning beyond the specific product Coca-Cola and would thus elicit fractional drinking responses from the majority of the subjects.

---

[1] Model GB manufactured by Scientific Prototype Corporation, New York, New York.

Each group was presented with its particular subliminal message 40 times over approximately 15 minutes. Each member of Group II saw and verbally stated the word COKE five times. Following these presentations, the subjects were questioned to insure that the messages were indeed subliminal. They then completed a fake Perceptual Health Inventory which, among other things, obtained the subject's estimate of the time-lapse since his last fluid intake and a subjective thirst-rating on a seven-point scale ranging from "not at all thirsty" to "very thirsty."

Findings

The basic analysis was to compare the subjective thirst ratings between the various groups, checking to ensure that any differences obtained could not be credited to a differential time lapse since the last reported fluid intake. The thirst rating scale data were treated as ordinal data, and nonparametric Mann-Whitney U tests were run between the appropriate experimental groups. Likewise, since the time lapse estimates were assumed to be related to increases in thirst by a direct but unknown function, they were also treated as ordinal data and compared by means of the Mann-Whitney U test. The five hypotheses based on the theory proposed earlier and the results of the U tests are summarized below. All except the last comparison are one-tailed tests.

1. The subliminal presentation of the stimulus word COKE will produce significantly higher thirst ratings than the subliminal presentation of a nonsense syllable.
   Thirst rating: $p = .022$
   Time lapse: $p > .10$
2. The subliminal presentation of the stimulus command DRINK COKE will produce significantly higher thirst ratings than the subliminal presentation of a nonsense syllable.
   Thirst rating: $p = .059$
   Time lapse: $p > .10$
3. The subliminal presentation of the stimulus command DRINK COKE will not produce significantly higher thirst ratings than the subliminal presentation of the stimulus word COKE.
   Thirst rating: Slight difference in the opposite direction from that used to refute the hypothesis.
   Time lapse: $p = .035$
4. The supraliminal presentation of the stimulus word COKE will produce significantly higher thirst ratings than the subliminal presentation of a nonsense syllable.
   Thirst rating: $p = .093$
   Time lapse: $p > .10$
5. Exploratory. A comparison of the effects of the supraliminal presentation of COKE with the subliminal presentation of the same stimulus.
   Thirst rating: $p > .10$
   Time lapse: $p > .10$

These findings indicate that: (1) a simple subliminal stimulus can serve to arouse a basic drive such as thirst; (2) a subliminal command to drink the beverage apparently will not greatly increase the influence of the message, and (3) a frequently presented, familiar subliminal cue may be as effective as the infrequent supraliminal presentation of the same cue in arousing a basic drive.

Experiment II

With the results of the first experiment indicating that subliminal messages can affect drive level, an experiment was designed to determine if choice behavior could be influenced by forming an association between two subliminal stimuli, one with positive and the other with neutral valence. Such an association would seem essential for any form of brand-specific promotion by subliminal messages.

The presentation of the subliminal stimuli took place during a cover experiment with the stated purpose of evaluating a series of outdoor scenes for use in an advertising campaign. The subliminal message, which was shown for 2.7 milliseconds as in the earlier study, consisted of the brand name (a single letter) of one of two identical bottles of perfume superimposed upon a seductive picture of a young woman. The seductive, seminude female was selected as the representative popular advertising theme for cosmetics, especially perfumes.

After each of the 20 male subjects had been exposed to the "advertisement" 35 times, he was asked, as a "pretest for another experiment," to sample each of two identical perfumes. Each bottle was identified by one letter on the label (F or L). Half of the subjects had been exposed to subliminal "advertisements" for Brand F and half for Brand L. The subjects then responded to the following question:

> Imagine that you have just picked up your blind date. She is exceedingly attractive and sexy. As she approaches, you notice her perfume. It is one of the two brands that you have just sampled. It is Brand ——.

This particular type of question was utilized because it allowed a degree of projection and thus may have freed the respondent from any inhibitory guilt feelings that may have been aroused by directly stating a preference for the brand associated with the nude. However, a chi-square analysis (in the table), showed no evidence of influence by the message.

Subliminal Brand Promotion and Brand Selection

Brand chosen	Brand promoted		Total
	F	L	
F	3	5	8
L	7	5	12
Total	10	10	20

$x^2 = .208.$ $p > .50.$

A preliminary test on female subjects was conducted to determine if further efforts on this particular experiment would be worthwhile. Ten female subjects were shown messages promoting Brand F in the same manner as the male subjects. Six chose the promoted brand in response to the following question: "Which of the two perfumes that you have just sampled would you expect Brigitte Bardot to prefer ———?" Such a selection has a chance occurrence probability of .377; therefore, it did not appear that a larger sample would prove useful and the experiment was ended. Apparently, this particular message was not being associated with the brand name, or, if it was, did not exert a significant influence on brand preference.

DISCUSSION

Berelson and Steiner, after reviewing the research on subliminal stimulation, concluded [3, p. 95] that there is:

> ...no scientific evidence that subliminal stimulation can initiate subsequent action, to say nothing of commercially or politically significant action. And there is nothing to suggest that such action can be produced "against the subject's will," or more effectively than through normal recognized messages.

This study does not support the first part of their conclusion. To the extent that the arousal of a drive can be expected to result in subsequent action to reduce that drive, subliminal stimulation can be said to initiate subsequent action. However, such action is of a general nature and not necessarily associated with the specific content of the subliminal message.

The question of whether associations with behavioral consequences can be induced with subliminal stimuli remains open. Perhaps a larger number of exposures or a more skillfully composed subliminal message could influence choice behavior. The present experiment merely demonstrates that such effects may be quite difficult (if even possible) to achieve and suggests that the associations that result in brand images may depend entirely on supraliminal stimuli, even if not necessarily on conscious cognitive processes.

REFERENCES

1. ADAMS, J. K., "Laboratory Studies of Behavior Without Awareness," *Psychological Bulletin*, 54 (May 1957), 383–405.
2. BARTHOL, RICHARD P. AND MICHAEL J. GOLDSTEIN, "Psychology and the Invisible Sell," in Harold H. Kassarjian and Thomas S. Robertson, eds., *Perspectives in Consumer Behavior*, Glenview, Ill.: Scott, Foresman and Company, 1968.
3. BERELSON, BERNARD AND GARY A. STEINER, *Human Behavior: An Inventory of Scientific Findings*, New York: Harcourt, Brace and World, Inc., 1964.
4. BEVAN, WILLIAM, "Subliminal Stimulation: A Pervasive Problem For Psychology," *Psychological Bulletin*, 61 (January 1964), 81–99.

5. BYRNE, DONN, "The Effect Of A Subliminal Food Stimulus On Verbal Responses," *Journal of Applied Psychology,* 43 (August 1959), 249–52.
6. ERIKSEN, CHARLES W., "Discrimination and Learning Without Awareness: A Methodological Survey and Evaluation," *Psychological Review,* 67 (September 1960), 279–300.
7. HILGARD, E. R. AND G. H. BOWER, *Theories of Learning,* Third Edition, New York: Appleton-Century-Crofts, Inc., 1966.
8. HULL, CLARK L., *Principles of Behavior,* New York: Appleton-Century-Crofts, Inc., 1943.
9. ————, *A Behavioral System,* New York: John Wiley & Sons, Inc., 1952.
10. KLEIN, G. S. AND R. R. HOLT, "Problems and Issues in Current Studies of Subliminal Activation," in J. G. Peatman and E. L. Hartley, eds., *Festschrift for Gardner Murphy,* New York: Harper and Row, Publishers, 1960.
11. MURCH, GERALD M., "Suggestion For Clarification of Terminology In Experiments On Subliminal Stimulation," *Perceptual and Motor Skills,* 19 (October 1964), 442.
12. NAYLOR, J. C. AND C. H. LAVSHE, "An Analytical Review of the Experimental Basis of Subception," *The Journal of Psychology,* 46 (July 1958), 75–96.
13. Scientific Prototype, *Three-Channel Tachistoscope Instruction and Maintenance Manual,* New York: Scientific Prototype Manufacturing Corp., 1964.
14. SECORD, P. F. AND C. W. BECKMAN, *Social Psychology,* New York: McGraw-Hill Co., Inc., 1964.
15. SMITH, G. J. W., D. P. SPENCE, AND G. S. KLEIN, "Subliminal Effects of Verbal Stimuli," *Journal of Abnormal and Social Psychology,* 59 (September 1959), 167–76.
16. SPENCE, DONALD P., "Effects Of A Continuously Flashing Subliminal Verbal Food Stimulus On Subjective Hunger Ratings," *Psychological Reports,* 15 (December 1964), 993–4.

7 OVERT SEARCH AND THE MEDIA SELECTION PROCESS

The evidence is clear that at least in some purchasing situations buyers do seek information, not only in the sense of paying attention by regulating their sensory receptors and moving their body so as to bring their receptors into closer affinity with a stimulus, but also by overtly seeking information, such as going to the public library to read a copy of *Consumer Reports*.

Bennett and Mandell (1969),* in a simple but well-designed study, present some interesting evidence on search behavior for a product class that we think of as highly involving, namely, cars. They found that people, after buying a car, recalled quite well what information sources they had used. Also, their findings indirectly supported the notion that people seek less information when their *confidence* in judging the brand is relatively high. First, the more prior purchase experience, and consequently the more confidence, the less *overt search* by buyers for auto information before making their latest auto purchase. Second, to the degree that their last several auto purchases were all of the same brand, *overt search* for auto information prior to the latest purchase was reduced.

Of considerable interest to all of us is the question, when an individual searches for information, where does he search? What sources does he use? We assume that the *arousal* variable energizes *overt search* behavior just as it does all overt behavior. To explain why he uses certain information and not others, we turn to an examination of the learning process. Presumably successful uncertainty-reducing or confidence-increasing searches are rewarding, unsuccessful searches are punishing.

Bauer and Wortzel (1966),* after carefully reviewing a number of earlier studies of how physicians obtain information about new drugs, put together a useful rationale to explain how the physician allocates his search effort among a number of information sources: detail men, drug advertising, and professional colleagues.

There is probably a second order of search that a buyer exhibits as well. Presumably, as we indicated, he learns to use some pieces of information instead of others. We hypothesize that by a comparable process, he also learns over time which types of information sources—media—are worthy of his attention. In other words, his *media patterns*—the magazines he subscribes to, the newspapers he buys, the TV stations he watches, and so on—are also partly determined by the extent to which he perceives them as serving his informational and entertainment needs. Once established, such media patterns will be strong determinants of *information exposed*.

14. Prepurchase information seeking behavior of new car purchasers—the learning hypothesis

peter d. bennett
& robert m. mandell

Learning theory suggests that the probability of achieving a correct response increases with the number of positively reinforced trials. Whether the subjects are rats in a simple T-maze, or human beings in more complex response settings, and under a variety of reward or punishment stimuli, many individual and most aggregated learning curves have the general shape shown in the figure.

Learning theorists disagree on several issues, including *what* is learned, i.e., habits or cognitive structures, and whether this learning occurs through trial and error or through ideation [5, Chapter 1]. On this "cognitive versus stimulus-response issue," Howard and Sheth

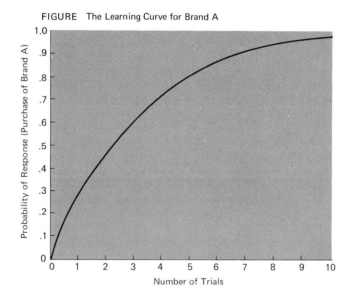

FIGURE The Learning Curve for Brand A

Probability of Response (Purchase of Brand A) vs *Number of Trials*

Reprinted by permission from *Journal of Marketing Research*, Vol. 6 (November 1969), pp. 430–433, published by the American Marketing Association.

Peter D. Bennett is associate professor and chairman, Marketing Department, The Pennsylvania State University. Robert M. Mandell is market development specialist, Corning Glass Works, and special lecturer in business administration, Corning Community College. The authors appreciate the support of their research given by The Pennsylvania State University.

[7] are eclectic.[1] Another important issue is the role of reinforcement. Guthrie [4] argues that responses are learned through contiguous association in time, but others, notably Hull [8] and Spence [12], insist that reinforcement, i.e., some reward or punishment, is essential to learning. The Howard-Sheth theory embraces the latter school of thought unequivocally.

Regardless of theoretical persuasions, learning theorists have always used some form of quantitative expression of response tendencies, e.g., latency, relative frequency, percentage of items recalled, etc. Recent developments in mathematical learning theory, principally Estes [2], Estes and Burke [3], and Bush and Mosteller [1], treat learning as a stochastic process and thus express response tendencies in probabilistic terms. Although Estes and Burke seem to depend more on Guthrie's theory of contiguous association, Bush and Mosteller declare that, ". . . our mathematical model is not committed to either reinforcement theory or contiguity theory" [1, p. 190].

As learning theory has been applied to consumer behavior, from Kuehn's classic work [9] to the elaborate Howard-Sheth model [7], the focus has been on response tendencies expressed in probabilistic terms. Howard [6] postulates a consumer brand choice "learning" function like that in the figure.

The form of the function is $P_A = M\ (1 - e^{-kt})$, where

P_A is the probability of purchasing Brand A
M is the maximum attainable loyalty to Brand A
k is a constant expressing the learning rate
t is the number of reinforced trials
e is the base of the natural logarithms.

Howard does not include the effects of non-reinforced trials or purchases of brands other than A.

Howard includes in his explanation of buying behavior a process of prepurchase information seeking. Before purchasing, the consumer actively seeks information from a variety of personal and impersonal sources. He also *attends* to more of the unsolicited information via the mass media. The "learning curve" is arbitrarily divided into segments of extensive problem solving behavior, limited problem solving behavior, and routinized response behavior [7, 257–8]. In the last two, the consumer has acquired some experience and does not actively seek information to the extent he does in the extensive problem solving stage. The concept of *stages* here, as elsewhere, is only meaningful as a rough guide to a process through which one passes. Howard and Sheth call this process the *psychology of simplification,* and hypothesize that the further "[the consumer] is along in simplifying his environment, the less is the tendency toward active search behavior" [7, p. 254]. In a recent five-week experimental study, Sheth and Venka-

---

[1] This statement, and those following, which place the Howard-Sheth theory with competing learning theories is based more on the authors' understanding of that model in its various published and yet unpublished forms, rather than on explicit statements by Howard and Sheth.

tesan [10] found subjects spent *less time* on information seeking as their repeat purchases increased.

Based on these central notions, the following hypotheses were formulated:

H_1: The buying experience itself is instructive, whether or not the choice is positively reinforced. As this experience increases, evidenced by the total purchases in the individual's history, the amount of effort expended on information search will decrease.

H_2: As the total number of reinforced purchases of a brand increases, the amount of information seeking before purchase of *that* brand will decrease.

H_3: As the number of *sequential* reinforced purchases of a brand increases, the amount of information seeking before purchase of *that* brand will decrease.

METHODOLOGY

The new automobile purchase was chosen as the consumer situation for several reasons:

1. The automobile was considered a sufficiently important product purchase for the consumer to recall his purchase history
2. The information sources available for prepurchase search are many and varied
3. Automobile purchases are made often enough to construct histories ranging from one to several "trials"
4. A frame from which to draw respondents was readily available from new car registration records.

The sample's respondents were chosen from all new car registrations in the greater Harrisburg, Pennsylvania, area between March 15 and April 14, 1967. Personal interviews were conducted during the period April 18–29, 1967. It was thus possible to interview the respondents soon enough after the purchase so they were able to recall their information seeking behavior. A 50 percent sequential sample of 180 was selected from which 148 questionnaires were completed, a response rate of 82 percent. The data included here are from 146 usable questionnaires. (Two respondents were employees of car dealers and thus eliminated.)

The purchase history was a critical set of data. The respondents were asked to reconstruct their entire automobile ownership history, were given ample time, and were encouraged to examine any legal or financial records that might assist their recall. An advance letter containing a form for recording the purchase history preceded the interview by approximately one week.

A second set of critical data was related to the extensiveness of information seeking behavior engaged in before purchase of the latest automobile. Nine different information sources were developed in a pretest of the questionnaire. An open-ended question was included, but was rarely answered. The ten information sources included were

TABLE 1   Sources of Information

Information source	Weight[a]
Consumer Reports	18
Dealer visit	18
Expert opinion[b]	12
Friends' opinion	10
Reading brochures[c]	10
Discussion with spouse	9
Auto show	7
Advertisements	7
News articles	6
Discussion with children	3
Total	100

[a] Weights indicate the relative amount of effort required to use the particular source.
[b] Expert could be mechanic or "purchase pal" with special knowledge of automobiles, either of a technical or economic nature.
[c] Indicates the actual reading of brochure, usually picked up at "Dealer visit."

those in Table 1. A number of socioeconomic variables were also included as were some questions not reported here.

It was obvious that some forms of information seeking involved more active search than others. Thus, a method for weighing the ten information sources became essential. Such an index was developed by a panel of 16 experts, 8 faculty members and 8 graduate students of the Marketing Department at The Pennsylvania State University. The panel was asked to use the criterion of the amount of effort each source called for. The consistency of the weighing schemes led the authors to trust the resulting scale as a sound if crude *ordinal* measure of information seeking behavior.[2]

RESULTS AND DISCUSSION

The histories ranged from 1 to 18 purchases and had a mean length of 6.4 purchases. The independent variable, "number of trials," was defined in three ways. The first definition (T_1) was the total number of automobiles purchased by the subject. It was hypothesized that experience, *per se*, would tend to reduce the need for information search before purchase. Both positive and negative reinforcement should increase the buyer's experience and cause him to rely more on his own judgment and thus less on his information search.

The other two definitions of trials are more in keeping with the main body of learning theory. T^2 is the number of purchases of the brand of automobile most recently purchased—regardless of sequence.

2 The authors' judgment is that the weighting schema has face validity. Siegel points out that, "A high or significant value of W [Kendall's coefficient of concordance] may be interpreted as meaning that the observers or judges are applying essentially the same standard in ranking the N objects under study" [11, p. 237]. For this panel of judges, $W = .3848$. $\chi^2 = 55.41$, $p < .001$ [11, pp. 229–38].

If we say that "1" represents the brand just purchased, and "O" any other brand, a history of 010010111 yields a value of $T_2 = 5$. (T_1 with this sequence is 9.)

The final definition of the number of trials (T_3) is the number of *successive* purchases of the brand just purchased. In the preceding purchase sequence, $T_3 = 3$. This last definition is the closest to the classical concept of response probabilities being a function of the number of successive positively reinforced trials.

The information seeking scale was used to classify the respondents by quartiles for testing the hypotheses by the chi-square statistic. For H_1, Table 2 shows that there is no significant relationship between the number of automobiles a consumer has owned and the amount of

TABLE 2   Information Seeking As Function of Number of Prior Purchases (T_1)

| Number of trials | Amount of information search effort (Quartiles) | | | | | |
	I (Lowest)	*II*	*III*	*IV (Highest)*	*Total*	*Base*
1–3	12.9%	32.3	25.8	29.0	100.0%	31
4–6	29.7%	25.9	25.9	18.5	100.0%	54
>6	26.2%	21.4	26.2	26.2	100.0%	61

$x^2 = 4.46$, $n = 146$, $df = 6$, $p < .62$.

information seeking he engaged in before his recent purchase. The null hypothesis cannot be rejected.

This result tends to deny the notion in the Howard-Sheth theory that all experience is instructive and reduces the need for information seeking. When consumers switch brands, they need the support provided by the information sought. If information seeking behavior is engaged in primarily for purposes of risk reduction [10], that risk seems not to be less for experienced than for inexperienced consumers.

H_2 was that the experience of buying and using a particular product brand would reduce the need to seek information before purchasing that particular brand. As is clear from Table 3, the null hypothesis

TABLE 3   Information Seeking As Function of Number of Prior Purchases of Brand Just Purchased (T_2)

| Number of trials | Amount of information search effort (Quartiles) | | | | | |
	I (Lowest)	*II*	*III*	*IV (Highest)*	*Total*	*Base*
1	10.0%	20.0	34.0	36.0	100.0%	50
2–3	26.8%	30.4	19.6	23.2	100.0%	56
>3	40.0%	25.0	25.0	10.0	100.0%	40

$x^2 = 17.80$, $n = 146$, $df = 6$, $p < .007$.

can be rejected ($p < .007$). Consumers tend to seek less information before purchase of a particular automobile make as a function of their prior experiences with that make.

Finally, the hypothesis (H_3) most closely related to classical learning theory is that information seeking behavior is a negative function of the number of *sequential* positively reinforced trials. The data presented in Table 4 clearly support that hypothesis ($p < .001$).

TABLE 4   Information Seeking As Function of Number of Sequential Prior Purchases of Brand Just Purchased (T_3)

Number of trials	Amount of information search effort (Quartiles)					
	I (Lowest)	*II*	*III*	*IV* (Highest)	*Total*	*Base*
1	17.7%	19.0	29.1	34.2	100.0%	79
2–3	21.0%	34.2	31.6	13.2	100.0%	38
>3	48.2%	31.0	10.4	10.4	100.0%	29

$\chi^2 = 22.12$, $n = 146$, $df = 6$, $p < .001$.

These results may have prescriptive value for marketing decision making. The essence of the study (H_2 and H_3) is solid empirical support for a major assumption in the Howard-Sheth theory of buyer behavior. It would be useful to see this evidence replicated with other products, including frequently purchased nondurables, which the Sheth and Venkatesan study [10] considers, if somewhat tangentially.

The "psychology of simplification" to which the Howard-Sheth theory refers is consonant with the main body of learning theory, whether of the reinforcement or contiguity persuasion; and this construct is supported here.

CONCLUSIONS

There has been ample evidence for some years to support the contention that brand choice behavior is a form of human behavior subject to learning through reinforcement. Many ramifications of this learning process have appeared in the numerous discussions of brand loyalty.

The pool of consumers who are loyal to Brand A at any particular time are either more susceptible to Brand A's marketing efforts or are harder to reach by competing brands. The findings here provide a basis in theory for the consistent empirical evidence of large numbers on the diagonal of period-to-period brand shifting matrices.

The Howard-Sheth theory of buyer behavior contains several constructs that provide a useful framework for research in consumer behavior. A whole series of efforts to support and clarify the theory with empirical evidence is needed.

REFERENCES

1. Bush, Robert R. and Frederick Mosteller, *Stochastic Models for Learning*, New York: John Wiley & Sons, Inc., 1955.
2. Estes, William K., "Toward a Statistical Theory of Learning," *Psychological Review*, 57 (March 1950), 94–107.
3. ———— and C. J. Burke, "A Theory of Stimulus Variability in Learning," *Psychological Review*, 60 (July 1953), 276–86.
4. Guthrie, Edwin R., "Association and the Law of Effect," *Psychological Review*, 47 (March 1940), 127–48.
5. Hilgard, Ernest R. and Gordon H. Bower, *Theories of Learning*, 3rd ed., New York: Appleton-Century-Crofts, 1966.
6. Howard, John A., *Marketing Management: Analysis and Planning*, Homewood, Ill.: Richard D. Irwin, Inc., 1963, Chapters 3–4.
7. Howard, John A. and Jagdish N. Sheth, "Theory of Buyer Behavior," in Reed Moyer, ed., *Changing Marketing Systems: Consumer, Corporate and Government Interfaces*, Proceedings, Winter Conference, American Marketing Association, 1967, 253–62.
8. Hull, Clark L., *The Principles of Behavior*, New York: Appleton-Century-Crofts, 1943.
9. Kuehn, Alfred A., "An Analysis of the Dynamics of Consumer Behavior and its Implications for Marketing Management," Unpublished Ph.D. dissertation, Carnegie Institute of Technology, 1958.
10. Sheth, Jagdish N. and M. Venkatesan, "Risk-Reduction Process in Repetitive Consumer Behavior," *Journal of Marketing Research*, 5 (August 1968), 307–10.
11. Siegel, Sidney, *Nonparametric Statistics for the Behavioral Sciences*, New York: McGraw-Hill Book Company, Inc., 1956.
12. Spence, Kenneth W., *Behavior Theory and Conditioning*, New Haven, Conn.: Yale University Press, 1956.

15. Doctor's choice: the physician and his sources of information about drugs

raymond a. bauer & lawrence h. wortzel

Enough has been written about the physician and his sources of information about drugs so that the picture should, by now, be reasonably clear. However, varying stereotypes still persist which, on the one hand, see the doctor as the helpless dupe of the pharmaceutical industry and, on the other hand, as a detached, devoted man of science who will have as little as possible to do with commercial sources of information about drugs. Perhaps one more look at the available evidence, approaching the problem from a variety of directions and considering a wider range of evidence than has been previously considered, will enable us to arrive at a reasonable description of the physician's behavior toward his sources of information, both commercial and noncommercial.

It is obvious, of course, that reality lies somewhere other than in the above stereotypes. We shall try to demonstrate that the advertising and promotion of drugs by and through commercial channels, *and* the dissemination of scientific information by and through noncommercial channels both serve useful functions for the physician. Exactly which sources of information will be preferred in a given instance is determined by certain aspects of the specific situation.

PHYSICIANS' VIEWS OF COMMERCIAL SOURCES OF INFORMATION ABOUT DRUGS: THEIR USES AND VALUES

Asking doctors where they learn about drugs has been a very popular activity over the past decade and a half.[1] A great many studies have been conducted and, since different samples have been used and somewhat different forms of questions asked, the results are not fully comparable. However, it is fair to say that, across the board, these

Reprinted by permission from *Journal of Marketing Research*, Vol. 3 (February 1966), pp. 40–47, published by the American Marketing Association.

Raymond A. Bauer is a professor of business administration, Graduate School of Business Administration, Harvard; Lawrence H. Wortzel is an assistant professor of marketing, Boston University.

  The present article is an extension of work done with Arthur D. Little, Inc., in conjunction with an overall study of the pharmaceutical industry.

[1] A curious exception is the past two or three years. The absence of reference to very recent studies in this article is not due to lack of diligence. We have conferred with a number of market researchers in the pharmaceutical field, and all agree that they know of no recent studies either published or private. Apparently, the topic has lost its fascination.

findings show that commercial sources of information form a major, and probably a predominant, part of the physician's means of keeping informed about new drugs.

The first study considered was conducted in 1951 by Caplow [3] who analyzed a sample of 129 practicing physicians in the Midwest. The study dealt only with physicians' *attitudes* toward different sources of information, both commercial and professional. Caplow's data indicate that physicians were favorably disposed toward commercial channels of communication and had indeed found them useful. For example, he reports that 93 percent of his sample read medical journals and that only three of the 129 physicians "expressed any strong negative attitudes toward journal advertising [3, p. 106]." Similarly, 69 percent of the physicians sampled were "favorably disposed" or "enthusiastic" in their attitudes toward detail men. Even direct mail was viewed favorably, although some considered its amount excessive, almost 50 percent of the sample.

Turning now to "scientific" (or noncommercial) sources of information, physicians in the Caplow study were asked to state whether personal contacts with other physicians or reading journal articles was more valuable to them. The results are almost a standoff: reading, 37 percent; personal contacts, 44 percent; and undecided 19 percent. Unfortunately, there are some limitations to Caplow's findings. This sample was both small and perhaps geographically (or otherwise) unrepresentative. Another limitation is stated by Caplow himself who reflects that "it is almost impossible [at least given the methodology he used] to elicit direct attitudes toward journal advertising since the presence of advertising in medical journals is taken entirely for granted . . . [3, p. 106]."

More importantly, distinctions were not made between influences on awareness and on prescribing, nor between information about new vs. existing products. Finally, the study offers no measure of the relative importance of commercial and noncommercial sources of information. In spite of these limitations, this study did establish the working hypothesis, subsequently confirmed by many other investigators, that physicians regard commercial sources of information as valuable. It also suggested some distinctions for later investigators to make.

Moving on now from simply attitudes to the usefulness of information from commercial sources, it might be well to ask first how physicians find out about *new* drugs, for this is the area in which information should be most important. In answering this question we shall turn first, and most importantly, to a study conducted by Ben Gaffin and Associates for the American Medical Association [8]. While this study was conducted in 1957–1958 and is, therefore, more than seven years old, it has certain outstanding features: It is virtually the only study which has been conducted using a national, representative cross-sectional sample of 1,001 practicing physicians. In addition, its data contain fewer ambiguities than do most other studies.[2] Furthermore, events of the past seven years should have served (as we shall show) only to heighten, rather than to change, the findings of this report.

---

[2] For example, in this study the categories "journal ads" and "journal articles" are carefully separated.

In the Gaffin study doctors were asked which sources of information "do you find most important to you personally in familiarizing yourself with new drugs?" and were requested to select two or three from a list presented to them. The results are shown in Table 1. Note that

TABLE 1   Physicians' Preferred Sources of Information

Source of information (ranked in order of frequency of mention)	Percent of physicians finding source useful
Detail men	68
Journal papers and articles	40
Medical journal advertisements	32
Direct mail	25
Doctor conversations	24
Drug samples	22
Staff meetings in:	
hospitals and clinics	16
national conventions	15

Source: [8].

commercial sources: detail men, journal ads, direct mail and samples received 147 mentions per 100 doctors, while noncommercial sources, including a few too minor to appear, only 96 mentions. Moreover, three of the first four sources mentioned: detail men, journal ads, and direct mail were commercial ones.

The physicians sampled by Gaffin were further asked which sources of information were important to "most doctors." Suppose we accept this device of offering the doctors a chance of distinguishing between themselves and "most doctors" as a method for detecting any bias in reporting their own behavior (e.g., they could have presented themselves as more "scientific" than "most doctors"). The physicians' replies to this question, however, were generally the same as those pertaining to themselves personally, with the slight exception that, on the average, fewer total sources were cited when physicians answered for most doctors. These findings, that the doctors sampled did not distinguish between their own behavior and that of most doctors, indicate that they have not weighted the report of their own behavior to make themselves look "better." It is evident, then, that physicians attach no stigma to the use of commercial sources in gaining information about new drugs. There is still the possibility, however, that there is a discrepancy between what they actually do and what they report. We contend only that they have not slanted their replies in a direction which would indicate an unfavorable or deprecating attitude toward commercial sources of information.

Further support for the Gaffin findings is offered in a study conducted about the same time by Ferber and Wales [6] using a sample of Chicago physicians. In this study, the physicians were asked where they *first* heard about pharmaceutical products they had recently adopted as well as "where else" they had heard about them. The responses are shown in Table 2.

One possible response to these data is: "Of course you would get

TABLE 2   Source of Notice of Recently Adopted Pharmaceuticals

Source	First	Other	All
Journal	24.6%	40.9%	31.5%
Detail man	37.7	14.2	27.7
Direct mail	19.2	22.4	20.5
Colleague	6.4	6.6	6.5
Convention, meeting	3.8	3.9	3.9
Sample	2.2	3.0	2.5
Hospital	2.2	2.6	2.4
Other	3.9	6.4	5.0
Total	100.0%	100.0%	100.0%
Total first mentions (products)	902		
Total other mentions		669	
Total mentions			1,571

Source: [7].

results like this. The sheer weight of commercial information *vis-a-vis* noncommercial would show that, on a probabilistic basis alone, a commercial source would have a much better chance of getting through." It is quite possible, however, to agree with this formulation as we do without concluding that the physician is a helpless dupe. These data indicate that doctors rely on commercial sources to make them *aware* of new drugs, but awareness and usage are not synonymous. In fact, it is our position (1) that information proferred by noncommercial, purely scientific sources does *not* necessarily induce awareness; and (2) that awareness, *no matter what its source*, does not necessarily induce trial.

Virtually everyone—marketer, consumer, and even social critic— recognizes the vital function of creating awareness of consumer goods. It is also widely recognized that awareness and trial or even "disposition to try" are separate phenomena. Yet, when it comes to discussions of physicians' sources of information about new drugs, very often there is a tacit assumption that the problem of awareness will take care of itself. That is, if the information is somehow, somewhere available physicians will seek it out.

We are fortunate that on this issue the Soviets have carried out a fairly well-controlled experiment.[3] They have a thoroughly "adequate" system of drug information: an official pharmacopea, announcements in the medical (and sometimes the lay) press and other media of communication, and simple one-page "flyers" describing new products which are sent to physicians. In addition to these sources there are exhibits of pharmaceuticals in the various Soviet clinics and representatives of pharmacies occasionally attend meetings of doctors to brief them on new drugs.

Nevertheless, in recent years there have been repeated official com-

[3] This view of the Soviet pharmaceutical industry is drawn from Raymond A. Bauer and Mark Field [2]. The fact that the Soviet data are now several years old is not relevant, since our intention is merely to illustrate what happens in a situation such as existed at that time.

plaints that doctors are unaware of the existence of new drugs, and official proposals for widespread advertising to create the initial condition of awareness that is taken so much for granted in our own promotional system.

It would thus seem that we have tended to overlook some of the functionality of our system of pharmaceutical promotion. We tend to take its speed and pervasiveness for granted. But the speed and pervasiveness of our system serves a function in alerting and reminding the physician, with a minimum of effort on his part, of the range of alternatives available to him for use in his practice.

We think we have, by now, argued sufficiently the case for the usefulness to the physician of the commercial promotion of drugs in making him aware of what is available. There still remains, however, the question of trial: Do physicians actually prescribe indiscriminately everything they hear about? If physicians discriminate in their prescribing habits, how and under what circumstances is discrimination effected? To answer these questions we should look at influences on physicians' prescribing habits as opposed to influences on awareness. Or, in the cynic's words, we might ask: How much subversion is really going on?

DETERMINANTS OF THE DECISION TO PRESCRIBE

A review of the full range of studies presently available will lead to the conclusion that doctors more or less uniformly, but with variations, report that both their first source of information about a drug *and* the source that convinces them to prescribe it is more likely to be a commercial than a noncommercial one.

Caplow and Raymond in 1953 conducted a survey among 182 midwestern physicians [4]. A total of 308 product-use histories was collected from this group, each of whom was asked to discuss a product type of his own choosing. Tables 3 and 4 present the authors' data with respect to the number of sources cited as inducing the physician's adoption of the product.

Caplow and Raymond's conclusions, based on the data reported in these tables, are that "ethical pharmaceutical products are normally adopted in response to the combined stimulus of several forms of advertising or communication [4, p. 20]." It is also obvious from these

TABLE 3   Number of Media Involved in 308 Pharmaceutical Product-use Histories

Number of media involved	Number of products	Percent
1	67	21.8
2	117	38.0
3	89	28.9
4 or more	35	11.3
Total	308	100.0

Source: [4].

TABLE 4   Distribution of Media in 308 Product-use Histories by Order of Mention

Media	First mentions	Second mentions	Third mentions
Primary:			
Detail men	31.1%	14.5%	11.9%
Direct mail	15.6	13.2	17.8
Journal advertisements	5.6	32.3	39.0
Journal articles	18.8	17.9	8.5
	71.1%	77.9%	77.2%
Secondary:			
Conventions	2.3%	2.1%	
Conferences	5.2	6.0	
Colleagues	14.0	8.9	22.8
Patients	2.9	0.9	
Druggists	0.3	3.4	
Other sources[a]	4.2	0.8	
	100.0%	100.0%	100.0%

Source: [4].

[a] Other sources include radio broadcasts, popular magazines, etc.

data that commercial sources predominate (despite the possibility of response bias which would lead to an under-reporting of these sources).

The Gaffin study again reports similar results. Physicians were also asked in this study to "think of a drug they had recently prescribed for the first time," and then to state where they had gotten the information which led them to prescribe the drug. Table 5 will show commercial sources again appear to predominate.

On the basis of a comparison of these data, it would be tempting to conclude that the sources influencing awareness and trial are one and the same and let the matter go at that. Fortunately, some data are available from the Ferber and Wales study which permit us to compare directly the sources leading to awareness with those influencing trial; (in other words, to compare the attention-getting source with the convincing source). Table 6 shows that the relationship is not 1:1.

TABLE 5   Source of Information Leading to Prescribing New Drug

Detail man	48%
Direct mail (advertisement)	20
Medical journal (undifferentiated between professional article and commercial advertisement)	17
Drug sample received:	
Other doctors	8
Other (not specified)	7
	100%

Source: [8].

TABLE 6   Relationship Between Source of First Notice and Source Leading to Prescribing New Drug

Convincing source	Source of first notice				
	Journal	Detail man	Mail advertisement	Other	All sources
Journal	63.6%	14.3%	22.1%	9.2%	28.6%
Detail man	4.6	51.2	5.5	2.3	21.3
Mail advertisement	5.0	11.6	44.8	5.4	15.5
Other[a]	26.8	22.9	27.6	83.1	34.6
Total	100.0%	100.0%	100.0%	100.0%	100.0%
Base:	220	293	163	130	806

Source: [7].

[a] Excludes products with a "don't know" or no answer in either classification. For this reason, column totals and imputed row totals in this table are not the same as the corresponding figures in Tables 3 and 5.

Two other observations should also be apparent by now: (1) physicians vary in their preferred sources of information (not all chose detail men, or journals, for example); (2) certain characteristics of the drug in question, and of the disease for which it is prescribed, will affect the amount of information a physician demands before prescribing a drug. Similarly, these characteristics will affect the source a physician goes to for information, for not all sources contain the same amount of facts (an advertisement vs. a journal article, for instance), nor will the same information be weighted equally regardless of its source.[4] In other words, the preferred source of information varies with the riskiness of the disease or drug and, unfortunately, in the studies so far cited, *we do not know what drugs physicians were referring to when they cited the sources of information which led to prescribing the drug in question.*

The primary observation, that physicians vary in their own source preferences, can be clarified rather quickly. Menzel and Katz, in the first of their now famous studies on new drug adoption among physicians [9], separated doctors who were frequently asked for advice by their colleagues from all other doctors. The former cited journal *articles* as the most important source of information about drugs, with detail men and mail from drug houses in tie for second place.

Those doctors who were not consulted by their colleagues cited detail men first and mail and periodicals from drug houses second. Thus, those physicians for whom it is most imperative to be *more fully informed* since they act as information sources for the others in the group appear to choose professional sources.

Turning now to the situational effects of drug and disease on

---

[4] The detail man's report of the incidence of side effects *vs* a trusted colleague's narration of his experience needed before prescribing, say, a new antihistamine-aspirin combination for a cold, varies in both amount and credibility from that needed before prescribing a new drug for a severe case of hypertension.

physicians' information sources, several studies can be cited. A group of Harvard Business School students, under the direction of Edward Bursk [6], asked a sample of doctors which source a hypothetical doctor would select for information on a drug used to treat three stages of severity. It was found that the doctors were increasingly likely to cite professional over commercial sources as the severity of the disease increased.

Coleman, Menzel and Katz [5] also found that professional, as compared to commercial, influences play a more important role in doctors' drug choice as the situation becomes increasingly indeterminate. Their criterion of "professional influence" was the tendency of a doctor to follow the prescription habits of his immediate colleagues. Their first evidence of the selective role of information sources was that doctors tended to rely on their colleagues early in a drug's history, *i.e.*, when knowledge about it was sparse.[5] Secondly, they concluded that doctors were more likely to rely on the judgment of professional associates in situations "where the physiology of illness is not well understood and treatment is subject to much trial and error." In the case in point, they compared doctors' treatment of hypertension with their treatment of a respiratory infection. There was more tendency for doctors to follow the lead of their colleagues in treatment of the former.

In the earlier study, Menzel and Katz had also found that the information sources doctors cited varied with whether any drug was generally applicable to acute or chronic conditions. For drugs applicable to acute (not long lasting) conditions, commercial sources outnumbered noncommercial sources by 56 to 33 percent. However, noncommercial sources were preferred in the proportion of 54 to 43 percent where difficult chronic conditions were involved [9].

Even within the domain of commercial sources, doctors have preferences. In a study conducted in cooperation with the Schering Corporation, one of the present authors found that doctors' preferences for drugs is related at least in part to their preference for particular companies and/or detail men [1]. These data indicated that more than "irrational favoritism" was involved. One may assume that personal considerations are very likely to play a role in the doctor's relation to the detail man rather than his preference for the company. Or, to put it another way, the doctor's preference for a drug company is more likely to be a result of his satisfactory experience with that company's products than is his preference for a detail man, which is more likely to be a function of his personal relations with that man. Consistent with this assumption was the finding that company preferences was likely to play a predominant role where risky drugs were involved. In other words, doctors were willing to let personal considerations enter

---

[5] Using a somewhat different methodology and confining his study to a large city (Coleman, Menzel, and Katz had made their study in medium-sized cities), Winick [11] failed to confirm the findings of Coleman, *et al.* [5]. Briefly, there was no correlation between the times at which doctors adopted a new drug and their reported association on either social or professional bases. Winick does *not* regard his findings as a necessary disconfirmation of the early ones. The failure to confirm may be due to differences: in methodology, of interaction patterns of doctors in medium and large cities, or in the two drugs studied.

into their drug choice where little risk was involved, but relied more on their appraisal of the company's reputation where there was appreciable risk; thus, in some sense relying on a "professional" rather than a "purely commercial" source.

Finally, we might note one rather ironic piece of evidence. It is common knowledge that the decade of the 1950s (the period in which virtually all the studies to which we have referred have been conducted) was marked by a continually increasing flood of new drug products and by a burgeoning of promotional activity on the part of the manufacturers. Thus, the pure volume of drug information with which a physician had to cope became ever larger. At the same time, the size of many physicians' practices was also increasing.

Common sense suggests that the more information that is available the more time one will spend ingesting it. Communications research, however, does not agree with this particular form of common sense. One of the most distinctive features of the behavior of any audience is its selectivity with respect to the information available. It is entirely conceivable that if a given channel of information becomes overloaded, attention to it will be completely turned off, or more generally, the amount of exposure may decrease with the amount of information potentially available. Noyes presented some data that suggest this may have happened with respect to pharmaceutical promotion as far back as 1956 (see Table 7) [10]. Noyes goes on to say:

TABLE 7   Hours Spent per Week on Each of Three Media (per 100 Physicians)[a]

	Hours spent in	
	1952	1956
Detail men	130	91
Journal advertisements	107	56
Direct mail[b]	102	58

Source: [10].

[a] This table shows that between 1952 and 1956, the average number of hours a doctor spent on the three media dropped from 3.4 to 2.2 per week.
[b] The third row is apparently mistakenly labeled "detail men" in the original. From the first, it is obvious that the correct labeling is "direct mail."

> An interesting sidelight to this comparison is the fact that whereas in 1952 no doctors reported *not* seeing detail men or *not* reading advertising, last month we found that 9% see *no* detail men, 36% read *no* journal ads, and 40% read *no* direct mail advertising.

Regrettably, Noyes is not very specific either about the source of her data or her methodology, and to the best of our knowledge there is no other time series that is addressed directly to this question. But assuming that we may take Noyes' data at somewhere close to their face value, it would appear that sometime in the early 1950s doctors took added initiative *vis-a-vis* their sources of information and began to use them with increasing selectivity.

But do these data constitute proof, or do they even suggest that there is too much pharmaceutical promotion, or that this promotion is not useful to the physician? This is almost like asking if the Sunday edition of the *New York Times* is too large. Patently, not every *Times* purchaser reads every word, nor is the Sunday *Times* constructed with this in mind. As a matter of fact, it is highly probable that as one gets better acquainted with the Sunday *Times*, he becomes more efficient at locating what interests him personally and consequently spends less time perusing it while possibly getting more information out of it. Remember that point we made in contrasting the Soviet and the American pharmaceutical systems: an *effective* informational system is not one that looks *efficient*, if we operate with simplistic notions about the initiative of the audience and about the possibility of targeting audiences with single messages. The above, however, is an aside. What is at stake here is whether there is evidence that doctors exercise critical judgment in using commercial sources of information. They are discriminating to the extent that the health of their patients and the use of their own time is concerned. Since time is not a "free good," they will rely more on the most available source when the issue is relatively free of risk.

The next question, then, is that of their overall opinions of these sources of information. (We are thus returning to the question raised by Caplow in the early 1950s but looking at it in more detail.)

PHYSICIANS' EVALUATION OF PHARMACEUTICAL PROMOTION

There are many criteria and many sources of information which can be brought to bear on the adequacy of drug promotion as an element in the professional scheme of communications. The most direct method is to consider the opinions of the men who use this information, the American physician population.

THE COST OF PROMOTION

There appears to be little doubt in physicians' minds that the major intent of drug promotion is a commercial one. A recently unpublished, privately conducted qualitative study (by the Schering Corporation) had these positive things to say about doctors' attitudes:

> In talking to these men about drug companies, their promotions and services, the major finding is that physicians identify very positively with the major drug companies. They feel, for the most part, that their research activities, promotions, and services are essential to the physician and his role.

Later on, however, the writer enters this firm qualification:

> These doctors are not naive and they are fully aware that all and everything the company does has contributed to its success, to keeping its name and its product to the forefront in the profession. Moreover, they are aware that they have made sizeable profit from this promotion.

Of the cross-sectional sample of doctors interviewed by Gaffin Associates in 1957–1958, two-thirds thought that pharmaceutical advertising increased the price of drugs [8, p. 16]. From this figure one might conclude that there was also strong agreement that the amount of money going into advertising was too high. In fact, it is interesting that it has generally been assumed that if a person says advertising raises prices, he believes prices are too high. The possibility that he believes advertising contributes to the actual value of the product has seldom been investigated. However, in both 1939 and 1940 Gallup found that approximately 70 percent of the American public thought advertising raised prices, and an identical percentage said they would be willing to pay more for "a nationally backed product!" Approximately the same is true of Gaffin's physician sample. Only 35 percent of the doctors thought that the percent of the average prescription price that goes into advertising was too high[6] [8, p. 16]. Furthermore, their ideas about how to go about reducing the cost of advertising were interesting. Suggestions by 46 percent of the doctors for cutting costs concentrated almost exclusively on reducing the volume of direct mail. Only three percent favored a decrease in visits by detail men, and another three percent thought journal advertising might be decreased.

Thus, virtually no one suggested cutting back journal advertising, or more importantly, detailing activities which, in most companies, is the major promotional cost. As a matter of fact, when doctors were asked directly what they would think of a company that tried to get along without detail men, a minority of seven percent said they would think better of it. For every one doctor who approved of curtailing detailing, more than seven disapproved.

Four out of five doctors interviewed in the Gaffin study had favorable attitudes toward the distribution of drug samples, although some did suggest modification of the procedure. About one in five would make no changes. Three out of 10 favored some policies which would reduce the volume of samples, such as making sure that physicians did not get samples they did not need. Slightly *more* than three out of 10 physicians favored an increase in sampling. If all these physicians' suggestions for "improvement" were followed, there would apparently be no overall reduction in the volume of sampling.

The *nature* of favorable attitudes toward sampling is reflected in statements of two doctors interviewed in the private survey referred to previously:

> Drug sampling is a service because it gives us a chance to evaluate the drug without burden of cost. It also helps us to treat indigents, to furnish the drug at no cost.

> Their sampling is quite important, but since Senator Kefauver it has been less. This is a disservice since the drug companies helped doctors to evaluate the drug and they were used in certain communities to help the indigent.

---

[6] In this connection it is worth noting that about the same proportion, 33 percent, thought that the percentage of the average prescription price that goes into advertising was 20 percent or over. This is about a 100 percent overestimation.

In sum, a cross-sectional sample of doctors seemed to have no doubt that drug promotion costs money nor, by implication, were they under any illusion about the pharmaceutical firms' intentions of earning profits from these promotions. But, these doctors are little inclined to cut back any of this promotional activity save for the volume of direct mail.[7] All in all, there is no evidence that doctors want to reduce promotional efforts across the board to save on drug costs. True, these data from Gaffin date back seven years, but they are the only data of which we are aware that permit this sort of analysis.

THE USE OF DISCRIMINATION

Data from a number of studies have already been introduced to indicate that physicians do in fact use their informational sources with discrimination. This circumstance is further reflected in the Gaffin data, where the doctors interviewed put themselves firmly on record as favoring the use of commercial sources of information, but with discrimination.

There was general disapproval in the proportion of 4 to 1 of a doctor who might depend *heavily* upon advertising for his information about new drugs and general, but not equally strong, disapproval of a doctor who might depend *heavily* on detail men. But, there was even more disapproval of a doctor who would refuse to use these sources of information. A doctor who might refuse to read pharmaceutical advertising was condemned by more than 3 for every 1 who approved of this behavior. A doctor who would refuse to see detail men was criticized in the proportion of 17 to 1 [8, p. 17]. The message is clear: Doctors feel that sources should be used with discrimination but that they should by all means *be* used.

THE PHYSICIAN AND PHARMACEUTICAL PROMOTION: AN OVERVIEW

Any serious consideration of the practicing physician's job situation, and of the amount of information about drugs which is available to him, quickly leads to the conclusion that communication channels leading to the physician are overloaded. There are several possible responses to a situation of this type. The physician could completely ignore all communication; he could randomly select those to which he will attend; or he could allocate his available time and effort in such a way as to gain the most useful information in the time available for this activity. The evidence presented in this paper strongly suggests that physicians *do* make decisions to allocate their time and effort usefully.

The most important way in which the physician accomplishes this is by letting the environment do his initial screening. He depends on

---

[7] Direct mail is a special case and probably draws a good deal of hostility because of its nuisance value, specifically the burden of screening out irrelevant material.

the environment (in this case, commercial promotion) to call his attention to those drugs which are worthy of further investigation. Furthermore, the physician is selective even in this regard, devoting time and attention insomuch as he can to sources of high information content such as detail men,[8] or to sources which can be quickly screened, such as journal advertising. One of the most important characteristics of mail advertising is that it is *relatively* difficult to screen as compared to journal advertising. This, we suspect, is the reason it generates so much irritation and, simultaneously, why it may be an effective promotional tool.

In this manner, the physician is able to allocate the bulk of his information—getting time for that which is *really* important: collecting further information about drugs which, *after screening*, look promising. And again, further selectivity takes place: If the condition which the drug is designed to treat is neither severe, nor the action of the drug particularly uncertain, the amount of information provided by commercial channels may be sufficient for the physician to make the decision to prescribe it. As the severity of the illness increases, and as the treatment becomes less well understood, more information is needed before prescribing, and it is here that professional sources come into play, we suspect, for two reasons: (1) The *amount* provided by commercial sources may be insufficient; and (2) its trustworthiness may, at this level of risk, be somewhat suspect.

In summary, the physician has managed to develop a system for coping with his environment by letting it do some of his work for him. This system reduces the amount of useless information the physician will have to collect, while freeing time to collect that information which he deems most useful. Furthermore, if we may take Noyes' data on face value, we have evidence that as the weight of pharmaceutical promotion increased in the early and mid-fifties, the physician population, rather than becoming increasingly burdened, became more selective and actually spent *less* time reading and listening to these sources.

It would be preposterous to argue that this system used by the doctor *vis-a-vis* commercial drug communications is in any sense "optimal," or that the entire system of pharmaceutical promotion is optimal for our society or even for the industry. The very notion of what an optimal system might be is utterly illusive, if only because we have no common metric by which to compare the values involved: the patient's health, cost of medical care to the patient, doctor's time and energy, doctor's peace of mind, social costs of illness, social benefits of health, cost to the society of the investment of men in money and promotion, costs of promotion to the pharmaceutical industry, profits of the industry, and so on. The most that we can do is analyze

---

[8] A prudent detail man will never belabor a physician with that which he already knows. We have heard this affirmed by both detail men and by doctors. But perhaps the most eloquent testimonial to this reluctance of detail men to approach doctors unless they have "something new to say" comes from the expressions of frustration of managers of detail forces when they discuss the difficulty of getting their men to detail an older, established product.

the situation as carefully as possible to make sure that various functions of this promotional system are not overlooked, and to check out the reactions of the people who use it to see how satisfied they are; this we have done. After that, each individual must make his own judgment.

Probably the worst that can be said with relative certainty of commercial promotion is that it may be wasteful. Given the variety of informational needs among physicians, it is at least a difficult task to feed each physician selectively that information—and only that information—which will be useful to him.

Waste, obviously, can be curbed. We could, for example, limit the amount of commercial promotion in which the pharmaceutical industry will be allowed to engage. In doing so, however, we would also be limiting physicians' awareness of new drugs. Fortunately, the pharmaceutical industry also has an interest in limiting waste, for as commercial promotion passes the point at which it induces knowledge of new drugs among physicians, it has also passed the point at which its returns begin to diminish. The problem, therefore, is not one of whether commercial promotion should *per se* be limited, *but* instead be one of developing more precise means of measuring and predicting knowledge producing levels.

REFERENCES

1. BAUER, RAYMOND A., "Risk Handling in Drug Adoption: Role of Company Preferences," *Public Opinion Quarterly*, 25 (Winter 1961), 546–59.
2. _____ AND MARK G. FIELD, "Ironic Contrast: US and USSR Drug Industries," *Harvard Business Review*, 40 (September–October 1962), 89–97.
3. CAPLOW, THEODORE, "Market Attitudes: A Research Report from the Medical Field," *Harvard Business Review*, 30 (November–December 1952), 105–12.
4. _____ AND JOHN J. RAYMOND, "Factors Influencing the Selection of Pharmaceutical Products," *Journal of Marketing*, 19 (July 1954), 18–23.
5. COLEMAN, JAMES, HERBERT MENZEL AND ELIHU KATZ, "Social Processes in Physicians' Adoption of a New Drug," *Journal of Chronic Diseases*, 9 (January 1959), 1–19.
6. Consumer Behavior Research Seminar, Harvard Business School, unpublished manuscript, Spring 1960.
7. FERBER, ROBERT AND HUGH G. WALES, *The Effectiveness of Pharmaceutical Promotion*, Urbana, Ill.: Bureau of Economic and Business Research, University of Illinois, 1958.
8. GAFFIN, BEN AND ASSOCIATES, *Attitudes of U. S. Physicians Toward the American Pharmaceutical Industry*, Chicago, Ill., 1959.
9. MENZEL, HERBERT AND ELIHU KATZ, "Social Relations and Innovation in the Medical Profession: The Epidemiology of A New Drug," *Public Opinion Quarterly* (Winter 1955–6), 337–52.
10. NOYES, DOROTHY, "Your Share of Disposable Professional Time," *Modern Medicine Topics*, 17 (June 1956), 5–7.
11. WINICK, CHARLES, "The Diffusion of an Innovation Among Physicians in a Large City," *Sociometry*, 24 (December 1961), 384–96.

8 STIMULUS AMBIGUITY AND PERCEPTUAL BIAS

Perceptual bias is a process variable made up of a number of mechanisms which explain the remarkable capacity a human displays of selecting from a massive flow of information that small portion that he considers relevant for his needs at the moment. "Selective perception" is a related term that has been used for many years; however, it too is a process construct and crudely describes but does not explain.

A major determinant of *perceptual bias* is the clarity, unambiguity, or certainty of the stimulus being viewed. To the extent that the stimulus is unclear or ambiguous the more likely is perceptual bias to occur. We refer to this characteristic as *stimulus ambiguity*. It incorporates all those effects of the stimulus—physical ambiguity, meaning ambiguity, credibility, and fantasy—other than its predictive value that Cox (1962)* so nicely distinguished from confidence value. *Perceptual bias* is the process by which the human filters and even imaginatively supplements his sources of information, so as to obtain an acceptable combination of predictive and confidence cues. The mechanisms that make up *perceptual bias* are complex and have not been well articulated for application in field conditions; they have been developed in the laboratory.

Perceptual bias occurs, in large part, only because cues are ambiguous, as we said earlier. But in the world of buyer behavior, most cues are ambiguous. Allison and Uhl (1964),* for example, suggest that people cannot discern differences among brands of beer—taste cues are ambiguous—and that as a consequence they use the brand label and their associations with it to evaluate the beer.

Price would seem to be one of the most unambiguous of cues, and in line with the Cox findings, buyers may use it to guide them in evaluating the quality of a product. Gardner (1971)* finds that price can affect the buyer's perception of brand quality, but only if it is the single cue. If it is a part of a multiple-cue situation, it does not appear to have much effect on perceived quality.

This ambiguity of brand cues would also seem to permit brands having some very fundamental psychological significance for the buyer. The self-concept—the idea that how we view ourselves in relation to other objects such as brands is important in explaining our behavior—is thought to shape buyer choices. Dolich (1969)* provides some positive evidence on this important issue.

16. The measurement of information value: a study in consumer decision-making

donald f. cox

How does a consumer evaluate a product? On what bases does the suburban housewife distinguish between high and low quality electric hand mixers, dishwashing detergents, or stereo amplifiers? Clearly the consumer must base her judgment on some type of information about the product. But what is the nature of the information she uses? Does she pick at random from the many pieces of information available to her? Or is she selective in using information? If she is selective, does she base her evaluation only on high value information?

A product can be conceived of as an *array of cues*. The array can include information such as price, color, scent, friends' opinions, taste, feel, salesmen's opinions, and so on. The consumer's task in evaluating a product is to use cues (information) from the array as the basis for making judgments about the product.

My thesis is that when presented with an array of cues, consumers will value some cues more than others. Furthermore, the higher the value a consumer places on a cue, the higher the probability that she will utilize that cue as the primary basis for evaluating the product.

In other words, the consumer is selective in her use of information about a product, and tends to base her evaluation primarily on high value information or cues. This remains to be demonstrated. But even if this were the case, in order to predict which cues a consumer would use in a given situation, it would be necessary to know how she assigns value to the various cues. That is, how does the consumer distinguish high value information from low value information?

SOME EXAMPLES OF PRODUCT EVALUATIONS

For some time, sophisticated marketers have been aware that consumers may judge a product on the basis of a few cues or bits of information. Consider the following examples of product evaluations.

In 1932, Laird[1] conducted an experiment in which housewives were asked to examine and evaluate four pairs of silk stockings which were as identical as possible in manufacture, but differed in scent. The scents were so faint, however, that only six of the 250 housewives tested noticed them. Nevertheless, one pair of stockings (with a

Reprinted by permission from William S. Decker, ed., *Proceedings of the American Marketing Association* (Fall 1962), pp. 250–257, published by the American Marketing Association.

[1] Donald A. Laird, "How the Consumer Estimates Quality by Subconscious Sensory Impressions," *Journal of Applied Psychology*, June, 1932, p. 241.

'narcissus' scent) was judged to be the best hosiery—on the basis of such attributes as texture, weave, feel, wearing qualities, lack of sheen, and weight—by 50% of the housewives. Another pair (with a 'natural' scent) was judged best by only 8%.

In a recent sales test,[2] two piles of nylons were placed on a counter in a retail store. The stockings in both piles were identical in price and manufacture, but differed in that one pile had been scented (with an 'orange' aroma), the other pile was left with the natural (from the factory) scent. About 90% of the women who purchased stockings from this counter selected the orange-scented stockings. When asked why, many replied that they seemed to be better quality stockings and would probably wear better and longer than the other brand.

An experiment conducted by a large dairy found that consumers considered a cream colored, 14% butterfat ice cream to be richer in flavor than white colored, 16% butterfat ice cream.

Detergent manufacturers have found that housewives tend to judge the cleaning power of a detergent on the basis of suds level and smell. Similarly, the color of a detergent and its package is a cue often used to judge mildness. (Thus it is neither accident nor chemical necessity which leads manufacturers of liquid dishwashing detergents to color their products pink.)

However, even given this awareness that consumers may base their evaluation of a product on a very small number of cues, it still would be highly useful to be able to predict, for a given product, which cues are most likely to influence consumer evaluations. Given this ability, problems such as the case of the noiseless mixer might be avoided. (A noiseless electric hand mixer was developed and marketed but did not sell. Why? Consumers thought it had insufficient power).[3]

In order to make such predictions it is necessary to measure the value consumers assign to various bits of information or cues. This in turn implies two requirements:

1. Isolating the dimensions on which consumers evaluate information; and
2. Developing measures of the value a consumer assigns to information on each of the value dimensions she uses.

THE DIMENSIONS OF INFORMATION VALUE

The first question to be resolved is the determination of the dimensions of information value. How many dimensions are used, and what is the nature of each?

Previous work in psychology[4] has been based on the assumption

[2] *Women's Wear Daily*, January 28, 1961, p. 15.

[3] Robert Froman, "Marketing Research, You Get What You Want," pp. 231–238, in Westing, J. H. (ed.), *Readings in Marketing*, (New York, Prentice-Hall, 1953).

[4] For example, see Jerome S. Bruner, Jacqueline J. Goodnow, and George A. Austin, *A Study of Thinking*, (New York, Wiley, 1956), and Leo Postman and Edward Tolman, "Brunswick's Probabilistic Functionalism," pp. 502–564, in Sigmund Koch, (ed.), *Psychology: A Study of A Science, Study I, Vol. 1, Sensory Perceptual, and Physiological Foundations*, (New York, McGraw-Hill, 1959).

that people tend to evaluate information on only one dimension. We might call this dimension the *predictive value* of a cue. Predictive value is a measure of the probability with which a cue seems associated with (i.e., predicts) a specific product attribute. For example, if I knew for certain that a stereo amplifier contained high quality internal components, I would say that there was a high probability that the amplifier was of good quality. Internal components, then, would be a high predictive value cue. On the other hand, the knobs on the front of the amplifier would be a low predictive value cue as far as I am concerned. That is, if I only knew for certain that the knobs were of good quality, the probability that the amplifier itself was good is not high.

The measurement of information value on the basis of predictive value seems like a sensible procedure. Maybe it is too sensible. In any event, it has been found that people don't always behave as if this were the procedure they followed. A number of studies have shown that consumers may base their evaluation of a product on low predictive value information (e.g., scent can affect evaluations of the wearing qualities of nylon stockings).

There are two possible explanations for this behavior. Either consumers do not always use high value information, *or* they do use high value information, but they measure information on some other dimension in addition to predictive value.

Hunch led me to reject the first alternative and to try to find an additional dimension on which consumers might assign value to information. I finally hit upon another dimension, and will call it the *confidence value* of a cue. Confidence value is a measure of how *certain* the consumer is that the *cue* is what she thinks it is. For example, consider an audiophile and a suburban housewife, both of whom were trying to form independent judgments of the quality of a stereo amplifier. Both might share the belief, that the internal components represent a high predictive value cue. That is if they knew for certain that the components were good, they would also feel that in all probability the amplifier itself was good. In addition, the audiophile presumably could tell with a high degree of confidence whether or not the components *were* of good quality. Thus the internal components would, for this audiophile, be both a high predictive value cue, and a high confidence value cue. The housewife, on the other hand, may be unable to discriminate with confidence between good and bad innards. For her, this is a low confidence value cue, even though it is high in predictive value.

HYPOTHESES

The first hypothesis established was that consumers assign value to information or cues on *two* independent dimensions—predictive value and confidence value. A further hypothesis was that when confidence value was held constant, the higher the predictive value of a cue, the higher the probability that it would be utilized as the primary basis for evaluating a product or product attribute. On the other hand, when predictive value was held constant, it was hypothesized that the cue highest in confidence value was most likely to be used. In the case where consumers were faced with a choice between a cue high in predictive value but low in confidence value, and a cue low in predictive value, but high in confidence value, the hypothesis was that they would tend to favor the latter cue, that is, the low predictive value—high confidence value cue.

THE EXPERIMENT

The following experiment was designed to test these hypotheses.

Three separate groups, totaling 414 lower and middle class housewives were asked to evaluate "two brands" of nylon stockings and to indicate how confident they were about their evaluation. The stockings were in fact identical, except for the identifying letters R and N. After making the evaluations (on 18 attributes) subjects heard a tape-recorded salesgirl's opinion that Brand R stockings were better on six attributes (feel, weight, texture, fit, weave, and versatility). The subjects then re-evaluated the nylons, evaluated the salesgirl, and indicated how confident they were about their evaluations of the salesgirl.

Subjects' ratings of the salesgirl on experience, reliability, etc., were taken as a measure of the predictive value of the salesgirl cue, on the assumption that an apparently experienced salesgirl is more likely to know the difference between good and bad quality nylons than an inexperienced salesgirl. Thus if a subject rated the salesgirl high, she was assumed to have assigned a high predictive value to this cue. If she was also very certain that the salesgirl *was* experienced and reliable, the subject was also assumed to have assigned a high confidence value to the salesgirl cue. The confidence value assigned to the other "cue" (the stockings themselves) was measured according to how confident subjects were about their evaluations of the nylons.

RESULTS

The results of the experiment, shown below in Table 1, supported the hypotheses.

Among subjects who were equally confident in their evaluations of the nylons and of the salesgirl, (i.e., when confidence value was held constant) those who rated the salesgirl high on experience, etc. (i.e., who assigned a high predictive value to the salesgirl cue) were significantly more likely to utilize the salesgirl cue and hence to change their evaluations of the nylons in the direction advocated by the salesgirl.

When predictive value was held constant, as for example, among subjects who rated the salesgirl high, those who were more confident in evaluating the salesgirl than in evaluating the nylons were most likely to change.

TABLE 1   Change in Evaluation in Relation to Salesgirl Rating and Relative
Degree of Confidence in Rating the Salesgirl vs. the Nylons

Salesgirl was rated:	Subject had greater confidence evaluating the:	Positive	None	Negative	Base
1. High	Salesgirl	68% *	18%	14%	119
2. High	Stockings	46	35	19	69
3. Low	Salesgirl	56	19	25	64
4. Low	Stockings	30	44	26	87
5. High	Equal confidence	46	42	12	41
6. Low	Equal confidence	18	64	18	34
	diff (1, 2) P < .003	diff (5, 6) P < .009**			
	diff (3, 4) P < .001	diff (2, 3) P < .16			

* e.g., Of 119 subjects who rated the salesgirl high, *and* who were more confident in evaluating the salesgirl than the stockings, 68% changed their evaluation of the nylons in the direction advocated by the salesgirl.

** e.g., Among those equally confident in evaluating the salesgirl and the stockings, the difference between 5), the proportion of those rating the salesgirl *high* who showed positive change in evaluation, and 6), the proportion of those rating the salesgirl low who showed positive change is statistically significant beyond the .009 level.

Finally, as hypothesized, subjects who rated the salesgirl low but who held the rating with a high degree of confidence were more likely to change than subjects who rated the salesgirl high, but who held the rating with a relatively low degree of confidence. In other words, a low predictive value–high confidence value cue was more likely to be utilized than a high predictive value–low confidence value cue.

DISCUSSION OF RESULTS

In sum, it was found that consumers use at least two dimensions in assigning value to information, and that the value assigned to one dimension can vary independently of the value assigned to the other. In other words, the same cue may be high in predictive value and low in confidence value, or vice versa. Furthermore, each dimension of information value has quite different operating characteristics as far as the utilization of information is concerned. If a person wanted to identify an object on a dark night, and had a choice between a high candlepower light and one low in candlepower, he would most likely choose the former. But only if he could turn the light on. If for some reason, possibly because of a faulty switch, he couldn't turn the high power light on, he would then use the low candlepower light. Predictive value seems to work much like candlepower in the process of cue utilization. Predictive value seems to be the basic force in determining information value, and hence cue utilization. We have seen that when confidence value is held constant, the higher the predictive value of the cue, the higher the probability that the cue will be utilized as the basis for evaluating the product. But confidence value, like the light switch, acts as a qualifying variable and carries a strong veto. Unless a consumer feels sufficiently confident about evaluating a cue she is not as likely to use it—no matter how high its predictive value.

The procedure makes good sense, even though it may violate "common sense." If I have to evaluate the quality of a stereo amplifier, and if I can't tell a condenser from a scratch filter, it would be foolhardy to try to base my evaluation on an assessment of the internal components. If no other information were available, I'd feel more confident about estimating the quality of the set on the basis of its external features, such as the knobs.

One of the consequences of the fact that information is valued on two different and independent dimensions and that information value is not a simple additive or multiplicative function of predictive value and confidence value, is that a good deal of high value information—when measured by predictive value—is never used, or at best is underutilized.

On the other side of the coin, low value information (again when measured by predictive value) is often overutilized because its confidence value is high. The consumer who estimates the quality of a stereo amplifier on the basis of its external appearance rather than its internal components is basing his evaluation on low (predictive) value information.

It is not surprising, then, that consumers make many errors in evaluating products. We have seen that they can be persuaded (or can persuade themselves) that one of two identical stockings is better than the other; that a noiseless mixer is powerless; that a cream colored, low butterfat ice cream is rich in flavor; that a detergent packaged in a violently colored box is harsh, while the same detergent packed in pleasing colors is mild.

Lest anyone think I have a low opinion of the consumer, I should point out that the same type of behavior has been exhibited by college admission boards—presumably learned men and women. The boards, according to one study[5] consistently (though unintentionally) underutilized all information about candidates except for their scores on scholastic aptitude tests.

The problem lies not in the consumer as much as in the enormous difficulty of evaluating a product. Faced with a bewildering array of information, a need to economize (her time if nothing else) and a desire for certainty, the consumer has little choice but to be selective in her use of information.

IMPLICATIONS FOR MARKETING ACTION

If the results of this study are valid, we can conclude that the information value of a cue is a function (but not a simple function) of the predictive value and the confidence value assigned to the cue.

---

[5] See David C. McClelland, "Encouraging Excellence," *Daedalus*, 1961, 90, pp. 711–725.

According to the concepts developed in this study, in order to change the image of a product or brand, the marketer has a choice between two main types of strategies. He may alter the characteristics of dominant cues, and/or he may alter the information value of the cues in the array in order to make some cues more (or less) dominant or to alter the nature of cue-attribute associations. To the extent that he can: a) identify dominant cues, and b) specify the factors which will alter the information value of a cue, his job will be that much easier, and his efforts that much more effective.

For a number of reasons, these tasks are very difficult, and it is likely to be some time before they can be accomplished in a precise manner in many practical situations. First among these reasons is the great difficulty of measuring the predictive value and confidence value of various cues.

The present study involved (not by accident) much easier and simpler measurement problems than one is likely to meet in the real world. In addition, the information value of a cue is by no means fixed. It may vary considerably for different consumers; hence an influential cue for one type of consumer may be unimportant to another. Furthermore, the array of cues associated with a product is rarely static. And a cue which is dominant in one array may become less important as new (higher information value) cues are added to the array. For example, many consumers formerly used size as a guide to the quality of high fidelity speakers, until a new cue—*Consumer Reports*—was added. This higher value cue then became the dominant cue for many people.

Another complicating factor, evident in the above example, is that not all of the cues associated with a product are controllable by the marketer. Outside sources of information such as word of mouth advertising, *Consumer Reports*, and competitors' advertising must also be taken into consideration, even though they cannot be controlled.

Finally, it should be pointed out that identification of dominant cues only indicates which cues are influential in affecting consumers' images of a product. It does not tell us whether the effect will be beneficial or detrimental to the product's image.

All of these complications add to the problems of measuring or estimating the information value of cues. But to the extent that these problems can be overcome, and information value and the factors which alter information value can be estimated, the payoff for marketing strategy could be quite handsome.

17. Influence of beer brand identification on taste perception

ralph i. allison
& kenneth p. uhl

As a company tries to find the factors accounting for strong and weak markets, typical consumer explanations for both tend to be about the physical attributes of the product. That is, the product quality often becomes both the hero and the culprit, like Dr. Jekyll and Mr. Hyde, but with the hideous reversal coming not by night but by market. The experiment presented in this paper was also designed to give rough measurements of the magnitude of the marketing influences. Unidentified and then labeled bottles of beer were delivered to homes of taste testing participants on successive weeks. The drinkers' taste test ratings provided the data for the study.

THE EXPERIMENTAL DESIGN[1]

The principal hypothesis subjected to testing through experimentation was this: "Beer drinkers cannot distinguish among major brands of unlabeled beer either on an overall basis or on selected characteristics." Beer drinkers were identified as males who drank beer at least three times a week.

The test group was composed of 326 drinkers who were randomly selected, agreed to participate in the study, and provided necessary classification data. Each participant in the experiment was given a six-pack of unlabeled beer, identified only by tags bearing the letters A, B, C, D, E, F, G, H, I, or J. The labels had been completely soaked off and the crowns had been wire brushed to remove all brand identification from the 12-ounce deposit brown bottles. Each six-pack contained three brands of beer with individual bottles randomly placed in the pack so no one lettered tag predominated in any one position.[2] There were six different pairs placed among the 326 participants. An effort was made to give each participant a six-pack that contained the brand of beer he said he most often drank. The groups and numbers were placed as follows:

Reprinted by permission from *Journal of Marketing Research*, Vol. 1 (August 1964), pp. 36–39, published by the American Marketing Association.

[1] The experimental design and the findings outlined are from one market area. However, similar experiments were conducted and similar results were obtained in several other markets.

[2] Pretesting gave no evidence of a positional or letter bias; *i.e.*, for participants to drink or rate the beer in any particular alphabetical or spatial order.

	Placed
Group 1 (AB, CD, EF)	53
Group 2 (AB, CD, IJ)	55
Group 3 (AB, CD, GH)	55
Group 4 (AB, EF, IJ)	55
Group 5 (AB, GH, IJ)	54
Group 6 (AB, EF, GH)	54
	326

A and B represented one of the company's beer brands; C and D represented one major regional beer brand; and E and F were one other major brand of regional beer. G and H were one national brand; and I and J were the fifth well-known brand used in the experiment. Among these five brands there were some taste differences discernible to expert taste testers.

The lettered tags (one around the collar of each bottle in the six-pack) carried a general rating scale from "1" (poor) through "10" (excellent) on the one side and a list of nine specific characteristics on the reverse side (see Exhibit #1). The specific characteristics, which

EXHIBIT 1   Rating Tags

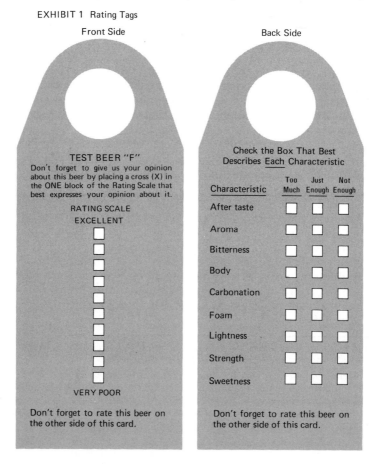

Front Side

TEST BEER "F"

Don't forget to give us your opinion about this beer by placing a cross (X) in the ONE block of the Rating Scale that best expresses your opinion about it.

RATING SCALE

EXCELLENT

VERY POOR

Don't forget to rate this beer on the other side of this card.

Back Side

Check the Box That Best Describes Each Characteristic

Characteristic	Too Much	Just Enough	Not Enough
After taste	☐	☐	☐
Aroma	☐	☐	☐
Bitterness	☐	☐	☐
Body	☐	☐	☐
Carbonation	☐	☐	☐
Foam	☐	☐	☐
Lightness	☐	☐	☐
Strength	☐	☐	☐
Sweetness	☐	☐	☐

Don't forget to rate this beer on the other side of this card.

included after-taste, aroma, bitterness, body, carbonation, foam, light-ness, strength, and sweetness, could each be rated as "too much," "just enough," or "not enough." These nine specific characteristics were selected from a much larger field. Their selection was based on both greater agreement on meaning among beer drinkers and on the ability of beer drinkers, in general, to identify and rate them.

One week after the distribution of the unlabeled beer, the empties, nude except for the rating tags, were picked up and new six-packs left behind. This time, however, the bottles were properly labeled with each six-pack containing six different brands of beer (the same five brands plus a sixth brand that was added for the labeled test). In addi-tion, each deposit bottle was tagged (as shown in Exhibit #1), but these tags were identified by the letters K through P. A week after the second placement the empties and rating tags were picked up.

THE FINDINGS

The experiment produced a number of useful findings. More specif-ically, evidence was available to answer these questions:

1. Could beer drinkers, in general, distinguish among various beers in a blind test?
2. Could beer drinkers identify "their" brands in a blind test?
3. What influence would brand identification have on consumers' evaluations of various beer brands?
4. What influence would brand identification have on consumers' evaluations of specified beer characteristics?

Taste Differences in a Blind Test

The data produced by the experiment indicated that the beer drinkers, as a group, could not distinguish the taste differences among the brands on an overall basis. Table 1 contains the evidence on these

TABLE 1   Blind Overall Taste Test—All Participants

Beer brand	Overall rating	Significantly different from other brands[a]
AB	65.0	No
CD	64.1	No
EF	63.3	No
GH	63.4	No
IJ	63.3	No

Source: Carling Brewing Company

[a] At the .05 level.

ratings. Basically, there appeared to be no significant difference among the various brands at the .05 level.

Beer drinkers when asked to rate the nine characteristics listed in Table 2 as "not enough," "just enough," and "too much," indicated a

TABLE 2   Blind Taste Test—Specific Characteristics (All Participants)

Characteristic	Per cent indicating "just right" by beer brands					Significant difference among brands[a]
	AB	CD	EF	GH	IJ	
After-taste	59	52	57	55	55	No
Aroma	64	68	63	62	62	No
Bitterness	58	54	53	54	54	No
Body	53	58	60	53	57	No
Carbonation	64	70	62	62	65	Only CD
Foam	62	66	63	59	66	No
Lightness	68	63	69	64	69	No
Strength	50	51	56	50	53	No
Sweetness	64	61	59	62	66	No

Source: Carling Brewing Company

[a] At the .05 level.

difference that was significant in "just enough" votes for one characteristic on one beer (carbonation of brand CD). Other than the one case, the reported differences among brands were so minor as to be not significant. A second analysis of the data, in which the "just enough" category was treated as a neutral or a zero and the "too much" and "not enough" positions as +1 and −1 respectively, in general, substantiated the percentage findings.[3] In addition, this analysis indicated that four of the characteristics—aroma, body, foam, and strength—were rated rather uniformly among the brands as "not enough" and one characteristic—bitterness—received a clear "too much" rating. Based on the overall taste test and the specified characteristics test, the conclusion was that beer drinkers could *not* distinguish taste differences among the beer brands presented in unlabeled bottles.

Could Drinkers Identify "Their" Brands?

The labeled test clearly indicated that beer drinkers would assign "their" brands superior ratings and, accordingly, it was assumed that if participants could identify "their" brands in the blind test that they would respond to them with superior ratings. The general ratings in the nude bottle test, by brand drunk most often, indicated that *none* of the brand groups rated the taste of "their" brand beer superior over all of the other beers (see Table 3). For example, regular drinkers of brand AB, indicated via their ratings that they preferred "their" brand over EF and CD, but they gave virtually similar ratings to brands IJ and GH as they gave to their own brand. Drinkers of the other brands

---

[3] This three-place neutral center scale is in need of further testing and comparison with four- and five-position scales to help determine the amount of bias it induces.

TABLE 3   Users Loyalty to "Their" Brand (Blind Test)

Brand drunk most often	Taste test ratings by brand rated					Own brand rated significantly higher than all others[a]
	AB	CD	EF	GH	IJ	
AB	67.0	62.4*	57.7*	65.0	65.8	No
CD	64.9	65.6	65.4	63.2	63.9	No
EF	68.8	74.5*	65.0	62.5	61.4	No
GH	55.4	59.2	68.7*	60.0	71.4*	No
IJ	68.4	60.5*	69.2	62.0	65.6	No

Source: Carling Brewing Company

[a] At the .05 level.

* Brands significantly different from user's own brand.

did not rate "their" brands as favorably in the blind comparison tests as did AB drinkers. Drinkers of brand EF rated beer CD significantly above "their" brand. Users of IJ rated all of the comparison brands except CD as equals and CD was rated as poorer tasting. Drinkers of brand GH must not have drunk the brand because they preferred its flavor—they rated two of the four comparison brands as superior in flavor and the other two are no less than equal to "their" brand. And based on the overall taste ratings, the regular drinkers of brand CD could just as well have drunk any of the other comparison brands—there were no significant differences among the assigned ratings.

Based on the data secured from the experiment, the finding appeared to be that most beer drinkers could *not* identify "their" brands of beer in a blind comparison test.

Influence of Brand Identification on Overall Ratings

A number of important findings arose out of comparisons of the data from the nude bottle phase with the labeled bottle phase. The overall ratings for all of the brands increased considerably with brand identifications. However, there was also much variation in the amount of increase registered among the various brands. And when beer drinkers were categorized according to the brand most frequently drunk, they consistently rated "their" beer higher than comparison beers in this positive identification taste test. Also, there was much variation in the amounts of increase—some brands received much higher ratings (*i.e.,* overall ratings) from their regular users than did other brands from their regular users. The differences in the ratings were assumed to be due to the presence of labels—the only altered conditions of the experiment.

The data that gave rise to the several statements about the effects of brand identification are examined in more detail below. In the *blind* test, none of the five brands received overall ratings that were sufficiently different from all of the others to be considered statistically significant. However, in the labeled test the differences in all but two of the overall ratings were significant (the ratings assigned to brands EF and IJ were relatively the same). Looking at some of the other figures, brand GH was rated significantly higher than all of the other brands and CD was rated higher than all brands but GH. Other differences that were judged statistically significant can be noted in Table 4.

TABLE 4   Comparison Taste Test—Blind vs. Labeled (Overall Ratings)

Beer brand	Blind test	Labeled test	Significant difference between blind and labeled test[a]
AB	65.0	70.6	Yes
CD	64.1	72.9	Yes
EF	63.3	67.8	Yes
GH	63.4	76.9	Yes
IJ	63.3	67.0	Yes
Significant differences between brands	None	Yes[b]	

Source: Carling Brewing Company.

[a] At the .05 level.

[b] All brands were significantly different from all others at the .05 level except EF and IJ relative to each other.

And as can be seen in this table, all five brands in the labeled test were rated significantly higher than the same brands in the blind test. Remember, these were the same brands of beer used in the nude test, but in the labeled test the participants could clearly identify each beer brand.

The loyalty of the participants toward "their" brands increased when positive brand identification was possible (see Table 5). All of the

TABLE 5   Users Loyalty to "Their" Brand (Label Test)

Brand drunk most often	Taste test ratings by brand rated					Own brand rated significantly higher[a]	Blind test ratings for own brand
	AB	CD	EF	GH	IJ		
AB	(77.3)	61.1	62.8	73.4	63.1	Yes	(67.0)
CD	66.3	(83.6)	67.4	78.3	63.1	Yes	(65.6)
EF	67.3	71.5	(82.3)	71.9	71.5	Yes	(65.0)
GH	73.1	72.5	77.5	(80.0)	67.5	Only over IJ	(60.0)
IJ	70.3	69.3	67.2	76.7	(73.5)	Only over EF	(65.6)

Source: Carling Brewing Company.

[a] At the .05 level.

labeled ratings assigned by regular users were significantly higher than the blind test ratings. In the blind test, participants indicated, at best, very little ability to pick "their" beers and set them off with relatively high overall ratings. For example, the regular drinkers of brand CD in the blind test awarded all of the brands about the same overall rating. However, in the labeled test, the CD drinkers awarded their beer brand an overall rating of 83.6, an 18 point increase over the blind test rating. This change was sufficiently above their overall ratings of all comparison brands to be statistically significant.

The gains in ratings were not uniform from one group to another. In the labeled test, brands GH, CD, and EF picked up more sizable gains than did AB and IJ. Comparison of the data in Table 5 with that in Table 3 will indicate other important rating changes from the blind to the label test.

Influence of Brand Identification on Specified Characteristics

The labeled test also produced some changes in ratings of specified characteristics of beer brands. In the blind test with the "just enough" category assigned a zero value, the participants tended to rate all of the beers as not having enough aroma, body, foam, and strength. All but one of the beers were rated on bitterness as "too much," and accordingly, not sweet enough. In the labeled ratings, "aroma" was greatly improved as was "body," "foam," and "strength." However, the ratings on "bitterness" and "sweetness" remained virtually the same as recorded in the nude test.

CONCLUSIONS

Participants, in general, did not appear to be able to discern the taste differences among the various beer brands, but apparently labels, and their associations, did influence their evaluations. In other words, product distinctions or differences, in the minds of the participants, arose primarily through their receptiveness to the various firms' marketing efforts rather than through perceived physical product differences. Such a finding suggested that the physical product differences had little to do with the various brands' relative success or failure in the market (assuming the various physical products had been relatively constant). Furthermore, this elimination of the product variable focused attention on the various firms' marketing efforts, and, more specifically, on the resulting brand images.

This experiment also has helped the Company measure and rank its brand image relative to competitive brand images and has offered base comparison marks for similar experiments, both in the same and other markets at later dates. Such information has helped in Company evaluation and competitive marketing efforts. And to the extent that product images, and their changes, are believed to be a result of advertising (*i.e.*, as other variables can be accounted for or held to be homogeneous among the competitive firms), the ability of firms' advertising programs to influence product images can be more thoroughly examined.

18. Is there a generalized price-quality relationship?

david m. gardner

There is much evidence that a relationship exists between a product's price and its perceived quality [8, 9, 12, 13]. However, no study gives evidence that the price-quality relationship can be generalized to various products with varying prices and consumer purchasing patterns. Furthermore, some studies [8, 13] have relied on an implied price-quality relationship derived from a forced choice situation, and only one study [12] did not use price as the sole determinant. The possibility that other factors influence the perception of quality is largely ignored.

THE STUDY

This study explored the degree to which the price-quality relationship can be generalized. To incorporate brand name as another possible determinant of quality perception, three studies were designed: (1) a laboratory experiment with quality estimates as the dependent variable, (2) a partial replication of an early price-quality study often used as a standard, and (3) a comparative ranking of purchase situation cues.

The Laboratory Experiment

Of a group of 20 products normally purchased by college students, three were chosen for the experiment: toothpaste, a man's dress shirt, and a suit. These best represented the extremes and the midpoint on a frequency of purchase-search time continuum, thus representing different shopping patterns and different relative price ranges. Then, following the plan of an earlier study [6], subjects were requested to make estimates of product quality after examining the three priced and branded products.

Prices were assigned to each product, using Gabor and Granger's approach [1]. Average high and low prices for each product were determined in a pretest by asking, "What is the lowest price at which you would still buy—the price below which you do not trust the quality?" and "What is the highest price you would be prepared to pay?" Prices between extremes were also chosen to give a more accu-

Reprinted by permission from *Journal of Marketing Research*, Vol. 8 (May 1971), pp. 241–243, published by the American Marketing Association.

David M. Gardner is Associate Professor of Business Administration, University of Illinois. This work was supported by a grant from the University of Illinois Research Board. The author acknowledges the assistance of James Hlavacek and Ollie Ahtola, doctoral candidates at the University of Illinois, in executing this study and analyzing the data.

rate picture of price differentials in inferring a price-quality relationship. Each product had five prices at each quartile value as shown in Table 1. In the actual study, a sixth nonprice condition was introduced, where no price was available to the subject.

TABLE 1   Product Prices (in Dollars)

Price	Toothpaste	Men's shirt	Men's suit
Low	$.53	$3.99	$60.00
Medium low	.58	5.25	67.50
Medium	.64	6.50	75.00
Medium high	.69	8.25	92.50
High	.75	10.00	110.00

Gabor and Granger's procedure has an essential advantage by eliminating extremely low and high prices, which are unrealistic and would bias results in favor of a price-quality relationship. Brands selected (Crest toothpaste, Arrow shirt, and Palm Beach suit) were those most widely known by the population studied and those able to cover the price range established.

The study design was a completely random 3×6×2 factorial. Each product was investigated at six price levels and two brand levels (with or without brand name). The three products comprised the third factor.

Subjects (juniors and seniors enrolled in the introductory marketing course at the University of Illinois, Urbana) were randomly selected from a larger subject pool, excluding females.

The dependent variables for the laboratory experiment were: product quality, willingness to buy, and attitude toward the product. The first two were measured on nine-point scales, from extremely high to low quality and willingness to buy. Attitude was defined and measured by 23 semantic differential scales [10], 11 highly loaded on the evaluative dimension, 7 scales on potency, and 5 on activity.

Subjects first examined one product accompanied by a show card describing its selling points, the price for the particular treatment, and a brand name or no brand identification. Then subjects filled out a questionnaire with the dependent measures. The procedure was repeated for a second and third product. Product, price, and brand were presented completely randomly except that all products presented to each subject either had to have brand and price designated or no brand and price. There were 120 exposures, with 10 subjects in each of the 36 conditions.

Replication Study

To give added meaning to the data from the laboratory experiment, a partial replication of an earlier study [13] was also conducted. Subjects here indicated which of three brands (A, B, C) they would purchase for a number of products. The only difference between the brands for each product was price.

For the replication, aspirin and liquid shampoo were selected from the earlier study and added to toothpaste, dress shirt, and suit, whose prices were the extremes and midpoint used in the laboratory experiment. Prices for aspirin and shampoo were established by an informal survey of current prices.

Fifty-nine subjects were randomly selected from the same subject pool reported above. They were asked to indicate which of three brands (A, B, C) they would purchase for each of the five products. As before, the only difference between brands was price.

Ranking of Purchase Situation Cues

To place the data gathered from the two studies in context, several purchase situation cues (most often mentioned in the relevant literature) were chosen to be ranked in degree of importance by the subjects. A paired comparison procedure was used in which 50 more subjects ranked six purchase situation variables (service and assistance, brand name, store reputation, product quality, price, and store location) for the three products used in the laboratory experiment.

RESULTS

The major dependent variable of the laboratory experiment was perceived product quality. If there was a price-quality relationship for these products, it should have been detected, since the nine-point scale was not a forced purchase decision. If price transmitted product quality information, there should have been a significant difference between the "no price" and at least one "price" treatment, and, hopefully, significant differences between "price" conditions.

Table 2 raises serious questions about any generalized price-quality

TABLE 2 *F*-Ratios for Dependent Variables (Laboratory Experiment)

Source of variation	d.f.	Perceived quality	Willingness to buy	Semantic differential
Products	2	7.51[a]	15.82[a]	5.70[a]
Price	5	.83	7.03[a]	.19
Brands	1	82.99[a]	14.79[a]	47.87[a]
Product × price interaction	10	1.37	2.02[b]	1.01
Product × brand interaction	2	4.19[b]	.23	7.34[a]
Price × brand interaction	5	1.26	1.11	.34
Product × price × brand interaction	10	1.24	.72	.55
Within replicates	324			

[a] Significant at the .01 level.
[b] Significant at the .05 level.

relationship. Since neither the price main effect nor an interaction involving price was significant for perceived product quality, it must be concluded from this study that price did *not* transmit information affecting perception of product quality on all three products, whether branded or not.

However, price did seem to affect willingness to buy the man's dress shirt. The Newman-Keuls multiple comparison test [7] showed these comparisons significantly different at the .05 level:

Unbranded shirt
No price vs. $10.00
No price vs.   8.25
$3.99 vs.   8.25
3.99 vs.   10.00
5.25 vs.   8.25
5.25 vs.   10.00
Arrow shirt
$3.99 vs. $10.00
3.99 vs.   8.25
5.25 vs.   10.00
5.25 vs.   8.25

There was no significant difference in willingness to buy between products. One significant difference between $67.50 and $92.50 was noted in willingness to buy unbranded suits.

It is clear that the brand name greatly influences perception of product quality (see Table 3), willingness to buy and attitude toward

TABLE 3   Marginal Means for Dependent Variables (Laboratory Experiment)

	Perceived quality	Willingness to buy
Products		
Toothpaste	4.14	4.43[a]
Shirt	3.64	4.85
Suit	4.23	5.85
Price		
No price	4.13	4.68
Low price	4.06	4.15
Medium low	4.17	4.72
Medium price	3.85	4.98
Medium high	3.80	5.78
High price	4.02	5.93
Brand		
Not branded	4.62	5.45
Branded	3.39	4.63
Overall mean	4.01	5.04

[a] The lower the value, the higher the perceived product quality and the higher the willingness to buy. Values range from 1 to 9.

the product as measured by the semantic differential. There was a notable difference between the presence or absence of brand name for these dependent variables at the .01 level of significance for all three products. In these cases, a brand name always resulted in a higher perceived level of product quality.

The result obtained in the partial replication of the earlier study was consistent with earlier findings. In the simulated purchase situation of this study, 34% and 55% of the subjects indicated, respectively, that they would choose one of the two higher-priced alternatives for aspirin and shampoo. Tull, Boring, and Gonsior reported 26% for aspirin and 49% for shampoo in their low reference price experiment. With the same procedure in this study, 61% indicated a preference for the two higher-priced alternatives for toothpaste, 75% for the man's dress shirt, and 81% for the suit.

Another group of subjects was asked to rank six purchase situation variables using the paired comparison procedure. The results are presented in Table 4. Price was *not* first for any of the three products used

TABLE 4   Rank Order of Purchase Situation Variables

Products	Mean values
Toothpaste	
Brand name	3.57[a]
Price	3.49
Product quality	3.40
Store location	2.37
Service and assistance	1.23
Store reputation	0.94
Men's dress shirt	
Product quality	4.06
Price	3.17
Brand name	3.17
Store reputation	2.14
Service and assistance	1.57
Store location	1.00
Men's suit	
Product quality	4.03
Price	3.34
Service and assistance	2.66
Store reputation	2.34
Brand name	1.86
Store location	0.83

[a] The higher the value, the higher the ranking of that variable compared to all others. The limits are 0 and 6.

in this study. For the suit and shirt, the rankings of product quality and price are significantly different at the .01 level using a *t*-test.

DISCUSSION

The results of this study cast serious doubt on the possibility of a generalized price-quality relationship. In the replication of the Tull, Boring, and Gonsior study, price was the only information cue, and thus a price-quality relationship could easily be implied. However, when other information cues are introduced (the merchandise itself, brand, and limited product information) this relationship is replaced by a brand-quality relationship. The ranking of price lower than, or at most equal to, other purchase situation variables is evidence for this finding.

Therefore, it must be concluded that price, except for unique but as yet unspecified circumstances, does not influence perception of product quality. However, this conclusion depends on the dependent variable and the definition of product-quality used. Until a definitive statement of perceived product quality is devised, any price-quality relationships must be closely examined to ascertain if they show unique situations where price does in fact influence quality perception or whether the study has been designed so that a price-quality relationship will be found.

REFERENCES

1. GABOR, ANDRÉ AND C. W. J. GRANGER. "On the Price Consciousness of Consumers," *Applied Statistics,* 10 (November 1961), 170–88.
2. _____. "Price as an Indicator of Quality: Report on an Enquiry," *Economica,* 33 (February 1966), 43–70.
3. _____. "Price Sensitivity of the Consumer," *Journal of Advertising Research,* 6 (December 1964), 40–4.
4. _____. "Foundations of Market-Oriented Pricing: The Attitude of the Consumer to Prices," *New Developments in Pricing Strategy.* Bradford, England: Management Centre, University of Bradford, 1967, 1–23.
5. _____. "The Pricing of New Products," *Scientific Business,* 3 (August 1965), 143.
6. GARDNER, DAVID M. "An Experimental Investigation of the Price-Quality Relationship," *Journal of Retailing,* 46 (Fall 1970), 25–41.
7. KIRK, ROGER E. *Experimental Design: Procedures for the Behavioral Sciences.* Belmont, Calif.: Brooks/Cole Publishing Company, 1968.
8. LEAVITT, HAROLD J. "A Note On Some Experimental Findings About the Meanings of Price," *The Journal of Business,* 27 (July 1954), 205–10.
9. McCONNELL, J. DOUGLASS. "The Price-Quality Relationship in an Experimental Setting," *Journal of Marketing Research,* 5 (August 1968), 300–3.
10. OSGOOD, C. E., G. J. SUCI, AND P. H. TANNENBAUM. *The Measurement of Meaning.* Urbana: University of Illinois Press, 1957.
11. SCITOVSKY, TIBOR. "Some Consequences of the Habit of Judging Quality by Price," *The Review of Economic Studies,* 12 (1944–45), 100–5.
12. STAFFORD, JAMES E. AND BEN M. ENIS. "The Price-Quality Relationship: An Extension," *Journal of Marketing Research,* 6 (November 1969), 456–8.
13. TULL, D. S., R. A. BORING, AND M. H. GONSIOR. "A Note on the Relationship of Price and Imputed Quality," *The Journal of Business,* 37 (April 1964), 186–91.

19. Congruence relationships between self images and product brands

ira j. dolich

This article examines whether products as symbols are perceived and organized into congruent relationships with the self concept.

The main points in developing psychological involvement are (a) the individual's perception of products as symbols and (b) existence of a self concept to which the individual relates the product symbol. Some success has been achieved in showing that individuals consider products to be symbols. Sommers [9], using Q-sort techniques, established that individuals were generally successful in using products to describe two different social strata.

Although Evans [4] unsuccessfully tried to classify Ford and Chevrolet owners by differences in personality variables, Tucker and Painter [10] showed some correlation of personality variables with product usage. Also, Birdwell [1] obtained significant relationships between the self concept and several automobile makes. Grubb [5], in a limited study, found congruence of self concept with brand of beer consumed.

Many studies on measurement and analysis of self concepts have been done by psychologists.[1] They have been especially interested in studying differences in perception of two important self concepts—the real self and ideal self. The real self is generally defined as an individual's perception of how he actually is, and the ideal self is that perception of how he would like to be.

Both Birdwell and Grubb used the real-self concept to test for congruency with product images. It is not known whether the real-self or the ideal-self image has greater influence on purchase behavior. Given the presence of psychological involvement, it is important to know which of these self images regulates behavior. It is possible that purchases of some products are influenced more by the real self and other products are regulated by the ideal self.

THEORY AND HYPOTHESES

The main concern here is the relevance of self theory to consumer choice decisions. Rogers [8] proposed that individual behavior was

Reprinted by permission from *Journal of Marketing Research*, Vol. 6 (February 1969), pp. 80–84, published by the American Marketing Association.

Ira J. Dolich is assistant professor of marketing, Pennsylvania State University. He wishes to thank Professor R. Clifton Andersen who supervised the dissertation on which this article is based.

[1] An extensive review of the literature can be found in [12].

regulated by each person's perceived similarities (or dissimilarities) of environmental conditions to the self image. Products and brands have images that are perceived by individuals as having various symbolic meanings. Therefore, products and brands are part of the environment (Rogers' phenomenal field) symbolized by the individual. Accordingly, only those products or brands symbolized as similar to the self concept will maintain or enhance the self. Thus, whether individuals accept brands with images similar to the self concept and reject brands with images dissimilar to the self concept is the main issue of this study.

With the realization that consumer choice is related to matching product or brand images to self images, two further points evolve. First, is there a difference in the brand images of socially consumed products (consumption in the presence of others) and privately consumed products (others not present during use) and second, does the ideal-self image indicate a dominant role in consumer brand selection?

These three concerns were formulated into the following hypotheses:

1. Self concept congruence is greater for most preferred product brands than for least preferred product brands.
2. Self concept congruence with socially consumed products differs from self concept congruence with privately consumed products.
3. Real-self image congruence with product brands differs from ideal-self image congruence with product brands.

Testing these hypotheses required measurement of self images and brand images and a method to determine statistical relationships.

THE RESEARCH DESIGN

The research design was established to determine the extent of congruence among self structures, products, and brands. Relevant to the design are product selection, measuring instrument used, administration of the test, and statistical analyses of the data.

Selection of Products

Four products were chosen for the study. The selection criteria were:

1. All products must be consumed by the population being sampled.
2. They must be readily available in a wide variety of outlets.
3. Brands within a product category must be similar in form, size, composition, and price.
4. Product consumption should be fairly rapid to develop a frequent purchase pattern.
5. An indication of advertising appeals that develop brand preferences based on social-psychological concepts should be present.

Finally, it was decided to use two products that are consumed publicly and two that are consumed privately. Four products meeting these requirements are beer and cigarettes (public consumption) and bar soap and toothpaste (private consumption).

Measuring Instrument

The semantic differential was used to measure evaluations by respondents of real-self image, ideal-self image, and brand images. It is described as "a combination of controlled association and scaling procedures" [7] and satisfies the requirement of measuring several concepts with the same instrument.

Magazine ads and television commercials were studied to get appropriate adjectives descriptive of the products. After several tests, the following adjectival pairs were selected, pretested and used in the measuring instrument:

Evaluative:	good-bad, safe-dangerous, superior-inferior, clean-dirty, tasty-distasteful
Potency:	hard-soft, robust-fragile, strong-weak, brave-cowardly, masculine-feminine
Activity:	active-passive, lively-calm, exciting-dull, impulsive-deliberate, complex-simple
Stability:	stable-changeable
Novelty:	modern-old-fashioned
Receptivity:	colorful-drab
Unassigned:	sophisticated-unsophisticated, expensive-inexpensive, reliable-unreliable, conforming-unconforming.

Individual scales were randomly assigned positions in the instrument. Each polar adjective of a scale was positioned to eliminate constant scale polarity.

The meaning of each concept to an individual subject is defined operationally as the set of scores for the scales representing that concept. The operational concepts are two brands of four products and the two self images. The same set of adjectival pairs was used to measure each concept mentioned.

Administration of the Test

The test was given to 200 University of Texas students, in an advanced undergraduate psychology course. Test results were screened to eliminate those who were not consumers of all four products.

Each test packet contained the same ten concepts to be evaluated. To reduce systematic bias in rating the concepts, a random distribution of eight concept orderings was used. Although subjects were restricted to specific products, they were free to exercise individual preferences for product brands most and least preferred.

Statistical Analysis

Congruence scores were analyzed using a 4×2×2 factorial analysis of variance design. The four products, two brands, and two self images were the main factors in the analysis of variance model. The statistical design was considered a Model I factorial analysis of variance model since all of the factors were fixed [11].

Data Compilation

The congruence between a self image and a brand image was obtained by computing the absolute arithmetic difference, scale by scale, between two semantic differential instruments. For example, scale ratings for an individual's real-self image and the brand of beer most preferred would be as follows:

The person I am[2]

Scale		(1)	(2)	(3)	(4)	(5)	(6)	(7)		Code
1	impulsive	___	___	X	___	___	___	___	deliberate	3
2	simple	___	___	___	___	X	___	___	complex	5
(to Scale 22)										

The brand of Beer I most prefer is _____

1	impulsive	X	___	___	___	___	___	___	deliberate	1
2	simple	___	___	___	___	X	___	___	complex	5
(to Scale 22)										

Congruence scores were calculated as shown:

Scale	Real-self image	Brand most preferred	Difference
1	3	1	2
2	5	5	0
Total			2

[2] The ideal-self image was measured similarly using the concept title, "the person I would like to be."

The absolute difference between example ratings was two and zero for Scales 1 and 2, respectively. Summing these differences gives a value of 2 that represents congruence of the real-self image with the brand of beer most preferred by the respondent. Thus, low scores indicate greater congruence than high scores.

One respondent's congruence scores are shown in Table 1. The

TABLE 1   An Individual's Congruence Scores of Self Images with Product Brands[a]

Product	Real-self image		Ideal-self image		Total
	Brand most preferred	Brand least preferred	Brand most preferred	Brand least preferred	
Beer	22	55	23	56	156
Cigarettes	24	68	21	75	188
Bar soap	23	61	26	70	180
Toothpaste	22	42	23	45	132
Total	91	226	93	246	656

[a] A low score indicates greater congruence (similarity) than a high score.

numerical arrangement in this table represents an individual's congruence scores between self images and product brands and was the basic data used in the analysis of variance tests for the three hypotheses.

RESULTS

Each hypothesis was operationalized into null and alternate hypotheses for statistical testing. The computed F ratios, T values and the corresponding computed occurrence probability or table value at the five percent level of significance are shown in Table 2.

Hypothesis 1

Using an occurrence probability of .05 as the significance level, rejection of the null hypothesis was indicated for each subject classification. Thus it was concluded that preferred brands of these products were perceived to be more similar to self concepts than least preferred product brands.

This result was expected since Birdwell showed self concept congruence existed for choice of automobiles, and Grubb indicated its presence in choice of beer. Cigarettes, bar soap, and toothpaste had similar relationships in this study.

Hypothesis 2

The results of this test suggest that the product classification schema was inappropriate for females but might have been acceptable for all subjects generally, and males specifically. The test, however, only indicated the presence of product differences; it did not describe those differences. Since the problem was identifying differences between products, the brand most preferred and brand least preferred product scores were tested for significant differences between products within each brand classification.

Correlate 2a. The product scores within the brand most preferred classification were statistically similar; therefore, the schema appear to be invalid when classifying *preferred brands* of products. If there were differences between products in the most preferred brand classification, the subtlety of the relationships was not revealed by the semantic differential.

Correlate 2b. The self concept congruence with *least preferred* brands did provide differences between products. The dissimilarity of self concept congruence with least preferred brands provided some support for Bourne's [2] schema as related to unacceptable or least preferred brands.

Less self concept congruence was found between beer, cigarettes, and bar soap than toothpaste. Furthermore, the total sample and female subjects showed socially conspicuous products (beer and cigarettes) to have significantly different self image congruence than privately consumed products (bar soap and toothpaste).

Hypothesis 3

The first analysis for Hypothesis 3 tested for differences between the real-self and ideal-self congruence scores without regard to brand

TABLE 2   Summary of Statistical Tests[a]

Analysis	Results		
	Total sample	Males	Females
Hypothesis 1: Self concept congruence with most preferred brands of products and least preferred brands of products are equal.	730.98[b]	511.83[b]	229.26[b]
Hypothesis 2: Self concept congruence with socially consumed products is equal to self concept congruence with privately consumed products.	5.10[b]	4.11[b]	1.90
Correlate 2a: Self concept congruence with *most preferred* brands of socially consumed products is equal to self concept congruence with *most preferred* brands of privately consumed products.	1.98	1.62	0.79
Correlate 2b: Self concept congruence with *least preferred* brands of socially consumed products is equal to self concept congruence with *least preferred* brands of privately consumed products.	13.09[b]	10.56[b]	3.96[b]
Beer and cigarettes	0.274	0.372	0.381
Beer and bar soap	2.183[b]	1.235	2.014[b]
Beer and toothpaste		2.919[b]	
Hypothesis 3: Real-self image congruence with brands of products is equal to ideal-self image congruence with brands of products.	26.93[b]	27.93[b]	2.44
Correlate 3a: Real-self image congruence with *most preferred* brands of products is equal to ideal-self image congruence with *most preferred* brands of products.			
Beer	0.00	0.00	
Cigarettes	1.51	1.63	
Bar soap	2.38	4.06[b]	
Toothpaste	1.51	1.62	
Correlate 3b: Real-self image congruence with *least preferred* brands of products is equal to ideal-self image congruence with *least preferred* brands of products.			
Beer	11.11[b]	8.13[b]	
Cigarettes	4.41[b]	4.07[b]	
Bar soap	9.66[b]	6.50[b]	
Toothpaste	7.15[b]	4.88[b]	

[a] Tests are at five percent level of significance. Figures shown are *F* ratio except for Correlate 2b where *t* ratios are shown.

[b] Indicates significant differences.

classification. Dissimilarity of image congruence for males and the total subject classifications are indicated in Table 2. Correlates 3a and 3b were not analyzed for female subjects since the initial test of

Hypothesis 3 indicated statistical similarity of relationships for these individuals.

The correlates of Hypothesis 3 were developed to explain significant differences between self-image base congruence scores by analyzing their relationships within brand classifications, i.e., most and least preferred brand categories. First, for each product, investigations were made between brand most preferred congruence with the real-self image and brand most preferred congruence with the ideal-self image. Second, an analysis was performed for each product on least preferred brand image congruence with the real-self and ideal-self images.

Correlate 3a. With respect to *brand most preferred*, only bar soap for the male subjects showed significant differences between real-self image and ideal-self image congruence scores. Also, for males the real-self image provided greater congruence than the ideal-self image for bar soap. Thus, the ideal-self image did not indicate a dominant role in consumer choice decisions for most preferred brands of the four products.

Correlate 3b. With respect to *brand least preferred*, the total sample and the male subjects showed significant differences between real-self and ideal-self congruence for all products. Also, the ideal-self image congruence score was larger (less congruent) than the real-self image congruence score in each case. Therefore, some subjects provided evidence to support the dominant role of the ideal-self image in consumer choice decisions.

Previous indications of greater importance of the ideal-self image in consumer choice decisions were not shown by the image relationships tested for female subjects. Also, the real-self image (not the ideal-self image) was found to provide greater congruence in most preferred brands of bar soap for male subjects. Thus, the ideal-self image was generally found to have the same image relationships for most preferred brands as the real-self image. Males did, however, substantiate relative differences in image congruences for least preferred product brands.

CONCLUSIONS

Results of the investigation appear to verify psychological theories that individuals tend to relate the brand symbol to self concepts. Subjects showed greater similarity of self concept and brand most preferred images than self concept and brand least preferred images. Favored brands were consistent with the self concept and thus reinforced it. Marketing strategies that are successful in establishing perceived psychological values for product brands seem to develop product acceptance or rejection by the similarity of these values to the self concept.

According to Bourne [2], reference group influence is strong in brand selection of beer and cigarettes and weak in selection of bar soap. Thus, individuals should be able to differentiate socially conspicuous products from private consumption products by self-image relationships. Differences between brands of products consumed socially and privately were not indicated in the analysis of most preferred brands. However, all groups differentiated least preferred brands of toothpaste according to Bourne's classification. Socially conspicuous products generally showed less congruence than private consumption products for *brands least preferred*. Thus, reference group influence, as related to the self concept, was revealed in least preferred brand relationships but not in most preferred brand relationships.

Douglas [3] and Martineau [6] consider the ideal-self concept to have greater operative influence in consumer choice. However, this study did not provide evidence that the ideal-self image was more closely related than the real-self image to consumer choice decisions for most preferred brands. Male subjects showed evidence in support of greater ideal-self than real-self image influence in consumer choice decisions on brand rejection. These males showed significantly less congruent ideal-self image than real-self image relationships for least preferred brands.

IMPLICATIONS

The subjects examined in this study indicated greater perceived product differences for least preferred brands than for most preferred brands. For the subjects investigated, the results indicate that promotional strategies based on psychological factors are more sensitive to self concept compatibility for least preferred than for most preferred brands. A conservative policy of developing an ambiguous brand image (with respect to real-self and ideal-self images) might result in more buyers because there will be less ideal-self sensitivity to rejection.

However, product differentiation based on psychological factors should increase discrimination in consumer choice rejection if related to ideal-self image relationships. Brand images referenced to the ideal-self image could significantly reduce the potential number of buyers if their ideal-self images were inconsistent with the product image. This study suggests that careful consideration should be given to consumers' psychology when psychological involvement is used as a promotional tool for brand differentiation.

REFERENCES

1. BIRDWELL, AL E., "A Study of the Influence of Image Congruence on Consumer Choice," Unpublished Ph.D. dissertation, University of Texas, 1964.
2. BOURNE, FRANCIS S., "Different Kinds of Decisions and Reference-Group Influence," in Perry Bliss, ed., *Marketing and the Behavioral Sciences*, Boston: Allyn and Bacon, Inc., 1963, 247–55.
3. DOUGLAS, JOHN, GEORGE A. FIELD, AND LAWRENCE X. TARPEY, *Human Behavior in Marketing*, Columbus: Charles E. Merrill Books, Inc., 1967, 66.
4. EVANS, FRANK B., "Psychological and Objective Factors in the Prediction of Brand Choice: Ford Versus Chevrolet," *Journal of Business*, **32** (October 1959), 340–69.
5. GRUBB, EDWARD L., "Consumer Perception of 'Self Concept' and its Relation

to Brand Choice of Selected Product Types," in P. D. Bennett, ed., *Marketing and Economic Development*, Chicago: American Marketing Association, 1965, 419–24.

6. MARTINEAU, PIERRE, *Motivation in Advertising*, New York: McGraw-Hill Book Company, Inc., 1957, 45.

7. OSGOOD, CHARLES E., GEORGE J. SUCI, AND PERCY H. TANNENBAUM, *The Measurement of Meaning*, Urbana: University of Illinois Press, 1957, 20.

8. ROGERS, CARL R., *Client-Centered Therapy*, Boston: Houghton Mifflin Company, 1965, 501.

9. SOMMERS, MONTROSE S., "Product Symbolism and the Perception of Social Strata," in Stephen A. Greyser, ed., *Toward Scientific Marketing*, Chicago: American Marketing Association, 1964, 200–16.

10. TUCKER, WILLIAM T. AND JOHN J. PAINTER, "Personality and Product Use," *Journal of Applied Psychology*, 45 (October 1961), 325–9.

11. WINER, B. J., *Statistical Principles in Experimental Design*, New York: McGraw-Hill Book Company, 1962, 155.

12. WYLIE, RUTH C., *The Self Concept*, Lincoln: The University of Nebraska Press, 1961.

Cognition Leading to
Purchase Satisfaction

4

9 BRAND COMPREHENSION AND EVOKED SET

In Part 4 we examine a selection of current knowledge concerning the cognitive chain leading from *brand comprehension* to *purchase, satisfaction*, and *confidence*. First we consider *brand comprehension* and a related concept, *evoked set. Brand comprehension* refers to the amount of nonevaluative or denotative information that the buyer possesses concerning a set of brands within a product category. This information serves two vital functions. First of all, the buyer must have some descriptive information of each brand before he can possibly arrive at a preference, or attitude, with respect to any given attribute of a brand. Secondly, his knowledge of denotative brand attributes serves as an input together with *motives* in the formation of attitude dimensions. Stated differently, *brand comprehension* provides information necessary for the formulation of a product class concept. Moreover, we know that the buyer pays more attention to certain brands within a product category than he does to others. It is typical to find him totally ignorant, or at least unable to spontaneously recall even the names of several brands within any product category. In order to cope with the volume of existing product information, relative to the importance he attaches to consumption within a given product category, the buyer will typically reduce his span of product knowledge to a subset within the product category, his *evoked set*. Thus, *brand comprehension* will include information on products within the buyer's *evoked set*, not necessarily all brands within the category.

The importance of the *evoked set* concept should be obvious. Cognition and ultimate purchase behavior can only occur among those brands for which the buyer has at least a working knowledge of their denotative attributes. The size of the *evoked set* thus sets a limit on the breadth of buyer choice at any point in time.

Investigation by Campbell (1969)* on the magnitude of *evoked set*, its determinants, and its impact on brand choice contains some interesting conclusions on how the buyer's simplification process operates. For the product categories of toothpaste and laundry detergent, no buyer was found to have an *evoked set* larger than 7 with the mean values for the two categories being 3.1 and 5 respectively. Moreover, buyers that had a relatively large *evoked set* in either one of the two product categories also had a relatively large *evoked set* for the other product category, and similarly for buyers with small *evoked sets*. Thus, *evoked set* size tended to be a buyer attribute. As one might expect, the size of the *evoked set* was found to vary inversely with the degree of brand loyalty exhibited in the given product category, while price sensitivity and *evoked set* size varied directly with one another. These findings are important in suggesting how the buyer copes with the problem of reducing a vast volume of product information to a manageable quantity. Nevertheless, many questions remain to be answered as to the conditions under which a brand is added or rejected from *evoked set* and how the concept operates in diverse product categories.

Very little is known about the process of committing information to memory and its subsequent retrieval. Involved in this process must be a cataloging function. The development of multidimensional scaling technique has aided the researcher in providing a somewhat mechanistic means for analyzing the structure of respondents' *brand comprehension* in terms of similarity mapping. The same technique can be applied with preference or attitudinal data. The example by Doehlert (1968)* presents the essentials of the technique in terms of mapping automobile colors. The fact that only three dimensions are necessary makes the article an excellent introduction to multidimensional scaling. While it should be understood that this technique is not meant to necessarily simulate the process underlying *brand comprehension,* it does suggest a means by which the denotative attribute dimensions important in a given product category can be assessed.

20. The existence of evoked set and determinants of its magnitude in brand choice behavior

brian milton campbell

This dissertation is an empirical study on the existence of evoked set and possible determinants of its magnitude in brand choice behavior. In theory, evoked set is defined as the set of brands of a product which the buyer actually considers when making a specific brand choice. It represents a significant simplification of the real world which is composed of all the brands of a product available to the buyer. More specifically, the purpose of this study is to discover (a) whether or not evoked set does, in fact, exist in brand choice behavior, (b) if evoked set exists, is there a numerical limit to the size of the buyer's evoked set, (c) whether or not there is at least a partial relationship between the magnitude of evoked set and the number of brands the buyer is aware of (other than the constraint that the evoked set can never be greater than what the buyer is actually aware of), and (d) whether or not there is an association between evoked set size and certain behavioral and demographic variables.

For purposes of the analysis the writer conducted 200 housewife interviews. The hypotheses were tested and relationships established by use of chi-square, Somers' D, regression, correlation and factor analysis.

The results of the study may be summarized as follows:

1. The concept of evoked set exists in brand choice behavior. It was found to be operating as an integral part of the brand choice processes for the two products considered in the study. In fact, the respondents' evoked sets contained only a minor proportion of all the brands which they were aware of for a given product. The evoked set represents a significant simplification of a complex decision situation and thus enables a buyer to select a preferred brand in at least a pseudo-rational manner.
2. For the two products researched, very few buyers demonstrated an evoked set greater than seven. The evidence strongly suggests that there is a numerical limit to the number of brands in a buyer's evoked set, across different products and different buying situations.
3. Buyers were consistent in their relative evoked set size. That is, respondents who showed a relatively large evoked set for toothpaste had a correspondingly large set for laundry detergent; and vice versa for those with small evoked sets. Consequently, evoked

Reprinted by permission of the author. A dissertation abstract.

set appears to be an individual phenomenon and not particularly related to the specific product in question.

4. In the two cases of toothpaste and laundry detergent, the size of the buyer's evoked set was not influenced by the number of brands she was aware of. Therefore, we may say that "relative awareness" was not a determinant of evoked set size.

5. The size of evoked set was found to be associated with "degree of brand loyalty" and "importance of price differences between brands of the same product." In essence, these two independent variables are partial determinants of the size of the buyer's evoked set.

6. The demographic characteristics measured in the study were not found to influence or determine the size of evoked set, to any appreciable degree. The number of brands the buyer considers was not conditioned by her age, income, education, family size, or socio-economic status.

7. Buyers rank their preferences for brands in the evoked set quite distinctly. The respondents tended to give such a brand either a very high probability of purchase, around 0.9 to 0.99, a medium probability of about 0.5, or a very low probability of about 0.01 to 0.1.

21. Similarity and preference mapping: a color example

david h. doehlert

THE SIMILARITY MAP

Du Pont is bringing out consumer products at an increasing rate. We have a large research and development effort to provide the consumer with the product he wants. We not only develop consumer products which we manufacture; we also provide end-use research for manufacturers who buy raw materials from us.

To guide our research and development on new and improved products, we must know what the consumer thinks. We must know what matters to the consumer and what he likes best. What we present to you today is the discovery that we can show by map what matters, and that we can show on the same map what each consumer likes best.

We claim that when a product is undergoing development, this kind of map can be used to assess where we stand relative to competition. And it can be used to measure our progress as we vary the product or its package or advertising. Finally, it can estimate market shares after development. So we say that at all stages it can provide guidance for research and development.

We have prepared 45 of these maps since 1963. Rather than use one of those cases for an example, we posed this problem: what colors of automobiles should be offered to the consumer? We could not test all kinds of colors, so we concentrated on some blues and greens and a gray and two browns.

We showed the colors, three at a time and asked these questions:

Which pair is most alike?
Which pair is least alike?

We also asked about preference. The second part of this paper discusses preference data.

Each pair of colors appeared on four different cards in the course of the test. Suppose colors 3, 11, and 18 appeared together. Then if the subject declared 18 and 11 most alike all four times that he saw 18 with 11, we can conclude that, relative to other color differences, this difference is a small one. On our map, then, these two colors would be put close together.

Another pair of colors might always be declared least alike; on the map those two would be placed far apart. We have no coordinates in advance on which to map the colors. We only have information from

Reprinted by permission from Robert L. King, ed., *Marketing and the New Science of Planning*, 1968, pp. 250–257, published by the American Marketing Association.

the subjects about which pairs are most alike and which are least alike. That is, we have a similarity score for each pair of items.

The map is prepared from this data by starting with an arbitrary scattering across the map of points to represent the nineteen colors. The computer program shifts the points until the pairs that were declared most alike are close together on the map and those less alike are farther apart. The program terminates iteration when further shifting of points cannot improve the map. This is the Kruskal-Shepard method of multidimensional scaling.

Figure 1 is the map of the nineteen colors shown in perspective. It is a display of how people see these 19 colors.

FIGURE 1 Similarity Map of 19 Colors

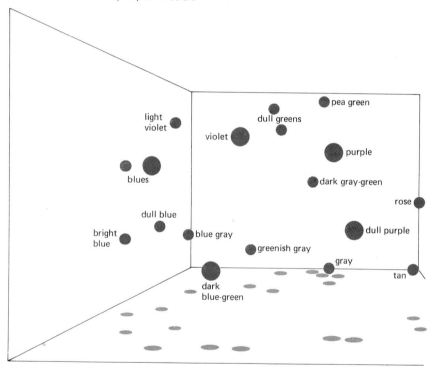

Later we will show which regions of this map are preferred. This will answer the question—which automobile colors should be offered. However, before discussing preference data, we will look closer at the process of developing this map.

THE DATA COLLECTING METHOD

We have standardized the data collection to make it fast, to reduce errors, and to make for quick analysis. Each set of three items is displayed on a single table. Three trays and six prepunched cards are provided for each person in the test to use in evaluating the three items. Suppose the subject has decided that 1 and 13 are most alike. She selects the card with 1 and 13 printed on the top edge, and drops that card in the tray labeled "most alike." The card for the least alike pair goes in the "least alike" tray, and the card for the third pair in the middle tray. Since the cards are prepunched with the subject's code number, the cards can go directly into analysis without any further handling. The cards are not marked by the subject, and can be used again for some other set of items.

There were nineteen such tables around the room in our experiment. The subjects went around the room twelve times in three hours. Less testing per person is needed when fewer than nineteen items are being tested. And in some applications, the testing can be divided among several groups of subjects so that it is less tiring for each subject.

DEGREE OF CONSENSUS ABOUT SIMILARITY OF THE COLORS

We checked our eighteen subjects for agreement about the similarities of these colors. That is, we computed correlation coefficients for all pairs of subjects. Then, using these correlations as measures of the similarity of subjects, we made a supplementary map (Figure 2).

It shows that subjects 2 and 12 are seeing the colors very differently from the others. We have checked their color vision, and we find that they are color blind. I expected to find that the others have normal color vision. Surprisingly, number 8 is also color blind. It is curious, indeed, that he gives data much like normal subjects, while 2 and 12 do not. Two and 12 are so different that we have made a separate map of the colors for them. Their map is different in that tans go over with greens. In other applications it might be possible to make just one map for all persons. We have always been able to do so. We invited trouble by using color for our example, because about 8% of all males have defective color vision.

THE NUMBER OF DIMENSIONS

We do not go into an analysis with a preconceived idea of the number of dimensions needed to make a good map. Color is unusual in this respect. If you know anything about color, you know that colors have been represented as three-dimensional for a long time. However, in this example, we acted as if there were no ideas available as to the number of dimensions needed to map colors.

This approach makes the example more realistic, because in all our 45 applications we have never had prior information as to how many dimensions to expect. The analysis is the means of discovering the number of dimensions needed. In this color analysis we tried all maps of 2 to 8 dimensions. Figure 3 shows a statistic like the residual error, plotted against the number of dimensions.

It says that when you go below five dimensions the residual error goes up despite an increase of nineteen degrees of freedom at every

FIGURE 2   A Map of Subjects

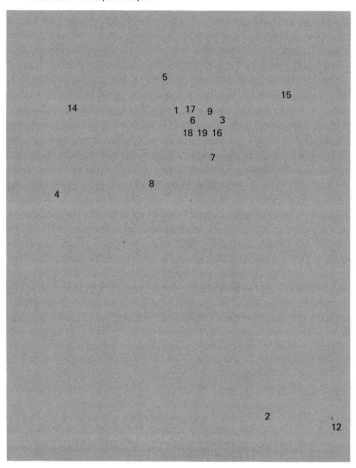

step. This is the equivalent of saying that real effects are being lumped with the noise, when the fifth and fourth dimensions are dropped.

So we conclude that these people see color in a five-dimensional way. We elected to show the three-dimensional result in Figure 1 to make the presentation and understanding easier. The three dimensions show most of the information in the data: they include 80% of the variance of the points.

THE PREFERENCE MAP

We have shown a method for detecting differences that consumers see between items. We also wish to know which items they prefer. That is, we want our goals for developing new products to be the preferences of the consumers. The experimenter's personal reaction doesn't matter. What does matter is the opinions of those who buy. Therefore, preference data are needed.

FIGURE 3 Lack of Fit Versus Dimensions

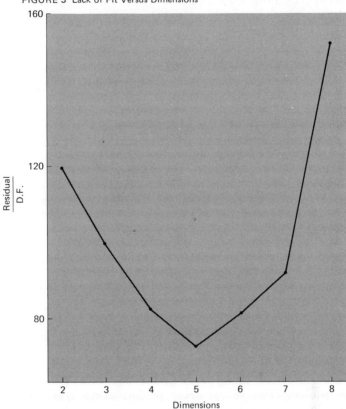

We would like to present the preference data in a way that is easily seen and interpreted. We will show that this can be done by relating the preference results to the similarity map.

DATA COLLECTION

The preference data were obtained at the same time that we collected the similarity data. A subject was asked to indicate which color he would like most for his next automobile, and which color he would like least for each group of three colors. He was asked to assume that the three colors were the only ones available. The preference data was recorded by voting with cards.

SUBJECT CONSISTENCY

The eighteen subjects in this test were highly consistent. Each made a few contradictory remarks, but not many compared to the total number of comparisons made.

We can also examine their consistency in repeating preferences. Was each subject able to repeat his data? Or did he change his mind about what items he preferred as he saw them more and more times?

Figure 4 shows that the correlation coefficients between tests for Person 18, for example, are quite high.

FIGURE 4   Correlation of Preference Scores,
Test to Test for Person 18

Test No.	Test No.			
	1	2	3	4
1		.81	.77	.76
2			.95	.92
3				.95

Each subject saw every pair of colors four times. The coefficient between the first two tests (.81) is large, and only slightly smaller than the coefficients between tests 2 and 3 and between tests 3 and 4 (.95). This indicates that in the early tests Person 18 was changing somewhat, but in later tests his preferences for colors were firmly fixed.

All of the subjects had correlation coefficients as large or larger than those seen here. Many were in the high 90's. Thus, we can say that the subjects can repeat their performances from test to test. Since our data are consistent, we can use all eighteen of the subjects in the preference analysis.

Not all people like the same colors. Therefore, we should allow each subject to display his individual preferences and we do this.

We display these individual preferences graphically as were the colors themselves. Preference scores assigned to the nineteen colors by a subject were used to find a point for him on the similarity map. The location of this point represents his ideal automobile color. It will be close to the colors he likes and further away from those he dislikes. To see how ideal points are located, let us look at Person 18 again.

First, consider Person 18's location on the similarity map. Figure 5 shows two of the three dimensions of the map; axes 1 and 2.

This is the top view of the three-dimensional map that you saw earlier. As you can see, Person 18 is very close to item 9. That is, the distance between the ideal point for Person 18 and item 9 is quite small. This is one of the colors that he preferred, one which he gave a large preference score. We see that there exists a medium distance between his ideal point and item 18, and we have a large distance to item 15. Item 15 is one of his less preferred items and one that he gave a small preference score.

Now consider Table 1, which shows the preference score, and the corresponding map distances for Person 18.

TABLE 1   Preference Scores and Corresponding Map Distances, Ideal Point to
Item Point, for Person 18

Items	Preference Score	Map Distance
1	66	.5
2	5	2.1
3	17	2.0
4	28	1.8
5	25	1.7
6	35	1.3
7	27	1.5
8	64	1.0
9	67	.4
10	45	1.2
11	35	1.5
12	21	1.8
13	20	1.8
14	12	2.2
15	11	2.0
16	56	.8
17	51	.9
18	40	1.1
19	59	.6

FIGURE 5   Similarity Map of 19 Colors Showing
Preference Point of Subject 18

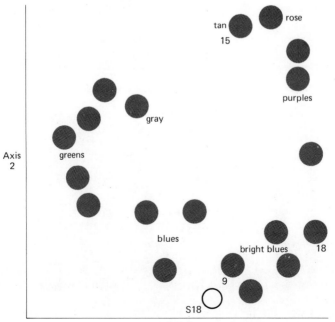

If our method of placing Person 18 on the similarity map is effective, then large preference scores will correspond to small distances. Notice that item 9 does have a large preference score and a small map distance. Item 18 has a smaller score and a larger distance, and the item 15 has a very small score and a still larger distance.

This tells us that the ideal point for Person 18 on the map represents his preference data quite well. That is, he is close to the colors he likes and far from those he dislikes. To show just how well his ideal point represents his data, we have plotted preference scores against distances in Figure 6.

As you can see the distances and scores are very well correlated. In fact, the coefficient of correlation is .97.

We have also included Person 9's scatter plot of distances and scores. His correlation coefficient is smaller (.78) than Person 18's. However, the correlation is very good except for item 7. Item 7 is the only gray that was included in the test. This indicates that we may need the fourth dimension to locate gray relative to the other colors.

The degree of correlation between the distances and scores is a

FIGURE 6   Preference Scores Versus Distances for Two Subjects

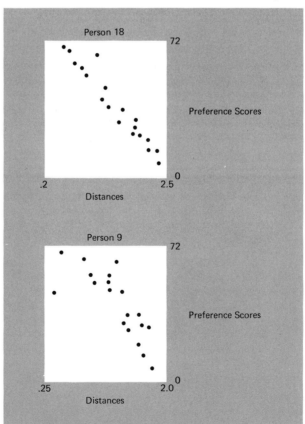

measure of the effectiveness of presenting the preference data on the similarity map. The correlation coefficients for all subjects were above .75, and most of them were in the high 80's and 90's. Thus, we can say that our method is effective.

Now we are ready to consider the total preference map. Each person has been placed on the similarity map at his optimum location within the range of the map. Perhaps the ideal color for a person was not included in the test. However, we may be able to conceive of it as some compromise between existing colors. If we could make this color, it would be preferred by him over all other colors, at least within the color space presented in the test.

If the person-points appear together in some region of the space, then the colors in or near that region are the best candidates to market. Looking at Figure 7, we can see that we have a very popular region with a large concentration of ideal points.

FIGURE 7   Preference Map Showing 19 Colors (Large Circles)
and 16 Person Ideal Points (Small Circles)

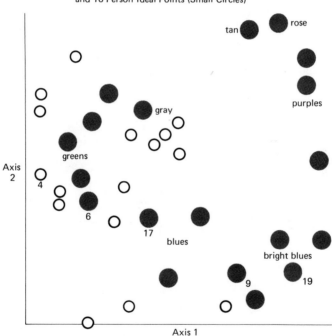

These are the colors (green, blues) that are most preferred by the majority of the subjects in our test. We also have a region preferred by a few people and we have a very unpopular region.

If we wished to choose colors to make or market for automobiles, we would want them to fall into the most preferred region of the map. In this case, we might try to make three or four that would satisfy the large region of ideal points and, perhaps, one that would fall into the zone preferred by a few people.

An interesting question might be posed here: "Does a subject consider items close to him distinguishably more preferred to those further away?"

For illustration, let us look at Person 4 and colors 6, 17, 9 and 19 on the map. You will notice that these colors range from more preferred to less preferred, respectively, for Person 4. Each pair of these items was seen four times by Person 4. For every pair, Person 4 consistently preferred the items in the order given above, all four times he saw the pair. This is significant at the .07 level. The differences shown on the map are, therefore, significant.

SUMMARY

A study of the preference map gives us guidance in research as to what items to market. If a preferred item does not exist, the similarity map indicates the directions in which we should move to make items that will fall into the preferred regions of the map.

We would, of course, be cautious about the conclusions drawn from this experiment as we had only 18 subjects. We would not expect to be able to predict the preferred color regions for the total population of automobile buyers from such a small sample. This was used just for the purpose of demonstrating our method. Larger samples of subjects can be readily tested and analyzed.

10 ATTITUDES

The theory of buyer behavior discussed in Chapter 1 distinguishes between two types of attitudes: *personal attitudes* and *situational attitudes*. Both concern evaluative perceptions of products, but each from a different perspective. *Personal attitudes* are the preference evaluations of the buyer considered merely from his perspective. However, since behavior seldom occurs in isolation from other people, the buyer may find it necessary to take account of what he assumes are the opinions of others important to him, that is, *situational attitudes*. A mental weighting process is assumed to go on, as described in Chapter 1, whereby priorities are attached to the individual *personal* and *situational attitudes* in a given purchase decision. Each purchase alternative will be positioned on each attitude dimension according to information from *brand comprehension*.

The term "attitude," however, has been used in research literature in several ways. Partly due to the resulting differences in operational measurement, inconsistencies have arisen as to the degree of reported association between attitudes and overt behavior. Bauer (1966)* carefully discusses this and other problems surrounding attitude measurement, concluding that the validity of the construct "lies in its usefulness to us . . . in understanding, predicting and influencing behavior toward that class of objects."

Assael and Day's (1968)* longitudinal study of attitudes and awareness related to market share for thirteen brands in three product categories yielded some interesting findings. For two of the categories, attitudes and awareness appear to be good predictors of market share, but this is not so for the third category. Of the two predictor sets, attitudes were more important than awareness. The data also supports the hierarchy of effects hypothesis. The results suggest possible usefulness of such longitudinal attitude measurements for incorporation in marketing information systems.

The thoughts of a practicing market researcher, Baber (1968),* pull together current practice with some evolving theory relevant to attitude measurement, and remind us that it is pointless to search for predictive attitude structures in product categories or among groups of people where such structures are likely to be weak or nonexistent.

22. Attitudes, verbal behavior, and other behavior

raymond a. bauer

Until quite recently students and practitioners of communication in marketing were occupied with establishing the sequence of communication effects that purportedly intervene between the communication and the hoped-for eventual behavior in the form of sales. An advertising campaign supposedly first makes a person aware that a product exists, communicates information about the product, gets him to like it, then gets him to prefer it to others, penultimately moves him to the point of deciding to buy it, and ultimately makes a sale. There are a considerable number of such models of the supposed steps in the communication process, each with some variation of its own. Without getting into the relative merits of each, we may pay attention to the features which they have in common. The most general assumption is that a communication or communication campaign of some sort, in order to affect behavior, must first produce some intermediate and presumably observable change in people. A corollary is that if the intermediate changes can be produced, there is presumably a good chance, although admittedly an imperfect one, that behavior can be influenced. Finally, it is assumed that there is an ordered sequence of changes, with awareness coming first, acquisition of information coming before attitude (or more literally "preference") changes, and attitude changing before behavior is affected. Depending on how many intervening stages a given author might want to conjure up, there is room for argument over the sequence of some of the minor stages; for example, the decision to buy a product for trial might come before one had decided he preferred it to other products. (As a matter of fact this could, in many circumstances, be a very reasonable step.)

I have treated this concern for models of communication effectiveness which posit a series of intervening steps as though it were something of the past, whereas in fact in many quarters it is still a very lively issue.

But in very recent years there have appeared a number of statements that bring these assumptions very much under scrutiny. While in one sense the models of effectiveness are *new*, they are already being questioned.

For many decades we have, of course, had the persisting concern over the relationship of attitudes to overt behavior. Various interpretations have been placed on the imperfection of this relationship over the long history of the problem. However, in the light of more recent writings, it is worth recording that researchers *have* generally found a

Reprinted by permission from Lee Adler and Irving Crespi, eds., *Attitude Research at Sea*, 1966, pp. 3–14, published by the American Marketing Association.

discernible, positive relationship between various measures of attitudes and the overt behavior with which one would assume they would be associated.

A number of authors have raised questions as to whether the communication process that has ordinarily been assumed actually occurs in any generally accepted sequence in all instances. A very good example would be Maloney's challenge to the notion that the most believable advertisement will necessarily sell more, or even as much as a less believable advertisement.[1] There are presumably circumstances under which a certain degree of implausibility will tease people into going out and trying a product.

But Festinger, Haskins, and Krugman, and most recently Appel have raised more fundamental questions about the relationship of attitudes to behavior. To use prevalent social science terminology, the question has been raised as to whether attitudes or more specifically attitude changes are either a necessary or a sufficient condition for behavior change.

Haskins[2] has reviewed all the studies he could locate which might reflect the usually assumed communication process with intermediate states anticipating if not causing changes in behavior. He describes what is at a first look something of a shambles. It would be difficult to say that the data he introduced support the notion of *any* regular sequence of effects. Festinger and Krugman address themselves to issues which are—for our purposes—somewhat more precise.

Festinger[3] professes to have read with incredulity a statement of Arthur R. Cohen that we have plenty of studies which show we can effect opinion change *via* communication, and that existing opinions (or if you prefer, attitudes) are correlated with behavior; but we have had virtually no studies which combine both steps. So, we don't understand if, and/or how, a *change* in opinion affects a change in behavior. Festinger, stimulated by these remarks of Cohen, found only three studies which *combined* the steps and studied the effect of opinion *change* upon behavioral *change* (in contrast to a simple correlation between *existing* opinions and behavior). For all practical purposes the three studies produced negative findings.

One may ask: How can this be? If there is a rather regularly observed correlation between attitudes and behavior, then there must perforce be a correlation between new attitudes (or if you will, attitude change) and behavior. One might argue that the matter simply has not been studied and that certainly a federal case cannot be made on the slim evidence that is available: three studies. However, there is the disturbing possibility—at which I feel Festinger only hints—that it is most possible to change people's attitudes precisely when they regard the topic as of so little importance that they are unlikely to do any-

[1] John Maloney, "Curiosity v. Disbelief in Advertising," *Journal of Advertising Research*, Vol. 2, No. 2, 1962.

[2] Jack B. Haskins, "Factual Recall as a Measure of Advertising Effectiveness," *Journal of Advertising Research*, Vol. 4, No. 1, March, 1964, pp. 2–8.

[3] Leon Festinger, "Behavioral Support for Opinion Change," *Public Opinion Quarterly*, Vol. 29, No. 3, Fall, 1964, pp. 404–417.

thing about it—except answer attitude questions; or, of equal interest and importance, there may be strong situational pressures to present a verbal version of some attitudes but not equal pressure to enforce the behavior.

In any event, Festinger raises the issue that attitude *change* may not be a sufficient condition for behavioral change or at least that there is no research to show that it is.

Krugman[4] approaches the matter from the other side. In attempting to understand how T.V. advertising has any effect, he argues that it may do so through the process of incidental learning, or by the type of learning that is characteristic of the study of meaningless material. Thus, without being particularly aware of what is going on, a person acquires sufficient knowledge about a product that when he is confronted by it, he is just sufficiently changed to buy it. However, no ordinary attitude test might detect an intermediate change in attitudes (by this Krugman apparently means product preference most specifically) between the time of exposure to the communication and the time of actual purchase. In fact, Krugman hypothesizes: the act of purchasing and the confrontation with the product may crystallize the events which have laid latent in the person's mind, and in a meaningful sense attitude change may follow behavior change. Note: This explanation is, among other things, competitive with the theory of cognitive dissonance which would argue that the person changed his attitude to make it consistent with the fact that he had purchased the product.

In any event, Krugman gives us at least some sensible way of looking at the fact that advertising campaigns have produced sales results when there was no evidence of intervening attitude change—as ordinarily conceived. Krugman thus asks whether or not attitude change is a necessary condition for behavior change!

While all this is going on, Charles Ramond is using every opportunity to push for well-designed and controlled experiments, using sales as the measure of success. Other researchers (Krugman and Yoell) are innovating in behavioral measures of attitudes—pupillary dilatation as a measure of interest, pulling of levers as a measure of interest, and so on.

It is fair to anticipate that we may be on the verge of a neobehaviorist revival which in turn will feed into the hands of those marketers who say: "I am interested only in sales and I don't care what else you measure." If this happens, we will be severely handicapped in our ability to study the process that intervenes between a communication and eventual action. We will also be deprived of the efficiency of being able to make at least a tentative evaluation of our communication tools —e.g., copy testing—without the extreme expense and time of full-scale experiments with sales as the criterion of effectiveness. And none of these consequences is warranted by our existing state of knowledge nor is it—to the best of my knowledge—desired by any of the men to whom I have referred above.

---

[4] Herbert E. Krugman, "The Impact of Television Advertising: Learning without Involvement," *Public Opinion Quarterly*, Vol. 29, Fall, 1965, pp. 349–356.

Hence, I would like to take a close look at the circumstances which lie behind these very recent developments and hopefully introduce at least a few ideas which may prove useful in our reactions to the material of the papers which follow.

You may have noticed that I used a number of words rather freely and interchangeably: attitude, opinion, intervening states, intervening stages, perhaps even intervening variable. This was deliberate since I wanted to avoid your getting any prematurely fixed idea of what I thought I meant when I used such words.

It might be useful for us to look back on how the concept of attitude got into psychology. It dates back well over half a century to experiments on reaction time. It was discovered that a person could push a key sooner after seeing or hearing a stimulus if he concentrated on pushing the key rather than on watching for the stimulus. This was first thought of as an actual physical phenomenon, a postural "set" or "attitude" that facilitated rapidity of response or inhibited it. Pretty soon the concepts of "set" or "Aufgabe" (task) lost their association with an actual postural state and came into the more general stream of psychological discourse. They were the direct ancestors of the concept of attitude which, as you well know, is most often defined (with appropriate or inappropriate modifiers) as a disposition to act.

What is important to us is that the concept of attitude came into psychology as an intervening variable to refer to a state of an organism in order to account for the fact that some people reacted differently than others, and that the same people reacted differently under different circumstances. It was also used as an aid to the prediction and control of behavior in that it led experimenters to give different instructions to their subjects (i.e., to attend either to the response or to the stimulus) in order to produce differences in reaction time.

Note further that an attitude, set, or what have you, was and is a *postulated* state of the organism that never has, and never will be, observed directly. It is a hypothetical construct which we infer from samples of the individual's behavior, be they samples of what he says, does overtly (free behavior or lever pulling and other behavior under experimental conditions), or readings of his physiological responses— skin conductance, skin temperature, eye blink, pupil size, or anything new that may come along. The concept of a "true expression of attitude" or "true attitude" or a "valid measure of attitude" as ordinarily discussed is *nonsense*. It is even conceptually difficult to imagine what we might mean by such a phrase as "true attitude." Ordinarily we think intuitively that we have a person's true attitude if he tells us what he would tell himself under the circumstances. But then, we turn right around and talk about "unconscious attitudes" or "unconscious components" of attitudes. The dilemma of even thinking about such a notion as a "true attitude" is that we can learn "what it is" only through the sorts of samples of behavior I have referred to above and the *inferences* we draw from that behavior. It is indeed difficult to use an unknown entity (the "true attitude") as the basis for assessing the validity of the inferences we draw from samples of behavior.

I am going to jump right into the middle of the fray and take the stand that the validity of our assessments of attitudes is *solely* the *utility* of the inferred concept for understanding, predicting, and influencing the behavior of individuals. Further, failure to recognize this conception of validity, and the concurrent failure to understand the full implication of the fact that an attitude is a hypothetical construct, leads us to confusion about the verbal behavior on the basis of which we often infer attitudes. Next, any of the usual distinctions between attitude, opinion, fact, sentiment, and like words stem from confusion between ordinary linguistic usage and that any one of these terms refers only to some such postulated dispositional variable and we may as well call them all "attitude" or "opinion." I have no opinion or attitude as to which is the preferable word, but they all refer logically to the same order of construct and we should not let the fact that our language is rich interfere with the logic of science.

I do not want to create the impression that I am claiming more originality than is my due. I acknowledge varying degrees of debt and grant varying degrees of precedent to such writers as Milton Rokeach, Paul Lazarsfeld, Smith, Bruner, and White, Donald Campbell, Krugman, and so on. I hope to take a little credit for the packaging and for the fact that Henry Riecken and I made many of these points back in 1949 but unfortunately in a defunct journal.[5]

Most attitude measurement is done by way of observing verbal behavior, yet few writers keep the distinction between the two clear. We have the age-old concern for the imperfect correspondence between "attitudes" and behavior, but the almost always dominant assumption that "attitudes" have to be validated against behavior. But as some authors have in fact pointed out, what we often are dealing with is not people's attitudes, but with what they said in one situation and what they did in another. The most hoary example of this is La Piere's "experiment" in which he wrote to innkeepers to ask if they would accept Chinese guests. They were almost unanimous in saying they would not. Yet when La Piere and his wife presented themselves with a pleasant looking Chinese couple they were invariably admitted. Is this, as is almost always assumed, an instance of a disparity between "attitude" and "behavior"? I submit that we are dealing with two separate kinds of behavior and that we have no evidence that the innkeepers in question were in any meaningful sense prejudiced against Chinese. *My* inference is that their underlying attitude was "avoid personal friction as much as possible" and that their intention in writing that they would not accept Chinese was to avoid a painful situation. When they were confronted with the Chinese, they did the least painful thing and admitted them.

There are many reasons that people say the things they do. In an interview situation they may be trying to ingratiate, dominate, infuriate, or confuse the interviewer. They may be trying to hide their feelings from themselves; or they may be trying to get the interview over as rapidly as possible. Or, we hope, they may be trying to tell the interviewer as accurately as possible how they feel and what they know

[5] Raymond A. Bauer and Henry W. Riecken, *International Journal of Opinion and Attitude Research;* Vol. 3, No. 4, Winter 1949–1950; pp. 513–529.

about the phenomenon in which the interviewer is interested. Of course, we systematically try to structure our interviews so as to create the last of these circumstances.

Where we believe attitudes are well crystallized and issues well drawn, we are often willing to accept rather terse bits of verbal behavior as sufficient for inferring a person's attitude. Expressions of preference in a Presidential race are, I suppose, a good example. However, there are very few issues and situations in which an interviewer can free the respondent of cultural expectancies and cultural norms. The respondent will look for them in the interview. Back and Gergen found that substantially identical questions produced more "o.k." responses when they were placed further toward the end of the interview. The authors reasoned that as an interview progresses, the respondent proceeds to identify the frame of reference, values, and so on, of the person who designed the interview or questionnaire schedule, or be sensitized to the prevalent cultural values apropos to the issue being studied.[6] Hence, even though our interview procedures may not in themselves produce a systematic response bias, the culture often favors one response over another.

The same line of reasoning holds for the three studies cited by Festinger in which there was apparent opinion or attitude change, but no subsequent behavioral change that correlated meaningfully with the attitude change. The topics, toilet training of children, management behavior of foremen, and oral hygiene were all ones on which the subjects were taught the proper answers desired by competent authorities. Yet it can be assumed that there are strong situational pressures on mothers to hurry the toilet training of their young, and on foremen to act in an authoritarian manner. (The oral hygiene issue is somewhat different.) Here we have situations in which there is a situational pressure favoring a "correct" verbal response and inhibiting a "correct" behavioral response. How can we say which is a better reflection of the individual's attitude on the question, or even whether the determinant of what was said and done was so much a reflection of how the person felt on the issue as compared to a desire to comply to the situational pressures?

What, then, are the implications of this distinction between verbal behavior and attitude that I have drawn for attitude measurement, and for our understanding of the process that presumably intervenes between exposure to a communication and possible eventual changes in behavior?

In the first instance, I have no desire whatsoever to downgrade the usefulness of verbal behavior for the inferring of attitudes. On the contrary I wish to affirm the usefulness of verbal behavior as a source of information and hope to bolster our confidence in it by spurring efforts to understand better the problems of inference involved. Verbal behavior is just as objective as physiological measures or observations

---

[6] Kurt W. Back and K. J. Gergen: "Idea Orientation and Ingratiation in the Interview: A dynamic model of response bias." *Proceedings of the Social Statistics Section of the American Statistical Association*, 1963; pp. 284–288.

of overt behavior. One can report with equal reliability and absence of bias what a person said as he can report the reading of a dial or a description of overt behavior. At the same time that physiological and behavioral measures are not more "objective," they are not devoid of problems of inference. No such measure with which I am acquainted does not present possible ambiguities. If a person's pupil dilates, we may feel perfectly confident that his interest is aroused. But: Is he pleased, frightened, disgusted, or what?

By being fully aware of the need to accept the situational influences on verbal behavior we can expand our ability to make inferences about the attitudes we assume to exist. For example, Greyser suggests that inverting the order and form in which propositions are presented can be used to infer the stability of attitudes.

While I am presently unprepared to say much about the problems of inference, it occurs to me that most of the inferences we make takes place in the process of analysis of our data. The common sequence in which we assign meaning to responses to a single question or to a scale score is: First, look at the overt nature of the response and then, based on our experience, judge whether or not the meaning is clear and unambiguous. Such a judgment will usually be based on our experience with similar answers or scale scores in previous studies we have done or read. If we feel the meaning of the answers may be unclear or ambiguous, we do one of two things: On the one hand, pass the problem of inference on to the reader by simply referring to our respondents as people who said something: thus "Of the people who said yes in response to . . . , x% also said yes in response to . . ." It is pertinent to note that the mark of a careful analyst is that he frequently finds it important to say, "those persons who scored high on our scale of 'isolationism' " rather than "isolationists." Or, we may, in the process of analysis, illuminate the meaning of the responses.

As an example of the use of analysis for the purpose of inferring the meaning to be attributed to responses, I offer a recent experience of my own. Respondents to a survey indicated a great deal of concern over the *cost* of food, but these same respondents thought that they got better *value* for their money when buying food than when buying other items in the cost-of-living index. If we stopped with the data at this stage, we might conclude that: (1) Respondents were ambivalent; (2) they drew a clear distinction between "cost" and "value;" or (3) some respondents were very concerned about costs, and others thought that they got good value when they bought food. The next step in analysis indicated that the third proposition was the most plausible one since people who reported strong feelings about the cost of food were considerably less likely to report that they thought it was a good value. Did this therefore mean that there is a close linkage in the consumer's mind between the overall cost of food as a category in their budget and the value of individual food items—when they rate such items separately. However, the distinction between cost and values gets confused when respondents answer a question about the value of food in general. From all this we may conclude that while concern over the cost of food may influence a person's response to the value of food as a general category in his cost of living, it will not carry over to his reaction to the *value* of specific food products.

In saying all this, I have in mind the fact that I am in categorical disagreement with no less an authority than Green[7] in his classic article on attitude measurement in the *Handbook of Social Psychology*. Green states that attitudes are inferred from samples of verbal behavior and that therefore we can make predictions *only* to similar samples of verbal behavior. Unquestionably prediction to the same universe as that from which the original construct was inferred is the safest type of activity in which to engage.

There is little utility to doing this in the case of attitudes, however. Where they have been studied it was with the implication that the inference of attitudes from verbal or other behavior was an efficient and feasible way of anticipating how a person might behave in some *other* situation and in which the *type* of behavior would be different than that presently available for observation. This type of inference is common throughout our life. If we were to take Green's position and apply it to quality control of the products we produce, only tests by destruction would be allowed. The only way to test a missile would be to fly it. But since we can fly it only once, sensible people make the best observations they can to infer what will happen when it is launched.

Among formal methods of attitude assessment, Lazarsfeld's Latent Structure Analysis is as compatible as any with the general position I have taken since it is most explicit in avoiding any implication that an attitude is a physically existent "thing." However, as is so often the case, a formal procedure is not a complete substitute for an alert mind. The most useful specific suggestion that I have to make is that when we are concerned with verbal behavior as the basis for inferring attitudes, we take into consideration the several functions that *expression* of attitudes may have.

Smith, Bruner, and White,[8] as Riecken and I did at an earlier period, draw an *explicit* distinction between the private functions which holding an opinion may have for an individual and the functions which may be served by verbal behavior related to that private belief. They suggest three broad functions served by *expression* of opinion: (1) A person may only be *externalizing* what he believes privately; (2) he may be involved in what they call *"object appraisal"* —namely, expressing a tentative formulation about some segment of the external world as a way of helping himself understand it; or (3) he may be involved in *social adjustment*—the sort of manipulation of the external world I suggested previously in which he may be ingratiatingly, bullying, deceiving the interviewer, and so on. Ordinarily we hope that the respondent is doing what Smith, Bruner, and White call "externalizing." However, this is precisely what cannot be taken for granted.

---

[7] Bert F. Green, "Attitude Measurement," Dr. G. Lindzey (ed.): *Handbook of Social Psychology*, Volume I, Cambridge: Addison Wesley, 1954, pp. 335–369.
[8] M. Brewster Smith, Jerome S. Bruner, and Robert W. White, *Opinions and Personality*. New York: John Wiley and Sons, Inc., 1956, pp. 41–43.

You may well contend that all I have been arguing is the ABC's of good interviewing and questionnaire design. I think, however, that I am going a full step beyond present good practice in that I am advocating that we consider the "unbiased answer" as only a limiting case and possibly a misleading one, since it is based on the assumption that there is a "true belief" which can be determined directly without intervening inference. But, more radically, I am trying to move us away from *any* fixed concept of "what an attitude is." So long as we continue to think, however implicitly, of all attitudes as having any necessary dimensions, we tend to lose sight of the purpose for which we employ the concept.

Permit me to return to the observations made by both Haskins and Krugman that behavioral changes have been observed without intervening attitude changes. If we are thinking of attitudes as conventionally measured, we must agree with them and this is an interesting circumstance with which to contend. However, Krugman specifically addresses himself to what is learned from advertising and what that learning process is. Therefore, he postulates a change which intervenes between exposure to a communication and the subsequent behavior. And, it is indeed impossible to think sensibly about a communication-behavior sequence which does not involve some intervening change in the person, whatever the nature of that change is. It then becomes a practical matter of whether we can in any way observe this intervening state for purposes either of better understanding the process or of anticipating or influencing the subsequent behavior. In this sense it is useful to assert that there *cannot* be behavior change without attitude change.

I say it is useful to make this assertion because I intend it as a programmatic statement much of the order of the popular phrase: "If a thing exists it can be measured." As long as *anything* remains unmeasured the truth of the statement cannot be confirmed, but cannot be refuted either, since failure to measure something can always be attributed to lack of diligence or aptitude. Obviously, it is the intent of the statement, "Get out and measure," that is important and not its truth or falsity. The recent commentators have done us a service by pointing out that the existing conceptions of and measurements of attitude do not identify the intervening states of the organism. My contention is that there is neither sense nor utility to conclude therefore that there are no such intervening states which are amenable to observation but rather that we should exercise our ingenuity in imagining what they may be (Krugman has some suggestions on this score) and how we may observe them.

If Krugman is right, and it is my guess that he is, the intervening change which takes place in cases of low salience is virtually exclusively a cognitive one. That is to say there is apparently no perceptible shift in product *preference* as a result of uninvolved exposure to T.V. advertising, but rather a slight restructuring of how the individual sees the world with perhaps some of the person's values being made slightly more salient than before. While preference for or antipathy toward an object or class of objectives has traditionally been regarded as one of the defining characteristics of the concept of attitude, it is senseless to argue that an "attitude is not changed" if one of the components with which we have traditionally been concerned remains stable while others change.

At this point, you may well be asking if I am preaching attitudinal imperialism in the sense of claiming that the concept of attitude may be conceived of so broadly as to embrace any internal state of a person. It is not my intention. Everything I have said is within the confines of the conventional definition of an attitude as a disposition to act toward an object, event, or class of objects or events. All I have insisted on is that we recognize that it is a *construct* which must be inferred, and that its validity lies in its usefulness to us, the investigators, in understanding, predicting, and influencing behavior toward that class of objects. The implications of my position are that we should not feel bound in our search for utility either by what previous investigators have found useful or by some metaphysical conception of "what an attitude is."

23. Attitudes and awareness as predictors of market share

henry assael
& george s. day

Recent studies of the predictive value of brand attitudes and attitude change have concentrated on their relationship with individual brand choice behavior rather than with aggregate market behavior (for example, see Achenbaum, 1966; Axelrod, 1968; Day, 1969). Logically, the individual level is the proper place to start, for if the value of attitudes cannot be demonstrated there, any conclusions about aggregate relationships must be suspect. Fortunately, the studies cited above have consistently found highly significant relationships, although the results are subject to important qualifications concerning differences between market segments.

This paper accepts the presence of a predictive relationship between attitudes and behavior at the individual level as given, and is concerned with the nature and strength of the relationship at the aggregate level.

Kristian Palda's recent study (1966) represents one of the few attempts at an aggregative approach. Yet his analysis of past data was limited by two factors. First, regressions of predictor variables on market share were run only for awareness; there was no measure of attitudes. Second, appropriate time series data from which to derive the relationships were not available. Palda's regressions were based on only three successive waves of interviews with inconclusive results regarding the appropriate lead-lag relationship.

The most obvious difficulty in taking an aggregate approach to prediction is the requirement that a sufficient number of data points exist to establish the appropriate lead-lag relationship. Ideally, time series data for the brand attitude and awareness predictors would be available over 15 or 20 reporting periods, and would be based on a series of independently drawn national probability samples. Moreover, a rigorous design would insure that market behavior was measured in a separate reporting system to avoid a spuriously high relationship to attitudes. Yet there are realistic constraints in building a predictive system on aggregate time series models. Very few companies have been willing to invest in the ongoing marketing information system required to collect attitudinal information systematically. Two years might be required before sufficient data points can be established.

This study first examines the relationship over time of the interven-

Reprinted by permission from the *Journal of Advertising Research*, Vol. 8, pp. 3–10, © copyright 1968, by the Advertising Research Foundation.

[1] This study was funded by the Graduate School of Business Administration, New York University and the Graduate School of Business, Stanford University. The authors wish to express their gratitude to C. E. Wilson of The Nestle Co., Inc. and Arthur S. Pearson of Bristol-Myers Company for contributing the data and assisting in the analysis.

ing variables of attitude and awareness to a measure of aggregate purchasing behavior—market share. Several time series models will be applied using alternative predictors in an attempt to establish the most reliable predictive system. This will also provide an opportunity to determine the extent to which attitude and awareness changes precede or follow changes in market share. (For a discussion of the difficulties in establishing temporal relationships between attitudes and behavior, see Ramond, 1965.)

A second major objective will be to examine the predictive power of the three intervening variables of attitudes, awareness, and previous brand usage in different product contexts. Palda's review (1966) of the conceptual pitfalls in using attitudes and awareness as predictors of behavior needs no elaboration. What requires further consideration is the possibility that the relative effectiveness of the intervening variables depends upon the product category or even the brand whose market performance is being predicted. It is not difficult to conceive of a product category where pure "visibility" may be more important in generating sales than the delivery of specific appeals which can change brand attitudes. Or, given a stable market with a low price-elasticity of demand, it is possible that variables relating to past usage will more precisely forecast future shifts in market share than cognitive or affective dimensions.

It is not apparent that easy generalizations can be made as to the best regression model using a stable set of predictors across brands or product categories. This paper will demonstrate that the model and predictor variables must be a function of the individual brand and product category.

THE DATA

In the last few years, two companies—Nestle and Bristol-Myers—have independently established the type of marketing information system required to implement an aggregate time series approach. Both companies have collected information on brand attitudes, awareness and reported usage over extended periods of time: Bristol-Myers on a monthly basis for 14 months, Nestle on a bi-monthly basis for two and one-half years. Each survey was an independently drawn national probability sample conducted by telephone interview. The Bristol-Myers survey collected data for four product categories, two of which —deodorants and analgesics—were used in this analysis. Nestle collected data on instant coffee. Due to the length and complexity of the Bristol-Myers questionnaire, a centralized Wide Area Telephone Service installation was used for maximum interviewer control (see Eastlack and Assael, 1966). Both companies interviewed approximately 1,200 respondents per reporting period.

Three predictor variables common to both sets of data were used in the analysis: Brand attitudes, unaided brand awareness, and the proportion of respondents using the brand in the last two months. Brand awareness was based on unaided brand recall. Brand attitudes for analgesics and deodorants were measured by agreement with a series of statements derived from advertising themes and product characteristics. For instance, "Analgesic X is the brand most recommended by doctors," or "Deodorant Y gives longer lasting protection." Attitudes for instant coffee were derived from statements based on the relative perception of each brand. For instance, "Brand X is one of the best brands." Judges were asked to rate each statement in accordance with the Thurstone judgment procedure (Edwards, 1957) so as to determine the scale positions of each statement along a favorable-unfavorable continuum. The proportion of respondents attributing the statement to a brand was weighted accordingly and the results summed across all statements. This produced an aggregate attitudinal score for the brand in each reporting period.

The three predictor variables were related to brand share measures collected by outside agencies. The reporting period for the market share measures had to conform to the survey. Since Nielsen share is reported on a bi-monthly basis, it was used as the dependent variable for the Nestle study. MRCA share is reported on a monthly basis and was used for deodorants and analgesics to insure conformity with the Bristol-Myers reporting cycle. The use of two different brand share reporting systems should not be too disturbing since a recent study demonstrated that where significant share movement occurs, both systems agree closely in measuring shifts in brand share (Assael, 1967).

METHODOLOGY

Time series regressions were run for 13 brands—four brands each for deodorants and analgesics—and five for instant coffee. Because there were 14 to 15 data points, it was decided that no more than three predictor variables should be used in the regressions. Adding more variables would mean an unacceptably sharp reduction in the amount of variance accounted for due to a loss in degrees of freedom.

Two basic sets of time series equations were used in this study: In the first set, attitudes, awareness and usage lead market share by one period. In the second, brand attitudes become the dependent variable and market share, awareness and usage lead attitudes by one period. This formulation raises the familiar question whether attitudes lead or lag behind changes in market share. The findings on this question alone are too voluminous to be dealt with here and will be considered in a later paper.

Three types of time series models were used in predicting market share and brand attitudes: a direct effect model and two types of cumulative effect models. The direct effect model assumes that the effect of the predictor variable on market share is confined to a single time period:

$$MS_{t+1} = a + bAtt_t + U_t \qquad (1.)$$

where MS_{t+1} is market share in period $t+1$, Att_t is brand attitudes in the preceding period, and U_t a random error term. This model was run for the 13 brands using awareness and usage as well as attitudes in predicting brand share. It was also used in the second set of regressions in predicting attitudes by share, awareness and usage in the previous period. Therefore, 78 regressions were run using this model.

The cumulative effects models assume either that the predictor variables "build up" to a change in behavior over several time periods or that there is a delay in the behavioral change because of environmental constraints. The first cumulative effects model is based on the following linear association:

$$MS_{t+1} = a + b_1 Att_t + b_2 Att_{t-1} \ldots + b_{n-1} Att_{t-n} + U_t \qquad (2.)$$

This linear-cumulative model was not run for usage due to data restrictions. It was used to predict share with awareness and attitudes, and to predict attitudes with awareness and brand share for a total of 52 regressions. Only the two immediately prior periods were used in applying this model due to the loss of degrees of freedom after adding more than two periods. Therefore, it differs from the direct effects model only in adding an Att_{t-1} term.

Koyck's distributed lag model was also introduced to account for cumulative effects (Koyck, 1954; Palda, 1964):

$$MS_{t+1} = a + bAtt_t + \lambda MS_t + U_t \qquad (3.)$$

The model assumes that the effects of the predictor variable will be greatest in the period immediately preceding a change in market share. The influence of earlier periods dies away to zero according to a logarithmic decay function with parameter λ. Through this function, the model considers the cumulative effects of all prior periods, whereas the linear-cumulative model only incorporates the two prior periods. It avoids much of the serial correlation ordinarily encountered when successive time periods of the same predictor are used in one equation. It also uses only two degrees of freedom, an important advantage with a limited number of data points. This model was used in predicting share and attitudes with the three predictor variables, for a total of 72 regressions.

In addition to the three basic models, a baseline regression equation was estimated for each of the 13 brands, demonstrating the degree to which changes in market share can be explained by previous share:

$$MS_{t+1} = a + bMS_t + U_t \qquad (4.)$$

This measure represents the simplest extrapolation model. As such, it provides a baseline for appraising the incremental contribution of the intervening variables to the prediction.

Other models were applied to the data as well. Semilog transformations of the predictor variables were run for both the direct effects and Koyck models. This assumes that a large shift in the predictor variable would be required to forecast a change in market share. First differences rather than the absolutes were also run for the direct effects and Koyck model. Finally, these models were applied to a measure of market share in dollars as well as units. These modifications did not appreciably improve the fit of the basic models. Therefore, attention will focus on the ability of the direct effects and distributed lag models to predict brand attitudes and market share in units.

FINDINGS

The predictive relationship of attitudes, awareness and usage to subsequent market share are presented for the 13 brands in Table 1. The adjusted r^2 values (coefficient of multiple determination) represent the percentage variance in market share explained by the particular independent variable. The first set of figures below each r^2 value give the standard error of estimate for each regression equation. Generally, the more variance in market share accounted for by the predictor variables, the lower will be the standard error. This figure is useful in comparing the power of the predictors and the relative fit of the various models within a given brand. Comparisons of standard errors should not be made between brands since the magnitude of the standard error is a function of the size of the brand's market share.

The second set of variables below each r^2 are the Durbin-Watson statistic (d). This measures the degree to which the successive random error terms (U_t) in time series data are independent as regression analysis assumes. The smaller the d value, the greater the serial correlation in the data. Asterisked values indicate the operation of significant serial correlation. (See Malinvard (1966) for a significant table for this statistic and a discussion of the possibility that it may underestimate the extent of serial correlation.)

Table 2 summarizes the results of the analysis by presenting the combination of the predictor and time series model accounting for the largest percentage of explained variance in market share for each brand.

Comparisons can be drawn from the pattern of results within each product class.

Analgesics

A feature of the time series predictions of market share common to all brands in this market is the very limited contribution of trend effects to an understanding of the variance in market share (Table 1A). Practically all of the variance was explained by the intervening variables. Beyond this, there was no pattern in the relative effectiveness of the three models. The direct, linear-cumulative and distributed lag models were each superior in some situations.

In the possible combinations of four brands and three time series models, there were only two instances where awareness and usage explained more variance than attitudes. Attitudes produced the best fit for Brand 3 using the linear-cumulative model. All three models performed well using attitudes for Brand 1. The distributed lag model was most effective in regressing attitudes on market share for Brand 4.

TABLE 1 Per Cent Variance Explained in Predicting Market Share

A. Analgesics

	Brand 1			Brand 2			Brand 3			Brand 4		
	Att.	Aw.	Use	Att.	Aw.	Use	Att.	Aw.	Use	Att.	Aw.	Use
Direct Effects (Equation 1)												
Adj. r^2 (%)	41	6	12	13	0	0	0	0	6	0	0	0
S.E.	1.42	1.82	1.77	1.39	1.50	1.53	.97	.96	.90	1.00	1.03	1.03
D.-W.	1.83	1.05	1.85	1.81	1.77	1.71	2.36	2.35	2.62	1.08	1.31	1.30
Linear-Cumulative (Equation 2)												
Adj. r^2 (%)	43	16	†	7	13	†	17	0	†	0	0	†
S.E.	1.42	1.71	†	1.41	1.37	†	1.00	.94	†	1.04	.99	†
D.-W.	1.86	1.24	†	2.07	2.46	†	2.36	2.46	†	.94*	.95*	†
Distributed Lag (Equation 3)												
Adj. r^2 (%)	38	22	4	4	0	0	0	0	0	24	4	3
S.E.	1.48	1.66	1.83	1.45	1.57	1.60	1.00	1.00	.94	.86	.97	.97
D.-W.	1.95	1.72	2.04	1.65	1.76	1.70	2.24	2.21	2.62	1.81	1.83	1.83
Baseline (Equation 4)	Market Share t-1			Market Share t-1			Market Share t-1			Market Share t-1		
Adj. r^2 (%)		5			0			0			12	
S.E.		1.84			1.54			.96			.93	
D.W.		2.09			1.67			2.24			1.81	

* Significant serial correlation exists in the model: Generally a Durbin-Watson value below 1.00. (A value between 1.00 and 1.50 indicates potential serial correlation.)

† Data not available.

TABLE 1 Per Cent Variance Explained in Predicting Market Share (Continued)

B. Deodorants

	Brand 5			Brand 6			Brand 7			Brand 8		
	Att.	Aw.	Use	Att.	Aw.	Use	Att.	Aw.	Use	Att.	Aw.	Use
Direct Effects *(Equation 1)*												
Adj. r^2 (%)	12	12	0	29	13	0	12	5	0	16	0	0
S.E.	1.91	1.90	2.07	2.54	2.80	3.07	3.48	3.70	3.72	.68	.77	.79
D.-W.	.54*	.60*	.48*	.77*	.42*	.38*	.69*	.61*	.64*	1.10	1.00*	1.00*
Linear-Cumulative *(Equation 2)*												
Adj. r^2 (%)	11	13	†	52	5	†	0	0	†	9	0	†
S.E.	1.91	1.88	†	2.07	2.89	†	3.62	3.60	†	.71	.78	†
D.-W.	.58*	1.12	†	1.16	.45*	†	.72*	.83*	†	1.03	1.03	†
Distributed Lag *(Equation 3)*												
Adj. r^2 (%)	64	60	55	73	63	61	38	39	39	30	12	12
S.E.	1.21	1.29	1.33	1.57	1.80	1.87	2.83	2.81	2.79	.62	.70	.70
D.-W.	1.68	1.99	1.65	2.68	1.45	1.94	1.45	1.65	1.82	1.59	1.93	2.03
Baseline *(Equation 4)*	*Market Share t-1*			*Market Share t-1*			*Market Share t-1*			*Market Share t-1*		
Adj. r^2 (%)	59			65			40			20		
S.E.	1.28			1.79			2.82			.67		
D.-W.	1.64			1.99			1.56			1.93		

* Significant serial correlation exists in the model: Generally a Durbin-Watson value below 1.00. (A value between 1.00 and 1.50 indicates potential serial correlation.)

† Data not available.

TABLE 1 Per Cent Variance Explained in Predicting Market Share (Continued)

C. Instant Coffee

	Brand 9			Brand 10			Brand 11			Brand 12			Brand 13		
	Att.	Aw.	Use	Att.	Aw.	Use	Att.	Aw.	Use	Att.	Aw.	Use	Att.	Aw.	Use
Direct Effects *(Equation 1)*															
Adj. r^2 (%)	17	7	33	74	70	15	26	12	18	36	20	28	28	4	18
S.E.	.46	.53	.42	.23	.22	.52	.74	.81	.78	1.03	1.15	1.08	.32	.37	.34
D.-W.	.92*	.70*	1.44	1.38	1.78	.73*	1.93	1.79	2.18	1.64	1.37	1.49	.92*	.68*	.77*
Linear-Cumulative *(Equation 2)*															
Adj. r^2 (%)	11	2	†	73	68	†	38	11	†	32	13	†	32	15	†
S.E.	.48	.51	†	.29	.31	†	.68	.81	†	1.06	1.19	†	.31	.35	†
D.-W.	.97	.95*	†	1.34	1.82	†	2.32	1.79	†	1.76	1.35	†	1.04	1.28	†
Distributed Lag *(Equation 3)*															
Adj. r^2 (%)	24	14	43	79	84	68	28	23	18	52	44	45	56	54	58
S.E.	.44	.47	.38	.26	.22	.32	.73	.75	.78	.89	.96	.95	.25	.26	.24
D.-W.	1.31	1.47	1.89	1.47	2.45	1.60	1.96	1.79	1.92	2.16	2.07	1.98	1.99	2.10	1.95
Baseline *(Equation 4)*	*Market Share t-1*			*Market Share t-1*			*Market Share t-1*			*Market Share t-1*			*Market Share t-1*		
Adj. r^2 (%)	20			69			15			34			57		
S.E.	.46			.31			.79			1.04			.25		
D.-W.	1.46			1.53			1.47			1.58			2.03		

* Significant serial correlation exists in the model: Generally a Durbin-Watson value below 1.00. (A value between 1.00 and 1.50 indicates potential serial correlation.)

† Data not available.

TABLE 2 Predictor and Model Explaining Most Variance by Brand

	Analgesics			Deodorants			Instant Coffee	
Brand	Predictor	Model	Brand	Predictor	Model	Brand	Predictor	Model
1	Attitudes	Linear-Cumulative or Direct	5	Attitudes	Distributed Lag	9	Usage	Distributed Lag
2	Attitudes Awareness	Direct or Linear-Cumulative	6	Attitudes	Distributed Lag	10	Attitudes or Awareness	Distributed Lag
3	Attitudes	Linear-Cumulative	7	Attitudes Awareness Usage	Distributed Lag or Baseline	11	Attitudes	Linear-Cumulative
4	Attitudes	Distributed Lag	8	Attitudes	Distributed Lag	12	Attitudes	Distributed Lag
						13	Attitudes Awareness Usage	Distributed Lag or Baseline

Deodorants

This market was different from analgesics because of the pronounced trend effects. That is, knowledge of prior share of market explained between 20 per cent and 65 per cent of the variance in subsequent share of market. As a consequence of the strong trend effect, the intervening variables only contributed a moderate improvement in the explained variance. According to Table 3, the average R^2 increased by only 5½ per cent with the addition of attitudes as a predictor.

The distributed lag model consistently produced the most explained variance for all four brands. This contrasts with the more varied performance of the three models for analgesics. Once again, attitudes were the most effective of the intervening variables. In only two of 12 possible situations was awareness or past usage superior to attitudes in explaining variance.

Instant Coffee

The nature of the results in this market generally paralleled those for analgesics and deodorants. There was a significant trend effect for all brands, although it was not as pronounced as in the deodorant market. Again, the most useful intervening variable was attitude. The only exception was Brand 9 where past usage was superior as a predictor whichever model was used. The distributed lag model was superior in explaining variance in all cases except Brand 11.

The general superiority of the distributed lag model using attitudes as a predictor was particularly gratifying because it appeared to eliminate most of the problems of serial correlation. Whereas both the direct effects and the linear-cumulative model failed the Durbin-Watson test on several occasions (particularly in the deodorant market), there were no signs of serial correlation with any of the distributed lag models.

Table 3 summarizes the degree of relationship between the predictors and market share. The average variance and standard error of estimate for each regression model in each product class was determined. An average score was also computed for all three product categories. The closer relationship between attitudes and subsequent market share is clear.

Relation of Predictor Variables to Attitude

Average r^2 values using attitude as the dependent variable and market share, awareness and usage as the independent variables are presented in Table 4. The explained variance was consistently lower than in Table 3. Market share was a much poorer predictor of attitudes than attitudes of market share. On the aggregate level at least, this would tend to support the hypothesis of a hierarchy of effects—attitude change precedes a behavioral change.

The extremely low level of explained variance does not permit any conclusion as to the best predictor of attitude change. Usage provided

TABLE 3 Per Cent Average Variance Explained in Predicting Market Share

	Avg. 3 Products			Analgesics			Deodorants			Instant Coffee		
	Att.	Aw.	Use	Att.	Aw.	Use	Att.	Aw.	Use	Att.	Aw.	Use
Direct Effects												
Adj. r^2 (%)	23.7	11.5	10.0	14.3	1.5	4.5	17.3	7.5	0	36.2	22.6	22.4
S.E.	(1.24)	(1.35)	(1.39)	(1.19)	(1.33)	(1.31)	(2.15)	(2.29)	(2.42)	(.56)	(.62)	(.63)
Linear-Cumulative												
Adj. r^2 (%)	24.2	12.0	†	16.8	7.3	†	18.0	4.5	†	37.2	21.8	†
S.E.	(1.23)	(1.33)	†	(1.21)	(1.25)	†	(2.08)	(2.29)	†	(.56)	(.63)	†
Distributed Lag												
Adj. r^2 (%)	39.2	32.2	30.3	16.5	6.5	1.8	51.5	43.5	41.8	47.8	43.8	46.4
S.E.	(1.04)	(1.11)	(1.13)	(1.19)	(1.30)	(1.34)	(1.56)	(1.65)	(1.67)	(.52)	(.53)	(.52)
Baseline	Market Share t-1			Market Share t-1			Market Share t-1			Market Share t-1		
Adj. r^2 (%)	30.5			4.3			46.0			39.0		
S.E.	(1.13)			(1.32)			(1.64)			(.57)		

† Data not available.

TABLE 4   Per Cent Average Variance Explained in Predicting Attitudes

	Avg. 3 Products			Analgesics			Deodorants			Instant Coffee		
	M.S.	Aw.	Use	M.S.	Aw.	Use	M.S.	Aw.	Use	M.S.	Aw.	Use
Direct Effects												
Adj. r^2 (%)	7.4	4.9	8.6	2.0	1.0	9.8	8.5	0	9.7	10.8	12.0	7.2
S.E.	(1.79)	(1.82)	(1.68)	(2.74)	(2.77)	(2.58)	(2.32)	(2.43)	(2.39)	(.59)	(.57)	(.58)
Linear-Cumulative												
Adj. r^2 (%)	10.2	9.8	†	10.5	5.0	†	7.5	1.0	†	12.2	20.8	†
S.E.	(1.74)	(1.80)	†	(2.58)	(2.72)	†	(2.34)	(2.48)	†	(.59)	(.52)	†
Distributed Lag												
Adj. r^2 (%)	8.5	9.5	10.2	0	6.5	5.2	11.8	4.3	15.7	12.6	16.0	11.0
S.E.	(1.79)	(1.78)	(1.70)	(2.79)	(2.71)	(2.67)	(2.27)	(2.36)	(2.34)	(.59)	(.58)	(.57)
Baseline	Market Share t-1			Market Share t-1			Market Share t-1			Market Share t-1		
Adj. r^2 (%)	5.9			2.0			7.5			7.6		
S.E.	(1.79)			(2.76)			(2.34)			(.58)		

† Data not available.

a marginally better fit for deodorants and awareness for instant coffee. The direct effects of aggregate behavior, awareness and usage do not explain shifts in attitude. Yet the cumulative effects models did not substantially increase the proportion of explained variance. The distributed lag model in particular produced a much higher proportion of explained variance when market share was the dependent variable.

Despite the low average r^2 values, several of the predictors did explain a reasonably high proportion of variance in attitudes for specific brands. Proportion of recent users explained about 25 per cent to 30 per cent of the variance in attitudes for the two leading brands in the deodorant and analgesic categories. Whether the greater attitudinal sensitivity to shifts in recent usage is due to the leading market position of these brands is open to question. Market share provided a good fit with attitudes for two brands in the deodorant and instant coffee categories. Market shares for both brands are low and volatile. Awareness was very closely related to attitudes for one instant coffee brand. Other than these relationships, the predictors contributed little to explaining variance in brand attitudes.

IMPLICATIONS

A number of significant implications have emerged from this study. On the behavioral side, it is apparent that the intervening variables in the purchasing process are important factors in explaining variance in aggregate behavior. Their importance varies by brand and product category. For deodorants, the marginal benefits accruing from measurements of attitudes and awareness—as compared with a straight extrapolation of market share—raise doubts regarding the predictive value of these variables. For analgesics and instant coffee, the cognitive and affective variables are in most cases superior to the extrapolation model. For these latter categories, a marketing information system involving the ongoing collection of data on attitudes and awareness becomes a reasonable investment should a major objective be the prediction of aggregate behavior.

The findings have consistently demonstrated that the affective dimension is significantly more effective in explaining variance in market share than the cognitive or usage dimensions. This would reinforce the importance that marketing analysts are placing on attitudinal analyses. It would also appear to support the proposition in the hierarchy of effects hypothesis that changes in attitudes are more closely related to subsequent behavior change, than are changes in awareness. Further support for this hypothesis is the finding that attitudes predict market share better than market share predicts attitudes. This suggests that attitudinal change precedes rather than follows a behavioral change.

These findings must be accepted with reservation in support of the hierarchy of effects hypothesis since they deal with aggregate data. It is possible that data on the individual level may not support these findings.

On the methodological side, the analysis has shown that generalizations concerning the nature of relationships within a product class can not always be made. For analgesics no single time series model proved superior. There were no consistent findings regarding the operation of direct or cumulative attitudinal effects within any product class.

Moreover, it is apparent that these relationships may be dependent on the relative market position and characteristics of the brands. For example, Brand 1 in the analgesic market was characterized by direct attitudinal effects, and Brand 4 by cumulative effects. Brand 1 is the leading brand with a widely fluctuating share, while Brand 4 is a new entry which has consistently improved its share in recent years. This may suggest the greater likelihood of direct attitudinal effects in volatile market situations; brand switchers may be more quick to translate an attitudinal change to a behavioral change. The consistently strong relationship between previous and current market share in deodorants and instant coffee compared with analgesics further illustrates the importance of product class. In short, predictive models must be built by product and by brand in forecasting changes in aggregate market response.

REFERENCES

Achenbaum, Alvin A. Knowledge Is a Thing Called Measurement. In Lee Adler and Irving Crespi (eds.). *Attitude Research at Sea.* Chicago: American Marketing Association, 1966, pp. 111–126.

Assael, Henry. Comparison of Brand Share Data by Three Reporting Systems. *Journal of Marketing Research,* Vol. 4, No. 4, November 1967, pp. 400–401.

Axelrod, Joel N. Attitude Measures That Predict Purchase. *Journal of Advertising Research,* Vol. 8, No. 1, March 1968, pp. 3–17.

Day, George S. *Buyer Attitudes and Brand Choice Behavior.* New York: The Free Press, 1969 (in press).

Eastlack, J. O. Jr. and Henry Assael. Better Telephone Surveys through Centralized Interviewing. *Journal of Advertising Research,* Vol. 6, No. 1, March 1966, pp. 2–7.

Edwards, Allen L. *Techniques of Attitude Scale Construction.* New York: Appleton-Century-Crofts, 1957.

Koyck, L. M. *Distributed Lags and Investment Analysis.* Amsterdam: North-Holland Publishing Co., 1954.

Malivard, E. *Statistical Methods of Econometrics.* Chicago: Rand McNally, 1966.

Palda, Kristian S. *The Measurement of Cumulative Advertising Effects.* Englewood Cliffs, N.J.: Prentice-Hall, 1964.

Palda, Kristian S. The Hypothesis of a Hierarchy of Effects: A Partial Evaluation. *Journal of Marketing Research,* Vol. 3, No. 1, February 1966, pp. 13–24.

Ramond, Charles K. Must Advertising Communicate to Sell? *Harvard Business Review,* Vol. 43, Sept.–Oct. 1965, pp. 148–161.

Smith, Gail. *A Preliminary Report on the General Motors Advertising Effectiveness Program.* Presented at the 1965 Spring meeting of the Association of National Advertisers.

24. If you think I care, you've got another thing coming

cecil baber

The title of this paper is not just a catchy title thought up for this occasion. Rather, it sums up what the majority of attitude research practitioners are now facing and measuring. My thesis is that practitioners think they are measuring attitudes but they are not.

Because of their skill and intuitive understanding of the marketing process they (the practitioners) are at times predictive. At other times they are not. They are intellectual entrepreneurs, not attitude researchers.

In this paper I will point out six areas of reference on attitude research which should be taken into account by the practicing marketing researcher. To my knowledge these areas are presently being ignored.

This paper is a practitioner's view of these reference points and will have, therefore, all of the misunderstandings inherent in such a presentation. I hope, however, in raising these points, which I imperfectly understand, that it will lead to discussion between academia and the practitioner—and therefore to clarification and, hopefully, to use. My apologies go in advance to the people whose names I will mention in the paper who feel I may have oversimplified or distorted their views.

The six reference points are:

1. What is the implication of Krugman's low-involvement—high-involvement theory for marketing research?
2. Is the Hovland work on persuasion relevant to marketing research?
3. What are the implications of the one-step and two-step theories of communication for the marketing and advertising researcher?
4. Are we ignoring multi dimensions of attitude? This is a problem raised by the work of Rokeach.
5. Where does an attitude scale start or finish? This refers to the works of Sherif and Sherif.
6. How do we cope with bias in attitude research?

KRUGMAN AND LOW INVOLVEMENT—HIGH INVOLVEMENT

Krugman tells us[1,2] that there are many products with which people are barely involved. They just don't care. Of if they care, they just don't care very much.

Now our measurement systems are devised to measure things that people care about. They were developed by psychologists for measur-

Reprinted by permission from Lee Adler and Irving Crespi, eds., *Attitude Research on the Rocks*, 1968, pp. 232–239, published by the American Marketing Association.

ing attitude shift. We marketing researchers are using a tool developed to measure things which are *important to people,* while Krugman tells us that many products (and of necessity this seems to me to be true) are not cared about by most people.

Let us look at this on the theoretical level. Rosenberg and Hovland[3] divide attitude into three component parts: affect, cognition and behavior. They tell us that "an individual's *affective* response toward another individual may be inferred from measures of such physiological variations as blood pressure or galvanic response, but is more typically inferred from verbal statements of how much he likes or dislikes him. Similarly how an individual will *act* toward a given situation may be evaluated by how he does respond when directly confronted with the situation but may also be inferred from what he says he will do in a given situation. *Cognitions* include perceptions, concepts and beliefs about the attitude object and these are usually elicited by verbal questions in printed or oral form."

The authors go on to tell us that "the basic question in studies of attitude dynamics is how, or under what conditions, responses in any or all of these three classes undergo relatively persistent alteration." And it is exactly on this point that Krugman makes his argument. He tells us that of the three dimensions of attitude-affect, cognition and behavior, only the cognition and behavior components become fully involved in "low-involvement" products, with the affective component weakly involved, if at all. Yet, on most occasions what do we marketing and advertising researchers measure? The affect component, that is, the "like-dislike" of a product.

If all of this is true we find ourselves in the uncomfortable position of measuring something that does not exist or, if it exists, is of a negligible value. We tell our clients and our principals all kinds of stories about their products and about how their customers like or dislike them, or how they perceive them, when in reality we have created a distortion of our own convenience, complete with a set of new rules (read statistics) on how to deal with it all.

Unless we are dealing with a high-involvement product, measuring the affect component is irrelevant. The title of this paper seems to sum up the whole point. We think we are measuring someone's caring (like-dislike) but we've got another thing coming. Probably indifference.

HOVLAND AND PERSUASION

The work of the late Carl Hovland and his group at Yale[4, 5, 6] has largely been ignored by practitioners. One of the reasons brought forth to explain this is that we are working in an area where the decay rate (the factor of time) must be taken into account while much of Hovland's measuring is directly after the stimulus. I wish to make the point, however, that much may be still relevant. Critical questions to an advertiser or to a salesman or sales manager are covered in such works as *The Order of Presentation in Persuasion*[4] where the authors are concerned with how to pattern communications in order to alter attitudes. Another published work *Personality and Persuasibility*[6] sought to find personalities or personal characteristics that are susceptible to persuasion. This latter work has in the last year or so become of particular interest to me. When I first came across it, I was interested from an academic or perhaps general point of view. I never realized at the time that it would be particularly relevant in a marketing situation. Since then we have used it as a guide in investigating and communicating to a certain segment of the retail trade—the retail carpet salesman. His characteristics are faithfully outlined in the volume and the work has proved to be not only fascinating but a valuable marketing guide.

A considerable amount of Janis' work[5, 6] was done with time as one of the factors. This part of the work should be reviewed by the advertising researcher.

The persuasion literature, given the initial impetus of the Hovland group, continues to grow. Haskins has been able to follow these new developments and point out their relevance to advertising.[7]

We had best look at the Hovland work again.

WHAT ARE THE IMPLICATIONS OF THE ONE-STEP AND TWO-STEP THEORIES OF COMMUNICATION FOR THE MARKETING AND ADVERTISING RESEARCHER?

Like most practitioners I am unsure of my terms. What I am talking about could perhaps best be termed diffusion theory—or how people learn about new things and then take action.

Up until about 25 years ago we thought that people interacted directly with the mass media and then either took action or did not. This is a sort of atomistic approach, with each man an island unto himself with information beamed directly at him. At about that time the mass communications researchers discovered a strong interaction in the community with a few members of the community whom we have since learned to call "opinion leaders" or "thought leaders." We have found that many products or services (or processes in the case of the agricultural studies) depend on the interaction with the opinion leader.

And when I use the term "opinion leader" here I don't mean the traditional, layman's view which sees the mayor, clergy, and prominent citizenry as that group. I mean that person uncovered for us by the pioneer studies of Lazarsfeld, Katz and Klapper.[8, 9] An "opinion leader" is a person with an extra-ordinary perception of group norms or values who is able to influence that group on a particular subject. These pioneering diffusion researchers have taught us that these people occur in all segments of society and are likely to be an opinion leader on one subject while not on another. We all find similar phenomena in our daily lives. There are those to whom we turn for advice when we wish to purchase a new car or new tires, or to solve a child behavior or cooking problem for us.

So the adoption of many products or processes depends on these people. What are the implications? Enormous, but I would like to discuss briefly only one major point here. Most pre-testing of advertising is done on a sample of a group of logical consumers. If two-step theory is true, then the tester is making a dangerous assumption. He is assuming that his sample's reaction is predictive of the results of the eventual interaction between thought leader and ordinary consumer. It may not be so. Mass communication researchers have taught us that opinion leaders are different. They, contrary to usual consumer behavior, are actively involved in searching out and accepting information on their specialty. They care. The researcher measuring ordinary consumers may be measuring people who care slightly—or *not at all*. He may by accident have one or two opinion leaders in the sample, but their questionnaires, mistakenly I contend, are given the same strength of count as the others.

So what is happening? We find that advertising is being tested on people who, very often, are not the people who will be reading and acting on the information. This "testing on the wrong people" may have a lot to do with the emptiness and "talking down to" of a lot of our advertising. Opinion leaders want information. They actively seek it out. Writing ads for the masses for many products is a mistake—certainly beyond the headline and/or illustration.

Richard Halpern has pointed out to me that a "one-step" theory may be meaningful in low-involvement products. People probably do not discuss these purchases, and interact, if at all, directly with the mass media.

Point: if you are going to pre-test your advertising you should find out quickly whether you have a low—or high—involvement product before designing your test.

ARE WE IGNORING MULTI DIMENSIONS OF ATTITUDE?

Milton Rokeach in an outstanding paper presented to The World Association For Public Opinion Research in Dublin in September 1965[10] explained why most "attitude measurement" does not work. He told us that people have not only an attitude toward an object but an "attitude toward a situation." Translated into marketing terms this might refer to attempting to understand a person and, let us say, toothpaste. Upon understanding the framework—the attitude toward the situation—oral hygiene, we can then try to measure his "attitude" toward individual brands.

Most of us do not do this. An example (among hundreds) of what we marketing researchers are practicing is a comparison of rating scales by Abrams.[11] He discusses various scales that were tested against each other as a predictor for consumer behavior opposite alternate brands of toothpaste and "scouring powder."

I am not criticizing the scales themselves. Certainly the author is ingenious. I would suggest that Rokeach's work implies that the questionnaire could be vastly improved were he to ask the qualifying questions of attitude toward the situation first and then ask his scaling questions and tabulate and interpret within the framework he has established.

In practice this is often hard to do. As clients, we tend to think everyone is as involved with the product as we are and in exactly the same way. The added expense and complexity of the situational questions can seem hard to justify when rigid time and money constraints are presented.

We practitioners are under the gun. We must produce information totally relevant to marketing decision-making. Often, therefore, we lose sight of the forest and start studying trees—our brand versus competitors' rather than the field itself and then—and only then—where we fit.

WHERE DOES AN ATTITUDE SCALE START OR FINISH?

We spend money and time developing scales. Despite this care, the truth is that we do not know where the scale starts, or where it ends. We also assume it is uni-dimensional, but is it? If we ever hope to improve our attitude research we have to start taking into account the common sense (very uncommon so far) of Sherif and Sherif.[12] They tell us that our present techniques lead us to measure only a part of the scale—and furthermore we do not know, as we are presently working, where on the scale we are measuring. They teach us how to understand the totality of the scale. Furthermore they give us an excellent sorting technique which can give us the answer as to whether our product is a low- or high-involvement product.

At Du Pont of Canada we have become extremely conscious of the limitations of our present attitude research especially in the area of anchor points. To improve, we have recently worked on a project with the Marketing Science Institute where we have tried to use their technique termed MAPP to try to understand the consumer's way of perceiving a product field and individual products within that field. Green's paper given at this conference describes the technique. Stephenson's Q technique also appears to accomplish the same end—that of anchor points and height of involvement.

HOW DO WE COPE WITH BIAS IN ATTITUDE RESEARCH?

This may be the one factor in our favor so far. Marketing and advertising research people tend to be highly skilled at probing a market. On the whole, we do not know what we are doing when we try to "research attitudes toward our product." However, our biased inputs and biased feedbacks often lead us to mature conclusions. Sometimes it may be because of our unique position in marketing. We are the only ones paid to listen patiently and watch the marketplace. From this time and money comes a feeling that often is more or less right. I feel best at describing us as intellectual entrepreneurs. If we are really going to make large business decisions on the basis of our present technology as it is practised I have little hope for scientific marketing.

If you doubt my charge of bias I suggest you read the recent book of Rosenthal[13] where he showed how experiments can be biased by the experimenter.

PROGNOSIS

I have tried to show how a few considerations injected into our present "attitude research" could improve it immensely. I can not offer any real gimmick or quick rule that will immediately cure all your ills. Perhaps the closest I can come is to relate one rule of thumb that helps me. James Becknell told me about a fellow named Fishbein whose criteria seem particularly suitable to our work. He asks two questions in either order, "What do you think about it?" and "Is it important to you?" These kinds of considerations matter.

I hope this paper will stimulate dialogue between the practitioner and the practicing theorist and thus narrow the knowledge gap. If nothing else I hope I have alerted you so that next time you come to measure my "attitude" toward your toothpaste or "scouring cleanser" you'll watch out. You think I care—but you've got another thing coming!!

REFERENCES

1. KRUGMAN, H. E., "The Impact of Television Advertising-Learning Without Involvement," *Public Opinion Quarterly,* Fall 1965.
2. KRUGMAN, H. E., "The Measurement of Advertising Involvement," *Public Opinion Quarterly,* Winter 1966–1967.
3. ROSENBERG, M. J., C. I. HOVLAND *et. al., Attitude Organization and Change,* New Haven: Yale University Press, 1960.
4. HOVLAND, C. I., W. MANDELL *et. al., The Order of Presentation in Persuasion,* New Haven: Yale University Press, 1957.
5. HOVLAND, C. I., I. L. JANIS, H. H. KELLEY, *Communication and Persuasion,* New Haven: Yale University Press, 1959.
6. JANIS, I. L., C. I. HOVLAND, *et. al., Personality and Persuasability,* New Haven: Yale University Press, 1959.
7. HASKINS, J., *The Role of the Spokesman in Mass Communications: A Review of the Literature,* U.S. Public Health Service, Injury Control Program, 1967.
8. KATZ, E. AND P. F. LAZARSFELD, *Personal Influence,* Glencoe, Ill.: The Free Press, 1955.
9. KLAPPER, J. T., *The Effects of Mass Communication,* Glencoe, Ill.: The Free Press, 1960.
10. ROKEACH, M., "Attitude Change and Behavior Change," *Public Opinion Quarterly,* Winter 1966–1967.
11. ABRAMS, J., "An Evaluation of Alternative Rating Devices for Consumer Research," *Journal of Marketing Research,* May 1966.
12. SHERIF, C. W., M. SHERIF, R. E. NEBERGALL, *Attitude and Attitude Change,* Philadelphia: W. B. Saunders Co., 1965.
13. ROSENTHAL, M., *Experimenter Effects in Behavioral Research,* New York: Appleton-Century-Crofts Co., 1966.

11 INTENTION: PLANNED PURCHASES

A buyer does some amount of planning, whether short or long term, for most purchases. In some cases this planning is rather casual, and in others, highly detailed. Considerable research has been done on the *intention* construct by product category or even larger groupings (appliances, housing), but not nearly enough on brand choice. Two virtues of intentions data are their generally respectable predictive power and the speed and economy with which they can be collected.

Rothman (1964)* investigates the relative predictive effectiveness for four commonly used measures of likely future purchase behavior. Granbois and Willett (1968)* examine some evidence concerning consumer major durables, considering the prediction of both purchase outcomes and purchase timing. Stapel (1968)* examines the role that advertising can play in affecting intention to buy a given brand.

As the construct is used in Chapter 1, we view *intention* as a set of probability assessments of purchase likelihood attached to each brand of an *evoked set,* obtained by collapsing the relevant *personal* and *situational attitudes* dimensions. Such a conceptualization is considered appropriate for any level of buyer decision-making from extended problem-solving to routinized response behavior. Where the probability assessments attached to each brand are relatively equal, the predictive value of *intention* as it concerns brand choice is correspondingly reduced. This situation may be common in extended problem-solving related to a major durable purchase. At the opposite extreme, perhaps common with routinized response behavior, the probability assessment would be high for a given brand, even approaching unity, suggesting that the purchase of that given brand is almost certain.

The *intention* construct has thus been operationally defined so as to enhance its predictive value in the light of what has been learned from the application of subjective probability intentions measures. The tight linkage between attitudinal dimensions and *intention* serves both theoretical and practical objectives. By this approach, an analysis of why a purchase does or does not take place can be extended back beyond the prepurchase intention measure to the attitudinal dimensions.

This conceptualization of *intention* is appropriate for purchases where some amount of planning has taken place prior to purchase. However, it is well known that buyers make some purchases with no apparent or measurable prepurchase deliberations. Chapter 12 gives the explanations for unplanned purchases.

25. Formulation of an index of propensity to buy

james rothman

We frequently wish to summarize in a single index the various attitudinal elements that exist towards a brand. Such an index should be chosen to suit the purpose for which it is required, most frequently that of measuring an individual's propensity to buy the brand. (To clarify a possible point of confusion it should be emphasized that an index of propensity to buy is not necessarily the same as an index of buying intention.) Such indices of propensity to buy can find application in many fields, such as the continuous measurement of attitudes towards brands, the determination of the characteristics of potential buyers of a product, and the copy testing of advertisements. However, although these indices are so useful and many alternative forms have been proposed and justified on *a priori* grounds, practically no research seems to have been done to assess by empirical techniques the relative effectiveness of different forms of a propensity to buy index. Consequently, pilot research was undertaken to compare the effectiveness of four main alternative methods of measuring propensity to buy.

CRITERIA EMPLOYED

The main criterion employed to assess the relative effectiveness of the different indices was to compare the results suggested by the indices with a behavioral response which could generally be agreed upon to be indicative of a high propensity to buy. One hundred and seventy-two housewives in the Greater London area, in 16 different sampling points, were interviewed, using an age and class quota control. During the course of the interview, scales which, on *a priori* grounds, might be supposed to measure propensity to buy, were administered for two brands in each of two product groups.[1]

After completion of the interviews, the respondents were divided into four matched groups. Each respondent received two letters. Each letter offered to send the respondent a postal order for a sum slightly less than the retail price of the product if the respondent returned a wrapper or box top from it. The letters were allocated to respondents in

Reprinted by permission from *Journal of Marketing Research*, Vol. 1 (May 1964), pp. 22–25, published by the American Marketing Association.

James Rothman is Chairman of Sales Research Services Ltd. Grateful acknowledgement is made to John Bound of Quaker Oats Limited for discussing the semantic differential scales for breakfast cereals. Their final form, however, is the sole responsibility of the author.

[1] The brands and product groups selected were Lux and Camay toilet soap, and two breakfast cereals, Welgar Shredded Wheat and Kelloggs Rice Krispies. These brands are well known in the United Kingdom. The manufacturers of these products were, however, not in any way responsible for this study.

such a way that each received a letter for one brand only in each of the two product groups. By plotting the proportion of respondents who accepted the offers against their propensity to buy them, as shown by each of the alternative indices, it was possible to see whether those who indicated a high propensity to buy the product on a given scale accepted the offer to a greater extent than those who showed a low propensity to buy on that scale.

We hypothesized that the steeper the regression line of proportions accepting the offer against propensity to buy, the better was the performance of that index as an indicator of propensity to buy.

SCALES TESTED

Four alternative scales were tested. These are described below:

1. Self-rating Scale
2. Gift Method
3. Guttman Scale
4. Distance Method

Self-rating Scale

This, the simplest of all scales, was selected because its use in market research questionnaires has frequently been reported. In this method, respondents are shown a card containing the following statements and are asked which one applies to them for each brand:

I *definitely will* buy it
I *probably will* buy it
I *might* buy it
I *probably won't* buy it
I *definitely won't* buy it

Gift Method

The second method is again one whose use has frequently been reported in market research. In this case, however, it was converted from the straight question (which is the normal form) into a scale question. This is the so-called "gift" question, where respondents are told that a draw will be held for a year's supply of the product and are asked to select the brand they would prefer to receive. To convert this into a scale question, we obtained from respondents not only the brand they would most like to have, but also a division of the remainder into brands they would not like to have at all, brands they would prefer not to have, brands they would prefer to have, and brands they would particularly like to have. In this way we were able once again to obtain a rating for each product on a five-point scale.

Guttman Scale

The third method involved the use of a Guttman scale [2, 3], one in which items can be ranked so that a positive response to one item will predict a positive response to any lower item. A Guttman scale of propensity to buy for Welgar Shredded Wheat was constructed, using 7 of an original set of 11 statements. This scale had a coefficient of reproduceability of 0.95, and the same scale was used for all the other brands. The eight positions on the scale were combined into five divisions prior to analysis.

Distance Method

The final method was chosen with some reservations. Though logically appealing, measurement errors could be so great as to overcome its discriminant value. However, it was felt that this decision should be made on the basis of experimental evidence, and so the method was included. The method itself can be called the "distance" method and requires more detailed explanation. Suppose we have a series of products which, in everybody's view, only differ from each other along a single dimension, say, relative sweetness. For each individual we can visualize the existence both of an ideal level of sweetness and an assessment for her of the level of sweetness of each product in the range. It is reasonable to suppose that for a given individual her propensity to buy the different brands will vary with the distance along the sweetness dimension that exists between each product and her ideal brand. This is demonstrated in the diagram below:

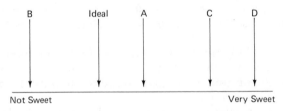

Brand A is the product closest to her ideal on the sweetness dimension, and is therefore the one that she would be most likely to buy, assuming that all prices were equal. Product B is farther away, and therefore her propensity to buy this product ought to be less than that for product A, but should still be relatively high compared with, for example, product D, which is a long way from her ideal. Consequently, we could use these distances as a measure of the individual's propensity to buy.

The same argument holds true for two dimensions, as is illustrated in the following diagram, which could be held to apply to a series of soft drinks which differed only in sweetness and in carbonation. Here however we are faced with a further difficulty. While it is feasible to produce an equal increment scale along the dimension of sweetness, and another equal increment scale along the dimension of carbonation, it is not possible to know whether a unit step along the sweetness scale is equivalent in distance to a unit step along the carbonation scale. To overcome this, experiments can be made employing different sets of weights, respondents can be asked to indicate the relative importance of each scale to them either directly or by means of paired comparisons. Alternately, as was done in this case, it can be assumed

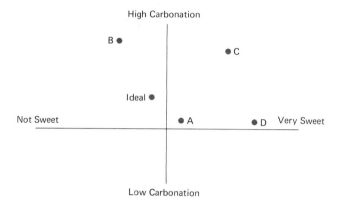

that the average distance between the brand usually bought and the ideal brand along each dimension should be the same. Hence, weights inversely proportional to the average score differences between the ideal and the usual brand can be used.

The true situation, of course, is that for any given product there are not just two dimensions along which they differ from each other, but a multitude of dimensions. One way of measuring the attitudes of people towards products on dimensions such as these is by the use of semantic differential scales, using dimensions which previous research and depth interviews, etc., have shown to be important. Attitudes shown on these scales are usually correlated with each other. To simplify the analysis, therefore, it is usual to extract from these results a number of mutually uncorrelated factors by the method of principal component analysis. These factors can be considered composite scores derived from the original scales, and serve to simplify the analysis and the presentation of results.

Ten five-point semantic differential scales were therefore administered for the brands under consideration. The items used for these scales varied between the two product groups and were selected from previous experience with the products.

Besides measuring attitudes towards the brands under consideration on these scales, we also asked respondents to rate an ideal brand—one that, as stated in the questionnaire, was perfect, in their opinion, from every point of view—in order to assess the position of the ideal brand in the same set of dimensions. Four orthogonal factors (with means of 50 and standard deviations of 10) accounting for the following proportions of the total variance were produced from these scales, using the method of principal component analysis with varimax rotations [1]:

Factors	Toilet soap	Breakfast cereals
1	29%	29%
2	16	11
3	12	11
4	10	11
Total variance explained:	67%	62%

For each respondent, the distances along each dimension between the brands under study and the ideal brand were calculated by the following formula:

$$\mathbf{D}_{ik} = \sqrt{\sum_j w_{jk} d^2_{ijk}}$$

where $\mathbf{D}_{ik}$ is the overall distance for the ith respondent on the kth brand and d_{ijk} is the calculated distance for her of the kth brand from her ideal brand along the jth dimension. Three sets of weights w_{jk} were used:

a. equal weights
b. the most important factor was given a weight of one and the rest of zero
c. the weights chosen for the brands were inversely proportional to the mean distances along the dimensions for their users.

In practice, the distances given by this last set of weights correlated so closely to the distances calculated by the equal weights method that analysis using this third set of weights was not carried any further.

RESULTS

Each measure of propensity to buy was transformed into five positions. These were given scores ranging from 5 for the highest position, down to 1 for the lowest, in each case. The means of these scores for the different brands are summarized in Table 1. Correlations were com-

TABLE 1   Scale Means for Propensity to Buy

Scale	Lux	Camay	Rice Krispies	Shredded Wheat
Self-rating	3.1	2.8	3.2	3.1
Gift	3.0	2.8	3.1	2.8
Guttman	3.0	2.7	3.2	3.3
Distance:				
Equal weights	3.1	2.8	3.0	3.0
Main factor	3.0	2.9	2.9	2.9
Number of interviews	172	172	167	167

puted between the ratings of an individual and her tendency to send things by mail or take advantage of special offers. If such correlations had been found it would have been necessary to re-weight by these characteristics before any further analysis could take place. In fact, no such correlation was found, so re-weighting was not carried out.

Table 2 shows the regression coefficients for the different methods in terms of the change in the percentage accepting the offer per unit change in scale position, calculated from the line of best fit (least squares) for the numbers in the different categories. In other words, these coefficients indicate the steepness of the graph of the percentage

TABLE 2   Regression Coefficients of Percent Returning per Scale Position and Their Significance Levels

Method	Lux	Camay	Rice Krispies	Shredded Wheat	Toilet soap combined	Breakfast cereals combined
Self-rating	3.7	4.3	4.4	4.6	4.0	4.2
	(.16)	(.13)	(.14)	(.11)	(.06)	(.06)
Gift	5.6	6.8	8.4	10.4	6.2	10.0
	(.06)	(.03)	(.03)	(.04)	(.01)	(.0004)
Guttman	0.3	2.2	4.6	5.6	2.3	3.5
	(.47)	(.32)	(.12)	(.09)	(.28)	(.08)
Distance:						
Equal weights	5.6	8.7	1.2	−1.1	5.2	−0.4
	(.07)	(.02)	(.38)	(.61)	(.03)	(.56)
Main factor	*	8.5	−0.5	2.2	4.5	0.8
	(.50)	(.01)	(.55)	(.38)	(.04)	(.38)
Base numbers	86	83	84	83	169	167
Mean proportion accepting offer	53%	52%	58%	46%	53%	52%

* Less than 0.005

accepting the offer against propensity to buy. Below each regression coefficient is shown the probability of obtaining a regression coefficient equal to or greater than this value on the assumption of a normal distribution.

It will be seen from these that, of the first three methods (self-rating scale, gift method and Guttman scale), the gift method gave the steepest slope and, on this criterion, is therefore the best.[2]

In view of our earlier reservations, the performance of the distance methods on the toilet soaps, particularly Camay, is very encouraging. With toilet soaps, the use of equal weights for the different dimensions would appear to be the most satisfactory method at present, though further experimentation could yield useful results. The failure of the distance methods on breakfast cereals requires explanation. Since the distance methods were most successful for Camay, known to be a toilet soap with a very strong image, it may be that the method only operates satisfactorily on brands with strong images, and that the failure for breakfast cereals is due to the greater fuzziness of their images.

Scales of propensity to buy are also of value in determining the attitude toward the brand of those who claim that they do not usually buy it. The sample sizes were too small to enable the non-usual buyers of a brand who were sent the offer to be studied separately. The bases for the combined figures for the two brands of toilet soap and of breakfast cereals were, however, sufficiently large to warrant analysis; see Table 3. It will be clear from Table 3 that, although the slopes in general are less steep for the non-usual buyers, the same pattern is apparent and the superiority of the Gift method is maintained.

FURTHER RESULTS

Other information on the performance of the scales and their inter-relationships is given in Tables 4 and 5, which show the between scale correlation coefficients and the within scale between brand correlation coefficients. It will be seen from Table 4 that all the between scale correlation coefficients are positive but that none is sufficiently high to make it a matter of indifference which of two scales is used. Table 5

---

[2] The poor performance of the Guttman scale method is somewhat disappointing. The scales themselves were quite satisfactory in terms of reproduceability, the coefficients being estimated as follows:

Lux	Camay	Rice Krispies	Shredded Wheat
0.92	0.91	0.96	0.96

The coefficient of reproduceability has, however, been criticised as an estimate of the effectiveness of a scale, as, indeed, has the scaling method itself. On this occasion, at any rate, the criticism would seem to be justified and these results emphasize the importance of employing external validity checks in the development of a scale, instead of merely relying on measures of internal consistency.

TABLE 3   Regression Coefficients and Their Significance Levels for Those Who Did Not Usually Buy the Brand for Which They Were Sent the Offer[a]

Method	Toilet soap combined	Breakfast cereals combined
Self-rating	2.1	−2.3
	(.27)	(.71)
Gift	3.5	8.6
	(.18)	(.02)
Guttman	−3.2	.18
	(.73)	(.48)
Distance:		
Equal weights	3.8	−4.8
	(.18)	(.90)
Main factor	2.4	−0.3
	(.24)	(.53)
Base numbers	113	104
Mean proportion accepting offer	50%	45%

[a] Since both these markets were ones in which one housewife bought more than one brand, respondents were asked to indicate all the brands they usually bought, and non-usual buyers of a brand were defined as those who did not mention the brand in answer to these questions.

shows that for the non-distance scales, scale checking patterns were not a significant factor. The equal weights distance method on the other hand appears to have suffered to some extent from this effect.

FOLLOW-UP SURVEY

Although the postal offer letters sent to the respondent gave no indication of being connected in any way with the earlier interview, it was felt possible that some respondents had decided to accept (reject) the postal offer because they had praised (criticised) it in the earlier interview. In particular, there might have been some confusion in respondents' minds between the gift question and the subsequent postal offer, thus explaining its superior performance. Recall interviews were therefore carried out with half the sample to verify this point, and also to ensure that respondents had not been indulging in any sort of fraud when they accepted the offer. When asked, "Why do you think you were sent the offer?" only 1 out of 86 respondents mentioned the gift question, and when asked, "why did you decide to accept/not to accept the offer?" none of the respondents mentioned the gift question. This supports the hypothesis that respondents did not confuse the postal offer with the gift question.

When asked if they had the product in the house at the time of interview, and if they had bought any more after the offer was received, four respondents in the case of cereals, and two in the case of toilet soap, who accepted the offer claimed that they had the product in the

TABLE 4   Between Scale Within Brand Correlation Coefficients

	Self-rating	Gift	Guttman	Distance	
				Equal weights	Main factor
Lux					
Self-rating	X	0.70	0.62	0.15	0.49
Gift		X	0.70	0.16	0.46
Guttman			X	0.11	0.49
Distance: Equal weights				X	0.47
Main factor					X
Camay					
Self-rating	X	0.67	0.58	0.48	0.52
Gift		X	0.61	0.31	0.48
Guttman			X	0.36	0.65
Distance: Equal weights				X	0.65
Main factor					X
Rice Krispies					
Self-rating	X	0.56	0.62	0.26	0.27
Gift		X	0.63	0.24	0.36
Guttman			X	0.26	0.43
Distance: Equal weights				X	0.57
Main factor					X
Shredded Wheat					
Self-rating	X	0.61	0.75	0.55	0.60
Gift		X	0.62	0.55	0.51
Guttman			X	0.48	0.46
Distance: Equal weights				X	0.68
Main factor					X

house and had not bought any more since. On the other hand, an equal number of respondents in both cases did not take up the offer, although they had the product in the house and *had* bought some more since. It will be seen from this that errors from "cheating" are slight and tend to be compensated by regular purchasers who did not bother to take up the offer. All the respondents who claimed to have accepted the offer and to have bought subsequently were able to provide as supporting evidence details of the place where they made the purchase.

TABLE 5   Between Brand Within Scale Correlation Coefficients

	Lux / Camay	Rice Krispies / Shredded Wheat
Self-rating	*	0.07
Gift	−0.15	−0.06
Guttman	*	0.16
Distance: Equal weights[a]	0.45	0.32

* Less than 0.005

[a] The correlation coefficients for the Distance-Main Factor method were not calculated.

CONCLUSION

The conclusion from the comparison would appear to be that the gift scale method has the greatest likelihood of yielding satisfactory results for a variety of brands and products. There would seem, therefore, to be no reason why this method should not be used in the future as an overall index of attitudes toward brands in place of the self-rating method.

We hope, therefore, to make use of this gift scale method in the future, both in ad hoc surveys and in continuous consumer surveys, and while doing this to obtain further information on the method's validity for other product groups and under other purchasing stimuli than postal offers. We feel, however, that the self-rating method, because of its high correlation with the gift scale method, can still be applied satisfactorily in circumstances where a question offering the opportunity to win a free gift cannot be employed. In addition, the self-rating method would also seem to be a satisfactory second scale where two different scales are required in order to determine attitude shifts.

The results from the distance method are sufficiently encouraging to warrant further development work, particularly for obtaining information about brands which have strong brand images. It may well be, however, that the importance of the distance method will not be so much as a measure of propensity to buy but as a method for estimating in advance the relative effectiveness of different advertising approaches.

REFERENCES

1. HARMAN, HARRY H., *Modern Factor Analysis*, Chicago: University of Chicago Press, 1960.
2. STOUFFER, S. A. and others, "Measurement and Prediction," *Studies in Social Psychology in World War II*, Vol. IV, Princeton: Princeton University Press, 1950.
3. *Attitude Scaling*, London: Market Research Society, 1960.

26. An empirical test of probabilistic intentions and preference models for consumer durables purchasing

donald h. granbois
& ronald p. willett

The instability of demand over time for consumer durable goods has encouraged widespread efforts to learn more about the effects of such determinants as income, credit, household situational factors, and attitudes and expectations, and to fit such variables into predictive models. One important approach to predicting demand for consumer durables has been based on periodic surveys measuring consumer buying intentions. The research reported here relates to a recent innovation in intentions research, the estimation of consumers' subjective probabilities of purchase.[1]

Several of the shortcomings of the usual intentions studies for predictive purposes are concisely stated by Juster in a summary of the findings of cross-section analyses of data yielded by intentions surveys.[2] Most significant here is the conclusion that, although intenders' purchasing rates are always higher than those of non-intenders, they never approach unity. Juster's work has demonstrated the feasibility of asking respondents to estimate on a simple 11-point scale their probabilities of purchase, during a specified future period, for one or more major durable goods. Furthermore, he has shown that such probability estimates provide a better forecast of the purchase rate than data drawn from standard intentions surveys.

We have attempted to study in somewhat greater detail the properties of similar probability estimates dealing with timing, brand, and store aspects of purchases as well as the act of purchase itself. The findings to be reported here are based on data drawn longitudinally from a small panel of families established for this specific purpose.

PROPOSITIONS TESTED

The present study was suggested by a number of recurring decision process questions experienced by the authors. One category of interest

The authors are grateful to the General Electric Company for support of the field work, and to the Indiana University School of Business for research grants during the summer of 1966, which allowed the development of the study.

Reprinted by permission from Robert King, ed., *Marketing and the New Science of Planning*, Proceedings of the 1968 Conference, pp. 401–408, published by the American Marketing Association.

[1] The major developmental work in this area is reported in F. Thomas Juster, *Anticipations and Purchases: An Analysis of Consumer Behavior* (Princeton, N.J.: Princeton University Press, 1964). For an interesting comparison of the results of a standard intentions study and a study of purchase probabilities involving the same households, see F. Thomas Juster, "Consumer Buying Intentions and Purchase Probability: An Experiment in Survey Design," *American Statistical Association Journal* (September, 1966), pp. 658–696.

[2] *Ibid.*

concerned the evolution of brand and store choices, and their relationship with the level of buyers' intentions. An associated question was how deliberation paralleled this decision process. Finally, past research suggested that the acts of choice and the execution of such decisions might be separate processes, subject to different influences.

This paper presents data relevant to the following propositions:

1. Probabilistic estimates of brands and stores to be patronized will more frequently predict purchase outcomes than will probabilistic estimates of purchase timing.
2. The dispersion of an individual's probabilistic estimates of purchase timing, brand, or store alternatives will predict purchase outcomes more frequently than direct measures of the probabilities themselves. In general, high dispersion will be related to high purchase rates.
3. Measures of deliberation, such as shopping, information seeking, and consideration of alternatives, will vary inversely with purchase timing.
4. There will be a mathematically predictable rate at which estimates of the likelihood of purchase will be fulfilled over time.

These propositions are all restricted to the particular group considered here—consumers stating a definite plan to purchase a major durable good within six months.

THE RESEARCH SETTING

During the academic year 1966–67, probabilistic intentions data with respect to timing of purchase, brand, and store were gathered from a panel of 167 Indianapolis households. These families were recruited with a mail instrument designed to identify families expressing a 50 percent or better chance of buying one of a specified list of major durables during the following six months. Only households where both husband and wife were present were included, and households in low-income central city locations were excluded. Husband and wife participated in a joint personal interview at the beginning of the study (Wave 0), and the wife was reinterviewed by telephone every eight weeks until purchase or until four follow-up interviews were completed (Waves 1, 2, 3, and 4). During the course of the study, sixty-two purchases occurred; forty-one couples definitely dropped their purchase plan; and sixty-four had neither purchased nor dropped the plan at the end of the study.[3]

Probabilities were obtained independently from husband and wife during the joint interview, and by telephone from wives during each follow-up interview. The probability scale used the following response set:

---

[3] We have recently conducted a mail follow-up study of the families who had dropped their purchase plan or who had not purchased at the end of the study: 37 additional purchases of the items originally planned were reported. Some of the analysis that follows will utilize these additional data.

10—certain we will
9—
8—very likely we will
7—
6—likely we will
5—
4—some chance we will
3—
2—little chance we will
1—
0—certain we won't

This scale was used for the following variables:

1. The chances of buying the product in question within the following six-month period.
2. The chances of buying in each of the following six months.
3. The chances that the brand bought would be one of those in the respondent's consideration class (determined in a separate question).
4. The chances of buying each of the brands in the consideration class.
5. The chances that the store from which the product would be purchased would be one of those in the respondents' consideration class (determined in a separate question).
6. The chances of buying from each of the stores in the consideration class.

Additional data gathered in the study included various measures of shopping and deliberation, situational factors involved in the planned purchase, and socio-economic characteristics. The present paper will deal with the six probability variables, various measures of deliberation, and the interrelationships between these sets of variables and the outcomes of the panel members' planning processes.

PROBABILISTIC ESTIMATES AND PURCHASE OUTCOMES AND TIMING

Three versions of the probability estimates for both husbands and wives were used as variables: the probability of purchase within the subsequent six months or purchase of a stated brand or store alternative; the highest probability for a single month, brand or store alternative, and the dispersion of probabilities across the alternative months, brands or stores (operationally, the relative dispersion of an individual's probability estimates for alternatives).

Table 1 summarizes the results of tests of the equality of means across purchase categorizations for all three sets of probabilistic estimates. An immediate inference from these data is that our first proposition cannot be supported. Probabilistic estimates of purchase timing were, without exception, significantly different across the outcome subsets of households, and, with the exception of wives' responses, also unequal across the purchase timing subsets of the purchasing

TABLE 1   Composite Results of Test of the Linear Hypothesis for Explanatory Variables Across Purchase Outcome and Timing Categories

	Significance Level of F Test of H_0	
Explanatory Variable	Purchase Outcome* Purchased by Follow Up Wave One, Two, Three or Four, No Purchase, Dropped Purchase Idea (d.f. = 4,162)	Purchase Timing** Purchase by Follow Up Wave One, Two, Three or Four (d.f. = 3,59)
Subjective Probabilities of Purchasing Timing:		
Probability of Purchase Within Subsequent Six Months		
Husband	.01	.01
Wife	.01	.01
Highest Probability for a Subsequent Month		
Husband	.01	.01
Wife	.01	n.s.
Dispersion of Probabilities Across Subsequent Six Months		
Husband	.05	.01
Wife	.025	n.s.
Subjective Probabilities of Purchase of Brands:		
Probability of Purchase of Brand in Consideration Class		
Husband	n.s.	n.s.
Wife	n.s.	n.s.
Highest Probability for Any Brand in Consideration Class		
Husband	n.s.	n.s.
Wife	n.s.	n.s.
Dispersion of Probabilities Across Brands in Consideration Class		
Husband	.05	n.s.
Wife	n.s.	n.s.

	*	**
Subjective Probabilities of Patronage of Stores:		
Probability of Patronage of Store in Consideration Class		
Husband	n.s.	n.s.
Wife	n.s.	n.s.
Highest Probability for Any Store in Consideration Class		
Husband	n.s.	n.s.
Wife	n.s.	n.s.
Dispersion of Probabilities Across Stores in Consideration Class		
Husband	n.s.	n.s.
Wife	n.s.	n.s.
Deliberation Variables:		
Longitudinal Deliberation Index	.01	.01
Sources of Information Overall	.01	.01
Sources of Information at Joint Interview	n.s.	n.s.
Stores Visited Overall	.01	n.s.
Stores Visited at Joint Interview	n.s.	n.s.
Store Visits Overall	.05	n.s.
Store Visits at Joint Interview	n.s.	n.s.
Brands in Consideration Class		
Husband	.01	—
Wife	.05	—
Stores in Consideration Class		
Husband	n.s.	n.s.
Wife	n.s.	n.s.
Months Between Intention and Joint Interview	n.s.	—
Months Between Intention and Purchase	n.s.	—

* Test of H_0 for equality of means of explanatory variables for outcome categories.

** Test of H_0 for equality of means of explanatory variables for timing categories.

households. Only one brand estimate—the dispersion of probabilities across brands considered by the husband—proved to be related to purchase outcomes at an acceptable level. None of the store estimates were sufficiently different across outcomes' subsets to be significant.

The apparent independence from outcomes of probabilistic estimates of brands and stores must be interpreted with caution because of the unusual distributions observed for these variables. Probabilities of purchase of a brand in the consideration class as given by husbands and wives were negatively skewed, with the probabilities .9 and 1.0 accounting for over 43 percent of both parties' responses. Similar patterns were observed for these probabilities for stores. An inference from this set of findings is that a limited number of brand and store alternatives had been defined well in advance of purchase, and respondents were confident that choice would be made from these alternatives. There is no evidence, however, that this confidence served as an indicator of likelihood of purchase.

Dispersion of probabilities across brand and store alternatives also took on an unusual form. This version of the probability variable—reflecting the inequality of odds across alternatives rated by respondents—was bimodally and U-distributed.

In the one instance where there was a significant relationship between dispersion and purchase outcomes (the dispersion of husbands' probabilities across brands in the consideration class), inequality of outcome means apparently occurred because of the disappearance of bimodality and emergence of positive skewness of the dispersion values in the non-purchasing group. We have not fully investigated the polarization of this probability measure for brands and stores as it relates to brand and store choice, but it does not appear to affect or be affected greatly by purchase timing.

TABLE 2   Means of Standard Deviates of Purchase Probabilities for Purchase Waves

Probability Dimension	Means of Standard Deviates of Probabilities*		
	Purchase by Wave 1	Purchase by Wave 2	Purchase by Wave 3 or 4
Probability at Wave 0 of Purchase Within Subsequent Six Months			
Husband	.83	.17	−.20
Wife	.75	.30	−.23
Highest Probability at Wave 0 for any Month of the Six Months			
Husband	.71	.11	−.30
Wife		(not significant)	
Dispersion of Probabilities Across the Six Months at Wave 0			
Husband	.51	−.20	−.32
Wife		(not significant)	

* Means for all husbands or wives equal zero.

Figure 1 demonstrates graphically the significant relationship between chances of purchase and purchase outcomes. Standard deviates
(X–X/S.D.) of chances of purchase within the next six months as estimated by husbands and wives during the joint interview show quite
similar relationships with purchase outcome. Purchasers systematically gave higher probability estimates than non-purchasers, and dropouts were evenly distributed among the probability categories.

Table 2 presents further evidence that the subjective probabilities
with respect to purchase timing were strongly related to purchase
outcomes. Standard deviates were computed for three versions of this
variable for both husbands and wives: the probability of purchase
within the subsequent six months, the highest probability for a single
subsequent month, and the dispersion of probabilities across the subsequent six months. Scores were consistently highest for early (Wave

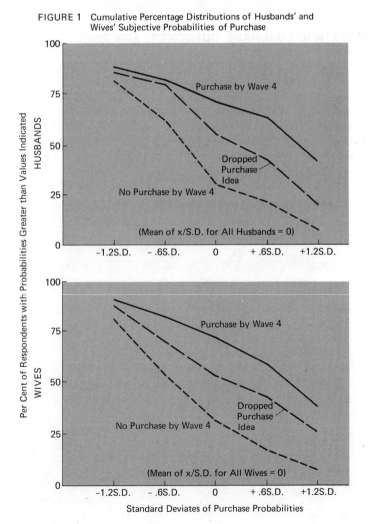

FIGURE 1   Cumulative Percentage Distributions of Husbands' and
Wives' Subjective Probabilities of Purchase

1) purchasers; somewhat lower for later (Wave 2) purchasers; and lowest for purchasers at Wave 3 or Wave 4.

Dispersion of probabilities across the subsequent six months for which probability estimates were taken at Wave 0 was significantly related to purchase outcomes, but was most interesting as it related to purchase timing. The mean of standard deviates of dispersion for husbands where purchase occurred by Wave 1 was isolated from the means for Wave 2, 3, and 4 purchasers which were similar (Table 2). It would appear that the dispersion measure as an indicator of purchase timing is operative only within weeks of purchase, although the evidence available is hardly definitive. Thus, although dispersion is related to propensity to buy, our second proposition—suggesting that dispersion of an individual's probabilities will predict purchase outcomes and timing—cannot be supported.

DELIBERATION, PURCHASE OUTCOMES, AND PURCHASE TIMING

Similar analysis of variance testing of the deliberation variables resulted in clear evidence that families purchasing between the joint interview and the first follow-up interview engaged in less intensive search and deliberation than did those purchasing later (Figure 2). Deliberation here is an index based on length of planning period, number of family discussions, number of contacts with information sources (stores, other people, printed material, and attention paid to

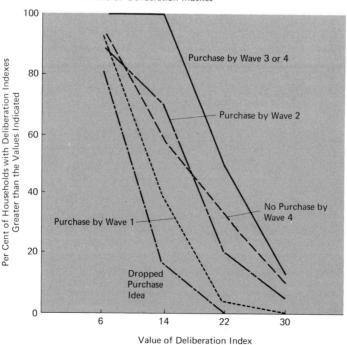

FIGURE 2 Cumulative Percentage Distribution of Households' Deliberation Indexes

Purchase by Wave 3 or 4

Purchase by Wave 2

No Purchase by Wave 4

Purchase by Wave 1

Dropped Purchase Idea

Per Cent of Households with Deliberation Indexes Greater than the Values Indicated

Value of Deliberation Index

price, different brands, and product features).[4] The deliberation index, number of sources used overall, and number of stores visited overall all rose over the three time intervals of purchase (See Table 3). The alternative explanation—that families varied systematically in deliberation before the first interview occurred—is refuted by the lack of significant differences among families in number of sources, stores, and visits that had occurred at the time of the joint interview. Furthermore, no significant differences existed among the various purchase outcome groups in terms of the number of months between their first intention of purchase (determined by a retrospective question in the joint interview) and the joint interview, or between their first intention of purchase and purchase itself. These findings offer substantial support for proposition three.

Market dropouts were not distinguishable from other families in terms of their degree of deliberation (number of sources, stores, or visits) at the time of the joint interview. They did engage in significantly less deliberation after the joint interview, as measured by the deliberation index, number of stores, and number of visits. Interestingly, before dropping their plans, these families had consulted about as many sources of information overall as did early buyers, suggesting that they had consulted other people, printed materials, and other sources before deciding to drop their purchase plan.

Respondents who had not purchased by the end of the study exhibited an interesting characteristic. In terms of overall deliberation (the deliberation index and total number of sources consulted), this group showed quite high deliberation, similar to that of later purchasers. This relatively high deliberation apparently involved sources other than stores, since the mean number of stores and visits was relatively low for the group. The conclusion suggested by both the market dropout and the non-purchase groups is that actual shopping through visits is a necessary (and often final) part of the deliberation process which non-purchasers do not often perform.

Both husbands and wives in the non-purchase group listed significantly more brands in their consideration class at the time of the joint interview than did either purchasers or market dropouts. In a sense, number of brands considered seemed to serve as an index of "nearness to purchase," the fewer brands considered, the more likely purchase was to occur. However, market dropouts were not distinguishable from purchasers in terms of the number of brands in their consideration class.

PREDICTING PURCHASE OUTCOMES

Individually, four variables (two probabilistic purchase timing estimates and two deliberation variables) appeared to be superior in

---

[4] This index follows very closely that developed by Katona and Mueller. See George Katona and Eva Mueller, "A Study of Purchase Decisions," in Lincoln Clark (ed.) *The Dynamics of Consumer Reaction. Consumer Behavior*, Vol. 1. (New York: New York University Press, 1954), pp. 30–87.

TABLE 3   Means of Selected Deliberation Variables for Purchase Outcomes and Purchase Waves

Deliberation Variables	Means by Purchase Outcomes				
	Purchase by Wave 1	Purchase by Wave 2	Purchase by Wave 3 or 4	No Purchase by Wave 4	Dropped Idea
Longitudinal Deliberation Index	13.4	16.8	22.2	18.4	10.4
Total Number of Sources of Information	2.9	4.7	5.6	5.3	3.0
Total Number of Stores Visited	4.5	4.8	5.7	3.3	2.5
Total Number of Store Visits	7.6	9.6	8.9	5.5	4.9
Number of Brands in Consideration Class at Wave 0, Husband	1.9	1.7	2.0	2.8	1.8
Number of Brands in Combination Class at Wave 0, Wife	2.2	1.8	2.2	2.4	.16

consistently differentiating among the groups of respondents who experienced different purchase outcomes. The four variables and their respective F ratios were:

1. Husband probability at Wave 0 of purchase within subsequent six months, $F = 12.2$
2. Deliberation index, $F = 10.3$
3. Wife probability at Wave 0 of purchase within subsequent six months, $F = 9.2$
4. Number of brands in the husband's consideration class, $F = 8.7$

Further, with the exception of the interrelationship of husband and wife probabilities ($r = .70$), correlations between the variables were low, suggesting the possibility that each variable was making an independent contribution to the determination of purchase outcomes. We tested this possibility by conducting linear discriminant analyses of both purchase outcomes and purchase timing, and a multiple correlation analysis of purchase timing.

Classifications resulting from the four variable discriminant functions appear in Table 4.[5] The function relating the four explanatory variables to purchase outcomes appears to have successfully discriminated among those households really intending to purchase and

TABLE 4   Four Variable* Linear Discriminant Analysis of Purchase Outcomes

Actual Purchase Outcome	Percentage Classification of Cases by Discriminant Functions			
	Purchase Within 6 Mo. of Wave 0	Purchase Within 7–21 Mo. of Wave 0	No Purchase Within 21 Mo. of Wave 0	Total Cases
	(Purchase Outcome Test)			
Purchase Within 21 Mo. of Wave 0	(	94.9	)	5.1	100.0
No Purchase Within 21 Mo. of Wave 0	(	13.2	)	86.8	100.0
	(Purchase Timing Test)			
Purchase Within 6 Mo. of Wave 0	75.9	24.1	—	100.0
Purchase Within 7–21 Mo. of Wave 0	34.1	65.9	—	100.0

* Variables included (and their F ratios from a test of the linear hypothesis of equality of group means) are:

1. Husband probability of purchase at Wave 0, $F = 12.2$
2. Deliberation index, $F = 10.3$
3. Wife probability of purchase at Wave 0, $F = 9.2$
4. Number of brands in consideration class, husband, $F = 8.7$

---

[5] These analyses include the additional 37 households completing purchase between Wave 4 and our recent follow-up study.

those whose intentions were marginal. Overall, the first discriminant function misclassified only seven percent of all cases. Analysis of the standardized coefficients of the function suggests that two variables, husbands' probabilities and numbers of brands considered by husbands, were the principal contributors to the classifications.

The four variables proved to be less successful predictors of even a crude categorization of purchase-timing, distinguishing households purchasing within six months of Wave 0 and those purchasing later. On this test, the discriminant function misclassified 28 percent of the cases. Husbands' estimates of the probability of purchase was the most influential variable in determining case classifications. Both of the above discriminant analyses must at this point be used provisionally, as we have not yet subjected them to further tests of predictive power.[6]

A second test of the concomitance of the four variables and purchase timing was conducted using as the dependent variable the number of months between the Wave 0 interview and the time of purchase. Multiple correlation analysis of these variables produced an explained variance of 21.2 percent ($R = .460$), of which 18.8 percentage points were contributed by two variables, husband probabilities and number of brands in the husband's consideration class. The multiple correlation coefficient of .460 (and standard error of 5.3 months) cannot be considered to be evidence of a good fit between the explanatory variables and purchase timing.

AGGREGATE RATES OF PURCHASE TIMING

While the outcomes of the multivariate analyses of purchase timing were not impressive, a final proposition was tested: that aggregate purchases—given the minimum probabilities of purchase required for entering the study—would accumulate systematically over time. To test this, the cumulative percentage of households purchasing by month after Wave 0 was fitted with an exponential growth curve of the form $Y_c = A + BR^x$. The result of this analysis, appearing in Figure 3, was a close fit of the modified exponential $Y_c = 67.73 - 51.19 \times .9197^x$ to the actual data. (The sum of squares around the curve was 6.5 percent of the total sum of squares around Y.)

Further analysis of the residuals around the curve suggests that they may be due to autocorrelation in the form of seasonality, giving additional credence to the calculated fit. Thus, there is some support for the fourth proposition, at least as it relates to the specific group of households studied. Only replication of the study will determine whether this fit is merely idiosyncratic of the group investigated.

---

[6] Additional tests to be applied to these functions include those suggested in R. E. Frank, W. F. Massy, D. G. Morrison, "Bias in Multiple Discriminant Analysis," *Journal of Marketing Research* (August, 1965), pp. 250–258.

FIGURE 3   Exponential Growth of Cumulative Proportion of Households Purchasing After
the Joint (Wave 0) Interview

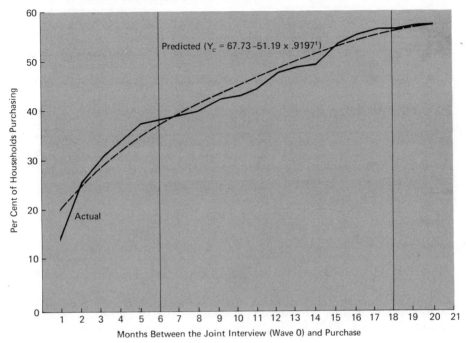

27. Predictive attitudes   jan stapel

A general theme of this conference deals with qualities and quantities. A conflict between qualities and quantities has been suggested by some. Is that a realistic view of things as they really are? "Qualitative" and "quantitative" are not the same for different people and things.

Let us take, as an example, some object uniquely qualitative, like a work of art, say a painting by a Dutch master like Rembrandt van Rijn or Vincent Van Gogh. It is well nigh impossible to put its unique qualities in words, let alone figures. But wait a minute: Does not this depend entirely on the way one looks at it? How does a frame-maker look at a Rembrandt or a Van Gogh? He is mainly interested in height and width. To a frame-maker, a masterpiece may be nothing but a set of inches.

And what about the marketing man in an art dealer's company? His main concern is about how to fetch the highest price. The frame-measurements reveal very little about the quality of the work of art. But the price does. It measures the quality as perceived and evaluated by the highest bidder in an auction, a likely retail outlet to be used for a Rembrandt or a Van Gogh.

Now one can put—and this has actually been done—a Rembrandt or a Van Gogh picture into an advertisement. The work of art thus becomes Art Work. The painting remains the same but its measurements take on a new meaning. The layout now takes the place of the frame-maker and the problem might be: Does it leave enough room for head-line and body copy in a full-page ad?

The marketing and advertising people now involved also look at works of art from another angle. Suppose Rembrandt's picture of the young Jewish Bride is put into a hope chest ad and Van Gogh's Potato-Eaters in ads selling potato chips. The advertisers involved would likely be concerned about readership (as measured by Daniel Starch, for instance), and recall (as measured by Gallup and Robinson). They would be highly interested in incremental sales of hope chests as a result of featuring Rembrandt's little bride. They would also like to know how many people, how often, were buying a certain brand of potato-chips as a result of featuring a Van Gogh in an advertising campaign.

What I am trying to say is that in research about what happens in marketing communications or in the market place the concern usually is not with unique qualities of objects but with attitudes toward and behavior about them.

Reprinted by permission from Lee Adler and Irving Crespi, eds., *Attitude Research on the Rocks*, 1968, pp. 96–115, published by the American Marketing Association.

SUMMARY ATTITUDE MEASURES

In one way of measuring such attitudes, the way that concentrates on the open-ended, more or less unstructured approaches, large quantities of verbal reactions can be gotten out of respondents. It is terribly difficult to read from such relatively unstructured verbiage unequivocal signals saying people will actually do something (like buying) or not. It is, in other words, hard to *sum up* qualitative research data in terms of clearly defined attitudes and likely behavior of respondents. There is nothing unnatural or artificial about that. People have to sum up every day, for practically every action they take. People have to sum up for buying decisions and brand choices. They have to take a stand about issues. They have to make up their minds constantly. (That's what minds are for.)

TELEVISION REDIFFUSION

The first case I am going to cite deals with consumers making up their minds about something with many more aspects and dimensions (though perhaps less cultural qualities) than a Rembrandt or a Van Gogh. It is about television-broadcasts, television from many stations, including some located abroad, piped into the home.

Before the Dutch equivalent of the Bell Telephone Company test marketed a new service (television rediffusion) in one small area of the city of The Hague, Holland, NIPO [Netherlands Institute of Public Opinion] was asked to test the concept, study attitudes and to estimate the number of future buyers.

The "pay off"-item in our interviews was a verbal buying intention scale[1]: Responses are shown in Table 1 together with two sets of figures:

TABLE 1

	(a) Sampling September 1963	(b) Percent of each reply-category having bought by end of year
	%	
Will certainly buy TV-rediffusion	19	64%
Very likely buy	27	39%
Probably, probably not, don't know	45	34%
Certainly not	9	5%
	(100)	

a. The results from sampling before the actual launching of the new rediffusion-service.
b. The results of checking subscriptions (four months after the sur-

vey) ordered by respondents after TV-rediffusion had been introduced.

The percentages show how many in each category had actually bought TV-rediffusion.

Although the respondent cannot have realised it at the time of the interview, those saying they would certainly buy TV-rediffusion in actual fact indicated a likelihood of doing so of 60%. People who said they would very likely buy indicated a likelihood of actual buying behavior of four out of ten, etc.

LIKELIHOOD OF BUYING A CAR

In February of 1966 we interviewed a nation-wide sample about buying plans for automobiles (new and used cars). We did not use a verbal buying intention scale but were once again testing a "percent chance" or "likelihood scale,"[1] asking:

> "Will you indicate how big you yourself estimate the chance of someone in this family buying a car, either new or used, *this year?* What percent chance?"

Results are shown in Table 2. The first column of figures are reply-

TABLE 2

Likelihood of BUYING a motor car, new or second hand	Original sample February 1966	Re-interviewing early in 1967, figures of re-interviewed respondents only
	%	
100% (One hundred percent sure)	3,9	79% of these had actually bought
90% (Almost certain)	1,7	
80% (Very big chance)	1,7	
70% (Big chance)	1,7	48% had bought
60% (Not so big a chance)	1,3	
50% (About even)	4,1	36% had bought
40% (Smaller chance)	0,4	
30% (Small chance)	2,8	
20% (Very small chance)	2,2	14% had bought
10% (Almost certainly not)	6,1	
0 (Certainly not)	58	
Nothing indicated	16	Not re-interviewed

marginals. The second column gives the percent of respondents who actually had bought a car since February, 1966, when re-interviewed early in 1967. (71% of respondents indicating a 10%-chance or higher have been re-interviewed.)

In both cases cited above respondents were asked to take a stand about their intention or likelihood to buy something. I use "taking a stand" advisedly. It is the way Sherif, Sherif and Nebergall talk about attitudes.[2]

The before and after-data also show that verbal behavior in the first wave of interviews definitely showed "predispositions to behave in specific ways to specific stimuli," as Crespi has defined attitudes[3]. If one agrees with Crespi's definition it necessarily follows that attitudes are *predictors* of future behavior. (Attitudes of course also help explain why specific behavior occurred in specific situations or in reaction to specific stimuli *after the event.* But if that is true, then again the attitude would have been predictive if it had been known *before* the event.)

An attitude as measured *only* by a buying intention question or likelihood-of purchases-scale does not help very much in explaining backgrounds or motives. Other interview observations of verbal behavior are needed to sort of see "the whole picture," or what we hope it is. But a pay off-item, whether voting intention or a simulated purchase for instance, is terribly useful in getting down to earth and to put a hard backbone of quantities into a conglomerate of qualitative data and insights.

We are not saying the softer element isn't extremely useful or necessary, but we will concentrate, in this paper, on the hardest sort of quantitative attitude data.

"ORDER COUPONS"

Illustrative of such data are those shown in Table 3, taken from a small

TABLE 3

(Respondents) Agreeing to statement:	Sample of 115 housewives after "forced exposure"	Control group of 120 cases, no exposure to ad
(a) You are sure you'll never buy AJAX	22	47
(b) You don't yet know whether you will ever buy AJAX	13	16
(c) You will probably buy AJAX before long	31	24
(d) You are certainly going to buy AJAX within a short time (OF WHICH:)	37 (31%)	13 (11%)
(e) You want me to send your name and address to the manufacturer so that they can send you a bottle of AJAX right away. Payment of f 1.45 at delivery	(15) (13%)	(2) (2%)
No reply	12	20
	(115)	(120)

advertising pre-test of an AJAX (print) advertisement featuring the internationally known "white tornado."

More interesting even than seeing forced exposure to a good ad producing attitude-change (31% "certainly buy" as against 11% amongst non-exposed matched sample) is that 13% of the exposed and

2% of the non-exposed respondents ordered a 40 cent-bottle of **AJAX** then and there even as **AJAX** was getting considerable distribution at the retail level. These housewives "validated" their verbal behavior with an actual purchase.

PLEASE DISCUSS TRADE-IN

Earlier this year we conducted an attitude study in one of the Scandinavian countries, interviewing 363 car owners. Questioning about one new model produced the replies that appear in Table 4.

TABLE 4

Respondents saying:	
I am certainly going to buy this car	4%
This car greatly interests me: I will probably buy one in the future	13%
This car interests me: I may think of buying one	30%
I am somewhat interested in this car, but I do not think I will ever buy it	25%
	(72)
I am not at all interested in this car	28%
	(100%)

Registering the reactions to this interest-scale was then followed by questioning about whether respondents would like their *name and address* to be given our client for any of the following purposes. The results of this questioning are shown in Table 5.

TABLE 5

Sending of brochure about new model by car company	33%	said yes and allowed address to be taken down for that purpose
Have dealer telephone as soon as new model in showroom	2%	said yes, gave telephone-number
Have dealer contact respondent for test drive	3%	said yes
Have salesman come to house to discuss trade-in car presently owned for new model	4%	Yes
	42%	
Showed interest (Table 4) but did not want any of the above	30%	
	(72)	
Not interested in this car (see Table 4), no action to be taken	28%	
	(100%)	

The 72% with some degree of interest (Table 4) produced 42% (almost six out of ten) who welcomed some form of sales activity and cooperated in allowing address and telephone-number to be relayed to the client.

"Taking a stand" about buying behavior can be considered both as the attitude towards buying a given object as well as the action related *summing up* of attitudes (preceding or underlying) towards the object.

With some luck an overall attitude, simply measured, turns out to be closely related to overt behavior. Here are two such cases.

SELLING CHOCOLATE BARS

In one study in another European market one sample tasted a new product (since then successfully launched) in a blank wrapper. In another monadic test a carefully matched sample tasted the biggest selling competitive product (a 10 cent chocolate bar) also in a blank wrapper.

The taste judgements on the "Stapel scale" are reported in Table 6.

TABLE 6   (Combined Results from Samples of Children, Women and Men)

Taste	New product	Main competitive product
	%	%
+ ☐	25	30
☐	18	18
☐	14	14
☐	5	5
☐	5½	3½
■	1½	3
■	½	1
■	3	1½
■	2	1½
− ■	1	—
Don't know	24½	22½
	(100)	(100)

After more questioning (in which we found out the major taste elements that made for high ratings) all respondents were queried about buying intentions with an order coupon-possibility of getting delivery before actual launching of the product. (Table 7)

Not surprisingly 65% of all order coupons for the new product came from those who rated the taste in the top white box (Table 6) and the same was true for 52% of all order coupons for the (anonymously wrapped) competitive chocolate bar.

TASTE (IN A 10 C.-CHOCOLATE BAR) EQUALS "INTERESTINGNESS" IN PRINT ADS

Amongst many experimental studies in post-and pre-testing of advertisements the following one may be of some interest. Respondents in

TABLE 7

	Respondents who tasted new product	Respondents who tasted competitive product (blank wrapper)
	%	%
Ordered direct delivery, gave name and address	5	6½
Said they would certainly buy as soon as in stores	23	25½
	(28)	(32)
Would probably buy	60	58
Would never buy	10	8
No answer	2	2
	(100)	(100)

one of NIPO's regular IMPACT-surveys of print advertising were, at the very end of the interview, asked to go through the magazine once more and rate how *interesting* or *uninteresting* they found the advertisements. (All 34 ads were post-tested.)

Recall (before looking in the book) and recognition had been established beforehand. The average recall and recognition scores of the 34 ads for each of the *interestingness*-ratings are given in Table 8.

TABLE 8   (Impact Survey Nr 424 "Margriet" magazine of April 22, 1967)

Interestingness of advertisement	Average Recall	Average recognition claiming ad Read
	%	%
+ ☐ (100%)	22½	44½
☐	13	32½
☐	8½	28
☐	7	24
☐	5	18
■	4	14½
■	6½	14
■	4½	14
■	5½	14
− ■	3	6

The reading behavior and the recall levels appear to be pretty closely related to readers' attitudes about the interestingness of advertisements. This tells a thing or two about what to do for getting readership and recall although unfortunately not how to do it.

SCALES IN TERMS OF MONEY

There is another way of expressing an attitude. Whilst the yes or no about buying is akin to what happens in the market place the following line of questioning is modelled on what takes place in the auction room. The following question was asked during a survey a short while before the introduction of color television in The Netherlands.

"Now about the price of color television sets. What do you think a new color TV-set (with a 59 cm tube) may cost? Would it be worth Dfl. 3,750 to you? Would it be worth Dfl. 3,300 to you? Dfl. 2,900 etc.?"

Table 9 shows the distribution of answers to this question.

TABLE 9   Color TV-set would be worth to respondent:

63%	Dfl. 1,150 or more
45	Dfl. 1,300 or more
38	Dfl. 1,450 or more
21	Dfl. 1,700 or more
14	Dfl. 1,950 or more
7	Dfl. 2,200 or more
4	Dfl. 2,500 or more
2	Dfl. 2,900 or more
1	Dfl. 3,300 or more
1	Dfl. 3,750 or more
(37%	Not worth Dfl. 1,150 or D.K.)
(1 $ US = Dfl. 3.60)	

This distribution (see Graph 1) is of a well known type. So, remark-

GRAPH 1 Willing to Pay for Color TV Set

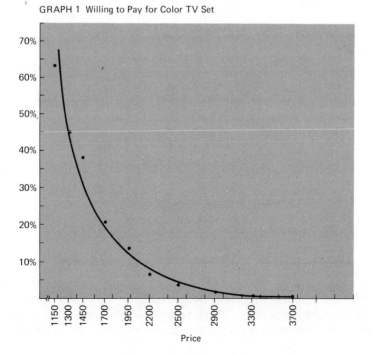

ably enough, is the frequency distribution of replies to the following question from a survey on development aid (Graph 2 and Table 10).

"Aid to underdeveloped nations cost money. Would you be willing to give a financial contribution, for example once a year? How many guilders a year are you prepared to give?"

GRAPH 2   Development Aid (p. annum)

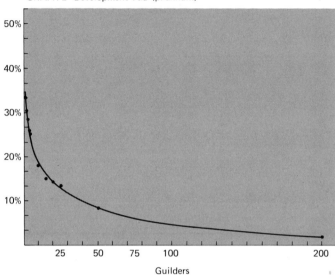

Guilders

TABLE 10   Development aid. Willing to pay per year:

57%	Nothing and no answer
43%	One guilder or more
40½	Two guilders or more
39	3 guilders or more
36	4 guilders or more
35½	5 guilders or more
28	10 guilders or more
15	15 guilders or more
14½	20 guilders or more
14	25 guilders or more
8	50 guilders or more
5	100 guilders or more
2	200 guilders or more

Both Tables 9 and 10 show perfect scales, the sequence in which respondents have ordered themselves is a very neat one. Parenthetically in this line of questioning respondents rank themselves as it were on a ratio-scale, which is a rare enough phenomenon in social research.
    Interesting vistas would seem to open up when we cross tab the amounts of money "promised" over the replies to a preceding question,

viz. the Stapel scale-ratings about development aid in the same survey. (Table 11)

TABLE 11   Question: "This question is about aid to underdeveloped countries. How do you feel about giving such aid by this country? Will you indicate your feeling on this scale? The more favourable your judgment the higher the white square you point out. The more unfavourable your opinion the lower the black square you point out."

	Question of Table 10		Other question same survey
	Mentioning one guilder or more	Mentioning Dfl. 25 or more	In favour of paying higher income tax for development aid
	%	%	%
+ □ (100%)	59½	21	44
□	51	17	28
□	50	13	18
□	44	9	14
□	42½	11½	16
■	32		
■	31		
■	28	10	12
■	12		
– ■	—		

"This question is about aid to underdeveloped countries. How do you feel about giving such aid by this country? Will you indicate your feeling on this scale? The more favorable your judgment the higher the white square you point out. The more unfavorably your opinion the lower the black square you point out."

(As in Table 8 percentages of actual behavior or "promises" of behavior seem to go up in fairly regular, sometimes exponential patterns along the seemingly equi-distant Stapel scale-positions.)

While these and some other first findings of a similar nature need a lot more experimentation and analysis, one summing up of the findings presented here seems pretty safe:

The more the attitudes checked are in the nature of summing up (like taste, "interestingness" of ads, overall quality) the closer they tend to be related to relevant behavior.

The more attitudes investigated deal with doing something about the object, paying a price for it, buying it (rather than the object "an und fur sich" as the Germans so beautifully put it) the closer one gets to *summing up* of perhaps conflicting attitudes and by the same token the closer one gets to what is likely to happen in the market place.

If one can agree with this there is an obvious moral: Always investigate *summing up*-type attitudes, if one possibly can.

TV-SPOT CHANGES ATTITUDES

NIPO has been doing just that for several years now in its regular post-testing of advertising. From our first IMPACT post-test of television advertising in The Netherlands come these data about a 30 second spot of FUZ washing powder (Procter & Gamble).

426 housewives in TV-owning families were interviewed whether they had looked on the evening of January 2, 1967 (the first day of Dutch TV advertising).

195 (46%) had been looking at the three minute break for advertising (at 8:15 p.m.) in which the FUZ-spot had been shown.

All respondents were questioned about their using FUZ (and all other (some 30) brands and products advertised) before the TV-programs were discussed. Most were *non*-users of FUZ. All non-users were asked to indicate whether they thought they would certainly or probably buy FUZ in the near future. The likely future users of FUZ numbered 6% amongst the non-users who had not looked at TV at 8:15 p.m. and 25% amongst the non-users who had looked and could recall and correctly play back the FUZ-commercial. The 19% difference is significant at the 0.05 level of confidence. ($X^2 = 5.55$)

This allows us to state that looking at the FUZ-spot with enough interest to play back its content some 20 hours later does produce a positive change in the attitude about buying the product even if only from unawareness to awareness and "let's try this once."

SUMMARY

As data reported earlier in this paper (and quite a few similar NIPO-studies) have shown, verbal indications of likely buying behavior tend to be valid indications of actual purchasing. That is why this intent-to-buy feature has become a standard element in all of our advertising post-testing and many of our pre-test activities.

Amongst all the qualitative data advertising post-tests produce (such as content of recall, feelings about it, type of interest aroused, etc.) the direct measurement of buying attitudes (amongst non-users) puts up a useful quantitative framework.

Qualitative data provide the useful insights, a sense of understanding of *how* and *why* something happens as it does. Quantitative data of the "pay off" kind tell *what* happens or is likely to happen.

REFERENCES

1. An almost identical device has been described by F. T. Juster, "Consumer Buying Intentions and Purchase Probability," *Journal of the American Statistical Association*, September 1966.
2. SHERIF, C. W., M. SHERIF AND R. E. NEBERGALL, *Attitude and Attitude Change*, Philadelphia: W. B. Saunders Co., 1965.
3. CRESPI, I., "The Challenge to Attitude Research," *Attitude Research at Sea*, eds. L. Adler & I. Crespi, Chicago: American Marketing Association, 1966.

12 UNPLANNED PURCHASES

For many purchases we make, particularly those that involve routinized response behavior, little if any deliberation immediately precedes the purchase. However, the term "impulse purchase" is somewhat misleading in its connotation if one concludes that such behavior is necessarily irrational. After all, there are certain purchase opportunities for which immediate action involving little or no hesitation merely amounts to prudent economy of motion. Such behavior may only represent purchases deferred until a more convenient time. Thus, in this chapter we consider the conditions under which apparently *unplanned purchases* commonly take place and the alternative explanations for such behavior.

In a study conducted over a three-week period, Shaffer (1960)* compared the differences between planned and actual food purchases for two samples of families. On the whole, he concluded that families do not necessarily spend more money for food because of "impulse buying." However, examining families individually, he found that this result was due to some families overbuying and some families underbuying in the absence of prior planning. Thus, one group canceled out the effect of the other group. Moreover, a high incidence of unplanned purchasing, disregarding brand choice, did not apparently affect the frequency of purchase for food items. Shaffer suggests that "the store may be the most rational place to make many food purchase decisions, since it is there that prices, quality, and availability of substitutes and complements may best be included in consideration." Thus, we have the first suggestion that apparently *unplanned purchases* may nevertheless be the resultant of an orderly decision process, at least so far as food items are concerned.

A field study by Kollat and Willett (1967)* concerning grocery purchases provides additional insight regarding the incidence of planned purchases relative to unplanned purchases, and personal characteristics and food shopping behavior variables related to unplanned purchasing. The results suggest that unplanned grocery purchases generally outnumber planned purchases, and the proportion of unplanned purchases is found related to only a few independent variables.

Elsewhere Kollat and Willett (1969) discussed the confusion that centers around the terms "impulse" or "unplanned" purchases and the alternative definitions that have been applied to the terms by prior researchers. Differences in definitions have arisen due to conflicting explanations for the phenomenon. Kollat and Willett set forth two possible explanations: the exposure hypothesis and the customer-commitment hypothesis. As the term implies, the exposure hypothesis would suggest that unplanned purchases result largely from in-store stimuli as the shopper uses product displays for reminders of shopping needs or is attracted by special promotional displays prompting her to envision a need for the given product. (Such factors as in-store display and shelf-position factors are taken up in greater detail in Chapter 13.) The alternative hypothesis, customer-commitment, maintains that "measured purchase intentions" differ from "actual purchase intentions" because the shopper is unwilling and/or unable to commit the time and/or cognitive energies to formulate accurate purchase intentions. The buyer may not consider it worth the time to develop highly specific buying plans, or, upon questioning by an interviewer, she may not articulate her shopping plans with great completeness. However, their data do not allow an assessment of which explanatory hypothesis—exposure or customer-commitment—most adequately accounts for the unplanned purchasing. This question, although an important one, remains unanswered. As Kollat and Willett conclude, unplanned purchases during a typical grocery shopping trip undoubtedly arise from a mixture of both explanations.

The interested reader is referred to criticisms by Pollay (1968) of the Kollat and Willett study, and to their reply (Willett and Kollat, 1968).

REFERENCES

1. KOLLAT, DAVID T. AND RONALD P. WILLETT. "Is Impulse Purchasing Really a Useful Concept for Marketing Decisions?" *Journal of Marketing*, Vol. 33 (January 1969), 79–83.
2. POLLAY, RICHARD W. "Customer Impulse Purchasing Behavior: A Reexamination." *Journal of Marketing Research*, Vol. 5 (August 1968), 323–325.
3. WILLETT, RONALD P. AND DAVID T. KOLLAT. "Customer Impulse Purchasing Behavior: Some Research Notes and a Reply." *Journal of Marketing Research*, Vol. 5 (August 1968), 326–330.

28. The influence of "impulse buying" or in-the-store decisions on consumers' food purchases

james duncan shaffer

The purpose of this study was to estimate the influence of "impulse buying" or in-the-store decisions on (1) total food expenditures and (2) the allocation of expenditures among particular foods and food groups.

The basic findings of this study may be summarized as follows:

1. A comparison between anticipated and actual food purchases for a week by individual families showed that less than half of the purchases actually made were anticipated. This indicates that a large percentage of food purchase decisions are made in the store.

2. A comparison between anticipated and actual food purchases for two random population samples showed there was little difference between anticipated and actual purchases for the population as a group. This indicates that total food expenditures and the allocation of expenditures among particular foods and food groups for the population as a whole are not substantially altered by the fact that many purchase decisions are made in the store.

DESIGN OF THE STUDY

Comparison Between Actual and Anticipated Purchases for Matched Samples

If "impulse buying" or in-the-store decisions have a significant influence on the food purchases of a population group there should be a significant difference between actual and anticipated purchases for a pair of matched samples. The difference in purchases between one random sample reporting actual purchases (which would have been subject to "impulse" and in-the-store decisions) and another random sample from the same population reporting what they anticipate buying while sitting in their living room not influenced by what they see in the store should give an upper estimate of the aggregate influence of in-the-store choices. Such a survey was conducted in Lansing, Michigan during the spring and early summer of 1958.

A probability sample of 1200 families was selected by taking, after a random start, every nth residential address from the address section of the City Directory.[1] Half of the sample was assigned, in an alternat-

Reprinted by permission from the *Journal of Farm Economics* (May 1960), pp. 317–324, published by the American Farm Economics Association.

Journal paper No. 2591 from the Michigan Agricultural Experiment Station.

[1] Published by R. L. Polk and Co., Detroit, Mich. Addresses were listed in numerical order by streets in alphabetical order. After no less than three call-backs, one of which had to be in the evening, substitution of the next address was made for those which could not be contacted.

ing manner, a questionnaire which asked for a record of all food purchases for the past seven days. The other half of the sample was assigned questionnaires which asked, "Assume that for some reason you had to order all of your food for the next 7 days right now by telephone—what would you order?" In each case the respondent was given a form listing, by classes, approximately 650 different food items with space to indicate quantities, prices and expenditures for each. Space was provided for writing in items not itemized in the form.

Approximately the same number of each type of schedule (actual or anticipated) was taken each week over a three month period. Thus the anticipated and actual purchases are for very nearly the same time period. The data are weekly observations but representative of a three month period, not a single week.

Comparison Between Actual and Anticipated Purchases for Same Families

A comparison between actual and anticipated food purchases for a single sample of families was also made to provide a further estimate of the influence of in-the-store decisions. This was done by asking the families reporting anticipated purchases to keep a diary the following week reporting purchases actually made for the same time period they had reported their anticipated purchases. They were asked to return this record by mail. They were offered no reward for keeping the record and there was no follow-up reminder. A total of 199 useable reports (about ⅓) were returned.

These two records from each family provided data for two types of comparisons. It is possible to determine the differences between actual and anticipated purchases for each individual family with these differences becoming basic data. This provides data for estimating the number of purchases (total or for individual products) which were unanticipated or unplanned. This is the essential data used in such "impulse buying" surveys as have been done by the Du Pont Company.[2]

An alternative tabulation is to sum the anticipated purchases and the actual purchases and compare the sums for the population. In this case if 10 families anticipated buying a pound of white sugar and instead brought brown sugar and another 10 families did the opposite the analysis would indicate no difference between actual and anticipated purchases of white and brown sugar. These estimates are comparable to those obtained from the two matched random samples. It is from this type of analysis that the impact of these "unplanned" purchases on total sales can logically be implied. It cannot be implied from the individual family differences.

---

[2] *Today's Purchase In Super Markets,* Film Department, E. I. Du Pont de Nemours & Co.

COMPARISON OF ANTICIPATED AND ACTUAL PURCHASES

Matched Samples

There was very little difference in the average per capita expenditures for all food or for each of 9 major food groups between the samples reporting anticipated and actual purchases, as shown in Table 1. There

TABLE 1   Comparison of Average Expenditures and Average Number of Purchases from Reports of Actual Purchases of Food for Past Week and Reports of Anticipated Purchases for Following Week from Matched Samples[1]

Product Class	Average Expenditure Per Capita		Average Number of Purchases Per Family	
	Anticipated	Actual	Anticipated	Actual
Total Food at Home	$7.00	$7.18	31.3	29.7
Dairy Products[a]	1.13	1.10	3.3	3.2
Fats and Oils[a]	.36	.38	1.8	1.8
Fruits	.73	.73	4.3*	3.8
Vegetables	.71	.72	6.3	5.9
Meat, Poultry and Sea Food[b]	2.39	2.50	6.7*	6.2
Bakery and Cereal Products	.75	.78	5.5	5.5
Sugar, Sweets and Nuts	.22	.25	1.6	1.4
Beverages[c]	.49	.51	1.3	1.4
Cooking Aids	.18	.16	.4	.4

[1] Based upon 600 families reporting actual purchases and 593 reporting anticipated purchases.
[a] Butter is included in fats and oils.
[b] Includes eggs.
[c] Not including fluid milk or fruit juices.
* "Anticipated" was significantly different from "actual" at 5 percent level.

were only minor differences in the average number of purchases per family between the two samples. The average number of purchases was significantly different according to statistical test for only two product groups, meats and fruits, and in each case the anticipated purchases exceeded the actual. (The differences, while statistically significant at the 5 percent level by *t*-test, were not large.)

A comparison was also made between the reports of the 600 families reporting actual purchases and the 593 families reporting anticipated purchases for each of 575 items which were reported purchased by one or more families.[3]

---

[3] Unfortunately the definition of a product or item is rather arbitrary and ambiguous—it could be provided precisely only by listing all of the items assigned a differentiating code. Items were *not* differentiated in respect to brand or size of package. In other words butter was treated as one item regardless of brand or type of package. In general items were differentiated in respect to method of preservation—fresh, canned and frozen peas would be three different items. The code was such that it identified at least 857 different food items.

For the great majority of products there was no significant difference in the percent of families buying between the two samples. For only 16 items was the percent of families actually purchasing significantly greater (at the 5 percent level by *t*-test) than the percent anticipating purchases. For 31 items the percent of families anticipating purchase was significantly greater than those actually purchasing.

Same Families

The comparison between the reports of actual purchases and antici-pated purchases for the same group of families for total food and each of nine food groups is summarized in Table 2. The results were essen-

TABLE 2   Comparison of Average Expenditures and Average Number of Pur-chases from Reports of Anticipated Purchases of Food and Reports of Purchases Actually Made for Same Week by Same Families[1]

Product Class	Average Expenditure Per Capita		Average Number of Purchases Per Family	
	Anticipated	Actual	Anticipated	Actual
Total Food at Home	$6.95	$6.94	31.2	33.7
Dairy Products[a]	1.22*	1.08	3.6	3.6
Fats and Oils[a]	.31	.31	1.6	1.5
Fruits	.68	.69	4.1	4.2
Vegetables	.68	.73	6.2	6.5
Meat, Poultry and Sea Food[b]	2.34	2.32	6.8	6.9
Bakery and Cereal Products	.76	.86	5.7*	6.8
Sugar, Sweets and Nuts	.23	.26	1.6*	1.9
Beverages[c]	.50	.45	1.2	1.4
Cooking Aids	.18	.19	.5*	.7

[1] Based on reports of 199 families.
[a] Butter is included in fats and oils.
[b] Includes eggs.
[c] Not including fluid milk or fruit juices.
* "Anticipated" was significantly different from "actual" at 5 percent level.

tially the same as found in the comparison of the matched samples. Average per capita expenditures for food and for each of the food groups showed very little difference between these families' antici-pated purchases and purchases actually made (although the difference for dairy products was significantly different at the 5 percent level[4]). A very close similarity also existed between the averages obtained from the matched samples and those obtained from the two reports from the same families. There was somewhat less correspondence

---

[4] One would expect one of these 20 averages to test significantly different at the 5 percent level simply on the basis of chance, so too much should not be made of this difference.

among the four samples in respect to the average number of purchases, but again the differences were not great.

This evidence indicates that "unplanned" or "impulse" purchases of food do not alter the average expenditures for food or the allocation of expenditures among these nine major food groups.

However, this does not mean that actual expenditures were the same as anticipated expenditures *for each individual family.* Quite the contrary was true, as is shown in Table 3. Actual expenditures for total

TABLE 3   Comparison of Anticipated and Actual Expenditures of Individual Families[1]

Product Class	Percent of Families with Actual Expenditures Differing from Anticipated by—		Percent of Families with Actual Expenditures Larger or Smaller than Anticipated by More than 10 Percent	
	Less than 10 Percent	More than 50 Percent	Larger	Smaller
Total Food at Home	19	20	39	42
Dairy Products[a]	22	32	31	48
Fats and Oils[a]	25	47	38	38
Fruits	12	51	46	43
Vegetables	15	43	47	38
Meat, Poultry and Sea Food[b]	16	34	42	42
Bakery and Cereal Products	12	35	53	35
Sugar, Sweets and Nuts	20	60	48	32
Beverages[c]	31	41	37	32
Cooking Aids	52	39	29	19

[1] Based upon two reports from each of 199 families.
[a] Butter is included in fats and oils.
[b] Includes eggs.
[c] Not including fluid milk or fruit juices.

food were within 10 percent of total anticipated expenditures for only 19 percent of the 199 families completing the two reports. Twenty percent of the families had actual food bills which differed from the anticipated expenditures by more than 50 percent. Actual expenditures differed from anticipated by more than 10 percent for more than two-thirds of the families for each product class except one. And actual expenditures differed from anticipated by more than 50 percent for more than one-third of the families for each product class.

The second part of Table 3 gives a clue to the reason for the apparent inconsistency of these data with those presented in Table 2 for the same families. About as many families actually spent more than they anticipated as spent less than anticipated. This was true of total food and more or less true for each of the nine food classes. *Thus the differences for individual families were compensating with the result that anticipated and actual expenditures were different for most individual families yet were not different for the population as a group.*

Data on the number of purchases were tabulated in the same manner as those for expenditures shown in Table 3. The pattern of results was very similar to that shown for expenditures.

A comparison of the percent of families actually buying with the percent anticipating buying for each item for the same families also provided results very similar to those for the matched samples. In both cases only about 7 percent of the items showed a significant difference (at the 5 percent level) between the percent of families anticipating the purchase and those reporting an actual purchase. Of the items which tested significantly different, the percent anticipating the purchase was greater for 12 items and the percent actually making the purchase was greater for 28 items. Only 12 items were significantly different for both the matched samples and the same-family comparisons.

This evidence indicates that "unplanned" or "impulse" purchases of individual food items, disregarding brand, alters the frequency of purchase of only a very small number of food items.

However, this does not mean that each individual family actually bought most of the items which they anticipated buying during the following week. An item-by-item comparison was made for each family between what they anticipated buying and what they reported actually buying. The average homemaker reported an actual purchase of 49 percent of the items which she anticipated buying. *Of the actual purchases made only 46 percent of the items were anticipated.*

Of those items purchased by 10 percent or more of the families, more than 70 percent of the actual purchases were anticipated for 15 items. These items, along with the percent of actual purchases which were anticipated, were: eggs, 92 percent; head lettuce, 90; white enriched bread, 89; butter, 86; cottage cheese, 81; frozen orange juice, 80; skim milk, 79; ground coffee, 77; soda crackers, 77; whole or cracked wheat bread, 76; oleomargarine, 74; pre-packaged ice cream, 74; wieners and franks, 72; homogenized milk, 72; and vegetable and meat soup, 71.

Of those items purchased by 10 percent or more of the families, less than 30 percent of the actual purchases were anticipated for 12 items. These were: plain cookies with frosting or marshmallow, none; frosted or sugared doughnuts, 4 percent; fruit filled cookies, 8; canned navy beans, 15; canned tomatoes, 18; brown sugar, 20; canned cucumber pickles, 24; plain or sugared cookies, 25; sausage, 27; salt, 29; plain boxed spaghetti or macaroni, 29; and canned pineapple, 29.

CONCLUSION

These data indicate that for this population neither total expenditures for food nor the distribution of consumer purchases among food groups or among individual foods is significantly altered by in-the-store decisions. This is indicated by the evidence that (1) there was little difference in food purchases between two matched samples, one of which reported actual purchases and the other anticipated purchases, and (2) there was little difference in actual purchases and anticipated purchases for a sample of families reporting both.

The majority of food purchases are in-the-store choices and are different than would be made by individual consumers at the time of purchase if food were ordered from home without "contact" with the store. This is indicated by the evidence that less than half of the actual purchases made by individual families were anticipated. This is consistent with the findings of other studies, which have indicated that a large proportion of food purchase decisions are made in the store.

These two apparently contradictory conclusions are not inconsistent if the influence of factors affecting consumer choices in the store cancel out over time or between families. The data provide evidence that this happens.

The data for this study were collected over a period of about three months so they are data "over time," not for a particular one-week period. Many studies have indicated that "in-the-store stimuli" influence purchases for a particular week or for particular stores. Such findings are not inconsistent with the results of this report. In-store promotions may substantially increase sales during the period of promotion. Also, an individual store may gain sales by its display techniques. However, this study suggests that such findings may reflect gains at the expense of competing stores or of future sales rather than indicating a significant increase in consumer expenditures over time.

It is also likely that past experiences in grocery stores influenced what consumers anticipated purchasing. Thus it is possible that in-the-store stimuli may have some longer-run influence on purchases.

These data indicate that the observation that many purchase decisions are made in the store does not justify the conclusion that many food purchases are based upon "impulse," that the purchases are irrationally made, and that consumers are subject to substantial manipulation through control of stimuli in the store situation. By referring to in-the-store purchase decisions as "impulse purchases" the implication is made that the purchases are inconsistent with the established preference pattern of the shopper. For if the word "impulse" is used in any ordinary sense it implies spontaneous action not governed by reason.

However, the store may be the most rational place to make many food purchase decisions, since it is there that prices, quality, and availability of substitutes and complements may best be included in consideration. Purchases decided upon in the store certainly need not be inconsistent with the long-run preference pattern of the family; the evidence of this study is that they are probably consistent.

This study did not deal with purchases of branded products. It may be that "impulse buying" and "in-the-store stimuli" are important in determining the allocation of expenditures among the different brands of a commodity. A study similar to the one of this report but distinguishing branded products should prove interesting.

29. Customer impulse purchasing behavior

david t. kollat
& ronald p. willett

Impulse purchasing is not confined to any type of marketing institution, but it probably most frequently refers to food purchasing decisions. Many studies have used impulse purchasing to view a segment of consumer behavior. Studies by du Pont [8] have measured the incidence of impulse purchasing and have shown how different kinds of products are affected by it. Other studies have investigated how type of store [7, 20], shelf location [16], shelf space [9], and display location [14] affect impulse purchasing. Others [5, 15] purport to have identified and measured various reasons for impulse purchasing, while another [19] has hypothesized circumstances that appear to be associated with the occurrence of the behavior.

Customers make impulse purchases, and it is surprising that most studies did not have the shopper as an independent variable.[1] Does impulse purchasing truly represent an impulsive choice by the shopper, or is the purchase merely unplanned. Does unplanned purchasing occur with equal frequency among all customers, or are certain shoppers more likely to make unplanned purchases? What kinds of customers are most susceptible to unplanned purchasing?

The objectives of the present study were: (a) to determine the degree to which customers differ in their susceptibility to unplanned purchasing; (b) to discover what customer characteristics are associated with differential susceptibility to unplanned purchasing; and (c) to identify some of the precipitating conditions that lead to an unplanned purchase.

METHODOLOGY

Conceptualization of Unplanned Purchasing

An unplanned purchase results from a comparison of alternative purchase intentions with actual outcomes. Accordingly, an intentions typology, an outcomes typology and the categorization that results from a pairing of the typologies were used to structure the research.

The intentions typology consists of the major stages of planning that presumably exist before the customer is exposed to in-store stimuli.[2] The major intentions are:

1. Product and brand—Before entering the store the shopper knows both the product and brand of product to be purchased.

Reprinted by permission from *Journal of Marketing Research*, Vol. 4, pp. 21–31, published by the American Marketing Association.

[1] There are isolated exceptions to the tendency not to investigate differential customer susceptibility to unplanned purchasing. For these exceptions see [5, 11, 12, 15, 17].

[2] Major refers to the presence or absence of a product or brand decision prior to entering the store. A more sophisticated typology would be N dimensional to reflect pre-shopping decisions concerning the amount to be purchased, the size and kind of package or container to be purchased, etc.

2. Product only—Before entering the store the shopper knows which product she wants, but has not decided on the brand, e.g., a plan to buy potato chips but not a particular brand.
3. Product class only—Before entering the store the shopper knows the class of product that she intends to purchase, but has not decided on the products in that class; e.g., intention to buy meat but must decide on steak or hamburger.
4. Need recognized—Before entering the store the shopper recognizes the existence of a problem or need, but has not decided which product class, product or brand that she intends to purchase, e.g., a need for something for dinner.
5. Need not recognized—Before entering the store the shopper does not recognize the existence of a need, or the need is latent until she is in the store and has been exposed to its stimuli.

The basis of the intentions typology is to specify the customer's planning prior to going to a supermarket. Or, the various stages indicate the kind and extent of in-store decision making.

The outcomes typology consists of the major kinds of behavior that could result from shopping; the outcomes are:[3]

1. product and brand purchased;
2. product and brand not purchased, i.e., no purchase;
3. product purchased, brand not purchased, i.e., brand substitution;

Conceptually there are 15 categories that result from the pairing of the above intentions and outcomes. Fortunately, this categorization can be compressed since several categories are not empirically identifiable.

When the conceptual intentions-outcomes matrix is modified to reflect the operational requirements of the study, the resulting matrix can be collapsed into nine categories, (Figure 1). Using this intentions-outcomes matrix, Category 9 becomes the definition of unplanned purchasing.

Research Design

The methodology in this study represents a modification and expansion of the du Pont [8] and West [20] approaches. The research plan consisted of two phases: (a) store interviewing, and (b) home interviewing.

The present investigation is a field study rather than a survey [13]. Therefore, it is more concerned with a comprehensive account of the investigated processes than with their typicality in a larger universe.

Since asking respondents to itemize purchase intentions might affect subsequent shopping behavior, a "Pretest-Postest, Separate Sample Postest Only Control Group" design was used [3]. Sampling fractions were used to identify those shopping parties eligible for the

---

[3] Again we are concerned with the major types of outcomes that occur. Consequently, the observations made in Footnote 2 are applicable. An additional type of outcome would be: product not purchased; brand purchased. This kind of outcome was omitted because it infrequently occurs.

FIGURE 1   An Operational Intentions-Outcomes Matrix

| | Outcomes | | |
Intentions	Product and brand purchased	No purchase	Product purchased; Brand not purchased
Product and brand mentioned	1	2	3
Product only mentioned	4	5	
Product class mentioned	6	7	
Need recognized	8		
Need not recognized	9		

study and to assign the eligible shopping parties to an experimental or control group. Shoppers in the experimental group were asked what they planned to purchase at the time they entered a supermarket,[4] while shoppers in the control group were not questioned about purchase intentions. Shoppers in both groups conducted their shopping, and purchases were recorded at the checkout. A 4×4 Latin square design was used to balance out systematic variation in unplanned purchasing attributable to type of store, time of day, and day of week. Eight units of a national supermarket chain were paired into four groups, and randomly assigned to Treatments A through D. In each cell, the stores were randomly assigned for either morning or afternoon-evening interviewing. Interviews were done on Friday, Saturday, Sunday and either Tuesday or Wednesday, with the occurrence of Tuesday or Wednesday randomly determined. A total of 596 interviews was obtained in a four-week period.[5]

Home interviewing was conducted to obtain the detailed information that could not be gathered during store interviews. This phase involved 196 follow-up interviews of the 596 original shopping parties. These respondents were interviewed within two days after their original interview.

Effects of the Store Interview

Since shoppers were systematically assigned to experimental and control groups and only experimental group respondents were asked to

---

[4] Experimental group respondents were first asked if they had a shopping list. If shoppers had a list, the interviewer copied it; and if a brand were not mentioned he asked if the respondent had decided on a specific brand. After the interviewer finished copying the list, she asked the shopper if there were anything else that she planned to purchase that was not included in the shopping list. If the respondent did not have a shopping list, the interviewer continued to ask the respondent for the products and brands that she planned to purchase until the shopper presumably exhausted her purchase intentions. A technique was used that minimized the probability that shoppers would know that their purchases would later be recorded.

[5] The number of experimental and control group interviews conducted in each store on each interviewing day was proportional to that store's customer traffic on the day relative to the total traffic of all eight stores during all interviewing days.

tell purchase plans, differences in purchasing behavior between the groups might be attributed primarily to the influence of the entry interview. The experimental and control groups were compared by using three indices of purchasing behavior: (a) grocery bill; (b) number of different products purchased;[6] and (c) mixture of products purchased.

The differences between the experimental and control group grocery expenditures are not significant at the .05 probability level. The entry interview did not appear to affect the amount spent during the shopping trip.

Since the grocery expenditure categories used in the study consist of $3 to $5 intervals, the entry interview could actually cause an increase in grocery expenditures up to $5 and still not appear in the data. To overcome this problem a more sensitive measure of transaction size was used—number of different products purchased.

The mean number of products purchased by experimental and control group shoppers was 13.1 and 12.9. This difference is not significant at the .05 probability level. Thus, the entry interview did not appear to affect the number of different products purchased.

Although the entry interview did not affect the transaction size, it could have precipitated an increase in the incidence of purchase of some items and a decrease in others. A final test assessed the effects of the entry interview on the mixture of products purchased.

Purchase frequencies[7] were computed for 64 product categories. For each product category, the experimental group purchase frequency was compared with the control group frequency. The coefficient of correlation between the product purchase frequencies of the experimental and control groups is .91. It appears that the entry interview could have only slightly distorted the mixture of products that customers purchased.

Thus, asking respondents what they planned to purchase did not affect either the money spent in the store or the number of different products purchased, and had little effect on the mixture of products purchased.

CUSTOMER DIFFERENCES IN UNPLANNED PURCHASING BEHAVIOR

Number of Purchases

The average customer made eight unplanned purchases while the average number of specifically planned purchases was only 2.5. The mean number of purchases for any of the other intentions-outcomes

---

[6] Number of different products purchased differs from number of products purchased in that it does not reflect multiple purchases of the same product. For example, if a shopper purchased two quarts of milk and one loaf of bread the number of different products purchased would be two.

[7] Here, purchase frequency is the number of purchases of a product divided by the sample size. Division by sample size is necessary to approximate experimental group-control comparability since the former consisted of 596 respondents and the latter 196 shoppers.

categories was less than 1.0. In absolute terms then unplanned purchasing was by far the more frequent.

Table 1 gives the dispersion of respondents for two major intentions-

TABLE 1   Distribution of Respondents by Number and Proportion of Purchases in Major Intentions-outcomes Categories[a]

Number of purchases	Intentions-outcome planned purchases[b]	Unplanned purchases[c]
0–7	93.8%	66.0%
8–15	5.7	16.4
16–23	.5	10.0
24–31	—	4.7
32–40	—	1.9
Total	100.0	100.0

Percent of Purchases	Intentions-outcome planned purchases[b]	Unplanned purchases[c]
0–11	36.3%	18.8%
12–23	22.0	3.2
24–35	17.9	10.0
36–48	6.4	9.3
49–59	8.6	14.4
60–71	2.9	21.1
72–81	1.0	11.5
82–93	—	8.8
94–100	4.9	3.0
Total	100.0	100.0

[a] 596 respondents.
[b] Corresponds to Category 1 in Figure 1.
[c] Corresponds to Category 9 in Figure 1.

outcomes categories. The maximum number of unplanned purchases made by a shopper was 40, the minimum 0 and the standard deviation 9.2. Both the ranges and standard deviations of the remaining intentions-outcomes categories are considerably smaller. It is apparent that the incidence of unplanned purchasing varies greatly for shoppers, absolutely and relatively, from the customer variation in other intentions-outcomes categories.

Percentage of Purchases

The intentions-outcomes categories can also be expressed in percentages. The percentage refers to the number of purchases in a given intentions-outcomes category for one respondent divided by the total of different products purchased by that respondent.

In terms of relative frequency, the average customer purchased 50.5 percent of the products on an unplanned basis. In contrast, the mean percentage of specifically planned purchases is 25.9 percent, and the highest mean for any of the remaining categories is only 8.2 percent. In percentage terms the incidence of unplanned purchasing is greater than the combination of all other intentions-outcomes categories.

The wide variation in the percentage of unplanned purchases is demonstrated by the nearly equal distribution of shoppers across the percentage categories (Table 1). Specifically planned and other intentions-outcomes categories display considerably less variation among shoppers.

Overall, then unplanned purchasing is the most common intentions-outcomes category, expressed in either absolute or percentage terms. Also, shoppers vary widely in the number and percentage of unplanned purchases.

Only the proportion of unplanned purchases will be the dependent variable. In this manner the effects of number of purchases are netted out, allowing number of products sought to be a possible explanatory variable.

Two stages of analysis are necessary for understanding customer unplanned purchasing behavior. The first stage is to determine which variables are associated with the occurrence of different rates of unplanned purchasing, but this stage does not explain how unplanned purchasing occurs or what it involves. The second stage attempts to reconstruct some of the precipitating conditions that lead to an unplanned purchase.

FINDINGS—CORRELATES OF IMPULSE PURCHASING BEHAVIOR

Many variables were used in an attempt to explain customer differences in unplanned purchasing behavior. The analysis produced three major kinds of variables: (a) variables that are not related to unplanned purchasing and do not affect it; (b) variables that are related to but do not affect unplanned purchasing; and (c) variables that are related to and affect unplanned purchasing.

Variables Not Associated with Unplanned Purchasing

Figure 2 itemizes variables that are statistically independent of customer differences in unplanned purchasing behavior. Economic and demographic variables—income, number of wage earners, occupation, and education—do not influence the rate of unplanned purchasing.

The personality variables used in the study have been used by Brim [6] and were derived from French's [10] factor analytic review of personality tests. *These personality variables are statistically independent of unplanned purchasing on the basis of chi-square and correlation coefficient tests of significance.* The highest correlation coefficient is only .09.

Finally, an array of general food shopping variables are independent of customer differences in unplanned purchasing. The presence of food budgets and the use of food coupons and trading stamps do not affect customer rates of unplanned purchasing.

FIGURE 2   Variables Not Associated with Unplanned Purchasing

A. *Economic and Demographic Variables*[a]
1. Income of the household
2. Number of full-time wage earners in the household
3. Occupation of the household head
4. Formal education of the household head

B. *Personality Variables*[b]
1. Impulsiveness
2. Dominance
3. Optimism
4. Self-confidence
5. Self-sufficiency
6. Belief in fate
7. Future time orientation
8. Desire for certainty
9. Belief in the predictability of life
10. Belief in multiple causation of events

C. *General Food Shopping Behavior Variables*[c]
1. Size of shopping party
2. Existence of a food budget
3. Frequency of food budget revision
4. Role of wife in determining food budget
5. Use of food coupons
6. Use of trading stamps
7. Recalled exposure to newspaper advertisements for grocery products
8. Frequency of discussion about grocery products

[a]596 Respondents. Variables are independent of the percentage of customer unplanned purchases at the .05 level of probability (chi square).

[b]196 Respondents. Variables are independent of the percentage of customer unplanned purchases at the .05 level of probability (chi-square and correlation coefficients).

[c]196 Respondents. Variables are independent of the percentage of customer unplanned purchases at the .05 level of probability (chi square).

Variables Associated with Unplanned Purchasing

Several variables are related to customer differences in unplanned purchasing only because they are related to another variable, the number of different products purchased. When the number of different products purchased is held almost constant, these variables do not influence the percentage of unplanned purchases.[8] Although these variables are related to customer variations in unplanned purchasing, they do not affect the behavior. These variables are:

A. *Demographic variables*
   1. Number of people living in the household
   2. Sex of the shopper
B. *General food shopping behavior variables:*
   1. Number of shopping trips made per week
   2. Distance traveled to the store
   3. Day of week
   4. Time of day
   5. Size of store

The shopper's sex does not affect unplanned purchasing behavior. Women purchase a higher percentage of products on an unplanned basis, because they usually make more purchases. When the number

---

[8] The analytical strategy of holding transaction size approximately constant as to remove one source of concomitant variation involved the following: (a) total number of different products purchased were divided into quartiles; (b) contingency tables and the resultant chi squares were derived for the relationship between the independent variables and the percentage of unplanned purchases for each of the four quartiles. Since this procedure leaves some intracell variation in the number of different products purchased, transaction size has been controlled rather than left as a continuous variable.

of purchases is held constant, men and women have the same degree of susceptibility to unplanned purchasing.

Day of week does not affect unplanned purchasing. In-store promotional activities are, of course, more intensive on Thursday, Friday, and Saturday. Percentages of unplanned purchases are higher on Friday and Saturday, only because more products are purchased on these days; when the number of products purchased is held constant, day of week is not related to unplanned purchasing.

Variables Affecting Unplanned Purchasing

Three categories of independent variables affect customer unplanned purchasing and are related to it. They are: (a) transaction size variables, (b) transaction structure variables and (c) characteristics of the shopping party.

This study used two measures of transaction size: number of different products purchased and grocery bill.

Figure 3 depicts the approximate area containing the 559 coordinates

FIGURE 3   Configuration of the Scatter Diagram of the Relationship Between the Number of Different Products Purchased and the Percentage of Unplanned Purchases[a]

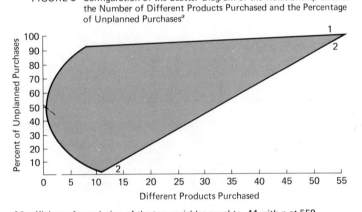

[a] Coefficient of correlation of the two variables equal to .44 with n at 559.

of number of different products purchased and the percentage of unplanned purchases. The relationship suggests that when the number of different products purchased is low, the proportion of unplanned purchases may be either high or low, but when the number of different products purchased is high, the percentage of unplanned purchases is also high. Generally, the greater the number of different products purchased, the greater the percentage of unplanned purchases.

Since the percentage of unplanned purchases is actually the number of unplanned purchases divided by the total number of different products purchased, Figure 3 shows the relationship between the number of unplanned purchases and the number of different products purchased.[9]

---

[9] In Figure 3 the y axis is equal to a/b, and the x axis is equal to b where a is the number of unplanned purchases, b is the number of different products purchased and a/b is the percentage of unplanned purchases.

If the number of different products purchased determined all varia-
ation in the number of unplanned purchases, then the relationship
would be Line segment 1 in Figure 3.[10] Given any number of different
products purchased, the vertical distance between the actual percentage of unplanned purchases and the percentage indicated by Line
segment 1 indicates the variation in the number of unplanned purchases that is not accounted for by the number of different products
purchased.

In Figure 3 all observations lie in the area formed by Line segments
1 and 2. As the number of different products purchased increases, the
vertical distance between Line segments 1 and 2 decreases. Therefore,
as the number of different products purchased increases, the unac-
counted variation in the number of unplanned purchases decreases.

Grocery bill is also a measure of transaction size. Figure 4 depicts

FIGURE 4   Relationship Between Grocery Bills and the
Percentage of Unplanned Purchases

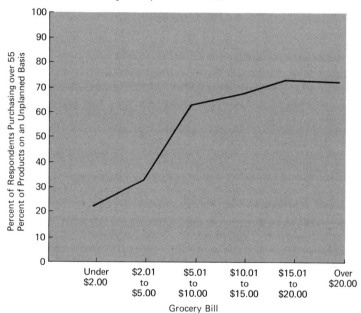

the relationship between unplanned purchasing and grocery bills. The
percentage of respondents purchasing over 55 percent of their total
purchases on an unplanned basis increases as the grocery bill increases
until the bill exceeds $20, then the percentage declines slightly.

Transaction structure refers to the mixture of products purchased.
Two measures of transaction structure affect customer unplanned
purchasing and are related to the behavior: (a) kind of shopping trip
and (b) product purchase frequencies.

---

[10] In Line segment 1 of Figure 3, the absolute change in the number of unplanned
purchases equals the absolute change in the number of different products purchased; that is, the number of different products purchased accounts for all of the
variation in the number of unplanned purchases.

Kind of shopping trip may measure some of the things that trans-action size measures, but some it does not. When transaction size is held constant, kind of shopping trip is still significantly related to the percentage of unplanned purchases. As Figure 5 indicates, major shop-

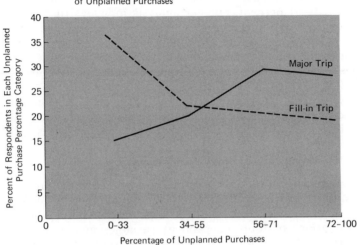

FIGURE 5   Relationship Between Kind of Shopping Trip and the Percentage of Unplanned Purchases

ping trips are generally characterized by a larger percentage of un-planned purchases than are fill-in trips.

Additional empirical measures of transaction structure are not avail-able; thus further study of the relationship between unplanned pur-chasing and transaction structures requires an indirect approach. One approach uses the unplanned purchase percentage for each product category as the dependent variable and attempts to find product char-acteristics that affect this percentage. Using some of the insights advanced by Stern [19], four product characteristics were tested: (a) product purchase frequencies, (b) price, (c) amount of product adver-tising, and (d) ease of product storage.

Only product purchase frequencies are significantly related to prod-uct unplanned purchase rates. The linear correlation coefficient of the 63 product purchase frequencies and product unplanned purchase rates is −.60. Products such as milk, bread, eggs, etc., which have a high frequency of purchase, tend to have a relatively low unplanned purchase percentage. In contrast, products having a low frequency of purchase like drugs, toiletries, and dessert items, tend to have a rela-tively high unplanned purchase percentage.

Given two customer transactions of the same size, one would expect an inverse relationship between the purchase frequencies of the prod-ucts included in the transaction and the percentage of unplanned purchases that comprise the transaction. For example, if the shopper purchased products having high purchase frequencies, she would be expected to be a relatively low percentage unplanned purchaser. If she purchased the same number of products, but the products pur-chased are not purchased frequently, she would be expected to make a higher percentage of unplanned purchases.

Only two of the shopping party characteristics affect customer unplanned purchasing. These characteristics are: (a) presence of a shopping list and (b) number of years the shopping party has been married.

The effect of a shopping list on unplanned purchase percentages is uncertain. In fact, the mean percentage of unplanned purchases for customers having a shopping list is the same as for those without a shopping list—51 percent. Further analysis indicates that the effect of a shopping list on unplanned purchasing depends on the transaction size. When more than 15 or 20 products are purchased, shoppers having a list make a smaller percentage of unplanned purchases. However, when less than 15 or 20 products are purchased, the shopping list does not affect the percentage of unplanned purchases.

Finally, couples married less than 10 years have the lowest rate of unplanned purchasing. Generally, the percentage of unplanned purchasing increases irregularly as length of marriage increases.

Composite Determinants of Unplanned Purchasing

Thus far the effects of only one independent variable on unplanned purchasing have been considered. Using the percentage of unplanned purchases made by customers as the dependent variable, the effects of all combinations of four independent variables and now examined.[11]

Since three of these four variables are discrete rather than continuous, the analytical device is analysis of variance. However, analysis of variance cannot be used in its most usual manner because the data violate assumptions of the procedure.[12] This, however, is not too debilitating since analysis of variance is not being used to test the significance of these variables, as this has already been accomplished using other statistical techniques. Rather, analysis of variance used here assesses the different effects of various combinations of variables. Accordingly, within cell or unexplained variation can be used as the criterion for determining which combination of independent variables accounts for the greatest portion of the variation in unplanned purchasing. Therefore, the smaller the within cell variation, the more the given independent variable combination accounts for the variation in unplanned purchasing.

Table 2 presents the within cell or unexplained variation for each possible combination of the four independent variables. The number of different products purchased accounts for more variation in unplanned purchasing than any other variable. Number of years married

---

[11] Product purchase frequencies cannot be included in this analysis since it requires the use of another dependent variable—product unplanned purchase rates. Number of different products purchased rather than grocery bill will be used as the measure of transaction size.

[12] The various classifications of the four independent variables result in a 48-cell table. When the 586 respondents are assigned to appropriate cells, cell sizes are neither equal nor proportional. The addition theorem for sum of squares does not hold in the four variable case when cell sizes are both unequal and disproportionate. Consequently the common significance test and estimation of components of variance are not possible [18, p. 379]. This limitation was overcome by separately calculating each within cell sum of squares.

TABLE 2 Analysis of Variance Applied to Independent Variables Significantly Related to the Percentage of Unplanned Purchases[a]

Independent variable combinations	Within cell variation mean square[b]
Number of different products purchased	693
Major or fill-in shopping trip	841
Presence of shopping list	861
Number of years shopping party has been married	793
1st order combinations	
Number of products purchased; major or fill-in	627
Number of products purchased; shopping list	615
Number of products purchased; years married	641
Major or fill-in; shopping list	772
Major or fill-in; years married	784
Shopping list; years married	799
2nd order combinations	
Number of products purchased; major or fill-in; shopping list	605
Number of products purchased; major or fill-in; years married	607
Number of products purchased; shopping list; years married	600
Major or fill-in; shopping list; years married	768
3rd order combination	
Number of products purchased; major or fill-in; shopping list; years married	574
Total	861

[a] Significantly related means: (a) relationships with chi-square tests of significance equal to or less than .05, or linear correlation coefficients that are significantly different from zero at the .05 level of probability and (b) relationships that apparently are not attributable to concomitant variation.
[b] Mean square is the within cell sum of squares divided by the appropriate degrees of freedom.

appears to be the second strongest variable followed by the kind of shopping trip. The fact that shopping lists do not produce any variation in unplanned purchasing is consistent with the earlier findings that shopping lists affect unplanned purchasing only when more than 15 or 20 products are purchased.

First and second order combinations again demonstrate the relative strength of number of different products purchased. The percentage of accounted-for variation is increased further as the other three variables are combined with the number of different products purchased. The least amount of unaccounted-for variation in customer unplanned purchasing results when all four variables are used together.

FINDINGS—CUSTOMERS' PRE-SHOPPING PURCHASE SITUATIONS AND UNPLANNED PURCHASES

The discussion of the relationships between unplanned purchasing and other variables is based on the usual definition of unplanned purchasing; a purchase is unplanned if the respondent did not indicate a plan to purchase it. Thus, all unplanned purchasing is considered as homogeneous behavior.

However, as some writers [19] have pointed out, there may be several kinds of unplanned purchases. The classification used in this study is an abbreviated version of Alderson's [1] classification of purchase situations. An unplanned purchase is classified on the basis of whether the product was purchased before, then further classified according to whether it represents out-of-stock or inventory addition purchases, and then according to whether the brand purchased is the same as the last brand purchased.

The classification consists of five categories of unplanned purchases. Each of 187 shopping parties, interviewed in Phase II, was asked to indicate the appropriate category for earlier unplanned purchases.

Pre-Shopping Need and Experience

Table 3 gives an analysis of unplanned purchases for the purchaser's experience with product and brand and his pre-shopping inventory

TABLE 3   Customers' Pre-Shopping Experience and Need for Unplanned Purchases[a]

Composition of unplanned purchases	Number of unplanned purchases	Percent of unplanned purchases
Purchased before		
Out-of-stock; same brand	813	63.6%
Out-of-stock; different brand	78	6.1
Inventory-addition; same brand	297	23.2
Inventory-addition; different brand	52	4.1
Not purchased before	39	3.0
Total	1279	100.0%

[a] 187 respondents.

situation. Of the unplanned purchases, 97 percent involved products purchased before. Of the unplanned purchases represented by products that had been purchased before, nearly 64 percent were out-of-stock same brand purchases, six percent were out-of-stock different brand purchases, 23 percent were inventory-addition same brand purchases and four percent were inventory-addition different brand purchases.

Nearly 86 percent of the unplanned purchases represent situations in which both product and brand have been purchased. Slightly over 10 percent represent a situation in which the product but not the brand has been purchased.

COMPETING EXPLANATIONS FOR UNPLANNED PURCHASING

Only competing explanations of the relationships will be discussed, they are: (a) the exposure to in-store stimuli hypothesis and (b) the customer-commitment hypothesis.

With one exception [2], previous investigations of unplanned purchasing have explained it as exposure to in-store stimuli. In fact, unplanned purchasing seems to be the same as in-store decisions or the effects of in-store suggestion. In-store stimuli apparently create new needs or remind the shopper of temporarily forgotten needs.

The customer-commitment hypothesis suggests that differences between purchase intentions and actual purchases are caused by incomplete measures of purchase intentions. Differences exist between measured and actual purchase intentions because the shopper is unwilling or unable to spend the time and effort necessary to itemize her purchase plans.

The customer may be unwilling to itemize her purchase intentions because she does not want to devote the time and thought necessary to give the interviewer a comprehensive list of her purchase plans. Instead she gives the interviewer only an incomplete itemization of her purchase plans.

Several plausible reasons explain why the shopper may be unable to itemize her purchase intentions. First, the shopper may know what she will purchase but may be unable to express her purchase intentions because of the nature of the interview. The methodology required the shopper, without a shopping list, to rely on her memory for purchase intentions. Unaided and nearly spontaneous recall is used to measure purchase plans. This procedure almost guarantees that measured purchase intentions will deviate somewhat from actual purchase plans. Also, the shopper may know what she will purchase but be unable to relate these intentions, regardless of the interviewer's assistance. Without exposure to in-store stimuli, the shopper may be unable to tell the interviewer what she will purchase.

The validity of these hypotheses is assessed by examining the degree to which each accounts of the findings of the present study and other investigations of unplanned purchasing.

Transaction Size

Figure 4 indicated that the percentage of unplanned purchases increased as the number of different products purchased increased. Further, as the number of different products purchased increased, it accounted for more variation in the number of unplanned purchases.

For the in-store stimuli hypothesis to apply, it is necessary to assume that the amount of customer exposure to in-store stimuli increases as the number of different products purchased increases. Then the greater the number of products purchased, the greater the exposure to in-store stimuli and, hence, the greater the percentage of unplanned purchases.

The customer-commitment hypothesis explains that as the number of different products a customer intends to purchase increases, the customer finds it increasingly more difficult and time consuming to itemize his purchase intentions. Consequently, as the number of products purchased increases, the difference between actual and measured purchase intentions also increases.

If the customer-commitment explanation has any validity, it would seem that measured purchase intentions should correspond more closely to actual purchase intentions when the customer's time and effort are minimized. In order to minimize customer commitment, each shopper was asked to indicate during the store entry interview how much she planned to spend. Spending intentions were then compared with actual grocery expenditures.

There is a strong tendency for actual expenditures to approximate spending intentions (Table 4). Shoppers are more likely to spend less than they anticipated than they are to spend more than they planned.

TABLE 4   Spending Intentions Compared with Actual Expenditures[a]

| Spending intentions | Grocery bill[b] | | | |
	Less than	The same	More than	Total
$ 2.00 or Less	—	76.1%	23.9%	100.0%
2.01–$5.00	19.3%	68.6	12.1	100.0
5.01–10.00	32.1	54.5	13.4	100.0
10.01–15.00	38.3	30.0	31.7	100.0
15.01–20.00	37.8	33.3	28.9	100.0
20.01–25.00	32.3	47.1	20.6	100.0
25.01–30.00	50.0	25.0	25.0	100.0
Over 30.00	56.3	43.7	—	100.0

[a] 596 respondents.
[b] Shown in percent of respondents.

Shopping Trip

Figure 5 shows that the percentage of unplanned purchases was larger during major shopping trips than during fill-in trips. The exposure hypothesis justifies this finding by asserting that during fill-in trips the shopper's needs are more clearly identified so that she is less susceptible to in-store suggestion. During major trips, however, the shopper's needs are not well defined, thus the shopper is more receptive to in-store stimuli.

The customer-commitment hypothesis also accounts for the relationship. Fill-in trips typically satisfy relatively urgent needs. Moreover, products purchased during fill-in trips probably have higher purchase frequencies and a longer purchase history than most products purchased during major trips. Therefore, fill-in trips probably involve smaller effort and time commitments than major trips, so that measured purchase intentions deviate less from actual purchase intentions.

Frequency of Purchase

The exposure hypothesis gives two reasons for the inverse relationship between product purchase frequencies and product unplanned purchase rates. First, products with high purchase frequencies usually receive less promotional emphasis than other products. Second, customers may be less susceptible to in-store promotions for products with high purchase frequencies.

The customer-commitment hypothesis uses a simple learning theory paradigm to account for the relationship [4]. Products having high purchase frequencies also usually have an extended purchase history. Thus during any shopping trip, a customer is more likely to purchase products with higher purchase frequencies. Thus, frequently purchased products have lower unplanned purchase rates; it is easier for the shopper to remember that she plans to purchase them.[13]

Shopping List

A shopping list influences unplanned purchasing only when more than 15 products are purchased; shoppers with a list have lower unplanned rates. The exposure hypothesis assumes that a shopper who expects to purchase a small number of items has clearly defined needs and is less susceptible to in-store stimuli. A shopping list does not affect this behavior. However, the shopper with plans to purchase a large number of products, according to the exposure hypothesis, uses in-store stimuli to identify shopping needs.

According to the customer-commitment hypothesis, when few products are purchased, the time and effort commitments involved in itemizing purchase plans are small and are only marginally reduced by a shopping list. If a large number of products are purchased, the effort and time commitments are high, and are greatly reduced by a shopping list.

Years Married

The exposure hypothesis can account for the increased rate of unplanned purchasing as years married increase. First, as years married increase and the children grow, both the quantity and variety of their food consumption increase. Pre-planning becomes more time consuming and difficult, so the shopper may rely more on in-store stimuli. Also, other household members may accept the housewife's purchases so that she can make more in-store purchase decisions. Finally, older shoppers have probably had more shopping experience and may feel better qualified to evaluate purchase alternatives in the store.

The customer-commitment explanation assumes that shoppers married for shorter times can give a more accurate itemization of purchase intentions. Since younger shoppers usually have smaller incomes, they may plan grocery expenditures. Younger households may have greater husband-wife participation in determining grocery expenditures, and their purchases may be thought out before the shopping

---

[13] This statement is consistent with purchase intentions data. Frequently purchased products are more likely to be mentioned as purchase intentions regardless of whether these products are actually purchased.

trip. Since the number and variety of purchases usually increase when the size of the household increases, it may be easier for younger couples to give a more complete listing of purchase plans.

Types of Unplanned Purchases

Most unplanned purchases represent either out-of-stock same brand or inventory-addition same brand purchases. In-store stimuli usually remind shoppers of present or future needs rather than evoking new needs.

Out-of-stock same brand unplanned purchases do seem consistent with the customer-commitment hypothesis. That is, most of these purchases are probably routine, so the customer could probably identify them as purchase intentions given an appropriate research design. However, inventory-addition same brand purchases may have actually been planned, others were probably precipitated by in-store stimuli.

Unplanned purchasing can be described as a blend of the hypothesis. Some unplanned purchases are probably precipitated by exposure to in-store stimuli. Others are not unplanned at all but are caused by the way in which the behavior is usually measured. These purchases are classified as unplanned because measured purchase intentions deviate from actual purchase plans because of the customer's inability or unwillingness to give the time and thought necessary to tell the interviewer her purchase plans. Unfortunately, the data do not seem to permit a conclusion about these two explanations for customer unplanned purchasing behavior.

REFERENCES

1. ALDERSON, WROE, *Marketing Behavior and Executive Action,* Homewood, Ill.: Richard D. Irwin, Inc., 1957.
2. APPLEBAUM, WILLIAM, "Studying Customer Behavior in Retail Stores," *Journal of Marketing,* 16 (October 1951), 172–8.
3. BANKS, SEYMOUR, *Experimentation in Marketing,* New York: McGraw-Hill Book Co., 1965.
4. BAYTON, JAMES A., "Motivation, Cognition, Learning—Basic Factors in Consumer Behavior," *Journal of Marketing,* 22 (January 1958), 282–9.
5. *Brand Switching and Impulse Buying,* New York: Point-of-Purchase Advertising Institute, 1963.
6. BRIM, ORVILLE, *et al., Personality and Decision Processes,* Stanford: Stanford University Press, 1962.
7. CLOVER, VERNON T., "Relative Importance of Impulse Buying in Retail Stores," *Journal of Marketing,* 15 (July 1950), 66–70.
8. *Consumer Buying Habits Studies,* E. I. du Pont De Nemours and Company, 1945, 1949, 1954, 1959, 1965.
9. COX, KEITH, "The Responsiveness of Food Sales to Shelf Space Changes in Supermarkets," *Journal of Marketing Research,* 1 (May 1964), 63–7.
10. FRENCH, JOHN W., *The Description of Personality Measurements in Terms of Rotated Factors,* Princeton, N.J.: Educational Testing Service, Princeton University Press, 1953.

11. *How People Shop for Food*, Market Research Corporation of America, manuscript.
12. *Impulse Buying*, Philadelphia: The Curtis Publishing Company Research Department, February 1952.
13. KATZ, DANIEL, "Field Studies," in Leon Festinger and Daniel Katz, eds., *Research Methods in the Behavioral Sciences*, New York: Holt, Rinehart, and Winston, 1953.
14. KELLY, ROBERT F., "An Evaluation of Selected Variables of End Display Effectiveness," Unpublished doctoral dissertation, Harvard University, 1965.
15. *One on the Aisle*, New York: Life Marketing Laboratory, manuscript.
16. PATTERSON, LAWRENCE W., *In-Store Traffic Flow*, New York: Point-of-Purchase Advertising Institute, 1963.
17. SHAFFER, JAMES D., "The Influence of Impulse Buying or In-the-Store Decisions on Consumers' Food Purchases," Michigan Agricultural Experimental Station Journal Paper No. 2591.
18. SNEDECOR, GEORGE W., *Statistical Methods*, Ames, Iowa: Iowa State College Press, 1961.
19. STERN, HAWKINS, "The Significance of Impulse Buying Today," *Journal of Marketing*, 26 (April 1962), 59–62.
20. WEST, C. JOHN, "Results of Two Years of Study Into Impulse Buying," *Journal of Marketing*, 15 (January 1951), 362–3.

13 BEHAVIOR AND COGNITION DURING PURCHASE

In this chapter, consideration is directed toward the physical and mental activity ongoing during the act of purchase. The mental activity, information-processing, can concern in-store stimuli and the evaluation of purchase alternatives. Moreover, there is the exchange of information between buyer and salesman, referred to as bargaining, wherein a good deal of gamesmanship may take place. Where joint purchase deliberations involving husband and wife are concerned, it is of interest to note the influence pattern or role specialization that may evolve.

Concerning in-store stimuli affecting purchase outcomes, we begin with a study by Frank and Massy (1970)* in which the importance of retail shelf position and relative display space to sales levels is investigated. In package-goods marketing, manufacturer salesmen serving the retail food outlet often devote a considerable amount of their time to securing favorable shelf position and display space for their brand in the belief that the items most easily seen and reached will sell in greater quantity. Rather than conducting controlled experiments, the researchers employed store recorded data over an extended time period with an analytical design intended to account for interactive effects among shelf rows and shelf levels for given brand–package-size combinations.

Although all of us have experienced bargaining behavior while engaged in discussions with salesmen, relatively little systematic research has been reported on the nature of give-and-take that transpires. Particularly for major purchases, such interaction is a very important source of new information that can alter or substantiate purchase intention. Pennington's (1968)* study presents a fascinating examination of bargaining variables related to eventual purchase outcomes, along with eleven variables that apparently affect the likelihood of a completed sales transaction.

With the repeated calls for consumerism legislation, there is a clear need to conduct research regarding the information that consumers genuinely need and can appropriately use. In order to provide additional information to the consumer, there is often additional cost that must ultimately be passed along in the price. If this information helps the buyer in better allocating his resources to products that satisfy his expectations, the additional cost may well be warranted. Friedman (1966)* conducted a study in which buyers were asked to select the "most economical package" for twenty different products sold in supermarkets. Given the considerable number of price-quantity combinations available, this task generally involves some difficulty. Friedman's objective was to devise measures of such confusion so as to identify those product categories wherein the objective task (select the most economical package) is most difficult to attain. He also suggests other applications of such confusion measures.

30. Shelf position and space effects on sales

ronald e. frank
& william f. massy

INTRODUCTION

The purpose of this investigation is to estimate the effects of selected retail shelf merchandising policies on the sales of particular brand/size combinations for a branded, frequently purchased grocery product. Though the effects of in-store merchandising practices such as shelf display have been intensively investigated in the case of farm products,[1] there is a lack of published research for branded, frequently purchased food products. A review of the literature showed only two studies of the effects of shelf position and/or facings on sales [1, 6]. This study is concerned with the answers to the following questions:

1. What is the effect of varying the number of rows (facings) of a brand's shelf display?
2. What is the effect of varying its height from the floor?
3. Is the effect of varying the number of rows different if an item is near the floor as opposed to being near the top (i.e., is there an interaction between the effect of shelf rows and the level of the shelf display)?

THE DATA

The grocery product studied here is purchased by the majority of United States households on an average of once every two weeks and is heavily promoted by both manufacturers and retailers.

Data were taken from a store audit run for sixty-three weeks in one of the nation's largest metropolitan areas. Twice each week thirty stores were audited. In each store a detailed weekly record of sales and supporting promotion was made for each brand and container size. This included the shelf price, whether or not advertised by retailer, advertised price, whether or not in-store signs or displays were used, the number of rows stacked, and the shelf level.

This study is based on data for the seven highest-volume brands in the market area. For each store in our sample in which one of these was distributed, a separate weekly record was made for each container size stocked for that brand. (There are three container sizes in which the product is typically packaged, hereafter referred to as small, medium and large size containers.) Although a maximum of 630

Reprinted by permission from *Journal of Marketing Research*, Vol. 7 (February 1970), pp. 59–66, published by the American Marketing Association.

[1] As early as 1958 a bibliography appeared listing over 200 references to in-store farm product merchandising studies [2].

(thirty stores times seven brands times three sizes) series, each sixty-three weeks in length, could conceivably have been generated, this investigation is based on only 385 store-brand-size specific time series because all stores did not stock all sizes of all brands.

THE RESEARCH DESIGN

Because the data have both time series (repeated weekly measurement in the same store over time) and cross-sectional (the measurement of different stores at a point in time) characteristics, the effects of the shelf policy variables might be inferred by relating their variation from one week to the next to the concomitant variation in sales for a particular brand and size. Alternatively, the same set of relationships could be analyzed by their variation from one store to another or, say, from one brand to another within a given store. A third possibility would be to combine these two approaches.

This analysis is cross-sectional, making no use of the time series aspect of our data because of the virtual lack of variation over time in the shelf policy variables under investigation. Store managers seldom changed the shelf level or significantly altered the number of rows allocated to a given brand and size. The absence of variation in these policy variables over time means that their effects cannot be inferred from historical time series data.

A Problem of Confounded Effects

Though we chose to base our findings on cross-sectional data, this approach is not without important problems, such as the direction of causation. Do changes in shelf policy variables lead to changes in sales or vice versa? Do store managers increase shelf space for a given brand/size in order to increase its sales or in response to historical sales differences?

Suppose we took our data and, for a given time period, cross classified each store/brand/size observation by the number of shelf rows and sales and found a positive relation between the two variables. What might have caused such a relationship? There are a number of alternative hypotheses:

1. The number of rows is a determinant of sales, to the full extent we observe in our data.
2. The effect of number of rows (whatever its magnitude) is confounded with the store manager's response to historical sales differences from one brand to another and/or from one container size to another.
3. The effect of number of rows is confounded with differences in store size (e.g., larger stores might provide more display space per item for the product).

Ideally, we would like to adjust for the possible confounding of brand/size and store effects with those of the shelf policy variables.

We could avoid store effects by analyzing our data one store at a time. This would mean conducting thirty analyses, one for each store; having, at best, only twenty-one observations (one for each brand/size combination) upon which to base our results within each store.

But brand or size effects would still not have been taken into account. An analysis controlling for brand or size effects would run into similar problems—"thin" data, and the inability to control for the other possible sources of confounding.

The problem was to find some way of specifying the relationship between shelf policy variables and sales that would permit the pooling of data across stores, brands and sizes and, at the same time, substantially mitigate the degree to which their effects would be confounded with those of the shelf policy variables.

The Models

Two basic models are used:

1. $NS_{ijk} = a + \sum_{l=1}^{3} b_l R_l + \sum_{l=4}^{9} b_l L_l + \sum_{l=10}^{37} b_l C_l$

2. $NS_{ijk} = a + \sum_{l=1}^{22} b_l I_l + \sum_{23}^{50} b_l C_l$

In the first model, normal sales (NS) for Brand i in container size j in the kth store are hypothesized to be a linear function of the following three *sets* of variables (represented by the letters, R, L and C):

1. R—measures the number of rows devoted to given brand and size.
2. L—measures the shelf level on which the particular brand and size is displayed.
3. C—measures the effects of brands, sizes and stores so that their association with sales will not be confounded with the estimated effects of the shelf policy variable.

The second model is identical to the first except that the R and L sets of variables are replaced by a set referred to as I (interactions). The I's also measure the main effects of shelf level and number of rows, but differ from the previous model in that they are defined to measure also the nature and extent of any interactions between shelf level and number of rows (i.e., any tendency for the effect of shelf rows to depend on shelf level or vice versa).

Multiple regression analysis was used to estimate the parameters of each model. (The first model will hereafter be referred to as the "main effects model," second as the "interaction model.")

Variable Specifications: Normal Sales

Weekly sales for the ijth brand/size combination in a given store can be defined as the sum of two components: (1) that part due to the effects of policy variables that remain unchanged for a substantial period of time, such as shelf level and number of rows, as well as product characteristics; and (2) that part due to the effects of short-run promotions such as special advertised-price offers, displays, premiums, etc.

The dependent variable used in this analysis (NS_{ijk}) is defined as the average sales for ijth brand/size combination in the kth store over those weeks during which that particular brand/size combination was not being promoted in the store under consideration. This variable is our operational definition of the first of the two components of sales described above.

In our opinion this constitutes a better measure of demand for evaluating the effects of shelf policy variables than the average of all sales[2] because:

1. It is "adjusted" for the extraneous effects (in the context of this investigation) of short-run promotions on sales.
2. The estimates of the effect of shelf policy variables will be less confounded with the effects of other forms of promotion than if average total sales are used as the dependent variable. This depends on the assumption that the rate of activity for the promotional policy variables (e.g., short-run advertised-price cuts) which determines the magnitude of the short-run component of total sales is correlated with the magnitude of the shelf policy variables as well as with sales for the brand itself (i.e., that stores with a relatively large number of rows for a given brand/size combination engage in above average short-run promotional activity with respect to it).

Although these assumptions were not formally tested, they are reasonable in the context of the market for the product under investigation as well as in the context of other branded, frequently purchased and promoted retail grocery items.

Shelf Rows

For the first set of independent variables defined in the exhibit, the shelf row variables, the original data base consisted of ten, of which the first few were deleted for reasons to be given below. Each was a dummy variable which measures whether or not ('1' if yes and '0' if no) the brand/size/store combination displayed a particular number of rows. For example, variable 3 in the exhibit would take a value of '1' if there were seven rows for that brand/size combination in a given store. Averaging the number of rows over the weeks for that brand/size/store combination (i.e., in which that brand/size combination was not being promoted in the store studied) gave the number of rows. The averaging could have been almost completely ignored as the shelf policy variable changed very infrequently from week to week. This same procedure was used for the other shelf policy variables.

Only six of the variables were included in our analysis. None of the observations displayed only one row. The variables measuring whether two, three or four rows were displayed were highly collinear with those reporting five or more rows, and therefore were deleted from the analysis.

---

[2] Though this is a better measure of sales for our purpose, it is not perfect. For example, it does not hold constant the effects of promotions for competing brands and sizes in the same store. This is impossible in the context of this product market in that in most stores at least one brand/size combination is being promoted each week.

Shelf Level

Dummy variables were also used to measure the shelf level on which a given brand/size was displayed. Originally there were four shelf level variables; only three are included in the analysis because one was eliminated due to collinearity.

Controls

As previously stated, differences in normal sales levels (*NS*) across stores, brands, and package sizes are apt to be confounded with the differences in normal sales associated with the shelf policy variables. The purpose of including the twenty-eight control variables in our analysis is to statistically control (adjust) for this confounding due to brands, sizes and stores. This is directly analogous to covariance analysis as used in experimentation.

How does the inclusion of these control variables in our analysis serve to adjust for their effects? Consider the series of normal sales figures for each observation. Shelf policy variables and the control variables are apt to cause normal sales to vary. We wish to adjust for the effects of the control variables in order to infer the effects of the shelf policy variables; the removal of their effects on sales can at the very least increase the precision of any subsequent estimates of the effects of the shelf policy variables and, at best, not only increase precision but also adjust for the effects of confounding.

Coefficients computed from a regression in which normal sales form the dependent variable and the 28 control variables are the independent variables, together with the raw data on which the run was based, could then be used to compute a series of *expected normal sales* figures for each observation. Variation in the magnitude of *expected normal sales* would be due only to the effects of control variables. If for each observation we subtract the *expected normal sales* computed from the results of our regression analysis from actual normal sales (i.e., compute the residuals about the regression surface), what variables are apt to cause the residuals to vary? If our model of the control variables adequately describes their relationship to normal sales, then the effects of the control variables on variation from one observation to another will *no longer be present in the residual series:* the residuals can be thought of as a *new* normal sales series adjusted for the effects of brands, sizes and stores and used as a dependent variable in a regression analysis with the shelf policy variables as independent variables.

This procedure would have reduced the original variation in normal sales from observation to observation with residuals varying less than the raw data. Estimates of the effects of shelf policy variables based on the residuals will therefore be more precise than with unadjusted normal sales, but without handling the problem of confounding. Confounding is due not only to the correlation of the control variables with normal sales, but also to their correlation with the shelf policy variables. The procedure using residuals adjusts for the correlation

FIGURE Independent Variables for Each Brand/Size/ Store Combination (All are Dummy Variables)

I. *Rows—R*
   Whether or not there are:
   1. 5 shelf rows
   2. 6 shelf rows
   3. 7 shelf rows
   4. 8 shelf rows
   5. 9 shelf rows
   6. 10 shelf rows or more
II. *Shelf Level—L*
   Whether or not the display is:
   7. 2 shelves from the floor
   8. 3 shelves from the floor
   9. 4 or more shelves from the floor (if 7, 8 and 9 are all 0, then the display is on the first or bottom shelf)
III. *Controls —C*
   Whether or not the brand being analyzed is brand
   10. B1
   11. B2
   12. B3
   13. B4
   Whether or not the size being analyzed is:
   14. The medium size container
   Whether or not the store being analyzed is:
   15.
   16.
   17. ⎫ One of the 23 individual stores represented by the dummy variables numbered 15 through 37
   ⋮
   37. ⎭
IV. *Interactions—I* *
   Whether or not the *ij*th brand/size combination is on the *first shelf* from the bottom and has:
   38. 6 shelf rows
   39. 7 shelf rows
   Whether or not the *ij*th brand/size combination is on the *second shelf* from the bottom and has:
   40. 2 shelf rows
   41. 6 shelf rows
   42. 7 shelf rows
   Whether or not the *ij*th brand/size combination is on the *third shelf* from the bottom and has:
   43. 2 shelf rows
   44. 3 shelf rows
   45. 5 shelf rows
   46. 6 shelf rows
   47. 7 shelf rows
   48. 8 shelf rows
   Whether or not the *ij*th brand/size combination is on the *fourth shelf* from the bottom and has:
   49. 2 shelf rows
   50. 3 shelf rows
   51. 6 shelf rows
   52. 7 shelf rows
   53. 8 shelf rows
   Whether or not the *ij*th brand/size combination is on the *fifth or higher shelf* from the bottom and has:
   54. 1 shelf row
   55. 2 shelf rows
   56. 3 shelf rows
   57. 6 shelf rows
   58. 7 shelf rows
   59. 8 shelf rows

*Only those interactions which occurred were given a code. This accounts for the apparently incomplete categories of shelf rows.

of the control variables with normal sales, but *ignores* the correlation between the control and shelf policy variables (the shelf policy variables are left out of the regression analysis including the control variables, and the control variables are left out of the analysis of the shelf policy variables).

The simultaneous inclusion of both the control and shelf policy variables in the same regression analysis adjusts:

1. For the direct effects of the control variables on normal sales, thereby increasing precision.
2. For the confounding of the effects of control and shelf variables, thereby reducing this source of bias.[3]

Twelve of the control variables originally measured in our data base were excluded from our analysis due to collinearity (three brand, two size and seven store variables).

Interactions

To determine if the effect of varying shelf rows differs depending on shelf level, or vice versa, the effects of every *combination* of these two shelf policy variables must be estimated. There were originally five shelf level variables and ten shelf row variables, implying a total of fifty dummy variables (one for each combination of the original variables).

Only twenty-two of these interaction variables were included in our analysis; twenty-five were deleted because their particular combinations of shelf level and facings never occurred in our data, and three because of collinearity. Each observation would have a '1' for one of these twenty-two variables and a zero for the other twenty-one.

RESULTS

In reporting the results of the comparison between the main effects and interaction models for the shelf policy variables, whichever of these models is "best" will be the basis for our discussion. The burden of proof is on the interaction model; it hypothesizes a greater degree of complexity about the effects of shelf level and rows on normal sales and is less parsimonious than the other. (Even in the world of the computer, parsimony is of value.)

Main Effects Versus the Interaction Model

Table 1 reports a comparison of the coefficients of determination (i.e., the proportion of the variation in normal sales accounted for by the full set of independent variables included in the analysis) for the main effects and interaction models.

Each row of the table reports a comparison of the models based on different groups of stores. Separate analyses were conducted on the data for high (fifteen stores with the highest total volume of the product's sales during the period of the audit) and low volume (remaining) stores as well as for all stores pooled together. These store categories

---

[3] For a more detailed discussion see Green and Tull [4].

TABLE 1   Coefficients of Determination[a] for Main Effects and Interaction Models

	Model	
	Main effects	Interaction
All stores	.41	.41
High volume stores	.46	.45
Low volume stores	.55	.52

[a] Adjusted for sample size

were used in an analysis of the effects of short-run retailer promotions. In that context, substantial differences in response to promotional variables were observed and were carried over as the basis for store stratification to this analysis.[4]

In none of the three comparisons did the interaction model outperform the main effects model in the proportion of variation in normal sales explained. In fact, in two of the three cases, the coefficients of determination for the interaction model (after adjustment for sample size) were *less* than those for the comparable main effects model. An analysis of the coefficients of the interaction and main effects models, together with these results, led us to the conclusion that the interaction model provides neither greater predictive efficacy nor increased insight into the way in which shelf level and rows affect normal sales. We could find no evidence that the effect of varying the number of shelf rows depends on shelf level or vice versa. Therefore, the main effects model was chosen as the one used for reporting the results of our analysis of the effects of shelf policy variables on normal sales.

Main Effects Model: Overall Performance

We will interpret the results from the main effects model in two stages. In this section we focus on:

1. Whether or not the contribution of the variables, included in a given regression analysis, to explaining variation in normal sales is significantly different from zero. The appropriate test of this hypothesis is an F test.[5]
2. Whether or not the *addition* of the shelf policy variables to the model contributes more to the prediction of normal sales than one might expect by chance. The appropriate test of this hypothesis we shall call the F-add test. These tests are especially important, for if the null hypothesis is accepted (that the contribution of the additional variables is due to chance), then there is little merit in concerning ourselves with the detailed interpretation of the coefficients.

[4] See Frank and Massy [3].

[5] For a statement of the theory underlying this as well as the other F-tests referred to in this section, see Johnston [5, 106–38].

3. Whether or not the differences between the coefficients observed in the high and low volume analyses are due to chance (i.e., whether or not the effects of the variables included in the model are the same in both store segments). In our discussion we shall refer to the appropriate test of this hypothesis as the *F*-diff test; as in the case of the *F*-add test, it provides a check against over-interpreting the data.

The sections which follow discuss in detail the pattern of effects within each set of shelf policy variables. For each of the three store classification (all stores, high, and low volume stores) three separate regression runs were made, based on all three sets of variables (*R*, *L* and *C*). In addition, within both the high and low volume store classifications, three other runs were made for the following container size categories: (1) small size containers; (2) medium size containers; and (3) small and medium size containers combined.

Store Volume Categories

The first analysis by store volume category was a run including only the control variables. The coefficient of determination for the low volume store analysis was .47; for the high volume store analysis it was .37. All of the *F*-ratios corresponding to each of the three regression runs with this model were significant at the .0001 level. These results are important only in that they serve as a comparison for the effect of adding the row and level variables to the analysis.

The coefficient of determination for all three groups of stores increases with the addition of the row and level variables, running from .37 to .46 and from .45 to .55 respectively. The fact that the coefficients of determination increased more when the sample was split (after adjusting for sample size) than when all stores were pooled, provides some evidence that the effects of the shelf policy variables may vary from one store segment to another. In testing this hypothesis, the *F*-add tests (which measure whether or not the contribution of the row and level variables is due to chance) are all statistically significant at the .0001 level. Clearly it is worth interpreting the exact nature of these effects in more detail.

Lastly, a test was performed on the main effects model with all four sets of variables included to determine whether or not the effects in the high volume store segment were different from those in the low volume segment to a degree greater than one might expect by chance. The *F*-diff ratio was significant at the .005 level.

As there appear to be differences in the effects of shelf policy variables from high to low store segments, our subsequent discussion will focus upon these results as opposed to those for the all stores segment. The effects of the shelf row and level variables clearly merit further discussion.

Container Size Categories

The principal reason for conducting the container size analysis was to determine the extent to which the effects of the shelf row and level variables differ from small to medium container sizes. (The data were too sparse for large size containers to be included.)

The F-ratios for each of the six regressions were all significant at the .0001 level. Two F-diff ratios were computed to test the hypotheses that the effects of the shelf policy variable are dependent on container size within both the high and low volume store categories. The F-diff ratio for container size effect differences in high volume stores was significant at the .005 level, whereas the F-diff for container size effects in low volume stores was significant at *only* the .30 level. Based on these results, our discussion of the effects of shelf policy variables by container size will be based on the results for the high volume category.

Shelf Rows

Table 2 reports the coded regression coefficients and t-ratios for the main effects model for all three store categories based on three sets of variables (shelf level and row as well as controls). The coefficients for the control variables are deleted from the table, as they were included in the model only to increase precision and reduce the bias of the coefficients for the shelf policy variables reported.

TABLE 2   Summary of Coded Regression Coefficients and T-Ratios* for Main Effects Model

	All stores	High volume stores	Low volume stores
Shelf facings			
5	100	100	100
	(0.48)	(0.41)	(2.80)
6	165	183	116
	(3.15)	(1.97)	(4.29)
7	177	222	115
	(3.34)	(2.59)	(4.28)
8	165	183	125
	(2.64)	(1.41)	(4.48)
9	271	395	115
	(4.32)	(4.36)	(2.73)
10 or more	252	428	128
	(4.34)	(3.79)	(3.46)
Shelf level			
2nd shelf from bottom	17	33	35
	(3.41)	(2.57)	(2.54)
3rd shelf from bottom	23	194	25
	(2.33)	(2.00)	(2.26)
4th shelf from bottom	66	89	—
	(0.37)	(0.32)	
R^2	.48	.53	.61
R^2 adjusted	.41	.46	.55
F	8.69	8.37	9.84
Degrees of freedom	(37, 385)	(25, 199)	(25, 186)

* t-ratios are in parentheses.

Because of the competitive nature of the results, the coefficients in this table (and Table 2) have been coded using the following formula:

$$b^* = \frac{b_{ij} + k_{.j}}{b_{1j} + k_{.j}}, \text{ where}$$

b_{ij} is the actual coefficient of the ith variable in the jth regression equation.

$k_{.j}$ is a constant which varies from one equation to the next (i.e., from one column to the next).

b_{1j} is the original regression coefficent for the first independent variable in the equation which for all of the results to be reported is 5 shelf facings.

This coding procedure leaves the t-ratios and the relative magnitude of effects within an equation unchanged. However, the resulting comparison of effects across sizes and store types is correct only in the direction of observed effects (e.g., that the effect of number of facings is greater in high volume than low volume stores).

The value of each coefficient for the shelf row variables is not important in itself, but the change in their magnitude from five to ten or more rows is. The effect of shelf rows on normal sales is measured by the relationship between the magnitude of the "coded" regression coefficients for each of the six dummy variables and the number of rows represented separately for both high and low volume store segments. Both relationships are approximately linear. The slopes of these relationships are our estimate of the effect on weekly sales of increasing the number of shelf rows by one unit for high and low volume store segments. The slopes are 60.0 and 3.0 percentage points.[6] That is, in high volume stores increasing the number of shelf rows by one unit (within the range of activity included in our analysis) results in a weekly sales increase of 60 percentage points; the same change in low volume stores results in only 3.0 percentage points.[7]

Table 3 reports the extension of the analysis by store volume category to small and medium container sizes. In the high volume category, an additional row for the medium container size is associated with an approximate 45 percentage point increase in weekly sales, but in the case of small size containers the addition of a row brings an increment of about 10 percentage points. In the low volume stores the corresponding figures are 2.0 and 0.0 percentage points for small and medium container sizes.

Shelf Level

The results for shelf level are considerably more tenuous than those for shelf rows. As in the case of the shelf row coefficients, the magnitude of the individual coefficients for the shelf level variables is not

---

[6] These estimates were computed plotting the two sets of coefficients and entering freehand linear functions on the graphs.

[7] In retrospect the number of shelf rows could have been treated as a ratio scaled variable in a linear regression model.

TABLE 3 Summary of Regression Coefficients and T-Ratios*—Main Effects Model by Container Size

	High volume stores			Low volume stores		
	Pooled small and medium size	Small	Medium	Pooled small and medium size	Small	Medium
Shelf facings						
5	100	100	100	100	100	100
	(0.49)	(0.82)	(0.35)	(2.91)	(0.59)	(2.27)
6	292	92	258	124	80	125
	(3.01)	(0.47)	(3.38)	(4.19)	(0.11)	(3.79)
7	353	124	240	121	111	111
	(3.45)	(2.24)	(2.52)	(3.98)	(0.88)	(2.99)
8	406	124	250	138	123	118
	(2.67)	(1.47)	(2.27)	(4.44)	(1.11)	(3.33)
9	630	120	364	127	125	81
	(5.32)	(1.01)	(4.82)	(3.01)	(1.15)	(1.04)
10 or more	550	152	400	141	114	126
	(4.92)	(3.38)	(4.05)	(3.67)	(0.92)	(2.40)
Shelf level						
2nd shelf from bottom	46	68	80	7	21	11
	(1.34)	(1.04)	(0.02)	(1.98)	(0.89)	(−0.40)
3rd shelf from bottom	31	16	150	0	27	2
	(1.28)	(1.84)	(0.89)	(1.68)	(0.41)	(−0.05)
4 or more shelves from bottom	108	8	160	—	—	—
	(0.04)	(1.55)	(0.63)			
R^2	.59	.68	.62	.64	.82	.65
R^2 adjusted	.52	.56	.48	.57	.74	.60
F	5.34	5.35	4.38	5.78	8.52	4.83
Degress of freedom	36, 130	23, 59	24, 60	37, 121	23, 52	24, 59

* t-ratios are in parentheses.

important. What is important is the change in value of the coefficients as a function of shelf level itself.

The dummy variables included in the model are for displays that are two, three and four or more shelves from the floor. Displays on the bottom shelf or one shelf above it were coded with three zeros for each of the three dummy variables.

The results for the effects of number of rows on sales (reported above) vary over store volume and package size categories in a logically coherent fashion (the effects are greater for large stores than for small and, in high volume stores, for the medium as opposed to the small container size) and t-ratios of 2.0 and 3.0 were frequent. In contrast, the results for the shelf level variables do not meet prior expectations, nor are the t-ratios frequently above 1.0 or even near the magnitude of those for the row variables. Using the results from Tables 2 and 3 one can come to two opposite conclusions with respect to the effects of shelf level:

1. The lower shelves are the most effective (Table 3—high volume stores, small container size).
2. The middle and upper shelves are most effective (high volume stores—Table 2—and high volume stores, medium container size—Table 3).

Due to the number of anomalies in the results, together with the low t-ratios, the most reasonable interpretation is that shelf level has an extremely modest effect on sales of this product, if any at all.

CONCLUSIONS

At the outset, we state our concern for the answers to several questions as to the effects of shelf policy variables on sales. Here in summary form is a list of the questions, together with the answers, based on the preceding analysis:

1. *What is the effect of varying the number of shelf rows allocated to a brand/size on sales?* Within the range of 5–10 rows, adding a row adds to proportionately greater increment to weekly sales in high (but not low) volume stores regardless of the container size involved.
2. *What is the effect of varying the shelf level on a brand/size's normal sales?* Only a modest effect, if any.
3. *Is there an interaction between the effects of shelf level and rows on normal sales?* No.

In designing this investigation we attempted to minimize the potential bias caused by the confounding of store, container size and brand effects on sales with the effects of the shelf policy variables in three ways:

1. By using normal as opposed to total sales as a dependent variable.
2. By using covariance analysis using stores, container sizes and brand dummy variables as covariates.

3. By containing the brands included in the investigation to the six with the highest volume in the market area under investigation (confounding should be less among those brands than if those with extremely small market shares had been included in the analysis).

Nonetheless these results probably to some degree overstate the effects of the shelf policy variable for two reasons:

1. We have attempted to adjust for the confounding of sales difference in stores, brands and size on the shelf policy variables. But to the extent we have not been successful, any remaining degree of confounding is apt to lead to an overstating of the effects of the shelf policy variable.
2. Our model of the effects of the shelf policy variables assumes that the full effect on sales of a given change in the magnitude of one of the shelf policy variables is felt instantaneously, where it is more reasonable to assume that the effects are cumulative over time (i.e., that initially there is a small effect on sales and that this gradually builds up to the full effect). Within the constraints of our data, we have no way of assessing how long it takes to attain the full effect of a change in number of rows on normal sales.

To mitigate the effects of the confounding variables, controlled store experimentation is usually superior to analyzing observational data such as we have reported. Experiments, however, typically are more expensive and time consuming than observational studies. How can one obtain the time and cost advantages of observational analyses with the assurance that confounding has been virtually eliminated, as in a controlled store experiment?

Ideally, in our opinion, observational and controlled store experiments should be conducted on the same or matched sets of stores to "validate" the results of observational studies. If this can be successfully done (and we think it can) then, in the long run, observational studies with appropriate controls (for stores, brands and sizes) can be used in place of controlled store experiments for decision making.

REFERENCES

1. Cox, Keith, "The Responsiveness of Food Sales to Shelf Space Changes in Supermarkets," *Journal of Marketing Research*, 1 (May 1964), 63–7.
2. Dominick, Bennett A., Jr., *Research in Retail Merchandising of Farm Products*, Washington: U.S. Department of Agriculture, Marketing Research Report No. 416, 1960.
3. Frank, Ronald E. and William F. Massy, *A Marketing Decision Model* (to be published sometime in late 1970 or early 1971).
4. Green, Paul E. and Donald S. Tull, "Covariance Analysis in Marketing Experimentation," *Journal of Advertising Research*, 16 (June 1966), 45–53.
5. Johnston, J., *Economic Methods*, New York: McGraw-Hill Book Co., 1962.
6. Progressive Grocer, *Colonial Study*, 1964.

31. Customer-salesman bargaining behavior in retail transactions

allan l. pennington

The transaction is a basic unit of analysis in any marketing activity. All agencies directly or indirectly involved in marketing a good or service share the trait of interacting, exchanging, negotiating, or transacting with other agencies. No single agency can stand apart from its suppliers, customers, and environment.

Yet surprisingly little research has explicitly adopted the transaction as the basic unit of analysis [10]. Instead, the research has tended to concentrate on only one party to the transaction, buyer or seller, without being overtly concerned with relative inputs and outputs of both parties, decision-making processes of both buyer and seller, and interaction of both parties to the transaction relative to its ultimate outcomes.

Several empirical studies, such as those in [1, 3, 8, 9, 12, 13, 14, 16], help clarify the simultaneous behavior of both parties to the transaction. Although each study was designed for a different purpose and concentrates on a different institutional setting, they all give some insight into the interactive effects of transactional behavior.

Most of them incorporated what Lazarsfeld calls the distributive approach to the study of action.[1] They focus on outcomes resulting from the transaction rather than the transaction per se. Virtually no research has measured and analyzed in depth the processes involved in transactional behavior between the parties to the transaction. Thus, a rigorous analysis of the transaction in an empirical setting, giving careful consideration to the behavior of *both* buyer and seller, appeared to be a meaningful and worthy venture.

Transactions comprise several separate but related processes, any of which could be meaningfully examined. The study results here focused on retail transactions for just one of these processes—the process of bargaining behavior.[2]

How much bargaining behavior and price negotiation occur in a retail setting will vary greatly across product types. Most purchases of goods and services are routine and involve little, if any, explicit bargaining behavior by either salesman or customer. However, trans-

Reprinted by permission from *Journal of Marketing Research*, Vol. 5 (August 1968), pp. 255–262, published by the American Marketing Association.

Allan L. Pennington is assistant professor of marketing, University of Minnesota. The author expresses his appreciation to Ronald P. Willett for his contribution in planning and supervising this study.

[1] Lazarsfeld also presents two alternative approaches, the morphological and the analytical, which have been used to a lesser extent. See [2].

[2] For examination of another transactional process—social interaction—see [17].

actions involving durable goods or other items in which price is a variable factor were presumed to involve bargaining and price negotiation strategies for both parties. Transactions between appliance salesmen and their customers were, therefore, chosen as a focal point for the present study. However, price is not the only marketing variable involved in the negotiation process. Product features, styling, delivery, and other similar variables are also important in the formal and informal negotiation process in such transactions.

Thus, this study analyzes, in depth, transactions between appliance salesmen and their customers. More specifically it:

1. identifies the presence or absence of a specific process of bargaining behavior in the selected institutional setting
2. determines how greatly bargaining behavior concentrates on price as compared with other variables
3. identifies specific components of bargaining behavior and their relative frequencies
4. determines how the mentioned factors relate to purchase outcomes.

METHODOLOGY

Conceptualization of Bargaining Behavior

Previous empirical research on bargaining behavior fails to specify measurable components of the bargaining process. In this study, four structural components of bargaining behavior were formulated for both customer and salesman. These components are derived from theoretical formulations of bargaining behavior, notably from Kuehn [11] and Schelling [15]. The components, which can be readily observed and interpreted in a natural setting and which are measurable with the methodology used, are:

1. *direct offers.* any concession by the salesman, such as reduction of price, more rapid delivery, or extended credit terms; the customer's offer to purchase for concessions such as the above.
2. *presentation of concession limits.* statement of expectations from the transaction by either salesman or customer, such as statement of prices, desired style, or service policies.
3. *determination of concession limits.* attempts to determine expectations of the other person in the transaction, such as a salesman's attempt to determine the customer's credit wishes or a customer's attempt to determine a salesman's delivery schedule.
4. *attempts to change concession limits.* attempts by either customer or salesman to get the other to change his expectations of the transaction.

These overt behavior patterns were seen as attempts by parties in the transaction to engage in bargaining activity. All of the structural components were equally weighted, and the frequencies' sums of each of the four components yielded both a customer total bargaining score and a salesman total bargaining score for each transaction.

Research Design

The methodology had two phases: (1) identification and measurement of the structural components of bargaining behavior for both customer and salesman and (2) telephone interviews with customers to generate additional data on shopping patterns and purchase outcomes.

Data collection took place in 11 appliance or department stores in seven midwestern cities. The total was approximately equally represented by department stores, multi-line stores, and stores specializing in only one full-line brand. Fourteen salesmen participated in the study.

The study was based on a detailed examination of about 15 transactions for each salesman, or 210 transactions. The transactions included in the study were the first 15 transactions in which the salesman participated after the study began. The time necessary to generate 15 transactions varied widely, depending on traffic patterns and salesman rotation systems, and ranged from part of a day to one week. In effect, then, the transactions represented a census of customers with whom the salesman interacted over time.

All transactions in which the salesman was able to make a presentation of the product to the customer were included. Salesmen were not allowed to qualify the customer as a "hot" prospect before inclusion in the study. The only transactions excluded were service calls, social calls, and transactions involving appliances priced under $50.

Measuring Instruments

To meaningfully identify the structural components of the bargaining taxonomy it was necessary to develop measuring instruments that could detect every verbal exchange between the customer and salesman. Therefore, a tape recording of the entire transaction was necessary.

Salesmen were equipped with a miniature wireless microphone that they could conveniently carry in a coat pocket. Pretests showed conclusively that this microphone did not interfere with the salesman's actions. It transmitted the verbal record of the transaction to a receiver and tape recorder behind a counter, in a storage room, or in some equally convenient place.

One member of the research team was located with the equipment and arranged to receive and record the verbal portion of the customer's and salesman's actions. The other member, from a distance, visually rated and coded the actions of the customer and salesman. This visual coding was systematically timed so that it could easily be correlated with the verbal recording. Pretests verified the feasibility and practicality of the verbal and visual recording.

Later, the recorded transactions were played back, and each of the bargaining acts was recorded. A bargaining act was defined as a single occurrence of any of the structural components of bargaining in the transaction. These structural components were recorded in both absolute and relative frequencies to generate the total bargaining scores of the customers and salesmen. Also, the referents to which the behavior was directed were recorded for each bargaining act.[3]

All customers in the study were presented with a ticket enabling them to register for a free door prize. Names, addresses, and phone numbers were secured from these registrations for the subsequent customer interviews.[4] Salesmen also filled out a brief check list indicating their impressions of the customer's intentions and characteristics.

All customers were telephoned by professional interviewers two or three days after the transaction was recorded. Interviews determined purchase outcomes, customers' intentions, opinions about appliance stores and salesmen, and demographic data. About two weeks later, all customers who had not completed a purchase by the first interview were interviewed again. These data were compared with salesmen's perceptions recorded earlier.

BARGAINING BEHAVIOR IN APPLIANCE TRANSACTIONS

Table 1 contains the mean number of acts and mean proportion of acts for each of the four structural components. The greatest focus of bar-

TABLE 1   Structural Components of Bargaining

Bargaining component	Mean number of acts per transaction	Proportion of acts per transaction
Presenting concession limits	17.9	58.8
Determining concession limits	7.0	23.1
Attempts to change concession limits	4.8	15.6
Direct offer	.8	2.5
All bargaining acts	30.4	100.0

gaining behavior was on presentation of concession limits—such as presentation of prices, delivery dates, product features—by the salesman, and statements of desired price ranges, styles, and product features by the customers. High frequencies of this structural component were positively related to strong customer intentions, greater shopping time, price oriented patronage motives, and previous ownership of the product.

Attempts to change concession limits were significantly higher when customers had shopped in several stores, considered several brands, contemplated purchase to replace an existing appliance, and obtained high-school educations. This component had significantly lower frequencies in department store transactions than in the other store types.

---

[3] Referents were defined in terms of the specific marketing content of each of the bargaining acts, such as price, delivery, or service.

[4] Previous research projects conducted by a member of the research team indicated that this approach was feasible and practical for identifying customers.

Finally, direct offers had no significant correlation with customer shopping behavior. However, frequencies of direct offers were significantly higher in multi-line operations than in either department stores or brand specialist operations.

Table 2 shows the mean number and relative dispersion of bargain-

TABLE 2   Frequencies of References for Bargaining Acts

Referent	Mean number per transaction	Coefficient of variation (percent)
Price	11.2	88.1
Product features	6.5	130.4
Timing of purchase	3.0	146.1
Brand	1.9	183.3
Terms	1.7	161.5
Delivery	1.7	136.9
Service	1.2	186.9
Guarantee	.9	150.6
Product quality	.6	191.5
Styling	.5	308.0

ing referents across all transactions. As expected, price was the most frequent bargaining referent, followed by product features and timing of purchase, respectively. The price referent also had the lowest coefficient of variation, thereby demonstrating more consistency than the other referents across all transactions.

SUMMARY OF PURCHASE OUTCOMES

Tables 3 and 4 show the distribution of purchase outcomes. More than half of the customers made a purchase within two or three days, and

TABLE 3   Purchase Outcomes

Purchase outcome[a]	Number of cases	Percent of cases
Purchase	132	62.9
When observed	58	27.6
Within three days of being observed	48	22.9
Within two weeks of being observed	26	12.4
No purchase	78	37.1
Total	210	100.0

[a] Purchase (or no purchase) refers to the shopper's completion (or failure to complete) a major appliance purchase within about two weeks of being in an appliance store.

almost 63 percent purchased a major appliance within two weeks after they were observed.

Notable also, almost 63 percent of the purchasers of major appli-

TABLE 4   Place of Purchase

Purchase outcome and place[a]	Number of cases	Percent of cases
Purchase—test store	83	62.9
When observed	58	43.9
Within two weeks of being observed	25	19.0
Purchase—elsewhere	49	37.1
Total	132	100.0

[a] Purchase (or no purchase) refers to the shopper's completion (or failure to complete) a major appliance purchase within about two weeks of being in an appliance store.

ances bought in the store where the transaction was recorded.[5] Most of the customers who purchased (56.1 percent) did so at some other time than when they were observed, and more than a third of this group returned to the test store to purchase.

BARGAINING BEHAVIOR AND PURCHASE OUTCOMES

Dimensions of Purchase Outcomes

Respondents were initially divided into two groups—purchasers and nonpurchasers. Purchasers included respondents who had purchased a major appliance at any of the stages of the study—T_0, T_1, T_2.[6] Nonpurchasers included those who had not purchased a major appliance when they were interviewed at T_2. There were 132 respondents in the first category and 78 respondents in the second. Also, the purchasers were divided into two groups: (1) those who had purchased at T_0 and (2) those who had purchased at either T_1 or T_2. Of the 132 purchasers, 58 were in the first category, and 74 in the second.

CUSTOMER VARIABLES AND PURCHASE OUTCOMES

An examination of the associations between customer variables and purchase outcomes revealed very few significant relationships. A notable exception is the highly significant relationship between customers' purchase intentions and total customer purchase outcomes. About 84 percent of the shoppers who had "definite plans to purchase an appliance soon" purchased either at the time they were observed shopping or within two weeks of that time. The proportion of pur-

[5] Do not be confused with the identical percentages in Tables 3 and 4; they were identical strictly by coincidence.

[6] To simplify citation of the various measurement points, this notation was adopted:

T_0 is time when the shopper was observed in an appliance store, and the transaction was recorded

T_1 is T_0 plus two or three days

T_2 is T_0 plus approximately two weeks.

chasers in each of the remaining intention categories declined consistently with the decline in intentions.

In contrast, intention differences between purchasers at T_0 and purchasers at T_1 or T_2 were not statistically significant. Thus, intentions appeared to be a generally necessary but insufficient condition for the successful transaction.

Number of stores shopped also affected purchase outcomes. Those shoppers who had not purchased by T_2 had shopped for an appliance in considerably fewer stores than those customers who purchased by T_2. In other words, the likelihood of purchase was greater as the number of stores shopped increased. In contrast, considering only purchasers, customers who purchased at T_0 shopped fewer stores than those who purchased at either T_1 or T_2.

These results suggest that, for most shoppers, a minimum amount of shopping and comparison was necessary before reaching a decision to purchase. However, the tendency of one-store shoppers to purchase at T_0 probably reflected a segment of shoppers who found extensive shopping too costly, who were indifferent about brands and stores, or who conducted their search for information before actually shopping.

Also, customers who purchased by T_2 were identified by two patronage motives: (1) model availability and rapid delivery and (2) dealer's reputation. Similarly, those who purchased at T_0 were more likely to express these reasons for patronage than purchasers at T_1 or T_2. The price-oriented customer was the most reluctant to purchase spontaneously, perhaps because of his hopes of finding still better alternatives.

None of the typical economic demographic variables, such as income, education, and age, were statistically related to any dimensions of purchase outcomes.

Incidence of Purchase

Measures of transaction bargaining behavior and shopping variables were tested for independence of classification with customers who purchased in the two-week period versus those who did not. The purpose of this analysis was to isolate those customers whose transaction behavior indicated that they were high-intentions shoppers.

Total transaction bargaining acts and salesman bargaining acts did not show a significant association with this classification of purchase outcomes. The number of customer bargaining acts, however, did appear to differentiate between high- and low-intentions shoppers. Customers who engaged in relatively high numbers of bargaining acts were more apt to purchase than those with low-bargaining scores.

A high frequency of determining concession limits appeared to be characteristic of the high-intentions customer. Transactions with high frequencies of this bargaining component produced substantially higher numbers of purchasers. Since this component was primarily customer-initiated, it was related to the number of customer acts, indicating some accompanying variation. Thus, it can be inferred that purchase outcomes were partially determined by the number of customer acts, the frequency of determining concession limits, or of both acting together.

Too, purchase outcomes were significantly related to both the absolute and relative frequencies of commitments to concession limits.[7] This factor was particularly important since it was not affected by transaction time or volume of acts. In other words, commitments to concession limits were related to purchase outcomes regardless of the transaction's length or the number of bargaining acts.

In both cases, transactions with purchasers evoked considerably more commitments than transactions with nonpurchasers. Commitment to concession limits indicated that either the customer or the salesman had taken a firm position on some factor or issue important to the transaction. Making these firm stands or positions clear to make communication effective was characteristic of high-intentions shoppers.

Surprisingly, the relative frequencies of reference to price in the transaction were inversely related to a purchase by T_2. Nonpurchasers elicited substantially higher relative frequencies of reference to price than did purchasers. Three plausible explanations exist for this phenomenon. Nonpurchasers may have been in the beginning stages of the deliberation and shopping process and, as such, were seeking price information to relate their needs to their budget. Purchasers, on the other hand, may have shopped more and, therefore, were focusing on model, brand, or other features. Alternatively, purchasers may have deliberately refrained from price considerations in the transaction to disguise the fact that they were very close to the purchase point. At best, this could improve the customer's bargaining position; at worst, it could avoid salesmen's pressure to complete the sale. A third explanation might be that nonpurchasers had a strong price orientation that reflected the unfulfilled price expectations of this group.

Purchasers had much stronger propensities to elicit references to delivery and terms than nonpurchasers. It is intuitively obvious that decisions involving delivery and terms would occur very close to the purchase point, and references to these factors would, thus, be more likely to occur in instances where purchases ultimately occurred.

Also, transactions involving customers who purchased by T_2 were associated with high frequencies of reference to product quality, service, and timing of purchase.

Timing of Purchase

Concentrating only on the purchasers, all of the transaction's dimensions of bargaining behavior were related to two other customer outcomes—purchase at T_0 and purchase at either T_1 or T_2. This analysis focused on manifestations of bargaining behavior of both customer and salesman in an attempt to infer those behavioral patterns that induced immediate purchase rather than purchase at a later time or at another retail store. These findings constitute additional indicators of the chances that a customer will purchase spontaneously and may identify causes of the successful transaction.

---

[7] Commitment to concession limits occurred when a salesman or customer either repeated the same concession limit a number of times or took an irrevocable stand relative to a concession limit.

FIGURE Realtionships of Bargaining Variables and Purchase Outcomes

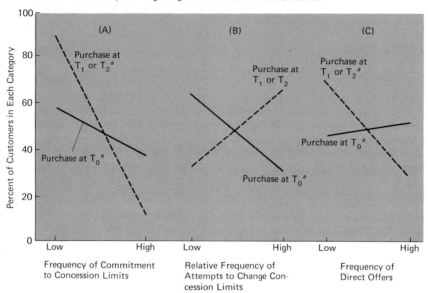

[a] T_0 is time when shopper was observed in an appliance store.
T_1 is T_0 plus two to three days.
T_2 is T_0 plus approximately two weeks.

In the figure, Section A shows the relationship between purchase outcomes and absolute frequencies of commitments to concession limits. The relationship between purchase outcomes and relative frequencies of commitments to concession limits is similar. In both cases, those who purchased at T_0 were more prone to commit themselves or induce salesman commitment than those customers who purchased later. Taking a firm position on something expected from the transaction (for example, price to be paid or time of delivery) and voicing such an expectation for the other's appraisal appeared to increase the chances of an immediate sale.

Section B shows the relationship between immediate purchase outcomes and relative frequencies of attempts to change concession limits. Transactions involving immediate purchasers were substantially low in this respect. Since changing concession limits was primarily a salesman-dominated act, perhaps salesmen were discouraging sales through attempts to brand switch, trade up, or in some other way change a customer's expectations from the transactions.

Similarly, frequency of attempts to change concession limits by devaluating the other's product[8] was negatively related to purchase at T_0. This subcategory of changing concession limits was a customer-dominated act, and usually took the form of criticism of the product, price, or store policies. Situations of this type put the salesman on the

---

[8] Product, in this sense, is not to be taken literally. It can refer to the other's brand, price, attitude, personality, or a host of other factors.

defensive and, thus, presented additional obstacles toward successful completion of the transactions.

Section C demonstrates the positive relationship between purchase at T_0 and frequencies of direct offers. This relationship was to be expected since a direct concession was typically the final act toward inducing the customer to purchase and was much more likely to occur with customers whom the salesman perceived were possible immediate purchasers. Several times the customer appeared to be more concerned with receiving a concession per se, than with its size. Several transactions involving large unit value products were observed where requests for marginal concessions as related merchandise, quicker delivery, or similar items were refused by the salesman, and this appeared to reduce the likelihood of a completed transaction.

Transactions generating purchases at T_0 had a much lower incidence of reference to price than did transactions producing later purchases. Just as purchasers differed from nonpurchasers in price aspirations and bargaining strategies, so might purchasers at T_0 be expected to differ from later purchasers. Purchasers at T_0 may have purposely refrained from price considerations to disguise their purchase intentions and, thus, improve their bargaining power. The heavy emphasis on price for nonpurchasers, however, may have reflected unrealistic or unfulfilled price expectations.

The likelihood of purchase at T_0 was inversely related to the frequency of reference to product quality. Thus, transaction participants that were not closed at T_0 referred to product quality more often than did participants in successful transactions. Immediate purchasers had probably already reached decisions on such general characteristics as quality level and price range before the transaction; thus, they had less need to refer to product quality and more need to refer to product features, delivery terms, or other more specific factors.

Additionally, significant relationships existed between timing of purchase and references to delivery, references to terms or payment facilitation, and references to guarantee. In these instances, transactions involving a spontaneous purchase had significantly higher incidences of these references. Reference to one or all of these typically occurred only in the final stages of deliberation. Certainly, they were not likely to be mentioned by customers who were not seriously contemplating a purchase. Information about delivery, payment facilitation, and guarantee probably reinforced the decision to purchase rather than caused it. Salesman-initiated references to delivery, payment facilitation, and guarantee were similarly more likely to occur with customers whom the salesman perceived to be in the final stages of deliberation.

Delayed Purchase Outcomes

All purchasers were also divided into two more groups for analysis. The first group contained those customers who purchased at the test store, whether they purchased at T_0, T_1, or T_2; this group comprised the original 58 customers who purchased while the transaction was being recorded and 24 customers who returned to the test store to purchase at a latter date, or 82 customers in all. The second group included the 50 customers who ultimately purchased outside the test store.

This classification may be more meaningful since, several times a customer's reason for not purchasing at T_0 was merely a mechanical detail such as getting credit approval or confirming the decision with the spouse. Other times, something that occurred before, during, or after the recorded transaction attracted the customer back to the test store.

Place of purchase was significantly related to both absolute and relative frequencies of commitments to concession limits, where transactions involving purchasers at the test store had a higher incidence of this bargaining component. This same relationship was found to distinguish between purchasers and nonpurchasers and between purchasers at T_0 and later purchasers, probably for the same reasons. Although the logic of the explanation remains the same in all three cases, the relationships were much stronger in the last two. Thus, from an operational viewpoint, commitment to concession limits appeared to be an important predictor of customer behavior.

Transactions with customers who did not purchase in the test store elicited considerably greater references to price than in the case of dyads that generated purchase at the test store. Again, this could be attributed to differences in bargaining strategies or in price aspirations for those customers close to the point of purchase. Another explanation might be that customers who decided to purchase at a given store might have shopped in other stores to reinforce their decision. In other words, to rationalize their decision to purchase from Store A, they shopped in Store B to compare Store A's prices.

INTEGRATION OF FINDINGS

Several explanatory variables appeared to be related to the successful transaction. Many of these variables, however, were not independent of each other, i.e., many of the variables were strongly related to other explanatory variables and to purchase outcomes. Thus, it was necessary to sort out the smaller number of variables that provided the greatest understanding and explanation for the successful transaction. Focusing on the differences between transactions that were closed immediately and transactions that were not completed at the time they were observed, two steps were taken to simplify the number of possible explanatory variables.

First, a test of independence was used to determine the relationships of the explanatory variables and purchase outcomes and to determine concomitance among the explanatory variables. Those variables that were not interrelated were then correlated with purchase outcomes to further refine the analysis and eliminate additional explanatory variables. Thus, a few key variables were isolated that appeared to strongly influence purchase at the time the transaction was observed.

Second, an attempt was made to test the efficiency of this limited number of variables in distinguishing between transactions completed when observed and those completed later.

KEY PREDICTORS OF SUCCESSFUL TRANSACTION

Eleven variables were identified that appeared to affect the likelihood of a completed purchase when transaction was observed. A summary of the results of the correlation analyses of these variables and purchase outcomes is in Table 5.

TABLE 5   Relationships Between Key Shopping and Bargaining Variables and Purchase at Time Observed

Shopping or bargaining variable	Correlation of variable with purchase at time observed (Point-Biserial r)
1. Number of stores shopped by customer	−.27[c]
2. Frequency of direct offers	+.18[b]
3. Relative frequency of attempts to change concession limits	−.25[c]
4. Frequency of commitment to concession limits	+.33[c]
5. Frequency of attempts to change concession limits by devaluating other's product	−.17[a]
6. Frequency of reference to product quality	−.17[a]
7. Frequency of reference to delivery	+.25[c]
8. Frequency of reference to styling	+.21[b]
9. Relative frequency of reference to price	−.24[c]
10. Relative frequency of reference to warranty	+.18[b]
11. Relative frequency of reference to brand	−.16[a]

[a] Significant at .05 level.
[b] Significant at .01 level.
[c] Significant at .001 level.

Efficiency of the Key Explanatory Variables

The preceding analysis did not reveal the effects on purchase outcomes of these key variables working in concert. The dependent variable—purchase outcomes—was dichotomous, preventing the use of multiple-correlation analysis to accomplish this purpose. Instead, the variables were tested together by using multiple-discriminant analysis, a statistical technique for making forecasts or estimating structural parameters in problems where the dependent variable appears in dichotomous form. Its use and interpretation are similar to those in multiple-regression analysis: a linear combination of numerical values for two or more independent variables was used to predict the behavior of the dependent variable [5].

Using the values of each of the 11 variables for a given transaction, this technique predicted whether a transaction should have been completed at the time observed, or whether it was not likely to be completed then. The predictions, based on the values of the explanatory variables for each transaction, were then compared with the true outcomes for the transactions. The extent to which the discriminant function had misclassified the actual outcomes of the transactions served as an index of the efficiency of the 11 variables in predicting purchase outcomes at the time they were observed.

The composite behavior of the 11 variables failed to accurately predict purchase outcomes in only 19.7 percent of the cases. Deleting the shopping variable from the analysis and considering only the ten bargaining variables, the percentage of misclassifications remained the same although the level of significance was less impressive (Table 6).

TABLE 6 Discriminant Analyses of Explanatory Variables and Purchase Outcomes at Time Observed

Explanatory variable	Percentage of misclassifications	F ratio
One shopping variable and ten bargaining variables	19.7	7.16[a]
Ten bargaining variables alone	19.7	6.58[a]

[a] Significant at .01 level.

Because variables were added, dropped, or used in different combinations as the research progressed, the possibility existed that the results somewhat reflected the fitting of the peculiar properties of the particular sample analyzed [6]. In other words, the search bias inherent in the multiple discriminant technique may have overstated the predictive power of the explanatory variables.[9] Nevertheless, the results were considerably more reliable than chance in their ability to identify the customer most likely to purchase when the transaction was observed. Future research efforts should attempt to validate these results in an atmosphere without search bias.

CONCLUSIONS

The transaction represents an infrequently used but potentially useful unit of analysis as a focal point for research efforts. The findings of this study show that individual processes incorporating the behavior of both buyer and seller can be meaningfully identified and analyzed. The study results also show that bargaining behavior between customers and salesmen, although not overwhelming in frequency or volume, exerts an important impact on ultimate purchase outcomes. Meaningful assessment of retail shoppers' bargaining behavior can have important ramifications in identifying the high-intentions customer, determining the time of purchase, and adapting the sales presentation to the unique characteristics of individual consumers.

[9] For a complete examination of search bias, see [7].

REFERENCES

1. BLAKE, JAMES M., "Sales and Purchasing: Here's How They Look at Each Other," *Dun's Review and Modern Industry*, 72 (June 1955), 45–7.
2. DAHL, ROBERT A., MASON HAIRE, AND PAUL F. LAZARSFELD, *Social Science Research on Business: Product and Potential*, New York: Columbia University Press, 1959, 95–155.
3. EVANS, FRANKLIN B., "Selling as a Dyadic Relationship: A New Approach," *American Behavioral Scientist*, 6 (May 1963), 76–9.
4. FERBER, ROBERT, "Research on Household Behavior," *American Economic Review*, 52 (March 1962), 19–63.
5. FRANK, RONALD E., ALFRED A. KUEHN, AND WILLIAM F. MASSY, eds., *Quantitative Techniques in Marketing Analysis*, Homewood, Ill.: Richard D. Irwin, 1963.
6. FRANK, RONALD E., WILLIAM F. MASSY, AND DONALD G. MORRISON, "The Determinants of Innovative Behavior with Respect to a Branded, Frequently Purchased Food Product," in L. George Smith, ed., *Reflections on Progress in Marketing*, Chicago: American Marketing Association, 1964.
7. ————, "Bias in Multiple Discriminant Analysis," *Journal of Marketing Research*, 2 (August 1965), 250–8.
8. FRENCH, CECIL L., "Correlates of Success in Retail Selling," *American Journal of Sociology*, 66 (September 1960), 128–34.
9. GADEL, M. S., "Concentration by Salesmen on Congenial Prospects," *Journal of Marketing*, 28 (April 1964), 64–6.
10. GRANBOIS, DONALD H. AND RONALD P. WILLETT, "Patterns of Conflicting Perceptions Among Channel Members," in L. George Smith, ed., *Reflections on Progress in Marketing*, Chicago: American Marketing Association, 1964.
11. KUEHN, ALFRED, *The Study of Society: A Unified Approach*, Homewood, Ill.: Richard D. Irwin and the Dorsey Press, 1963.
12. LOMBARD, GEORGE F. F., *Behavior in a Selling Group*, Boston: Graduate School of Business Administration, Harvard University, 1955.
13. MILLER, STEPHEN J., "The Social Base of Sales Behavior," *Social Problems*, 12 (Summer 1964), 15–24.
14. RICH, STUART U., *Shopping Behavior of Department Store Customers*, Boston: Graduate School of Business Administration, Harvard University, 1963.
15. SCHELLING, THOMAS C., "An Essay on Bargaining," *American Economic Review*, 46 (June 1956), 281–306.
16. WHYTE, WILLIAM F., *Human Relations in the Restaurant Industry*, New York: McGraw-Hill Book Co., Inc., 1948.
17. WILLETT, RONALD P. AND ALLAN L. PENNINGTON, "Customer and Salesman: The Anatomy of Choice and Influence in a Retail Setting," in Raymond M. Haas, ed., *Science, Technology, and Marketing*, Chicago: American Marketing Association, 1966.

32. Truth in packaging in an american supermarket[1,2]

monroe peter friedman

The matter of truth in the packaging and pricing of products in the American marketplace has been a subject of public controversy in recent years. Much of the current attention stems from the introduction in the 87th Congress of the so-called Truth-in-Packaging Bill by Senator Philip A. Hart of Michigan. The Senate hearings associated with this proposed legislation have stimulated nationwide interest, which has found expression in the mass media in the form of numerous newspaper and popular magazine articles.

Three basic assumptions of the Truth-in-Packaging Bill are as follows:

1. A state of consumer confusion exists in the United States with regard to the true contents and prices of many common retail products.
2. This confusion has resulted from improper packaging and labeling practices by American manufacturers and packagers of consumer products.
3. The remedy for these improper practices is a change to the federal law by which greater authority would be given to the Food and Drug Administration and the Federal Trade Commission in the regulation of packaging and labeling practices.

These assumptions are supported by the testimony of many witnesses in the Senate hearings concerned with packaging practices. As might be expected the hearings also produced testimony of witnesses who challenged one or more of the basic assumptions of the bill.

In large measure the testimony relating to the bill's assumptions was based not on empirical studies of consumer behavior in the American marketplace, but rather on the individual experiences of the witnesses or their organizations with packaging and labeling practices. A notable exception was an attempt to examine the first assumption of the bill, dealing with consumer confusion, by Nelson (1962), the

From U.S., Congress, House, Committee on Interstate and Foreign Commerce, *Part 1 Fair Packaging and Labeling, Hearings on H. R. 15440, S. 985*, 89th Cong., 2d sess., 1966, pp. 154–160.

[1] This research was supported in part by a grant from the College of Arts and Science of Eastern Michigan University. Volunteers from The Ypsilanti, Michigan Chapter of the American Association of University Women, together with two students, Alice Gretzler and Margaret Keck, assisted in the data collection phase of the research.

[2] A briefer version of this paper was presented at the 1965 annual meeting of the American Psychological Association.

Consumer Counsel for the state of California. In her study, Nelson instructed five college educated housewives to purchase the most economical package (largest quantity for the price) for each of 14 common supermarket products. All purchases were made in a Sacramento, California supermarket. The principal result of this study was that the housewives succeeded in selecting the most economical package in only 36 of the 70 purchasing decisions.

As a scientific endeavor the Nelson study has serious shortcomings, e.g., an extremely small number of subjects and the absence of experimental controls for important variables such as product and store familiarity. However, when the study is considered in light of Nelson's background and intentions, namely as an attempt by a concerned non-scientist to seek empirical evidence for a perceived problem for which scientific evidence did not exist, a more tolerant view is surely in order. In any case the Nelson study appears to be the only attempt, by scientist or non-scientist, to deal directly with the empirical problem of consumer confusion in today's marketplace.

The current study attempts to objectively define the issues in the truth-in-packaging controversy by treating consumer confusion as a psychological variable capable of measurement. It is believed that this approach to the problem will permit an empirical evaluation of the first two of the three stated assumptions of the Truth-in-Packaging Bill.

METHOD

Subjects

Thirty-three young married women who were either students or the wives of students at Eastern Michigan University served as subjects (Ss). All Ss had attended college for at least one year and in addition had been married for one or more years. The Ss were tested in a local supermarket with which they were familiar through previous shopping; indeed most Ss were regular customers of the store. Recruitment of Ss took the form of personal requests of the Ss through visits to their homes (mostly apartments in the married student complex of Eastern Michigan University). The Ss were paid for their time.

Procedure

The Ss were instructed to select the most economical (largest quantity for the price) package for each of 20 products on sale at the selected supermarket. A time limit was enforced for each product decision, a limit based on the number of packages on display for the product. More specifically, 10 seconds was allowed for each of the packages in the product category, unless either (1) there were less than six packages to a product class, in which case a one-minute time limit was used, or (2) there were more than 24 packages to a product class, in which case a four-minute time limit was employed.

In addition to stating which package she believed to be the most economical for each of the 20 products, each S reported to the experimenter (E) accompanying her, the information which she used in making her decision.

Each of the 20 products employed in the study had the following characteristics:

1. Two or more different size packages of the product were on sale at the supermarket.
2. Two or more different brands of the product were on sale at the supermarket.
3. The two or more brands for each product appeared to be comparable with regard to the nature of their contents. Thus dry cereals were not selected as a product since corn flakes and raisin bran do not appear to be comparable; on the other hand the different brands and varieties of family flour were considered comparable.
4. The products appeared to be widely used by American families.
5. The products were significant contributors to total supermarket sales. Thus table salt, which qualifies on the basis of the first four criteria was not used in the study since it represents only about .1% of total supermarket sales.

Finally, a characteristic not of any one product, but of the whole group of 20 was that the set of products appeared to be a balanced representation of the packaged products available at American supermarkets.

The testing of the 33 Ss took place over a two-day period. To aid in the testing a map of the supermarket was constructed with a specified route which touched upon the location of each of the 20 products. Ss were then tested in groups of five to ten. Each member of a group was randomly paired with an E and the two were randomly assigned to one of the 20 product locations as their starting point in the test sequence. After S had responded to E's questions at the first location, the two proceeded along the route to the next product location, and continued in this manner until S had been tested at all 20 product locations. This experimental design not only permitted the testing of many Ss simultaneously but also allowed the effect of a variety of product sequences (20 in all), to be reflected in the results of the study.

Thirteen of the 33 Ss were retested two days after their original testing, thus permitting the determination of test-retest reliability coefficients for the experimental measures employed in the study. Concurrent validity coefficients for the measures were ascertained from correlations with the Ss' pretest ratings of the 20 products. The pretest consisted of a brief story about a housewife who is undecided which of two packages of a particular product to purchase. The two packages are equally appealing to her on a number of grounds, such as appearance and quality of contents. She finally decided to purchase the package which gives her more of the product for the price. It was pointed out to the Ss that the housewife's task of determining which of the two packages is more economical would vary in difficulty for the 20 products. The Ss were instructed to rank the 20 products, using an alternation ranking procedure, with respect to the estimated difficulty the housewife would have in determining the more economical of two packages containing the product.

At the time the pretest was administered the Ss were asked to indicate which of the 20 products were not usually found in their household.

Measures

Three behaviorally based, quantitative measures of confusion in unit price information are used in the analysis of the data. The first, Confusion Measure 1, simply indicates the number of Ss who made incorrect choices for each of the 20 products. Confusion Measure 2 calculates for each product the mean percentage increase in unit price for the Ss' selected packages compared with the most economical package. Confusion Measure 3, which employs data from a supermarket trade magazine study dealing with the total sales for each of the 20 products provides an estimate of the increase in price which an economy-minded household unit with a specified budget would pay over a constant time period, say a year, if its purchases reflected the values found for Confusion Measure 2.

The rationale behind Confusion Measure 1 is reasonably clear. We want to know whether Ss are able to select the most economical package for each of the 20 common products; indeed, the number of Ss who fail in this task should be an indication of the degree of confusion associated with consumer attempts to purchase supermarket products on the basis of economy. The second measure of confusion simply reflects the magnitude of the selection errors expressed for each prodduct as a percentage of the unit price of the most economical package. It is assumed that the larger the value found for a particular product, the greater the error which an economy-minded consumer would be expected to make when purchasing the product.

The last measure to be considered, Confusion Measure 3, represents an interaction of the estimated consumer expenditures for a supermarket product and the percentage error given by Confusion Measure 2. This third measure of confusion provides for each product a dollar-and-cents estimate of the additional expenses which an economy-minded shopper would bear due to errors in package selection. To give substance to this measure it is necessary that the actual records of consumer expenditures or estimates of such expenditures be available for processing. A search by the writer for a detailed product-by-product breakdown of the supermarket expenditures for some statistically average, or otherwise well-specified household unit, proved to be unsuccessful. Indirectly relevant data were found, however, in the *Progressive Grocer Colonial Study* (1963), which reports the percentage contribution to total sales made by each of several hundred products for six supermarkets in the southeastern United States. The six markets were members of a larger chain called the Colonial Stores.

It seems clear that the results of the Colonial Study do not reflect American supermarkets or consumers as a whole. The study was conducted over an eight-week winter period within a single chain of supermarkets in one region of the country. Thus there are seasonal, regional, and probably socio-economic reasons for suspecting differences. However, in the absence of any suitable national data dealing with either supermarket sales or consumer expenditures on an individual product basis, the results of the Colonial Study are employed in the analysis of the Ss' responses of the present study. The reader is cautioned that the Colonial Study results serve only as an estimate, with strongly suspected biases, of the corresponding national data.

The percentage contributions to total supermarket sales for the 20 products of the present study are perhaps made more meaningful when applied to a consumer's annual budget of say, $1,000 for supermarket expenditures. Thus the Colonial Study figure of 1.1% for powdered detergents assumes a value of $11.00 for this hypothetical budget. For this budget, Confusion Measure 3 is simply the portion of the individual product expenditure which can be assigned to error in package selection. The actual amount assigned would depend upon the value of Confusion Measure 2. Thus a household unit with economical shopping habits and a $1,000 annual supermarket budget might spend $11.00 for powdered detergents. Given a value of 24% for powdered detergents on Confusion Measure 2, we would find $^{24}/_{124}$ of the $11.00, or $2.13, as the amount over and above the minimal amount of $8.87 which our economy-minded household unit would pay if it always succeeded in purchasing the most economical package of powdered detergent. For this case then the value for powdered detergent on Confusion Measure 3 would be $2.13.

Values for other products were found in a manner similar to that described above. One first constructs a ratio consisting of the value of Confusion Measure 2 over an expression made up of the Confusion Measure 2 value plus 100. The next step is to multiply this ratio by the estimated consumer expenditure for the product. To find the value for a total supermarket expenditure different from the base of $1,000 employed here simply construct a ratio of the new total expenditure over the base of $1,000 and multiply the Confusion Measure 3 value by this fraction.

RESULTS

Of the total of 660 decisions made by the 33 Ss, 47 represented products which the Ss stated were not usually found in their homes. Since the proportion of errors for these 47 decisions did not differ significantly from the corresponding proportion for decisions involving more familiar products, the two classes of selections (familiar and unfamiliar) were pooled for the purposes of analysis.

The three measures of confusion in unit price information were applied to the 20 products employed in the study and were found to have substantial validity when correlated with the experimental pretest (Spearman rank correlations of .58, .62, and .70 for Confusion Measures 1, 2, and 3 respectively). Likewise substantial reliability coefficients were found (Spearman rank correlations of .91, .93, and .91 for the three numbered measures). These reliability values may be somewhat too high, reflecting the unavoidably short interval of two days between first and second testings. The complete list of 20 products and their associated values on the three confusion measures are presented in Table 1. Also presented in Table 1 are the estimated consumer expendi-

TABLE 1   Confusion Values and Estimated Consumer Expenditures for 20 Supermarket Products

Product	Confusion measure 1 [1] (total errors)	Confusion measure 2 (percentage error)	Confusion measure 3 [2] (weighted error in dollars)	Estimated annual consumer expenditures [2] (dollars)
Canned peaches	8	2	0.06	3.10
Canned peas	5	5	.20	4.10
Catsup	23	13	.28	2.40
Evaporated milk	2	0	0	6.60
Family flour	6	2	.13	6.70
Frozen orange juice	6	6	.36	6.40
Granulated sugar	0	0	0	10.70
Instant coffee	11	10	.92	10.10
Liquid bleach	32	32	.70	2.90
Liquid detergent	8	4	.24	6.20
Liquid shampoo	14	63	1.01	2.70
Mayonnaise	8	16	.46	3.30
Paper towels	30	12	.48	4.50
Peanut butter	7	2	.06	3.20
Potato chips	22	1	.05	5.30
Powdered detergent	33	24	2.13	11.00
Soft drinks (cola)	27	17	2.01	13.80
Solid shortening	0	0	0	5.50
Toilet tissue	22	5	.37	7.70
Toothpaste	22	16	.69	5.00
Sum			10.15	121.20
Mean	14.3	11.5	.507	6.06

[1] N-33.

[2] Based on a total annual supermarket expenditure of $1,000.

tures for the 20 products for a hypothetical consumer budget of $1,000.

Examination of the values for Confusion Measure 1 reveals extremely wide variation for the set of products, with a tendency for food products to have lower values than non-food products. Significant differences were found for the set of 20 products on Confusion Measure 1 (Cochran Q=283, P<.001). The mean value of 14.3 yields an error rate of 43% for the 33 Ss. Significant differences were also found for the set of ranked product values on Confusion Measure 2 (Friedman X^2_r= 214, P<.001) and Confusion Measure 3 (Friedman X^2_r=242, P<.001). It is of interest to note that of the total estimated annual consumer expenditure of $121.20 for the 20 products the sum of $10.15 can be accounted for by errors in consumer selections. Thus, if it were possible for an economy-minded consumer with a $1,000 supermarket budget to always select the package giving her the largest quantity of a supermarket product for the money, she would pay an estimated $121.20 minus $10.15, or $111.05. It is estimated then that a more typical economy-minded shopper, who makes her selections in conformance with the Ss' selections in the current study, would spend $10.15 more than the errorless figure of $111.05, or in other words she would spend 9.15% more than the hypothetical consumer who was always able to select the most economical package.

DISCUSSION

It is important to note that the plan and procedures of this study deal not at all with the day-to-day purchases of American consumers. It may be that economy plays a small role in many of these purchases. However for the purposes of this study the question of what actual criteria are employed by consumers at large in their supermarket shopping is largely an irrelevant one. The question of concern is the following:

Is it possible for consumers to select, within a reasonable period of time and without the aid of paper and pencil or of computing devices, that package of a particular supermarket product which offers the largest quantity of the product for the money?

If large numbers of consumers can not make correct selections when so instructed, and particularly if their errors are large, it would seem that the task is a confusing one. If in addition their errors are costly, there is real reason for concern.

Of course it does not necessarily follow that a confusing task results from improper packaging practices. However for the present study significant differences were found for the set of 20 products on all three measures of confusion, and it seems unlikely that these differences can be attributed in any large part to factors other than the differences in package characteristics. For example the possible influences of warm-up or fatigue effects were off-set by the experimental variations in order of product presentation. Also level of illumination appeared to be fairly constant for the 20 product locations. In addition, in several instances packaging practices were identified which required calculations which could not be performed without great difficulty, if at all, in one's head. For example the quantity of paper towels was presented in terms of number of sheets but the size of a sheet was not standard across brands. Indeed in the current study they ranged from a small of 7.5 by 11 inches to a large of 11 by 11 inches. Furthermore the number of sheets in a roll varied from 75 to 200. And finally, some rolls were packaged singly and others two to a package. Liquid bleach was a second product characterized by difficulties which were apparently influenced by packaging practices. In particular one brand of this product which formerly was made up with the commonly employed 5.25% concentration of sodium hypochlorite, the active ingredient in bleach, had been reduced in concentration to 3.25% a short time before the data were collected; the selling price of the product, however, had not been reduced, nor for that matter had there been a change to the label or package in any manner other than the listing of the new concentration on the back of the bottle. Since most of our Ss were regular shoppers at the supermarket employed in the study it appears that rather than examining the bottle closely, they assumed the concentration had not been changed. With the original 5.25% concentration of sodium hypochlorite this bottle would have been the most economical selection; however with the change in concentration this was no longer the case.

Since the results of this study were influenced in no small way by the time allotted for each package selection it might be well to explain the basis for selecting the unit of 10 seconds. Since the S's task was considerably more demanding than day-to-day supermarket shopping it was felt that time should be provided above and beyond the normal shopping time. A recent study (Fitzsimmons and Manning, 1962) found that it takes a shopper approximately one minute to select an item in a supermarket. This one minute period includes walking time in the store but not time at the check-out counter. The Ss of the current study were given an average of 2.35 minutes at each product location; with the addition of walking time they had available about three times as much time as they would be expected to take for their supermarket shopping.

It is of interest to inquire what generalizations might be made from the present findings to other Ss and other settings. First with regard to the Ss of the study it seems clear that they represent a combination of qualities that should make for extremely low confusion scores. As a group they are characterized by considerable education and by the financial strains usually associated with young married college couples. These two ingredients suggest not only strong interest in economy as a criterion for supermarket shopping, but also considerable success in meeting this criterion. It would seem then that other individuals in general, and less educated individuals in particular, would not perform as well as the Ss of the present study.

Although superficially it might appear that the results of this study would transfer readily to other supermarket settings there are differences between markets which should be considered. Although many markets carry the major brands for common products they differ in the extensiveness of sizes available, and in the particular store brands which they carry. Also differences in shelf space and position for a product might well influence the ease with which a shopper could make comparisons. Problems arise too when one attempts to generalize the results for the 20 products employed here to other supermarket products. That sweeping generalizations are clearly inappropriate is indicated by a Colonial Study finding that about 30% of the consumer's supermarket expenditures are allocated to meat and produce, two foods which are not packaged beyond a simple brown bag or cellophane wrapper. With regard to more typically packaged supermarket products, again problems arise. The selection criteria for the 20 products employed in the present study have provided us with a clearly non-random sample of packaged products. A particularly strong bias was introduced by selecting products with a record of relatively high total sales, which would imply relatively high familiarity among shoppers.

Two natural next steps of research are suggested by the data. The first would be a systematic study of what factors make for confusion in consumer selection. For example, packaging practices which are frequently claimed by consumer spokesmen to be confusing include the following:

1. Poorly presented information concerning both the nature of the contents and the quantity of contents. These deficiencies in display may take many forms; e.g., too small print, weak contrast between the printed information and the background, and failure to present the information at a prominent location on the package.
2. Misleading information concerning both the nature of the contents and the quantity of contents. "Giant quart" is a typical example of the latter practice.
3. Misleading information concerning price. Often cited here is the so-called cents-off specials. Representatives of consumer groups claim that these "specials" are often not acknowledged by super-market managers in their pricing policies.
4. The use of unnatural numbers to indicate quantity. An example here would be the use of fractional or mixed numbers instead of whole numbers.

With a larger number of products than the 20 of the current study, regression analyses could be performed to determine which, if any packaging characteristics serve as good predictors of the confusion measures.

A second potentially valuable research step would involve the development and evaluation of training guidelines for consumers. With a larger and more heterogeneous group of Ss than the one employed here one could attempt to identify the distinguishing package information employed by high-scoring (as compared to low-scoring) Ss in their performance of the experimental task. A natural application of the results of such a study would be to consumers at lower socio-economic levels.

CONCLUSIONS

Within the confines of the particular experimental setting employed, the following conclusions appear to be in order.

1. The three measures of confusion in unit-price information have substantial validity and reliability.
2. The 20 products differ significantly on all three measures of confusion.
3. There is reason to believe that these differences reflect, at least in part, differences in packaging practices.

REFERENCES

FITZIMMONS, CLO, AND SARAH L. MANNING. *Purchases of Nonfood Items in Selected Retail Stores.* Lafayette, Ind.: Cooperative Extension Department in Agriculture and Home Economics at Purdue University, 1962.

NELSON, HELEN. *Packages and Prices.* Sacramento: Consumer Counsel Office, State Capitol, 1962.

Progressive Grocer Colonial Study. New York: Progressive Grocer Publications (420 Lexington Avenue), 1963.

14 SATISFACTION AND AFTER PURCHASE EFFECTS

Casual observation and data from many psychologists suggest that people do what they are rewarded for doing, and so we would expect that a buyer is more likely to buy a brand that has previously given him satisfaction. There is a great amount of laboratory evidence to confirm this. Unfortunately, in the laboratory reward has been measured by its consequences, whereas in a natural setting, difficulties in objectively specifying the reward before it is received can bias the results.

To complicate matters further, dissonance research (Brehm and Cohen, 1962) hypothesizes that if dissonance arises (which can result when a buyer has overestimated the quality of a given brand), the buyer may (among other possible courses of action) suddenly inflate his perception of the brand's quality far beyond that justified by its true quality. The dissonance could presumably also arise merely because he was unsure after the purchase whether he had been successful in making a good purchase. Unfavorable information about the chosen brand and favorable information about an unchosen competing alternative is also predicted to cause dissonance. Thus, so many possible antecedent situations can give rise to so many possible manifestations of dissonance that precise prediction from dissonance theory is difficult to attain.

As with so much of dissonance research, the studies included in this book show inconsistent findings. Kassarjian and Cohen (1965)* report confirmation of their dissonance hypothesis. Hunt (1970)* attempted to structure a "real life" experimental design to investigate if the cognitive dissonance hypothesis can be used by a retailer in dealing with recent customers and obtained mixed results. Oshikawa (1969)* reviews many of the past cognitive dissonance studies and raises questions concerning certain built-in biases and alternative explanations for the observed behavior. He goes on to suggest the circumstances under which the theory of cognitive dissonance may explain and predict behavior.

The theory of buyer behavior discussed in Chapter 1 includes post-purchase *satisfaction* rather than dissatisfaction or cognitive dissonance. *Satisfaction* is posited to affect the level of *confidence* that the buyer will have in his judgment during similar future purchases.

REFERENCE

1. BREHM, JACK W. AND ARTHUR R. COHEN. *Explorations in Cognitive Dissonance.* New York: Wiley, 1962.

33. Cognitive dissonance and consumer behavior harold h. kassarjian & joel b. cohen

The field of human behavior and its various subsets, especially consumer behavior, is fully as complex and as confusing as the jargon with which we attempt to describe it. From among the bewildering array of proposed answers, partial evidence and, occasionally, impartial evidence, is it possible to assemble some sort of meaningful theoretical system? A possible approach to understanding and predicting consumer behavior might be to look at the various needs, motivations, and goals underlying pertinent behavioral patterns.

Among the underlying needs which may have a substantial effect on a consumer's acts and decisions is the need for cognitive consistency. Although the human organism is continually receiving stimulus information through its perceptual apparatus, the individual tends to interpret it in a meaningful manner to reduce the ambiguity and uncertainty that would result from either an absence of relevant information or a jumble of unassociated or conflicting information. This cognitive reinterpreting process and its search for consistency deserve further analysis, since the individual is often faced with inconsistencies in everyday life.

For example, in the face of undeniable and overwhelming evidence that cancer is directly attributable to cigarette smoking, why is it that people continue to smoke cigarettes? Why is it that an advertiser has greater difficulty in reaching and convincing people who are not using his product than people who are already his customers?

A social psychologist, Leon Festinger,[1] has developed a theory that may hold a solution to these kinds of questions and many others which businessmen have pondered for some time. This theory should have broad application in the field of consumer behavior and may make important contributions in communications and advertising. In the pages that follow, the essential elements of his theory of cognitive dissonance will be explored as to their applicability to consumer behavior. An empirical test of the theory is furnished by a study of the reactions of the public to the Surgeon General's report on smoking and health.[2]

The theory claims that the individual—the consumer—strives toward consistency within himself. His attitudes, values, and beliefs are ordered into clusters that are internally consistent, and consistent with his behavior. Hence a person who feels that college education is worthwhile will encourage his children to go to college. Yet when we discover inconsistencies—and they may be quite dramatic—they capture our interest primarily because they stand in sharp contrast against a world of consistency. We pay little attention to the person who refuses to buy a Mustang because it is a Ford product for which

he has a dislike. The person who is of interest is the one who purchases a Ford in spite of negative attitudes toward the Ford line.

Prior to making any major decision or taking a significant action,
one is often faced with conflicts between two or more alternatives.
The consumer must choose between a Ford or a Chevrolet, or an
employee must decide whether to leave a rather secure position for
the advantages and greater potential of a new job with its concomitant
lack of security. Unfortunately, however, even after making the decision the individual is often faced with uncertainty as to its wisdom.
"Maybe I should have bought a Chevy instead of a Ford."

These postdecision and postaction states have been termed states of
"dissonance" by Festinger. This feeling of inconsistency or dissonance
is a state of discomfort, disequilibrium, or tension that demands
reduction. Few are the occasions when one is certain he has made
either a completely "right" or a completely "wrong" decision. Even the
worst of alternatives usually has some positive features, and, the
moment a decision is made the positive features of the rejected
alternative and the negative features of the selected alternative are
inconsistent or dissonant with his action. However, once the choice is
enacted, cognitions about the behavior, inconsistencies that do exist,
are generally brought in line with the behavior pattern. The consumer
begins to feel his choice was the best possible decision that could have
been made. To put it another way: states of dissonance are transformed into states of consonance, and the inconsistencies are eliminated.

Although there are many dissonance reduction pathways, a few
widely used methods of reducing dissonance can be categorized.

> An individual can reduce dissonance by eliminating one of the cognitive
> elements or his responsibility or control over an act or decision. Physi-
> cal dissociation can be accomplished by selling a newly purchased car
> for the identical amount one paid for it.

Dissociation of responsibility or control over an act or decision is a
fairly common occurrence. One may come to believe that his choice
was inevitable or unavoidable, or wise because a similar choice has
been made by others. Projecting the blame for consequences of these
decisions then becomes a relatively "painless" method of dissonance
reduction. Advertising which employs the "band wagon" approach
may often be successful because it possibly enables the individual to
submerge his actions in mass behavior.

> Information can be denied, distorted, or forgotten in the service of
> dissonance reduction. Selective forgetting is a process by which un-
> pleasant or unreconcilable elements are dismissed from awareness.

An effort to deny the existence of an element can be seen in the
behavior of an angry man who feels anger is an inappropriate response
to a particular situation. The man, whose face is flushed, whose ges-
tures border on the violent, and whose voice is strained may exclaim,
"Me angry! Why I'm perfectly calm!"

Perhaps the most fascinating of the dissonance studies revolved
about the activities of a group of people who were strongly committed

to the belief that a cataclysmic flood would soon engulf North America. The group's leader, who had been in "communication" with people from outer space, had been promised that the group would be rescued by a flying saucer. Elaborate preparations had been made for their departure. Members proceeded to cut their material ties with earth by discarding possessions, quitting jobs, saying their goodbys, etc. When the predictions failed to come about—there was no saucer, no flood, but presumably a great deal of dissonance—the group did not disband or attempt to hide from publicity as they had done earlier. Instead they told their story to the press and virtually anyone who would listen in an attempt to recruit additional members. Their explanation for what had happened was that the group's sincere and devoted behavior was responsible for God's saving the world. Dissonance was reduced by altering their perception of reality and by attempting to convince others that this perception was accurate. In this way the reality of a failure in prophecy was made consonant with the behavior of the individuals concerned.[3]

Not as spectacular, yet involving similar processes, are many distortions of reality we make every day. People can and do believe those facts which are palatable to themselves while disbelieving and distorting unpleasant facts.

Out of the great multitude of stimuli impinging upon a person at any given moment, one of the more important criteria used to guide the perceptual processes is the desire for consonance. Hastorf and Cantril's[4] study of a bitterly contested football game between Dartmouth and Princeton shows that the game was perceived quite differently by undergraduates devoted to opposite sides. Both teams had been accused of unnecessarily rough and dirty play. The authors found, through subsequent questioning and showings of the game film, that students found the opposition to be guilty of undesirable acts to a greater degree than the school with which they identified. In this way the dissonance which would exist when a positively regarded group performed negatively regarded acts was held to a minimum.

Advertisers have long known that an audience will seek out information that is consonant with the views the individuals themselves hold. Product and political advertising, speeches, and propaganda are usually couched in vague, ambiguous terms that will allow the listener to interpret the comments made in his own way. The consumer will often control his own exposure to information and advertising to support what he wants to believe. Undoubtedly, the primary audience for advertising is comprised of the advertiser's present customers.

To gain insight into the utility of advertising for consumers who have already purchased the advertised product, one can refer to an experiment designed and conducted by Brehm.[5] The object of the experiment was to measure the change in attractiveness between two objects before and after a decision between them was made. After each person had inspected a group of products, she was handed a sheet of paper and asked to rate each item in terms of how attractive it was to her, on a scale from "definitely not at all desirable" to "extremely desirable."

The subject was then informed that she would be given a gift for participating in the study and was offered her choice of two of the items she had rated. Before the subject left, she was presented with "research reports" mentioning the good and bad characteristics of the product and asked once again to rate each of the products she had seen. Subjects seemed to re-evaluate existing information and interpret the information contained in the reports, making the chosen object better than it might be and the rejected object worse than it might be, in order to gain support for their choice.

> Dissonance can also be effectively reduced by minimizing the importance of the issue, decision, or act that led to the dissonant state.

If an issue is perceived as unimportant by an individual looking back upon it, he may find it easier to excuse his ineffective efforts in evaluating whatever alternatives were present. He may call attention to the many more important issues with which he was concerned at the time. Failures may be explained away as due not to his own inadequacies, but to his lack of interest or effort.

> Selective exposure to new information avoids a dissonance confrontation. A person will tend to avoid exposure to dissonant information and, instead, will tend to expose himself to information which adds consonant elements, weakens existing dissonant elements, and reduces the importance of the issue which led to dissonance, or a combination of these.

It is here that advertising provides a great source of relief from postpurchase dissonance. The man who has chosen the Ford over the Chevrolet has the opportunity to select biased communications supporting his decision. A study supporting this contention indicated that new car owners, on the average, noticed magazine automobile ads featuring the car they had just purchased nearly twice as often as ads for automobiles they had considered but not purchased.[6]

This is not to say that people will necessarily avoid unpleasant information. A study of public awareness of a campaign conducted by the American Cancer Society helps to give perspective to both selective exposure and acceptance of unpleasant information. Those who named cancer as a "most dangerous disease" tended to expose themselves to the campaign to a greater degree than those not so naming cancer. The fact that these people named cancer as being dangerous indicated a fear of the disease. This fear being well grounded in supporting facts was a cognitive element strongly resistant to change. As such, new information was sought that was consonant with this fear—information which would help an individual avoid the disease.[7]

The seeking out of unpleasant and even frightening information is an appropriate step in problem-solving where that information is useful in coping with the environment. Since in all cases it is the least resistant cognitive element that will change in response to dissonance, it is well to examine the importance of each element for the individual's coping with his environment. Essential elements are apt to be highly resistant ones.

The pressure of events and people interacts with the individual's needs and predispositions to determine the importance of any belief or value to him. In a dynamic society, these forces are constantly changing. Predicting the direction of dissonance reduction by estimating which of the relevant cognitive elements is most resistant to change is exceedingly complex. In cases where those engaged in changing attitudes have been successful, they have been effective in engaging cognitive elements such that the more essential element causes a change in the less essential element.

Dissonance theory has provided hypotheses regarding possible reactions of individuals to inconsistent cognitive elements where the relative importance of each element to the individual is uncertain. In summary, consonance can be achieved by:

1. Eliminating one of the elements or disassociating his responsibility or control over that element.
2. Denying or distorting the reality causing the dissonance.
3. Minimizing the importance of the issue.
4. Selectively exposing himself to new information that will tend to reduce dissonance by adding only consonant information.

From this theoretical point of view, it should be possible to investigate the reactions of cigarette smokers to the dissonant information linking cigarette smoking with lung cancer and other medical abnormalities. It can be assumed that with the wide dissemination afforded the Surgeon General's findings in the mass media of communication, cigarette smokers are in a state of dissonance. The smoking behavior is clearly dissonant with the need to survive or stay healthy. Hence we can hypothesize one or more of the following reactions:

1. Change the behavior pattern of smoking by: stopping smoking or attempting to stop smoking; or switching to a less dangerous product.
2. Deny or distort reality by refusing to believe the "scientific" evidence linking cancer to smoking, at least as it pertains to one's own chances of becoming ill.
3. Minimize the importance of the issue.
4. Add new cognitions by: seeking social support for the dissonant smoking behavior; or seeking new information supporting smoking.

METHOD

In order to test these hypotheses, a public opinion study was conducted in April 1964, some three months after the release of the Surgeon General's report. The study was done in conjunction with a class marketing research project. Because of classroom exigencies, no attempt was made to make the study representative of the country; rather a medium-sized city was chosen for data collection. The thirty students in the class were trained in interviewing techniques and each completed twelve to twenty interviews.

SAMPLE

The community chosen for the study was Santa Monica, California, an incorporated city contiguous to Los Angeles. The approximately 85,000 residents represent a wide range of incomes, occupations, market value of homes, age, education, and ethnic groups.

The sample was selected on a probability basis by listing the blocks from the 1960 U.S. Census of Housing along with the total number of occupied dwelling units. The dwelling units were then cumulatively totaled, and, starting at a random point, the block in which every nth dwelling unit was located was chosen for the study. Each block was then assigned a separate random starting position.

The instructions to each interviewer were such that interviewing was started at a given position and continued in a clockwise direction until he completed five interviews on each block. To prevent a preponderance of female respondents, each interviewer was instructed to obtain approximately half men and half women in his sub-sample. In most cases, interviewing was carried on over several days. In each case where an interviewer returned to the same block to complete his cluster, he was requested to start at the same dwelling unit in an attempt to minimize "not-at-home" bias so that any given block had from 0 to 2 call-backs. No provisions were made for a "refused to be interviewed" bias, but rather the interviewers were instructed to go next door.

RESULTS

As previously mentioned, dissonance theory would predict that when a smoker is confronted with dissonant information linking cigarette smoking with cancer, one of the possible, but naturally not exclusive, reactions he may engage in is to change the behavioral element and stop smoking or attempt to stop smoking. Table 1 presents the re-

TABLE 1   Per Cent of Sample Stating They Made Serious Attempts to Stop Cigarette Smoking During the Previous Year

	Heavy Smokers (132)	Moderate Smokers (50)	Light Smokers (39)	Total Smokers (221)
No. of attempts				
None	79.5	66.0	69.2	74.7
One	12.1	22.0	12.8	14.5
Two or more	8.4	12.0	18.0	10.8

sponses to the question: "Have you ever made a serious attempt to stop smoking? (IF YES) Within the last year how many times would you say you have made an attempt to stop smoking?"

Among the respondents who were smoking at the time of the study, 75 per cent stated they made no serious attempt in the previous year to stop smoking while about 25 per cent had made one or more serious attempts at dissonance reduction in this manner during the same period.[8] Table 1 further presents the data broken down by "Heavy Smokers" (those smoking one or more packages of cigarettes per day), "Moderate Smokers" (those smoking 10–19 cigarettes per day), and "Light Smokers" (less than 10 cigarettes per day). One might expect that heavy smokers are in a greater state of dissonance than light smokers and hence would make a more concerted effort at attempting to stop. The results indicate that heavy smokers do not differ significantly[9] from moderate or light smokers in this respect. Apparently, a majority of all smokers are too heavily committed to their smoking behavior to be influenced by persuasive communication, no matter how strongly worded or impressively documented.

In the light of these results, one can only wonder once again if an advertiser spending untold dollars can possibly expect to be successful in changing consumer habits and attitudes against the prevailing tide of consumer behavior, especially since his advertising is often viewed with distrust rather than esteem, his motives are suspect, and his claims are poorly if ever documented. However, when advertisers set more modest goals and give reasons which tend to reduce dissonance in a less threatening direction, their success should be far greater. For example, in an ancillary aspect of this study, 43.3 per cent of the cigarette smokers stated that filter tip cigarettes are healthier, safer, better for you, as compared with 18.3 per cent of the nonsmokers. In addition, 34.2 per cent of the nonsmokers felt they were just as bad, as compared to 21.4 per cent of the smokers. A chi square analysis indicates these differences are significant well beyond the .001 level of confidence ($x^2 = 26.8 \cdot df = 1$).

Table 2 offers further evidence that changes in consumer behavior

TABLE 2   Per Cent of Ex-smokers (67) with Date They Quit Smoking*

Per cent saying they stopped smoking:	
Since January 1964	9.0
In 1963	19.4
Before 1963	71.6

* Data were collected in April 1964.

contrary to a long-standing behavioral pattern are extremely difficult to achieve. These data represent responses to the question: "When did you last stop smoking?" asked only of ex-smokers.

Approximately 9 per cent had quit since January 1964, the date of release of the Surgeon General's report. This coincides with reports that cigarette smoking in California fell 8 to 10 per cent during the first quarter of 1964. As this paper is being written, a few months later, the trend is reversing.[10]

A second possible approach to reducing dissonance by changing the smoking behavior would be to switch to a less dangerous product. Table 3 presents responses to the question: "Over the past few years have you changed your smoking habits, that is, have you switched from any one tobacco product to another, say from———to———?" The results indicate that there has been very little switching, again supporting the thesis that smoking behavior is a very resistant element, and if the cancer linkage does create any change, generally it is not in the area of a behavioral change. The differences between light, moderate, and heavy smokers are not significant, although they would have been predicted so by dissonance theory. Amount of smoking does not seem to be a critical variable in creating change—heavy and light smokers are equally resistant.

Since the behavioral element seems to be quite resistant to change, the theory of cognitive dissonance would predict that there might be a perceptual distortion of the cognitive element concerning the believability of the "scientific" evidence relating lung cancer to smoking. Table 4 contains the responses to the question: "Recently there has been a great deal of discussion about the linkage or relationship between cigarette smoking and lung cancer and various other medical problems. Do you feel this linkage has been definitely proven, probably proven, probably not proven, or definitely not proven?"

The results lend overwhelming support to the theory: the more a person smokes the less he believes that the cigarette-cancer linkage is proven.[11]

It would be of interest to see if education is related to believability of the Surgeon General's report. It was expected that the more educated person might better understand the implications of the health report; and credibility is higher among them. Table 5 presents the results of the believability question broken down by level of education.

As can be seen, among smokers, persons with higher education show a greater tendency to feel the cigarette-cancer linkage is proven.[12] However, the dissonance hypothesis is supported for both respondents of lower and higher education (Lower education: $x^2 = 23.12. p < .001$; Higher education: $x^2 = 12.24. p < .001$).

It is interesting to note that, although behavior is quite resistant to change, opinions regarding the believability of the cancer linkage seemed to have increased significantly over a decade. Comparing the present results of this study with a study in Minneapolis[13] in 1954 (shown in Table 6), showing the same relationship between amount of smoking and acceptance of the cancer-linkage, indicates a potential over-all increase in the believability of the health danger. If the comparison is not unreasonable for many smokers, the smoking behavior was the most resistant element while cognitions about health were modified more easily.

The possibility that there is today a greater believability in the cancer linkage than a decade ago further complicates the problem of reducing dissonance for these particular individuals. As long as the person could believe the linkage was not proven, little dissonance remained to be eliminated.

TABLE 3   Per Cent of Smokers Who Switched Tobacco Products

	Heavy Smokers (126)	Moderate Smokers (45)	Light Smokers (39)	Total Cigarette Smokers (210)	Exclusive Pipe/Cigar Smokers (36)
Tobacco switch from:					
Cigarette to pipe	1.6	9.4	2.6	2.4	19.4
Cigarette to cigar	—	—	—	—	13.9
Other	0.8	2.3	5.1	2.0	2.8
No change	97.6	93.3	92.3	95.6	63.9

TABLE 4   Relationship of Smoking to Believability of Health Report

	Heavy Smokers (132)	Moderate Smokers (48)	Light Smokers (39)	Total Cigarette Smokers (219)	Pipe/Cigar Smokers (37)	Non-smokers (240)
Per cent saying linkage is:						
Proven	52.2	58.3	77.0	58.0	83.8	80.4
Not proven	40.9	37.5	20.5	28.8	13.5	10.8
Don't know	6.8	4.2	2.5	5.5	2.7	8.7

TABLE 5   Relationship of Health Report Believability to Education

| | Level of Education | | | |
| | High School or Less | | Some College or More | |
	Cigarette Smokers (126)	Non-smokers (122)	Cigarette Smokers (91)	Non-smokers (109)
Per cent saying linkage is:				
Proven	50.0	73.8	70.3	88.0
Not proven	43.7	11.5	25.3	7.3
Don't know	6.3	14.7	4.4	4.7

TABLE 6   Opinions of Respondents Concerning the Linkage Between Cigarette Smoking and Lung Cancer (1954 Minnesota Poll)

	Heavy Smokers (41)	Moderate Smokers (105)	Light Smokers (59)	Non-smokers (348)
Per cent saying linkage is:				
Proven	7	16	20	29
Not proven	86	75	68	55
Don't know	7	9	12	16

The growing body of apparently undeniable evidence has served to magnify the dissonance for smokers whose behavioral patterns tended to remain fixed. Hence, dissonance theory might predict some further reactions. For example, we might expect that these dissonant people attempt to minimize the importance of the issue, dissociate their control over their smoking behavior, feel that smoking is less dangerous than the alternatives, or seek social support for their behavior. To tap these hypotheses, a series of questions was asked: "In recent years there have been many articles and stories about the connection between cancer and smoking. Some of the articles claim the linkage is very clear that smoking does lead to medical problems; other articles throw doubt on this relationship. Why do you feel there is this discrepancy?"

The outstanding finding in Table 7 is that considerably more smokers (.001 level of confidence) gave a denial type of response in which they attempted to minimize the importance of the health issue by claiming such things as: "Many smokers live a long time," "Lots of things are a hazard."

To seek reactions from a slightly different point of view, only those smokers who believed that smoking is a health hazard were asked: "Many people believe that smoking is in fact a health hazard and yet continue to smoke. For example, you mentioned that you have not stopped smoking. Why do you feel there is this discrepancy?"

TABLE 7   Responses to Question Asking Why a Discrepancy Exists in Articles on Cancer-Smoking Linkage

	Total Cigarette Smokers (221)	Total Non-smokers (239)
Per cent saying the discrepancy is because:		
Two sides to every issue—research methods differ	4.1	10.9
Lots of hazards in life—facts are not clear—many smokers live a long time—both get lung cancer	35.7	14.2
Linkage is proven—industry influences pro-smoking stories—smoking causes cancer	31.2	42.7
People want pro-smoking stories to believe	2.3	9.2
Smoking does not cause cancer—not harmful in moderation—smoking hurts some and not others	11.3	8.3
Publicity—conspiracy	1.4	1.3
Other response	0.4	0.4
Don't know—refused to answer	13.6	13.0

The responses of this particular sub-sample are in Table 8. Again it will be noticed that about one-fifth of the sample stated that "there

TABLE 8   Responses Why Health Hazard Believers (179) Have Not Stopped Smoking

Per cent saying they have not stopped smoking because:	
Can't stop—like to smoke—won't stop	31.3
Lots of hazards in life—can die of many things—not much of a threat for me (rationalization)	22.3
Smoking is better than alternatives—better than being a nervous wreck—better than taking pills—better than excessive drinking	13.4
I don't care about my health—pleasure is more important than health	6.7
I will soon stop or switch	1.7
Moderation is OK—pipes/cigars OK	8.4
No guts—lack of self control—I feel bad and have guilt feelings	5.6
Other responses	3.4
Don't know—refused to answer	7.3

are many hazards" in life and attempted to minimize this issue. Well over one-third stated that "they can't stop," "won't stop," suggesting in a sense that control of smoking is beyond their realm of control and that they are attempting to dissociate their cognitions regarding smoking from their ability to do anything about it. In addition to comments such as "I am unable to stop," "It takes too great an effort to stop," some respondents go so far as to state openly their inadequacies with statements such as "I'm an idiot," "No guts," and "I feel bad about it."

The important additional contribution of this question is the emergence of evidence that new consonant cognitions are added to the cognitive organization of the individual as a method of dissonance reduction. Approximately 20 per cent of the sample made such statements as "Better than taking pills," "Smoking is better than excessive eating or drinking," "Pleasure is more important than health," "Smoking is better than being a nervous wreck." Here one can interpret the responses as an attempt on the part of the consumer to convert a dissonant relationship into one that is quite consonant with his total belief pattern.

As still another measure of the opinions and attitudes of both smokers and nonsmokers, a series of sentence completion type questions was asked of respondents. Tables 9 to 13 present data derived from these instruments.

TABLE 9   Responses to Question: "Adults Who Smoke Are. . . ."

	Cigarette Smokers (210)	Non-smokers (240)
Foolish/harming themselves/crazy/stupid/abnormal/bad/ nuts	28.6	52.9
Nervous/anxious	4.8	7.1
Normal/OK/in the majority	25.2	10.8
Within their rights/doing what they want/content/satisfied	14.3	10.0
Acting on habit/hooked/addicts	4.3	4.6
Need something to do/bored	0.9	1.2
Other	0.9	0.8
Don't know/no answer	21.0	12.6

TABLE 10   Responses to Question: "Teenagers Who Smoke Are. . . ."

	Cigarette Smokers (210)	Non-smokers (240)
Concerned with social approval/trying to get along with crowd/want status	3.3	5.4
Foolish/crazy/uninformed/not smart/ruining health/stupid	57.6	55.4
Showing off/trying to act older/trying to be sophisticated	7.1	11.7
Wrong/rebels/immature	14.3	15.4
Like anybody else/it's their business/normal/seeking pleasure	11.0	3.4
Other	1.9	2.4
No answer/don't know	4.8	6.3

Summarizing the results of this line of questioning, many of the findings lend further support to the hypothesized consumer reactions. The seeking of social support—the "forty million Frenchmen can't be wrong" idea—among the smoker population is indicated in such statements as: "Adults who smoke are . . . normal, in the majority, happy, satisfied, etc." "Teenagers who smoke are . . . it's their business, normal, like everybody else, etc." "If a man/woman felt he/she had to

TABLE 11   Responses to Question: "People Who Never Smoke. . . ."

	Cigarette Smokers (210)	Non-smokers (240)
Are nonsmokers/don't have habit	22.4	14.6
Are better off/healthier/happier/more relaxed	34.9	40.0
Are smarter/wiser/better educated/more informed/think more	28.1	28.3
Die sooner from something else/are nervous/frustrated/mean	2.9	1.2
Don't get much out of life	4.3	0.4
Other	2.4	3.3
No answer/don't know	8.0	12.2

TABLE 12   Responses to Question: "If a Man Felt He Had to Smoke, He Should. . . ."

	Cigarette Smokers (210)	Non-smokers (240)
Smoke/start smoking/go ahead/continue	62.9	37.1
Smoke pipe/cigars	19.0	17.9
Smoke filter cigarettes/few cigarettes	2.8	2.9
Drink/eat, chew something/evade it/forget it/drink milk/pray/don't smoke/fight it/control it	8.1	29.6
It's up to him/whatever he thinks best	2.4	2.1
Other	2.4	2.9
No answer/don't know	2.4	7.6

TABLE 13   Responses to Question: "If a Woman Felt She Had to Smoke, She Should. . . ."

	Cigarette Smokers (210)	Non-smokers (240)
Smoke/start smoking/go ahead	66.2	39.6
Smoke pipe/cigarillos	1.0	0.4
Smoke filter cigarettes/smoke fewer cigarettes/use cigarette holder	8.1	5.0
Eat something/drink something/forget it/evade it/chew gum/ignore it	18.6	41.7
Other	1.9	4.1
Don't know/no answer	4.2	5.9

smoke, he should . . . smoke, go ahead, continue." Responses of this type were evoked from far fewer nonsmokers than from smokers, possibly suggesting that if one has company in his misery, he may not be so miserable.

Similarly, fewer smokers than nonsmokers felt that: "adults who smoke are . . . harming themselves, foolish, crazy, stupid, and bad." In response to the question: "If a man/woman felt he had to smoke, he should . . . ," smokers less often than nonsmokers said: "Fight it, control it, drink, eat, chew, and don't smoke."

Dramatically, 57 per cent of the smokers, in talking about teenagers stated: "Teenagers who smoke are . . . not smart, ruining their health, showing off, foolish, crazy, uninformed, etc." This response may well indicate that the belief clusters held by the smoker that allow him to continue smoking are precariously held—that it is too late for him to change but "For heaven's sake, prevent the teenagers from ruining their health."

CONCLUSIONS

Many of the hypothesized reactions of the consumer to dissonant information have been borne out. As inconsistent as smoking must seem to the logical analyst who realizes that the smoker is aware of the published reports on its potential health hazard, the behavior of the smoker is not irrational to himself. With rare exceptions, the confirmed smoker appears to be behaving consistently with his belief system by continuing to smoke. He has justified its rationality either by dissociating his responsibility over the decision; by denying, distorting, misperceiving, or minimizing the degree of health hazard involved; and/or by selectively drawing out new cognitions and new information that will reduce the inconsistency of his behavior and achieve consonance in his own cognitive world.

The dissonance theory clearly opens up avenues for understanding why the consumer—or for that matter any individual, whether he be buyer or seller, employee or manager—behaves as he does. Festinger's theory is definitely not a panacea to all business problems. Certainly it does not explain all behavior; it does not allow for unequivocal predictions nor has it been offered by the social scientists as a complete answer. However, it may provide the businessman and the researcher with a broader frame of reference for understanding human behavior.

REFERENCES

Appreciation is expressed to the Division of Research, UCLA Graduate School of Business Administration, and to the UCLA Bureau of Business and Economic Research for financial assistance in this study.

1. FESTINGER, LEON, *A Theory of Cognitive Dissonance* (Stanford, Calif.: Stanford University Press, 1957).

2. U.S. Department of Health, Education, and Welfare, *Smoking and Health: Report of the Advisory Committee to the Surgeon General of the Public Health Service*, Public Health Service Publication No. 1103 (Washington, D.C.: Superintendent of Documents, 1964).

3. FESTINGER, L., H. RIECKEN, AND S. SCHACHTER, *When Prophecy Fails* (Minneapolis: University of Minnesota Press, 1956).

4. HASTORF, A. AND H. CANTRIL, "They Saw a Game: A Case Study," *Journal of Abnormal and Social Psychology*, XIX (1954), 129–134.
5. BREHM, J., "Post-decision Changes in the Desirability of Alternatives," *Journal of Abnormal and Social Psychology*, LII (1956), 384–389.
6. EHRLICH, D., I. GUTTMAN, P. SCHONBACH, AND J. MILLS, "Post Decision Exposure to Relevant Information," *Journal of Abnormal and Social Psychology*, LIV (1957), 90–102.
7. *The American public discuss cancer and the American Cancer Society campaign: A national survey* (Ann Arbor: Survey Research Center, University of Michigan, December 1948).
8. The assumption has been made that at the time of the study all smokers had been exposed to and were aware of the possibility of a smoking-cancer linkage and hence were in a state of potential dissonance. In fact, 89 per cent of the smokers and 82 per cent of the nonsmokers claimed they had heard about the 1964 Surgeon General's report and were able to identify the specific medium in which they were exposed to that particular source of information alone.
9. A 3 × 3 chi square statistic was 6.08 with 4 *df*, $p < .20$. For tests of significance, it was assumed that the sample was statistically random. In fact the sample selection, rather than pure random, was one of using clusters with only occasional call-backs. This tends to increase the standard error such that some significance levels must be interpreted with caution.
10. *Wall Street Journal*, April 9, 1964.
11. A chi square analysis produced a statistic of 48.93 with 3 *df*. This is significant well beyond the .001 level. Naturally, these results can also be interpreted in the obverse direction such that the less a person believes in the smoking-cancer linkage the more he smokes. The implication of this point of view, however, is that beliefs and attitudes about cancer preceded the smoking behavior. The authors feel that it is more likely that the behavior is first enacted and cognitions about the behavior are then brought in line to be consonant with the behavior pattern.
12. A 2 × 2 chi square applied to the data is significant at the .01 level ($x^2 = 8.65$). In Tables 1, 3, 4, and 5, it would have been of interest to know how recent "quitters" felt about these questions. Unfortunately, only 6 respondents had quit smoking since publication of the Surgeon General's report and hence were not processed separately. These persons have been grouped with the nonsmokers.
13. Minneapolis *Sunday Times*, March 21, 1964. Reported in Festinger, *A Theory of Cognitive Dissonance, op. cit.*

34. Post-transaction communications and dissonance reduction

shelby d. hunt

Few theories have been developed in the behavioral sciences which have sparked as much empirical research as Leon Festinger's theory of cognitive dissonance.[1] Although research in the area has been voluminous, much of it is not directly applicable to marketing. The research of interest to marketers (e.g., Ehrlich, et al., Engel, Bell, Kassarjian[2]) has almost without exception used survey designs in an attempt to determine whether cognitive dissonance was present. "What should the firm *do* about cognitive dissonance" was not the specific focal point for their investigations. The purpose of this study is to evaluate experimentally some of the decision-oriented marketing implications of the theory of cognitive dissonance. The author presents a brief review of the theory and its marketing implications before describing the experimental design.

REVIEW OF THE THEORY AND MARKETING IMPLICATIONS

Definition 1: Cognitions are the bits of knowledge one has about himself, about his behavior, and about his surroundings.

Definition 2: Two cognitions are in a *dissonant* state if, considering these two alone, the obverse of one cognition would follow from the other.

Definition 3: Two cognitions are *consonant* if one cognition does follow from the other.

Definition 4: Two cognitions are *irrelevant* if one cognition implies nothing at all concerning the other.

With the above definitions in mind, Festinger presents the core of the theory of cognitive dissonance with respect to a decision.

1. There may exist dissonant or "nonfitting" relations among cognitive elements.

Reprinted by permission from the *Journal of Marketing*, Vol. 34 (July 1970), pp. 46–51, published by the American Marketing Association.

[1] Leon Festinger, *A Theory of Cognitive Dissonance* (Stanford, California: Stanford University Press, 1957).

[2] D. Ehrlich, I. Guttman, P. Schonbach, and J. Mills, "Post-Decision Exposure to Relevant Information," *Journal of Abnormal and Social Psychology*, Vol. LIV (1957); James F. Engel, "Are Automobile Purchasers Dissonant Consumers?" *Journal of Marketing*, Vol. 27 (April, 1963), pp. 55–58; G. D. Bell, "The Automobile Buyer After the Purchase," *Journal of Marketing*, Vol. 31 (July, 1967), pp. 12–16; Harold H. Kassarjian, and Joel B. Cohen, "Cognitive Dissonance and Consumer Behavior: Reactions to the Surgeon General's Report on Smoking and Health," *California Management Review*, Vol. 8 (Fall, 1965), pp. 55–64.

2. The existence of dissonance gives rise to pressures to reduce the dissonance and to avoid increases in dissonance.
3. Manifestations of the operation of these pressures include behavior changes, changes of cognition, and circumspect exposure to new information and new opinions.[3]

Gerald Zaltman suggests the following as policy implications of the theory of cognitive dissonance:

> Since the consumer seeks means to reduce dissonance after the sale, it might be wise not to "oversell" him on the product. It is preferable for the product to exceed consumer expectations rather than merely satisfy them or fall short of them.... When post-decision dissonance is reduced the initial decision becomes difficult to reverse. Thus, there is a likelihood of complete adoption, that is, repeat sales. . . . Post-decision dissonance is likely to be greatest after the purchase of recently established products from lesser known companies.[4]

The following prescription for action is typical of suggestions based on cognitive dissonance theory.

> The existence of possible negative postpurchase feelings indicates the marketer might benefit from directing some of his communications to the recent buyer, rather than all of them to the potential buyer. The recent buyer may need assurance that he has made the right choice. If he is in a dissonant state, he will be looking for supportive evidence in the forms of advertising and other communications.[5]

STATEMENT OF THE PROBLEM

The theory of cognitive dissonance would lead one to conclude that the consumer should be very receptive to communications from the retailer or manufacturer immediately after an *important* purchase. The present experiment was designed to investigate the following questions:

1. Are communications from retailers to recent purchasers *effective* in assisting these consumers to reduce cognitive dissonance?
2. What is the *relative effectiveness* of different types of communications in assisting consumers to reduce cognitive dissonance?
3. If the communications are effective in assisting consumers to reduce dissonance, what benefits will the retailer derive from supplying these communications?

RESEARCH DESIGN

The basic design of the experiment was an "after only-with control." There were two experimental groups and one control group with all measurements being taken after the "treatment."

---

[3] Same reference as footnote 1, p. 31.

[4] Gerald Zaltman, *Marketing: Contributions from the Behavioral Sciences* (New York: Harcourt, Brace and World, Inc., 1965), p. 62–64.

[5] Philip Kotler, *Marketing Management: Analysis, Planning and Control* (Englewood Cliffs, N.J.: Prentice-Hall, Inc., 1967), p. 75.

Sample Selection Procedure

A major department store in the Detroit metropolitan area cooperated by supplying daily a list of names and addresses of customers who had purchased refrigerators on the previous day. Recent purchasers of refrigerators were used because:

1. Refrigerators are one of the most expensive items sold by department stores. Therefore, if price is a manifestation of *importance,* then a refrigerator would be as *important* a purchase decision as one would make in a department store. (The greater the *importance,* the greater the probability that dissonance will develop.)
2. The particular department store carried several brands of refrigerators. Therefore, the customer had to decide not only in which store to make the purchase, but also which brand to purchase in which store. This increased the possibility of the occurrence of dissonant cognitions.
3. Refrigerators have a bewildering array of special features; e.g. colors, special compartments, revolving shelves, automatic defrosting, and rollers. In many cases a consumer might be forced to accept a unit which will not have *every* specific feature she desires. This again will introduce dissonant cognitions.
4. Appliance department personnel believe purchasers of refrigerators experience more post-transaction anxiety than purchasers of other comparably priced merchandise.

The following types of customers were *excluded* from the above described list of refrigerator purchasers:

1. Corporate, professional, and other business customers.
2. Customers residing outside the greater Detroit metropolitan area.
3. All employees of the department store.
4. Purchasers of "built in" appliances.

The remaining customers were divided, on a random basis, into a control group and two treatment groups.

Treatment Procedure

Each of the three groups received a different post-transaction message:

1. Group I was a control group and, therefore, received no post-transaction message from the department store.
2. Group II received a personal letter from the department store with the following characteristics:
   a. Department store letterhead stationery.
   b. Signed by the appliance department manager.
   c. A sentence expressing appreciation for the customer's purchase.
   d. Several sentences reassuring the customer that:
      (1) Her decision to purchase in this particular store was "correct."
      (2) Her selection of the particular brand-model was "correct."
      (3) The service requirements for that particular brand-model were minimal.
      (4) The department store "stands behind" its merchandise.

3. Group III received a telephone call from the researcher, representing himself as an employee of the department store. The message delivered orally to Group III was the same message used in the letter sent to Group II.

Interview Procedure

All interviews were conducted by a team of professional interviewers in the respondents' homes approximately one week from the transaction date. Some delay was necessary between transaction and interview in order for Group II to receive their messages.

Interviewing continued until a total sample size of 152 completed interviews had been obtained. The interview completion rate was 45%. Almost half of those not interviewed were "not at home"; the other refusals included: "too busy," "don't want to be bothered," and "illness in the family."

The Questionnaire

The basic measurement tool selected for the research was a modified form of the semantic differential.[6] The semantic differential requires respondents to make repeated judgments of how they perceive a particular concept along a seven-point scale between two bipolar statements. The questions in the instrument attempted to measure three key variables—cognitive dissonance, store image, and predisposition to purchase.

Cognitive Dissonance

No validated instrument is presently available for measuring directly the level of dissonance a consumer is experiencing. This research used the level of *post-transaction anxiety* as an indicator of the level of dissonance. A similar technique was used by Gerald Bell in a study on automobile purchasers.[7]

Several of the questions attempted to determine how confident the consumer was about her purchase; i.e., had she purchased the "right" brand at the "right" store. Respondents indicated on a seven-point scale their preference for statements such as: "I should have spent more (less) time in shopping around for this appliance"; "There is no doubt (considerable doubt) in my mind as to whether I should have made my purchase in *this* store."

The mean of the scores on these questions was operationally defined as the *perceived dissonance* for each subject. Statements were randomly dispersed in the questionnaire to prevent a position bias, and the scale was constructed so that low numbers always implied lower anxiety than high numbers.

---

[6] C. E. Osgood, G. J. Suci, and P. H. Tannenbaum, *The Measurement of Meaning* (Urbana, Ill.: University of Illinois Press, 1957).

[7] Bell, same reference as footnote 2.

Store Image

The study postulated one of the benefits that would accrue to retailers for providing post-transaction reassurances would be that the subjects who received the reassurances would have more favorable attitudes toward the store than the control group. The five attitudes used were:

1. Merchandise Suitability.
2. Store Services.
3. Store Congeniality.
4. Sales Personnel.
5. Locational Convenience.

Attitudes 1, 3, 4, and 5 were used by Robert G. Wyckham in his study of aggregate department store images. They were adapted from a previous article by George Fisk.[8]

Once again a modified semantic differential was used as a measurement tool and the mean of the responses to the several statements comprising each attitude was operationally defined as the subject's attitude. The scales were constructed such that low numbers always reflected a "more favorable" attitude than high numbers when viewed from the store's perspective.

Predisposition to Purchase

A second benefit retailers would derive from providing post-transaction reassurances was that the consumers who received the reassurances would be more predisposed to shop at the store than the control group. Subjects were asked to indicate their preference on a seven-point scale for the following statements:

> "In the future I plan to do a much higher (much lower) percentage of my shopping in this store than I have done in the past."

THE FINDINGS

Hypothesis 1

The subjects who received the post-transaction reassurances will have lower perceived dissonance scores (i.e., will be less dissonant) than the subjects in the control group.

In order to obtain an indication of the general tendency of the perceived dissonance scores in each group, the group mean perceived dissonance was computed for each group; i.e., the arithmetic average of the perceived dissonance scores of all subjects in each group. Since the assumption of scale intervality for the semantic differential is

---

[8] R. G. Wyckham, "Aggregate Department Store Images: Social and Experimental Factors," unpublished doctoral dissertation, Michigan State University, Department of Marketing and Transportation Administration, 1968; George Fisk, "A Conceptual Model for Studying Store Image," *Journal of Retailing*, Vol. XXXVII (Winter, 1961–62), pp. 9–16.

questionable, the group means are presented in Table 1 only as descriptive statistics. All statistical tests were performed on the underlying data.

TABLE 1   Group Mean Perceived Dissonance

Group	N[a]	Overall Mean Perceived Dissonance[b]
Control Group	66	2.11
Letter Group	43	1.90
Telephone Group	43	2.31

[a] Number of subjects in each group.
[b] The arithmetic average of the perceived dissonance scores of all subjects in each group.

Since low numbers in Table 1 indicate less dissonance, one would expect that the overall mean perceived dissonance scores for Group II (the group which received the letter) and for Group III (which received the telephone call) would be lower than the score for Group I (the control group). The scores in Table 1 only partially support this hypothesis. As expected, the group which received the letter had a lower dissonance score than the control group. Contrary to expectations, Group III had the highest dissonance of all the groups. Therefore, not only was the telephone call an ineffective device in assisting consumers to reduce dissonance, but also it apparently increased their post-transaction anxiety.

To test the significance of these general tendencies, a Kruskal-Wallis one-way analysis of variance by ranks was conducted on the underlying data. This is a test for determining whether "K" independent samples have come from the same population. Only ordinal data are required.[9]

Table 2 summarizes the results of the Kruskal-Wallis test with the

TABLE 2   Summary of Kruskal-Wallis H and Associated Probabilities with the Null Hypothesis That the Perceived Dissonance Scores of the Three Groups Came from the Same Population

Kruskal-Wallis H	p[a]
5.3513	.0680

[a] Probability of a true null hypothesis.

null hypothesis that there are no real differences in the perceived dissonance scores of the three groups. Since the test statistic does not quite meet the customary .05 level of significance, the findings that the dissonance scores of the telephone group were higher than the dissonance scores of the control group, which were in turn higher than the scores of the letter group, must be taken to be tentative.

[9] Sidney Siegel, *Nonparametric Statistics for the Behavioral Sciences* (New York: McGraw-Hill Book Company, Inc., 1956), pp. 184–194.

Hypothesis 2

*The subjects who received the post-transaction reassurances will have
more favorable attitudes toward the store than the subjects in the
control group.*

To obtain an indication of the general tendencies for the attitude
scores, the group mean for each attitude for each group was computed;
i.e., the arithmetic average of the attitude scores of all subjects in each
group for each of the five attitudes. Once again, the group means in
Table 3 are presented only as descriptive statistics, with all statistical
tests having been performed on the underlying data.

TABLE 3   Overall Mean for Each Attitude for Each Group

Group	N	Overall Group Mean[a]
Merchandise Suitability:		
Control	66	2.03
Letter	43	2.00
Telephone	43	2.26
Store Services:		
Control	66	1.88
Letter	43	1.94
Telephone	43	2.19
Sales Personnel:		
Control	66	2.14
Letter	43	1.90
Telephone	43	2.35
Store Congeniality:		
Control	66	1.95
Letter	43	1.85
Telephone	43	2.40
Store Location:		
Control	66	1.97
Letter	43	1.93
Telephone	43	2.11

[a] The arithmetic average of the mean scores of all subjects for each attitude in each group.

In general, the results paralleled the dissonance findings. The group
which received the letter did react according to expectations and had
the most favorable position for every attitude with the exception of
store services (low numbers are "more favorable" than high numbers).
The telephone group, contrary to expectations, had the *most unfavorable* position for each of the five attitudes. Not only were the post-
transaction reassurances given to the telephone group ineffective in
improving the consumers' attitudes toward the store, but also these
reassurances apparently had a negative effect on their attitudes.

Table 4 is a summary of the Kruskal-Wallis test on the underlying
data to determine whether the overall differences among the groups
for each attitude were significant. Since the test statistics indicate that
only the differences among the groups for the attitude of store congeniality were significant at the customary .05 level, the above findings

TABLE 4   Summary of Kruskal-Wallis H and Associated Probabilities with the Null Hypothesis That for Each Attitude the Scores of the Three Groups Came from the Same Population

Attitude	Kruskal-Wallis H	p[a]
Merchandise Suitability	2.7712	0.2502
Store Services	5.3079	0.0704
Sales Personnel	4.4020	0.1106
Store Congeniality	8.6811	0.0130
Store Location	0.9597	0.6189

[a] Probability of a true null hypothesis.

that the telephone group had the most unfavorable attitudes and that the letter group had the most favorable attitudes must be taken as tentative.

Table 4 also shows that the least significant of all differences was for the attitude of store location. Since store location is perhaps the most "objective" of the five attitudes, it would, therefore, be expected to be the most resistant to change.

Hypothesis 3

A second benefit the retailer might derive from providing dissonance reducing reassurances was that the consumers who received the reassurances would be more predisposed to purchase from the retailer than the control group.

Table 5 presents the mean predisposition to purchase for each group

TABLE 5   Mean Predisposition to Purchase for Each Group

Group	N	Predisposition to Purchase[a]
Control Group	66	2.92
Letter Group	43	2.70
Telephone Group	43	3.30

[a] The arithmetic average of the scores of all subjects in each group.

with low scores indicating high intentions of future purchases. As hypothesized, the letter group had the highest expectations of future purchases. Contrary to hypothesis, however, the telephone group had the lowest expectations of future purchases.

A Kruskal-Wallis test was conducted on the underlying data. The results are summarized in Table 6 and indicate that the overall differences among the groups are not significant at the .05 level.

SUMMARY AND CONCLUSIONS

To simply theorize that consumers experience cognitive dissonance is of little assistance to the marketing practitioner unless he has guidance

TABLE 6   Summary of Kruskal-Wallis H and Associated Probabilities with the Null Hypothesis That the Predisposition to Purchase Scores of the Three Groups Came from the Same Population

Kruskal-Wallis H	p[a]
3.9676	0.1375

[a] Probability of a true null hypothesis.

as to what he *can do* about dissonance, what he *should do* about dissonance, and what benefits will accrue to him if he *does do* something about dissonance. In short, research must address itself to the decision-oriented implications of the theory of cognitive dissonance.

This research has attempted to ascertain in a "real life" experimental design whether certain post-transaction messages from a retailer to recent purchasers would be effective in assisting the purchasers in their efforts to reduce cognitive dissonance. Also, the research examined the potential benefits the retailer might derive from providing post-transaction reassurances.

When compared with the control group, the subjects who received the post-transaction letter experienced *less* dissonance, had *more* favorable attitudes toward the store, and had *higher* intentions of future purchases. It would appear that at least some types of post-transaction reassurance would be effective.

Unfortunately, when compared with the control group, the subjects who received the post-transaction telephone call experienced *more* dissonance, had *less* favorable attitudes toward the store, and had *lower* intentions of future purchases. This post-transaction message appeared to be not only ineffective, but also actually counter-productive. The message actually aggravated the situation.

Neither theory nor the other findings of the study explain why the results of the telephone group were contrary to expectations. The author offers the following conjectures as possibly contributing to the findings:

1. The subjects who received the telephone call may have suspected some ulterior motive for its purpose.
2. The telephone call may have interrupted some of the subjects at inopportune times.
3. Some of the subjects may have been annoyed by firms that sell over the telephone, and therefore interpreted the telephone call as a sales device.

The above conclusions would imply that retailers and or manufacturers should exercise great caution before embarking on a program designed to help reduce the dissonance of recent purchasers. The program might not only be ineffective in helping the recent purchasers, but it could also aggravate the situation by actually increasing the dissonance of recent purchasers. Certainly, extensive pretesting of any specific program would be advisable.

35. Can cognitive dissonance theory explain consumer behavior?

sadaomi oshikawa

More than a decade has passed since the publication of Festinger's original book on the theory of cognitive dissonance.[1] Marketing researchers and psychologists have conducted numerous experiments to test the theory. Whether dissonance theory can be applied to marketing is a question which has raised considerable interest among marketing writers.[2] The theory asserts that a person has certain cognitive elements which are "knowledges" about himself, his environment, his attitudes, his opinions, and his past behavior. If one cognitive element follows logically from another, they are said to be consonant to each other. They are dissonant to each other if one does not follow logically from the other.

Dissonance can be aroused in three ways and can motivate the person to reduce this tension in a variety of ways. Dissonance may be aroused 1) after making an important and difficult decision, 2) after being coerced to say or do something which is contrary to private attitudes, opinions, or beliefs, and 3) after being exposed to discrepant information.

The theory does not specify the mode of dissonance reduction but indicates that there are many possible ways to reduce dissonance. Attitude change, opinion change, seeking and recall of consonant information, avoidance of dissonant information, perceptual distor-

Reprinted by permission from *Journal of Marketing*, Vol. 33 (October 1969), pp. 44–49, published by the American Marketing Association.

[1] Leon Festinger, *A Theory of Cognitive Dissonance* (Stanford, California: Stanford University Press, 1957).

[2] James F. Engel, "Are Automobile Purchasers Dissonant Consumers?" *Journal of Marketing*, Vol. 27 (April, 1963), pp. 55–58; James F. Engel, "Further Pursuit of the Dissonant Consumer: A Comment," *Journal of Marketing*, Vol. 29 (April, 1965), pp. 33–34; Robert J. Holloway, "An Experiment on Consumer Dissonance," *Journal of Marketing*, Vol. 31 (January, 1967), pp. 39–43; Harold H. Kassarjian and Joel B. Cohen, "Cognitive Dissonance and Consumer Behavior," *California Management Review*, Vol. 8 (Fall, 1965), pp. 55–64; Gerald D. Bell, "The Automobile Buyer After the Purchase," *Journal of Marketing*, Vol. 31 (July, 1967), pp. 12–16; Donald Auster, "Attitude Change and Cognitive Dissonance," *Journal of Marketing Research*, Vol. 2 (November, 1965), pp. 401–405; Gerald D. Bell, "Self-Confidence and Persuasion in Car Buying," *Journal of Marketing Research*, Vol. 4 (February, 1967), pp. 46–52; and James F. Engel and M. Lawrence Light, "The Role of Psychological Commitment in Consumer Behavior: An Evaluation of the Theory of Cognitive Dissonance," in *Applications of the Sciences in Marketing Management*, Frank M. Bass, Charles W. King, and Edgar A. Pessemier (eds.), (New York: John Wiley and Sons, Inc., 1968), pp. 179–206.

tion, and behavioral change are some of the common modes of dissonance reduction.[3]

Since the theory does not designate the expected mode of reducing dissonance, most researchers have adopted the experimental method in which subjects could reduce dissonance in only one predetermined way. When the subjects responded to the experimental manipulation in the manner predicted by dissonance theory, the dissonance researcher took the results as evidence for the support of the theory. However, some psychologists have suggested that many of the findings are the results of built-in artifacts (or biases) or can be explained by other competing theories, and that the affirmative result is not necessarily unequivocal evidence for the theory.[4] This article will attempt to assess this possibility.

This article will also attempt to examine theoretical issues and experimental findings for each of the three dissonance arousal conditions mentioned above to determine the relevance of the theory to the study of consumer behavior. In general it appears that the findings are contradictory and are not always supportive of the theory; however, an attempt will be made to sort out and evaluate the evidence.

POST-DECISION DISSONANCE

A review of literature on the psychological study of decision making led Festinger to hypothesize that decision making almost always provokes dissonance because, after a decision is made to choose one alternative, a person has to cope with the cognitive elements concerning the attractive attributes of the rejected alternatives.[5]

Since decision making entails the rejection of alternative(s), the theory asserts that post-decision dissonance is an inevitable consequence of decision making. The magnitude of dissonance depends upon the importance of the decision and the relative attractiveness of the rejected alternative(s). Therefore, the more important the decision and/or the more attractive the rejected alternative(s), the greater the dissonance.

One derivation of the theory is that the greater the number of alternatives a consumer considers before his purchase decision and/or the more equal the positive and negative attributes of the alternatives, the greater the post-purchase dissonance.

---

[3] Jack W. Brehm and Arthur R. Cohen, *Explorations in Cognitive Dissonance* (New York: John Wiley & Sons, Inc., 1962), pp. 306–308.

[4] S. E. Asch, "Review of L. Festinger, A Theory of Cognitive Dissonance," *Contemporary Psychology*, Vol. 3 (July, 1958), pp. 194–195; Milton J. Rosenberg, "When Dissonance Fails: On Eliminating Evaluation Apprehension from Attitude Measurement," *Journal of Personality and Social Psychology*, Vol. 1 (January, 1965), pp. 28–42; Alan C. Elms, "Role Playing, Incentive, and Dissonance," *Psychological Bulletin*, Vol. 68 (August, 1967), pp. 132–148; Karl E. Weick, "When Prophecy Pales: The Fate of Dissonance Theory," *Psychological Reports*, Vol. 16 (June, 1965), pp. 1261–1275; Howard L. Fromkin, "Reinforcement and Effort Expenditure: Predictions of 'Reinforcement Theory' Versus Predictions of Dissonance Theory," *Journal of Personality and Social Psychology*, Vol. 9 (August, 1968), pp. 347–352.

[5] Same reference as footnote 1.

Equivocal Evidence for Post-purchase Dissonance

The experimental evidence frequently quoted to support the existence of post-purchase dissonance was reported by Ehrlich *et al*. They found that the larger number of alternative automobiles the consumer considered before his purchase, the greater the frequency of reading the automobile advertisements of the make he bought. This finding supported dissonance theory. They also found, however, that both recent and not-recent purchasers noticed and read more advertisements of considered-but-rejected makes of automobiles than those of not-considered makes. This evidence cast doubt on the hypothesis that purchasers experienced dissonance. According to dissonance theory they should have avoided the advertisements of the rejected makes.[6]

It may be that, soon after the purchase of a new automobile, Ehrlich *et al's* consumers read automobile advertisements not because they experienced dissonance but because automobile buying was an infrequent undertaking and the topic of automobiles was relevant and useful to them. An experiment by Berkowitz and Cottingham supports the view that people tend to be interested in the topics which are relevant to themselves.[7] They found that safety-belt users were more interested in communication on safety-belts than were nonusers because the topic was relevant to them, their interest having been aroused previously.

Canon, Freedman, and Lowe and Steiner found that when information is dissonant but also useful, utility outweighs dissonance and the information will not be avoided.[8] However, Berkowitz and Cottingham's relevance hypothesis and Canon's utility hypothesis explain the finding equally well and the evidence is not unequivocally supportive of dissonance theory.

In an attempt to reconcile the Ehrlich *et al* finding with dissonance theory, Mills hypothesized that automobile purchasers liked considered-but-rejected makes better than not-considered makes. He reasoned further that, if they preferred to read ads of a chosen (and liked) product to those of a considered-but-rejected (less liked) product, then the Ehrlich *et al* finding that considered-but-rejected makes were noticed more frequently than not-considered makes could be explained by their liking for the former makes.[9]

[6] Danuta Ehrlich, Isaiah Guttman, Peter Schonbach, and Judson Mills, "Post-Decision Exposure To Relevant Information," *Journal of Abnormal and Social Psychology*, Vol. 54 (January, 1957), pp. 98–102; Table I.

[7] L. Berkowitz and D. Cottingham, "The Interest Value and Relevance of Fear Arousing Communications," *Journal of Abnormal and Social Psychology*, Vol. 60 (January, 1960), pp. 37–43.

[8] L. K. Canon, "Self-Confidence and Selective Exposure to Information," in L. Festinger (ed.), *Conflict, Decision, and Dissonance* (Stanford: Stanford University Press, 1964), pp. 83–95; Jonathan L. Freedman, "Confidence, Utility, and Selective Exposure: A Partial Replication," *Journal of Personality and Social Psychology*, Vol. 2 (November, 1965), pp. 778–780; Rosemary H. Lowe and Ivan D. Steiner, "Some Effects of the Reversibility and Consequences of Decisions on Postdecision Information Preferences," *Journal of Personality and Social Psychology*, Vol. 8 (February, 1968), pp. 172–179.

[9] Judson Mills, "Avoidance of Dissonant Information," *Journal of Personality and Social Psychology*, Vol. 2 (October, 1965), pp. 589–593.

In an experiment Mills proceeded to show that consumers preferred to read advertisements of the chosen product to those of the unchosen product. However, in this experiment the consumers had been promised that they would receive the chosen product as a free gift, but had not received it when they expressed their ad preferences. Consequently, their preference may have been influenced by their curiosity about the free gift. His findings would have been less ambiguous if the consumers had, in fact, received the gift. Even granting that Mills proved his hypothesis, the Ehrlich *et al* experiment showed that their consumer subjects did not experience strong enough dissonance to overcome the interest-in-the-liked product tendency.

Ehrlich and others ascribed their unexpected finding to the possibility that some recent purchasers sought the advertisements of unchosen makes in order to find faults and reduce dissonance. This, however, is not a satisfactory explanation regarding the behavior of the purchasers in their attempts to reduce dissonance. If the experimenter is allowed to do this, the findings will always support predictions and there is no room for the rejection of the theory. A better research approach would have been to clearly specify the predicted mode of dissonance reduction and to block other possible modes before the execution of the experiment.

Problems in Experimental Design

One of the criticisms raised by Chapanis and Chapanis and Janis and Gilmore was that some of the experimental findings in support of the theory were the results of built-in bias. They argued that some experiments were designed and manipulated in such a way as to produce supporting results. Consequently, the findings could not be accepted as evidence for dissonance theory.[10]

An experiment reported by LoSciuto and Perloff illustrates this problem. Dissonance theory postulates that if a person, given a choice between two equally desirable products, chooses one and rejects the other, he will experience dissonance. Such dissonance will lead the person to evaluate the chosen product more favorably and the rejected product less favorably. In their experiment, LoSciuto and Perloff had their subjects rank nine phonograph records according to desirability. To arouse strong dissonance, one group of subjects was given a choice between the third- and fourth-ranked albums; the other group was given a choice between the third- and eighth-ranked albums.[11]

The experimenters found that the first group of high-dissonance subjects tended to rerank the chosen albums as more desirable and the rejected albums as less desirable. The low-dissonance group did

[10] Natalia P. Chapanis and Alphonse Chapanis, "Cognitive Dissonance: Five Years Later," *Psychological Bulletin*, Vol. 61 (January, 1964), pp. 1–22; I. L. Janis and J. B. Gilmore, "The Influence of Incentive Conditions on the Success of Role Playing in Modifying Attitudes," *Journal of Personality and Social Psychology*, Vol. 1 (January, 1965), pp. 17–27.

[11] Leonard LoSciuto and Robert Perloff, "Influence of Product Preference on Dissonance Reduction," *Journal of Marketing Research*, Vol. 4 (August, 1967), pp. 286–290.

not show this tendency as strongly. According to dissonance theory, a greater proportion of high-dissonance subjects would show divergent changes in ranking (that is, reranking of the chosen albums as more desirable and the rejected ones as less desirable), while a greater proportion of low-dissonance subjects would show convergent changes. A chi-square test supported this prediction at the .001 level of significance.

Analysis of the design showed that the experiment was set up in such a way as to make it easier for high-dissonance subjects to show divergent changes and for low-dissonance subjects to show convergent changes. Since high-dissonance subjects chose between the third-ranked and fourth-ranked albums, the third-ranked albums had two places to move up, and the fourth-ranked albums had five places to move down, totaling seven places to move divergently. Seven (44%) of the total 16 movements would be considered divergent and the remaining nine movements (56%) would be convergent. For the low-dissonance subjects, 13 of the possible 16 movements (81%) contributed to convergent changes and only three (19%) to divergent changes.

If all subjects reranked the albums randomly, a greater proportion of low-dissonance subjects would show convergent changes and a greater proportion of high-dissonance subjects divergent changes. Although dissonance theory indicates that cognitive dissonance produces the above pattern of changes, an alternative explanation is that the observed pattern of changes is the result of the experimental design.

A Replication of the Experiment

This writer conducted an experiment to test this possibility.[12] One hundred fifty-four undergraduate students were told that he was conducting a survey among college students on the popularity of nine record albums. The students were asked to rank each of the nine albums. One week later they were given the impression that the first preference questionnaires had been misplaced and were asked to rank the same albums again. Because the subjects were not asked to choose between any two albums, dissonance was not provoked.

The pattern of changes for the third-, fourth-, and eighth-ranked albums from the first to the second survey was studied. The chi-square test rejected the null hypothesis of independence between the pattern of changes and the initial location of albums at the .0005 level of significance ($x^2 = 25.58$). This finding showed that the experimental design ensured the statistically significant outcome even when subjects did not experience cognitive dissonance. Sheth's experimental findings in support of dissonance theory can be largely explained as the result of the same built-in bias of using changes in rank positions as the dependent variable.[13]

---

[12] Sadaomi Oshikawa, "The Theory of Cognitive Dissonance and Experimental Research," *Journal of Marketing Research*, Vol. 5 (November, 1968), pp. 429–430.

[13] Jagdish N. Sheth, "Cognitive Dissonance, Brand Preference, and Product Familiarity," in Johan Arndt (ed.), *Insights into Consumer Behavior* (Boston: Allyn and Bacon, Inc., 1968), pp. 41–53.

Summary: Post-decision Dissonance

The Ehrlich *et al* study did show that new car owners sought out dissonance-reducing information, and supported dissonance theory. The difficulty, however, is that alternative explanations (or theories) predict the same results. Consequently, the findings were not unequivocal in support of dissonance theory. Furthermore, dissonance theory also postulates avoidance of dissonance-increasing information. Although some experiments supported this postulate, many others failed to do so. Thus, the theory has not fared too well in the area of information seeking and avoidance. In addition, problems associated with the experimental design may have produced a "built-in" bias for many post-decision dissonance studies.

FORCED COMPLIANCE

Another way to create dissonance is to have a person verbalize or behave in a manner which is contrary to his original attitude, belief, opinion or conviction. In most experiments, subjects were forced to comply with the request of the experimenter to create dissonance. Hence, this process is called "forced compliance."[14] The theory has some support in forced compliance experiments.

As applied to automobile-purchasing behavior, forced compliance resulted in dissonance when a consumer clearly knew that a particular make was superior to other makes in relevant attributes but was induced, *on his own volition*, to buy an inferior make. The knowledge of superior attributes of rejected makes is dissonant with the knowledge that he bought an inferior make. The less the amount of inducement to buy the inferior make and the greater the freedom he had in rejecting superior makes, the greater his post-purchase dissonance.

The importance of volition cannot be overemphasized. Without it, the person will not experience strong enough dissonance to motivate a dissonance-reducing behavior. Its importance was well illustrated in the Festinger and Carlsmith experiment.[15]

Forced Compliance in Consumer Behavior

When the forced compliance paradigm is applied to consumer behavior, the consumer has to be induced to buy the make he knows is inferior if his dissonance is to be aroused. If he believes that one alternative is not a good one but is forced to choose that alternative, he will not experience dissonance because he can explain the poor choice as forced upon him. If, on the other hand, he has complete freedom in making the decision and chooses the wrong alternative, then he will experience dissonance as he cannot ascribe his poor choice

---

[14] Same reference as footnote 3, pp. 84–91.

[15] Leon Festinger and James M. Carlsmith, "Cognitive Consequences of Forced Compliance," *Journal of Abnormal and Social Psychology*, Vol. 58 (March, 1959), pp. 203–210.

to the force imposed upon him. The problem, however, is that in a realistic market situation it is impossible to force a customer to buy a product which he knows is inferior.

One methodological problem of the forced compliance experiment is that the subjects were induced to comply and those who did, in fact, comply reduced dissonance in a variety of ways as predicted by the experimenters. Even in the artificial experimental situations, however, experimenters have been plagued by a loss of subjects who refused to comply. In the Festinger-Carlsmith experiment, 11 out of 71 subjects had to be discarded because of their refusal to comply. In another experiment, only 72 of the original sample of 203 subjects could be used.[16]

Experimenters must strike a balance between exercising too much force and not exercising enough. The implication of this methodological problem to marketing is that, in a natural setting, consumers are not likely to experience post-purchase dissonance via forced compliance because they will not behave in ways which they know will later arouse dissonance.

EXPOSURE TO DISCREPANT INFORMATION

Another set of circumstances under which dissonance may occur is when the consumer is exposed to *new* information not available to him at the time of decision making and which is obverse to the information he already has. This condition is called cognitive intrusion because new dissonant cognitions "intrude" upon one's cognitive structure.[17]

For example, suppose a consumer studied extensively and carefully the attributes of different makes of automobiles and purchased a particular make which he judged to be the best. Will he experience dissonance when he is later exposed to new information describing unfavorable attributes of the chosen make and/or favorable attributes of unchosen makes?

Whether exposure to discrepant information will arouse dissonance depends upon a variety of factors. The most important of these is the degree of commitment and ego-involvement.

The findings of several experiments suggested that when the discrepant information is not salient and the degree of public ego-involvement is small, dissonance will not occur. For example, Rosen found that when students made decisions individually *without* announcing publicly, more (67%) sought dissonance-*producing* information regarding the decisions made and less (33%) sought dissonance-reducing information.[18]

On the other hand, dissonance may be provoked because the con-

---

[16] Chapanis and Chapanis, same reference as footnote 10.

[17] Bruce C. Straits, "The Pursuit of the Dissonant Consumer," *Journal of Marketing*, Vol. 28 (July, 1964), pp. 62–66.

[18] Sidney Rosen, "Postdecision Affinity for Incompatible Information," *Journal of Abnormal and Social Psychology*, Vol. 63 (July, 1961), pp. 188–190.

sumer has publicly committed himself to the position that the choice he made is a good one. Public commitment results in ego-involvement which in turn increases the importance of that cognitive element on which one has committed himself.[19] "The magnitude of dissonance is a function of the ratio of dissonant to consonant cognitions, where each cognitive element is weighted for its importance to the person."[20] Consequently, public commitment tends to increase the magnitude of dissonance by increasing the relative weight of the dissonant cognitions.

Relating the above discussion to the Ehrlich *et al* study, it should be noted that most automobile purchasers are not put in a position to publicly defend the adequacy of their purchase decision, and discrepant information which they read in the newspaper will not arouse strong enough dissonance to make them resort to a dissonance-reducing behavior.

Alternative Theory Supported

To test if dissonance theory can be applied in a more natural situation where individuals do not commit themselves publicly, this writer conducted an experiment and examined whether, after being exposed to dissonant information, strong dissonance leads individuals to convince themselves that the original decision was correct.[21] Students were given the choice of essay type, objective type or any combination of both tests for midterm and final examinations. After indicating their preference, some were exposed to consonant information which supported their original choice while others were exposed to dissonant information.

They were also told either that they were committed to their original preference or that they could change their preference after reading the information. Dissonance theory predicts that those who were committed to the original preference and were exposed to discrepant information would try to reduce dissonance by becoming more convinced of the wisdom of their original decision. Kurt Lewin's field theory asserts, on the other hand, that discrepant information reduces the desirability of the chosen test and increases that of the rejected test and predicts the opposite outcome from dissonance theory.[22]

Experimental evidence supported Lewin's theory, showing that the students were positively influenced by both the discrepant and the consonant information regardless of their commitment. It appears that, under a natural circumstance, individuals do not respond to discrepant information in the way dissonance theory predicts.

[19] A. R. Cohen, J. W. Brehm, and B. Latane, "Choice of Strategy and Voluntary Exposure to Information under Public and Private Conditions," *Journal of Personality*, Vol. 27 (March, 1959), pp. 63–73; same reference as footnote 3.

[20] Same reference as footnote 6.

[21] Sadaomi Oshikawa, "Consumer Pre-decision Conflict and Post-decision Dissonance," *Behavioral Science*, Vol. 15 (March, 1970).

[22] Kurt Lewin, *Field Theory in Social Science* (New York: Harper & Brother, 1951), p. 274; same reference as footnote 3, p. 234.

EVALUATION OF THE THEORY AND APPLICABLE CIRCUMSTANCES

An attempt has been made to examine the experimental findings on the theory of cognitive dissonance. Many findings concerning exposure to discrepant information and post-decision dissonance arousal have been shown to be equivocal. In the forced compliance experiments, the artificial conditions under which compliance was obtained and some subjects' refusal to comply have reduced the usefulness of the experimental findings to the analysis of consumer behavior. It was shown, however, that if the subjects did comply, they attempted to reduce dissonance in a predicted manner.

Analysis of the theory and experimental findings suggested that the necessary condition for provoking dissonance strong enough to motivate dissonance-reducing behavior is that one be *committed on his own volition* to an undesirable product, position, or behavior and be unable to retract this commitment. However, consumers are unlikely to experience strong dissonance since they will not knowingly commit themselves to undesirable or inferior products in a natural market setting.

Role of Advertising as Dissonance Reducer

Dissonance theory sheds new light on the role of advertising of increasing the repurchase probability of the advertised product. A seller's product advertisement reassures the consumer as to the wisdom of the purchase by emphasizing its desirable features and therefore helps to reduce post-purchase dissonance. Dissonance reduction, in turn, reinforces his purchase. It may increase the probability of his purchasing the same brand.

Dissonance reduction may not operate as a strong reinforcer in the case of frequently-purchased merchandise. The more frequently the product is purchased, the less important becomes the question of which brand is purchased at any one time, and the less the post-purchase dissonance. The consumer who has purchased a convenience good usually would not experience strong dissonance because he knows that he is not irrevocably tied to that particular choice, but can easily switch brands. Since his dissonance is not strong, advertising's role in reinforcing the purchase is diminished.

On the other hand, the consumer who has just purchased an expensive specialty good is likely to experience strong dissonance if his purchase is irrevocable and if it is important in some psychological sense. For example, if a substantial financial outlay is involved or if his taste and intelligence are judged by the purchase, strong dissonance may be present. Under these circumstances, an advertisement which emphasized the desirable features of the chosen brand can reduce the dissonance which may lead the consumer to form a more favorable attitude toward the brand.

Wearing-Out of Reinforcing Effect

However, the longer the time lapse before product replacement, the less reinforcing will be the effects of the advertising. In the meantime, the seller's advertising must compete with that of his competitors, and it may not operate effectively as a reinforcing agent long after the purchase. By the time he is ready to replace the product, the effect of the firm's original advertising may have worn off and the attitude and preference of the purchaser may have been influenced by the more recent advertising efforts of the firm's competitors. Since dissonance is reduced over time,[23] it is reasonable to expect that the greater the post-purchase dissonance, the longer the period during which the seller's advertisement operates as a reinforcer.

Thus, for the consumer who purchased an expensive product, advertising can act as a reinforcement for some period of time following the purchase. This reinforcing effect, however, does not necessarily insure a repeat purchase because of the counteracting effects of competitive advertisements.

In summary, the theory of cognitive dissonance is designed to explain and predict post-decisional behavior, but in most instances it is not adequate to explain consumer behavior *before* a purchase decision.

---

[23] Same reference as footnote 6, p. 416.

15 CONFIDENCE

Confidence is the buyer's certainty in his judgment of a brand. The construct is brand-specific in focus, instead of applied to a total product category. Moreover, it definitely is not simply an individual mental or personality characteristic of the respondent. Regardless of the motives the buyer is acting upon when considering a set of brands, the confidence he has in appraising each brand on his set of attitude dimensions will vary by brand. This is true for several reasons, most important of which is that his prior experience and informational exposure relevant to each brand will almost never be identical.

The idea that buyers should have varying degrees of confidence in their judgments of brands is simply common sense. In psychological literature, the same notion is often referred to as the strength, or firmness, or conviction of an attitude. Its counterpart in decision-theory literature is the probability aspect of risk.

We believe that the *confidence* construct is an essential element of a complex theory of buyer behavior. Its role in affecting information-processing as well as ultimately the *intentions-purchase* link makes it indispensable. Very little study, however, has been devoted to *confidence*, except as it concerns persuasibility or confidence toward a total product category. The persuasibility studies, such as by Cox and Bauer (1964), have applied the term "specific self-confidence" to the confidence concept, which serves to emphasize its task-specific nature. The findings concerning persuasibility or conformity to an influence source are not of major interest for this chapter, and will not be discussed. The interested reader, however, is directed to additional studies cited in Cox and Bauer (1964), Shuchman and Perry (1969), and Bauer (1970). In this chapter, we examine the literature supporting the *confidence* construct and its relationship to product purchase.

Through an approach referred to by psychologists as construct validation, Howard (1969)* examines the existence and nature of *confidence* as a theoretical variable. The paper should be studied both for what it says concerning *confidence* and as an example of what construct validation is all about, because construct validation is usually essential in theory development.

In the second paper, Ostlund (1972)* investigates the relationship of *confidence* and *intention*. Remember, of course, that confidence builds as information-processing continues over what may be several iterations through the theory described in Chapter 1. In the Ostlund study, *confidence*, measured according to two goal orientation definitions borrowed from communications research, is found to relate

closely with the *intention* measure. The study is of particular significance since it included six quite different and genuinely new products.
First of all, the pattern of results was very consistent across these six
products. Secondly, the use of new-concept consumer products serves
an additional purpose, since, from a theoretical perspective, confidence
in one's judgment of product attributes for new concept products
should play a particularly vital role in determining intention and,
subsequently, purchase.

REFERENCES

1. BAUER, RAYMOND A. "Self-Confidence and Persuasibility: One More Time."
   Journal of Marketing Research, Vol. 7 (May 1970), 256–258.
2. COX, DONALD F. AND RAYMOND A. BAUER. "Self Confidence and Persuasibility
   in Women." *Public Opinion Quarterly*, Vol. 28 (Fall 1964), 453–466.
3. HOWARD, JOHN A. "Confidence as a Validated Construct." Paper presented
   at the Third Annual Conference on Buyer Behavior, 22–23 May 1969,
   Graduate School of Business, Columbia University. Mimeographed.
4. OSTLUND, LYMAN E. "Product Specific Self-Confidence Related to Buying
   Intentions." 1972. Written for this volume.
5. SHUCHMAN, ABE AND MICHAEL PERRY. "Self-Confidence and Persuasibility
   in Marketing: A Reappraisal." *Journal of Marketing Research*, Vol. 6
   (May 1969), 146–154.

36. Confidence as a validated construct   john a. howard

INTRODUCTION

Confidence in making a brand choice, we postulate, is a central construct in explaining buying behavior. In this role it explains both the buyer's *search effort*—the amount, source, and timing—and his probability of overt action of *purchasing* the brand. It regulates his information input, and it influences his purchase act (Howard and Sheth, 1969).

Our purpose here is to assess the extent to which confidence can be viewed as a validated construct. Although it is perhaps belaboring the obvious, we ask, "Why is the validation problem important to those of us researching the buyer?" The answer, of course, is that the things we work with are so often not observable. Take attitude, for example; whoever observed—touched, tasted, smelled, heard, or saw—an attitude? Confidence has the same unobservable characteristic. To create substantial knowledge with such idealistic constructs—concepts representing things that we are not willing to say necessarily do exist in some physiological sense—does indeed complicate the task of research. However, unless we are willing to pay attention to validating these constructs, research on buyer behavior is a hopeless task, and we should transfer our energies to more productive pursuits.

On the other hand, if we do recognize the validation problem and attempt to deal with it, we should not be unduly discouraged with our difficult task of creating knowledge about unobservables. The great developments in atomic energy, for example, have been based on a construct postulated more than two thousand years ago by Democritus, but not until very recently could the physicist have any real hope of observing—seeing, smelling, feeling, tasting, or hearing—an atom.

As an aid to the reader, all postulated constructs will have the first letter of the label capitalized. The operationally defined counterpart of this construct—sometimes termed "an intervening variable"—will be identified by the same term but followed by an asterisk.

DEFINITION OF CONFIDENCE

At the grossest level, Confidence is the buyer's subjective certainty—his state of feeling sure—in making his judgment of the quality of a particular brand. One of the central complications in defining the term is time. Because we wish to predict the purchase act some time before it occurs, we are interested in knowing the buyer's Confidence prior to the purchase act. The longer this period the greater the num-

Reprinted by permission from John A. Howard, *Third Annual Conference on Buyer Behavior*, Columbia Business School, May 22–23, 1969.

ber of aspects of the decision that are involved in his Confidence in contemplating the future act. To add concreteness to the discussion it is helpful to distinguish between his buying a brand in a product class with a short purchase cycle such as a food item, which may be as little as a week, versus his buying a large consumer durable such as a refrigerator for which the purchase cycle may be longer than five years.

With a short purchase cycle, logically the buyer could be uncertain about (1) his ability to judge the *current* value of the brand (the current dimensions of the evaluative beliefs that constitute his Attitude), and (2) his ability to judge the current value of those elements that constitute the inhibitors that underlie his Intention (to buy). By inhibitors we mean those factors in his purchase situation that constrain him from following the direction of behavior implied in his Attitude for each of the brands in the product class.

When we turn to the more complicated case of the durables, he could in addition be uncertain about (1) the future values of his inhibitors, and (2) the future values of the dimensions that enter into his Attitude.

Given these complications, the question then is: "What is the best way to simplify in order to conceptualize Confidence so that it can be a useful construct?" I suggest that we use three dimensions of certainty with respect to his (1) evaluation of the brand (current Attitude), (2) judgment of the current values of inhibitors, and (3) estimates of future values of inhibitors (future Intention) and omit his estimates of the future values of the dimensions of Attitude.

CONSTRUCT VALIDATION

Having postulated Confidence, we must ask, "Is it a valid construct?" Or, "Is it an ad hoc, isolated, and even meaningless concept?"

One might attempt to answer these questions in terms of whether the thing represented by the construct exists, for example, is there some physiological counterpart that we have not as yet measured? I would not care to take this realistic position, however. Instead, I would attempt only to answer it at a more idealistic level, namely, whether it is a useful construct here and now in guiding our research and interpreting our data for policy purposes, both public and private. Even if one is more realistic, and interested in *Confidence* in some physiological but currently unobservable sense, its construct validation is still a problem, because he must rely upon indirect measures.

How does one evaluate a concept? How does one say that it is good or bad, useful or not useful, satisfactory or unsatisfactory? The answer to these questions is to make use of the process of construct validation.

The importance of construct validation is that if the construct has been validated, the researcher can predict performance with respect to a measure that has not yet been employed in empirical studies. The lack of construct validations is the enormous weakness of current market research. In market research, we discover a measure and use it repeatedly in an habitual, mechanical way. We do not attempt to validate the construct that lies behind it so that we will be capable of making predictions about what values we will obtain on new measures of it. In market research, for example, we take an "attitude" measure that, in fact, is merely the buyer's verbal statement to a question over the telephone. The question is often, "Tell me how well you like this brand. Very much? Some? Not at all?" Then, we take the consumers' responses to these questions and begin to theorize from them—to conjecture about what causes attitude to have the value it has or about the extent to which attitude influences purchase—but the theorizing is almost always implicit, seldom explicit.

One of the consequences of lack of validation is shown by the practice sometimes observed among practicing market researchers of using "attitude" to refer both to a measure of the buyer's *evaluation* of a brand and to his *intention* to buy that brand some time in the future.

There are certain rules according to which we can say that we have or have not validated a construct (Cronbach and Meehl, 1955).

1. We need to make clear what the construct is. To "make clear what something *is*" is to describe the laws according to which it occurs. These laws are contained in an interlocking system or set of relations that make up a theory and that are called a nomological network where "nomological" has to do with laws of the mind.
2. We must specify the nature of these laws for our construct. These laws relate (a) observable attributes to each other, (b) hypothetical constructs to each other, or (c) hypothetical constructs to observable attributes.
3. At least some of the laws must pertain to observable attributes.
4. In the process of validating a construct we learn more about our construct. "Learning more about" a hypothetical construct involves either (a) elaborating the nomological network, or (b) increasing the definiteness of the components by providing more empirical evidence on the existing links.
5. Validation can be furthered by elaborating the nomological network. The network can be elaborated, for example, by adding a construct or a relation (a) if it generates nomologicals that are confirmed by observation; or (b) if it reduces the number of nomologicals required to predict the same observations.
6. We must be able to identify the case where quantitatively different measurement operations are measuring the same construct. Measurement operations that appear quite different "measure the same thing" if their positions in the nomological network tie them in to the same construct. Our confidence in making this identification is determined by the amount of empirical support for that particular region of the overall network that contains this construct.

Thus, the necessary conditions for a construct to be validated are that in the network containing the construct the links make contact with observable reality and that these links exhibit explicit, public steps of inference. The construct must, in other words, be *behavior relevant*.

With these essential conditions in mind let us describe the nomological network surrounding Confidence and then examine some of the empirical evidence on the links in the network.

NOMOLOGICAL NETWORK OF CONFIDENCE

It is perhaps helpful in discussing the links that constitute the networks surrounding Confidence to distinguish them according to the direction of causality. Let us first examine the outbound links, the consequences of Confidence. Confidence is positively linked to Intention and through Intention exerts an effect on overt action, upon purchase of the brand. It is also linked as a feedback inversely to the arousal aspect of the buyer's Motives, which in turn regulates search effort. When the Motives satisfied by this product class are operative, the value of Confidence will be one of the influences upon the intensity of those Motives. By "search" we mean those of the buyer's activities that affect the amount of information he takes into his nervous system. Search activities extend all the way from merely opening and closing his sensory receptors in response to certain stimuli to talking with other people and to performing such acts as obtaining *Consumer Reports* from the public library.

The inbound links—those constructs influencing the level of Confidence—are, first, the buyer's comprehension of the denotative or descriptive aspects of the brand concept (Brand Comprehension), and, second, the feedback from Satisfaction to Confidence. It is the degree of Satisfaction resulting from the purchasing act and the consumption of that brand. These two links are positive.

Often it is even more important to say what a construct is not than what it is. This delimiting role of theory is sometimes neglected. Confidence postulated is not to be Attitude nor any component of it. Some scientists view confidence as merely another way of describing the intensity of Attitude. We believe it will be more fruitful to treat it as being separate from Attitude.

Confidence illustrates the benefit of juxtaposing cognitive theory and behavior theory from psychology. Cognitive theory, by leaning very heavily on attitude, has developed a comprehensive system that can be manipulated but that is difficult to make operational because so many of the variables are unobservable. Behavior theory has been highly operational, but at the price of being an exceedingly complex system, one that is far more implicit than explicit, so that for our kinds of complex problems that system becomes impossible to manipulate. Thus, I believe we must break apart some of the cognitive concepts to achieve greater operationality. We are here breaking apart the usual concept of attitude into its evaluative (Attitude) and Confidence components.

Not only will this separation give us greater operationality, but it will give us the opportunity to sort out the differential effects of the great variety of stimuli impinging upon the buyer. As we know, the marketer is far more interested in some of these stimuli—advertising, for example—than others.

EMPIRICAL EVIDENCE FOR NETWORK

Now we move to the observable counterparts of the hypothetical constructs, the variables that link the nomological network to reality. We postulate that an intervening variable and its hypothetical counterpart are at least monotonically related. The reader should bear in mind the problem of surplus meaning: a hypothetical construct contains meaning that is never fully captured by its intervening counterpart.

To validate Confidence we must determine whether relations among observables (intervening variables) conform to the postulated relations among the hypothetical constructs. As will be recalled from the discussion of the nomological network, Confidence has certain causes and certain consequences. Let us first examine the consequences and then the causes.

Consequences of Confidence*

Confidence* is hypothesized to influence both overt purchase behavior and behavior directed to obtaining information about the brands in the buyer's evoked set of the relevant product class.

EFFECT ON OVERT BEHAVIOR

Our evidence from buying behavior is as yet limited, but research is underway. Johnson (1968) found confirming evidence in a purchase panel established in the test market for a new food product. Consumers with a given level of Intention* (intention to buy within some given time period) were more likely to execute that Intention*—to purchase—if their Confidence was high.

Farley and Ring (1969) in an 11-equation model of the system found a clear relation between Confidence* and Intention,* and the proportion of variance explained in this particular equation was better than any of the other ten equations.

That confidence in Intention as contrasted with the more general confidence in judging a brand also makes a difference in behavior is shown by Juster (1964) in evaluating consumers' plans to buy groups of consumer durables, such as houses, automobiles, refrigerators, television sets, and radios. The usual intention question is:

Do you expect or plan to buy a car in the next six to twelve months?
DW_____ (Definitely will)
PW _____ (Probably will)
DK _____ (Don't know)
No _____

Juster argues that the replies are estimates of the probability that the item will be purchased within the specified time. He believes a more direct approach should be used and he asks:

Taking everything into account, what are the prospects that some member of your family will buy a _____ sometime during the next _____ months, between now and next _____?

Certain, practically certain	(99 in 100)	10
Almost sure	(9 in 10)	9
Very probable	(8 in 10)	8
Probable	(7 in 10)	7
Good possibility	(6 in 10)	6
Fairly good possibility	(5 in 10)	5
Fair possibility	(4 in 10)	4
Some possibility	(3 in 10)	3
Slight possibility	(2 in 10)	2
Very slight possibility	(1 in 10)	1
No chance, almost no chance	(1 in 10)	0

In the case of automobiles, the probability scale predicts purchase considerably better than does the intention measure. For household durables, it improves the predictions but not by nearly so much.

SEARCH EFFORT

Let us now turn to the evidence on the effects of Confidence upon search behavior where we postulate an inverse relation between the level of Confidence and the tendency to look for information. Actually the relationship is more complicated than this, but except for the extremes, an inverse relation is satisfactory.

In a related way and in the buyer behavior area, Bauer and his group under the rubric of perceived risk have presented extensive ideas and findings (Cox, 1967). The results, however, do not bear closely on the issue here because the measures were conceptualized in terms of the product class, not brand choice. In terms of more general human behavior, Berlyne (1963) has assembled a great amount of evidence in simple laboratory experiments. Lanzetta (1967), following Berlyne, has done some of the most extensive laboratory work.

To validate his measure of subjective uncertainty, Lanzetta uses the information theoretic concept of uncertainty:

$$H = -p_i \log_2 p_i$$

where H is the amount of uncertainty and p_i is the probability of occurrence of the ith response. This equation provides an objective estimate of the amount of uncertainty in the stimulus (response uncertainty) since p_i is obtained by computing the relative frequencies of response from a sample of people who are asked to interpret each stimulus in the set of stimuli of varying complexities. He finds that subjective uncertainty measured by the subject's magnitude estimation of "felt degree of uncertainty about the choice" varies directly with this objective measure of uncertainty. Then, having validated his measure of subjective uncertainty, he goes another step and finds that subjective uncertainty (the inverse of Confidence) varies directly with the person's preference for additional information. Later work has carried the analysis further.

On the other hand, in data from a food product in a test market, O'Brien (1969) found that level of word-of-mouth discussion and level and Confidence* vary directly, instead of inversely. O'Brien's analysis was especially relevant because by his methodology he was able to trace causality from Confidence* to word-of-mouth. How can these contradictory findings be reconciled? It can be hypothesized, first, that in a naturalistic setting a certain level of Confidence must be attained before the person feels he knows enough about it to discuss it. This conclusion is prompted in part by Arndt's (1966) finding that there is a bit of game playing in word-of-mouth discussion where the receiver tries to minimize revealing his ignorance. Second, and also in a naturalistic setting, even after the person has acquired adequate information, he continues to talk about the new product because he is now telling others about it: he is an "opinion *leader*" and he thus enhances his status. His motives for talking have changed.

Causes of Confidence

Finally, it is important to examine the empirical evidence on the postulated causes of the level of Confidence in order to assess the validity of the construct. The reader will recall that we postulated in the nomological network two causes of confidence: Brand Comprehension* and Satisfaction. Farley and Ring (1969) found a positive relation between Brand Comprehension and Confidence.*

We should ask about the effects of informational input since it is a central issue. O'Brien (1969) found a clear relation between word-of-mouth and Confidence.* Word-of-mouth affected unaided brand awareness, which in turn affected level of knowledge about the brand, and I would accept these two measures as the equivalent of Brand Comprehension. This finding suggests that information can affect Confidence without first changing Attitude or Intention.

The finding that Attitude seemed to be by-passed by information in changing Confidence is important because of the common belief that Confidence is a dimension of attitude as usually defined. Clearly Confidence and Attitude as defined here are correlated, perhaps with r=0.4. If the line of argument being pursued here that they are separate entities is correct, then we conclude that the same things are not causing both.

CONCLUSIONS

We have formulated a nomological network that contains Confidence as one of its elements (Howard and Sheth, 1969). The relation among the constructs that make up the network have been specified as to direction of causation. Some empirical evidence on these relations among observables has been assembled. In this way we have conformed to the rules of construct validation. Perhaps the most accurate statement to make is that Confidence as a hypothetical construct appears to be partially validated.

If Confidence can be fully validated, significant progress will have been made because Confidence appears to serve an equilibrating role in buyer behavior. Assuming the buyer is experiencing a need for the new product in the market—that is, he is experiencing motivational *dis*equilibrium with respect to this product class—his Confidence is less when he is first confronted by the new product. This low Confidence motivates search effort, but as he receives information, his Confidence rises and his motivation to collect information recedes. His Confidence rises particularly as he buys the product and consumes it. Thus, he attains an informational equilibrium where he no longer needs information. This equilibrium will be most likely if the item is a frequently purchased one and he buys additional units of it. He will develop brand loyalty, which we can think of as a state of purchase equilibrium. Hence, we can say he has achieved information-purchase-equilibrium, which presumably will continue through repetitive cycles of motivational disequilibrium-equilibrium, until some external event such as another new product or possibly his internally generated need for variety "pushes him off dead center."

REFERENCES

1. ARNDT, J. (1966). "Word of Mouth Advertising: The Role of Product-Related Conversations in the Diffusion of a New Food Product." Unpublished Ph.D. dissertation, Graduate School of Business Administration, Harvard University.
2. BERLYNE, D. E. (1963). "Motivational Problems Raised by Exploratory and Epistemic Behavior." In *Psychology: The Study of a Science*, edited by Sigmund Koch, pp. 284–364. New York: McGraw-Hill.
3. COX, D. F. (1967). *Risk Taking and Information Handling in Consumer Behavior*. Cambridge, Mass.: Graduate School of Business Administration, Harvard University.
4. CRONBACH, L. J. AND P. E. MEEHL (1955). "Construct Validity in Psychological Tests," *Psychological Bulletin*, Vol. 52, 281–302.
5. FARLEY, J. U. AND W. L. RING (1969). "Devising an Empirically Testable Version of the Howard-Sheth Model of Buyer Behavior." Unpublished manuscript, Graduate School of Business, Columbia University.
6. HOWARD, J. A. AND J. N. SHETH (1969). *The Theory of Buyer Behavior*. New York: Wiley.
7. JOHNSON, R. P. (1968). *Study of Intentions vs. Behavior*. Unpublished manuscript, Graduate School of Business, Columbia University.
8. JUSTER, F. T. (1964). *Anticipations and Purchases: An Analysis of Consumer Behavior*. Princeton, N.J.: Princeton University Press.
9. LANZETTA, J. T. (1967). "Uncertainty as a Motivating Variable." Mimeographed. Vienna, Austria: Conference on Experimental Social Psychology.
10. O'BRIEN, T. V. (1969). "Information Sensitivity and the Sequence of Psychological States in the Brand Choice Process." Preliminary draft, Ph.D. dissertation, Graduate School of Business, Columbia University.

37. Product specific self-confidence related to buying intentions

lyman e. ostlund

"*Confidence* plays a major role in the buyer behavior system," according to Howard and Sheth (9). They postulate that *confidence* is "positively related to *intention* and negatively related to *motives*, which in turn affects the buyer's information input by way of *attention* and *overt search.*" Confidence is said to be "the extent to which the buyer believes that he can estimate the net payoff, that is, the reward from buying a given brand." Stated differently, confidence could be defined as one's degree of certainty in his judgment or evaluation of a brand of product or service in terms of his *personal attitudes*.

Essentially, no published empirical support is cited by Howard and Sheth for the postulated relationships of confidence to intention and motives. Farley and Ring (6), in their test of the Howard and Sheth model did, however, find a close relationship in one of the ten equations between confidence and intention. Beyond that single study, no other published research has centered on the relationships that Howard and Sheth postulate for confidence.

For other purposes, concepts closely akin to confidence have been investigated, principally as they relate to communication effects. Within a marketing context, Cox and Bauer (5) distinguish between two types of self-confidence: generalized and specific. General self-confidence, or, more commonly, self-esteem, is a mental characteristic, measured apart from any particular task or social situation. On the other hand, specific self-confidence is defined by Cox and Bauer as "confidence in performing a specific task or in solving a specific problem." Cox and Bauer are concerned with how these two types of self-confidence relate to persuasibility. Of greatest relevance for this paper are their conclusions regarding specific self-confidence.

First, when respondents were engaged in judging the merits of two identical but allegedly different pairs of nylons, their likelihood of attitude change varied inversely with their expressed specific self-confidence. Second, this was found true regardless of their level of general self-confidence. Shuchman and Perry (14) have criticized aspects of the Cox and Bauer study and pointed out certain contradictions that exist between it and a later study by Bell (3). Bauer (2) has responded to these criticisms and has referred to additional evidence in the Barach (1) and Gergen and Bauer (7) studies. The questions that remain among Bauer and his critics do not constitute an obstacle for the discussion that is to follow. Except for that by Bell, all of the above studies show the same results for specific self-confidence, which indeed agree with a good many earlier studies by researchers such as Hochbaum (8), Janis (10), Kelman (12), and Mausner (13).

The two concepts, confidence from Howard and Sheth and specific self-confidence from Cox and Bauer, are essentially the same. Both are task-specific and both should result from the interaction of mental characteristics, notably self-esteem, and task characteristics, with the latter set of determinants likely to dominate. Confidence, by Howard and Sheth, is brand-specific, whereas specific self-confidence by Bauer has been treated as category-specific. However, this distinction is not critical for this study.

The study about to be discussed directly investigates the relationship of confidence to purchase intention for a set of new products where presumably confidence in one's judgment of a product should be quite important. Based upon Howard and Sheth, confidence is hypothesized to relate positively with intentions. It was not possible in the same study to relate confidence to intensity of motives.

RESEARCH METHODOLOGY

A quota sample of 605 Boston area housewives examined six new products and completed self-administered questionnaires. The products were carefully selected to avoid "me-too" copies of existing products; however, they were all on sale in test markets outside the Boston area. The products were therefore previously unknown to the subjects, yet were not merely in the form of premarket prototypes or concept cards. Moreover, all the products were relatively inexpensive, so as to avoid products whose purchase might usually be joint husband-wife decisions. The products were:

Product 1: a plastic bandage, with antiseptic, in an aerosol can, which when sprayed on a minor wound provides a flexible, waterproof, and perspiration-resistant protective covering

Product 2: a disposable female undergarment

Product 3: a self-layering dessert mix

Product 4: a biodegradable sanitary napkin

Product 5: a hot foam aerosol shampoo

Product 6: a fabric treatment solution giving permanent press characteristics to any washable fabric

While the brand names cannot be identified here, respondents were aware of them and freely examined other labeling information on the package. Purchase intention was measured on the basis of how likely (a 0 to 100 subjective probability scale) each person said she was to buy each of the products shortly after it was to go on sale in the Boston area. The scale used is a later version of that reported by Juster (11). For purposes of data presentation, the scale was broken at two points —intentions scores of under 30, 30 to 70, and over 70—according to what appeared to be the most natural break points across all six products.

MEASURES OF CONFIDENCE

Wilding and Bauer (15) have demonstrated that it can be useful to distinguish among consumers as to their goal orientations during decision-making. The effect of a persuasive message was found to depend upon the degree to which subjects were operating under problem-solving or under social goals. That is, subjects may favor a given alternative either because they see it as inherently the correct solution to a problem, or instead because they see it as a way to win social approval or psychosocial rewards. Confidence in this study was therefore assessed according to both goal orientations, using questions similar to those by Cox (4), Barach (1), and Bell (3). The questions were:

1. How confident are you in evaluating how (*product name*) will perform?
2. How confident are you in evaluating the reactions of your friends if you bought (*product name*)?

A six-point response scale was used for both questions.

The first question measures confidence in assessing product performance risks, strictly a problem-solving goal orientation. The second question measures confidence in assessing psychosocial risks surrounding a product and concerns strictly a social goal orientation. Tables for both measures are presented (Tables 1–12) as well as a summary table (Table 13) where the responses from each respondent to both questions, related to the intention measure, are combined. The results that follow hold for all levels of respondent general self-confidence, thus agreeing with related findings of Cox and Bauer (5).

ANALYSIS AND DISCUSSION

For greater clarity, the confidence scales on the tables that follow have been collapsed from six to three categories. The original categories of "completely unconfident" and "mostly unconfident" were combined and labeled "unconfident." "Slightly unconfident" and "slightly confident" were included in "neutral." "Mostly confident" and "completely confident" became simply "confident."

Given asymmetric ordinal data, Somer's D statistic was selected as the measure of association since it allows one to state in probability terms the degree to which knowing a respondent's confidence aids in predicting his intention score. The level of statistical significance is given in terms of the Kendall's S distribution as well.

Confidence Regarding Product Performance Risk

For all six products, confidence regarding product performance risk related positively with purchase intentions. Examining Table 1 for the first product, Somer's D statistic equals .355. In probability terms, a high confidence level will correspond with a high intentions score 35.5 percent of the time. A similar relationship repeats itself for the remaining five products even though the distributions of intention scores vary considerably for the six products (Tables 2–6). Statistical significance beyond the .001 level is attained for all six products. The Somer's D statistics range in magnitude from .355 to .219.

Confidence Regarding Psychosocial Risks

Once again, for all six products a positive statistically significant relationship (.001 level) is obtained between the intention score and confidence, this time with respect to psychosocial risks (Tables 7–12). The degree of association between the two variables is lower, however, for each product, with the Somer's D statistic ranging from .284 to .170. Nevertheless, these relationships are strongly supportive of the Howard-Sheth hypothesis.

Combining the Two Confidence Measures

Since Howard and Sheth have not drawn a distinction between types of confidence in positing the confidence-intentions relationship, one may ask what happens when the above confidence components are combined for each respondent. Rather than present a detailed analysis in answer to this secondary question, Table 13 provides the Somer's D statistics from Tables 1–12 plus those for a combined confidence measure and intentions, all calculated from 3×3 collapsed tables. As would be expected, the degree of association on the combined confidence measure generally falls between those for the two components for all products except product 6, where by combining components Somer's D statistic rises.

It would appear that for these products respondents slightly favored a problem-solving orientation centered on product performance risks, rather than a psychosocial orientation, given the generally higher levels of association.

Measurement Error of the Confidence Scales

Some comments are in order concerning possible error with the confidence scales. When the study was planned, it was felt that the two questions selected represented the best ones available, judging from prior studies of specific self-confidence and persuasibility. However, there is some evidence to suggest that the questions are far from perfect operational extensions of the two concepts.

First of all, note the usable sample sizes among Tables 1–6 (from 594 to 601) and Tables 7–12 (from 590 to 596). From an original sample of 605, these losses are not monstrous. However, based upon an inspection of the completed questionnaires, the losses resulted from apparent respondent difficulty or frustration with the confidence questions. All the blanks came on the confidence questions. Furthermore, cryptic comments in the margins attested to respondent frustration with the naive tone of the questions. These observations suggest that subjects may not have expended respectable cognitive effort in responding to the questions.

A second piece of evidence is the distribution of respondents on the confidence scales for each of the six products. Since the sample was drawn according to a quota plan, there is no particular reason to believe that the distributions generated are in any basic way distorted by the sampling design. Nevertheless, the distributions on both self-confidence measures are seriously skewed toward the upper ends of the scales. This result could mean that the confidence scales are at fault in not producing a flatter distribution of respondents. Alternatively, it could mean that all six products are considered by respondents as rather easy to evaluate.

From only this body of data, one can not draw a firm conclusion on this issue. It is certain, however, that if the scales are subject to serious measurement error, this would only serve to conceal the degree to which the two confidence concepts relate to intentions, certainly not heighten it. Thus the high significance levels in Tables 1–12 are all the more impressive.

CONCLUSIONS

From this study, it is fair to conclude that confidence does indeed relate positively with at least purchase intention, as Howard and Sheth contend. This was found true for both Wilding and Bauer (15) goal orientations. Moreover, the Juster intention scale has demonstrated its success in predicting purchases with broad product groups. Juster (11) has stated that, if anything, the scale understates, rather than overstates purchase incidence. Thus, there is every reason to believe that the two types of confidence should relate positively to subsequent purchase behavior.

The matter of measurement error with the confidence scales deserves additional examination, however, particularly in view of the Shuchman and Perry (14) criticisms.

TABLE 1   Product 1: Confidence Regarding Product Performance Risks

Intention Score	Unconfident	Neutral	Confident	Percent	Total
Under 30	69%	22%	9%	18%	105
30–70	19	38	23	29	174
Over 70	13	40	68	53	319
	100%	100%	100%	100%	
Total	32	244	322		598

Somer's D = .355.

Kendall's S statistic significant at .001 level.

TABLE 2   Product 2: Confidence Regarding Product Performance Risks

Intention Score	Unconfident	Neutral	Confident	Percent	Total
Under 30	88%	52%	45%	53%	316
30–70	10	30	26	25	152
Over 70	3	18	29	22	132
	100%	100%	100%	100%	
Total	72	218	310		600

Somer's D = .223.

Kendall's S statistic significant at .001 level.

TABLE 3   Product 3: Confidence Regarding Product Performance Risks

Intention Score	Unconfident	Neutral	Confident	Percent	Total
Under 30	33%	20%	9%	12%	73
30–70	44	36	22	26	153
Over 70	22	44	69	62	372
	100%	100%	100%	100%	
Total	9	135	454		598

Somer's D = .272.

Kendall's S statistic significant at .001 level.

TABLE 4   Product 4: Confidence Regarding Product Performance Risks

Intention Score	Unconfident	Neutral	Confident	Percent	Total
Under 30	73%	33%	24%	29%	169
30–70	9	34	21	24	145
Over 70	18	32	55	47	279
	100%	100%	100%	100%	
Total	22	172	399		593

Somer's D = .249.

Kendall's S statistic significant at .001 level.

TABLE 5   Product 5: Confidence Regarding Product Performance Risks

Intention Score	Unconfident	Neutral	Confident	Percent	Total
Under 30	85%	43%	39%	45%	269
30–70	13	41	28	33	195
Over 70	2	16	33	22	133
	100%	100%	100%	100%	
Total	52	275	270		597

Somer's D = .219.

Kendall's S statistic significant at .001 level.

TABLE 6   Product 6: Confidence Regarding Product Performance Risks

Intention Score	Unconfident	Neutral	Confident	Percent	Total
Under 30	79%	36%	29%	37%	224
30–70	11	38	23	29	172
Over 70	10	26	48	34	202
	100%	100%	100%	100%	
Total	62	276	260		598

Somer's D = .282.
Kendall's S statistic significant at .001 level.

TABLE 7   Product 1: Confidence Regarding Psychosocial Risks

Intention Score	Unconfident	Neutral	Confident	Percent	Total
Under 30	36%	26%	11%	18%	104
30–70	40	37	24	29	173
Over 70	24	37	65	53	316
	100%	100%	100%	100%	
Total	25	215	353		593

Somer's D = .284.
Kendall's S statistic significant at .001 level.

TABLE 8   Product 2: Confidence Regarding Psychosocial Risks

Intention Score	Unconfident	Neutral	Confident	Percent	Total
Under 30	80%	54%	48%	53%	313
30–70	16	29	24	25	150
Over 70	4	17	28	22	130
	100%	100%	100%	100%	
Total	56	213	324		593

Somer's D = .170.
Kendall's S statistic significant at .001 level.

TABLE 9   Product 3: Confidence Regarding Psychosocial Risks

Intention Score	Unconfident	Neutral	Confident	Percent	Total
Under 30	47%	19%	8%	12%	71
30–70	20	32	24	26	152
Over 70	33	49	68	62	369
	100%	100%	100%	100%	
Total	15	145	432		592

Somer's D = .231.
Kendall's S statistic significant at .001 level.

TABLE 10   Product 4: Confidence Regarding Psychosocial Risks

Intention Score	Unconfident	Neutral	Confident	Percent	Total
Under 30	63%	31%	25%	28%	168
30–70	23	35	20	24	144
Over 70	13	35	55	47	279
	100%	100%	100%	100%	
Total	30	162	399		591

Somer's D = .236.
Kendall's S statistic significant at .001 level.

TABLE 11   Product 5: Confidence Regarding Psychosocial Risks

Intention Score	Unconfident	Neutral	Confident	Percent	Total
Under 30	86%	45%	40%	45%	264
30–70	11	38	31	33	192
Over 70	3	17	29	22	132
	100%	100%	100%	100%	
Total	36	241	311		588

Somer's D = .186.
Kendall's S statistic significant at .001 level.

TABLE 12   Product 6: Confidence Regarding Psychosocial Risks

Intention Score	Unconfident	Neutral	Confident	Percent	Total
Under 30	79%	39%	31%	37%	223
30–70	10	36	25	29	170
Over 70	10	24	44	34	202
	100%	100%	100%	100%	
Total	39	237	319		595

Somer's D = .241.
Kendall's S statistic significant at .001 level.

TABLE 13   Levels of Association for Confidence and Intention
(Somer's S Statistics)

Intentions Related to:	Confidence		
	Regarding Product Performance	Regarding Psychosocial Risks	Combined
Product 1	.355	.284	.326
2	.223	.170	.207
3	.272	.231	.246
4	.249	.236	.256
5	.219	.186	.214
6	.282	.241	.306

REFERENCES

1. BARACH, JEFFREY A. "Self-Confidence and Reactions to Television Commercials." In *Risk Taking and Information Handling in Consumer Behavior*, edited by Donald F. Cox, pp. 428–441. Cambridge, Mass.: Harvard Business School, Division of Research, 1967.
2. BAUER, RAYMOND A. "Self-Confidence and Persuasibility: One More Time." *Journal of Marketing Research*, Vol. 7 (May 1970), 256–258.
3. BELL, GERALD D. "Self-Confidence and Persuasion in Car Buying." *Journal of Marketing Research*, Vol. 4 (February 1967), 46–53.
4. COX, DONALD F. "Information and Uncertainty: Their Effects on Consumers Product Evaluations." Unpublished Ph.D. dissertation, Harvard Business School, 1962.
5. ———— AND RAYMOND A. BAUER. "Self-Confidence and Persuasibility in Women." *Public Opinion Quarterly*, Vol. 28 (Fall 1964), 453–466.
6. FARLEY, JOHN AND WINSTON RING. "An Empirical Test of the Howard-Sheth Model of Buyer Behavior." *Journal of Marketing Research*, Vol. 7 (November 1970), 427–438.
7. GERGEN, KENNETH J. AND RAYMOND A. BAUER. "The Interactive Effects of Self-Esteem and Task Difficulty on Social Conformity." In *Risk Taking and Information Handling in Consumer Behavior*, edited by Donald F. Cox, pp. 411–427. Cambridge, Mass.: Harvard Business School, Division of Research, 1967.
8. HOCHBAUM, GODFREY M. "The Relations Between Group Members' Self-Confidence and Their Reaction to Group Pressures to Uniformity." *American Sociological Review*, Vol. 19 (June 1954), 678–687.
9. HOWARD, JOHN A. AND JAGDISH N. SHETH. *The Theory of Buyer Behavior*. New York: Wiley, 1969, pp. 143–144.
10. JANIS, IRVING L. "Personality and Susceptibility of Persuasion." *Journal of Personality*, Vol. 22 (June 1954), 504–518.
11. JUSTER, F. THOMAS. "Consumer Buying Intentions and Purchase Probability: An Experiment in Survey Design." *Journal of the American Statistical Association*, Vol. 61 (September 1966), 658–696.
12. KELMAN, HERBERT C. "Effects of Success and Failure on 'Suggestibility' in the Autokinetic Situation." *Journal of Abnormal and Social Psychology*, Vol. 45 (April 1950), 267–285.
13. MAUSNER, BERNARD. "The Effect of Prior Reinforcement on the Interaction of Observed Pairs." *Journal of Abnormal and Social Psychology*, Vol. 49 (January 1954), 65–68.
14. SHUCHMAN, ABE AND MICHAEL PERRY. "Self-Confidence and Persuasibility in Marketing: A Reappraisal." *Journal of Marketing Research*, Vol. 6 (May 1969), 146–154.
15. WILDING, JOHN AND RAYMOND A. BAUER. "Consumer Goals and Reactions to a Communication Source." *Journal of Marketing Research*, Vol. 5 (February 1968), 73–77.

Cumulative Phenomena

5

16 PURCHASE PATTERNS

In Part 5, our primary interest shifts from the prediction of individual behavior at one point in time to that of behavior across a given group of individuals or events, that is, cumulative behavior. We begin with an examination of purchase patterns, which have in the past been generally described in terms employing the word "loyalty." With respect to consumer products, brand loyalty has referred to the consistency or regularity with which buyers apparently favor a given brand over others or close substitutes. More recently, attention has been directed to the extent to which industrial purchasing agents apparently tend to favor certain suppliers over others. As is often the case, the initial labeling of a phenomenon is not neutral with respect to an implied explanation, even though virtually nothing is known, more than some descriptive comments, of an explanatory nature. To be specific, the word "loyalty" at least implies an explanation as to why a given consistency or regularity in pattern exists, namely, that the buyer favors the brand or manufacturer out of conviction or commitment to the brand or manufacturer superiority over "substitutes." At least with respect to brand loyalty, alternative explanations have been set forth that account almost as well for variability in the data as does any hypothesis relating to buyer conviction.

The study by Tucker (1964)* demonstrates that a consistent pattern of brand choice behavior can arise even where the buyer is choosing from virtually identical brands. Thus, it is clear that such purchase patterns have not arisen from strong preferences for comprehendable product attributes. An explanation of at least equal relevance would be that consumers confronted with relatively indistinguishable brand alternatives will, due to inertia, settle into a pattern that suggests "loyalty" of a conviction sense when really their only objective is to simplify a cluttered, relatively unimportant task. Stated differently, if brands within a given product category are essentially identical, "rational buyer behavior" would suggest a strategy predicated upon inertia, rather than one of vacillation approaching random behavior. "If it doesn't make any difference, I don't worry about it."

Farley (1964)* found, through the use of regression analysis, that apparent differences in "brand loyalty" across product categories can be accounted for on the basis of structural variables concerning the market in which the products are sold, apart from specific characteristics of the products or buyer attitudes toward them. Thus, we have another possible explanation for a consistent or regular pattern of purchase behavior.

Many studies have centered their attention on isolating the characteristics of buyers exhibiting consistent purchase patterns. One of the few studies to obtain positive results is that by Carman (1970).* Nevertheless, his findings reinforce those of Farley concerning store loyalty.

Do consistent purchase patterns also exist among industrial buyers? Yes, according to research by Wind (1970).* Although his research was conducted using data from only one company, a high degree of consistent purchase behavior, or source loyalty, was found. Moreover, four sets of variables accounted for an average of 80 percent of the variance in source loyalties, a higher proportion than generally obtained in studies of "brand loyalty" among consumers.

In summary, more recent research with regard to consistent purchase patterns has finally focused on the underlying explanations rather than merely attempting to document the degree of such consistency. Without knowing why purchase patterns exist, one is not justified in reaching for marketing strategy implications concerning such patterns.

38. The development of brand loyalty

w. t. tucker

Most studies of brand loyalty have involved the measurement and description of loyalties to existing brands of merchandise. From these studies it can be safely concluded that there are rather wide variations in loyalty among individuals and that brand loyalty is at least in part a function of the frequency and regularity with which a brand has been selected in the past [5] and in part a function of the type of product involved [6]. Rather sophisticated analyses have suggested that some sort of Markov process best describes the growth of brand loyalty [3, 4]. One of the primary characteristics of the relevant research is its reliance on maximum realism and the minimal distortion of the context of consumer behavior [2]. Even efforts such as Pessemier's study measuring the strength of brand loyalty are ingenious in their efforts to maintain the semblance of realism under difficult circumstances [7].

Valuable as such methodological techniques are, they cannot be brought to bear on some critical aspects of brand loyalty. In order to discuss these meaningfully, it is necessary to define brand loyalty, despite the apparent simplicity of the terms. For purposes of this paper, brand loyalty is conceived to be simply biased choice behavior with respect to branded merchandise. If there are two cola drinks offered to a person a number of times, his degree of brand loyalty can be stated in terms of the relative frequency with which he chooses one brand rather than the other. If he selects Pepsi Cola rather than Coca Cola (and both are equally available) enough of the time to persuade the statistically sophisticated observer that the difference in frequency is not due to chance, he may be said to be brand loyal. No consideration should be given to what the subject thinks or what goes on in his central nervous system; his behavior is the full statement of what brand loyalty is.

It is always dangerous to fragment molar behavior into theoretical sub-systems, but the obviously complex character of brand loyalty demands some further analysis if it is to be fully useful either theoretically or to practical marketers. The loyalty may be to some subset of characteristics: the shape of the bottle, the sweetness of the drink, the colors on the cap, the brand name, or whatever. Now imagine that the loyalty to Pepsi Cola described above existed during that time when Pepsi was marketed in 12 oz. export beer bottles and the only bottled Coca Cola contained 6 oz. Imagine further that a single change was made: a new 12 oz. bottle of Coca Cola (there was such an experi-

Reprinted by permission from *Journal of Marketing Research*, Vol. 3 (August 1964), pp. 32–35, published by the American Marketing Association.

mental size at one time) was available to him as an alternative to the 12 oz. Pepsi. This might change his choice so that he would subsequently choose Coca Cola more frequently than Pepsi.

It is tempting to suggest that the individual was never really brand loyal to Pepsi at all, but merely preferred a larger drink. But chaos lies in this direction. Suppose for instance that the Pepsi Cola formula or drink is next placed in the Coca Cola bottle capped with the red, white and blue Pepsi Cola cap and the Coca Cola is placed in the old export beer bottle with a Coca Cola cap—and that the individual shifts back to the Pepsi. What becomes of brand loyalty? In fact brand loyalty is always a biased response to some combination of characteristics, not all of which are critical stimuli. This way of looking at brand loyalty may not be congenial, but something much like it (the gestalt approach suggests variations) seems required either for research on the nature of brand loyalty or practical questions regarding changes in product, packaging, or advertising.

One of the hypotheses that the experiment reported here undertakes to support is the notion that brand loyalty will grow in an almost completely infertile field, that biased choices will develop even when products are virtually identical and brand names are close to meaningless. Clearly, this hypothesis is an outgrowth of the preceding view of brand loyalty. It also stems from a confirmed belief that the stochastic learning model is not wholly satisfactory as a description of brand choice.

The stochastic learning model is based on an historical sequence of psychological experiments in which there were always right (rewarded or unpunished) responses and wrong (unrewarded or punished) responses. (Those few experiments not of this nature seem to have received little independent attention until recent years.) There seem to be two underlying problems in the learning model: (1) it assumes that a reinforced (usually a rewarded) response will have an increased probability of recurring; (2) it seems to imply that reinforcement, or differentials in level of reinforcement, form the sole basis for choice. It is possible that a rewarded choice (say the selection of a brand of shaving cream by the first-time user at age 15) may in fact decrease the likelihood of a repeat purchase if the individual is interested in finding out more about different kinds of creams or soaps. This could be referred to as search behavior. And, further, it seems possible that this boy could become brand loyal even if he could perceive no advantage whatsoever in any particular preparation, since such behavior would at least decrease the effort of decision making. More positive influences may be in the connotative meanings and associations that naturally grow around objects one uses, the activities he engages in, and people with whom he interacts. It is too easy an assumption to declare that brand loyalties established in this fashion would be fragile or transient. Psychological theory, if not learning theory, suggests that one may learn to like what he chooses as readily as he may learn to choose what he likes. Such possibilities seem worth investigating.

The present experiment differs from most of the previous work in that it suffers the disabilities of obvious artificiality at the same time that it gains the capacity to examine some of the above aspects of brand loyalty not open to observation in the "real" world. The experiment consisted simply of twelve successive consumer choices of bread from among four previously unknown brands. Forty-two women participated in the experiment. They were selected by two-stage random sampling from a single census tract in order to minimize delivery problems. Each woman was told that the study was designed to find out how women went about purchasing when they moved to a new location and were faced with unfamiliar brands. She was then asked to select one of four loaves of bread marked "L," "M," "P," and "H." Packaging was otherwise identical. Letter designations were chosen for ease of memory. And, although all are consonants from the middle of the alphabet and have approximately the same frequency of use in the English language, it is not assumed that they are "neutral" symbols. In fact, it seems probable that no set of symbols which are discriminable can be neutral or equally pleasing or have common meanings for all individuals.

The position of the brands on the tray was varied in Latin square design so that no brand was in the same position two times in a row and so that each brand occurred in each position with equal frequency. The bread used for all brands was identical, sandwich-loaf, thin-sliced bread, taken from a single oven on the morning of delivery.

In order to determine the strength of any brand loyalties formed during the experiment, once a panel member chose the same bread three times in succession, a premium was placed on another brand. The brand selected for the premium was that brand most seldom selected previously. Where two or more brands satisfied this requirement a random selection among them of the brand for the premium was made. The premium used was a new penny fixed to the brand label. If the woman did not select the brand with the premium on the first trial, the premium was increased by one penny per trial for each subsequent trial until the panel member selected the desired brand or the experiment ended.

It was anticipated that the experiment would begin with a period of search or exploratory behavior, during which the selection of any brand would decrease the probability that the same brand would be selected again. Following this period, it was believed that the selection of any brand would increase the likelihood that the same brand would be selected on the following trial. It was further anticipated that brand loyalty would be established despite homogeneity of product and that the degree of loyalty indicated by three successive choices of the same brand might be measurable in terms of the number of cents required to cause a change in selection.

THE PERIOD OF SEARCH

The evidence for a period of search or exploratory consumer behavior is clear. During the first several choices, the sequence of two choices of the same brand was far below that expected by chance. Twenty-nine of the forty-two women systematically tried each of the brands in order during their first four selections. Of course, it should be remembered that the nature of the experiment seems to suggest that a complete exploration is the sensible thing to do. Several of the panel members indicated in advance that they had already made the decision to try each of the four brands.

There is no clear indication when the period of search ends for an individual. Some of the housewives completed 12 successive choices without ever selecting the same brand twice in succession. Such behavior could equally well be described as extended search or indifference. At the same time, patterns for the entire group suggest that the first four choices were qualitatively different from the remaining selections. Table 1 shows the relative frequency of repeating a choice on each of

TABLE 1   Relative Frequency of Selecting X Brand, Given the Preceding Selection of X, but Not XX

Trial number	Relative frequency
2	.048
3	.050
4	.026
5	.210
6	.300
7	.346
8	.288
9	.240
10	.136
11	.261
12	.105

the 12 trials. Included in the data are only those persons who have not become brand loyal and who have a brand run length of one.

Clearly something happens after the fourth choice in terms of willingness to repeat the selection of any given brand. The indication is not, however, that search activity has ended for all participants. The relative frequency of repeating the fourth choice on the fifth trial (given no earlier repeat of the third choice on the fourth trial) remains below the expected value of .25, although not significantly so. (The relative frequency of a repeated choice of this sort up to the fourth trial is significant far above the .10 level, is in fact about 31 standard errors *below* the expected.)

The tailing off in the relative frequency of a repeated selection during the later trials is in part the consequence of growth in brand loyalty. Women who had become brand loyal no longer have brand run lengths of one except under the influence of premiums. Therefore, persons who had become brand loyal (had selected the same brand three times in a row) were eliminated from the data shown in Table 1 for all trials subsequent to the establishment of brand loyalty.

THE EMERGENCE OF BRAND LOYALTY

Exactly half of the women engaged in the experiment reached the criterion of brand loyalty by the end of twelve trials. These loyalties emerged at every possible point. Table 2 shows the frequency with which brand loyalty emerged on the various trials.

TABLE 2   The Trials on Which Women Completed Their Third Consecutive Selection of Any Brand

Trial number	Number of women
3	1
4	2
5	1
6	3
7	1
8	3
9	3
10	2
11	1
12	4

It can undoubtedly be presumed that additional women would have reached the criterion of brand loyalty with further trials. Two of the women not previously brand loyal selected the same brand on trials eleven and twelve. The probability of selecting a brand the third time given two consecutive selections throughout the experiment was .396, significantly above chance at the .05 level.

While it is impossible to state conclusively the stage of brand loyalty reached by those women who had not selected any brand on three consecutive trials, there were suggestions that some women had established a relative loyalty to two of the brands (ending trials of M, H, M, H, M and P, H, P, H) and that some had essentially eliminated one of the brands from further consideration (six of the non-loyal women selected one of the brands only once in the twelve trials).

The extremes in non-loyalty to brand were provided by four women who developed position loyalties of considerable duration. Position loyalties were not simple to judge, since participants could perform exploratory behavior among brands by the simple expedient of selecting from the same tray position for consecutive trials. Where continuous selection from a single position continued for a long period or where it emerged as an apparent solution to the decision process during the later trials, there seems rather conclusive evidence for stating that position loyalties did emerge. (It should be pointed out that all position loyalties were for the tray position at the participant's extreme left.)

A conclusion that seems almost inescapable is that women vary greatly in their susceptibility to brand loyalty. In some, the sort of behavior referred to as brand loyalty seems to have become functionally autonomous and may be a preferred form of behavior in any applicable situation.[1] At the other extreme there appear to be those

---

[1] Cunningham's position that no important number of shoppers is prone to brand loyalty is based on quite different data [1] and does not really contradict this position.

(suggested here by the position-loyal participants) to whom brand differences unaccompanied by product differentiation are inconsequential. This variation among women in susceptibility to brand loyalty may may be one of the major consumer variables which face the marketer of certain kinds of products.

THE STRENGTH OF LOYALTIES

There is a strong temptation to believe that when a woman encounters a preferred brand and another brand at a reduced price (simulated in this experiment by the addition of one or more pennies to a competing brand) her choice is somehow limited to those alternatives. Of course, behavior in the marketplace constantly demonstrates that this is not the case. In the present experiment, six of the women who switched from the brand to which they had become loyal, switched first to a brand that did not contain the premium of one or more pennies. Four of these switched to a non-premium brand when the first penny was placed on the premium brand. One switched after two cents was applied, one after three cents. Undoubtedly a gestalt psychologist would suggest that the addition of a premium to any brand restructured the entire situation. As one woman who changed, but not to the premium brand, said, "No wonder you put the special on brand 'P.' It's the worst one of all." To her the premium apparently was a signal to do something, but anything rather than the encouraged action.

Six of the brand-loyal women switched to the premium brand for premiums varying from 2–7 cents. The average value of these accepted premiums was 3½ cents. Eight women were still selecting their favorite brand when the experiment ended. Premiums that they refused on the last opportunity varied from 1–7 cents. Their average was 3½ cents.

Even the women who had established position loyalties showed resistance to change. Three of these women were offered premiums. Two who were offered premiums on a different position after five consecutive choices from the same position switched to the premium position for premiums of one cent and two cents. The third woman, for whom premiums were begun after eight successive selections from the same position, shifted to a choice from another location when the premium reached three cents. She did not select a loaf from the premium position at any time, although a total of five cents was placed on the brand in that position at the time of her last choice.

Obviously because of the variation in response to premiums and the small number of women involved, it is impossible to draw any general conclusions about the average strength of brand or position loyalties that developed during the experiment. At the same time, it is clear that such loyalties are more than trivial, even though they are based on what may seem trivial distinctions.

OTHER FINDINGS

While there is no satisfactory evidence that the order of choice affects the likelihood that a particular brand will be the one to which a woman becomes loyal, Table 3 shows the relevant distributions.

TABLE 3   Order of Trial of Brands to Which Participants Became Brand-loyal

Rank order in which brand was chosen	Number of women who became loyal
First	8
Second	6
Third	2
Fourth	5

CONCLUSIONS

An exploratory experiment such as the one reported here is more often suggestive than conclusive. The following conclusions are, therefore, tentative:

1. Some consumers will become brand loyal even when there is no discriminable difference between brands other than the brand itself.
2. The brand loyalty established under such conditions is not trivial, although it may be based on what are apparently trivial and superficial differences.
3. Consumers vary greatly in their susceptibility to brand loyalty.
4. Brand loyalty and preference for particular product characteristics are quite different considerations that together make up what is normally referred to as brand loyalty.
5. While it is difficult to identify exploratory consumer behavior, it seems clear that some consumer selections are largely exploratory in nature and may indicate that a repeat purchase is highly unlikely.

REFERENCES

1. CUNNINGHAM, ROSS M., "Brand Loyalty—What, Where, How Much?" *Harvard Business Review*, 34 (1956), 116.
2. FRANK, RONALD E., "Brand Choice as a Probability Process," *Journal of Business*, 35 (1962), 43.
3. HARARY, FRANK AND BENJAMIN LIPSTEIN, "The Dynamics of Brand Loyalty: A Markovian Approach," *Operations Research*, 10 (1962), 17.
4. HERTINER, JEROME D. AND JOHN F. MAGEE, "Customer Behavior as a Markov Process," *Operations Research*, 9 (1961), 105.
5. KUEHN, ALFRED A., "Consumer Brand Choice—A Learning Process" in Ronald E. Frank, Alfred A. Kuehn and William F. Massy, *Quantitative Techniques in Marketing Analysis*, Homewood, Ill.: Richard D. Irwin, 1962.
6. PECKHAM, JAMES O., "The Consumer Speaks," *Journal of Marketing*, 27 (1963), 21.
7. PESSEMIER, EDGAR A., "A New Way to Determine Buying Decisions," *Journal of Marketing*, 23 (1959), 41.

39. Why does "brand loyalty" vary over products?

john u. farley

Both businessmen and market researchers are vitally interested in the nature of demand for individual brands of products. This interest was whetted by the empirical studies of George H. Brown [1] and Ross M. Cunningham [2], who studied summary measures of brand purchase patterns reported by consumer panels. Both found marked consistencies in the patterns in which consumers buy brands of various products, and both concluded that people exhibit both strong and operative "brand loyalty." Frank has verified this conclusion using data on a single product class [5], as has Kuehn in the course of building complex models of consumer brand choice in certain markets [8] and the author in research on family behavior in several markets [4].

But Cunningham and Brown, both of whom studied more than one product, also reported that there are significant differences over products in measured brand loyalty, and Telser also found differences over products in estimated brand cross-elasticities and estimated product elasticities [12]. Brown and Cunningham, who concerned themselves with these cross-product differences, concluded that buyers are differentially loyal to different products; the authors seem to attribute this to differences in the products themselves or to differences in consumer attitudes towards different products. However, material from a number of fields suggests reasons why consumer behavior might well differ over markets, and it seems desirable to consider some alternative explanations before concluding simply that people are different and products are different. This paper develops a series of hypotheses about what variables in a market may affect summary measures of purchase sequences. Two such summary measures are used: One cross-sectional (summarizing activity within a given time period) and one based on time series (measuring changes in behavior over time). The cross-sectional statistic is this:

N_m = the average number of brands bought by families of product m during the period sudied.

And the time series statistic is this:

S_m = the percent of families in market m whose favorite brand is different in the first half of the period studied than in the second half.

Reprinted by permission from *Journal of Marketing Research*, Vol. 1 (November 1964), pp. 9–14, published by the American Marketing Association.

John U. Farley is assistant professor of industrial administration, Graduate School of Industrial Administration, Carnegie Institute of Technology. The study on which this paper is based was partially supported by the Ford Foundation, but the views expressed are not necessarily those of the Foundation. The author feels indebted to Professors Lester G. Telser, Hans Thorelli and John Jeuck for their help on a significant portion of this project, but accepts the errors as his own.

Small values of each statistic indicate brand loyalty, and larger values indicate relatively frequent brand switching. The empirical tests are made on the sixteen household and grocery products listed in Table 1.

TABLE 1   Products Studied

Canned peas	Toilet soap
Rice	All-purpose flour
Scouring cleanser	Frozen orange juice concentrate
Canned tuna and bonita	Cake mixes (white, yellow and chocolate)
Liquid bleach	Margarine
Canned peaches	Regular coffee
Frozen biscuits	Instant coffee
Toilet tissue	Canned citrus juice

Data cover purchases of 199 families from the Chicago Metropolitan Area in 1957 and were provided by the Market Research Corporation of America. To control inter-regional differences in consumption patterns that might swamp within-market effects [9], the study was limited to one small geographic area. In order to have the notion of sequences of purchases make sense, only those households purchasing more than four times were included in the sample for each product class.

WHAT MIGHT CAUSE VARIATION IN MEASURED BRAND LOYALTY?

Suppose that consumers consider various brands of a product good substitutes for one another. A number of factors might influence them to purchase several brands in a time period or change favorite brands over time. One such influence is a key economic variable—price. The important thing, though, is price activity and not necessarily price level [12]. Relative prices are constantly changing in a market as large and complex as Chicago, and prices may not be equally active in all markets. One way to measure price activity is to look at how often average monthly prices paid by consumers for each size of various brands of each product change position in a ranked array of such prices. The more flexible prices are, the higher the number of changes in ranks; and a change in ranking should bring switching in favor of the new lower-priced brands.

To measure price activity, average monthly prices were arrayed for each size of each brand with an observed average price for every month. A rank analysis of variance statistic was used to study changes in ranks in this array. The Friedman rank analysis of variance statistic, used to test whether n matched sets of k observations each are drawn from the same population, can be normalized to describe price activity. The basic statistic is this:

$$W = \frac{12 \sum_{i=1}^{k} R_i{}^2}{nk(n+1)} - 3n(k+1).$$

The observations in each month are ranked 1 to k. Then the sum of ranks over all twelve observations (R_i) is computed for each of the k samples. W ranges from 0 (when sums of ranks are equal for all brands) to $n(k-1)$ (when each item retains its initial rank over the 12 observations), and a normalized statistic, W_s, ranging from 0 to 1, is obtained by dividing the observed W by $n(k-1)$. In case more than one size class produced a value of W_s for a product, the values were simply averaged to get the overall measure for that product. Values of W_s close to 0 imply frequent exchange of rank and frequent change of relative prices. Values of W_s close to 1 indicate little exchange of rank. Thus small values of W_s should be associated with large values of the brand-switching measures.

A second influence, suggested by the economics of information [11], involves the hypothesis that people put more effort into shopping for products important to them than they do for relatively unimportant products. "Importance" of a product has two key dimensions in the consumer's resources: Time spent and money spent buying the product. A measure of the relative importance of an item in buyers' budgets is the amount spent by the family purchasing the median quantity of that item. A measure of time going into purchase of an item is the average number of purchases made of that item in a time period. In each case, large values of the measure should be associated with large values of the brand-switching indices.

A third influence is almost tautological and is intimately related to problems of defining a "product." Consumers may be stably loyal to a number of brands for different users or uses in the home. (The panel only records purchase, not use or user.) Also, families may prefer different brands for different flavors and/or varieties of a given product like bread. Three of the products studied here are most likely to be affected in this way. The measure is a dummy variable with a value of 1 for hand soap (multiple use or user), and cake mix and canned citrus juice (flavor or variety differentiation); the variable is zero for all other product classes. Brand-switching measures should be positively related to this variable.

A fourth potential influence is the extent to which brands are distributed in a market. We know that consumers tend to spread purchases of household products over a number of stores in a period as long as a year [3]. This, coupled with marked tendencies for consumers to repeat purchase of the brand bought last time, means that the buyer is much less likely to switch brands if many brands are widely available. An average of the market share of brands of a product stocked by various stores weighted by those stores' sales of the product measures the tendency of all brands of a product to be widely distributed. For each brand, the share of sales of the product class accounted for by the various chains and classes of stores explicitly coded by the panel at which the brand was purchased at least once are summed. These brand distribution statistics are weighted by the market share of the brand and summed within the market to produce a measure of the extent to which all brands are distributed. Or,

$$D_m = \sum_{i=1}^{r} (MS_i \sum_{j=1}^{s} (SS_j \Delta_{ij}))$$

where D_m is the index of distribution in the market,

> MS_i is the market share of brand i for the r available brands,
> SS_j is the share of sales of the product class in store j of the s store classes,
> $\Delta_{ij} = 1$ if brand i was sold in store j during the year,
> $= 0$ otherwise.

The statistic ranges from 1 (when all the Δ's are 1) to small values when stores tend to stock brands representing only a small share of the total market. The wider the extent of distribution of brands in a market, the lower should be measures of brand switching.

A fifth influence is due to supply constraints on how the consumer is able to spread his purchases over brands. If there are only a few brands available in some markets or if one brand has a very dominant market share, the consumer is simply constrained more in his choices than he would be under a situation in which the number of alternatives is larger and the power more equally divided. (The very interesting question of what *causes* differences in brand structure—whether such differences are dominated by strong and unyielding preferences on the demand side or by conditions of entry on the supply side—will be touched on later.) Measured brand switching should be positively associated with the number of brands available (the measure of the number of available alternatives) and negatively related to the market share of each market's leading brand (the measure of concentration of power).

EMPIRICAL RESULTS

A convenient starting point for analysis is to look at the simple correlation coefficients of the seven independent variables and two measures of brand switching intensity. The correlation coefficients, shown in Table 2, are rather promising. Thirteen of fourteen signs of the coeffi-

TABLE 2   Simple Correlation Coefficients Between Two Measures of Brand Switching and Seven Independent Variables

	Correlation coefficient with	
Independent variable	*Percent switching favorite brands*	*Average number of brands bought*
Price activity index	−.3849[b]	−.1521
Median expenditure	.0714	.3893[b]
Multiple use products	.3055[a]	.3355[b]
Aggregate distribution	−.4161[b]	−.4879[c]
Number of brands available	.5607[c]	.7620[d]
Market share of leading brand	−.6466[d]	−.6821[d]
Average number of purchases	.5882[c]	−.0152

[a] Significant $\propto = .2$
[b] Significant $\propto = .1$
[c] Significant $\propto = .05$
[d] Significant $\propto = .01$

cients are as expected. Further, three are significant at the .01 level of
a one-tailed test of the expected effect against a zero null hypothesis,
three at the .05 level, and four more at the .10 level. Each independent
variable is significant for at least one of the loyalty measures, although
the variables associated with distribution and brand structure appear
to have the strongest marginal relationships.

Unfortunately, as is often the case, good marginal relationships cause
trouble for multivariate analysis. The independent variables are themselves so highly correlated with one another that regression equations
(Table 3) using all seven independent variables produce significant

TABLE 3 Regression Coefficients of Equations Predicting Two Measures of
Brand Switching

Independent variable	Dependent variable	
	Average number of brands bought	Percent switching favorite brands
Percent distribution	.34582	−.29649
	(2.26714)	(.3209)
Dollar value of median expenditure	−.015024	.0083752[a]
	(.034304)	(.0048564)
Price activity index	.53243	−.12913
	(.76067)	(.10768)
Multiple use products	.423097	.054185
	(.39240)	(.05555)
Number of brands available	.044847[a]	.009239[b]
	(.032112)	(.004546)
Market share of leading brand	−1.462671	−.15677
	(1.16948)	(.1655)
Average number of purchases	.0532750	−.022674[c]
	(.050850)	(.0071924)
Constant	1.1992	.7838
Multiple correlation coefficient	.7683[c]	.6439[c]

[a] Significant $\alpha = .2$
[b] Significant $\alpha = .1$
[c] Significant $\alpha = .05$

multiple correlation coefficients, but have a total of only two regression coefficients significant at $\alpha = .1$. Also, the signs of coefficients show
little pattern. This is clear evidence of multicollinearity, and something must be done to try to distill out of the data some underlying
variables affecting the system.

USING FACTOR ANALYSIS TO CONSTRUCT NEW VARIABLES

One convenient way to handle this problem is to use factor analysis
to extract from the actual independent variables new summary variables to be used in regressions [10]. With this technique, a set of data

is summarized so that the problem is reduced from one involving a large number of variables to one with only a few variables in such a way that little information included in the original data is lost. The basic factor model expresses the value of any observed variable as a linear function of the following form:

$$(1) \qquad\qquad Z_j = \sum_{i=1}^{n} a_{ji} F_i + u_j$$

where the a_{ji}'s are called "factor loadings," the F_i's are the n common "factors" or "scores" associated with the measured value of the variable Z_j, and u_j is an error term. If the factors are uncorrelated, an important relationship follows: The correlation between two variables Z_i and Z_k is equal to a simple function of factor loadings:

$$(2) \qquad\qquad r_{ik} = \sum_{j=1}^{m} a_{ij} a_{kj}$$

for the m observed values of Z_i and Z_k. In addition, the square of any loading, a_{ij}, is the proportion of the variance of variable i explained by Factor j. These relationships plus standard least squares criteria permit solution for the loadings (often the final product of a factor analysis) and also for the values of the factor scores themselves. A number of computational routines are available for solving for the factor loadings, and an infinite number of systems of factors and loadings are consistent with a given set of observed correlations. The normal procedure is to choose some one method for obtaining an initial set of loadings and then to "rotate" these loadings. Rotation involves performing a linear transformation on the loadings to produce a new set which maintains the initial requirements of the factor model but which is more meaningful for the analysis.

The principal components extraction routine is used here. It is based on the requirement that each succeeding factor extracted account for the maximum amount of residual variance of the set of variables, given mathematical requirements of the factor model. The mathematics of this procedure are rigorous (if statistical inference on factor analysis itself is not) and are associated with a constrained maximizing solution of a set of linear equations. The number of factors extracted, which must of course be less than or equal to the number of variables, is also in the researcher's control. It can be decided beforehand, chosen on the basis of sequential contribution of additional factors to explanation of variance, or picked with the help of complex mathematical criteria.

The basis for rotation of the loadings into a new set, chosen for this analysis from a number of possibilities [7], is the varimax criterion. By this criterion, the transformation tends to simplify the expression in equation (1) by moving the loadings towards zero or one while maintaining the properties of the basic factor model. As a result, each observed value of a variable, Z, is largely explained by only a small set of the factors—that is, the structure is "simple."

Table 4 shows the factor loadings that resulted from applying these techniques to the data discussed earlier. It shows the matrix of vari-

TABLE 4   Rotated Factor Loadings for Three-Factor Model

Independent variable	Loading		
	Factor 1	Factor 2	Factor 3
Percent distribution	.10811	−.21008	.94277
Dollar value of median expenditure	−.94350	.09442	−.08127
Price activity index	−.16247	.60676	.13303
Multiple use products	−.00023	−.86364	.20397
Number of brands available	−.52411	−.11152	−.73696
Market share of leading brand	.20066	.53982	.67493
Average number of purchases	−.87864	.10012	−.33977

max rotated loadings for a three-factor model, where the model was chosen because of a sharp drop-off in cumulative explanation of variance by additional factors. (The model includes variables adding fifteen percent or more to the cumulative proportion of variance explained in a principal components extraction routine.) Since the dependent variables are not used in calculating factor scores for later use in regressions, the factors summarize only the information included in the independent variables. The loadings from the three-factor model show some pattern. Factor one is heavily loaded on variables associated with the importance of the item in the consumer budget—the amount spent on the product and the average number of purchases. Both loadings have the same sign as expected. The second factor is heavily loaded on price activity and multiple use of products. The signs are opposite as expected, since larger values of the first variable and small values of the second are associated with brand switching. The third factor is heavily loaded on variables associated with market structure—the number of brands available, aggregate distribution and the market share of the leading brand. The number of brands has a different sign from the other variables. The structure is simple at a cut-off point of .6 for the loadings and is only slightly more complex if the cut-off is lowered to .35.

The next step is to estimate the factor scores themselves with regression equations (still not using the dependent variables) of the following type:

$$X_{1p} = a_{11} F_{1p} + a_{12} F_{2p} + a_{13} F_{3p} + u_{1p}$$
$$\vdots \qquad \vdots \qquad \vdots \qquad \vdots$$
$$X_{7p} = a_{71} F_{1p} + a_{72} F_{2p} + a_{73} F_{3p} + u_{7p}$$

where the X_{ip}'s are independent variables, the F_{ip}'s factor scores, the a_{ij}'s factor loadings taken from Table 4 and the u_{ip}'s random error terms. The first subscript on the X's, a's and u's denotes the seven independent variables listed in Table 4. The second subscript on the a's and the first on the F's indicates the factor under consideration. The p subscript (constant in each regression) refers to the product class. There are thus sixteen separate regressions each estimating three factor scores for a market. The factor loadings are common to all sixteen regressions. Least-squares estimates of the scores are required because the system of equations shown above is overdetermined.

Table 5 shows the estimated factor scores and Table 6 shows the

TABLE 5   Estimated Factor Scores for a Three-factor Model

Product	Factor		
	1	2	3
Canned peas	−10.8230	−1.0667	−5.8494
Rice	− 6.8408	− .4680	−2.7310
Cleanser	− 6.2587	− .2790	−1.2277
Margarine	−14.4181	− .8272	−3.6516
Tuna	−10.9168	− .5817	−2.4352
Toilet soap	− 9.7637	−1.1643	−2.1071
Toilet tissue	−10.0416	− .0116	− .2396
Flour	− 8.6509	− .1329	−1.1172
Citrus juice	−10.0301	−1.5035	−3.7757
Frozen orange juice	−18.1904	− .8289	−3.5101
Regular coffee	−29.8031	− .9724	.7569
Instant coffee	−15.7285	.6264	−1.1715
Bleach	− 9.1039	.1359	.7352
Canned peaches	− 9.48871	− .4858	−2.6940
Cake mixes	− 9.9739	− .8906	−1.5162
Frozen biscuits	− 8.0336	.1691	− .3266

TABLE 6   Regression Coefficients of Equations Using Factor Scores to Predict Measures of Brand Switching

	Dependent variable	
	Average number of brands bought	Percent switching favorite brands
Factor 1	−.06844[d]	−.001745
	(.02210)	(.004067)
Factor 2	−.006142	−.04864[a]
	(.24264)	(.0282)
Factor 3	−.20533[c]	−.02158[a]
	(.08983)	(.01516)
Constant	1.5286	.20501
R^2	.631[d]	.512[c]

[a] Significant at $\alpha = .2$
[b] Significant at $\alpha = .1$
[c] Significant at $\alpha = .05$
[d] Significant at $\alpha = .01$

regressions using these scores to predict values of the two brand switching measures. (Remember that neither dependent variable was used in the factor analysis.) These results are more promising than the full-scale regressions (Table 3), even though there are still collinearity problems with the factor scores. Of the six regression coefficients, one is significant at the .01 level, another at the .05 level and two more at the .2 level. The total fit is significant at the .01 level for the first equation and at the .05 level for the second. The loss of predictive power relative to the equations using all the raw variables (Table 3) is small and the gain in terms of inference is large. The signs of the regression coefficients indicate the expected relationships among the raw variables. In the first factor, variables associated with the importance of the item in the family budget are loaded (Table 4) negatively, and the negative signs of the regression coefficients mean that the raw variables affect the dependent variables positively as expected. In Factor 2, the combination of loadings and negative regression coefficients indicates the dependent variables are associated positively with active prices and with multiple use of products. The third factor is positively loaded with percent distribution and market share of leading brand and negatively loaded with the number of available brands. The negative regression coefficients in each case imply the expected relationships— positive association of brand switching with the number of brands available and negative associations with broad brand distribution and market share concentration.

An alternative to estimating factor scores for use in regression is to use factor analysis to identify the raw independent variables which tend to summarize a large proportion of the information contained in a larger set of collinear independent variables. For this purpose, variables with the largest loadings in absolute terms were found in a rotated seven-factor principal components analysis. (These large loadings all occurred in the first four components, and it happened that all the loadings were greater than .9.) The summary group of variables looks reasonable; it is made up of the percent distribution statistic and the market share of the leading brand (structural variables), the price activity index and multiple use measure. The coefficients of regressions using only these variables are shown in Table 7. All signs are as expected, but since choosing a smaller set of variables does not necessarily dispose of the collinearity, only three of the coefficients are statistically significant at even the .2 level. In exchange for pattern in the signs of the coefficients, about a third of the explanatory power of the regressions using all seven dependent variables (Table 3) is lost. Of course, the predictive power is lower than that of regressions using the factor scores which summarize all the independent variables.

SUPPLY OR DEMAND PHENOMENON?

Variables associated with market structure showed high marginal correlations with the dependent variables and high loadings in the factor analysis. However, the question remains whether the observed values

TABLE 7   Regression Coefficients of Reduced Set of Independent Variables

Independent variable	Dependent variable	
	Average number of brands bought	Percent of buyers switching favorite brands
Percent distribution	−2.5243[a]	−.32148
	(1.7870)	(.2939)
Price activity index	.684829	.15317
	(.87924)	(.1446)
Multiple use products	.57960[a]	.061084
	(.39411)	(.064819)
Market share of leading brand	−1.84378[a]	−.24132
	(1.2846)	(.21128)
Constant	4.8548	.7355
R²	.581[c]	.423[b]

[a] Significant at $\propto$ = .2
[b] Significant at $\propto$ = .1
[c] Significant at $\propto$ = .05

of these structural variables are associated with barriers to entry (supply) or with strong consumer preferences (demand). Some marginal relationships among independent variables are interesting in this regard. The complex of percent distribution, the number of brands available and the market share of leading brands are strongly related to one another. The simple correlations are these:

percent distribution with no. brands	= −.70661
percent distribution with market share of leader	= .50452
market share of leader with no. brands	= −.56384

In the case of the leader's share and the number of brands, the results are almost tautological. In the other two cases, however, there are indications that concentration of market share is associated with wide distribution and a large number of brands with narrow distribution. The number of brands is explained to some extent by the extent of the market (the correlation between the number of brands and median expenditure is .496, and between the number of brands and the number of purchases .663). Multiple use is also associated with percent distribution but not with the number of brands available. This is tantalizing evidence that, given the extent of the market, the supply structure rather than consumer preferences tends to dominate the brand structure. Of course, longer-term study of brand and firm entry, exit, and survival are needed to really give this hypothesis a good test.

Another tantalizing relationship is a relatively weak tendency of prices to be more stable in markets with high concentration of market share. This tendency is strengthened in the partial relationship of price activity and the market share of the leading brand holding the average number of purchases (the extent of the market) constant. This partial correlation coefficient is .2861 and the simple coefficient is .2251. Consistent with this result, the relationship between price stability and the number of brands available is negative but weak in both the simple pair-wise relationship and in the partial relationship holding the extent of the market constant.

SUMMARY

A series of hypotheses about why measured brand loyalty might vary over product classes in the same geographic market were tested on data reported by consumer panel members. Given the small sample size, some potentially imperfect measurements, and collinearity problems, the results are quite encouraging. Consumers, as expected, tended to be less loyal (on the basis of marginal correlations) towards products with many brands available, where number of purchases and dollar expenditures per buyer are high, where prices are relatively active, and where consumers might be expected to simultaneously use a number of brands of the product. As expected, consumers are brand loyal in markets where brands tend to be widely distributed and where market share is concentrated heavily in the leading brand. Direct regression analyses failed because of multicollinearity, but regressions on scores estimated from a factor analysis and on limited sets of variables were also consistent with the hypotheses. Some weak evidence that the supply side tends to dominate the nature of the brand structure was presented, as was some evidence that price stability tends to be associated with concentration of market share in one brand and more weakly with few brands available in a market.

Much of the apparent difference over products in some important aspects of brand choice can apparently be explained on the basis of structural variables describing the markets in which the products are sold, and does not depend on specific characteristics of the products or on attitudes of consumers towards products. To be sure, this does not deny importance of specific or attitudinal variables in some cases [6], but it does indicate that markets such as those studied are similar enough on some dimensions that models built for the study of one product might be readily transferable to the study of others. Further, the results again suggest the importance of variables associated with the structure of markets in analysis of patterns of consumer behavior.

REFERENCES

1. BROWN, GEORGE H., "Brand Loyalty—Fact or Fiction," *Advertising Age*, 23 (June 9, 1952), 52–55, margarine; (June 30, 1952), 46–48, flour; (August 11, 1952), 82–82, headache tablets; (October 6, 1952), 82–86, soaps and sudsers; (December 1, 1952), 76–79, frozen orange juice concentrate; 24 (January 26, 1953), 75–76, summary.
2. CUNNINGHAM, ROSS M., "Brand Loyalty—What, Where, How Much?" *Harvard Business Review*, 34 (January-February 1956), 116–128.
3. ———, "Customer Loyalty to Store and Brand," *Harvard Business Review*, 39 (November-December 1961).

4. FARLEY, JOHN U., "Testing a Theory of Brand Loyalty," *Proceeedings of the American Marketing Association* (December 1963), p. 298–306.
5. FRANK, RONALD A., "Brand Choice as a Probability Process," *Journal of Business*, XXXV (January 1962), 43–56.
6. HAIRE, MASON, "Projective Techniques in Marketing Research," *Journal of Marketing*, 14 (April 1950), 649–56.
7. HARMAN, HARRY H., *Modern Factor Analysis*, Chicago: University of Chicago Press, 1960, 233–261.
8. KUEHN, ALFRED A., "Analysis of the Dynamics of Consumer Behavior and Its Implications for Marketing Management," Carnegie Institute of Technology, May, 1958.
9. LeBOVIT, CORRINE AND FAITH CLARK, *Household Practices in The Use of Foods—Three Cities, 1953*, Washington, D.C.: U.S. Government Printing Office, 1956.
10. MASSY, WILLIAM F., "Applying Factor Analysis to a Specific Marketing Problem," *Proceedings of the American Marketing Association* (December 1963).
11. STIGLER, GEORGE, "The Economics of Information," *Journal of Political Economy*, LXIX (June 1961), pp. 213–225.
12. TELSER, LESTER G., "The Demand for Branded Goods as Estimated from Consumer Panel Data," *Review of Economics and Statistics*, XLIV (August 1962), 300–325.

40. Correlates of brand loyalty: some positive results

james m. carman

Many recent empirical studies have investigated the correlation of a variety of characteristics of the housewife's behavior in the market place—such as brand loyalty, deal-proneness, and private brand-proneness—with her demographic, social, economic, and psychological characteristics. For the most part, these studies have met with negative results [8, 9, 10, 12]. The research reported here follows in the same spirit but ends on a somewhat more optimistic note.

This project dates from 1962 so that the direction taken in analysis, i.e., the relating of some notion of brand loyalty with socioeconomic variables, could have been changed when the disappointing results of others began to appear. No change in direction was made because two major weaknesses exist in all previous studies which we hoped could be overcome in this study. First, with a few exceptions, these empirical studies employed data from a large commercial consumer panel such as the *Chicago Tribune* or the Market Research Corporation of America. These panels have the advantage of having a large number of families who participate over fairly long periods of time. They have the disadvantage, however, of reporting on only a few demographic characteristics of panel members. Our hypothesis was that those characteristics were not rich enough to yield insights into personal determinants of brand loyalty.

Second, the large volume of data generated by those panels leaves the analyst with a strategy decision. How much simplification should he make in his analytical model merely to accommodate data reduction? Usually the sheer volume of data has forced the analyst into a simple model, usually linear regression. Our hypothesis was that more detailed analysis would yield more positive results. In sum, the conclusion was that empirical analysis was showing no significant relationships between brand loyalty and the characteristics of the shopper —not because none existed, but because these analyses were made on an inadequate data base, using overly simple models.

The conclusions of this paper support both of these hypotheses. A definite link can be established between personal characteristics, the shopping process, and brand loyalty. These results should aid in the construction and testing of more specific models of the consumer choice process and should be useful in market segmentation for grocery products.

Reprinted by permission from *Journal of Marketing Research*, Vol. 7 (February 1970), pp. 67–76; published by the American Marketing Association.

METHODOLOGY

The data for this study are from the Berkeley Food Panel, a panel on food purchases by Berkeley housewives conducted for fifteen weeks during 1966 by members of the Berkeley marketing faculty [5]. While more information was collected about the characteristics and attitudes of participants than has ever been done previously in longitudinal consumer research, the fifteen-week period provided much less information on buying sequences than is available from commercial consumer panels. Consequently, the interest of this paper is in a static concept of loyalty rather than in the dynamic study of changes in loyalty through time.

If loyalty is to be defined in a static sense, that is if the probability of purchasing each brand on each buy during the study period remains unchanged, it is necessary to either assume this zero order Markov property or make a test to see if it is true. Elsewhere the author has reviewed the tests that have been made for this purpose and has suggested another test which makes use of the Kruskal-Wallis H statistic [7]. This test was employed on the present data to screen out those households whose buying behavior, on each test product, was not stationary. Also excluded were households whose purchase activity on any particular product was very low. Thus, while the panel contained 249 continuously reporting households, the number available for analysis in this study was less. Not surprisingly, low activity losses varied between products. The nonstationary test results, on the other hand, are of some interest. The Kruskal-Wallis test rejected (with $\alpha \leq .10$) the hypothesis of stationarity in from 13 to 17% of the households in all product groups analyzed, except regular coffee. In this latter group, only 5% showed nonstationary patterns. This characteristic of relatively stable coffee brand preferences is important in considering not only the present finding, but also those of other studies of coffee brand loyalty.

For all but one product, the analyses of the loyalty of the stationary panel group were made using the Carman-Stromberg Entropy Loyalty Measure, θ, as a criterion. This measure is described in the Appendix to this article. With this measure, zero indicates perfect loyalty, and increasing values of θ indicate increasing degrees of disloyalty.

For the analysis of loyalty in the purchase of six ounce cans of frozen orange juice, the proportion of dollar purchases going to the favorite brand, P, was the dependent variable. The change was made solely as a matter of convenience in data handling. In most respects, θ and P are very similar and are highly correlated, but θ has the advantage of not being bounded so severely.

Four analyses are discussed here. The first is the study of loyalty to particular food chains in which θ is based on the total number of store visits for all types of purchases. Different stores of the same chain have been grouped together, and specialty stores of the same type (bakeries, butcher shops, dairies) have been treated as a single chain even though they are independently owned. The second analysis is of loyalty toward brands of regular, ground coffee. All sizes and brands are included. The third analysis is of canned fruit. All canned fruit is included, regardless of variety. The fourth analysis covers only the popular six ounce size of frozen orange juice. Of the 21 products covered by the panel, these three were selected because they were frequently purchased by a large number of panel families and thus provide a large data base for analysis.

The principal descriptive model and algorithm used in this study are derived from the binary branching model of the Morgan-Sonquist Automatic Interaction Detector (A.I.D.) schema [13, 18]. This approach is well suited for the data of the Berkeley Food Panel where we have a mixture of interval, ordinal, and nominal data, and where nonlinearities, nonorthogonality, and interactions are to be expected. The entropy loyalty measure is also an ideal dependent variable for A.I.D. in that it is neither severely bounded nor skewed.

The aim of the A.I.D. algorithm is to find those binary splits in each predictor where the between sum of squares of the dependent variable is greatest, and then to branch on the split with the highest ratio of between sums of squares to total sum of squares. This process is repeated after each split until the program can do no more splitting without violating one of three stopping rules. The stopping rules used in this study were: (1) a branch containing less than 20 observations could not be split; (2) a branch containing less than 2% of the original total sum of squares could not be split; and (3) a branch could not be split if the maximum between sum of squares in the proposed branch split was less than 1% of the original total sum of squares.

Runs made with looser stopping rules tended to form branches with only one or two observations and no logical explanation. Even with the stopping rules used, the validity of some splits is in doubt.

After the final A.I.D. tree was constructed for each product, a dummy regression model was run which contained, as predictors, those characteristics which the branching technique indicated were important. Some of the predictors which were used to form branches were not significant in the regression. This may be an indication that the stopping rules were not overly restrictive. On the other hand, the results from the two models should not be identical, since the regression approach assumes additivity and is a simultaneous solution, while the branching approach does not assume additivity and is sequential. When one adjusts to the quantity of data being considered, the tree diagrams are more meaningful than the regression results. However, because of editorial restrictions, only trees 1 and 4 for chain loyalty are reported here.

The regression results suffer from one other serious shortcoming. Because the predictors being tested were suggested largely by the results of the A.I.D. analysis, the regressions represent a second pass over the same set of data. This practice violates a fundamental assumption of the significance tests, and therefore the tests cannot be considered valid measures of statistical significance and predictive efficacy. There were insufficient observations to make an independent test of validity by the split sample technique.

The A.I.D. analysis on each product was divided into four sequential passes. The value of the dependent variable on the second pass is equal to the deviation of the actual value of the dependent variable for each respondent (i) about the mean of the branch (θ_j) in which it resides at the end of Pass 1 ($y_i = \theta_i - \theta_j$); the value of the dependent variable for each respondent in Pass 3 is the value of the deviation of the actual value about the mean of the branch in which it resides at the end of Pass 2; and so on.

The reasons for dividing the problem in this way are: first, with less than 200 households in the sample, stopping Rule 1 will prevent many predictors from having an opportunity to enter in a single pass; second, one strategy for identifying interaction effects is to enter predictors in time order of occurrence for the respondent. For example, the first pass over each product contains predictors which relate to the respondent's childhood experience and her present and past cultural and economic environments; the second pass contains predictors which relate to her personality, perceived role, and mobility; the third pass contains predictors which relate to her gregariousness, media exposure, shopping awareness, and geographic location; the fourth pass contains predictors which relate most directly to her shopping behavior and attitudes. Thus, the selection of sequence involves reasonably weak assumptions about the direction of causality. For example, perceived role (in Pass 2) may be caused by childhood experience and cultural and economic environment (in Pass 1), but it is assumed that the causality could not flow in the opposite direction. Because of the sequential nature of the procedure, a branching on perceived role in Pass 1 could mask an explanation of how this role was established if the causes of perceived role were not introduced until subsequent passes.

Throughout this paper variables are identified by the same set of variable numbers. A summary of the predictor variables is given in Table 1. These predictors were all constructed from questions which

TABLE 1 Summary of Predictors

Predictor X	Description
Childhood Training; Economic, Demographic, and Cultural Variables	
2 or 3	Two different scores measuring religious commitment
4 or 6	Two different scores measuring use of credit by respondent's parents
7	A score on complexity of personal investment portfolios which can be interpreted as a measure of wealth
8	Annual personal income
9	Question of source of money when respondent was a child
10	Measure of extent of training in financial responsibility when respondent was a child
22	Carman Cultural Class [6]
23 or 24	Life cycle
25	Employment status of principal female in household
51	Extent of non-U.S. influence in respondent's past experience
Personality, Perceived Role and Mobility Variables	
15	Home-oriented role perception score

TABLE 1   Summary of Predictors—continued

Predictor X	Description
16	Employment-oriented role perception score
17	Maternal-oriented role perception score
18	Community-oriented role perception score
19	Cooking interest factor score
26	Measure of proximity of mother-in-law
27	Years respondent has lived in Bay area
28	Years respondent has lived in current residence
29	Measure of perceived permanence in neighborhood
40	Figures prices while shopping score (Trier Item 5)
42	Meals not like those of parents score (Trier Item 16)
45	Shopping is a chore score (Trier Item 20)
52	Intergenerational occupation and education mobility score
55	Wells' Yeasay-Naysay 2 score
56	General conservatism score
58	Conservative on civil rights issues item
59	Political interest score
	Variables on Personal Sources of Information, Media Exposure, Geographic Location, and Food Shopping Awareness
20 or 44	Two measures of extent to which respondent reads food store advertising
21	Score on awareness of brands of dairy products carried by leading food stores
30	Number of stores in which respondent claims to know store employees
31	Total number of food store employees respondent claims to know
33	Frequency of use of Intersection "b," competing center southwest of study area
34	Frequency of use of Intersection "d," study center
35	Frequency of use of Intersection "g," competing center on western edge of study area
36	Area of residence
37 or 38 or 41	Identification of trusted personal sources of food shopping information
46	Frequency of television exposure
47	Frequency of radio exposure
48	Frequency of home entertainment
50	Frequency of formal socialization with neighbors
	Food Shopping Variables
12	Mean number of different stores visited per week
13	Mean number of food shopping trips per week
14	Mean expenditures on food per week
60	Image score for chain with aggressive price policy
61	Image score for largest West Coast chain
62	Webster Deal Proneness Index [20]
65 or 68	Number of different chains and independent stores visited during entire 15 week study period

may be found in the Appendices of [5]. Space does not permit a discussion of the construction of each predictor. Definitions of the dummy variables constructed from these predictors may be found in the trees or in the regression results.

RESULTS FOR CHAIN LOYALTY

The results of the analysis of loyalty to particular food chains are shown in Table 2 and Figures 1 and 2. The strongest correlation exists

TABLE 2   Dummy Regression Results for Static Chain Loyalty

Variable		Regression coefficient	Beta coefficient
12	(continuous)	.28	.82
36C	(Area 7)	−.24	−.16
36C	(Area 2)	−.18	−.10
36C	(Area 3)	−.10**	−.06
36	(Area 4)	−.19	−.12
30B	(know employees in 2+ stores)	−.16	−.16
23D	(young married)	.15	.14
23C	(over 45, children)	.10**	.07
23E	(unmarried with children)	.11**	.06
31B	(know 3+ employees)	.15	.11
58A	(civil rights conservative)	.10	.09
8	(continuous in thousands of dollars)	.01*	.09
41B	(neighbors are trusted source of information)	.10	.08
7B	(complex investment portfolio)	.11*	.08
48BC	(frequency home entertainment)	.08*	.07
13	(continuous)	−.03*	−.07
19B	(low cooking interest)	−.07*	−.06
25CD	(working wife)	−.07**	−.06
4B	(parents didn't use credit)	−.07**	−.05
9B	(received allowance)	.05**	.05
26A	(mother-in-law lives near)	−.08***	−.05
35A	(no use of intersection "g")	.05***	.05
28B	(in home 5+ years)	.06***	.04

$R^2 = .748$ $\bar{\theta} = 1.279$ $\sigma_{\theta x} = .264$ Constant = .442 $n = 197$ $F = 26.3$
Regression coefficients reject null hypothesis in t test with α risk of .05 or less unless indicated as follows:
*.05 $< \alpha \leq$ .10   **.10 $< \alpha \leq$ .20   ***.20 $< \alpha \leq$ .30

between loyalty and the mean number of different stores visited per week. Patently, these two variables will be correlated because they are both derivatives of the same event, a store visit. The predictor has been left in the analysis to emphasize the close relationship between loyalty and a concept developed later in the paper—shopping proneness. Note in Figure 2, however, that the loyal shopper is not necessarily a well-organized shopper. Of all shoppers, the most loyal are those who make an average of four or more trips per week to a single store. Likewise, the loyal shopper is not necessarily one for whom the markets are inaccessible. The most loyal shoppers are those who live in neighborhoods (Areas 2, 3, 4, and 7) with the greatest

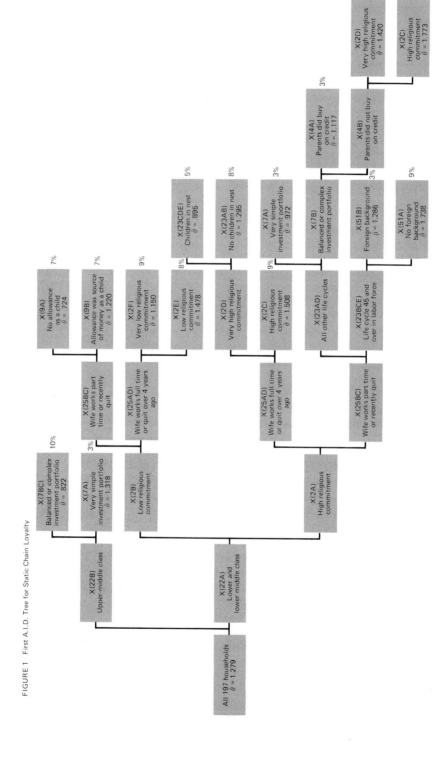

FIGURE 1   First A.I.D. Tree for Static Chain Loyalty

FIGURE 2   Fourth A.I.D. Tree for Static Chain Loyalty

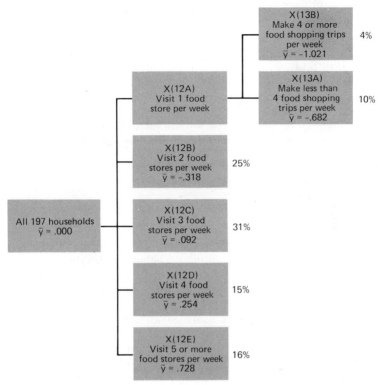

number of competing stores nearby and are familiar with employees in these competing stores (Variable 30B).

What are the personal characteristics of these loyal shoppers? Could it be that the characteristics of the residents of these neighborhoods and not the location of the neighborhoods are responsible for their loyalty? These are not the most exclusive neighborhoods in the study area. We find that among the lower-middle class, loyals are those housewives who work. There is also an inverse correlation between income and loyalty. These results, interacting with life-cycle effects (shown in Figure 1), indicate that the most loyal housewives in this area are busy mothers with a job and children still in the nest. These busy women also do less entertaining than their less loyal counterparts. Also, they are newer in the neighborhood and know fewer food store employees.

Another related subset of predictors is concerned with the perceived role and interests of the loyal housewives. They are less interested in being homemakers than are less loyal respondents. Also, they do not read food store advertising. Schapker reported that in 1965, 72% of all supermarket shoppers read food store advertising [15]. In our sample, nonloyal shoppers were those who read food store advertising "very often" or "always." This group made up less than 35% of the panel.

There are other predictors which entered the trees which have not been discussed and are more difficult to interpret, such as the effect of religious commitment on store loyalty. However, the most important predictors do present a profile of the store-loyal and nonloyal shopper which is meaningful and internally consistent. The nonloyal consumer is a full-time housewife with a strong interest in cooking and shopping and with the time and means to shop. The loyal consumer is the busy woman who typically is working to help support a family. She values her time in such a fashion as to devote little attention to entertaining, cooking, and being a careful shopper. Next we will see if these profiles become any clearer with regard to brand loyalty, rather than store loyalty.

RESULTS FOR PRODUCTS

Because the influence of personal characteristics on consumer behavior is subtle and elusive, it is necessary to study the A.I.D. trees in order to find plausible explanations of behavior. In this section some of the apparent influences will be described. Their relative importance in explaining variance in loyalty is suggested by the statistics in Table 3.

The overwhelming influence store loyalty has on the brand loyalty for all three products is apparent. For coffee, the number of different food chains visited during the study period (Variable 65) explains 63.5% of the total variance in loyalty. All other variables explained only 13.6%. For canned fruit, Variable 65 explained 66% of the variance in the loyalty variable. For frozen juice, store loyalty explains 63% of total variance and all others only 5%.

The shopper who restricts the number of stores she visits thereby restricts her opportunity to be disloyal to brands of specific food products. Thus, store loyalty is a regulator of brand loyalty and a necessary link in explaining the relationship between shopper characteristics and brand loyalty. The existence of strong store brands plays a role in this relationship for canned fruit but not for the other two products.

The significance of deal proneness (Variable 62) in all three products is not surprising, as coffee and frozen juice are both popular products to use for promotions. Food-store advertising is often read in order to learn of coffee promotions. What is surprising is that for canned fruit, shopping-prone consumers are loyal, deal-prone, and do not respond to newspaper specials. The explanation is that, unlike coffee, the shopping-prone consumer is inclined to buy relatively large quantities of private-label fruits on specials. High canned fruit loyalty scores thus are associated with those who do not find shopping a chore (Variable 45), those who calculate prices while shopping (Variable 40), those with big food budgets (Variable 14), and those who are deal-prone (Variable 62).

The next most important, and large, group of predictors of loyalty has social connotations. For coffee, we hypothesize that consumers

TABLE 3 Dummy Regression Results for Products

Product	Regular coffee		Canned fruit		Frozen juice	
Statistic	Regression coefficients	Beta coefficients	Regression coefficients	Beta coefficients	Regression coefficients	Beta coefficients
n	110		138		187	
R^2	.77		.78		.68	
F-ratio	21.4		25.9		24.8	
Mean loyalty	.72		.97		77.2%	
Standard deviation of regression	.26		.28		13.2%	
Constant	.49		.48		94.9%	
Predictor						
68 (Continuous)			1.54	.30	−13.2%	−.78
65D (9 or more stores)	1.19	.51	1.04	.67		
65C (6–9 stores)	.66	.46	.66	.49		
65B (4–5 stores)						
41B (Neighbors trusted source)	−.26	−.21			−3.5**	−.07
38B (Personal sources not trusted)	−.19	−.14				
38D (Household member least trusted)					9.6	.09
37D (Household member most trusted source)					5.6*	.08
48A (Low home entertainer)			.24	.14		
48AB (Medium home entertainer)					10.4	.09
48BC (High home entertainer)	.08**	.07				
42B (Meals not like parents)	−.16	−.13				
45B (Shopping is a chore)						
40B (Calculate price in store)			.21	.14	7.3*	.08
17B (High maternal role score)	.27*	.15	−.15	−.11		
15B (High home role score)					5.8*	.09

TABLE 3   Dummy Regression Results for Products (continued)

Predictor						
16B ((High employment role score))	.08***				3.4**	.07
18C (High community role score)	.18	.06	.15			
20B (Read food ads)						
44B (Don't read food ads)			.13	.10		
62B (Deal prone)	.16	.14	.13		-5.7*	-.08
14B (Spend $30 or more per week)			-.14	-.09		
36 (Live area 8 or 9)	-.17	-.13	-.14	-.10		
36 (Live area 8)						
36B (Live area 5 or 6)	-.18	-.13	.08**	.06	-3.6***	-.05
56B (Conservative)					-5.0	-.11
29B (Plan to stay in neighborhood)	-.14	-.13	-.12	-.10		
9C (No work for money as child)	.20	.11				
9B (Received allowance as child)			-.08**	-.07		
2A (High religious commitment)			-.19	-.15		
3CD (High religious commitment)	-.14***	-.11	-.14	-.10		
34B (Use intersection "d")			.16	.10		
33B (Use intersection "b")			.11*	.09		
46A (Never watch TV)					-8.7	-.10
46B (Watch very little TV)						
25B (Recently stopped working)			.14	.09	-5.5	-.09
25C (Working part time)	.14*	.09				
52C (High mobility score)	-.08**	-.07				
8B ($9–$15,000 income)	.08**	.07				
61B (Favorable Safeway image)			.09**	.07		
58A (Conservative on civil rights issues)			.09**	.07		
50A (Never socialize with neighbors)			.08***	.05	3.3**	.07
60B (Favorable image for aggressive store)					-4.5*	-.09
23E (Head over 45, children in nest)					-5.1**	-.07
26A (Mother-in-law lives near)					3.3**	.06

Regression coefficients reject null hypothesis in t test with α risk of .05 or less unless indicated as follows:

* $.05 < \alpha \leq .10$ ** $.10 < \alpha \leq .20$ *** $.20 < \alpha \leq .30$

think that the taste of the coffee they serve to guests has social importance and the probability of good coffee is increased by the use of a proven brand. The significant social predictors may be summarized by describing the characteristics of the brand-loyal coffee buyer.

She respects the food-shopping opinion of her neighbors (Variable 41), but, in general, trusts technical sources of food information more than personal sources (Variable 38). Her perceived maternal and community role scores are low, indicating a stronger home or career orientation (Variables 17 and 18). She lives in the better, eastern-tier neighborhoods of the shopping area (Variable 52), and she does not cook the kind of meals served in her parents' home (Variable 42). However, she considers herself a permanent part of the neighborhood (Variable 29). Loyal coffee buyers have a higher income consistent with the neighborhood than the nonloyal group (Variable 8). These results appear to be in agreement with the hypothesis of Brody and Cunningham [3] that brand-loyal coffee consumers should have high specific self-confidence. One would expect the loyal consumer just described to have high self-confidence.

In brief, the nonloyal coffee buyer is similar to the woman described above as nonloyal to stores, a shopper who shops for deals. However, this tendency to shop around is offset by the social and status importance placed on coffee, which leads to the formation of brand attitudes which often override the promotions of manufacturers and retailers.

Brand-loyal canned fruit buyers also seem to be bigger socializers than their nonloyal counterparts. They do more home entertaining (Variable 48), watch television (Variable 46), and socialize with their neighbors (Variable 50). The sociopolitical-economic variables in this analysis suggest that a part of the finding on canned fruit loyalty may be unique to the particular study area. The dominant chain in the study area is a consumer cooperative, which has come to be an important social and political institution in the community. This cooperative has a long line of canned fruits which it promotes strongly. Coop-loyal shoppers in our study were almost always loyal Coop canned-fruit buyers. Thus, some predictors of fruit-brand loyalty are, in reality, describing the loyal Coop shoppers.

Somewhat more difficult to interpret are the correlations between loyalty and low religious commitment and involvement (Variable 2). This variable enters the analysis of all products and, in the case of fruit, is also strongly significant in the regression analysis. Our hypothesis is not that belief in the value of a specific brand is inversely related to belief in a Supreme Being. Rather, our hypothesis is that church involvement is a part of the total family, community, social, shopping milieu and that, as such, it correlates with brand loyalty. To date, either the analyst has not been clever enough or the data have not been rich enough to establish any general structure for these relationships.

In comparing the results for frozen orange juice with those for the other products, it should be remembered that the dependent variable in this case is the proportion of purchases, in dollars, going to the favorite brand. Thus, large percentages and positive deviations show loyalty.

It is the nonloyal juice buyer who frequently entertains and socializes with neighbors (Variables 48 and 50). After removing the effect of store loyalty, what remains is a description of the nonloyal juice purchaser. In general, the data describe a consumer who has the desire and ability to shop for good buys. She lives near a competing shopping area (Variable 36) and often travels through the main shopping area (Variable 33); she trusts home economists and neighbors as sources of food shopping information (Variables 37 and 41); she has a high opinion of the market in the area with the most aggressive pricing policy; and she has a high deal-proneness index (Variables 60 and 62). This nonloyal juice purchaser is a housewife with considerable experience. Although her children are still in the nest, she is not a new mother. She is not now working, but probably did in recent years. Her primary responsibility, she feels, is to her home and children (Variables 15 and 16).

CONCLUSIONS

The results just described represent the culmination of an extended period of analysis of a very great quantity of data. Despite attempts to report only the most significant results, a large number of findings, occasionally contradictory, are condensed in the preceding tables and figures. To further summarize the findings and to resolve some of the contradictions, the following conclusions should apply generally to a large class of frequently purchased consumer products. Since experiments to prove these conclusions should be more tightly designed, they are stated in the form of hypotheses.

Hypothesis 1:

The single most important predictor of brand loyalty is store loyalty.

When the shopper makes her choice in a single store, she restricts the number of brand alternatives available to her. Thus, the store-loyal consumer will have higher brand loyalty scores simply because the number of possible outcomes in her brand-choice experiment is less.

However, our hypothesis is that store loyalty indicates more than a simple decrease in possible outcomes of the brand-choice experiment. This hypothesis is supported by Massy, Frank and Lodahl [12].

Hypothesis 2:

Consumers who are not "shopping-prone" will shop in a very small number of stores and, within those stores, will remain loyal to a very small number of brands rather than make careful choices between the values being offered by those stores.

The consumers in this study who fall into the "non-shopper" category make up about 20% of the panel. (Remember, the panel is not representative of all consumers.) While no attempt has been made to construct a statistical function to measure shopping-proneness, it is possible to describe the "non-shopper" by those characteristics which repeatedly proved to be significant in the analyses reported above. The non-shopper:

visits four or fewer different food stores during the entire fifteen-week period and, on the average, visits two or fewer stores per week;

has low scores on the Webster Deal Proneness Index;

has strong commitments outside the home (a job or an expression of lack of interest in homemaking);

infrequently entertains at home;

does not read food store advertising in the newspaper;

does not live in a block immediately contiguous to a cluster of competing food stores.

Some important characteristics cannot be used to discriminate between shoppers and nonshoppers. Except for shoppers whose physical condition restricts their ability to shop, age and life cycle are not useful in separating the two groups. Nonshoppers were found in all income classes and in all cultural classes.

While the identification and description of shopping-proneness is a major finding in this analysis, no claim of originality can be made since the concept can be traced, to Alderson in 1957 [1] and similar hypotheses have been suggested by Tate [19], Simon and Marks [17], and Frank, Green, and Sieber [8]. Using the more heterogeneous national MRCA panel, Tate finds nonshoppers have lower incomes than shoppers. In all other respects, the present study corroborates Tate's findings.

Hypothesis 3:
Personal characteristics of consumers will explain differences in store loyalty.

This conclusion is important because it is the basis of the efficiencies which are believed to flow from market segmentation and because it is contrary to Frank's conclusion, based on the analysis of commercial panel data [10].

Hypothesis 4:
Loyalty is positively correlated with the extent to which the housewife socializes with her neighbors.

The effect of socialization with and trust in neighbors as a source of food-shopping information (Variables 41 and 50) is somewhat difficult to unravel in the results presented above. At least one of these two variables entered into each of the analyses. For all but juice, brand- and chain-loyal consumers report moderate or heavy socialization with their neighbors and state that neighbors are a trusted source of food-buying information.

Hypothesis 5:
The characteristics of consumers which are associated with brand loyalty differ between products.

The notion that different products play different roles in the life of the consumer is a generally accepted concept [11, 12, 21]. In our analysis, the reference-group influence on coffee loyalty is most obvious. Consumers most interested in status were the most loyal. The brand of canned fruit purchased is evidently not as strongly influenced by reference groups: buying good values proved to be more important than buying specific brands. For frozen orange juice, where chain loyalty accounted for almost all of the explained variance, there are no obvious reference-group influences.

The present analysis is not designed to specifically investigate the influence of various products' status on loyalty. Such an investigation would require matching the status image of various brands with the status needs of consumers loyal to each. We did not consider here the particular brand to which a consumer is loyal. This point was clearly made by Brody and Cunningham [3].

The Iceberg Effect

Other scholars have commented on a bias in scientific journals to report only positive results. This paper has concentrated on those predictors which were useful in explaining differences in loyalty. No information has been given on which variables were not useful. At this point, it may be helpful to mention a few of these. One may think of this problem as an "iceberg effect." A look at Bucklin and Carman [5] will give some idea of the richness of the original data. For this study, the number of predictors was reduced to sixty-three. Table 1 shows that fifty-four of these entered the trees or regressions.

One group of predictors which remained largely below the surface was that measuring mobility. A great amount of effort went into construction of measures of geographic mobility, intergenerational mobility, and aspiration for social mobility. Only in the case of coffee did a mobility variable enter, and the significance of the predictor is in doubt. A special subsidiary analysis yielded similar results. Bucklin, in his analysis of consumers who shopped at a new market in the area, found a slight mobility effect—but in a direction opposite to that which he expected [4].

Another group of variables which remained largely below the surface was those dealing with personality. Some care was used in choosing the general personality indicator used in the study. None of the Myers-Briggs scales were significant, and the Wells' Yeasay-Naysay 2 Scale entered marginally on two of the analyses [5, pp. 37–8]. Thus, these findings add to a growing body of research which has had little success in predicting consumer behavior using general personality batteries. The emphasis must be placed on the word "general" [2, 3, 6, 12], for this study did uncover a significant personality characteristic—shopping-proneness. It is a personality construct in the sense that it describes the interest in and satisfaction received from shopping. Unfortunately, this or similar scales do not appear on any of the standard personality batteries. Perhaps we in consumer behavior now have enough information to begin construction of our own personality scales.

APPENDIX

An Entropy Measure of Brand Loyalty

The author and John L. Stromberg have suggested a new measure of loyalty, θ, derived completely in [7].

$$\theta = -\sum_{i=1}^{k} p_i \log p_i$$

where p_i is the true proportion of purchases going to brand i;
   k is the number of brands available on the market.

As a measure of loyalty, θ has a number of properties worthy of mention:

(1) Its derivation is a natural extension of a likelihood ratio test of the null hypothesis for complete nonloyalty. In other words, if a consumer gave no evidence that she distinguishes between brand, she could be classified at one (negative) extreme of the loyalty spectrum. When the process can be assumed to be zero order, a test for complete nonloyalty would be to test the hypothesis in the multinomial model, H_0: $p_1 = p_2 = \cdots = p_k = 1/k$.

(2) It is defined for all values of the parameters of the underlying multinomial model.

(3) It has maximum value for the completely "nonloyal" state, $p_1 = \cdots = p_k = 1/k (\theta = -\log 1/k)$, and minimal value for a state that could reasonably be considered most loyal, namely $p_i = 1$ for some $1 \leq i \leq k$ ($\theta = 0$).[1]

(4) It is independent of brand; that is, if $p_1, \cdots p_k$ are a set of fixed numbers such that $0 < p_i \leq 1, \sum_{i=1}^{k} p_i = 1$, then no matter how the $[p_i]$ are relabeled, θ remains the same; e.g., if one universe is characterized by $p_1 = \frac{1}{2}$, $p_2 = \frac{1}{6}$, $p_3 = \frac{1}{3}$, and another by $p_1 = \frac{1}{6}$, $p_2 = \frac{1}{3}$, $p_3 = \frac{1}{2}$, then the two have the same value of θ.

(5) It is a function of all the parameters of the underlying multinomial model; that is, implicit in this definition of loyalty is the idea that loyalty is a measure of a consumer's relative preferences among brands. Mathematically, it stems from the fact that the parameters $p_1, \cdots p_k$ are not independent of each other; in economic terms it reflects the fact that different brands of the same product are (by definition) strong substitutes. As an example, this definition of loyalty distinguishes between the following two situations (universes), $p_1 = \frac{1}{2}$, $p_2 = p_3 = p_4 = \frac{1}{6}$, and $p_1 = \frac{1}{2}$, $p_2 = 0$, $p_3 = \frac{1}{2}$, $p_4 = 0$ (the first is "less loyal" than the second) whereas a measure that only considered p_1 would not make this distinction.

This example leads to the observation that if a dummy brand, $k+1$, is added, $p_{k+1} = 0$ and $\theta = \sum_{i=1}^{k+1} p_i \log p_i$ is unchanged. (We adopt the convention that 0 log 0=0.) Behaviorally, this means that a shopper who "tries" many brands one time, but always returns to a favorite, will be more disloyal than one who divides her purchases between a favorite and only one or two minor brands, even though the proportion of purchases of "favorite" are the same in both cases. This property seems to be quite desirable from a theoretical standpoint.

(6) For a sample, the maximum likelihood estimate of θ is given by $\hat{\theta} = -\sum \hat{p}_i \log \hat{p}_i$, where $\hat{p}_i = n_i/n$ is the maximum likelihood estimator of $\hat{p}_i$, $i = 1, 2 \cdots k$, derived from observing n_i purchases of brand i in n trials.

(7) θ is a function that appears in a number of other widely differing contexts. In thermodynamics it is a measure of entropy; in communications

---

[1] The measure θ can be made to vary from 0 to 1 simply by dividing it by $-\log 1/k$. This would seem to make it independent of k, the number of brands; however, further theoretical justification is needed to show that this step is desirable; k should be the number of brands available in the marketplace. A comparison of θ for consumers with different products or different markets, where the number of brands available is not the same, probably is not justified. Thus, while comparison between a city shopper and a country shopper may not be justified, a comparison between two city shoppers in different metropolitan areas may be.

theory it is the amount of information in a source; in statistics it is a measure of discriminatory information. The implications of the generality of this variable for the concept of loyalty are not immediately obvious. However, this is an area that certainly deserves further investigation.

To explore more fully how this measure compares to other measures of loyalty, the chain loyalty of the 197 panel members discussed in the body of this paper was investigated. These 197 subjects did not reject the test of hypothesis for stationarity (multinomial model). A simple correlation matrix of key purchase characteristics was constructed.

It supports the findings reported by Massy and Frank [12]. The new "Entropy Loyalty Measure" is most highly correlated with the proportion of purchases going to the favorite chain ($-.785$), even though the former is measured in trips and the latter in dollars. In fact, the correlation with total runs (.648), not highly regarded by others, is slightly greater than the correlation with average run length in trips ($-.636$).

Correlations of θ with measures of activity, dollars per trip ($-.203$), and interval between trips ($-.286$), are slightly lower than are the correlations between these measures and the proportion going to the favorite chain. The number of different chains patronized has a greater effect on $\hat{\theta}$ than on any other measure (.865). Thus, the new measure seems to be more sensitive to "shopping around" than the other measures—a desirable property. In general, our work suggests that it is a sensitive measure of loyalty (defined statistically) and merits further attention.

However, using θ as a definition of loyalty still leaves some unanswered questions:

(1) In some cases, a preference between θ and p_i is not obvious. Consider the case of only two brands and the same number of purchases. The proportion of purchases going to the favorite will be linear between .5 and 1.0. To make this a measure of nonloyalty, we consider one minus this proportion, $1-p_i$, which ranges between 0 and .5; θ increases from zero at a faster rate and then reaches a maximum of the natural logarithm of 2.0 or .693. These two measures are plotted as a function of p_i in the graph below. In this example, there seems to be little basis for preference of one measure over the other.

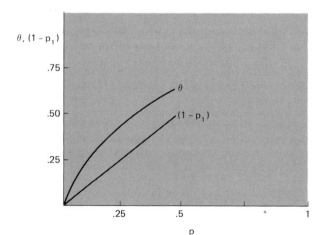

There are other situations for which the intuitive concept of loyalty is nebulous or even nonexistent; for instance, which of the following two cases is more loyal:

$$p_1 = \tfrac{1}{9},\ p_2 = \tfrac{2}{9},\ p_3 = \tfrac{1}{9}, p_4 = \tfrac{4}{9},\ p_5 = \tfrac{1}{9},$$

or

$$p_1 = \tfrac{3}{18},\ p_2 = \tfrac{5}{18}, p_3 = \tfrac{3}{18},\ p_4 = \tfrac{6}{18},\ p_5 = \tfrac{1}{18}?$$

Because Brand 5 adds very little to disloyalty, θ says the second is slightly more loyal. Is this reasonable? The proportion going to the favorite and the proportion going to the two favorite brands are both greater for the first case. Is it useful to extend the concept of loyalty to a point where our intuition and theory are both fuzzy?

(2) While θ does have the advantage of considering all brands, its application to purchases in dollars, rather than units, has not been tested for those products where differences in quantities per purchase are great.

Although θ is a continuous function of the parameters of the underlying multinomial model, $\hat{\theta}$, the sample estimate of θ, for fixed sample size is discrete, i.e. can take on only a finite set of values. This is a problem in every case of sampling, almost without exception; but for the small sample sizes characteristic of our data it becomes more serious. An interval estimate of θ may be appropriate.

REFERENCES

1. ALDERSON AND SESSIONS, INC., "Basic Research Report on Consumer Behavior: Report on a Study of Shopping Behavior and Methods for Its Investigation," in Ronald E. Frank, A. A. Kuehn, and W. Massy, eds., *Quantitative Techniques in Marketing Analysis.* Homewood, Ill.: Richard D. Irwin, Inc., 1962, 129–45.

2. BIRDWELL, AL, "A Standard of the Influence of Image Congruence on Consumer Choice," *Journal of Business,* 41 (January 1968), 76–88.

3. BRODY, ROBERT P. AND SCOTT M. CUNNINGHAM, "Personality Variables and the Consumer Decision Process," *Journal of Marketing Research,* 5 (February 1968), 50–7.

4. BUCKLIN, LOUIS P., "Competitive Impact of a New Supermarket," *Journal of Marketing Research,* 4 (November 1967), 356–61.

5. ———— AND JAMES M. CARMAN, *The Design of Consumer Research Panels: Conception and Administration of the Berkeley Food Panel,* Berkeley: Institute of Business and Economic Research, University of California, 1967.

6. CARMAN, JAMES M., *The Application of Social Class in Market Segmentation.* Berkeley: Institute of Business and Economic Research, University of California, 1965.

7. ———— AND JOHN L. STROMBERG, "A Comparison of Some Measures of Brand Loyalty," Research Program in Marketing Working Paper No. 26, Berkeley: Institute of Business and Economic Research, University of California, July 1967.

8. FRANK, RONALD E., PAUL E. GREEN AND H. F. SIEBER, JR., "Household Correlates of Purchase Price for Grocery Products," *Journal of Marketing Research,* 4 (February 1967), 54–8.

9. FRANK, RONALD E., "Is Brand Loyalty a Useful Basis for Market Segmentation?" *Journal of Advertising Research,* 7 (June 1967), 27–33.

10. ————, "Correlates of Buying Behavior for Grocery Products," *Journal of Marketing,* 31 (October 1967), 48–53.

11. GLOCK, CHARLES Y., in F. S. Bourne, "Group Influences in Marketing and Public Relations," *Some Applications of Behavioral Research*, R. Likert and S. P. Hayes, Jr., eds., Paris: UNESCO, 1957, 218.
12. MASSY, WILLIAM F., R. E. FRANK, AND T. M. LODAHL, *Purchasing Behavior and Personal Attributes*, Philadelphia: University of Pennsylvania Press, 1968.
13. MORGAN, J. N. AND J. A. SONQUIST, "Problems in the Analysis of Survey Data and a Proposal," *Journal of the American Statistical Association*, 58 (June 1963), 415–35.
14. RIZZO, J. R. AND J. C. NAYLOR, "The Factorial Structure of Selected Consumer Choice Parameters and Their Relationship to Personal Values," *Journal of Applied Psychology*, 48 (August 1964), 241–8.
15. SCHAPKER, BEN L., "Behavior Patterns of Supermarket Shoppers," *Journal of Marketing*, 30 (October 1966), 46–9.
16. SHETH, JAGDISH N., "A Review of Buyer Behavior," *Management Science*, 13 (August 1967), B718–56.
17. SIMON, LEONARD S. AND MELVIN R. MARKS, "Consumer Behavior During the New York Newspaper Strike," *Journal of Advertising Research*, 5 (March 1965), 9–17.
18. SONQUIST, J. A. AND J. N. MORGAN, *The Determination of Interaction Effects*, Monograph No. 35, Ann Arbor, Michigan: Survey Research Center, University of Michigan, 1964.
19. TATE, RUSSELL S., "The Supermarket Battle for Store Loyalty," *Journal of Marketing*, 25 (October 1961), 8–13.
20. WEBSTER, FREDERICK E., "The 'Deal-Prone' Consumer," *Journal of Marketing Research*, 2 (May 1965), 186–9.
21. WOODS, W. A., "Psychological Dimensions of Consumer Decisions," *Journal of Marketing*, 24 (January 1960), 15–9.

41. Industrial source loyalty

yoram wind

INTRODUCTION

The degree of customers' loyalty to brands and stores and the correlates, or determinants, of this loyalty are of major importance in
designing marketing strategies in both consumer and industrial markets. Yet whereas wide interest converted this area into one of the
principal areas of marketing, in which rigorous theoretical and a
variety of empirical approaches have been brought together to study
consumer loyalty behavior and its determinants [2, 3, 6, 7], no attempt
has previously been made to examine the loyalty of industrial buyers.

The present study attempts to fill this gap by analyzing source loyalty
by a West Coast electronics firm. In particular, it examines the purchase of industrial components and the various factors which influence source loyalty. In the purchase of industrial components the
buyer (purchasing department) selects a source (a manufacturer, dis-
tributor, or even a machine shop within his company) to supply the
needed parts specified, by brand or detailed specification, by the R & D
engineer or production control manager.

The study was conducted in two phases [9]. A preliminary investigation developed a number of research hypotheses. This phase consisted
of a number of interviews with, and protocols from, various organizational members who make or influence purchase decisions. The findings of this phase were summarized in a model of source loyalty and
number of hypotheses, which were tested in the second phase by
multiple regression and discriminant analyses of data collected from
company records and interviews with members of the firm.

A MODEL OF INDUSTRIAL SOURCE LOYALTY

The model developed in the first phase (the figure) hypothesizes that
source loyalty in the purchase of industrial components is a function
of four major sets of variables:

1. The "traditional" task variables of price, quality, delivery, quantity
   and service, commonly considered in the purchasing literature to be
   the sole determinants of decisions.
2. The buyer's past experience with the various sources, assumed to be
   summarized in his attitudes toward the various sources.
3. The organizational variables, reflecting the effect of the specific
   organizational setting on the buyer's decisions and behavior.
4. The factors perceived by the buyer to simplify his work.

Reprinted by permission from *Journal of Marketing Research*, Vol. 7 (November
1970), pp. 450–457, published by the American Marketing Association.

One other possible set of variables—the special relations of a buying firm with a given supplier (standing supplier contracts and reciprocity)—was not included in the model. Controls were exerted by excluding from the analysis all those cases in which standing supplier

A Simplified Model of Industrial Source Loyalty

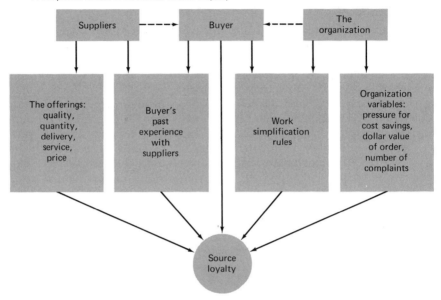

contracts existed. Reciprocity, the policy of buying from the company's customers, may of course affect the results, but since buyers were reluctant to talk about it, it was excluded from the model.

Each of the remaining four sets of variables and their hypothesized relationships to source loyalty are next described.

The Traditional Task Variables

Traditionally, the quality of products, the availability of the appropriate quantity, and the capacity to deliver at the right time have been viewed as key factors in determining source selection. Yet these requirements do not determine which suppliers will be selected and are therefore not significant determinants of source loyalty. Consequently, price was the only traditional task variable included directly in the model. Specifically, it was hypothesized that the greater the discrepancy between the price of the current source and others, the greater the probability of changing a source and the greater the discrepancy in prices of the current source over time.

The Organizational Variables

A buyer's past experience, which is likely to influence his loyalty, will tend to be reflected in (and can be measured by) his attitudes toward the source [10]. Source loyalty is hypothesized, therefore, to be greater the more favorable the buyer's attitudes toward a source.

Although most studies on industrial buyer behavior have not been concerned with organizational variables, the exploratory study suggested that these have an important influence. In particular, following the author's reward-balance model [11], it was hypothesized that the organizational setting affects the buyer via the pressure exerted on him for cost savings, the dollar value of the order, and the number of complaints from the using departments. The greater the pressure for cost savings, the larger the value of the given order, and the more complaints are transmitted, the greater the probability of switching to another source. It is expected, therefore, that these organizational variables will be inversely related to source loyalty. In addition, two other factors stemming from the organizational environment, the recommendation of a sole brand by the user and the identity of the buyer, were also expected to affect the degree of source loyalty.

Work Simplification Variables

Industrial buyers are in most cases under tremendous pressure to complete their routine of selecting and contacting sources of supply in a given period of time. Therefore, they tend to prefer alternatives that might simplify their work and save them extra effort and time. This phenomenon of work simplification is the industrial buyer's equivalent of the consumer's tendency to increase his shopping convenience [5]. It is thus hypothesized that:

1. Buyers tend to prefer sources which are located geographically closer to them, since this simplifies communication.
2. Buyers tend to remain with their favorite source as long as no strong pressures are exerted for a shift. A new order to the established source requires less effort than looking for a new source.

VERIFYING THE MODEL

The Data

The data for this study were derived from three major sources:

1. *The purchase history cards of components bought by an advanced electronics firm.* The sample of components was drawn from all components for which there were no standing supplier contracts and with at least seven purchases each. The total number included in the sample were about 1,200 for determining the degree of source loyalty, 314 for the first regression runs, 80 for the fresh set of data to test the model arrived at in the first runs, and 120 for the discriminant analysis. These cards provided information on the vendor selected, the date of purchase, other feasible suppliers, the quantity ordered, price, identity of the buyer, the brand recommendation if any, the location of the vendors and the terms of each purchase. These data provided the information needed for the construction of all variables, with the exception of the pressure for cost savings and attitude variables.

2. *The cost savings weekly memo.* This memo, distributed weekly to all purchasing agents, specified the cost saved by each division during the foregoing week. These data were used to construct the measures of pressure for cost savings.
3. *Data on the buyers' attitudes toward the various sources of supply.* These data were derived from an attitude study using the semantic differential scales.

The Research Approach

Before undertaking the quantitative analysis, measures for the dependent and independent variables had to be defined. Since there are no a priori criteria on the appropriateness of each measure, a number of alternative measures were tested in a series of regressions. From this the most appropriate measures of the dependent variables and the corresponding independent variables comprising the best regression equation—with the highest statistical explanatory power—were determined. In all, six measures of source loyalty were examined; of these, four were selected for further analysis. The definitions of these variables are given in the Appendix. Two other measures were eliminated, since their results were consistent with the other four and did not add to understanding of the initial 45 independent variables (5 of price, 11 of buyers' attitudes, 4 of dollar value of order, 17 of cost savings, 3 additional organizational variables, and 4 work simplification variables). Eleven independent variables were found to compose the best regression equation for three measures of source loyalty and nine for the fourth equation. These variables and the hypothesized direction of their relation to source loyalty are summarized in the Appendix. The selected variables were then tested on a fresh set of data using both regression and discriminant techniques [8].

The Findings

Does source loyalty exist? The purchase history cards indicated clearly that there is a high degree of source loyalty for both fabricated and standard industrial components. Only about 6% of the purchase history cards reported an instance of an isolated source (granted only one order). Thus, even on these grounds alone, some degree of loyalty is apparent.

The determinants of source loyalty. The four sets of variables hypothesized in the model were examined by multiple regression and discriminant analysis. The objective of the multiple regression was to estimate the strength of the relationship between source loyalty and the hypothesized explanatory variables. The discriminant analysis was designed to test the power of the selected variables in predicting the various degrees of source loyalty.

The regression analysis showed a significant relationship between the various measures of source loyalty and the four sets of independent variables with an R^2 ranging from .94 for the equation with SL_1 as the dependent variable to .73 for SL_4. The results thus tend to support the model. There were, however, substantial differences in the relative explanatory importance of the various independent variables.

Since the dependent and independent variables were in different dimensions, prices, attitudes, etc., the partial regression coefficients could not be compared directly. A standardized parameter estimate [4][1] was therefore computed to analyze the relative importance of each variable. The first column of Table 1 shows the standardized

TABLE 1   Regression Standardized Coefficients, t, F, and R^2 Values for SL_1

Independent variables[a]		Number of purchases from favorite source as percentage of total number of purchases from all sources (SL_1)	
		Best model	Best reduced model
Price:	P_1	−0.0215 (−0.477)	—
	P_2	−0.2069 (−2.971)	−0.3154 (−3.078)
Attitude:	A_1	−0.0068 (−0.125)	—
	A_2	0.1058 (2.038)	0.1910 (3.734)
Organizational:	DLV_1	−0.2146 (−2.378)	−0.2235 (−2.681)
	CS_1	0.2626 (3.505)	0.3429 (4.535)
	CS_2	−0.1582 (−1.909)	—
	ORG_1	0.1145 (2.208)	0.2036 (3.815)
	ORG_2	0.0074 (0.170)	—
Work simplification:	WS_1	0.0399 (0.947)	—
	WS_2	0.1162 (2.504)	0.1310 (2.593)
	R^2	.9412	.9409
	F	48.039	70.269

[a] Definitions are summarized in the Appendix.

[1] The standardized parameter estimates were derived by converting each variable into units of standard deviation. The computation of the standardized coefficient (β) and its relation to the regression coefficient (b) are indicated by the following equation:

$$\beta_{yi \cdot j} = b_{yi \cdot j} \frac{S_i}{S_y},$$

where
 β = standardized regression coefficient
 b = regression coefficient
 S = standard deviation
 y = dependent variable
 i = the specific independent variable studied
 j = all other independent variables.

coefficients for the equation with SL_1 as a measure of source loyalty. The equations with SL_2 and SL_3 as dependent variables showed a slightly lower explanatory power overall, but led to similar conclusions and are not discussed separately. An examination of these partial coefficients suggested that not all variables used in the regression were significant. Further testing on a trial and error basis enabled the elimination of certain variables without reducing the explanatory power of the equation. The resulting equation is presented in the second column of Table 1. It shows that a small number of key variables representing the four sets of variables explain source loyalty almost as well as the whole equation. In particular, cost savings (CS_1), price (P_2), and the dollar value of the order (DLV_1) emerged as the most important single determinants of source loyalty. Attitude (A_2), recommendation of a brand (ORG_1) and previous purchase history (WS_2) were slightly less significant.

The regression with SL_4 as dependent variables showed a similar tendency for a few variables to explain source loyalty, although in this case different variables were significant. The results of the equation with the nine selected variables as well as the best regression equation for a subcombination of these variables are listed in Table 2. These show that four variables alone account for an R^2 of .7295 with an F-value of 21.32.

TABLE 2   Regression Standardized Coefficients, t, F, and R^2 Values for SL_4

Explanatory variables[a]		The relationship between source decision at time $t-1$ and time t (SL_4)	
		Best model	Best reduced model
Price:	P_3	−0.1165	0.1210
		(1.500)	(1.509)
Attitude:	A_3	−0.2041	−0.2154
		(−2.609)	(−2.640)
	A_4	0.0285	—
		(0.044)	
Organizational:	DLV_2	0.1955	0.1899
		(2.528)	(2.293)
	CS_3	−0.2892	—
		(−3.708)	
	CS_4	−0.4290	−0.5300
		(−5.553)	(−6.486)
	ORG_1	0.0122	—
		(−0.163)	
	ORG_3	0.0628	—
		(0.830)	
Work simplification:	WS_3	0.1144	—
		(1.544)	
	R^2	.7171	.7295
	F	13.553	21.327

[a] Definitions are summarized in the Appendix.

Cost savings were the most important single expanatory variable with SL_4 as a measure of source loyalty. When both measures of the set—CS_4 and CS_3—were included, they had the highest and second highest standardized b, respectively. Following, but quite a bit behind, was A_3, the better of the two attitude measures examined in the second regression study. Of smaller importance, but still significant, were the dollar value, price, and work simplification variables.

The major findings of the analysis were such that all four sets of variables had a statistically significant effect on source loyalty, irrespective of the specific measure of loyalty used. All variables were related linearly to source loyalty and in the direction hypothesized by the model. The only exceptions were the few cases regarding the measure of dual loyalty. An analysis of the effect of each of the independent variables on source loyalty showed that some measures had more explanatory power, in particular P_2, DLV_1, CS_1, A_2, and WS_2, in explaining source loyalty as measured by SL_1, SL_2, and SL_3, and CS_4, A_3, DLV_2 and P_3 as the major explanatory variables of SL_4.

Apart from the customary problem of causality inference in a regression analysis, the findings are subject to a number of limitations due to the nature of the data. First, there was some heteroscedasticity and multicollinearity in the data, so that the statistical significance of some of the regression coefficients may therefore have been overstated. Second, a number of variables expected to influence source loyalty, such as complaints about the buyer's performance, promotion activity, and persuasiveness of certain salesmen, were not included in the model. Their effects will therefore be distributed among the other variables and result in some spurious association between them and source loyalty. Finally, the data related only to components purchased by a highly advanced electronics firm, within a price range of $.07 to $117.00. Hence the findings, while believed representative for this type of firm and components, may not apply to other types of components, other types of firms, or components outside this price range.

The discriminant analysis [9] was intended to test the ability of the four sets of variables to discriminate between cases of perfect source loyalty ($SL=1$) and some other degree of source loyalty ($SL<1$) and between $SL>.5$ and $SL\geq.5$.[2] In both cases the variables were able to discriminate effectively, although less effectively between $SL>.5$ and $SL\leq.5$ than between $SL=1$ and $SL<1$.

The discriminant function for $SL=1$ and $SL<1$ had a D^2 of 10.746 with an F-value of 29.781, implying a high degree of statistical significance. The function also exhibited a high predictive power, since it classified approximately 85% of the cases into the correct loyalty group.

---

[2] The dividing line between loyal (but not $SL=1$) and nonloyal is arbitrary. There is no theoretical justification for classifying these cases, and as loyalty is a matter of degree, it was decided that if 50% or more of all purchases were made from one source, these sources would be classified as having a high degree of loyalty. On the other hand, if less than 50% of all purchases were bought from any one source, this product was said to have a small degree of loyalty (a quasi-nonloyalty). Further study in this direction of determining an operationally significant boundary line between high and low source loyalty is required.

An examination of the ability of each individual set of variables to discriminate between $SL=1$ and $SL<1$ showed a clear superiority of the organizational variables over the others. Their discriminatory power was, however, lower than that of all four sets of variables taken together.

The D^2 of the discriminant function for $SL>.5$ and $SL\leq.5$ indicates that while the four sets of variables had some ability to discriminate between the two groups, it was less than in the case of perfect source loyalty. Similarly the ability of separate sets of variables to discriminate was smaller. In this case the attitude variables had a slightly higher discriminatory power than the organization or work simplification variables.

Thus it may be concluded that the four sets of variables taken together can discriminate effectively between $SL=1$ and $SL<1$ and somewhat less effectively between $SL>.5$ and $SL\leq.5$.

The interpretation of the results of the discriminant analysis should take into account, however, the limitations due to the nature of the data used and the relatively small sample size.

CONCLUSIONS

The preceding analysis provided substantial evidence of the existence of source loyalty in the purchase of industrial components by an advanced electronics firm. Furthermore, it indicated that the four sets of variables, suggested in the industrial source loyalty model, are important determinants of source loyalty, explaining on the average about 80% of the variance in source loyalty at a high level of statistical significance. While the variables included in the model are by no means the only ones which may affect industrial source loyalty, and while no one set of variables can be considered as the only or major determinant of source loyalty, the organizational variables were the single most significant set in both the regression and discriminant analyses.

Further research is needed to validate the results of this study. It does, nonetheless, suggest a number of managerial and research implications. The managerial implications, which should be viewed more as hypotheses for further research than as direct guidelines for action, are:

1. In designing the marketing strategies aimed at buyers of industrial components, one should take explicitly into account the organizational characteristics of the buying firm. In the specific firm studied, the effect of the organizational setting was through the pressure for cost savings and the dollar value of the order, although these variables might not be important in other organizations. One should assess the ways in which the organization affects the buying process.
2. Establishing only the statistical association between a number of variables and source loyalty provides no conclusions as to the specific causes of changes in sources of supply (lack of source loyalty).

It may be inferred, however, that a change in a source is less likely to occur (high degree of source loyalty is strongly probable) when some or all of the following conditions are met:

a. The price of a given source at time t is lower than it was at $t-1$. The buyer achieves his desired cost savings without engaging in a search for alternative ways to save. Hence he has no apparent motive to be disloyal to the given source.

b. The dollar value of the order is small. No significant cost savings are expected, and hence the buyer would tend to prefer not to change the source, since that would involve costs which are not likely to be offset by the expected savings.

c. The past cost savings of the given division are high (above their long-run average savings in relation to other divisions), reducing the current pressure for cost savings. Hence there is less motivation to engage in a search for cost savings that might lead to a change in source.

d. The specific brand is recommended by the user. In most cases the user specifies either no specific brand or a number of possible brands. In those few cases in which he specifies a particular brand, the buyer tends to accept his judgment and remain loyal to this source.

In addition to these substantive conclusions, the study suggests a number of important implications for further research in industrial marketing:

1. The industrial buying process can be studied. Even complex variables such as the organizational effect can be studied and quantified.

2. The data for studies of industrial buying behavior can be generated quite easily both from the people involved (buyers, users, purchasing managers, and salesmen) and from records of the buying firm. The latter source is of great importance and simplifies to some extent, studies of industrial buying behavior.

3. Among the data collection methods the protocol technique [1] has been most fruitful in providing insights into the organizational buying process. In this method the relevant organizational members who have something to do with purchase were asked to think aloud [12].

4. Quantitative techniques such as multiple regression and discriminant analyses can be utilized in the study of industrial buying behavior. There is a need to limit the study of industrial buying behavior to descriptive studies which avoid the use of multivariate statistical techniques.

In short, whereas the study of industrial buying behavior has lagged behind that of consumer behavior in both the number of studies and the research methods employed, the present study demonstrates the possibility of conducting a quantitative rigorous study of industrial buying behavior. It is thus hoped that this modest start will encourage further studies of industrial buying behavior.

APPENDIX

DEPENDENT AND INDEPENDENT VARIABLES INCLUDED IN THE MODEL

I. *The Dependent Variables*
SL_1 = Number of purchases from favorite source as percentage of total number of purchases.
SL_2 = Number of purchases from the two most favorite sources as a percentage of the total number of purchases from all sources.
SL_3 = Number of source shifts as a percentage of the total number of purchases.
SL_4 = The relation between source decision at times $t-1$ and t.

II. *The Independent Variables*
A. *For Regression Equations with* SL_1, SL_2, SL_3

Variables	Definition	Direction of hypothesized relationship with source loyalty
P_1 = Price of favorite source relative to others.	$$\dfrac{\dfrac{P_F}{AP_t} + \dfrac{P_F}{AP_{t-1}} + \cdots + \dfrac{P_F}{AP_{t-n}}}{n+1}$$ where: P = Price of favorite source AP = Average price of all other relevant sources (excluding F at trial t).	Minus
P_2 = Price at time t relative to previous price.	$$\dfrac{\dfrac{p_t}{p_{t-1}} + \dfrac{p_{t-1}}{p_{t-2}} + \cdots + \dfrac{p_{t-n}}{p_{t-n-1}}}{n+1}$$	Minus
A_1 = Attitude toward a given source relative to the ideal source (i.e., the buyer's dissatisfaction gap).	$$\sum^{k} (aW_I - aW_F)$$ where: a = Buyer's attitude toward a given source k = Number of attributes of the buyer's attitude W = Weight of each attribute—its relative importance for the buying decision I = Ideal source F = Favorite source.	Minus

APPENDIX—Continued

A_2 = Attitude toward a given source relative to other sources (i.e., buyer's relative dissatisfaction gap).

$$\frac{\sum\limits_{k} (aW_l - aW_F)}{\sum\limits_{k} (aW_l - aW_{SF})}$$

where: SF = The second favorite source.

Plus

DLV_1 = Dollar value of an order.

$$\left[\begin{matrix} PQ_l \geq 100 \to 1 \\ PQ_l < 100 \to 0 \end{matrix}\right] + \left[\begin{matrix} PQ_{l-1} \geq 100 \to 1 \\ PQ_{l-1} < 100 \to 0 \end{matrix}\right] + \left[\begin{matrix} PQ_{l-n} \geq 100 \to 1 \\ PQ_{l-n} < 100 \to 0 \end{matrix}\right]$$

where: P = Price per unit
Q = Quantity ordered
100 = Value of order in dollars, e.g., \$100

Minus

CS_1 = Divisional cost savings relative to cost savings of other divisions.

$$\frac{\dfrac{DIVCS_{t\,1-1W}}{TCSO_{t\,1-1W}}\left|\dfrac{AVDIVCS_t}{AVTCSO_t}\right| + \cdots + \dfrac{DIVCS_{tn-1W}}{TCSO_{tn-1W}}\left|\dfrac{AVDIVCS_t}{AVTCSO_t}\right|}{n}$$

where:
$DIVCS_{t\,1-1W}$ = Divisional cost savings at the week prior to the given trial t
$TCSO_{t\,1-1W}$ = Total cost savings of all other divisions
$AVDIVCS_t$ = Average weekly divisional cost savings for the whole period
$AVTCSO_t$ = Average weekly total cost savings of all other divisions for the whole period
$\dfrac{AVDIVCS_t}{AVTCSO_t}$ = Surrogate for a standard acceptable performance of the division.

Plus

CS_2 = Cumulative divisional cost savings relative to cumulative cost savings of all other divisions.

$$\frac{DICVCS_{t\Delta1-2W}}{CCSO_{t\Delta1-2W}} - \frac{CDIVCS_{t\Delta1-1W}}{CCSO_{t\Delta1-1W}}\begin{matrix}\leq 0 \to 1 \\ > 0 \to 0\end{matrix} + \cdots + \frac{CDIVCS_{t\Delta K-2W}}{CCSO_{t\Delta K-2W}} - \frac{CDIVCS_{t\Delta W-1W}}{CCSO_{t\Delta W-1W}}\begin{matrix}0 \to 1 \\ 0 \to 0\end{matrix}$$

where:
$CDIVCS$ = Cumulative divisional cost savings
$CCSO$ = Cumulative cost savings of all other divisions
Δ = Change in source.

Plus

APPENDIX—Continued

Variables	Definition	Direction of hypothesized relationship with source loyalty
ORG_1 = Recommendation of brand by user.	Measured as a dummy variable that takes the value of one—if a specific brand is recommended, zero—if no brand or more than one brand is recommended.	Plus
ORG_2 = Identity of buyer.	Number of times a buyer changed when a source was changed.	Minus
WS_1 = Movement to a geographically closer source.	WS_1 was defined as the following dummy variables that equal one —if the first change in source was to a source that is geographically closer to the buyer, zero—if it was not.	Plus
WS_2 = Previous purchase history.	$$\frac{\text{Average length of source run for FS}}{\text{Average run length of all other sources}}$$ where: FS = Favorite source. Length of source run = number of consecutive purchases from the same source. For example, in the sequence $XXXYY$ there are two runs —a run with 3 purchases (length 3) of Source X and 2 purchases (length 2) of Source Y.	Plus
B. For Regression Equation with SL_4		
P_3 = Price of preferred source relative to the average price of all other feasible sources at time $t-1$.	$$\frac{P_{St-1}}{AP_{t-1}}$$	Minus
A_3 = Relative dissatisfaction gap.	$$\sum^k \frac{aw_F}{k} \bigg/ \sum^k \frac{aw_{SF}}{k}$$	Minus
A_4 = Relative dissatisfaction gap.	$$\sum^k \frac{aw_{St}}{k} \bigg/ \sum^k \frac{aw_{St-1}}{k}$$	Plus

Variables	Definition	Direction of hypothesized relationship with source loyalty
DLV_2 = Dollar size of order.	DLV_2 is a dummy variable that takes the value of one when $PQ_t \geq 100$ and zero when $PQ_t < 100$ where: \$100 is assumed to be the critical value above which change in source is more likely to occur.	Plus
CS_3 = Divisional cost savings relative to cost savings of all other divisions in same time period.	$\dfrac{DIVCS_{t-1,w}}{TCS_{t-1,w}}$	Plus
CS_4 = Cumulative divisional cost savings relative to cumulative cost savings of all other divisions, based on standard of divisional cost savings.	$\dfrac{CDIVCS_{t-1,w}}{CCSO_{t-1,w}} \bigg/ \dfrac{ACDIVCS_t}{ACCSO_t}$	Plus
WS_3 = Length of source run.	This equals the number of source runs greater than one, when a run is defined as a consecutive sequence of purchases from the same source.	Plus
ORG_3 = Identity of buyer.	This was defined as a dummy variable that takes the value of one if a buyer changed when a source was last changed, and a value of zero if not.	Plus

REFERENCES

1. CLARKSON, GEOFFREY P. E., *Portfolio Selection: A Simulation of Trust Investment*, Englewood Cliffs, N.J.: Prentice-Hall, 1962.
2. CUNNINGHAM, ROSS M., "Brand Loyalty: What, Where, How Much?" *Harvard Business Review*, 34 (January–February 1956), 116–28.
3. _____, "Customer Loyalty to Store and Brand," *Harvard Business Review*, 39 (November–December 1961), 127–37.
4. MORDECAI, EZEKIEL AND K. A. FOX, *Methods of Correlation and Regression Analysis*, New York: John Wiley & Sons, 1959.
5. KELLEY, EUGENE J., "The Importance of Convenience in Consumer Purchasing," *Journal of Marketing*, 23 (July 1958), 32–8.
6. LIPSTEIN, BENJAMIN, "The Dynamics of Brand Loyalty and Brand Switching," *Proceedings*, 5th Annual Conference of the Advertising Research Foundation, New York, 1959.
7. MASSY, WILLIAM F., "Brand and Source Loyalty as Bases for Market Segmentation," in J. W. Newman, ed., *On Knowing the Consumer*, New York: John Wiley & Sons, 1966, 169–72.
8. RULON, P. J., "Distinction Between Discriminant and Regression Analysis and a Geometric Interpretation of the Discriminant Function," *Harvard Educational Review*, 21 (Spring 1951), 80–90.
9. WIND, YORAM, "Industrial Buying Behavior: Source Loyalty in the Purchase of Industrial Components," unpublished doctoral dissertation, Stanford University, 1966.
10. _____, "Integrating Attitude Measures in a Study of Industrial Buyer Behavior," in Lee Adler and Irving Crespi, eds. *Attitude Research on the Rocks*, Chicago: American Marketing Association, 1968, 58–77.
11. _____, "A Reward-Balance Model of Buying Behavior in Organizations," in George Fisk, ed., *Essays in Marketing Theory*, Boston: Allyn & Bacon, in press.
12. _____, "A Case Study of the Purchase of Industrial Components," in Patrick J. Robinson and Charles W. Faris, eds., *Industrial Buying and Creative Marketing*, Boston: Allyn & Bacon, 1967.

17 DIFFUSION

In this chapter we take up the study of how innovations, or, specifically, new products, are adopted by individuals and diffuse or permeate through a society. Research on these questions has gone on for over sixty years and thus represents a very long research tradition within the relatively young behavioral sciences. Only within the last five to ten years have students of marketing actively examined the diffusion process model for its usefulness in predicting the fate of new products.

This chapter begins with an overview of the diffusion literature and an attempt to relate the adoption and diffusion process models to the buyer behavior model (Ostlund, 1972).* It is hoped that the student will thereby see their extensive similarity and will not be prompted to consider the diffusion research literature as specialized and remote from buyer behavior research.

The reading by Robertson and Kennedy (1968)* focuses on the characteristics of innovators, or early adopters, of "Touch Tone" telephones. Their work demonstrates that, for at least this consumer appliance, innovators have a rather distinctive profile. Information of this sort has value to the marketer in that it can help in identifying prospective innovators for selective media attention, or it may better describe them as people and thus help in shaping appropriate advertising message content that should appeal to them.

The perceived characteristics of innovations, product perceptions, were investigated by Ostlund (1970)* for six different consumer innovations. In all cases, the product perception dimensions were considerably superior predictors of buying intention than were the characteristics of the perspective innovators. The success of Robertson and Kennedy in correctly predicting adoption of "Touch Tone" telephones based upon personal characteristic dimensions differs from the conclusion by Ostlund. It is, however, too early to draw firm conclusions. First of all, as Robertson and Kennedy acknowledge, their discriminate function was validated on the same body of data from which it was derived, which would tend to inflate its apparent predictive merit, but by what amount is difficult to estimate. However, it may well be that the type of innovation that they studied was in some way one that would bring out manifest differences between the characteristics of adopters and nonadopters, while those innovations studied by Ostlund might not. Clearly, replication of both studies is needed particularly within other product categories.

While most of the research concerning diffusion of innovations within a marketing context has involved consumer products, the same concepts and methodology should apply to industrial buying behavior.

Work by Ozanne and Churchill (1968)* furnishes an example of such research.

REFERENCES

1. Ostlund, Lyman E. "Predictors of Innovative Behavior," a revision of a paper presented at the Annual Conference of the Association of Consumer Research, University of Massachusetts, Amherst, August 30, 1970.
   _____. "Diffusion: A Dynamic View of Buyer Behavior," 1972. Written for this volume.
3. Robertson, Thomas S. *Innovative Behavior and Communications.* New York: Holt, Rinehart and Winston, 1971.

42. Diffusion: a dynamic view of buyer behavior

lyman e. ostlund

A systematic study of factors affecting the adoption and diffusion of innovations has been underway for over sixty years, in a variety of social science disciplines. This effort thus precedes by several decades an orderly flow of research centered on buyer behavior aimed at deriving comprehensive theory. Only within the last five to ten years has research been focused on the adoption and diffusion of new products as innovations, in the context of buyer behavior. Although such research has been slow in coming, the alarmingly high rates of new product failure may have stimulated attention to the literature on the adoption and diffusion of innovations, in the hope of reducing this fatality rate. Branches of sociology have made the major contributions to diffusion literature, and thus diffusion has come to be treated as a process of propagation in reference to patterns of behavior, ideas, tastes, processes, and products.

Adoption refers to the multistage mental and behavioral process assumed to take place in an individual, leading from awareness of the innovation to ultimate adoption, or commitment to that innovation. Diffusion can be looked upon as a dynamic social process, heavily dependent upon interpersonal information sources, occurring over extended time periods, and culminating in some maximum level of penetration or adoption across a specific, defined population. While the theory of buyer behavior (Chapter 1, this volume) applies beyond only new products, it is likewise a multistage mental and behavioral process incorporating hypothetical constructs, many of which are analogous to those within the generally accepted diffusion model by Everett M. Rogers (1962) to be discussed later. A key difference, however, is that the diffusion model specifically acknowledges not only the adoption process but also the rejection process. That is, while a new product or other form of innovation might initially be accepted or adopted by a given person, it can as well be rejected in a later cycle of deliberation, and in either case—adoption or rejection—this decision and the interpersonal communications flow that may surround it can go on to influence behavior on the part of friends or associates. A second difference is that while the emphasis in the study of buyer behavior is essentially on the prediction of individual behavior and mental stages leading to it, in diffusion literature at least equal emphasis has been placed on the prediction of ultimate diffusion levels and adoption rates per unit of time. In this sense, the emphasis is placed on aggregative rather than disaggregative data. As an innovation diffuses throughout a defined population, a cumulative S-shaped curve is traced such as that in Figure 1. This curve, assumed to be normal, depicts the rate of adoption or penetration of an innovation at any given time, perhaps ultimately reaching 100 percent. Students of marketing will recognize this same S-shaped curve as the one used to

FIGURE 1 Cumulative S-Shaped Diffusion Curve

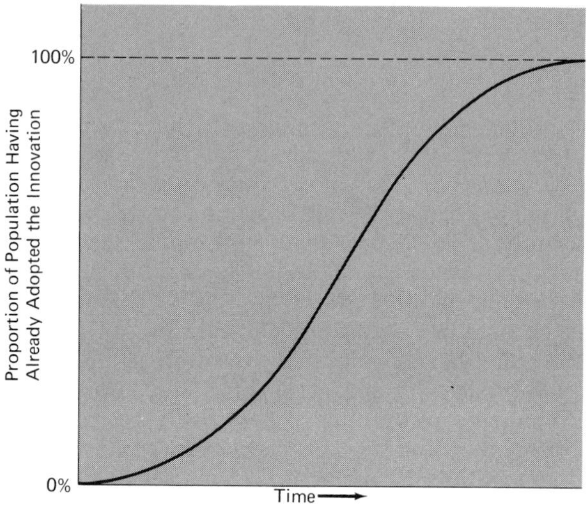

represent the life cycle of a product, and clearly the two concepts are related, but not identical.

It would be wrong to conclude that research that is labeled "buyer behavior research" is necessarily removed from that concerning the diffusion of innovations, or vice versa. An attempt is made here to draw parallels between the two schools of research and suggest the means of bringing them together. But before this can be undertaken, an overview of diffusion research findings is needed.

THE ORIGINS OF DIFFUSION RESEARCH

British and German anthropologists present us with the earliest evidence of serious research into factors related to diffusion of innovations. Their prime areas of interest were in diffusion processes that surrounded ethnic movements, revolutions, cultural transfers, religious movements, and finally technological and commercial change. This research went on in the nineteenth and early twentieth centuries and has been summarized by Kroeber (1927). The interest in diffusion research accelerated as sociologists and economists became interested in solving one of two general types of problems: (1) the identification of factors that would aid in promoting "socially good" products or ideas, or (2) finding ways of reducing the social cost represented by unsuccessful new product developments. It was not until the 1920s when the United States Department of Agriculture, with its farm extension service, began pouring money into the coffers of rural sociology departments in land grant universities that major research flows began. The Department of Agriculture was interested in learning all it could about why certain farming innovations whose development it had financed were rapidly adopted by farmers and others were rejected or adopted only after long resistance.

The diffusion research pursuit expanded beyond rural sociology and economics to include educational and medical sociology, modern anthropology, industrial engineering, geography, psychology, and communications, particularly the mass media. Voting studies done by the Bureau of Applied Social Research of Columbia University, under Paul Lazarsfeld, produced major contributions to our understanding of how the mass media and informal communications interact. In fact, to some social scientists the findings of voting studies such as those conducted in Erie County, New York (Lazarsfeld, Berelson, and Gaudet, 1948) and in Decatur, Illinois (Katz and Lazarsfeld, 1955) had great social import in documenting the strong influence of informal communications relative to the mass media on important public issues.

The definitive work by Ryan and Gross (1943) on factors related to the diffusion of hybrid seed corn and the long list of studies by Lionberger (1949, 1951, 1952, 1953, 1955, 1959, 1960) and others in the 1950s did much to build upon the early work in rural sociology. However, without a doubt the work that is most frequently referenced today in marketing literature is *Diffusion of Innovations* (1962) by Everett M. Rogers, which integrates findings from a wide variety of disciplines, all concerning the diffusion of innovations, and which contains Rogers' conceptual model of adoption as part of the diffusion process. We examine that model in detail after completing our overview. Rogers has gone on to establish the Diffusion Documents Center at Michigan State University as a central depository of over a thousand diffusion research studies. It is interesting to note that of that number, less than 5 percent have been conducted by market researchers (Rogers and Stanfield, 1968). Past studies were conducted by sociologists on such innovations as health insurance, synthetic fabrics, various durable goods including black-and-white television, and even fall-out shelters; these studies are, however, certainly relevant to our interest in the diffusion of new products. Table 1 summarizes the different research traditions (research streams on a similar topic) that have centered on the study of diffusion.

The diffusion process is generally described in terms of four sets of dimensions: the innovation, the communications process concerning the innovation, characteristics of the social system, and the passage of time (Rogers, 1962, pp. 12–20). In the vast majority of diffusion studies, the term "innovation" has been applied to highly unique, advanced ideas, often based upon significant technological achievement. However, as market researchers have been drawn into the diffusion research fold, varying definitions have been applied to the term. For example, several market researchers such as Frank, Massy, and Morrison (1964), Arndt (1967), Pessemier, Burger, and Tigert (1967), and others have applied the term to relatively mundane new products such as new brands of coffee and laundry detergents. Moreover, two researchers have suggested that "a product is an innovation if less than 10 percent market penetration exists in a given geographic location" (Lazer and Bell, 1966). Notice that this definition says absolutely nothing about what an innovation is; it refers only to its degree of market penetration.

As a result of this license in applying the term "innovation" to

TABLE 1   A Comparison of the Diffusion Research Traditions

Tradition	Main Disciplines Represented	Main Method of Data Gathering and Analysis	Main Unit of Analysis	Major Types of Findings
1. Anthropology	Anthropology	Participant observer combined with descriptive analysis	Societies or tribes	How idea diffuses from one society to another; consequences of innovation
2. Early sociology	Sociology	Data from secondary sources, and a type of statistical analysis	Mainly communities but also individuals	S-shaped adopter distribution; correlates of innovativeness
3. Rural sociology	Sociology	Personal interviews and statistical analysis	Individual farmers	Correlates of innovativeness, characteristics of ideas related to their rate of adoption; source of information at adoption process stages; S-shaped adopter distribution
4. Education	Education	Mailed questionnaires and statistical analysis	School systems	Correlates of innovativeness; S-shaped adopter distribution
5. Industrial	Industrial economists; Industrial engineers	Case studies and statistical analysis	Industrial firms	Correlates of innovativeness
6. Medical sociology	Sociology; Public Health	Personal interviews and statistical analysis	Individuals	Opinion leadership in diffusion; correlates of innovativeness
7. Marketing	Marketing; Social Psychology	Personal interviews and statistical analysis	Individuals	Same as is rural psychology, plus opinion leadership in diffusion

Reprinted with permission of the Macmillan Company from *Diffusion of Innovations* by Everett M. Rogers. © by The Free Press, 1962. (Row 7, Marketing, added.)

almost any product that comes on the market, increased variability and even conflicting results have been introduced among studies that, for example, attempt to draw a profile of early buyers of innovations. Robertson (1971, p. 7) has suggested that innovations should be classified in accordance with three general categories: (1) Continuous innovation—a product that is a minor variation of existing products, requiring little adjustment on the part of the buyer or the seller as to their established behavioral patterns. An example would be menthol cigarettes. (2) Dynamically continuous innovation—a product having somewhat disruptive effects on established buyer and seller behavioral patterns, although not requiring harsh readjustment. An example, investigated by Robertson, would be "Touch Tone" telephones. (3) Discontinuous innovation—an innovation that represents a sharp break from the past, requiring the establishment of new behavioral patterns. Examples would include television and computers. Most new products that we encounter are, by this classification, either continuous or dynamically continuous innovations. In fact, the researcher typically has difficulty in locating even dynamically continuous innovations for study.

While the definition of innovation is not trivial, it should be understood that the extent and speed of diffusion depends on how an innovation is actually perceived by potential adopters. Having sifted through a large number of diffusion studies, Rogers (1962) arrived at a set of product characteristic dimensions that appear frequently in marketing literature: (1) Relative advantage—the degree to which an innovation is perceived as superior to the product or idea it supersedes. (2) Compatibility—the degree to which a product is consistent with past experiences or habits of the potential adopter. (3) Communicability—the degree to which the innovation, or results from using the innovation, are visible and readily communicated to others. (4) Complexity—the degree to which an innovation is difficult to understand and/or use. (5) Divisibility—the degree to which an innovation can be tried without large financial or psychological commitment. The likelihood of adoption of an innovation will vary positively with all the above product perceptions except complexity, with which it will vary negatively.

While these dimensions sound appealing, they have received relatively little research attention. Work by Kivlin (1960) related several of these dimensions, plus some others, to the rate of diffusion for selected dairy innovations. Unfortunately, his measurement of these dimensions was not in terms of perceptions from dairy farmers confronted with the innovations, but rather from a separate judging panel of "farming experts" (none that were dairy farmers), who rated the selected dairy innovations on a set of scales.

The only work in a marketing context that employed the Rogers product characteristic dimensions was by Ostlund (1969, 1972), along with a sixth dimension, perceived risk, as conceptualized by Bauer (1960). The six new products studied by Ostlund would be classified as dynamically discontinuous innovations, using Robertson's (1972, p. 7) classification scheme. Among the sample of housewives, the five

Rogers dimensions plus perceived risk were found to be far better predictors of purchase intentions and behavior than predispositional factors, socioeconomic and demographic data (personal characteristics), with an average proportion of explained variance (R^2) of .50 across the six products. Although this initial work in applying product perception dimensions to the prediction of new product purchase is encouraging, replication in other product categories is needed before any firm conclusions can be drawn.

The communication process surrounding the diffusion of an innovation has been studied both in terms of mass media and word-of-mouth. The voting studies by Lazarsfeld and others referred to earlier attempted to sort out the relative importance of the two communication forms (Lazarsfeld, Berelson, and Gaudet, 1948; Katz and Lazarsfeld, 1955). It was found that a small portion of the population was apparently in close contact with the mass media and tended to pass along the information that they obtained to the remaining relatively more passive citizens. The term "opinion leader" was applied to these communicators, and the notion that communication flows in two steps— first to opinion leaders, then to the remaining population—was an outgrowth of this work and has received considerable attention in marketing literature. Katz and Lazarsfeld (1955) concluded that opinion leaders have a relatively narrow scope of interest, for example, opinion leaders for fashion are not likely to be opinion leaders for new movies. While reanalysis of the Katz and Lazarsfeld data by Marcus and Bauer (1964), plus work by Silk (1966) and Silk and Montgomery (1969), argue for statistically significant overlap, the levels are nonetheless pragmatically low and can generally be dismissed as of little importance. Moreover, studies suggest that the typical opinion leader has influence over a relatively small group of people, generally no more than ten in number, and the influence is not complete by any means.

It is more important to note the situations under which the mass media and word-of-mouth communication have each been found important. Generally, the mass media are most important in establishing initial awareness that the innovation exists. If, however, adoption of an innovation is an issue of some consequence, the potential adopter tends to turn toward word-of-mouth informational sources to obtain opinions from family, friends, and acquaintances before formulating his judgment of the innovation.

Since diffusion takes place within a social system, the characteristics of that system will likewise influence the extent and rate of diffusion. So-called traditional societies exhibit resistance to adoption, and those few brave souls who adopt the innovation early may be perceived as crackpots (Rogers, 1962, pp. 57–75). Thus, cultural differences can have a strong influence on the speed with which an innovation penetrates a society. As we go on to discuss the mental process of adoption by an individual, one should keep in mind that collectively it is the characteristics of perspective adopters that define the society.

The last determinant of the diffusion process is, of course, time. It is the one variable that researchers have not been able to confuse with conflicting definitions.

THE ADOPTION PROCESS

Thus far we have discussed factors that determine the degree and rate of diffusion. Now we turn our attention to the mental process that goes on as an individual in a given society ponders the adoption of an innovation. Some of the same factors just discussed, plus a few others, determine the likelihood that the individual will adopt the innovation and contribute one more point on the S-shaped cumulative curve. The adoption process has been conceptualized as a multistage mental and behavioral process leading from awareness of the innovation to interest in it, evaluation of it, trial, and final adoption (Figure 2). This is a

FIGURE 2   Paradigm of the Adoption of an Innovation by an Individual Within a Social System

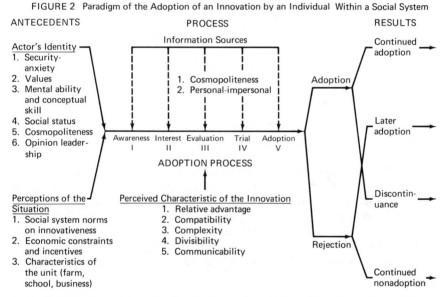

Source: Reprinted with permission of The Macmillan Company from *Diffusion of Innovations* by Everett M. Rogers. © by The Free Press, 1962. p. 306.

hierarchical model, not unlike that advanced by Lavidge and Steiner (1961) in discussing advertising effects (Figure 3). The adoption process model lacks close and consistent ties with current theoretical representations of the cognitive decision processes.

Awareness of an innovation can obviously come about from accidental exposure to it or from a diffusion process involving either word-of-mouth or mass communications. It has already been stated that for most new products, awareness is established by mass communications. At the interest stage in the adoption process the individual perceives indications of attractiveness or usefulness attached to the innovation. At this point, he may be stimulated to seek additional information. If his interest is maintained, he moves on to the evaluation stage where the perceived characteristics of the innovation, or product perceptions, such as relative advantage, compatibility, com-

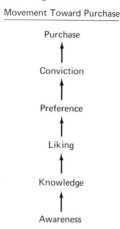

FIGURE 3 The Lavidge and Steiner Hierarchical Model of Advertising Effects

Movement Toward Purchase

Purchase

↑

Conviction

↑

Preference

↑

Liking

↑

Knowledge

↑

Awareness

Source: Reprinted from Robert J. Lavidge and Gary A. Steiner, "A Model for Predictive Measurements of Advertising Effects," *Journal of Marketing,* Vol. 25 (October 1961), p. 59, published by the American Marketing Association.

plexity, divisibility, communicability, and perceived risk, may be used to structure his thinking about the innovation's appeal. Based upon this evaluative process, the individual can arrive at one of two decisions: adoption or rejection. His adoption, however, may not be complete in that he may treat the initial purchase of the product as only a trial, and then subsequently adopt the innovation by registering commitment to it through repurchase if it satisfies his original expectations. On the other hand, the trial period may prove disappointing, bringing on rejection. As time passes, he will have additional opportunities to reevaluate each adoption or rejection decision.

Superimposed on this total adoption process is the informational flow, the perceptions of the situation in terms of social norms and economic factors, and the individual's own identity or characteristics; predispositional factors, socioeconomic and demographic variables.

CHARACTERISTICS OF INNOVATORS

Perhaps the two major areas of investigation in diffusion literature have been the word-of-mouth communication process and characteristics of the innovator. Once again, definitions of "innovator" vary among researchers, but in any case the term refers to an individual who adopts the innovation at a very early stage on the S-shaped cumulative curve. Since it is often found that the innovator initiates word-of-mouth communications as would an opinion leader, or is approached by later adopters for opinion, the establishment of his characteristics in an identifiable sense has been regarded by many researchers as the key to speeding up the diffusion process. Perhaps due in part to conflicting definitions as to what constitutes an innovation, along with a multiplicity of research settings, the same profile for the innovator has not emerged in all studies. For the most part, however, innovators do appear to have certain characteristics, although these characteristics may not function as adequate predictors of behavior. Robertson and Kennedy (1968) applied measures of venturesomeness, social mobility, privilegedness, social integration, concern for status, interest polymorphism, and cosmopolitanism in multiple discriminate analysis for the prediction of adopters and nonadopters of "Touch Tone" telephones. The difference between the means for the two groups was found to be statistically significant (p<.05, "T" test) for the first four variables. The discriminant function correctly classified 75 percent of the sample as innovators or noninnovators.

In terms of socioeconomic status, two recent studies serve as adequate examples of what are generally found to be the characteristics of innovators for relatively costly products or services. Gorman and Moore (1968) found that innovators of color television sets displayed higher family income and other up-scale signs such as relatively high education and occupational status by the husband, high valuation of residence, and ownership of other entertainment appliances. A similar socioeconomic profile was found by Robertson (1967) for "Touch Tone" telephone adopters and by Boone (1970) for adopters of community antenna television system (CATV) service. The same profile was not found, however, for innovators of a new brand of coffee investigated by Frank, Massy, and Morrison (1964), where no distinct profile in terms of socioeconomic variables was evident. The study by Pessemier, Burger, and Tigert (1967) found a relatively low income blue-collar socioeconomic profile for innovators of a new brand of laundry detergent. Given the substantial difference between the innovations studied by Gorman and Moore, (1968) Robertson, (1967) and Boone (1970) relative to those studied by Frank, Massy, and Morrison (1964) and Pessemier, Burger, and Tigert (1967), the conflicting results should come as no surprise. All innovations are not equivalent units.

Market researchers have generally taken 10 percent penetration as an appropriate point of division on the cumulative S-shaped diffusion curve for dividing innovators from noninnovators. However, several studies have used a higher percentage, such as that by King (1964) in which the cutoff was approximately one-third. This lack of consistency in the definition of an innovation dilutes the comparability of results across studies. Rural sociologists have imposed more structure on their thinking by setting up standardized definitions for both innovators and later adopter groups. Figure 4, again from Rogers (1962), indicates the conventions that have been adopted. The normal curve of relative time of adoption has been divided in terms of plus or minus one and two standard deviations. The first 2½ percent of adopters are classified innovators and the next 13½ percent are classified as early adopters. The areas within minus and plus one standard deviation are labeled early majority and late majority respectively. The final last 16 percent are referred to as laggards. These definitions

FIGURE 4   Adopter Categorization on the Basis of Relative Time
of Adoption of Innovations

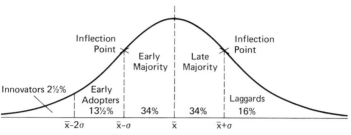

Time of Adoption of Innovations

The innovativeness dimension, as measured by the time at which an individual adopts an innovation or innovations, is continuous. However, this variable may be partitioned into five adopter
categories by laying off standard deviations from the average time of adoption.

Source: Reprinted with permission of The Macmillan Company from *Diffusion of Innovations* by
Everett M. Rogers. © by The Free Press, 1962. p. 162.

do not assume that differences at the cutoff points are necessarily
distinct in terms of anything other than time of adoption. As discussed
by Rogers (1962), certain general differences between adopter groups
in terms of predispositional factors and other measurements have
been found, but not consistently across studies. Because these same
adopter group definitions are not commonly followed in studies conducted in marketing, we will not involve ourselves in a discussion of
profile differences.

Admittedly, if the term "innovator" is applied to only the first 2½
percent of adopters, the researcher is compelled to have a relatively
large sample from a population in order to include enough innovators
to make the entire effort worthwhile. It is perhaps largely for this
reason that cutoff points such as 10 percent are more common in
marketing studies. In any case, it should be recognized that as the
cutoff point is increased, the chances of finding unique characteristics
for innovators are commensurately reduced.

RELATING DIFFUSION THEORY TO BUYER BEHAVIOR THEORY

In Chapter 1, a distinction was made as to levels of problem-solving:
routinized response behavior, limited problem-solving, and extended
problem-solving. Similarly, when considering the adoption of innovations the level of problem-solving that is assumed should be made
clear. Robertson's (1971, p. 7) classification of innovations as to continuous, dynamically continuous, and discontinuous is helpful in this
regard. If the innovation is merely a new brand of coffee (a continuous
innovation), the problem-solving may be little more than routinized
response behavior. If instead the innovation is a new product form
and thus a dynamically continuous innovation, such as perhaps permanent press shirts, limited problem-solving might arise. And finally, if
the innovation represents a new concept, a discontinuous innovation,
extended problem-solving would generally be involved. It must be
emphasized, however, that the three levels of problem-solving and the

three classes of innovations will not always match up as neatly as the above examples suggest. Exceptions will be abundant, but at least the pattern should generally hold.

It is only fair to say that the buyer behavior model applies mainly, although not exclusively, to cases where an established product category concept exists, which is not likely with discontinuous innovations. On the other hand, the accumulated body of diffusion research studies applies primarily, although again not exclusively, to discontinuous innovations. The buyer behavior model can, however, readily be extended to serve as the basis for discussing all classes of innovations, as will be shown.

A further point of distinction should be made between diffusion theory and buyer behavior theory. An important objective in many past diffusion studies has been the identification of causal factors in diffusion so as to predict ultimate levels of diffusion or penetration. This same objective is generally not present in buyer behavior theory, where instead we are attempting to predict the purchase actions of individuals based upon state-of-mind measurements.

There have been efforts made by Kelly (1967a), Fourt and Woodlock (1960), and Barclay (1963) to develop so-called penetration models for predicting ultimate purchase levels. Many of the concepts involved in these attempts have been borrowed from diffusion research literature. Figure 5 is a diagram from Kelly's study, which concerned

FIGURE 5   Hypothetical Configurations of the Penetration, Patronage, and Abort Functions

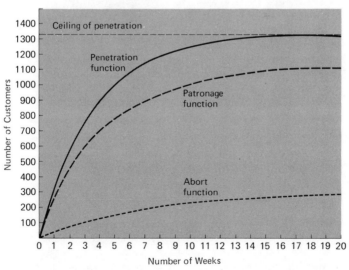

Source: Reprinted from Robert F. Kelly, "Estimating Ultimate Performance Levels of New Retail Outlets," *Journal of Marketing Research,* Vol. 4 (February 1967), p. 14, published by the American Marketing Association.

ultimate patronage levels for new retail stores. Kelly (1967b) also adapted the Rogers adoption process model to derive a patronage decision model for a new retail store (Figure 6).

Source: Reprinted from Robert F. Kelly, "The Role of Information in the Patronage Decision: A Diffusion Phenomenon," p. 121, 1967 June Conference Proceedings, published by the American Marketing Association.

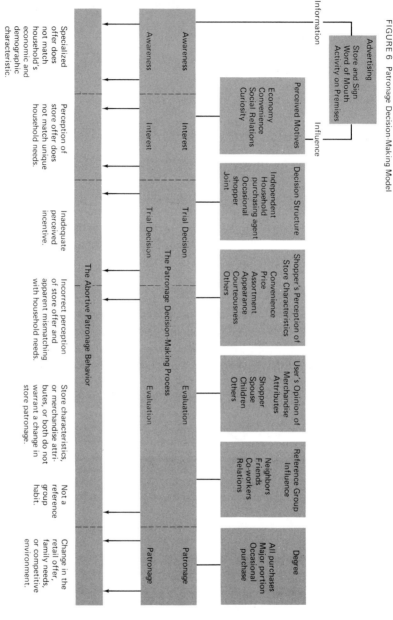

FIGURE 6 Patronage Decision-Making Model

It will indeed be unfortunate if diffusion research literature is treated in isolation from buyer behavior theory, as has been done in the past. For the purposes of advancing buyer behavior research, whether it concerns new products or old, it is of interest to draw upon diffusion research literature for all the knowledge it contains and to tie the two schools of thought together so that the current gap is gradually narrowed. Research efforts are wasted if this gap is perpetuated, thereby causing future researchers to choose between the two areas as to where they will expend their energies, when in fact no choice need be made. The author's bias in this connection is to position diffusion research within what is considered to be a broader and more useful framework of buyer behavior theory. In fact, the fit is rather more comfortable than first expected. The theory of buyer behavior discussed in Chapter 1 is reproduced in Figure 7. Let us begin by considering the adoption process.

The Adoption Process Model

The adoption by an individual of an innovation is a function of:

1. his perceptions of the situation
2. the communication surrounding the prospective adopter
3. perceived characteristics of the innovation
4. the characteristics of the prospective adopter

In relating the adoption process model to buyer behavior theory, let us begin by considering the exogenous variables, that is, the *institutional environment*, the *societal environment*, and *personal characteristics*. Exogenous variables in buyer behavior theory furnish us with a convenient starting point so as to consider an individual thinking and behaving within an environment. Part of the situational environment surrounding the adoption process concerns social system norms on innovativeness, as perceived by the prospective adopter. Such norms would be treated within the *social-organizational setting* construct of the buyer behavior theory. In particular, it has been noted in rural sociology that for an individual going through the adoption process, his traditional versus modern orientation toward methods of farming will determine in part his likelihood of adoption, and that comparable norms held by the surrounding social system will inhibit or encourage his early adoption (Rogers, 1962, pp. 62–72). Literature concerning adoption has considered two aspects of how social or cultural norms affect adoption. First of all, the existing social or cultural norms will affect the likelihood of adoption for prospective adopters, as indicated above. Secondly, providing adoption takes place by at least a venturesome few, the speed and extent in which additional adopters are attracted will depend significantly upon the degree to which the social or cultural norms are perceived as favoring such venturesome behavior. To the degree that such cultural and societal norms affect *motives*, buyer behavior theory adequately addresses the first of these influences. As for the second, that of how social or cultural norms are perceived as favoring or discouraging the adoption of an innovation, once again an important set of causal variables can comfortably be treated within buyer behavior theory. Specifically, such perceptions of social or cultural norms would reflect themselves in the construct *situational attitudes*, both with respect to their content and to their application in evaluating an innovation in a preference sense.

Buyer behavior theory contains much more detail with respect to information processing on the part of an individual than is contained

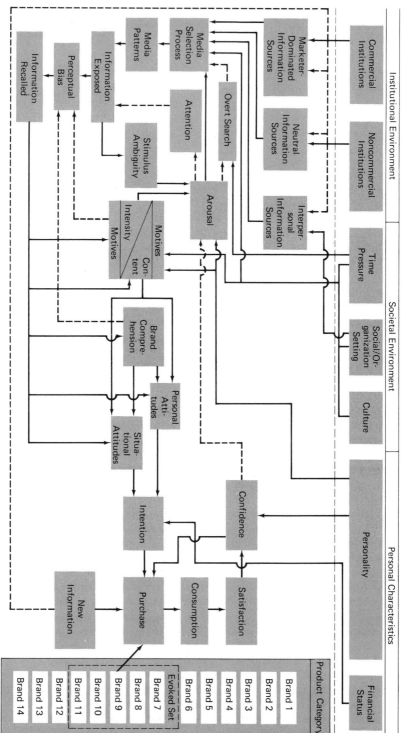

FIGURE 7   Theory of Buyer Behavior

in the adoption process model. Adoption process studies have distinguished between mass media effects, or formal communication, and word-of-mouth, or informal, communication. It has been recognized that the two forms of information play different roles as the diffusion curve is traced. At the foot of the S-shaped diffusion curve, prospective adopters are affected primarily, if not exclusively, by formal communications of some sort even if from a change agent who may not be considered disinterested. Within marketing, the change agent is thus the representative of a *commercial* or *noncommercial institution,* and in the context of buyer behavior theory, would be treated as a *marketer-dominated* or possibly a *neutral information source.* On the other hand, *interpersonal information sources,* or word-of-mouth, arise primarily from the *societal environment,* being a function of the *social-organizational setting.* Rural sociologists have demonstrated that commercial change agents are most influential at the trial stage of the adoption process (Rogers, 1962, p. 263). It is at this point that the prospective adopter looks to the commercial change agent for information on how and why to use the innovation. It is likely that this same conclusion would emerge whenever extensive problem-solving is engaged, regardless of the particular buyer context, so long as a commercial change agent is at all present. A second conclusion drawn by rural sociologists concerning commercial change agents is that their importance is greater for earlier adopters than for later adopters at the trial stage. The reason for this is that as the diffusion of an innovation proceeds, *interpersonal information sources* become relatively more abundant and more influential since their credibility is also perceived as higher than that of commercial change agents. While there is no separate consideration of so-called *neutral information sources* in the adoption process model, it is likely that certain noncommercial change agents, such as county agricultural extension agents in the context of rural sociology, would be perceived by some prospective adopters as relatively neutral. In a broader context, it should be understood that the change agent need not literally be a single individual but can be any flow of formal communication from an institution, commercial or noncommercial, urging the adoption of an innovation.

As the diffusion process unfolds, emulation sets in such that later adopters are adopting largely because of what they see happening around them, namely other people adopting. This becomes the most important form of communication content, whether delivered visually or verbally. In a relative sense, the perceived characteristics of the innovation become less important, and, instead, the perceived characteristics of the first adopters along with communications that emulates from them grow in importance. Thus, in relating the adoption process model to buyer behavior, one must bear in mind that a shift in importance from formal communications (*marketer-dominated information sources*) to informal communications (*interpersonal information sources*) is bound to occur with the passage of time, except possibly for those few innovations that have inconspicuous and/or highly private usage contexts.

With regard to information processing and types of information, the adoption process model does not clearly label the types of information that are injected at each stage. However, perhaps it is not unreasonable to suggest that they should parallel the divisions posited in the buyer behavior model. That is, information that merely describes the innovation, comparable to *brand comprehension*, would enter at the awareness stage. Information that suggests how needs can be satisfied could be thought of as influencing the *content* of *motives*. Connotative information, particularly from *interpersonal information sources* (word-of-mouth), would enter the adoption model at the evaluation stage and, for the buyer behavior model, would be assimilated in the formation of *attitude* dimensions and evaluations.

What does this shift in information sources suggest for *overt search*? Obviously, the first prospective adopters of an innovation can turn almost only to formal communications in order to receive additional information and are thus highly dependent upon its content in reaching a decision on whether or not to adopt. But for later prospective adopters, *overt search* will more likely center on the observation or query of earlier adopters (or rejectors). In that sense, the content of the communication should shift as the diffusion process continues, particularly if the change agent is cognizant of this transition in prospective adopter *overt search* strategy. That is, while early formal communications might tend to be rather substantive in order to aid the first adopters in their deliberations, subsequent communications, particularly after at least half of prospective adopters have joined the fold, might instead emphasize the developing popularity of the innovation, in order to stimulate a bandwagon effect. The primary ingredient missing in the buyer behavior model in order to apply it to the study of diffusion generally is a factor concerned with the legitimating impact of the progressively enlarging adopter group upon remaining prospective adopters. As the innovation permeates a society, its obvious presence legitimates its ownership, and more hesitant or conservative prospective adopters are drawn into the adopter camp. Stated differently, the theory of buyer behavior is missing a mechanism that would explain changes in *information exposed* in such a way as to encompass all forms of stimuli and their shifting emphasis with the passage of time. This mechanism would need to recognize the importance of visual display or evidence of the innovation in use as a part of the *interpersonal information source* construct, even when the exposure was accidental and not the result of *overt search*. At this point, far too little is known about the information processing function to formulate such a mechanism. A far better understanding of the *media selection process* is needed before one can set forth a mechanism governing *information exposed*.

As for the perceived characteristics of the innovation, it is not clear whether generalized dimensions, such as those by Rogers (relative advantage, compatibility, complexity, divisibility, and communicability), are adequate predictors of behavior across a wide variety of product categories or whether more specific dimensions must be employed, each set being specific to a given product category. The results by Ostlund (1972) are encouraging, however, and suggest at a minimum that these dimensions can provide a suitable starting point even if individual items or components in their measurement must be defined with an eye toward relevancy to the product category under consideration.

The Rogers perceived characteristics of an innovation are particularly appealing in a theoretical sense, owing to their conceptual distinctiveness and generality. It should be understood, of course, that each of these dimensions is rather encompassing as to the information it can contain, and thus in an empirical sense might need to be divided into several components in order to adequately describe the adopter's perception of absolute product characteristics. It should be recognized that people's perceptions of a product will influence not only their attitudes or intention toward it, but also their information search and processing functions. To the degree the innovation is difficult to appraise because of perhaps its complexity, one would also expect that messages concerning it would be difficult to appraise thus bringing about *stimulus ambiguity*, or an inability to adequately perceive and comprehend a message. In the event the *stimulus ambiguity* is great, buyers may feel frustrated and suspend further *overt search* toward gaining clarification. At the opposite extreme, if the innovation and messages concerning it are straightforward and readily understood, *stimulus ambiguity* will be low or nonexistent and the need for further *overt search* mitigated. Thus, it is likely that some, if not all, of the perceived product characteristic dimensions would affect mental constructs such as *confidence* and *stimulus ambiguity*, in addition to *personal* and *situational attitudes*. Obviously, in the case of a discontinuous innovation, extended problem-solving would be engaged, which would typically result in *overt search* for additional information in order to cope with the complexity of the innovation along with the *stimulus ambiguity* of messages concerning it. Clearly, this information processing function would be affected by the prospective adopter's level of *confidence* in appraising the given innovation.

How can the product perception dimensions be integrated into the motive-directed cognitive process leading to purchase satisfaction? The product perception dimensions concern primarily connotative or evaluative information and thus are most relevant to the *attitude* constructs. The same product perception dimensions could function either as *personal attitude* or as *situational attitude* dimensions. With the passage of time, the relative importance of these two sets of attitudinal dimensions would generally shift. Early in the diffusion curve, with the innovation being relatively unknown, innovators would be acting primarily out of their own evaluation (*personal attitudes*) of the innovations, not their perceptions of other people's attitudes (*situational attitudes*). However, as the diffusion process continues, adopters would increasingly be acting out of their assessment of other people's attitudes through a process of emulation, and thus *situational attitudes* would become evermore important.

The last set of adoption determinants concerns the prospective adopter's identity or characteristics. Most such variables can readily be accommodated within the *personality* construct of buyer behavior theory. However, certain of the adopter characteristic variables used in rural sociology are not, strictly speaking, psychological characteristics. Rather, they concern the adopter's propensity to engage in social interaction or opinion leadership, or display an interest orientation beyond one's local environment. Such variables reflect not only one's personality but also one's environment, and can be handled instead as the resultant of interaction between *personality* and *social/ organizational setting* variables in the buyer behavior theory. Regardless of what variables are chosen to describe the characteristics of adopters, they should not be employed as isolated predictors of adoption. Instead, they should be thought of as one set, along with the remaining three sets of variables (communication variables, innovation-characteristic variables, and situational variables) that interact to determine the likelihood of adoption.

Having related the determinants of the adoption process model to constructs in buyer behavior theory, let us consider the multistage process itself, which is divided into the following steps: awareness, interest, evaluation, trial, and adoption.

The awareness stage is roughly equivalent to the *information exposed* construct in buyer behavior theory. The feedback of *motives* to *perceptual bias* operates upon *information exposed* to yield a filtered, possibly distorted, view of the given innovation, resulting in *information recalled*. Different types of *information recalled* will in turn affect *motives, brand comprehension,* and *attitudes,* as discussed in Chapter 1. The evaluation stage in the adoptive process model as analogous to what goes on in the *personal attitude* construct, based upon perceived innovation characteristics, or *brand comprehension* data. An explicit recognition of how *personal attitudes* can be overwhelmed by the opinions of others is, however, absent in the adoption process model since no element comparable to *situational attitudes* is posited. The opinions of others must be taken into account in the evaluation stage and the buyer behavior theory does a better job at suggesting how this takes place.

The trial stage in the adoption process model has no direct counterpart in the theory of buyer behavior. Instead trial is handled as the first cycle through the buyer behavior model. In the case of innovations requiring large financial and/or psychological commitment (e.g. buying a color television set), the first purchase represents not trial but adoption since reversing the purchase decision would be difficult without very major costs. On the other hand, where the innovation is relatively inexpensive and/or involves a rather short repurchase cycle, the first purchase would indeed represent a trial and one would not expect a state of true adoption (commitment) to become manifest until repeated purchases of the product had resulted in continued high *satisfaction.* This distinction as to the type of innovation and the resulting problem-solving process affects not only the purchase deliberations but also postdecision cognitive and behavioral processes that arise from the resulting level of *satisfaction.* The theory of buyer behavior is a good deal more detailed in specifying the cognitive processes that immediately surround purchase. The adoption process model contains no counterpart of *intention, new information,* and *evoked set.* *Intention,* if it were added to the adoption process model, would fall between evaluation and trial, and could be a valuable predictor in tying state-of-mind measurements to behavior. Similarly, *new information* would be specified as a definite input prior to the trial stage.

The concept of *evoked set* may or may not be relevant to the adoption process model, depending upon the type of innovation under consideration. Where the innovation represents only a minor departure from existing product forms, a product class concept would presumably be firmly held by the prospective adopter and the innovation would be positioned within that product class concept, thus within the prospective adopter's *evoked set.* On the other hand, if the innovation represents a major or discontinuous shift from past product forms, there may be no convenient existing product class concept, and thus the *evoked set* would contain only one product, namely, the innovation under consideration.

The adoption process model eventually carries us to the final stage where adoption or rejection takes place. Additional cycles through the adoption process model are assumed, and regardless of the original outcome, continued use or nonuse of the innovation can result. However, while the adoption process model is continuous over time, it does not explicitly treat two important postpurchase constructs: *satisfaction* and *confidence.* Without these constructs there is no tie between postdecision processes and the information processing functions, including the generation of word-of-mouth communications by the adopter. Because the flow of interpersonal communications is important to the diffusion process model, these omissions in the adoption process model make it awkward to tie the adoption of an innovation by an individual and the ensuing communication to the impact of such word-of-mouth on subsequent prospective adopters.

The greater detail given to the cognitive processes within the theory of buyer behavior makes it superior to the adoption process model for both generating testable hypotheses and relating states-of-mind to behavior. However, the adoption model itself represents only part of the research that is contained within diffusion literature. We must next focus our attention on the diffusion process model: an aggregation of separate adoption processes by individuals over time.

The Diffusion Process Model

As was stated earlier, the four basic elements of the diffusion process model are:

1. characteristics of the innovation
2. the total communications process concerning the innovation
3. the characteristics of the social system
4. the passage of time

The first three elements are meant to be descriptive of aggregative phenomena and, as contrasted to the adoption process model, do not focus on an individual adopter. With the interaction of these four basic elements, the diffusion of an innovation takes place and the cumulative S-shaped diffusion curve is generated. It is this aggregative dynamic aspect of the diffusion model that is missing from the theory of buyer behavior, since the latter places emphasis upon the cognitive and behavioral process of individuals in a manner analogous to the adoption process model.

How could the buyer behavior model be employed in the study of an aggregative phenomenon such as diffusion? Bear in mind that a customary objective in diffusion research is to arrive at predictions of the maximum diffusion or penetration for a given innovation and rates of adoption, relative to time, at preselected intervals. In marketing terms, we want to predict the maximum eventual sales level, and so as to derive the shape of the sales (S-shaped) curve, we also want to estimate sales rates (per unit of time) at selected points in the future. In order to accomplish this, first, we must have aggregative measures of how buyers in a given target market (our defined population segment) evaluate the characteristics of the innovation. Second, we need aggregative measures of the volume and character of the communication process concerning the innovation. That is, how many people are talking about the innovation, and what proportion of the conversations are generally favorable to the further diffusion. Third, in aggregative terms, we need some measures of what our selected social system, or target market, is like as to those norms and values that may affect further diffusion. Fourth, we must record all measures according to time so as to "date the variables," since merely the passage of time will determine in part the degree of diffusion.

Returning to buyer behavior theory, how can it provide the four sets of determinants just discussed? In discussing the adoption process model, it was suggested that the dimensions of relative advantage, compatibility, complexity, communicability, and divisibility by Rogers can serve as *personal* and *situational attitude* dimensions at the disaggregate level. Now this argument is taken a step beyond to suggest that these dimensions can also be employed to compile aggregative data concerning perceptions of the innovation. For example, an index can readily be formed for relative advantage across a sample of respondents drawn from the target market. Once such indexes exist for all five product perception dimensions, there remains only to relate these measures to benchmark scores in order to judge the degree to which the aggregative product perception dimensions will contribute to a given diffusion level. The benchmark scores would be derived from all prior applications of the same dimensions to innovations evaluated by samples drawn from the same target market. Computationally, this could be accomplished through the use of a multiple regression equation where the coefficient for each product perception dimension used as a predictor variable was obtained from the prior applications of the dimensions on innovations evaluated by respondents of the given target market, with corresponding sales data.

Aggregative measures of the communication volume and character would need to be developed in an analogous manner. However, as discussed in Chapter 1, operational measures for *interpersonal informa-tion sources* are difficult to design. Recall measures, although imperfect, have been used commonly in diffusion studies within both rural sociology and some buyer behavior studies. Once again, any such communication measures would need to be related to benchmarks derived from prior studies before prediction of the ultimate diffusion level and adoption rates would be possible.

The characteristics of the social system, or the *social-organizational setting*, would be relatively easy to assess since scales such as tradi-tional-modern orientation have been in use for some time. Aggregative scores from a sample of target market respondents would again be related to benchmark scores in estimating the contribution of *social-organizational setting* variables to the prediction of ultimate diffusion levels and adoption rates.

The last prime determinant of the degree and extent of diffusion is that of time, a variable not specifically recognized in the buyer behavior theory although its testing has been done with panel data so as to "date the variables" and thus deal empirically with the theory as a dynamic system. A similar approach could be taken to study a diffu-sion process. Second, time can be included as a separate predictor variable, as is often done in economic forecasting.

CONCLUSIONS

A very brief overview of the vast body of diffusion research literature has been presented. While only a small portion of the work was con-ducted within the marketing setting, the interest in diffusion research among students of marketing is gaining momentum and can be ex-pected to provide valuable insights for new product marketing in the future.

It is important that this literature not be left in isolation, apart from efforts to formulate and test buyer behavior theories. Obviously both schools of thought focus on highly similar mental processes. It is with this consideration in mind that an attempt was made to relate the elements of the adoption process model and the diffusion process model to buyer behavior theory. It is the author's contention that both the adoption and diffusion process can and should be studied within the framework of a comprehensive cognitive framework so as, both to provide anchoring points for empirical work and to generate a larger number of testable hypotheses. Nothing in what has been stated should be taken as demeaning the work of diffusion research-ers. It is perhaps somewhat presumptuous to position a large and long standing body of research within a newer and less tested theoretical framework. Nevertheless, it is felt that the adoption and diffusion models are rather limiting, particularly as concerns information processing and other perceptual processes. This deficiency can and should be corrected by their integration into a broader cognitive theoretic model. On the other hand, buyer behavior can benefit con-siderably from past diffusion research. In particular, the product perception dimensions, namely, relative advantage, compatibility, complexity, communicability, and divisibility, appear very appropriate for use as attitudinal dimensions and, at the same time, could hopefully shed some explanatory light on the distortions that occur in the information processing functions.

REFERENCES

ARNDT, JOHAN. "Role of Product-Related Conversation in the Diffusion of a New Product." *Journal of Marketing Research*, Vol. 4 (August 1967), 291–295.

BARCLAY, WILLIAM P. "Probability Model for Early Prediction of New Product Market Success." *Journal of Marketing*, Vol. 27 (January 1963), 63–68.

BAUER, RAYMOND A. "Consumer Behavior as Risk Taking." In *Dynamic Marketing for a Changing World*, edited by Robert S. Hancock, pp. 389–398. Chicago: Proceedings of the 43rd Conference of the American Marketing Association.

BOONE, LOUIS E. "The Search for the Consumer Innovator." *Journal of Business*, Vol. 43 (1970), 135–140.

FOURT, LEWIS A. AND JOSEPH W. WOODLOCK. "Early Prediction of Market Success for New Grocery Products." *Journal of Marketing*, Vol. 25 (October 1960), 31–38.

FRANK, RONALD E., WILLIAM F. MASSY, AND DONALD G. MORRISON. "The Determinants of Innovative Behavior with Respect to a Branded, Frequently Purchased Food Product." In *Reflections on Progress in Marketing*, edited by L. George Smith, pp. 312–323. Chicago: Proceedings of the 1964 Winter Conference of the American Marketing Association.

GORMAN, WALTER P., III AND CHARLES T. MOORE. "The Early Diffusion of Color Television Receivers into a Fringe Area Market." *Journal of Retailing*, Vol. 44 (Fall 1968), 46–56.

KATZ, ELIHU AND PAUL F. LAZARSFELD. *Personal Influence: The Part Played by People in the Flow of Mass Communications.* Glencoe, Ill.: Free Press, 1955.

KELLY, ROBERT F. "Estimating Ultimate Performance Levels of New Retail Outlets." *Journal of Marketing Research*, Vol. 4 (February 1967a), 3–19.

————. "The Role of Information in the Patronage Decision: A Diffusion Phenomenon." In *Marketing For Tomorrow . . . Today*, edited by M. S. Moyer and R. E. Vosburgh, pp. 119–129. Chicago: Proceedings of the American Marketing Association, 1967.

KING, CHARLES W. "The Innovator in the Fashion Adoption Process." In *Reflections on Progress in Marketing*, edited by L. George Smith, pp. 324, 339. Chicago: Proceedings of the 1964 Winter Conference of the American Marketing Association.

KIVLIN, JOSEPH E. "Characteristics of Farm Practices Associated with Rate of Adoption." Unpublished Ph.D. dissertation, Pennsylvania State University, 1960.

KROEBER, A. L. "Diffusionism." In *Encyclopedia of the Social Sciences*, edited by G. Elliot Smith. New York: Norton, 1927.

LAVIDGE, ROBERT J. AND GARY A. STEINER. "A Model for Predictive Measurements of Advertising Effects." *Journal of Marketing*, Vol. 25 (October 1961), 59–62.

LAZARSFELD, PAUL F., BERNARD BERELSON, AND HAZEL GAUDET. *The People's Choice.* 2d rev. ed. New York: Columbia University Press, 1948.

LAZER, WILLIAM AND WILLIAM BELL. "The Communication Process and Innovation." *Journal of Advertising Research,* Vol. 6 (September 1966), 2–7.

LIONBERGER, HERBERT F. *Low-Income Farmers in Missouri: Their Contacts with Potential Sources of Farm and Home Information.* Columbia, Mo.: Experiment Station Research Bulletin 441, 1949.

_____. *Sources and Use of Farm and Home Information by Low-Income Farmers in Missouri.* Columbia, Mo.: Agricultural Experiment Station Research Bulletin 472, 1951.

_____. "The Diffusion of Farm and Home Information as an Area of Sociological Research." *Rural Sociology,* Vol. 17 (1952), 132–140.

_____. "Some Characteristics of Farm Operators Sought as Sources of Farm Information in a Missouri Community." *Rural Sociology,* Vol. 18 (1953), 327–338.

_____. *Information Seeking Habits and Characteristics of Farm Operators,* Columbia, Mo.: Agricultural Experiment Station Bulletin 581, 1955.

_____. "Community Prestige and Choice of Sources of Farm Information." *Public Opinion Quarterly,* Vol. 23 (1959), 111–118.

_____. *Adoption of New Ideas and Practices: A Summary of the Research Dealing with the Acceptance of Technological Change in Agriculture, with Implications for Action in Facilitating Social Change,* Ames, Iowa: State University Press, 1960.

MARCUS, ALAN S. AND RAYMOND A. BAUER. "Yes: There Are Generalized Opinion Leaders." *Public Opinion Quarterly,* Vol. 28 (Winter 1964), 628–632.

OSTLUND, LYMAN E. "The Role of Product Perceptions in Innovative Behavior." In *Marketing Involvement in Society and the Economy,* edited by Philip R. McDonald, pp. 259–266. Chicago: Proceedings of the 1969 Fall Conference of the American Marketing Association.

_____. "Identifying Early Buyers." *Journal of Advertising Research,* Vol. 12 (April 1972).

PESSEMIER, EDGAR A., PHILLIP BURGER, AND DOUGLAS TIGERT. "Can New Product Buyers Be Identified?" *Journal of Marketing Research,* Vol. 4 (November 1967), 349–354.

ROBERTSON, THOMAS S. "Determinants of Innovative Behavior." *Proceedings of the 1967 Educators' Conference.* Chicago: American Marketing Association, pp. 328–332.

_____ AND JAMES N. KENNEDY. "Prediction of Consumer Innovators: Application of Multiple Discriminant Analysis." *Journal of Marketing Research,* Vol. 5 (February 1968), 64–69.

_____. *Innovative Behavior and Communication.* New York: Holt, Rinehart and Winston, 1971.

ROGERS, EVERETT M. *Diffusion of Innovations,* New York: Free Press, 1962.

_____ AND J. DAVID STANFIELD. "Adoption and Diffusion of New Products: Emerging Generalizations and Hypotheses. In *Applications of the Sciences in Marketing Management,* edited by Frank Bass, Charles King, and Edgar Pessemier, pp. 227–250. New York: Wiley, 1968.

RYAN, BRYCE AND NEAL C. GROSS. "The Diffusion of Hybrid Seed Corn in Two Iowa Communities." *Rural Sociology,* Vol. 8 (1943), 15–24.

SILK, ALVIN J. "Overlap Among Self-Designated Opinion Leaders: A Study of Selected Dental Products and Services." *Journal of Marketing Research,* Vol. 3 (August 1966), 255–259.

_____ AND DAVID B. MONTGOMERY. "Patterns of Overlap in Opinion Leadership and Interest for Selected Categories of Purchasing Activity." In *Marketing Involvement in Society and the Economy,* edited by Philip R. McDonald, pp. 377–386. Chicago: Proceedings of the 1969 Fall Conference of the American Marketing Association.

43. Prediction of consumer innovators: application of multiple discriminant analysis

thomas s. robertson & james n. kennedy

INTRODUCTION

The successful diffusion of new products depends on an understanding of the consumer innovator. This article reports on using multiple discriminant analysis to predict innovators and to assess the importance of several innovator characteristics.

Two multiple discriminant equations are generated. The first, a short-cut method permitting manual calculation, is based on the assumption that the variables studied are independent. The second requires a computer but considers whatever interdependence is present.

The findings here are based on an empirical inquiry into the adoption of a new small home appliance product. The characteristics studied came from literature on new product diffusion from various academic disciplines.

INNOVATOR CHARACTERISTICS

The characteristics of consumer innovators are illdefined. Although some 800 studies on the diffusion of new ideas and practices have been reported in sociology, direct application of these findings to the marketing on consumer products is questionable.

As defined in sociology, innovators are the first 2.5 percent of the community's potential adopters to purchase. In marketing, a 10 percent figure has gained some recognition. An innovation is loosely defined as any product that consumers perceive to be new. Adoption or innovative behavior is the process of accepting and purchasing the innovation. Diffusion means the spread of the item from the manufacturer to ultimate users.

A model of innovator characteristics follows. This model is based on

Reprinted by permission from *Journal of Marketing Research*, Vol. 5 (February 1968), pp. 64–69, published by the American Marketing Association.

Thomas S. Robertson is assistant professor of business administration, University of California, Los Angeles. James N. Kennedy is general supervisor of statistics, Illinois Bell Telephone Company. The research for this article was supported by the Illinois Bell and Michigan Bell Telephone Companies and the Bureau of Business and Economic Research, UCLA. Prof. Douglas J. Dalrymple and Daniel Greeno of UCLA, C. T. Smith and E. N. Asmann, business research administrators of A. T. & T. and Illinois Bell Telephone Company, respectively, gave helpful criticism.

agricultural findings summarized by Everett M. Rogers [18], on a major research effort tracing a new drug's diffusion in the medical community [6], and on four innovative behavior studies in the marketing discipline [1, 4, 10, 16]. The characteristics selected are not exhaustive but are of most general importance in previous research.

Venturesomeness

Rogers uses venturesomeness as a summary concept to characterize agricultural innovators.

> "The major value of the innovator is venturesomeness. He must desire the hazardous, the rash, the daring, and the risking" [18, p. 169].

Venturesomeness is operationally defined in this study as willingness to take risks in the purchase of new products. Risk-taking by consumers has been investigated in several recent marketing studies [3, 8].

Social Mobility

The Tastemaker studies by Opinion Research Corporation conclude that innovators are the mobiles in society [1]. Social mobility means movement on the social status hierarchy. Here, upward social mobility is measured and defined by prior and anticipated movement on the social class ladder.

Privilegedness

Income level frequently has correlated with innovative behavior [4, 19]. Privilegedness is financial standing *relative* to other community members. Richard P. Coleman applied the privilegedness concept to the compact car and color television markets and found, for example, that color television innovators were overprivileged members of each social class [7].

Social Integration

Social integration is defined as the person's degree of participation with other community members. This variable has been important in the agricultural studies and the medical diffusion study [18, 6], but it has not been directly tested in the consumer goods' area.

Interest Range

Katz and Lazarsfeld found degree of interest in a consumption area to be "strongly related" to opinion leadership [14]. A common assumption has been that innovators are more interested in the consumption area in which they innovate [22]. The Tastemaker studies further suggest that innovators may be committed to a wider range of interests or values than non-innovators [1]. The hypothesis of interest range will be studied here.

Status Concern

Status concern is the person's need to be noticed and admired. The variable is not explicitly derived from diffusion research but from Veblen's treatise on conspicuous consumption [20]. The conspicuousness of innovations and the resulting attention may prompt innovative behavior. Air-conditioners, for example, were a highly conspicuous item and this affected their pattern of diffusion in the Philadelphia neighborhood studied by Whyte [21]. Bourne, on reference group influence, cites the product's conspicuousness as perhaps the main attribute in whether purchase will be susceptible to reference group effect [5].

Cosmopolitanism

How oriented the person is beyond his community is referred to as cosmopolitanism. Findings from the agricultural and medical studies emphasize that innovators have cosmopolitan outlooks. The physician innovator, for example, subscribed to more medical journals, attended more out-of-town professional meetings, and visited more out-of-town medical institutions and teaching hospitals [13].

Hypotheses

Innovators will have distinguishing characteristics from non-innovators. The formulation and direction of each hypothesis is based on previous research findings. Innovators will be:

1. more venturesome in their consumption behavior than non-innovators,
2. more socially mobile,
3. relatively more financially privileged,
4. more socially integrated,
5. interested in a wider range of consumption areas,
6. more status concerned,
7. more cosmopolitan in outlook.

RESEARCH DESIGN

Research was done in one reasonably well defined social system, the middle class suburban community of Deerfield, Illinois. Innovators were operationally defined as the first ten percent of the community's members to adopt the small home appliance innovation under investigation. Penetration of this product in the community was 11 percent at the time of the study, one year after the product's introduction. Non-innovators were those who did not purchase the product.

The sample had 60 innovators and 40 non-innovators. This breakdown was preferred to allow more opportunity to trace the flow of information that innovators used. Innovators were chosen systematically from the community's geographic areas where the product's penetration was greatest. The sampling procedure selected every other household owning the innovation for inclusion in the sample. By a random number procedure, non-innovators were selected from each block on which an innovator was chosen. Thus it was hoped that certain demographic variables would be controlled for the innovator and non-innovator subsamples.

A telephone street-address directory was used in sample selection and interviews were arranged by telephone. Under these controlled procedures, response rate was about 80 percent. The only known biases are the exclusion of unlisted telephone number households, no telephone households, and some working wife households.

In-home personal interviews, lasting about 90 minutes each, were done by professional interviewers. The female head of household was the spokesman for each family consumption unit because she represented the family's opinions best and she was more open to depth interviewing.

Table 1 gives the questionnaire items measuring venturesomeness

TABLE 1   Examples of Questionnaire Items

Characteristic	Measurement components	Questionnaire items
Venture-someness	Attitude toward innovative behavior	How do you feel about buying new things that come out for the home?
	Actual adoptions of home appliances	Which of the following items do you have for your home?
	Willingness to buy hypothetical innovations	How willing would you be to buy the following items immediately after they come on the market?
	Self-perception on represented innovator characteristics	In regard to new products on the market, I am: (last-first . . . leader-follower, etc.)
Social mobility	Continuity or change in friendship patterns	What about *your* friends and the friends that *you and your husband* have together. Where do you know them from? How long have you known them?
	Neighborhood mobility patterns	What do you dislike about your neighborhood? If you move, what kind of neighborhood would you like to move to? Why?
	Occupational mobility	What is your husband's occupation? What position did your husband hold before this one?
	Locational mobility	How long have you lived at this address? How often have you moved within the last five years?
	Organizational mobility	How often do you give up one organization and join another?

and social mobility characteristics. For example, the venturesomeness characteristic is assessed by four measurement components. The answers to these components can all be arranged on seven-point scales from highly venturesome to highly non-venturesome. The mean of the several components gives an overall venturesomeness score for the person. The same procedure was followed for the remaining variables.

Four coders handled the coding of the open-ended material. Over 90 percent consistency was obtained using guidelines set by the head researcher.

LINEAR DISCRIMINANT FUNCTION

The objective of the multiple discriminant analysis is to produce a linear function that will distinguish innovators from non-innovators. Weights are assigned to the variables such that the ratio of the difference between the means of the two groups to the standard deviation within groups is maximized. The discrete nature of the dependent variable suggests discriminant analysis rather than regression analysis, which has as an assumption that the dependent variable is a random variate.

The linear discriminant function can be expressed as [9]:

1. $$Z = w_1 x_1 + w_2 x_2 \ldots + w_n x_n.$$

Here, $x_1 \ldots x_n$ represent the independent variables while $w_1 \ldots w_n$ represent the discriminant coefficients, or *weights*, to be applied to the independent variables. Z will be called the person's point score. Based on the point score, it should be possible to predict innovators and non-innovators.

Discriminant analysis also allows the researcher to determine the relative importance of the independent variables. The importance value, proposed by Mosteller and Wallace [17], measures the contribution of each variable to the difference in the average point scores between the two groups $(\bar{Z}_I - \bar{Z}_N)$.

Given that one mean value is exactly at the average of the innovator group and another at the average of the non-innovator group, then the difference in score is a measure of the importance $[Y_i]$ of the variables, indicating the contribution it makes to the total difference in innovator versus non-innovator point scores.

2. $$Y_i = w_i \bar{x}_{i_I} - w_i \bar{x}_{i_N} = w_i (\bar{x}_{i_I} - \bar{x}_{i_N}).$$

Here, w_i is the discriminant weight for the variable under consideration while x_{i_I} is the mean score of the innovator sample for this variable and x_{i_N} is the mean score of the non-innovator sample. The discriminant weight may be determined manually if the covariance of the variables involved is assumed to be zero. Otherwise, the computations should be made using a regression analysis or discriminant analysis program.

Thus, if independence of the variables is assumed, the weights may be computed directly from the relationship:

3. $$w_i = (\bar{x}_{i_I} - \bar{x}_{i_N}) / (\sigma^2_{i_I} + \sigma^2_{i_N})$$

where $\bar{x}_{i_I}$ is the average for the *ith* characteristic in the innovator sample and $\bar{x}_{i_N}$ is the average in the non-innovator sample. The respective variances of the *ith* characteristic are represented by $\sigma^2_{i_I}$ and $\sigma^2_{i_N}$ [17].

Significance of the point-score distributions is tested using the difference between the average point scores for innovators and non-innovators.

4. $$D = \bar{Z}_I - \bar{Z}_N$$

Using this value and the appropriate degrees of freedom, the various significance tests can be approximated [12, p. 379].

APPLICATION

Manual Technique

The first step in the analysis was to compute discriminant weights using (3), assuming zero covariance among the variables. The objective was to quickly identify the important variables and to provide guidelines for the final computer analysis.

Mean scores and manually computed weights for innovators and non-innovators are summarized in Table 2. Means are based on a

TABLE 2   Mean Values of Characteristics, Discriminant Weights, and Importance Values[a]

Characteristic	Innovator mean (N=60)	Non-Innovator mean (N=40)	Manual computations	
			Weight	Importance
Venturesomeness[b]	4.88	4.12	3.59	2.73
Social mobility[b]	3.93	3.20	2.02	1.47
Privilegedness[c]	3.68	3.25	1.77	0.76
Social integration[c]	4.13	3.78	1.97	0.69
Status concern	2.00	1.73	1.72	0.46
Interest range	5.27	5.00	1.25	0.34
Cosmopolitanism	2.77	3.03	−1.41	0.37
Unweighted total	26.66	24.11	Difference	6.82

[a] Mean values based on a seven-point scale except status concern where a three-point scale was used.
[b] Difference between means significant at p < .01 (t test).
[c] Difference between means significant at p < .05 (t test).

maximum possible score of 7, except for the status concern variable, where the maximum possible score is 3. Differences in mean scores from variable to variable may be comparable; yet, as will be seen, the importance values resulting can vary significantly as a function of the variances.

The discriminant function is designed to give high point scores (Z values) to the innovator group and to give low point scores to the non-innovator group. These Z values represent the combination of weighted characteristics for each person. It is possible to set a cutoff point so that the cost effects of misclassifying innovators and non-innovators are minimized. This cutoff point can then be used to predict innovators and non-innovators from other samples. The model's functioning, therefore, gives maximum significant difference between the means of the two groups by assigning optimum weights to the independent variables.

Based on the manually derived discriminant function and optimum cutoff points, 82 percent of the innovator group and 63 percent of the non-innovator group could be correctly classified. This discriminant function also gave importance values for the several variables, which indicated that venturesomeness and social mobility together accounted for about 62 percent of the point score difference between innovators and non-innovators.

The manually derived discriminant function, therefore, proved useful for gaining insight concerning the data. Its value is that of an approximating device. It is also helpful in evaluating the effects of various methods of coding and parameterizing the variables.

Computer Technique

The input data for the computer analysis was respondent scores on the seven characteristics (independent variables) and a dummy dependent variable. The dependent variable was assigned values of (100) $(n_2)/(n_1+n_2)$ for innovators and (100) $(-n_1)/(n_1+n_2)$ for non-innovators. A regression analysis program was then used to generate discriminant function weights (actually regression coefficients), the coefficient of multiple correlation, and a test of significance (F test). The covariance among the variables was, of course, considered. Discriminant function weights and importance values are in Table 3. Each

TABLE 3 Discriminant Weights and Importance Values by Computer

Characteristic	Weight	Importance	Relative importance
Venturesomeness	3.59	2.73	35%
Social mobility	3.08	2.25	29
Privilegedness	2.04	0.88	11
Social integration	2.44	0.85	11
Status concern	0.95	0.26	3
Interest range	0.59	0.16	2
Cosmopolitanism	−2.86	0.74	9
Total		7.87	100%

importance value is also transformed into its relative importance compared with the other variables.

Venturesomeness makes the greatest contribution in discriminating between the two groups. Its importance value, 2.73, may be interpreted as the contribution this variable makes toward overall innovative behavior, or, more strictly, the contribution toward the overall difference between the average point scores of innovators and non-innovators. Its relative value is 35 percent.

The social mobility characteristic with an importance score of 2.25 accounts for 29 percent of the point score difference between innovators and non-innovators, while privilegedness and social integration each have relative contribution values of 11 percent. Status concern and interest range account for only 3 percent and 2 percent, respectively, of the difference between innovator and non-innovator point scores, and are of minor importance here.

Cosmopolitanism, finally, has a negative weight with an importance value of .74. This value can be interpreted as a positive localism score and accounts for 9 percent of the difference between group point scores. A high cosmopolitanism score reduces the likelihood of innovative behavior.

The Z score distributions are in Table 4. The cutoff point that mini-

TABLE 4   Point Score Distributions

Point score range	Innovators		Non-Innovators		Density ratio P_I/P_N
	Percent P_I	Cumulative	Percent P_N	Cumulative	
57.6–60.0	1.7				∞
55.1–57.5	5.0	6.7			∞
52.6–55.0	8.4	15.1			∞
50.1–52.5	11.7	26.8	7.5		1.56
47.6–50.0	18.3	45.1	5.0	12.5	3.66
45.1–47.5	23.3	68.4	20.0	32.5	1.17
42.6–45.0	18.3	86.7	17.5	50.0	1.05
40.1–42.5	10.0	96.7	7.5	57.5	1.33
		a			
37.6–40.0	0.0	96.7	20.0	77.5	0.00
35.1–37.5	3.3	100.0	7.5	85.0	0.44
32.6–35.0			7.5	92.5	0.00
30.1–32.5			5.0	97.5	0.00
27.6–30.0			0.0	97.5	0.00
25.1–27.5			2.5	100.0	0.00

a Cutoff score that minimizes misclassification cost if the population contains 10 percent Innovators and the ratio of costs, C_c/C_{LP} is .10.

mizes cost effects of misclassification is dependent on: (a) the proportion of innovators and non-innovators in the population and (b) the cost of misclassifying a member of either group. The two misclassification costs may be considered as: (1) the loss of profit from not selling an appliance to an innovator and (2) the cost involved in canvassing a nonbuyer. Members of a population are classified as innovators if the following relationship is satisfied [2]:

5. $$p_{I(Z)}/p_{N(Z)} \geqslant (C_c/C_{LP})(q_N/q_I).$$

The values $p_{I(Z)}$ and $p_{N(Z)}$ are the percentages of innovators and non-innovators in the sample with point score Z. The frequency or *density ratios*, $p_{I(Z)}/p_{N(Z)}$, are in the last column, Table 4, for each of the groupings. The proportion of innovators and non-innovators are represented by q_I and q_N, respectively; the canvassing and loss-of-profit costs are C_c and C_{LP}.

For example, if the ratio of canvassing cost to loss-of-profit is .10, and ten percent of the population are innovators, the value for the right-hand side of (6) is .90. The ratios, computed in Table 4, exceed this value in the class intervals for point scores above 40. The estimated cutoff that minimizes the cost of misclassification is, therefore, 40. That is, if the point score of a particular respondent is above 40, he would be called an innovator and canvassed; if his score is 40 or below, he would be called a non-innovator and not canvassed. This strategy minimizes the cost effects of misclassification for the sample estimates.

The cutoff point that minimizes the number of respondents misclassified in the sample can also be determined by (6). Here, the cost effects are considered to be equal, and the ratio C_c/C_{LP} is, therefore, 1. Since the sample has 60 innovators and 40 non-innovators, the ratio of q_N/q_I is assumed to be .67. The optimum cutoff point, minimizing misclassification in the sample is also 40 since the ratios for point scores above 40 in Table 4 exceed .67.

It can also be seen that the density ratios do not decrease steadily, as might be expected, because of the relatively small sample number of innovators and non-innovators.

The significance of the discriminant function was evaluated by an F test [15]. The F value obtained, 2.767, suggests that the discriminant function could discriminate between innovators and non-innovators ($P<.05$). The multiple correlation coefficient was .417.

The task of validation is not yet finished, however. As shown by Frank, Massy, and Morrison [11] and by Mosteller and Wallace [17], bias can occur in multiple discriminant analysis if the discriminant function is applied to the same sample data used to estimate the function.

> "The primary cause of this bias is due to errors of sampling when estimating the means of the population, upon which the discriminant coefficients are based" [11, p. 252].

A further possible source of bias is search bias which enters when a researcher seeks the best predictive variables. This bias is of no significance in this study because all hypothesized variables were used in the discriminant function.

The method for validation consists of splitting the sample data and using one-half the data to derive the discriminant function and then applying this function to the remaining data [11]. This procedure can help isolate the effect of sampling errors by the decrease in discriminant power from the analysis subsample to the applied subsample.

Here, two validation runs were made. Data were divided into two series—odd and even. A linear discriminant function was computed for each series and applied against the analysis series and the applied series. Thus four combinations emerge: odd-odd, odd-even, even-even, and even-odd.

Results (Table 5) show a drop in the percentage of correct classifications when the discriminant function is applied to new data. This is caused by sampling variation in the original computation of the weights. The F tests were not significant because of reduced sample sizes. Overall results based on the discriminant function should be regarded as tentative rather than conclusive. There is evidence that predictive ability was improved. Each percentage improvement can potentially translate into an increase in sales volume.

DISCUSSION

Review of the innovative behavior literature from several disciplines suggested probable characteristics of consumer innovators. These characteristics were measured for consumer innovators and non-innovators, and discriminant analysis was applied to test the value of the composite of characteristics for predictive purposes and the discriminating value of each characteristic.

Results of manual and computer techniques did not differ greatly, despite the assumption of zero-covariance in the manual method. The manual method is a good approximating device and at an early stage in a research project can be used to test the value of the hypotheses in discriminating ability.

For the present set of findings, it appears that two variables, venturesomeness (willingness to take new product risks) and social mobility (movement up the social class hierarchy) account for most of the innovative behavior difference between innovators and non-innovators of new home appliances. The astute marketer of such product innovations would seem to have his best chance for initial sales success with an appeal to venturesome, socially mobile people.

Characteristics also important are social integration (degree of participation with others), privilegedness (financial standing relative to other community members), and cosmopolitanism (orientation beyond the local community), the only negatively related variable. The status concern and interest range variables are of minor importance here. The marketing program for an appliance innovation should perhaps further emphasize the socially integrated, privileged, and non-cosmopolitan characteristics of innovators.

The present set of findings about adoption of new home appliances suggests, therefore, promotional and market segmentation strategies. Achieving initial market penetration would seem to depend on appeals to the characteristics of importance. A revised marketing strategy would be needed after the innovator penetration level was secured in order to appeal directly to the characteristics of non-innovators. In fact, varying promotional appeals might be appropriate throughout the buildup of market share.

TABLE 5 Results of Validation Tests

Percentage correctly classified	Total	Even data		Odd data	
		Even-even	Even-odd	Odd-odd	Odd-even
Innovators (N=60)	96.7%	83.3%	76.7%	100.0%	93.4%
Non-innovators (N=40)	42.5	65.0	60.0	45.0	30.0
Total (N=100)	75.0	76.0	70.0	78.0	68.0
F value	2.767	1.004		0.928	
Multiple correlation coefficient	.417	.379		.366	

REFERENCES

1. *America's Tastemakers,* Research Reports Nos. 1 and 2, Princeton, N.J.: Opinion Research Corporation, 1959.
2. ANDERSON, T. W., *An Introduction to Multivariate Statistical Analysis,* New York: John Wiley & Sons, Inc., 1958, 130–1.
3. BAUER, RAYMOND A., "Consumer Behavior as Risk Taking," in Robert S. Hancock, ed., *Proceedings of the American Marketing Association,* Chicago, June 1960, 389–98.
4. BELL, WILLIAM E., "Consumer Innovators: A Unique Market for New-ness," in Stephen A. Greyser, ed., *Proceedings of the Winter Conference of the American Marketing Association,* Chicago, 1963, 85–95.
5. BOURNE, FRANCIS S., "Group Influence in Marketing and Public Relations," in Rensis Likert and Samuel P. Hayes, Jr., eds., *Some Applications of Behavioral Science Research,* Paris: UNESCO, 1957, 217–24.
6. COLEMAN, JAMES S., ELIHU KATZ, AND HERBERT MENZEL, *Medical Innovation: A Diffusion Study,* Indianapolis: The Bobbs-Merrill Company, 1966.
7. COLEMAN, RICHARD P., "The Significance of Social Stratification in Sell-ing," in Martin L. Bell, ed., *Proceedings of the 43rd National Conference of the American Marketing Association,* Chicago, December 1960, 171–84.
8. CUNNINGHAM, SCOTT M., "Perceived Risk as a Factor in the Diffusion of New Product Information," in Raymond M. Haas, ed., *1966 Fall Proceedings of the American Marketing Association,* Chicago, 1966, 698–721.
9. FISHER, RONALD A., *Statistical Methods for Research Workers,* London: Oliver and Boyd, 1958, 285–9.
10. FRANK, RONALD E. AND WILLIAM F. MASSY, "Innovation and Brand Choice: The Folger's Invasion," in Stephen A. Greyser, ed., *Proceedings of the Winter Conference of the American Marketing Association,* Chicago: 1963, 96–107.
11. _____ AND DONALD G. MORRISON, "Bias in Multiple Discriminant Analysis," *Journal of Marketing Research,* 2 (August 1965), 250–8.
12. GOULDEN, CYRIL H., *Methods of Statistical Analysis,* New York: John Wiley & Sons, Inc., 1952, 378–93.
13. KATZ, ELIHU, "The Social Itinerary of Technical Change: Two Studies on the Diffusion of Innovation," *Human Organization,* 20 (Summer 1961), 70–82.
14. _____ AND PAUL F. LAZARSFELD, *Personal Influence,* Glencoe, Ill.: The Free Press, 1955.
15. KENDALL, MAURICE G., *A Course in Multivariate Analysis,* London: Charles Griffin and Co., Limited, 1957.
16. KING, CHARLES W., "Fashion Adoption: A Rebuttal to the 'Trickle Down' Theory," in Stephen A. Greyser, ed., *Proceeedings of the Winter Conference of the American Marketing Association,* Chicago, 1963, 108–25.
17. MOSTELLER, FREDERICK AND DAVID L. WALLACE, "Inference in an Authorship Problem," *Journal of the American Statistical Association,* 58 (June 1963), 275–309.
18. ROGERS, EVERETT M., *Diffusion of Innovations,* New York: The Free Press, 1962.
19. _____, "Characteristics of Agricultural Innovators and Other Adopter Categories," *Studies of Innovation and of Communication to the Public,* in Wilbur Schramm, ed., Stanford: Stanford University Press, 1962, 63–97.

20. VEBLEN, THORSTEIN, *The Theory of the Leisure Class*, New York: The Macmillan Company, 1912.
21. WHYTE, WILLIAM H., JR., "The Web of Word of Mouth," *Fortune*, 50 (November 1954), 140–3, 204–12.
22. ZALTMAN, GERALD, *Marketing: Contributions from the Behavioral Sciences*, New York: Harcourt, Brace & World, 1965, Ch. 3.

44. Adoption research: information sources in the industrial purchasing decision

urban b. ozanne
& gilbert a. churchill

The last four years have witnessed an outpouring of studies on the adoption and diffusion of consumer product innovations. A number of researchers have even gone beyond product studies to the application of diffusion theory to such areas as new store patronage. However, the diffusion and particularly the adoption of *industrial* innovations remains largely unexplored. In outlining a set of diffusion research questions at the Fall Conference two years ago, Charles W. King concluded with a judgment that still holds:

> Many of these conceptual questions are generally applicable to the industrial product setting. Research from the other traditions relevant to industrial product adoption and diffusion, however, is extremely limited. Research by marketers is essentially nonexistent. The application of diffusion theory in industrial product acceptance is an unexplored field.[1]

While a limited amount of industrial diffusion research has been completed by Carter and Williams, Sutherland, Enos, Mansfield, and a few others, virtually no one has looked into the industrial *adoption* process.[2] The industrial adoption process is that set of activities and decisions through which decision makers in an individual firm move from awareness of the industrial innovation to its final adoption or rejection. We have completed a pilot study of this process and are initiating the field research for the second phase of a five-year study of industrial adoption behavior. The present paper reports on some of the problems of the pilot study and presents findings from one of its parts.

The balance of this paper is organized into three major sections. The first section sets forth an *a priori* model of the industrial adoption process. The second section describes the methods and problems of the pilot study and discuss the applicability of the traditional five-stage

---

Reprinted by permission from Robert L. King, ed., *Marketing and the New Science of Planning*, Proceedings of the Fall Conference, 1968, pp. 352–359, published by the American Marketing Association.

[1] Charles W. King, "Adoption and Diffusion Research in Marketing: An Overview," in Raymond M. Haas (ed.), *Science Technology, and Marketing*, Proceedings of the Fall Conference of the American Marketing Association, 1966, pp. 665-684, at p. 684.

[2] C. F. Carter and B. R. Williams, "The Characteristics of Technically Progressive Firms," *Journal of Industrial Economics* (March 1959), pp. 87–104; Alister Sutherland, "The Diffusion of an Innovation in Cotton-Spinning," *Journal of Industrial Economics* (March 1959), pp. 118–135; John L. Enos, "A Measure of Rate of Technological Progress in the Petroleum Refining Industry," *Journal of Industrial Economics* (June 1958), pp. 180–197; Edwin Mansfield, "The Speed of Response of Firms to New Techniques," *Quarterly Journal of Economics* (May 1963), pp. 290–311.

adoption model to the industrial setting. The last section of the paper presents the results of that part of the pilot study that deals with the function of information sources in the industrial adoption process.

A MODEL OF THE INDUSTRIAL ADOPTION PROCESS

A conceptual model of the industrial adoption process served as a framework for organizing the pilot study. The model helped to indicate relationships among the variables and to suggest possible questions for research. The work of rural sociologists suggested much of the conceptual foundation of the industrial model. In fact, Rogers outlined an adoption model that provided the basic elements of the Industrial Adoption Process Model.[3] Figure 1 presents a diagram of the "Model."

The Model contains three primary elements: (1) antecedents, (2) process, and (3) results. The antecedents include the adopting-firm's identity, the decision-group's identity, and the participants' perceptions of the situation. The firm's identity influences the adoption of new items; it is composed of such variables as: the firm's age, its research and development commitment, its rate of growth, its industrial environment, its economic constraints, and its profitability.

With the exception of those anthropological studies that focus on the acceptance of an innovation by a tribe or by some comparable social group, adoption and diffusion research takes the *individual* farmer, housewife, doctor, or consumer as the relevant adopting unit. The individual may be the appropriate unit of analysis in much of this research. However, there are instances—the acceptance of an industrial product or process by a company purchasing group, for example —where focusing on a group as the unit of adoption produces more meaningful results.

The Industrial Adoption Process Model implicitly recognizes that a decision-making *group* is the most likely unit of adoption in the diffusion of industrial innovations. The characteristics of individual decision-group members are aggregated to form the decision-group identity variables. Among these characteristics of the members are age, education, cosmopoliteness, mental ability, length of company service, level in the organizational hierarchy, previous experience, and technical orientation.

The perception of the situation held by each member of the decision-making group influences his adoption behavior. The norms of the member's social groups function as incentives or restraints on his actions. Individuals in a social system with a modern norm behave differently from those who are members of groups with traditional norms.

The second major element of the Model is the process itself. To assist analysis, rural sociologists have broken the adoption process into a series of *stages* with a different activity occurring during each

---

[3] Everett M. Rogers, *Diffusion of Innovations* (New York: The Free Press, 1962), pp. 305–307.

FIGURE 1   Industrial Adoption Process Model

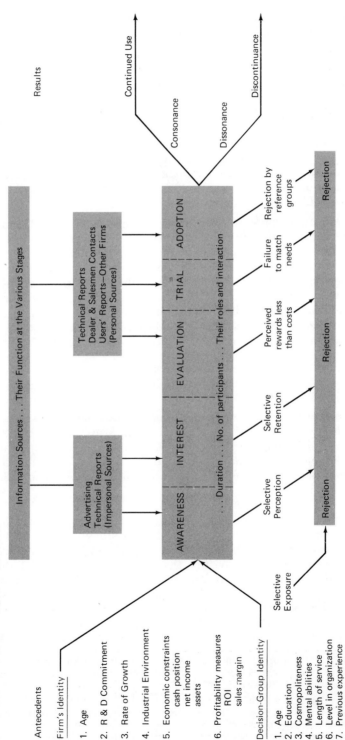

Source: Adapted from Everett M. Rogers, *Diffusion of Innovation*, New York: Free Press, 1962, p. 306.

stage. The five stages of the traditional adoption model serve as the stages in the model of the industrial adoption process.[4]

1. Awareness. At the awareness stage the adopting unit (or a member of it) is exposed to the new idea.
2. Interest. At this stage the adopting unit seeks additional information about the innovation.
3. Evaluation. At the evaluation stage the potential adopter weighs the advantages of the innovation against its costs. If the advantages are perceived to outweigh the costs, the process will continue.
4. Trial. The potential adopter employs the innovation on a limited scale in order to test its application to his particular situation.
5. Adoption. At the adoption stage the adopting unit decides to continue full use of the innovation.

A question that underlies our research on industrial adoption is: How well does the agricultural five-stage model fit the industrial adoption process? The next·section will discuss this question.

The third and final element of the Industrial Adoption Process Model is the results. The process concludes either in adoption or rejection of the innovation. The firm may accept a new idea at the end of the process and may employ it continuously, or the firm may reject the innovation at a later date—this delayed rejection is called a "discontinuance." The firm also may continuously reject the innovation.

RELEVANCE OF THE A PRIORI MODEL

The Pilot Study

The pilot study focused on the adoption of a new automatic machine tool by a sample of Midwestern industrial firms. The machine tool was not a radical departure from its predecessors, but its automatic control system and certain other features represent a readily observable improvement. Due to the magnitude of the investment ($35,000 to $70,000, depending on machine size and the selected accessories), a company purchasing group was expected to be the typical decision unit.

This predicted (and observed) prevalence of a group as the unit of adoption suggested one part of the pilot study. In this part we were concerned with the characteristics of the decision-making group, particularly those characteristics that in some way affected the dimensions of the process. Included in this examination were such process dimensions as the duration of the industrial adoption process, the use of information sources, the consideration of alternatives to the subject innovation, the functions performed by members of the decision-making group, and the interaction among decision-group members.[5]

---

[4] North Central Rural Sociology Sub-Committee for the Study of Diffusion of Farm Practices, *How Farm People Accept New Ideas*, Ames, Iowa, Iowa Agricultural Extension Service Report 15, 1955, pp. 3–6.

[5] In dealing with a decision *group* and in examining such process dimensions as the decision-group's functional arrangement and its members' interaction, the pilot study of necessity borrowed heavily from the literature of organization theory. For an excellent review of this literature, see: Philip B. Applewhite, *Organizational Behavior* (Englewood Cliffs: Prentice-Hall, Inc., 1965).

A second part of the pilot study investigated the influence of the firm's identity on these same dimensions of the industrial adoption process. The third part of the pilot study, the focus of the latter half of this paper, examined the function of information sources in the industrial adoption process, particularly the function of information sources at the individual stages.

Field Procedure

The pilot study took the form of an exploratory field study directed at a sample of 52 firms that recently purchased the innovation. The machine-tool manufacturer that developed the innovation divides its national market into six divisions. Out of the total list of customers, the population of interest was limited to those customers in the Upper Midwestern Division. From this geographical subpopulation, a probability sample of 52 firms was selected.

The field study employed semistructured depth interviews to secure the basic data. Special effort was made to interview every individual who was directly involved in the decision to purchase the new machine tool. Compared to a consumer interview situation where the subject is asked to reconstruct a behavior or process from memory, the validity of these industrial interview results may have been substantially better. Almost invariably the industrial decision-makers were able to produce a complete file on the purchasing process. The file served to establish dates and the order of events, and to jog the respondents' memories on other aspects of the purchasing decisions. Moreover, it was possible to compare the responses among the two or three members of the decision group.

Of the 52 firms selected in the sample, three refused to cooperate, giving pressure of business as their major reason for nonparticipation. In five of the selected firms, one or more of the major decision-makers had died, retired, or left the company, and the remaining decision-group members (if any) were unable to provide adequate answers to a majority of our questions. Decision-makers in three industrial firms did not view the automatic machine tool as an innovation. They considered the machine as nothing more than a normal replacement for obsolescent equipment. In the remaining case omitted from the analysis, the major decision-maker agreed to the interview but, when interviewed, refused to answer many of the questions put to him. Thus, of the original sample of 52 firms, we were able to obtain satisfactory information on 40. Within these 40 firms, we interviewed a total of 90 decision-makers. The omitted cases did not appear to differ significantly from the included cases in such obvious characteristics as amount of sales or assets, industry, age of firm, and so forth.

Relevance of the Five-Stage Model

With the exception of one stage, the trial, the traditional five-stage adoption model fits the industrial adoption process rather well. To be sure, there are some problems in defining the stages and in collecting data associated with the stages. These problems will be discussed as we analyze the appropriateness of each stage of the *a priori* process model.

Operationally, the awareness stage closely approximated its conceptualization. In other words, the notion of first coming into contact with the innovation and the idea of an information source that brought this awareness were meaningful to the respondents. Nevertheless, the respondents had a great degree of difficulty in dating this stage and in specifying the precipitating information source. This difficulty was, in part, a function of the time span from awareness to the interview, and of the lack of any data for awareness in the companies' purchase files.

The interest stage proved quite relevant and was far easier for the respondents to specify. Often a particular incident such as a salesman's call remained in the respondent's mind to remind him of the beginning of the interest stage.

Evaluation is an extremely difficult stage to define operationally and to investigate. Rogers has noted that "the evaluation stage is probably least distinct of the five adoption stages and empirically one of the most difficult about which to question respondents." During the six pretest interviews, it became apparent that most respondents initiated their evaluation of the machine tool upon receipt of the formal "price quotation and tooling proposal." Thus, the date of the receipt of this proposal was allowed to specify the beginning of the evaluation stage. While the use of this operational specification of the evaluation stage may have strayed from the conceptual definition in a small number of cases where some evaluation of other alternatives already had taken place, this convention had some obvious advantages to recommend it. The idea was simple to communicate to respondents, consistency in questioning was improved, and information in their files enabled the respondents to report the data of receipt of the proposal exactly.

The trial stage in the adoption process offers an obstacle to the application of the traditional five-stage model to the industrial setting. This obstacle may not arise in investigating a process involving an innovation that embodies the quality of "divisibility" or one that is purchased frequently. The potential adopter is able to employ the latter kinds of industrial innovations, a new ceramic material or a new hand tool for example, on a limited scale at the trial stage. This is not so with a "lumpy", expensive innovation like an automatic machine tool.

We had supposed that with indivisible industrial products the potential adopter would improvise a trial. He could bring samples of his materials or special jobs to the supplier's plant for a test demonstration. This was done in a few cases but only *after* the decision had been made and the machine ordered. This demonstration appears to have been used by these purchasers to reduce post-decision dissonance. For very large industrial firms that eventually could utilize five to ten or more of these automatic machine tools, the purchase of the first machine may have functioned as a trial. However, for the overwhelming majority of small to medium-size firms in the sample, this form of trial was too expensive.

The conclusion suggested by these findings is that, for expensive capital equipment such as an automatic tool, the trial stage is impractical or impossible. However, for raw materials, fabricating materials and parts, operating supplies, certain types of accessory equipment, and other *divisible* industrial products, the trial stage may well be a distinct and useful stage.

At the adoption stage the decision-makers in the firm not only purchase the innovation but also decide to continue its use throughout the organization. This definition of adoption seems compatible with the reality of the industrial adoption process. However, the pilot study did not intentionally measure events and decisions that occurred after the delivery of the first automatic machine tool.

Definition of the Decision-Making Group

A problem arose during the field work centering on how to define the firm's decision-making group. The question became just who is a member of the decision-making group? Is the president of the firm a member when he merely reviews the purchasing proposal and signs his name? Is the engineer in the methods department a member when he simply gathers the information about the alternative machines? Generally, the members of the decision group were allowed to define the group's membership for the purposes of the study. Occasionally, we made a decision to eliminate from consideration an individual who was not directly involved in deciding the central questions surrounding the adoption of the innovation.

THE FUNCTION OF INFORMATION SOURCES

As noted previously, part of the study focused on the function of information sources at the different stages of the industrial adoption process. Previous studies have suggested that impersonal sources of information are more important in the early stages of the adoption process, while personal sources of information are relatively more important in the latter stages of the process. The pilot study sought to examine this general hypothesis. However, due to reasons discussed above, the analysis will be limited to the function of information sources at three stages, at awareness, interest, and evaluation.

Table 1 suggests the range of information sources encountered in the pilot study. The table classifies the information sources into the categories employed in the subsequent analysis. The information sources first are separated into personal and impersonal categories, and then into such familiar subcategories as personal influence, personal selling, advertising, and so on. Table 1 also introduces two non-standard sources of information: technical sources, which turned out to include only the price quotation and tooling proposal, and the past experience of decision-makers with other automatic machine tools.

Most Important Information Sources

The respondents were asked to specify the most important information source at each stage in the adoption process. In other words, they

TABLE 1   Classification of Information Sources

A. Personal Sources
   1. Personal influence
      a. Visit to machine user's plant
      b. Company associate
      c. Business associate
      d. Friend
   2. Personal selling
      a. Salesman
      b. Engineer
      c. Distributor
      d. Visit to supplier's plant

B. Impersonal Sources
   3. Advertising—Trade journal advertisement
   4. Publicity
      a. Magazine article
      b. Newspaper article
   5. Sales promotion (non-media advertising)
      a. Product brochure
      b. Product testimonial
      c. Trade show exhibit
      d. Demonstration movie
   6. Technical sources—Price quotation and tooling proposal
   7. Previous experience

---

indicated which sources of information brought awareness, aroused their interest, and proved most helpful in evaluating the innovation. Table 2 provides a breakdown of the most important information

TABLE 2   Stage in the Adoption Process Versus Most Important Information Source

	Awareness	Interest	Evaluation	Total
Personal influence	0	1	4	5
Personal selling	20	33	12	65
Advertising	8	0	0	8
Publicity	0	0	0	0
Sales promotion	9	3	0	12
Technical sources	0	2	21	23
Experience	0	1	3	4
Total	37[a]	40	40	117

[a] Only 37 most important information sources are listed at the awareness stage because respondents in three firms could not recall the precipitating source.

source as a function of stage in the adoption process. Personal selling, the most frequently mentioned *personal* source of information, was prominent at all stages in the process, but especially in generating interest. The price quotation and tooling proposal, the most used *impersonal* source, saw only token service at the early stages in the process, but was the single most important source at the evaluation stage. Many companies placed almost exclusive reliance on the proposal at the evaluation stage.

A χ^2 test of the assumption of independence is employed to examine the relationship between stage in the process and most important information source. Table 3 arranges the data in the form of a contingency table for this computation.

The null hypothesis to be tested is that the use of personal or impersonal sources of information is independent of the stage of the process. The calculated χ^2 value is 17.604. When compared to a table value for two degrees of freedom, the result is seen to be significant at the .005 level. The evidence suggests that the two bases of classification are *not* independent. Rather, the use of personal or impersonal sources of information appears to depend on the stage in the adoption process.

The raw data of Table 3 are converted to proportions in Table 4. Viewing the proportions as conditional probabilities provides a clearer look at the inherent association. Table 4 suggests that the probability that personal contacts were the most important information source given that the decision group is at the awareness stage is 0.541. The probability of personal sources being most important rises to 0.850, given that the group is at the interest stage, and then declines to 0.400 given the evaluation stage. Impersonal information sources behave in an opposite fashion. The probability that they are most important given that the group is at the awareness stage is 0.459, given the interest stage is 0.150, and given the evaluation stage is 0.600.

TABLE 3   Most Important Information Source Versus the Stages in the Adoption Process

	Personal	Impersonal	Total
Awareness	20	17	37
Interest	34	6	40
Evaluation	16	24	40
Total	70	47	117

TABLE 4   Conditional Probabilities of the Use of Information Source Versus Stages in the Process

	Personal	Impersonal	Total
Awareness	.541	.459	1.000
Interest	.850	.150	1.000
Evaluation	.400	.600	1.000

Thus, at least for this study (and possibly for adoption processes involving other industrial innovations), the hypothesis that information sources become increasingly personal as the final adoption decision approaches is not necessarily true. Rather, the data suggest that personal information sources reach their pinnacle of importance at the interest stage and that impersonal sources are most important at the evaluation stage. This latter phenomenon is explained by the importance of the price quotation and tooling proposal in the industrial purchasing decision. In the adoption process associated with consumer products, there is no impersonal source of information that has a function comparable to the proposal.

These findings imply that marketers of industrial products must employ different timing of personal selling efforts than those selling farm and consumer innovations. Industrial salesmen must contact potential adopters earlier, and must play a greater role in generating interest than those selling in farm and consumer markets. Conversely, as the adoption decision approaches, industrial adopters are more prone to turn to impersonal but technical sources of information, such as the price quotation and tooling proposal.

Number and Variety of Sources

Closely related to the question of the most important information source at each stage are the dual considerations of number and variety of information sources used at each stage. Number of sources simply refers to all the sources mentioned by a decision group at a process stage. A salesman, for example, could make three calls at the evaluation stage, and this could count as three separate sources. The variety measure is derived from the classification of sources into seven subcategories in Table 1. The three visits of the salesmen would be considered as a variety of one at the evaluation stage, while a salesman's visit and the use of the price quotation and tooling proposal would count as two.

Our practical experience in industrial marketing suggested that the further along a decision group is in the adoption process, the greater is its need for informational inputs. Two hypotheses derived from this generalization were examined.

1. A decision group employs a greater *number* of information sources at the later stages of the adoption process than at the early stages. It uses a greater number of information sources at the interest stage than at the awareness stage, and a still greater number of sources at the evaluation stage.
2. A decision group employs a greater *variety* of information sources at the later stages of the adoption process than at the early stages. It uses a greater variety of information sources at the interest stage than at the awareness stage, and a still greater variety of sources at the evaluation stage.

Table 5 contains the number and variety of information sources used at each stage of the process by the 37 decision groups that could recall their information inputs at each stage. As is evident from the table, companies employed informational inputs in different amounts. The total number of information sources used ranged from three for Companies T, X, and BB to thirteen for Companies F, N, and P.

It is necessary to control the differing total number of information

TABLE 5   Number and Variety of Information Sources Used at Each Stage of the Adoption Process

Company	Number			Variety		
	Awareness	Interest	Evaluation	Awareness	Interest	Evaluation
A	2	2	3	2	2	2
B	1	1	2	1	1	2
C	3	2	3	2	2	2
D	2	1	2	2	1	2
E	3	2	4	2	2	1
F	3	4	6	2	3	5
G	1	1	2	1	1	2
H	1	3	4	1	3	2
I	2	3	3	2	2	3
J	3	2	4	2	2	2
K	1	2	4	1	2	4
L	3	3	3	2	3	3
M	4	4	4	2	4	3
N	4	2	7	3	1	3
O	3	2	2	2	1	2
P	4	5	4	3	2	3
Q	2	1	1	2	1	1
R	1	1	3	1	1	2
S	1	3	2	1	3	2
T	1	1	1	1	1	1
U	1	2	1	1	1	1
V	1	4	3	1	3	2
W	2	3	3	2	3	3
X	1	1	1	1	1	1
Y	3	1	4	1	1	3
Z	1	1	5	1	1	4
AA	1	3	1	1	3	1
BB	1	1	1	1	1	1
CC	3	2	2	2	2	2
DD	4	2	3	3	2	3
EE	1	2	3	1	2	3
FF	1	3	2	1	2	2
GG	1	2	2	1	2	2
HH	2	3	2	2	3	2
II	1	2	4	1	2	3
JJ	2	2	3	2	2	3
KK	2	3	2	2	2	2

sources per company in order to test the hypothesis that a greater number would be used at the later stages of the process. The awareness stage serves as the standard of comparison. The number of sources employed at the interest and evaluation stages are contrasted to the number employed at the awareness stage, and the deviations are calculated on a company by company basis. For example, Company A used two sources of information at the awareness stage, two at the interest stage, and three at the evaluation stage. The deviations for Company A are $N_I - N_A = 0$, $N_E - N_A = +1$ were N_i stands for the number used at the ith stage.

Table 6 summarizes these deviations. This procedure is predicated,

TABLE 6   Deviations for Number and Variety of Information Sources Using Awareness as the Standard

Company	Number			Variety		
	Awareness	Interest	Evaluation	Awareness	Interest	Evaluation
A	0	0	+1	0	0	0
B	0	0	+1	0	0	+1
C	0	−1	0	0	0	0
D	0	−1	0	0	−1	0
E	0	−1	+1	0	0	−1
F	0	+1	+3	0	+1	+3
G	0	0	+1	0	0	+1
H	0	+2	+3	0	+2	+1
I	0	+1	+1	0	0	+1
J	0	−1	+1	0	0	0
K	0	+1	+3	0	+1	+3
L	0	0	0	0	+1	+1
M	0	0	0	0	+2	+1
N	0	−2	+3	0	−2	0
O	0	−1	−1	0	−1	0
P	0	+1	0	0	−1	0
Q	0	−1	−1	0	−1	−1
R	0	0	+2	0	0	+1
S	0	+2	+1	0	+2	+1
T	0	0	0	0	0	0
U	0	+1	0	0	0	0
V	0	+3	+2	0	+2	+1
W	0	+1	+1	0	+1	+1
X	0	0	0	0	0	0
Y	0	−2	+1	0	0	+2
Z	0	0	+4	0	0	+3
AA	0	+2	0	0	+2	0
BB	0	0	0	0	0	0
CC	0	−1	−1	0	0	0
DD	0	−2	−1	0	−1	0
EE	0	+1	+2	0	+1	+2
FF	0	+2	+1	0	+1	+1
GG	0	+1	+1	0	+1	+1
HH	0	+1	0	0	+1	0
II	0	+1	+3	0	+1	+1
JJ	0	0	+1	0	0	+1
KK	0	+1	0	0	0	0

of course, on the assumption that a firm employing more information sources during the entire process is also likely to employ more sources at the awareness stage. Although the assumption may not hold for all cases, it held for most cases, and it represents a more reasonable approach to the data than one where the confounding factor of differing total number of sources is left completely uncontrolled. A similar approach is used to handle information source variety and these results are also summarized in Table 6.

The above hypotheses are examined using the analysis of variance technique. Table 7 represents the analysis of variance table for the

TABLE 7   Analysis of Variance Table for Number of Information Sources

Source of Variation	Sum of Squares	Degrees of Freedom	Mean Square	Variance Ratio
Between Columns	31.24	2	15.62	8.95[a]
Residual	112.38	108	1.94	
Total	143.62	110		

[a] Significant at 0.005 level

number of information sources. The calculated F value equals 8.95, a result which is significant at the 0.005 level. The evidence suggests that the number of information sources depends on the stage of the process.

$$\text{Mean}\frac{0}{37}=0.000; \quad \frac{9}{37}=0.243; \quad \frac{33}{37}=0.892$$

$$\frac{0}{37}=0.000; \quad \frac{12}{37}=0.324; \quad \frac{26}{37}=0.703$$

To determine which stage deviations in particular contributed to this significant result, comparisons were run between pairs of means using the Least Significant Difference criterion. The standard error of the difference between means ($s_{\bar{D}}=\sqrt{\dfrac{2s^2}{n}}$) is seen to be equal to 0.322. Theoretical z for the 5% level of significance in a one-way test (it was hypothesized that *more* sources would be used at the later stages) is 1.645. Thus, any difference between a specific pair of means is significant if it exceeds 1.645 (0.322) = .530. The calculated values are: $\bar{x}_1=0$, $\bar{x}_2=0.243$, and $\bar{x}_3=0.892$. The difference u_2-u_1 is not significant, but u_3-u_1 is and so is u_3-u_2. The data therefore suggest that the initial hypothesis should be reformulated to read: The number of information sources used in the adoption process is approximately the same at the awareness and interest stages, but increases at the evaluation stage as the final decision becomes more imminent.

A stronger conclusion is warranted for the variety of information sources. Table 8 contains the basic analysis of variance information. The computed F of 17.35 is significant at the 0.001 level, suggesting that information source variety depends on the stage of the process. The Least Significant Difference criterion in this case is 0.304 = 1.645

TABLE 8   Analysis of Variance Table for Variety of Information Sources

Source of Variation	Sum of Squares	Degrees of Freedom	Mean Square	Variance Ratio
Between Columns	22.28	2	11.4	17.35[a]
Residual	69.38	108	0.64	
Total	91.66	110		

[a] Significant at 0.001 level

$(0.185) = zs_{\bar{D}}$, where $s_{\bar{D}} = \sqrt{\dfrac{2s^2}{n}}$ and where $s^2 = 0.642$, $\bar{x}_1$ is again 0, $\bar{x}_2 = 0.324$, and $\bar{x}_3 = 0.703$. With variety of sources, the difference $u_2 - u_1$ is significant as again are $u_3 - u_1$ and $u_2 - u_1$. The evidence indicates that a greater variety of information sources are employed as the decision group moves from awareness to interest, and then to evaluation.

SUMMARY AND CONCLUSIONS

This paper has presented evidence suggesting that the traditional adoption process model can be applied in the industrial setting. An analysis of this evidence leads to the conclusion that the trial stage may not exist for indivisible innovations. However, where industrial products can be employed on a limited scale, the potential adopter may well go through a trial stage. We have also examined the function of information sources at three stages in the adoption process. Contrary to predictions, personal sources (in particular personal selling) were more important at the early stages, while impersonal sources (especially the price quotation and tooling proposal) were paramount at the evaluation stage. The available evidence also suggests that as the final decision approaches, the need for informational inputs increases. At the evaluation stage the industrial decision-makers employ a larger number and a greater variety of information sources than at the earlier stages.

Most studies of industrial purchasing behavior have concentrated on the relationships between economic and organizational factors and the *results* of the purchasing process. Until the last few years, what went on during the process of deciding was largely ignored. Without adequate information on the internal dynamics of the industrial adoption process, an evaluation of different influences on the process was nearly impossible. Thus, researchers have tended to overlook the effects of the supplier's promotional efforts on purchasing behavior. The goal of improving the effectiveness of promotional efforts requires a research approach capable of assessing the impact of these efforts on purchasing decision making. Research such as described in the present paper, that focuses on the decision *processes* rather than on the results of these processes, should be potentially valuable for making this assessment.

In particular, insights into the function of information sources in the industrial adoption process can be used to evaluate the promotional efforts of the supplier. These insights may help to determine whether the messages, the media, and the timing of the persuasive communications are suitable. The question of suitability centers on whether the information transmitted meets the needs of the potential adopters. From this kind of analysis may come a communications mix that will serve more effectively the objectives of suppliers and the needs of potential adopters.

45. Predictors of innovative behavior

lyman e. ostlund

INTRODUCTION

Most research on the adoption and diffusion of new products has centered on either the communication process [1, 14] or the characteristics of the innovators or early adopters of the product [12, 9, 6, 13]. Virtually no research has been reported in diffusion literature on the role of perceptual variables in predicting innovative behavior. However, applications of perceptual mapping techniques in marketing literature have demonstrated the importance of such variables [19]. Diffusion researchers, by ignoring perceptual variables concerning the characteristics of the innovation, have, without saying so, treated all innovations as equivalent units.

In work reported earlier [11], both perceptual and predispositional variables were employed to predict innovative behavior as it concerns initial trial by use of a surrogate measure. Multiple regression applied to the data indicated that perceptual variables for all six new products in the study were better predictors of innovative behavior than predispositional or socioeconomic-demographic variables. But with the use of only regression analysis, no conclusions could be drawn concerning any interaction or nonlinearity among the predictor variables. In this paper, both the predictive strength of the independent variables and any interaction or nonlinearity are examined.

THE DATA

Predictor Variables

A survey of prior studies that have aimed at defining the profile of the innovator provided the predispositional and socioeconomic-demographic variables employed in the study [11]. The predispositional variables selected have been used in an earlier study by Robertson [13]. Problem-solving and psychosocial general self-confidence, investigated by King [9] and Bylund [6], were added to the list. Because a literature survey had revealed conflicting findings with respect to several socioeconomic and demographic variables, only four that appeared to be most important were included: age and education of respondent, family income, and occupational status of husband.

A survey of diffusion studies by Rogers [15] indicated that very little attention has been devoted to developing and applying perceptual variables for the prediction of innovative behavior. From examining several studies, however, he concluded that the following variables might be relevant and worthy of research: relative advantage, compatibility, complexity, divisibility, and communicability. One additional perceptual variable was added to the study, perceived risk, based upon the original conceptualization by Bauer [5] and work that has followed by Cunningham [7], Arndt [1], Bylund [6], and Sheth [17]. The definitions of these variables and their expected relationship to the dependent variable, a surrogate measure for innovative behavior, are given in Table 1.

The Surrogate Measure

Since it was not possible with the nature of the new products studied to record actual purchase behavior, a surrogate measure was employed. This measure was a modified version of a buying intention scale developed by Juster [8]. This modified scale, referred to here as "innovative willingness," was a 0 to 100 subjective probability scale on which each respondent in the study indicated how likely she was to buy any one of the six test products within the first few weeks after going on sale in the test area. Only the end points of the scale were labeled: 0 = I absolutely will not buy; 100 = I absolutely will buy.

The Test Products

A great many products are claimed by marketers to be new when they are first introduced to the market. Most of these products, however, are merely minor modifications of existing products and do not satisfy the definition of the term "innovation" as used in diffusion research literature. While this definition is difficult to satisfy whenever consumer products are involved, considerable effort was expended to locate a group of products regarded as appropriate products, which the housewife (respondent) might normally buy on her own, without the husband jointly involved, yet which were previously unknown to the sample of respondents. Any new product with which the respondents were already familiar would naturally be inappropriate, since their prior purchase deliberations, whether purchases resulted or not, would likely bias the perceptual data later obtained.

With these considerations in mind, six new products were gathered from metropolitan areas remote from the test area, Boston. These products and their descriptions are given below:

Product 1: a plastic bandage, with antiseptic, in an aerosol can, which when sprayed on a minor wound provides a flexible, waterproof, and perspiration-resistant protective covering.
Product 2: a disposable female undergarment
Product 3: a self-layering desert mix
Product 4: a biodegradable napkin
Product 5: a hot foam aerosol shampoo
Product 6: a fabric treatment solution giving permanent press characteristics to any washable fabric.

TABLE 1   Definitions of Variables and Hypothesized Relationships

Variable	Definition	Expected Relationship with Surrogate Measure of Innovative Behavior
Predispositional:		
Venturesomeness	Willingness to take risks in buying new products	positive
Cosmopolitanism	Degree of orientation beyond a particular social system	positive
Social integration	Extent of social participation with other members of the community	positive
Privilegedness	Perceived financial well-being relative to peers	positive
Interest polymorphism	Variety and extent of one's personal interests	positive
General self-confidence in problem-solving	Perceived ability to cope with day to day problems	positive
General self-confidence in psychosocial matters	Perceived ability to cope with others' opinions of one's decisions	positive
Socioeconomic-Demographic:		
Family income	Total family income	positive
Respondent education	Years of formal education	positive
Occupational status of husband	Social-occupational status, measured by the Duncan scale*	positive
Respondent age	Respondent age in years	not specified
Product perception:		
Relative advantage	Degree to which an innovation is perceived as superior to ideas it supersedes (both economic and noneconomic considerations)	positive
Compatibility	Degree to which an innovation is perceived as consistent with existing values, habits, and past experiences of the potential adopter	positive
Complexity	Degree to which an innovation is perceived as difficult to understand and use	negative
Divisibility	Degree to which an innovation is perceived as available for trial on a limited basis, without a large commitment	positive
Communicability	Degree to which results of an innovation will be apparent and possible to communicate to others	positive
Perceived risk	Degree to which risks are perceived as associated with the product	negative

* Reiss, Albert J. Jr., Otis Dudley Duncan, Paul K. Hatt, and Cecil C. North. *Occupations and Social Status.* New York: Free Press, 1961, Appendix.

Research Setting

In a laboratory setting, a sample of 605 Boston area housewives first completed questionnaires involving the predispositional, socio-economic-demographic variables. They next proceeded to examine individually each of the six test products. The sample was divided into six groups and each portion examined the products in a different rotated sequence. After examining all six products, the respondent was asked to indicate on the 0 to 100 innovative willingness scale her likelihood of buying each of the six products soon after it might come on the market.

HYPOTHESES

The relationships expected to exist between the predictor variables and the surrogate measure of innovative behavior are indicated in Table 1. Examination of earlier studies presented a rather conflicting view of how age should relate to innovative behavior, suggesting that it is perhaps idiosyncratic to the product studied.

The most important hypothesis, however, concerned the relative importance each set of predictors was expected to display. It was expected that product perception variables would exhibit stronger relationships (greater predictor power) with innovative willingness than would the predispositional or socioeconomic-demographic variables. Since there was no prior work to go on, it was not possible to proceed beyond this and suggest any prior model of how the variables should relate in a structural sense. That is, although the perceptual variables were expected to bear closer relationships to innovative willingness than the remaining predictor variables, there was no basis for postulating any hierarchical configurations.

ANALYSIS DESIGN

Through the use of n-way cross-classification tables, it is sometimes possible to gain an understanding for the relative importance of predictor variables, related to a dependent variable. The same is true with the use of step-wise regression where one can at least rank order the variables in terms of entry into the regression equations or by their partial correlations coefficients. These methods clearly do not, however, go any further than this in exposing interaction or non-linearity among variables.

An article by Bass, Tigert, and Lonsdale [4] concerning market segmentation pointed out how multiple regression can understate the importance of demographic-socioeconomic variables in distinguishing between consumer segments with regard to usage rates. They suggested that multiple regression first be used to identify the two or three most powerful predictor variables, and then proceed with cross-classification of those two or three variables to arrive at estimates of consumer segment usage means. Following up on this work, Assael [2] agrees with the shortcomings of relying exclusively on multiple regression, but disagrees with Bass, Tigert, and Lonsdale that their approach was best. He goes on to discuss two applications of a computer program generating a tree diagram that is multivariate and has several advantages. This computer program, Automatic Interaction Detector (AID), developed by Sonquist and Morgan [18] has been extensively described by both its developers and others [2, 3, 16], therefore only a brief description will be given here.

AID, through a series of iterations, attempts to manipulate variables and categories within variables so as to produce the greatest discrimination between group means of the dependent variable. The program seeks to find the division of the classes of any characteristics such that the partitioning of a given respondent group into two subgroups on this basis provides the largest reduction in the unexplained sum of squares. The number of respondents and the sum of the dependent variable for any subgroup are sufficient to estimate how much reduction in error sum of squares (i.e. amount of variance) would result from separating it from the parent group. With the standard constraints of the program, as applied in this study, if the actual reduction in unexplained sum of squares is not larger than 1 percent of the total sum of squares for the whole sample, the next most promising group for possible subdivision is examined, and so on, until all possibilities are exhausted. The number of iterations is limited by three constraints: (1) a minimum subsample criterion (set at n=5 in this study); (2) before a group can be split into two subgroups, it must contain no less than 2 percent of the total original sum of squares (this constraint prevents groups with only minor variation to be subdivided); and (3) if the group is eligible for subdivision, the size of the between group sum of squares for the particular group has to be a given minimum percentage of the original sum of squares. Since AID makes no assumptions of linearity, homoscedasticity, and normality it has particular strengths in detecting interactions between variables. As opposed to the use of extensive cross-classification, AID has the advantage of cutting rapidly into a mass of data, identifying the most important independent variables, making dichotomous breaks at the most opportune points, and eliminating the need for successive passes through the data by the researcher. The output of the program, consisting partly of a tree diagram, indicates clearly which independent variable(s) are important in determining the shared characteristics of each subsample [10].

The AID program is not perfect of course. As Assael [2] has observed, limitations do exist. First of all, the program produces only dichotomous splits. However, since the two subgroups produced by any split can in turn subdivide, a further reduction in unexplained variance may occur by that means. Second, an attribute of the program that can cause difficulties, depending upon the data, has to do with the fact that succeeding splits are contingent upon the subgroups produced by the first split. If a variable producing the first split had only slightly greater discrimination than that variable involved with the second split, the total diagram could look considerably different than if the second variable had entered first. Of course, this potential problem with the program can be overcome with a second run, this time omitting the variable that entered the program first in the previous run. In the case of the study reported here, it was known from prior regression analysis that the variable producing the first split in the tree diagrams for all six products had decidedly greater predictive power than dimensions entering second. Related to this, a third limitation, discussed by Assael [2], concerns the case where independent variables may be closely interdependent. The result of this may be spurious splits, particularly toward the terminal point of the tree. Prior intercorrelation analysis did not indicate this to be a significant problem with the data in this study.

Given the nature of the output from AID, its advantages mentioned earlier, and the fact it can handle nominal variables as well as scaled variables, it is well suited to studies involving socioeconomic-demographic variables.

FINDINGS

Earlier work with regression analysis indicated that the variables in this study, in predicting innovative willingness, would enter regression equations for the six products in the orders indicated in Table 2. It was found that for all six products, the expected relationships with the product perception variables to innovative willingness were supported by the data. However, for the predispositional and socioeconomic-demographic variables, the relationships with innovative willingness were often counter to those expected and usually not consistent across the six products. Note that relative advantage enters the six regression equations first, but beyond the first variable, the order of succeeding variables is different for each of the six products. However, in looking at the overall ranking, across all six products, we find that the first six positions are all occupied by product perception variables.

Starting with product one, the aerosol bandage (Figure 1), it is first necessary to give some instructions on how the tree diagrams are interpreted. Box one (the first on the left) represents the total sample (100 percent) amounting to a useful sample of 584. The average innovative willingness score from the 0 to 100 scale is 66. The mean index scores for each of the independent variables are in themselves meaningless except for a base point in comparing the two subgroups formed by a split. Looking at box two, this subgroup consists of 45 percent of the sample, having an average innovative willingness score of 43 and for whom the relative advantage index ranges from 2 to 8. Thus, the subgroup consists of respondents who perceived low relative advantage in product one. As would be expected, their average innovative willingness score of 43 is considerably below the average innovative willingness score for the total sample, which is 66.

Looking at box three, which represents a subgroup of 55 percent of

TABLE 2   Rank Order of Entry of Independent Variables in Stepwise Regressions

Variable	Products						Rank Total	Overall Rank
	1	2	3	4	5	6		
Product perception								
Relative advantage	1	1	1	1	1	1	6	1
Divisibility	5	10	9	5	4	5	38	4
Compatibility	3	2	2	2	2	2	13	2
Complexity	7	5	8	11	13	7	51	5
Communicability	2	17	4	18	3	10	54	6
Perceived risk	4	4	7	4	5	4	28	3
Predispositional								
Venturesomeness	(18)[b]	3	10	17	6	6	60	8
Cosmopolitanism	15	6	6	16	10	8	61	9
Social integration	10	12	13	7	9	15	66	11
Social mobility	6	7	(18)[b]	9	15	9	64	10
Privilegedness	9	8	16	13	16	11	73	13–14
Interest polymorphism	13	11	3	14	14	(18)[b]	73	13–14
Problem-solving general self-confidence	12	13	(18)[b]	10	7	14	74	15
Psychosocial general self-confidence	11	16	14	15	(18)[b]	3	77	16
Socioeconomic-Demographic								
Respondent education	16	15	12	12	11	12	78	17
Respondent age	8	9	11	3	12	13	56	7
Family income	17	14	15	8	17	(18)[b]	89	18
Occupational status of husband	14	(18)[b]	5	6	8	(18)[b]	69	12
R^2 for rank order variables	.537	.544	.417	.482	.490	.593	Average R^2 = .510	
F-ratio	(37.77)[a]	(38.79)[a]	(24.67)[a]	(28.65)[a]	(31.25)[a]	(53.48)[a]		

[a] Significant beyond the 0.1% level.
[b] Variable did not enter regression equation and was assigned a ranking value of 18.

FIGURE 1   Product 1

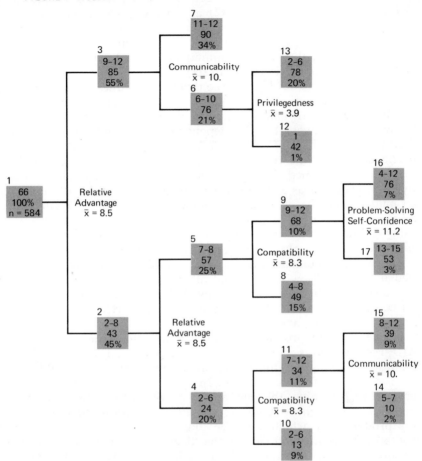

the total sample, we see that this group saw higher relative advantage in product one (an index of 9–12) and likewise indicated rather high innovative willingness, 85. Moving from left to right on the upper half of the tree diagram, we see that after the first split on relative advantage, succeeding splits are on communicability (dividing group three) and privilegedness (dividing group six).

Referring back to Table 2, we see that privilegedness is the ninth variable to enter the regression equation for product one. We can now see, based upon AID analysis, that it plays a role in the prediction of innovative willingness, but this depends upon responses to the product perception variables of relative advantage and communicability. In particular, unless the respondent perceives high relative advantage in the product, modified slightly by perceptions regarding communicability, privilegedness as a predispositional factor will evidently not exert an influence on the prediction of innovative willingness. Figure 1 also provides an example of a split on one variable (relative advantage) being followed by a second split on the same variable generating two subgroups (four and five) from the earlier subgroup (two).

The splits by compatibility of both groups four and five are of particular interest. They suggest that all the respondents found in group two can be further distinguished by their perceptions of product one on compatibility (how they see the product as relating to their past experiences, values, and habits).

For the second product, the disposable female undergarment, the AID tree diagram is more complicated (Figure 2). The average level of innovative willingness for the total sample is 36, considerably lower than was found for product one. In spite of this, there are later subgroups, such as nine, thirteen, and twenty-five, for which the average innovative willingness score exceeds 80. It should be understood that for products for which the tree diagram is complex, higher order splits to the right hand side of the diagram may not have a strategic importance from a marketer's viewpoint and may well be spurious. Two variables, relative advantage and compatibility, dominate Figure 2 in that succeeding subgroups in no case account for more than 9 percent of the sample. Thus, the remaining variables, although appearing on the tree diagram and bearing significant relationships with the dependent variable, tend to have no impact for over 60 percent of the sample.

For the third product, the self-layering dessert mix, average innovative willingness for the sample was highest among the six products, 73 (Figure 3). For most of the sample displaying high innovative willingness toward the product, relative advantage, communicability, and compatibility furnish the major splits before subgroups become rather small.

In the regression equation for product three, interest polymorphism entered the equation as the third variable (Table 2). However, in the tree diagram for the same product the variable is not present. A similar omission occurred for venturesomeness on product two. This indicates that the two analysis techniques, taking different approaches and making different assumptions in approaching the data, can gener-

FIGURE 2   Product 2

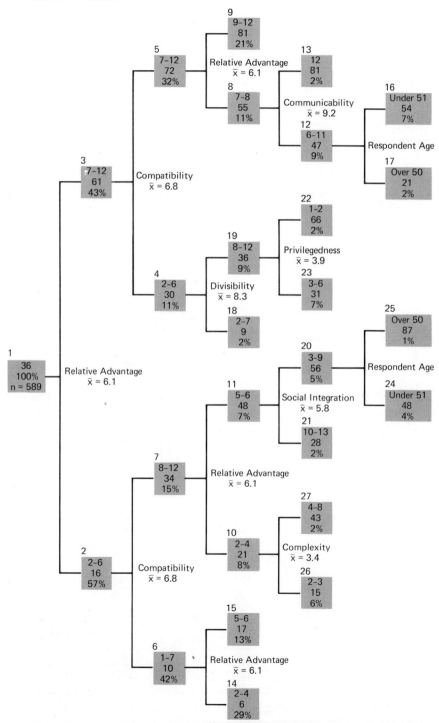

FIGURE 3 Product 3

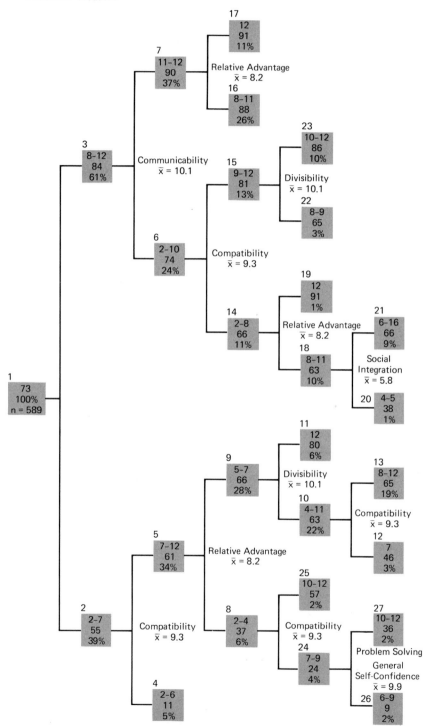

ate different results. In general, it would appear that multiple regression has overstated the role of predispositional factors relative to results from AID. Chances are, these conflicting results are due to curvilinearity among some of the independent variables. If this is true, it would follow that AID is in a better position to cope with these non-linear effects than is regression analysis. AID would suggest that for product three, predispositional factors, represented only by social integration and problem-solving self-confidence, play a negligible role as predictors of innovative willingness, for they succeed only in establishing terminal subgroups.

Product four, the biodegradable sanitary napkin, is the type of product for which one might expect respondent age to affect who will buy the product. Multiple regression analysis suggested that this was true since the variable entered the equation third. Looking at the top half of the tree diagram for the same product (Figure 4) one sees that respondent age does determine three splits. These splits occur among respondents who perceive high relative advantage and compatibility in the product. Nevertheless, the resulting subgroups of any size (eighteen, eight, and twenty) all have average innovative willingness scores exceeding that of the total sample. Once again it is seen that how the product is perceived has far more to do with the level of innovative willingness generated than the characteristics of the respondent, either in terms of predispositional or socioeconomic-demographic variables.

The lowest average innovative willingness score among all six products occurred for product five (Figure 5), the hot foam aerosol shampoo. For this product, the average innovative willingness score amounted only to 38. Relative advantage furnishes most of the group splits of any consequence here. Compatibility, which entered the multiple regression equation (Table 2) as variable two, succeeds in making its impact felt almost entirely on the top half of the diagram. In general, one can say that compatibility will have an impact in predicting the innovative willingness score only if the respondent also perceives high relative advantage for the product. Divisibility, found to enter the regression equation as the fourth variable, depends not only on the perception by the respondent of the product's relative advantage, but also its compatibility.

For the last product (Figure 6), the permanent press fabric treatment solution, the average innovative willingness score, 47, is third lowest. For those respondents who expressed high innovative willingness toward the product, and are therefore generally in the top half of the tree diagram, their assessment of relative advantage, and to a lesser degree complexity, appears to be the cause. However, since 63 percent of the sample fell into subgroup two, indicating low perceived relative advantage for the product, it is of greater interest to look at the lower half of the diagram. Multiple regression analysis (Table 2) had indicated that compatibility should be the second most important predictor variable. Since compatibility does cause the split in subgroup five amounting to 40 percent of the sample, the variable is important. Of particular interest is the fact that compatibility is thus producing

FIGURE 4 Product 4

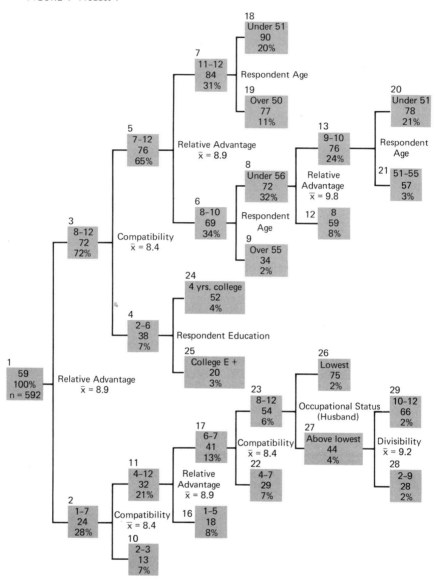

a split among a subgroup where the relative advantage score ranges from 6–9, encompassing the average relative advantage score given by the total sample.

Psychosocial general self-confidence, which was the third variable to enter the regression equation for product six (Table 2), established only two terminal subgroups in the tree diagram. Once again, regression analysis appears to overstate the importance of predispositional and socioeconomic-demographic variables, at the expense of perceptual variables, relative to the results obtained by tree diagram analysis.

FIGURE 5   Product 5

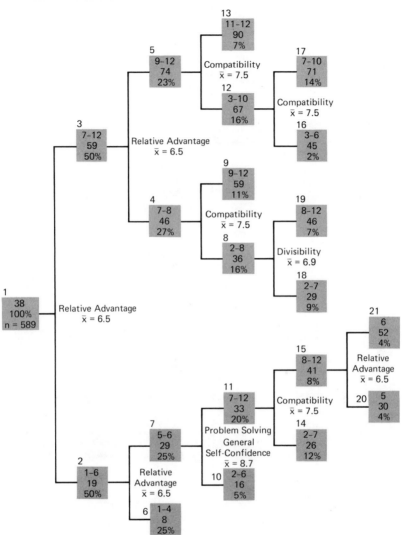

TABLE 3   Comparison of Coefficients of Determination

	Products						Average Across Products
	1	*2*	*3*	*4*	*5*	*6*	
From Regression	.537	.544	.417	.482	.490	.593	.510
From AID	.559	.572	.476	.547	.520	.621	.549

FIGURE 6   Product 6

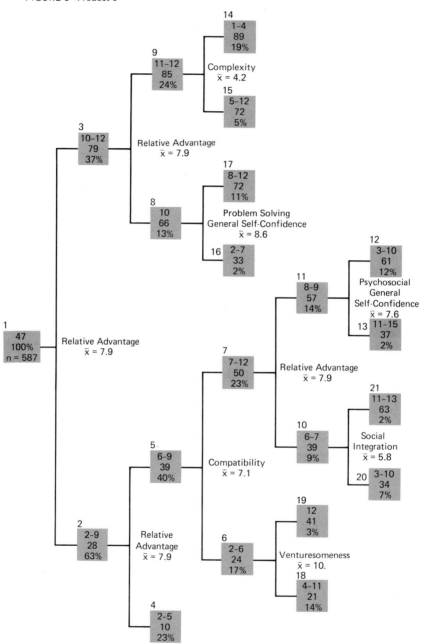

As can be seen from Table 3, the proportion of explained variance using AID is virtually no different from that explained by multiple regression. This is due primarily to the dominance of early variables entering either the multiple regression or AID analysis.

CONCLUSIONS

It has been shown that by the use of the Automatic Interaction Detector program (AID), it is possible to gain additional insight into the data obtained from the use of a large number of independent variables. Multiple regression, yielding only statistics as to the relative strength of relationships between the independent variables and the dependent variables, does not serve to indicate the important inter-active relationships. Given the absence of certain assumptions contained in multiple regression analysis, AID analysis can cope with curvilinear and interactive effects, which in this study appear to result in greater predictive importance being attached to the perceptual variables, even more so than true with multiple regression.

As has been concluded earlier [11], the relative importance of perceptual variables, overshadowing that of predispositional and socio-economic-demographic variables, suggests once again that diffusion studies aimed at the prediction of innovative behavior would do well to devote less measurement effort to the latter variables and more to perceptual variables.

REFERENCES

1. ARNDT, JOHAN. "Word of Mouth Advertising: The Role of Product Related Conversations to the Diffusion of a New Food Product." Unpublished Ph.D. dissertation, Graduate School of Business Administration, Harvard University, 1966.
2. ASSAEL, HENRY. "Segmenting Markets By Group Purchasing Behavior: An Application of the AID Technique." *Journal of Marketing Research*, Vol. 7 (May 1970), 153–158.
3. ————, JOHN H. KOFRON, AND WALTER BURGI. "Advertising Performance as a Function of Print Ad Characteristics." *Journal of Advertising Research*, Vol. 7 (June 1967), 20–26.
4. BASS, FRANK M., DOUGLAS J. TIGERT, AND RONALD T. LONSDALE. "Marketing Segmentation: Group Versus Individual Behavior." *Journal of Marketing Research*, Vol. 5 (August 1968), 264–270.
5. BAUER, RAYMOND A. "Consumer Behavior as Risk Taking." In *Dynamic Marketing for a Changing World*, edited by Robert S. Hancock, pp. 389–398. Chicago: Proceedings of the 43rd Conference of the American Marketing Association, 1960.
6. BYLUND, H. BRUCE. "Social and Psychological Factors Associated with Acceptance of New Food Products." *Bulletin 708* (December 1963). University Park: Pennsylvania State University, Agricultural Experiment Station.
7. CUNNINGHAM, SCOTT M. "Perceived Risk as a Factor in Product-Oriented

Word-of-Mouth Behavior: A First Step." In *Proceedings of the 1964 Educators' Conference, American Marketing Association,* edited by L. George Smith, pp. 229–238.

8. JUSTER, F. THOMAS. "Consumer Buying Intentions and Purchase Probability: An Experiment in Survey Design." *Journal of the American Statistical Association,* Vol. 61 (September 1966), 658–696.

9. KING CHARLES W. "The Innovator in the Fashion Adoption Process." In *Reflections on Progress in Marketing,* edited by L. George Smith, pp. 324–339. Chicago: Proceedings of the 1964 Winter Conference of the American Marketing Association.

10. MONTGOMERY, DAVID B. AND J. SCOTT ARMSTRONG. "Consumer Response to a Legitimated Brand Appeal." In *Insights Into Consumer Behavior,* edited by Johan Arndt, pp. 151–171. Boston: Allyn & Bacon, 1968.

11. OSTLUND, LYMAN E. "The Role of Product Perceptions in Innovative Behavior." In *Marketing Involvement in Society and the Economy,* edited by P. R. McDonald, pp. 259–266. Chicago: Proceedings of the 1969 Fall Conference of the American Marketing Association.

12. PESSEMIER, EDGAR A., PHILLIP BURGER, AND DOUGLAS TIGERT. "Can New Product Buyers Be Identified?" *Journal of Marketing Research,* Vol. 4 (November 1967), 349–354.

13. ROBERTSON, THOMAS S. "Determinants of Innovative Behavior." In *Changing Marketing Systems,* edited by Reed Moyer, pp. 328–332. Chicago: Proceeding of the 1967 Winter Conference of the American Marketing Association.

14. ROBERTSON, THOMAS S. AND JOHN R. ROSSITER. "Fashion Diffusion: The Interplay of Innovator and Opinion Leader Roles in College Social Systems." Working paper, U.C.L.A., Graduate School of Business, 1968.

15. ROGERS, EVERETT M. *Diffusion of Innovations.* New York: Free Press, 1962.

16. ROSS, JOHN. "Predicting the Adoption of Family Planning." *Studies in Family Planning,* The Population Council, No. 9 (January 1966), 8–12.

17. SHETH, JAGDISH N. "Perceived Risk and Diffusion of Innovations." In *Insights Into Consumer Behavior,* edited by Johan Arndt, pp. 173–188. Boston: Allyn & Bacon, 1968.

18. SONQUIST, JOHN A. AND JAMES MORGAN. "The Detection of Interaction Effects." *Monograph No. 35.* Ann Arbor: University of Michigan, Survey Research Center, 1964.

19. STEFFLRE, VOLLNEY, J. "Some Applications of Multidimensional Scaling to Social Science Problems." In *Attitude Research Reaches New Heights,* edited by Charles W. King, Jr. and Douglas J. Tigert, pp. 300–311. Chicago: American Marketing Association, 1971.

18

46. Applying buyer behavior theory to public policy

john a. howard & lyman e. ostlund

The character of business-government relations on the marketing front appears on the verge of a profound change. Scarcely a day goes by without front page reports in both the business press and the general newspapers concerning opinions or actions regarding so-called "consumerism" issues. Public opinion is running increasingly in favor of legislative changes. A poll by the Opinion Research Center of Princeton, New Jersey, in 1965 found 47 percent of the sample in agreement that new laws were needed to aid the consumer in obtaining his money's worth. The same poll conducted in 1968 found the percentage had risen to 58 percent, and by 1969 to 68 percent.

Consumers are not alone in thinking that some changes are in order. A survey of 1,400 American Marketing Association members (94 percent response rate) indicated that marketing practitioners and educators alike believe that the consumer is not adequately protected in a wide range of areas, from health hazards to the quality of product information. In particular, 83 percent agreed that the Federal Trade Commission "should assume a more active role in requiring manufacturers and retailers to provide more information of value to the consumer in making purchase decisions." Only 16 percent agreed with the statement that "the 'consumer movement' is likely to result in more harm than good for society." Perhaps most remarkable was the agreement by 71 percent of the respondents that "individuals should be allowed to bring class-action suits against companies from which they feel they have not received fair treatment" (A.M.A., 1971). According to Bazil J. Mezines, Federal Trade Commission activity has been increasing, almost one-third in fiscal 1971 over fiscal 1970 (Grocery Manufacturers Association Monitor 1971).

Up until recently, conflicts between business and government have centered on the maintenance of competition. In public statements both parties have sung the praises of competition. Yet, as Bauer and Greyser (1969) observe, competition does not always mean the same thing to both parties. At their extreme positions, the government spokesmen and other critics of American business appear to regard competition only as price competition. On the other hand, the businessman spends a good deal of his energies avoiding head-on price competition, preferring instead to compete via product differentiation through research and development or promotional activity and related devices.

Our marketing system has existed within a philosophical framework of Western economic liberalism under which two key assumptions are made: first, that companies are in fact competitive in prices and other aspects; and second, that consumers are both capable and well-informed decision-makers, which is usually referred to as the "doctrine of consumer sovereignty." It is the businessman who often inflates the potency of consumer sovereignty as a sufficient controlling mechanism over the marketplace while at the same time complaining privately about the difficulty of penetrating the clutter of advertisements in the overloaded mass media and the deteriorating consumer-perceived credibility of advertising. The would-be defender of "consumer rights" often makes the opposite exaggeration, portraying the consumer as a mere pawn having been stripped of rationality by the marketers' incessant emotional appeals and rendered incapable of defining and defending his own interests.

The first assumption, that of competition among companies, has long been a focal point of public policy toward business. In part, this has been due to the input of economists in arguing for structural changes and restrictions on certain practices within the marketplace in order that competition can be increased and with this, public policy objectives attained. Except for perhaps a few like Edward S. Mason (1958), economists have been conspicuously silent on the "facts" surrounding the consumer sovereignty doctrine, whereas their fact-finding and definitional guidance concerning standards of competition have been elaborate and highly commendable.

It is our contention that, in a relative sense, issues of business-government relations will henceforth center increasingly on the facts and definitional questions of consumer sovereignty. The burden of this role now appears to be falling primarily on the Federal Trade Commission. This is not to say that the maintenance of competition will be ignored. In fact, it seems altogether likely that competition can and will be fostered through governmental actions primarily aimed at enhancing consumer sovereignty. Our marketing system will be valued according to the degree to which it "aids" the consumer in pursuing his own consumption goals.

To repeat what was stated earlier, consumer sovereignty has to do with consumers being capable and well-informed decision-makers. For this to be true with a large proportion of the buying public, the informational flow within the marketplace must be "compatible" with the buyer's information-processing machinery and with his willingness to use it. Secondly, the information must be "adequate" to allow well-informed decision-making.

Consumer sovereignty extends far beyond the mere elimination of deceptive practices, which is essentially a legalistic and eventually an ethical question. There is some evidence in support of our conclusion that future F.T.C. action will center on another aspect of consumer sovereignty. In an address before the 1971 annual conference of the Association for Consumer Research, Federal Trade Commissioner Mary Gardiner Jones (1971, p. 16) stated: "In today's marketplace with its greatly increased technical and legal complexities, consumers are correspondingly and increasingly less able to rely solely on their own efforts to achieve their purchasing goals whatever they may be." Note what Jones has said: consumer sovereignty is incomplete and worsening. Her next statement, however, indicates how consumer sovereignty, an economic concept, could be recast within the statutory limitations of F.T.C. authority (1971, p. 16): "The imbalance of power and know-how between consumer and businessman has steadily widened. As a result the Commission in recent years has been placing increasing attention on its mandate to eliminate the 'unfair' as well as the 'deceptive' practice." An imbalance of power and know-how, or stated differently, an imbalance of information-processing capability and relevant information may become the basis for a working definition of "unfair" that the F.T.C. is charged to work against. Quoting Jones again (1971, p. 16): "Yet, the concept of unfairness is a much more subjective and less verifiable term than deception or untruth. Here again, therefore, the Commission is in need of new insights into what constitutes unfairness in terms of consumer behavior in the marketplace." If, as Commissioner Jones suggests, the F.T.C. devotes considerable regulatory effort toward enhancing consumer sovereignty under a doctrine of unfairness, the Commission may come to depend primarily upon empirical assessment of unfairness in terms of information-processing capabilities and information availability, rather than legal statutes and precedents as with deceptive practices. The F.T.C. may come to depend upon buyer behavior research for questions regarding unfairness, much as it has depended upon economic analysis of industrial concentration and market power for antitrust regulation. While several court tests of any unfairness doctrine will undoubtedly be necessary before its full effect will be felt by marketers, we consider it important to advance a framework within which the necessary buyer behavior research needed to guide F.T.C. policy can be positioned.

To begin with, one must keep in mind the Commission's statutory responsibilities. The model of the consumer in *F.T.C.* v. *Standard Education Society*[1] was in terms of protecting the credulous, the trusting, and even the wayfaring fools. As Commissioner Jones stated in her speech before the Association for Consumer Research (1971, p. 7): "Indeed, in determining the impact of any given representation or practice on consumers, it is undoubtedly essential that the Commission look to the least sophisticated consumer if it is to carry out its statutory mandate effectively." This model of the consumer concerns information-processing capability, albeit a minimized assessment. As a practical matter, it is unlikely the Commission would attempt to push this model to its extreme, except possibly in protection of certain market segments considered particularly subject to injury through limited information-processing capability, such as minority groups and the aged. Even here, while such distinctions may have political appeal, measurement difficulties may preclude demonstrating to a court's satisfaction that the differentials in information-processing capability are that substantial.

With respect to information availability, following the above model would lead to an understatement of informational needs for the typical consumer. Thus, it is highly unlikely that the same model would ever

---

[1] *F.T.C.* v. *Standard Education Society*, et al., 302 U.S. 112 (1937).

be applied to the problem of specifying that minimum kind and amount of information that the marketer of a given type of product would be required to provide. Instead, it is likely the Commission would follow a model that assumes higher consumer information-processing capability, as it has in defining the practices that restrain trade and in its relief to eliminate practices that are deemed to mislead this type of consumer. However, to assume that the consumer is in all cases exhaustively analytical and concerned only with functional product attributes would be naive indeed. Such a position would ignore a considerable body of knowledge that shows that, if anything, consumers characteristically underutilize available information, tend to conduct only a limited search for additional information, and are, of course, symbol-using animals in general and most definitely in selecting among branded merchandise.

The Commission must, however, aim primarily at correcting those cases of unfairness, that is, information imbalance, that will result in a behavioral change by the consumer. No purpose is served in requiring the marketer to disseminate information a given consumer segment will not or cannot use. To do so would represent a waste of resources by both the F.T.C. and the marketer. Rather, the Commission should first attempt to establish through consumer behavioral research the types of information that consumers currently use, or would use if available, and a clear understanding of the decision-making process in a given product category before drafting regulations or legislative recommendations. We will now set forth a framework that we believe best positions the research task that would face the Commission in attempting to establish a doctrine of unfairness based upon information imbalance.

A FRAMEWORK FOR RESEARCHING UNFAIRNESS

Even if deceptive and unfair practices were somehow totally absent, society would still decide that the sale of some products or certain business practices should be regulated or eliminated. Certainly dangerous products of different forms have been subjected to such limitations as have actions that cause restraint of trade. For the future, ecological issues may bring about further constraints. These possibilities are deemed beyond the scope of this article, however.

A comprehensive model of buyer behavior has been under development at Columbia University for several years. The most recent version is diagramed in Figure 1 from "The Model: Current Status of Buyer Behavior Theory" in this volume. The reader may find it helpful to refer to this diagram when considering the discussion that follows. Space limitations do not allow its elaboration here.

Issues of unfairness, if they come to be defined as Jones (1971) has suggested, will be concerned principally with what shall be termed "information shortages" and "information complexities." Using Table 1, we shall discuss examples of each.

Information shortages can be thought of as taking two forms: low quality due to low factual content and low relevance. Quality can be

TABLE 1   Forms of Informational Imbalance

Information Shortages	Information Complexities
1. Low quality due to low factual content	1. Establishing discriminating product attribute dimensions and weighting each
2. Low quality due to low relevance	2. Relating facts and opinions to product attribute dimensions
	3. Coping with the redundancy of both product attribute dimensions and product facts
	4. Excessive product offerings

lacking, either due to an outright intent to deceive the buyer, which falls outside the scope of unfairness, or to a factual content lower than desired by the consumer. As with information actually being deceptive, factual content is low only when perceived as low by the consumer. The issue cast in these terms is empirical, not legalistic. One would need to specify for what proportion of consumers serious factual inadequacies existed in the representations of a marketer. Referring to Figure 1, low factual content has to do with the construct *brand comprehension*, meaning the buyer's inventory of nonevaluative, or factual, information on each brand within his definition of the product category. To the degree that the consumer's decisions go on despite a self-perceived lack of factual product information, when such information could reasonably be provided by the marketer, there would be an issue of unfairness.

The F.T.C.'s recent decision to require substantiation of advertising claims may well cause some advertisers to drop the use of allegedly factual claims in favor of nebulous puffery bordering on fantasy. That possibility serves to highlight the second form of information shortage, namely information having low relevance to the manner in which the brands within a product category are customarily evaluated by consumers. According to the buyer behavior model in Figure 1, brands are evaluated on various attitude dimensions, weighted according to their perceived importance, to reflect both personal preferences among products and situational factors, such as the assumed preferences of family or friends. If, through empirical investigation, it is found that a certain set of attitude, or product attribute, dimensions are employed by most consumers when deliberating purchases within a given category, marketers might be required to make a reasonable effort in their representation to provide facts relevant to those dimensions; that is, to talk on those dimensions, and not, through design or ignorance, to talk around them. Clearly there would be many practical difficulties connected with regulatory action to mitigate unfairness defined in this manner. Perhaps the most major is that often the attitude dimensions will not be homogeneous within a consumer population. Rather, separate segments will exist, differentiated by, among other things, valued attitude, or personal preference, dimensions. It would be unreasonable to ask that the marketer provide relevant

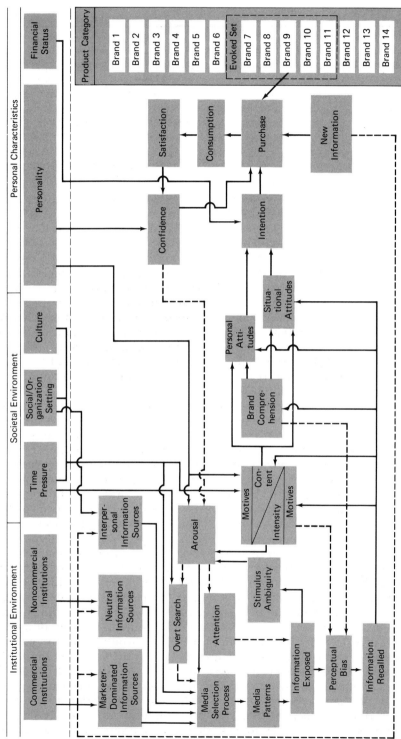

FIGURE 1 Theory of Buyer Behavior

information for all such segments, even those to which he makes no serious marketing effort. However, the opposite extreme might likewise be considered unreasonable, where no particular attempt is made at supplying relevant information. Nothing in what has been said denies that for many product categories nonfunctional, or "emotional," product attributes are important, however. Thus, the exclusive use of puffery might still be quite legitimate in categories such as perfumes, for example. The point remains the same. As stated earlier, the issue of unfairness would be an empirical one and, as such, specified differently across different product categories. To resist this conclusion while still requiring advertising substantiation leaves only two rather undesirable alternatives: running the distinct risk of allowing the marketplace to sink into an unhelpful cloud of puffery and empty communications; or running the risk that marketers will resort to appeals based upon clearly irrelevant but somehow impressive-sounding facts that would confuse, not help, the consumer in his decision-making. Relevancy is at least as important to secure as would be sufficiently high factual content. They are inseparable.

Information complexity addresses the matter of the consumer's information-processing capability. The question here is to what degree can the available information be sorted and manipulated by the consumer with sufficient ease to facilitate decision-making in furtherance of his self-selected purchase goals. First, and to repeat what was stated earlier, this capability will vary among population segments. Second, since this capability will be a function of the consumer's willingness to invest sufficient cognitive effort, it becomes a function of the perceived importance of the purchase. Stated differently, information-processing capability will vary across both population segments and product categories. The two determinants can be expected to interact as well. For example, differing levels of importance could be attached by various population segments to purchases within a given product category. Thus, perceptions, attitudes, and intention—in fact, the entire decision-making process—will vary both by population segments and by product category. Decision-making processes can vary according to the degree of genuine problem-solving that is engaged, from a minimal level described as "routinized response behavior," through limited problem-solving to extended problem-solving (see article one).

One avenue toward the enhancement of consumer sovereignty through improved information-processing capability would be by way of formal educational programs aimed at upgrading the quality of consumer decision-making. For the most part, such an approach falls outside the scope of F.T.C. activity. However, much the same objective can be pursued by addressing the information complexities outlined in Table 1. The first of these concerns the dimensions upon which purchase alternatives are evaluated. Out of a multitude of informational cues, and one's own motives, a consumer settles upon a set of attitude dimensions for structuring preferences among purchase alternatives. These dimensions, and their relative importance, or weighting, may continually shift as information from marketer-dominated informational sources, interpersonal (conversations with friends and family, reference-group influence) informational sources, and experience from actual consumption accumulates. Examples of such dimensions might be price, style, durability, and quality. The number of such dimensions actually used in decision-making will depend upon many factors, such as the nature of the proposed purchase, the individual's ability and willingness to think along several dimensions, and the availability of corresponding informational cues regarding each purchase alternative. From the standpoint of public policy, it is essential for intelligent consumer decision-making that the latter factor be considered carefully. Recent efforts by the F.T.C. to require the marketer to disclose certain product performance and ingredient data reflect this conclusion. But far more can be done by first investigating the manner in which consumers currently formulate attitude dimensions, and learning which ones they would use if the corresponding facts for their use were available. Second, product labeling and advertising could be required to provide data on certain prescribed dimensions that had been predetermined as both revealing and comprehendable by the consumer. Note here that product testing and research into the consumer decision-making process must go hand-in-hand. Advertising copy would thus reflect the attitude dimensions codetermined by current consumer decision-making practice plus the output of such product testing and consumer decision-making research. In this way, the institution of advertising would directly serve the informational needs of consumers.

It is important to bear in mind that consumers will fall back on faulty attitude dimensions if more accurate ones are not available. Except under conditions of extreme frustration over inadequate information, consumers will continue to make decisions, although certainly not the wisest ones from their viewpoint. Cox (1962) discusses the circumstances under which this occurs, distinguishing between the predictive value and the confidence value of informational cues to the consumer. Briefly stated, the consumer will seek out those cues of high perceived predictive value, but only so long as he has confidence in his ability to appropriately evaluate them. If the confidence value of a cue to him is relatively low, he will prefer instead to rely upon some other cue of lower predictive value, so long as its confidence value is high. This sort rule by Cox provides further implications concerning the second type of information complexity (Table 1). Let us suppose that a consumer has settled upon quality as the most important of the four attitude dimensions he will use in evaluating brands within a given product category. He may confront many informational cues that bear on quality, but not all such cues will point consistently toward one brand as clearly superior. He must therefore sort out which cues to rely upon in positioning the brands upon the quality dimension.

Cox uses the example of high-fidelity sound equipment quite effectively in illustrating his predictive-confidence distinction. The consumer, not being an electrical engineer, lacks confidence in cues concerning electronic specifications of the chassis even though such cues may well be appreciated as having high predictive value. He must cast aside electronics cues and seek other quality cues in which he has confidence, such as external appearance of the equipment, even though he appreciates the lower predictive value of such cues. The sort process here is not unlike the car buyer examining the paint job or slamming the doors in order to judge the car's overall quality. For major appliance purchases, most consumers can be expected to value a comprehensive product warranty of long term. Regardless of the weight placed upon that attitude dimension, their efforts to relate the facts of several warranty agreements to that valued dimension will depend largely upon the language of each warranty. If coched in abundant legal jargon, the consumer may have no confidence in his ability to evaluate such informational cues and may instead rely upon the salesman's opinion of which is best. Thus, from a research perspective, the question is: How can the facts, the information cues relevant to commonly used important attitude dimensions, be expressed in such a way that their predictive value is retained while their confidence value is increased?

The third form of information complexity concerns the general redundancy of both product attribute dimensions (attitudes), and product facts (informational cues in some product categories), particularly those where the products are both rather complex and/or heavily promoted. Setting aside all differences of quality, the mere quantity of informational cues may present processing difficulties for any consumer, and certainly more so for consumer segments of below average capabilities. High informational densities can also exist due to excessive alternatives of choice, to be discussed later. (Possible limitations on the quantity of advertising for reasons of social costs are not within the scope of this discussion.) For whatever reason, the quantity of informational cues contributing to information-processing difficulties may call for limitations. It is not our purpose to suggest the nature of such possible limitations, but only to identify the problem and discuss how its scope might be investigated.

Consumers seem on the whole quite well equipped to filter out vast quantities of informational cues, committing only a very small proportion of available cues to even short-term memory (see article one). Their selectivity and purposefulness in this filtration process is itself a marvel. However, this general capability still does not exclude the existence of product categories where excessive informational densities call for corrective measures. We would judge the burden of proof, however, as major. In any case, the research question concerns the likelihood of faulty consumer decision-making in the face of attempting to digest very high quantities of information. Stated differently, does the high information density bring on such frustration that suboptimization becomes the favored means to cope with the problem? This is a question for the researcher.

The fourth and final information complexity concerns excessive product offerings. This problem already exists in many packaged goods categories due to a proliferation of sizes and brands. Usually the marketer has attempted to maximize his revenue by catering to carefully defined consumer segments, each displaying marginally different preferences as to size, product application, product performance, or personal characteristics. The practice is most obvious in the household cleaner area, with the large number of specialized cleaning agents, each allegedly better suited to a given task than those general cleaning agents that consumers relied upon in the past. And, usually each such specialized cleaner is offered in more than one container size, both as a convenience to the consumer and as a vehicle to increase the brand's exposure to the consumer on the supermarket shelf. Regardless of the marketer's logic, the result is a complicated array of products and sizes among which it is often difficult to distinguish as to purpose and value. Given the huge size of United States markets, such market segmentation has been an obvious and practical business strategy to increase profits and has brought about some genuine technical advances for the consumer's benefit as well. But still, for those products of trivial inherent difference, differentiated only by what advertising says about them, and for those size differences where value per unit does not rise with container size, the consumer is clearly in danger of drawing false conclusions. For example, Friedman (1966) demonstrated in a laboratory study that even college-educated housewives were unable, by his criterion, to successfully cope with the single task of identifying the best value among different sizes of selected packaged goods. Although no research has been published on the question, an analogous conclusion is likely to emerge if the subject's objective is instead to match the most appropriate brand to a specifically defined task or application. Again, this issue is an empirical one and can be researched.

Let us relate the matter of excessive product offerings to a concept that has been the object of some research. For a given product with many brands, a consumer is likely to be aware of an incomplete subset of these brands. And, assuming the consumer has or is likely to make purchases from that category, he will seriously consider only a smaller subset of those of which he is aware. We call this last subset his *evoked set* (see article one). Campbell (1969) has investigated determinants and correlates of evoked set and has concluded, for example, that for even universally used products the average size of evoked set varies across consumers (e.g., with educational level), presumably as a reflection of information-processing capability. Since evoked set is also a function of the number of brands in a category, one might conclude that the relationship of average evoked set size to category size is at least a crude measure of brand proliferation. If that ratio measure is found to vary decidedly across consumer segments for a given product category, this can be taken as evidence of information-processing difficulties stemming from excessive product offerings, or brand proliferation. While the research issues can be handled readily, the remedies if needed may be far more awkward to devise.

IMPACT ON THE MARKETPLACE

What impact on the marketplace would result if the informational imbalance between the marketer and the consumer were significantly reduced? We have already stated that such disclosure should have a healthy effect on the maintenance of competition. But other effects can be expected as well.

To the degree that an entire product category is now benefiting from general consumer ignorance of true product performance attributes, the availability of better information could have a depressing effect on price levels and cause a contraction of total product category unit sales. For example, most if not all mouthwash products have made references to germicidal qualities, even tying them to alleged prophylactic and/or therapeutic effects against the common cold. As such nonsense abates, one reason for using mouthwashes, perhaps thought to be important by some consumers, is put to rest, and the remaining product appeals will tend to center on cosmetic advantages of the products' use. One would expect from this change a reduction in product category unit sales, most likely accompanied by direct or camouflaged price reductions. In more extreme cases, the availability of higher quality information could cause certain brands to fail. But there is a very positive aspect to this question as well. Worthy brands whose advantages had not been as widely appreciated in the past could benefit considerably if rival brands trading off consumer ignorance were to suffer. In particular, one would expect this result in product categories where the smaller, but worthy, brands were being swamped by the much heavier but rather uninformative promotional campaigns of major brands.

In general, where the informational imbalance was corrected, improved consumer decision-making should serve to place increased emphasis on functional, or performance, aspects of products, along with their price. First, we would expect this to stimulate greater real technical advancement in consumer products. Second, higher quality information could bring about a resurgence of private labels in some product categories. Surely, the more expensive proprietary analgesics would be thrown for a loss if their communications quoted exact ingredients and clinical performance relative to essentially identical but much cheaper private label brands.

CONCLUSIONS

We have identified what we believe to be the dawn of a new phase in business-government relations during which the concept of consumer sovereignty will finally be given operational meaning. The availability of information and the consumer's capability for its appropriate processing determine the degree of consumer sovereignty in a product category or, expressed inversely, the degree of information imbalance between the consumer and the marketer. Information imbalance can take many forms, as discussed, and its magnitude can and should be empirically assessed prior to attempts at devising remedial directives. In this way the resources of both enforcement agencies and the marketer are not squandered on informational requirements that produce no desirable behavioral change among consumers.

REFERENCES

American Marketing Association. "Consumers Not Well Protected, Back Standards if Safety Periled." *The Marketing News,* Vol. 5 (November 1971), 1.

BAUER, RAYMOND A. AND STEPHEN A. GREYSER. "The Dialogue that Never Happens." *Harvard Business Review* (January–February 1969), 122–128.

CAMPBELL, BRIAN M. "The Existence and Determinants of Evoked Set in Brand Choice Behavior." Unpublished Ph.D. dissertation, Columbia University, 1969.

COX, DONALD F. "The Measurement of Information Value: A Study in Consumer Decision Making." Chicago: *Proceedings of the American Marketing Association* (Fall 1962), 413–421.

FRIEDMAN, MONROE PETER. "Consumer Confusion in the Selection of Supermarket Products." *Journal of Applied Psychology,* Vol. 50 (December 1966), 529–534.

G.M.A. Monitor (August 26, 1971), 2.

JONES, MARY GARDINER. "The FTC's Need for Social Science Research." Address before the Second Annual Conference, Association for Consumer Research, University of Maryland, September 1, 1971.

MASON, EDWARD S. "The Apologetics of Managerialism." *Journal of Business,* Vol. 31 (1958), 1–11.

A Note on the Type

The text of this book was set on the Linotype in Aster, a typeface designed by Francesco Simoncini for Ludwig and Mayer, the German type foundry. Starting out with the basic old-face letterforms that can be traced back to Francesco Griffo in 1495, Simoncini emphasized the diagonal stress by the simple device of extending diagonals to the full height of the letterforms and squaring off. By modifying the weights of the individual letters to combat this stress, he has produced a type of rare balance and vigor.

This book was composed by Cherry Hill Composition, Pennsauken, New Jersey. Printed and bound by The Halliday Lithograph Corp., West Hanover, Mass.